Proceedings
of the
United Nations Conference
on
Trade and Development

SEVENTH SESSION
Geneva, 9 July-3 August 1987

Volume II
Statements and Summary Records

UNITED NATIONS
New York, 1991

NOTE

Symbols of United Nations documents are composed of capital letters combined with figures. Mention of such a symbol indicates a reference to a United Nations document.

The designations employed and the presentation of the material in this publication do not imply the expression of any opinion whatsoever on the part of the Secretariat of the United Nations concerning the legal status of any country, territory, city or area, or of its authorities, or concerning the delimitation of its frontiers or boundaries.

For the recommendations, resolutions, declarations and decisions adopted by the United Nations Conference on Trade and Development, see:

First session: *Proceedings of the United Nations Conference on Trade and Development*, vol. I, *Final Act and Report* (United Nations publication, Sales No. E.64.II.B.11), pp. 17-65;

Second session: *Proceedings of the United Nations Conference on Trade and Development, Second Session*, vol. I and Corr.1 and 3 and Add.1 and 2, *Report and Annexes* (United Nations publication, Sales No. E.68.II.D.14), annex I, A, pp. 27-58;

Third session: *Proceedings of the United Nations Conference on Trade and Development, Third Session, Report and Annexes* (United Nations publication, Sales No. E.73.II.D.4), annex I, A, pp. 51-114;

Fourth session: *Proceedings of the United Nations Conference on Trade and Development, Fourth Session*, vol. I and Corr.1, *Report and Annexes* (United Nations publication, Sales No. E.76.II.D.10), part one, sect. A. 1, pp. 6-44;

Fifth session: *Proceedings of the United Nations Conference on Trade and Development, Fifth Session*, vol. I, *Report and Annexes* (United Nations publication, Sales No. E.79.II.D.14), part one, sect. A. pp. 6-50;

Sixth session: *Proceedings of the United Nations Conference on Trade and Development, Sixth Session*, vol. I, *Report and Annexes* (United Nations publication, Sales No. E.83.II.D.6), part one, sect. A, pp. 6-45.

*

* *

For the check-list of documents before the Conference at its seventh session, see *Proceedings of the United Nations Conference on Trade and Development, Seventh Session*, vol. I, *Report and Annexes* (United Nations publication, Sales No. E.88.II.D.1), annex VIII.

For the list of participants in the seventh session of the Conference, see TD/INF.25.

TD/352 (Vol. II)

UNITED NATIONS PUBLICATION

Sales No. E.88.II.D.2

ISBN 92-1-112241-4

CONTENTS

PART ONE

Statements by heads of State or Government, heads of intergovernmental bodies, and other representatives and observers who addressed the Conference during the general debate

---

a Speaking as representative of the Head of State of the Republic of Cuba, to present the results of the Sixth Ministerial Meeting of the Group of 77.

---

[b] Speaking also on behalf of the European Economic Community and its member States.

iv

C. United Nations Secretariat

*

* *

D. Specialized agencies, GATT, International Trade Centre UNCTAD/GATT

---

c The text of the statement is reproduced in volume I, annex III.

PART TWO

Summary records of plenary meetings

ABBREVIATIONS

ACP	African, Caribbean and Pacific States
ANC	African National Congress of South Africa
CMEA	Council for Mutual Economic Assistance
DAC	Development Assistance Committee (OECD)
ECA	Economic Commission for Africa
ECE	Economic Commission for Europe
ESCAP	Economic and Social Commission for Asia and the Pacific
ESCWA	Economic and Social Commission for Western Asia
FAO	Food and Agriculture Organization of the United Nations
GATT	General Agreement on Tariffs and Trade
GDP	gross domestic product
GNP	gross national product
GSP	generalized system of preferences
Habitat	United Nations Centre for Human Settlements
IDA	International Development Association
IFAD	International Fund for Agricultural Development
ILO	International Labour Organisation
IMF	International Monetary Fund
ITU	International Telecommunication Union
LDCs	least developed countries
MFN	most favoured nation
MTNs	multilateral trade negotiations
OAU	Organization of African Unity
ODA	official development assistance
OECD	Organisation for Economic Co-operation and Development
OPEC	Organization of the Petroleum Exporting Countries
SDR	special drawing right
SWAPO	South West Africa People's Organization
TNCs	transnational corporations
UNCITRAL	United Nations Commission on International Trade Law
UNDP	United Nations Development Programme
UNEP	United Nations Environment Programme
UNESCO	United Nations Educational, Scientific and Cultural Organization
UNICEF	United Nations Children's Fund
UNIDO	United Nations Industrial Development Organization
UNU	United Nations University
WHO	World Health Organization
WIDER	World Institute for Development Economics Research

EXPLANATORY NOTES

References to "volume I" and "volume III" are to *Proceedings of the United Nations Conference on Trade and Development, Seventh Session*, vol. I, *Report and Annexes* (United Nations publication, Sales No. E.88.II.D.1) and *ibid.*, vol. III, *Basic Documents* (United Nations publication, Sales No. E.88.II.D.3).

The summaries of statements reproduced in part one of the present volume appeared in the relevant summary records (TD/SR...) and incorporate corrections from delegations and editorial modifications.

The report of the UNCTAD secretariat entitled "Revitalizing development growth and international trade: Assessment and policy options" (TD/328/Rev.1) and the report of the Secretary-General of UNCTAD entitled "Reviving multilateral co-operation for growth and development" (TD/329/Rev.1) are contained in volume III.

Meetings, conferences, declarations, programmes, etc., mentioned in the present volume

Addis Ababa

Twenty-first ordinary session of the Assembly of Heads of State and Government of the Organization of African Unity, Addis Ababa, 18-20 July 1985

Africa's Priority Programme for Economic Recovery 1986-1990 (AHG/Decl.1 (XXI), annex) (see A/40/666, annex)

Berlin

Session of the Political Consultative Committee of the States parties to the Warsaw Treaty, Berlin, 28-29 May 1987

Statement on the Elimination of underdevelopment and the establishment of a new international economic order (see A/42/354-E/1987/110)

Harare

Eighth Conference of Heads of State or Government of Non-Aligned Countries, Harare (Zimbabwe), 1-6 September 1986 (see A/41/697)

Havana

Sixth Ministerial Meeting of the Group of 77, Havana, 20-25 April 1987

Havana Declaration and Assessment and proposals by the Group of 77 relating to the seventh session of the Conference (see volume I, annex V)

Lagos

Second extraordinary session of the Assembly of Heads of State and Government of the Organization of African Unity, Lagos, 28-29 April 1980

Lagos Plan of Action for the Implementation of the Monrovia Strategy for the Economic Development of Africa (A/S-11/14, annex I)

Lima

Second General Conference of UNIDO, Lima, 12-26 March 1975

Lima Declaration and Plan of Action on Industrial Development and Co-operation (ID/CONF.3/31, chap. IV)

Punta del Este

Special Session of the Contracting Parties to the General Agreement on Tariffs and Trade, Punta del Este, 15-20 September 1986

Ministerial Declaration on the Uruguay Round, adopted on 20 September 1986 (GATT, *Basic Instruments and Selected. Documents, Thirty-third Supplement* (Sales No. GATT/1987-1), p. 19)

Pyongyang

Extraordinary Ministerial Conference of Non-Aligned Countries on South-South Co-operation, Pyongyang, 9-13 June 1987

Pyongyang Declaration and Plan of Action on South-South Co-operation (see TD/339)

Venice

Meeting of the heads of State and Government of seven major industrial countries, Venice, 8-10 June 1987

Economic Declaration (see A/42/344)

*

* *

OECD

Meeting of the Council of OECD at ministerial level, Paris, 12-13 May 1987

Communiqué (see TD/334)

*

* *

Declaration on the Establishment of a New International Economic Order (General Assembly resolution 3201 (S-VI) of 1 May 1974)

Programme of Action on the Establishment of a New International Economic Order (General Assembly resolution 3202 (S-VI) of 1 May 1974)

Charter of Economic Rights and Duties of States (General Assembly resolution 3281 (XXIX) of 12 December 1974)

International Development Strategy for the Third United Nations Development Decade (General Assembly resolution 35/56 of 5 December 1980, annex)

United Nations Programme of Action for African Economic Recovery and Development 1986-1990 (General Assembly resolution S-13/2 of 1 June 1986)

Agreement Establishing the Common Fund for Commodities, concluded at Geneva on 27 June 1980 (United Nations publication, Sales No. E.81.II.D.8 and corrigendum)

Substantial New Programme of Action for the 1980s for the Least Developed Countries (*Report of the United Nations Conference on the Least Developed Countries*, Paris, 1-14 September 1981 (United Nations publication, Sales No. E.82.I.8) part one, sect. A)

The Set of Multilaterally Agreed Equitable Principles and Rules for the Control of Restrictive Business Practices (United Nations publication, Sales No. E.81.II.D.5)

Decree No. 1 for the Protection of the Natural Resources of Namibia, enacted by the United Nations Council for Namibia on 27 September 1974 (*Official Records of the General Assembly, Thirty-fifth Session, Supplement No. 24* (A/35/24), vol. I, annex II).

*
* *

STABEX

System of stabilization of export earnings established by the First Lomé Convention, concluded between the EEC and 46 ACP States (28 February 1975), and reinforced by the Second Lomé Convention, concluded between the EEC and 58 ACP States (31 October 1979) and the Third Lomé Convention concluded between the EEC and 66 ACP States (8 December 1984) (see *Official Journal of the European Communities*, vol. 29, No. L 86 of 31 March 1986)

*
* *

Advisory Opinion of the International Court of Justice of 21 June 1971

Legal Consequences for States of the continued presence of South Africa in Namibia (South West Africa) notwithstanding Security Council resolution 276 (1970), Advisory Opinion, *I.C.J. Reports 1971*, p. 16.

*
* *

World Commission on Environment and Development, under the chairmanship of Gro Harlem Brundtland

Report: *Our Common Future* (Oxford, University Press, 1987)

**AGENDA OF THE SEVENTH SESSION
OF THE UNITED NATIONS CONFERENCE
ON TRADE AND DEVELOPMENT**

as adopted by the Conference at its 201st plenary meeting, on 9 July 1987

1. Opening of the Conference.

2. Election of the President.

3. Constitution of sessional bodies.

4. Election of Vice-Presidents and the Rapporteur.

5. Credentials of representatives to the Conference:
   (+) Appointment of the Credentials Committee;
   (b) Report of the Credentials Committee.

6. Adoption of the agenda.

7. General debate.

8. Revitalizing development, growth and international trade, in a more predictable
   and supportive environment, through multilateral co-operation: assessment of
   relevant economic trends and of global structural change, and appropriate formulation of policies and measures, addressing key issues in the following interrelated areas:
   (a) Resources for development, including financial, and related monetary ques-
       tions;
   (b) Commodities;
   (c) International trade;
   (d) Problems of the least developed countries, bearing in mind the Substantial
       New Programme of Action for the 1980s for the Least Developed Coun-
       tries.

9. Other business.

10. Adoption of the report of the Conference to the General Assembly.

Part One

**STATEMENTS BY HEADS OF STATE OR GOVERNMENT, HEADS OF
INTERGOVERNMENTAL BODIES, AND OTHER REPRESENTATIVES
AND OBSERVERS WHO ADDRESSED THE CONFERENCE
DURING THE GENERAL DEBATE**

Part One

STATEMENTS BY HEADS OF STATE OR GOVERNMENT, HEADS OF
INTERGOVERNMENTAL BODIES, AND OTHER REPRESENTATIVES
AND OBSERVERS WHO ADDRESSED THE CONFERENCE
DURING THE GENERAL DEBATE

PART ONE

Statements by heads of State or Government, heads of intergovernmental bodies, and other representatives and observers who addressed the Conference during the general debate

A. HEADS OF STATE OR GOVERNMENT AND OTHER SPEAKERS ABOVE MINISTERIAL RANK

Statement made at the 202nd plenary meeting, 10 July 1987,
by Mr. François MITTERRAND, President of the French Republic*

To be one of the few Heads of State of the so-called industrialized countries to address this Conference is an honour I appreciate to the full.

I know that speeches have already been made, and I imagine that more will be made, which will prompt reflection, fill in the background to difficult problems, and urge mankind to close ranks in an endeavour to solve the problems raised. I know also that, among those speeches, the statement made by the Secretary-General of the United Nations in particular pointed out the directions in which to go.

At a time when the world crisis is worsening, when unemployment is limitless, when the debts owed by many countries have reached a level that could never have been imagined, no speech can hope to affect reality or bring about an immediate change in the course of events. Even though the will of the international community to take the opportunity afforded by this Conference to launch a decisive attack on underdevelopment is open to doubt, the Conference should nevertheless enable substantial progress to be made in the matters dealt with, namely trade and development.

I see you here before me, ladies and gentlemen, representing the countries of the world or qualified by your own choices, your own responsibilities, one rarely sees thus assembled in one place so many political, diplomatic and technical authorities capable of dealing with so much information. Beyond trying to provide impetus, it is up to you to give significance to a political will too often absent, in particular, from North-South relations, which in recent years have met with more setbacks than they should have and caused more disappointment than is reasonable. In order to understand what ought to be done, let each of us make his contribution: then, from the whole, it will be possible to draw useful conclusions. Let us also try to analyse recent history and the present situation of our world. Let us be aware of the illusions of the past in order to avoid them in the future.

Who among us did not hope when the Second World War was over that we would be capable of ensuring peace through the United Nations? Heaven knows, I am a keen enough supporter of the Organization; I wish that it was even better respected, and that all the countries of the world which belong to it would meet one another there more. But who is to blame? It would probably take too long to dwell on that point; there has not been a day in the past 40 years when our planet has been spared.

Who has not hoped that the benefits of medical science, for example, would lighten the burden of endemic disease and leave the human race free to develop its full potential? What arrangements have been made to cater for the extraordinary growth of the human race: 5 billion today, 10 billion tomorrow? In many places, the splendid promise is turning into a threat to everyone, to the environment, to the food supply and to political stability. Because of the failure to match these advances, lives are being saved which famine will cut off with the passing seasons.

Who has not hoped that the unprecedented, historic economic growth we have experienced would inevitably draw the poorest nations, peoples and individuals towards prosperity? And yet entire social strata, if not continents, have so far missed their appointment with development.

Who has not hoped that the works, machinery, technologies, universities and information systems of the North would go everywhere, reach the remotest places in the South, and succeed in increasing the capacity of the South to produce more, to know and to organize, since that is the situation in the world? (My remarks in no way reflect on the degree of cultures, which are no less rich there than here even though they are different, and even though material resources remain grossly unequal.) Forty years and more have shown us that, with a few exceptions, the technological gap between the most developed and the less developed is widening instead of shrinking.

* Initially issued as TD/L.291.

Who has not hoped that the erratic variations in primary commodity prices would be brought under control? Yet those prices have perhaps never been as low as they are today, to the great detriment of the producing countries and at no appreciable gain to the consumers. Whereas, as you know, raw materials account for four fifths of the third world's exports, their real prices fell by 20 per cent between 1984 and 1985 and by 15 per cent in 1986, and have fallen in 1987 to the lowest level since the war. And the compensatory machinery in place covers only 10 per cent of the loss sustained.

Who has not hoped that, by favouring international trade, those who have less would be favoured above those who have more? It is a further paradox that passive or active protectionist measures have been steadily strengthened, afflicting the semi-industrialized countries of the South while playing an adverse role for the world economy as a whole.

In short: over the past five years, to go no further back, the developing countries, with the exception of the Asian countries, have seen a decline in their per capita product, and this year the per capita product of sub-Saharan Africa—to take a specific case—will be 13 per cent less than it was in 1980.

Such a decline has two consequences which are immediately apparent: the vital needs of the poorest populations are less and less well covered, and the countries where they live cannot develop; they cannot even develop their productive investments. Many cannot devote to their productive investments 10 per cent of what is already a very small gross national product. In some of the least developed countries, the figure is less than 5 per cent, or even a negative quantity.

That is a description which others have made and yet others will make. I do not claim to add anything, especially for those who are living through what I am trying to describe; but I thought it was up to a representative of the industrialized countries to speak out when his turn came, without hiding any of this cruel truth. The aim being, of course, to strive with you to find remedies for these ills. For the decline I just mentioned is worsening in three ways as I speak to you now.

In the first place, we are witnessing a break in the connection which has long existed between the abundance of raw materials and the development of industry. The food sector apart, manufacturing industry is tending to economize on materials. Many more articles are being made nowadays with far fewer primary commodities. I do not say this as a complaint—it is merely the way things are developing—but it must be included among the factors to be considered.

The atom is supplanting oil and power stations; cars are running on less and less petrol; copper is being ousted by new materials in the laying of our networks. Let us realize this; let us not lament it; let us have the capacity to adapt our societies to industrial circumstances and find the right place for raw materials without necessarily speeding up the flow, but by giving the matter enough thought to know what to do.

You know, too, that less manpower is needed to produce a greater result: computer technology, automation and robotics are replacing men's labour by that of machines. In the nineteenth century, machines replaced muscles, now memory and judgement are being replaced. Computers are writing programs, robots are making robots which in turn will make articles. The deciding factor is not necessarily manual dexterity—even though work done by hand is an essential element of any human civilization, giving form to the spirit—but the creativity of intelligence.

There is a third factor to be placed alongside those I have just mentioned: the creation of wealth, which I said was less and less connected with industrial development but more and more connected with financial and monetary ploys. The movement of capital generates more profits than industry and trade. Consequently, the financial department of enterprises is becoming more important than the workshops or the building sites, and productive investments are decreasing in favour of financial operations which, it must be said, are often speculative.

This threefold evolution is penalizing the South while appearing to favour the North, which would be greatly mistaken if it believed that on the whole that profit would be a lasting one. It is true that the South—whose wealth lies in its subsoil and its countless hands—lacks, or possesses only marginally, the capacity to join in the grand manoeuvres of the great financial centres. In short, even more than yesterday, there is a risk that everything will happen outside its sphere of influence.

You will have noticed that I have several times used two terms which are somewhat too simple and which do not convey my ideas: the North and the South. Ought we still to speak of the North and the South? I am the first one to find these terms inadequate. We should speak in the plural. Within each of the two hemispheres the situation varies widely: there are several Norths and several Souths. In cases like these, because trade and development are at issue, differences in circumstances are immediately apparent and necessarily call for differences in approach and differences in response. I nevertheless believe that global problems call for global solutions: by that I mean comprehensive solutions to the common problems of the countries of the South. That is one way of tackling the problems of the North.

If we should not manage this—I should make it clear that I am addressing the countries of the North, those in the North which are industrialized and which can influence the economic evolution of the world—their own future, their own destiny (they are not sufficiently aware of this) would also be at stake. They might well exhaust their own sources of wealth if they failed to understand that the world has become a shrunken planet and that the terms of trade affect every man, woman, producer and consumer on Earth. If we do not take care—forgive me for labouring the obvious, but when the obvious does not seem to be understood it must be repeated—the crisis will overwhelm the whole world. Everything that changes anywhere in the world has repercussions elsewhere in a powder train, a chain of successive reactions and adaptations. No one escapes it. We are in a situation of forced solidarity when we do not want to choose our solidarity.

Imagine that one or other continent is left out, forgotten, reduced to its poverty and its disorder: what will happen to the others? For we are all responsible, whether directly or not, for the tiniest patch of the living earth, struggling against the desert in all its forms, those of nature and those of the mind. We are responsible for our biosphere, that is assailed by pollution of every kind; for every area of sea that is threatened by us, by man; and for the most beaten-down of our fellow-men—the individual in his family or his town—beset by the familiar enemies: hunger, poverty and death.

So what are we to do? Are we to fold our hands—you are not here for that; on the contrary—are we to let the laws of the market prevail? Are we to organize, or should I say submit to, the law of the jungle? Are we merely to stand by while inevitable clashes occur? Of course not. Then we must go to the heart of things. And the time for this came long since. What a lot of time has been wasted! In short, the time has come to lay down a system of rules, to think of a concerted effort first of all by those who escape the worst of the damage, in the West as in the East, in the North as in the South. This effort should engage not only States, institutions and international organizations but also opinions, economic forces and voluntary organizations. This effort is worth making only if the developing countries stop being regarded as welfare cases, if they are treated as—and at the same time can prove themselves to be, or gain recognition as—responsible partners.

Before the last meeting of the seven major industrialized countries at Venice, and after that meeting, I said on behalf of my country that although the world's economic problems were complex—as we are well aware—their solutions were complex as well. But they can be grasped and defined by the intellect. Words can precede action; in the beginning was the word, as the Good Book says.

I wonder, however, whether what is most lacking in order to apply those solutions is not the political will—a political will equally shared.

A progressive solution, or progressive solutions, depend on dogged international action. So we must talk about that. You will be doing that in the days to come, but it has not been done enough over the years, at any rate for the past five or six years; I shall come back to this later.

I think it will be of use in your discussions to suggest a number of lines of approach which I put forward on behalf of France; these will certainly duplicate the statements and proposals made by many others; but let no one claim to be original, that is not the problem.

My first suggested line of approach is this. The rich countries in particular, those whose trade surpluses leave them some room for manoeuvre, should stimulate world growth. I am thinking of countries whose successes and character I admire, such as Japan. I am thinking of Europe, of which my country is part, and of the European organizations which are increasingly taking shape. They should launch out more boldly into major growth-producing projects. To take an example which will seem somewhat trifling when set against the scope of the problem, but which nevertheless has its importance: as you know, France and the United Kingdom, after discussions going back several decades and perhaps centuries, have decided to set about building a Channel tunnel. For our two countries, and for neighbouring countries too, that will entail laying an infrastructure of roads, telecommunications and high-speed rail links—a whole range of new programmes which will contribute to the growth of this part of the world.

The European Community itself has proposals before it and has studied them, while research facilities pooled by enterprises are being developed between 18 European countries, with the public authorities making their own contribution. I am telling you about what I know of. There are many other examples you yourselves could mention. All that ought to rally and stimulate world growth. Let those who can do that, do it; those who can, do not always do so—to put it politely.

Secondly, an international monetary system should be instituted to stabilize rates of exchange more effectively and to set interest rates at a reasonable level.

I recall that France spoke about this—I believe it was the first to do so after the events of 1971—in 1982 at a summit of the industrialized countries held at Versailles. Since then, what progress has been made on those lines? What we wanted as long ago as 1982 was to go further and keep the principal currencies within reference zones. We are not there yet, but the direction followed at a number of meetings which have been held in the United States of America, France and elsewhere is the right one. The recent Venice agreements went in that direction in reaffirming the need for surveillance and co-ordination of the industrialized economies and emphasizing the serious threat which the budgetary and external deficits of the biggest countries represent not only for themselves but for every country on Earth. What can you hope to do if the foundations on which the growth plans of countries struggling against poverty are destroyed in the space of a few days; if those countries, already making heavy sacrifices, see their efforts wiped out merely because a particular rate of interest remains inaccessible and attracts capital to only one place while denying it to the least developed and even the developing countries, many of which are making remarkable efforts? They just cannot stay the course.

My third suggestion is that we should combat protectionism. We should open the rich countries' market more widely to the products of the less-rich countries. I am well aware that this is a kind of refrain that is chanted from all international rostrums. I sometimes find myself telling people, including my own people, that protectionism is something we all practise. We shall not succeed in reducing this mortal threat to international trade, and to development in particular, unless we lay all facts on the table. It is no use pointing to this one rather than to that. Comparisons can be made—I could make them from this rostrum but, out of discretion, shall refrain from doing so—to show that in reality protectionism in one place is more hypocritical, better concealed while in another it is more open but no less harsh. One could give a description of the whole situation. You may speak of Europe, you may speak of the United States of America, you may speak of Japan: in a word, you may speak of all those who think that protection should be reduced where they want to sell and that their own should be increased when they have to buy—a symptom of selfishness which is well known but which will not be bearable much longer. Negotiations have started in the so-called Uruguay Round. These are for the specific purpose of combating protectionism. But let us be clear about it: there is protectionism everywhere. We cannot keep this Conference confined solely to subjects of interest to you.

Agriculture is very topical today. It is true that this is primarily the concern of a number of big, much more modest developing countries which could be or already are producers of grain, for example, and which see foreign markets being closed to them behind high barriers. In the same way we find certain categories of farmers being subsidized, for domestic political reasons, in order to withstand world competition and distort prices. There are organizations in existence—and I am very proud to belong to the organization of the European Community—which have been founded on the need to expand their markets to 6, 10, 11 or 12 countries while protecting themselves to a certain extent against others. All the facts must be laid on the table. We cannot hope to speak of agriculture without also speaking of industry and without also speaking—even if that embarrasses a number of the countries represented here—of services, on the pretext of making faster progress in one or another field. When it is proposed, as it has been, that we should distance ourselves from the programme of work accepted by common consent at the Punta del Este meeting and recently reaffirmed at Venice, that merely delays the time when direct and indirect forms of protection will be dismantled. I ask you and I ask our partners: let us go faster. France is ready to do so and wants to do so. It is ready to search its own conscience, but obviously cannot embark on that course without an assurance that the channels of international trade will be open to it under the same conditions.

My fourth suggestion is that action should be taken to stabilize raw material prices. I know as you do that there is controversy on this issue as a result of the experience of the past 20 years. It is true that the problem arises. Can it be solved? Is it even reasonable to look for a solution? At all events I shall observe in your presence that, for example, the commodity agreements on coffee, cocoa and rubber affect a large number of the poorest countries. Let us continue to encourage them. It is desirable that we should succeed in attaining the objectives of the Integrated Programme for Commodities, while taking into account the evolution of economic realities. For example—this is just a suggestion—why should we not take, without further delay, the actions prescribed to diversify and upgrade production? I am inventing nothing. It has already been decided; it has already been proposed. The plans are perfect; but the follow-up is not happening. Why should we wait? I am thinking of the early use of the resources provided in the second window of the Common Fund for Commodities. These are the terms the specialists use; often one does not understand very much; they have to be translated a number of times; but with a little application they can eventually be understood. Indeed, we must add to the variety of languages represented here the coded languages of a few specialists who indulge in them in order to keep up the prestige of their speciality. Even in my own Council of Ministers I find acronyms and abbreviations being used, some of which, such as UN, are fairly well known whereas others attain a degree of refinement that leaves everyone afraid to admit that he has not understood anything.

I admired the Minister for Foreign Affairs of Italy, who at the last European summit, after two hours of extremely learned discussion—and that Minister for Foreign Affairs is one of the most cultured men I know—said "When it comes down to it, you have talked a lot, but I did not grasp even a stray word of what was said".

My fifth point: the debt. It seems to me a matter of common sense that the financial policies deriving from agreements between international agencies and States should not threaten development. To be able to invest—and they must invest—the countries of the South need net inflows of capital.

A debt is a debt. I speak for a creditor State: a debt is a debt. The indebted countries know how important it is to be trusted by others and what a moral and practical commitment a debt represents. Often the indebted country must turn in upon itself in order to see whether it cannot do more to overcome its bureaucracy and adapt itself more closely to modern conditions of production and trade. But let us avoid reading a lesson to some and not to others. We have already seen, in the history of banking, many lenders make adjustments in their claims as a simple precaution, in order not to be ruined along with their debtors, and I do not really believe that we have yet explored all the avenues leading in that direction.

We must be fair: the countries of the North, directly or through the international institutions, have already made a far from negligible effort of transfer, but the results remain disappointing.

At Venice, the latest international meeting of a general nature in which I have taken part, France brought out a proposal concerning the Structural Adjustment Facility of the International Monetary Fund. (I have inadvertently fallen into the verbiage I was just inveighing against, but you understand anyway. Generally speaking, when we say "adjust" we mean "increase".) Our proposal was to adjust structurally the resources of the International Monetary Fund, especially for the poorest countries which are most affected by the decline of raw materials. Well, the Fund should be able to approach a trebling in the next three years. Nine billion special drawing rights would then be earmarked for loans which might be at 0.5 per cent for 10 years, and in that context the commercial banks would be able to increase their loans to those countries, while the capital of the World Bank would itself be increased as soon as possible.

My sixth and last point: the South needs lasting, long-term aid. I was very satisfied to find that, at the Venice meeting I just mentioned, the French delegation managed to secure from its neighbours, the richest countries, an undertaking which till then had been avoided, even in international assemblies, with regard to the third world. At that meeting—a decisive meeting—the objective of increasing official development assistance to 0.7 per cent of gross national product was affirmed and put in writing, at my country's request, for the first time. What is needed now is to attain it within a reasonable time. Of the seven countries there present I was, I must admit, proud—modestly proud—to find that France was the first, considering that that effort had to be continued, not to waver, as might have been feared, in attaining the 0.7 per cent in a few years. In 1981 our level was slightly under 0.3 per cent, where countries like the United States or Japan still are; they have reached only a little over 0.2 per cent. For the first time they consented to recognize the objective already proclaimed by the international agencies.

Now we have ceased keeping silent, as though sitting in an international assembly and keeping silent did not mean making a commitment; and the commitment has been made. You know that for the least developed countries it is 0.15 per cent but, we made that commitment at a conference in Paris. Such an increase in official aid, and in multilateral aid in particular, represents, as you well know, practically a vital necessity.

I have, I must admit, some reservations about certain emergency aid policies when they tend to confuse what ought to be done in specific famine situations with what ought to be done as a matter of lasting policy. Naturally, when a person or a population is in danger, there is a duty to assist, and a number of countries unfailingly do so by making their agricultural surpluses available when necessary. But that kind of first aid should not be confused with long-term policy.

What is important is that producers should learn to produce better; to spread production more effectively over the year regardless of season; to diversify production; to learn the techniques for attaining those objectives and related techniques, such as those of irrigation in order to be able to seed the land: in short, to protect balances that would not withstand what would be a misunderstood charity and a harmful form of assistance.

Well, we shall have to talk again about all that. I am coming to the end of my statement, which has gone on long enough. I merely wish to say this: France is ready to receive, in 1990 for example, the conference to review the progress of the Substantial New Programme of Action for the Least Developed Countries.

I think—and I say this in my capacity as President of the French Republic—that it would be useful to participate in any meeting which brought together leaders of North and South, at the highest level, on such subjects. It has been too long since anyone has talked about that.

I do not claim to have supplied a miraculous solution here. There is no such solution to the problems you are going to study. But there are, or there can be, continuous will, clear analysis and a degree of daring in flouting conventions and bypassing interests often misunderstood by those who refuse to practice solidarity.

I am dreaming for a moment: if 1989 should be for the third world and the developing countries what 1789 was for my country and then for several others and for the Third Estate, that would be a sign that history had changed course. Liberty, equality, fraternity: this was the theme nearly two centuries ago in a famous declaration inspired by other new departures inherited from eighteenth century philosophy. Liberty, equality, fraternity: we are a long way from them if we look at the stage we have reached, and especially if, as I think, those words should contain, beyond the political rights and guarantees so often lacking, a cultural, social and economic reality without which they are meaningless. It will, of course, be a long process. That is another reason to start without further delay.

It is up to us to take the chances available to us. The greatness of success is often a matter of modesty of aims, but also a matter of perseverance. Let us realize that the most serious problems you have to deal with have not been mastered by human intelligence or by our political societies. If that has been understood, let us apply correctives. But let us go forward; and I must express to you the hope I place in the outcome of your efforts.

Statement made at the 202nd plenary meeting, 10 July 1987, by Mr. Mohammed Hosny MUBARAK, President of the Arab Republic of Egypt

It is a pleasure for me to accept your kind invitation to attend the seventh session of the Conference, and to participate in its work and deliberations. It is my hope that we can contribute towards the emergence of a common perception to get the world economy out of the present deadlock, which is inflicting much suffering on the peoples of the developing countries at a time when they have been hoping to reap the benefits of decolonization and eradication of exploitation and to enter the stage of comprehensive social and economic development.

It is a source of pride for us that this session of the Conference is being chaired by a loyal son of the great African continent; a continent, we are proud to say, to which we belong by culture, civilization and destiny. Under his stewardship, and thanks to his wide and long experience in international economic affairs, we have no doubt that the high expectations attached to this session can be fulfilled. Indeed, his presidency is but a continuation of the great job carried out by his predecessor, the President of the sixth session, our dear friend President Lazar Mojsov.

I have attended those two sessions of the Conference because I believe in the importance of concerted action by all member States to deal with the heavy problems facing the world economy. Moreover, my country has been in the forefront of the States which attach importance to this aspect of international activity, as demonstrated by our hosting of the first Conference on Economic Development in 1962, a Conference that paved the way for holding the first session of this Conference in 1964. In all fairness, no one can deny that UNCTAD did play a positive and concrete role in the management of the North-South dialogue, on the basis of the interrelation among international economic problems and of the interdependence of the economies of all countries. In view of the important responsibilities of UNCTAD and the direct impact on the economic condition of many States, we are endeavouring to strengthen this organization, increase its effectiveness and enhance its role. But we have to admit that, so far, all efforts made on the international level have failed to yield concrete results capable of redressing the structural imbalance of the world economy, halting the persistent deterioration of the situation in the developing countries, achieving greater justice and ensuring equal opportunities for all nations and peoples.

It is certain that you will consider, at this session, many questions that require a great deal of consultation and exchange of views and experiences in order to adopt co-ordinated and harmonious positions so that we can bring about the necessary changes before it is too late. That is why I propose to concentrate on two basic issues, which I believe deserve special attention and high priority, on account of their great influence in shaping the contemporary international situation. Although much has been said about those issues during the last few years, the situation, as far as they are concerned, still needs decisive action and a speedy remedy.

The first issue is the problem of debt, which has reached such serious proportions that it cannot be ignored, threatening grave consequences unless the international community, debtors and creditors alike, takes effective action.

There is no need to go into the details of this problem to demonstrate its quality and destructive implications. Suffice it to say that it has been worsening every day and has reached unbearable limits. Against a debt of $971 billion in 1985, the corresponding figure one year later was $1,005 billion. And while the debt volume of the developing countries amounted to 198 per cent of their total exports of commodities and services in 1985, he corresponding percentage was 210 a year later. The percentage is much worse for the African countries south of the Sahara where it reaches 270 per cent. These are figures that demonstrate the inherent dangers of the present situation.

The second issue I would like to raise before you is the question of the deteriorating terms of trade because of the shrinking share of the developing countries in world exports. While this share was 28 per cent in 1980, it shrank to 23 per cent by the end of 1985, at a time when commodity prices, including those of petroleum, resulted in over $100 billion of profits for the developed nations. This phenomenon has been accompanied by a decline in the real flow of development assistance from the rich industrialized nations and a rise in interest rates resulting in a reverse flow of financial resources from the developing to the developed countries in an amount exceeding $31 billion. The serious nature of this situation becomes apparent if account is taken of the fact that the developing countries have continued to absorb a substantial portion of the exports of the developed industrialized nations, accounting for 44 per cent of Japan's exports, 36 per cent of American exports, and 19 per cent of EEC exports. These exports created 10 million new job opportunities in the affluent countries, which accumulated surpluses from their trade with

the developing countries amounting to $100 billion from manufactured products alone in 1985.

In spite of these obvious facts and their serious significance, no adequate efforts have been made to change the situation. On the contrary, we observe two other facts which aggravate it. The first fact is that the developed countries did not act seriously to encourage exports from the developing countries. Rather, they applied restrictions and tariff barriers against such exports. Moreover, they imposed protectionist measures instead of providing incentives and facilitating access to their markets. All this resulted in a further deterioration of the international terms of trade and an increasingly dangerous situation. The second fact is that, so far, the North-South negotiations have not led to any tangible changes in the situation. This makes it imperative for UNCTAD to intensify its efforts in favour of growth and development and for the elimination of protectionist and discriminatory restrictions against the exports of the developing countries. We would even expect that the developing countries be given special and preferential treatment, particularly at this stage, to help them face the crushing economic crisis. Therefore, I invite the Conference at this session to adopt a set of recommendations which could be used as an input and a catalyst in multilateral trade negotiations.

The current situation imposes a specific task, namely, to act together for the sake of change in a spirit of solidarity and out of an awareness of the common destiny of the larger international family.

It is of no use to exchange accusations and recriminations. What is required is that we live up to the challenge. We should fully understand that this state of affairs, resulting from the collapse of the export earnings of the developing countries to their lowest level since the economic crisis of the 1930s, cannot go on forever.

Our response should rise to the occasion. We have to agree on a number of facts which are indispensable for our collective endeavour to face the situation. The point of departure, in my view, is that all parties should recognize that the world, East and West, North and South, is one united whole. No particular group of nations can continue to develop and prosper while other nations are enduring increasing economic pressures. If the situation remains as it is, it will become inevitable for developing countries to reduce their imports from the developed nations, for it will not be possible for the developing countries to maintain the same level of imports from the industrialized nations when net external transfers from the developing countries amounted to $31 billion in 1985. In other words, an economic collapse in any part of the world will engulf all nations, sparing none, even the powerful. No nation or group of nations can aspire to live as an independent island in total isolation.

Furthermore, it is our collective duty to realize that no remedy for this deteriorating situation is possible without recognizing that the objective of the world community should be to facilitate the continuation of the process of integrated development in the developing countries, a process involving interwoven political and economic dimensions. Failing this, our efforts will be in vain. We should realize that development cannot be sustained in a particular continent because its nations have been successful in mastering modern technology and reaping the fruits of scientific progress, while the development efforts of other continents are stifled by faulty international economic policies and adverse conditions, combined with natural disasters, drought and desertification. It is a foregone conclusion that the developing countries, whatever may be their good intentions and resolutions, cannot reconcile their external obligations resulting from their debt and deteriorating terms of trade on the one hand with their development requirements on the other. It would be fallacious to argue that this problem concerns the developing countries, who alone should bear the entire burden and responsibility. Theoretically, this assumption is wrong, and practically it can have negative consequences.

On the other hand, this situation is unacceptable at a time when arms expenditures are increasing at an incredible rate. Suffice it to recall—if recalling is useful—that the world spends $2 million on arms every minute; that out of every 100,000 people there are 556 armed soldiers against only 5 physicians. How is this possible? Moreover, the average expenditure per soldier is $20,000 against an average of $380 per annum for the education of a child. Finally, the volume of economic assistance from the developed to the developing countries barely exceeds 5 per cent of their arms expenditure.

Can such conditions be allowed to continue? Can stable and balanced growth of the world economy and equitable development of the developing countries take place under these circumstances?

Can the developing countries break the deadlock through self-reliance in the absence of a tangible improvement in the world economic environment?

What can self-reliance achieve in conditions dominated by fluctuating exchange rates, rising interest rates, increasing protectionist policies, increasing restrictions and barriers, and, finally, diminishing international liquidity? The situation is indeed serious. We must start by admitting that we are all in the same boat and if it is left to drift, none of us, whatever his might or power, will survive. We have to close ranks. We have to co-ordinate our action. We have to look at the situation, not in terms of profits and losses, but rather from the perspective of the success of mankind in facing the ultimate challenge: to be or not to be.

We have no alternative but to act together earnestly and sincerely to break out of the impasse and overcome the crisis.

If we fail to do so, we will have abdicated our responsibility in making history and creating progress. This generation, which has scored the greatest scientific achievements in human history, cannot let fall the torch or allow the march of civilization to come to an end. The challenge is immense, and the responsibility great, but the flame of hope will not die and the standard will not fall if we are resolved to continue united our march forward.

Statement made at the 203rd plenary meeting, 10 July 1987, by Mrs. Gro HARLEM BRUNDTLAND, Prime Minister of Norway and Chairman of the World Commission on Environment and Development

Let me start by congratulating you, Mr. President, upon your election. I do so with a very special knowledge of your personal qualifications after having worked closely with you on the World Commission on Environment and Development. Let me also express my sincere gratitude to the Secretary-General of UNCTAD for inviting me to address this assembly and to present the report of the World Commission, entitled *Our Common Future*.

I do so with a keen awareness that there is a very strong relationship between UNCTAD's present agenda and our report and call for action. The Commission is ending its work, but UNCTAD will continue to serve as a constant reminder of the weaknesses, the deficiencies and the injustices inherent in the world economic system. UNCTAD should remain a centre for global understanding and solidarity—a common conscience in particular with regard to the weakest and the poorest.

Today, we are becoming increasingly aware that development depends upon the environmental resource base, and that development also affects the environment. Many development trends have a devastating impact on environment. These interactions clearly stand out as the major concern on the international political agenda, on par only with the vital issues of disarmament and security. The interlinkages are close between these issues. In our report, we have also pointed at the non-military threats to peace and the military threats to the environment, topics that are highly relevant, also for the United Nations Conference on the Relationship between Disarmament and Development to be held later this year.

Few would have anticipated a quarter of a century ago that environment and development would be ascending to the very top of international priorities.

We remember the 1960s, when development optimism prevailed globally. Growth rates were high in all countries. There were success stories of a number of newly independent States who gained self-confidence as free nations, and made ambitious leaps to catch up economically with the industrialized countries.

At the end of that decade we saw the heavy impacts of the first generation of severe pollution problems. The Stockholm Conference on the Human Environment in 1972 was met with scepticism among many developing nations. What was the intention of the North? Was it yet another quest for luxury? Were we, in fact, trying to slow development in the interest of protecting exotic scenery and species? Was conservation to be achieved at the expense of economic and social development in developing countries? Many of the environmental concerns of the industrialized nations seemed far removed from the preoccupation which the majority of humanity had with basic living standards and, in some cases, with survival itself.

In the 1970s, we witnessed discussions on the question of actual limits to growth. In that period, North and South seemed to be fighting completely different battles. Frustrations about the inabilities of our institutions to deal effectively with the most crucial issues were growing. The conferences on water supply, food, women, human settlements, new and renewable energy sources, those involving people's rights to choose the size of their families, all offered hope of improved co-operation on major issues. Yet, the sense of frustration prevailed. The world was growing closer, but the gaps between us seemed to be widening.

It was against this kind of background that the General Assembly gave the Commission its ambitious task. And the call from the General Assembly was an urgent one. Our report back to the General Assembly *Our Common Future*, is a political document that covers the whole global political agenda and which carries the consensus signature of Commissioners from 21 countries, most of them from developing countries.

Our report contains a strong message of warning and of urgency. We found that present trends and policies cannot continue. They will destroy the resource base on which we all depend. There are presently few signs that we are about to win our battle against poverty, which continues to tie hundreds of millions to an existence irreconcilable with requirements of human dignity and solidarity. We also found that there could be no question of environment versus development. Environmental degradation and the unequal distribution of wealth and power are in reality different aspects of the same set of problems.

Our second, and equally important message, is one of hope and of optimism. We believe very strongly that changes are not only necessary, they are also possible. Humanity has the knowledge, technology, ingenuity, and resources. If we use them correctly, we can adjust the course of development so that it enhances the resource base rather than degrades it. Never before in human history have we had similar capacities. But for the necessary decisions to be made, we need a new vision, a new courage, and a stronger political will and determination. We need a new global ethic—a practical ethic—one that can transcend governments, non-governmental organizations, the scientific communities, financial institutions, trade unions, and human thinking and behaviour.

The overriding political concept of *Our Common Future* is the concept of sustainable development. It goes beyond sustainability in the environmental sense. It is a broad concept for social and economic progress which we believe can provide new insights and inspiration for global co-operation.

We define sustainable development in simple terms as paths of progress which meet the needs and aspirations of the present generation without compromising the ability of future generations to meet their needs. In a world ridden by poverty, the goal of sustainable development can only be pursued successfully under conditions created by a new era of economic growth. Our report clearly recognizes that there are natural limits which we cannot exceed without dire consequences. It thus sets requirements for the content of growth, but no limits to growth itself.

I shall not repeat here the painful list of environmental disasters and grim statistics which have alerted us to the grave crisis facing our planet. Suffice it to remind us that the atmosphere is a fragile and closed system, not a limitless garbage sink for by-poducts of industrialization. Global heating, and the threat of climatic change must be countered in a joint determined effort in view of the risks of rising sea-levels and ensuing severe impacts on food-production and on settlement patterns. Acidification, perceived as a disease of the rich countries, is also making its impact felt in many newly industrialized areas in the developing world. The loss of tropical rain forests, which continues at alarming rates, not only threatens vast numbers of living species with extinction, but affects the global climate as well. Over 11 million hectares of forest are destroyed yearly, which means forests the size of Denmark are lost every 12 weeks. Each year six million hectares of productive dryland are turned into worthless desert; this means that dryland the size of Switzerland is turned into desert every nine months. Soil erosion is regarded as problem No. 1 by FAO.

The Commission focused on poverty as one overriding issue—not least as a major cause and effect of environmental degradation. This is not to say that the developing world is the main source of present global pollution. Severe threats to the global environment come from excesses of affluence in many countries in the North which consume the earth's resources at rates that can lead to their rapid depletion. But international economic inequalities are a root cause of the environment-development stalemate. Clearly, the developing countries will have little opportunity to follow sustainable paths of progress unless external conditions allow them to develop their human and economic potential.

The environment and natural resources of developing countries, the very capital on which they depend, has become the ultimate victim in a world economy troubled by serious imbalances. That victim must now become instead an ally.

A new era of economic growth, which the Commission so strongly calls for, can create the capacity to solve environmental problems and to alleviate mass poverty. It must be based on international economic conditions that can enhance the resource base rather than degrade it. Trends have all too long been working against this kind of objective. Slow growth in the industrialized countries, the collapse of commodity prices, the debt crisis and the decline in financial flows have caused immense problems for developing countries. The pressures on budgets have forced many countries to axe environmental programmes. The pressure to export more in order to service debts and finance imports has led to over-exploitation of natural resources, that only in the short term can alleviate payment problems and current-account deficits.

To pursue a new era of economic growth we need a revival of the multilateral approach. We need to realize that it is in our own self-interest, in developed as well as developing countries, to chart a new course for action.

The industrialized world will have to accept an obligation to ensure that the international economy helps rather than hinders the possibilities for global sustainable development.

The present level of debt service in many countries, in particular in Latin America and Africa, is a serious obstacle to sustainable development itself. Urgent action is necessary to alleviate debt burdens in ways that represent a fairer sharing between debtors and lenders. The massive drain of resources from developing countries has increased the pressures on the environment and dramatically increased the numbers of urban and rural poor in desperate struggle for survival.

Let us be frank about this: much of the debt will not be paid back in any real sense. To maintain such a demand will entail political disturbances in many countries of such magnitude that they would be completely unacceptable. What is needed is new lending on concessional terms, new investments and economic and social reforms. Major debtors also need more loans on commercial terms. New policies must comprise debt relief, long-term rescheduling and conversion to softer terms.

But we all know that lending alone will not suffice. Aid must be expanded after years of decline or stagnation. Developing countries need significant increases in financial and other contributions. But even internationally agreed targets are far from being met. The 0.7 per cent GNP target, reiterated at the summit of the seven major Western industrialized countries, now must be followed by concrete commitments by all major donors. Additional resources must be forthcoming for projects that aim at sustainable development.

Aid and lending efforts are obviously essential. In the longer term, measures to secure increased income from commodity exports and the abolishment of protectionism in international trade are equally important. Real commodity prices have never been so low since the 1930s. A growing number of developing countries are making notable success in expanding into manufacture and high technology. But the basis for diversification must be provided by a fair income from the traditional and current exports. We need to consolidate and improve commodity agreements and establish new ones.

UNCTAD has been dealing with these issues for more than two decades. The negotiations which will take place in UNCTAD, in GATT, the World Bank and IMF, regional development banks, UNIDO, UNDP, WHO, and FAO, to mention some very key agencies, will be at the core of the process of change that the Commission calls for. Sustainable development must become a goal and a guideline for international cooperation. Sustainability criteria must be integrated into policies and programmes.

In the light of recent debate about our report, where some scepticism came out about the implications of what some conceived as new conditionality as an underlying element, it is necessary to underscore some important elements of the Commission's thinking.

It is more than understandable that it would give rise to considerable resentment if environmental assessments of international organizations and other aid agencies were conceived as imposing yet another condition or pretext for delaying or cutting aid flows. I em-

phasize very strongly, therefore, that the Commission was quite emphatic in coupling its demands for a higher quality of more environmentally sensitive aid with increased aid flows, and wider international economic exchange. Developing countries will evaluate their own needs and define their own priorities. External conditions must be designed to allow them to make choices that will keep options open for the future.

I have a clear impression that the World Bank is looking at its own structure and capacity to be able to take on this kind of challenge. It is a challenge that it should be given by the international community. What is needed is the bridging of the knowledge and experience at the grassroots level in many countries with the broader economic assessments of the institutions of the Bretton Woods system. The integration of sustainable development into the various organizations must come in response to hopes, expectations and priorities of the developing countries.

Policy adjustments are clearly needed that allow the developing countries to grow at rates far beyond the present ones. This will have consequences for many important sectors.

The impacts of agricultural policies are examples of the world-wide interlinkages. The Commission calls for a shift in global agricultural production patterns to where the demand is. The production of enough food to feed a doubled world population is within reach. The real problem is securing access to food for those who need it and ensuring environmentally sound agricultural practices in all countries, North and South.

Therefore, northern subsidy-driven agricultural production systems must be reconsidered. Much greater resources are needed to promote sustainable agriculture in the third world, using techniques adapted to local conditions. The income of the small subsistence farmer must be a common objective.

The fuelwood crisis is a reality with which hundreds of millions of people grapple. The only solution in many areas is to launch vast afforestation campaigns involving people more strongly in that process. Policies, including industrial and trade policies, must be adjusted to treat trees as a subsistence crop.

The role of women is indeed crucial. In many countries they are the ones who have to meet the daily needs for food and fuelwood. They are the ones who first of all suffer the consequences of agricultural conditions and forestry practices and who have to work even more hours to provide for their families.

An important priority is to slow population growth. It is difficult to see how a disastrously declining living standard and further deterioration of the environment can be averted if present trends continue. However, there is no short-cut to lower birth rates. Population strategies must deal with the underlying social and economic conditions of underdevelopment, and must be based on improved health service and education. In many countries little can be done until the status of women is raised, their economic contribution recognized and their literacy increased. Only in a world which is safer and which gives the poor more self-respect and hope for their own future, will they have real choices, including the choice of being able to limit the size of their families.

But let us not forget that the population issue is not one of numbers alone. It is also one of consumption patterns and lifestyles. We know only too well how some people—many of them in the North—use the world's resources at rates that cannot be sustained, while hundreds of millions consume far too little.

Energy is of vital importance. The Commission recognizes that developing nations will require far more energy, while the industrialized world must aim at stabilizing and reducing its consumption. Energy efficiency must now become the cutting edge of national strategies. Still energy efficiency is not a final solution. No present mix of energy sources is available that is dependable, safe and environmentally sound. Large-scale research in renewable energy and transfer of energy technology to developing countries is therefore imperative indeed.

The Commission advocates a full integration of environmental considerations in economic decision-making, at all levels, public and private. Environment and economics are not in contradiction but should be seen as mutually supportive allies. We must break away from our traditional sectoral approach. Sectoral organizations tend to pursue sectoral objectives, and to treat the impacts on other sectors as more or less irrelevant for their own. Sustainable development requires that such fragmentation be overcome.

There is no alternative but to attack the problems at their source. We must clearly recognize that the policies of sectoral ministries such as Ministries of Finance, Industry, Energy, Agriculture are the ones that determine the state of the environment and consequently our options for the future. Sustainable development objectives must be integrated into the goals of all branches of public administration as well as the legislative bodies.

A new deal in international co-operation is called for. The process of integration must also take place at the global level. International organizations must be made responsible and accountable for ensuring that their policies support sustainable patterns of development.

Our hope is that the United Nations and the Secretary-General will provide guidance and leadership and that the coming General Assembly will respond responsibly and constructively to *Our Common Future*.

The report from the World Commission on Environment and Development is, above all, a strong call for renewed international co-operation. At this juncture, where multilateral co-operation, particularly in the North-South field, is at a low ebb, we need countries or governments infused with a moral vocation which goes beyond pursuance of narrow-minded national interests. The time has come to restore the credibility and authority of the international institutions that we have ourselves created.

Mutual interests bind us all together, and nowhere is it more easily seen than with regard to poverty. The interrelationships between national actions and their international implications are becoming all the more obvious. The environment respects no boundaries. We cannot act as if it did.

I have little doubt that as we approach the twenty-first century, our perceptions of the future will increasingly cease to be defined essentially in national terms. The stability of human progress will depend on our realization that we are all neighbours on a fragile planet and that "our common future" depends upon how we subordinate our separateness to our oneness.

The conference will during the next three weeks deal with many of the crucial issues that the Commission has taken up. The setting is urgent. The development crisis is real. UNCTAD and the whole international community are at a cross-roads. Business as usual will not do. We must all join forces in a new partnership between North and South in the fight against poverty and for a sustainable development. At the seventh session the Conference could make a fresh start for invigorated multilateral co-operation. Following a decade and a half of stand-still and even decline in our ability jointly to address the real and crucial issues of our time—the time has now come to act together.

**Statement made at the 203rd plenary meeting, 10 July 1987, by Colonel Denis Sassou NGUESSO,
President of the People's Republic of the Congo, current Chairman of the Assembly of
Heads of State and Government of the Organization of African Unity***

It is right here, at Geneva, whose very name evokes peace, the will to peace, co-operation among nations, that, after long years of discussion, the negotiations were completed which had started on 24 March 1948 at Havana on the necessity of creating as part of the United Nations system a body responsible for regulating international trade.

For us, that time marked the beginning of a North-South dialogue, the point of departure of a great hope—permanent concertation on the urgency and

necessity of joint management of the future of humanity.

On this solemn occasion, I have been given the responsibility of speaking to you on behalf of the Organization of African Unity and of my own country. Africa believes in the virtues of international co-operation. That is why it places so much hope in meetings of this kind.

I have pleasure in congratulating the President of the Conference, whose brilliant election reflects our esteem for him and the prestige enjoyed by his country. I am also pleased to congratulate and to thank the Secretary-

---

* Initially issued as TD/L.294.

General of the United Nations, whose convictions concerning the virtues of international co-operation fortify us in these critical hours for multilateralism.

If there is an institution whose aims and purposes meet the concerns of States, large and small, rich and poor, it is certainly UNCTAD, which was established to seek a better and more effective system of international economic co-operation, whereby the division of the world into areas of poverty and plenty may be banished and prosperity achieved by all; and to find ways by which the human and material resources of the world may be harnessed for the abolition of poverty everywhere.[1]

The creation of UNCTAD thus already foreshadowed the new order of international relations and negotiations that was to dominate the discussions in the United Nations system in the mid-1970s.

And it is quite right that the analyses and claims which question the prevailing economic order should constantly refer to this institution.

The seventh session of the Conference is being held in a context of crisis of the international economy unprecedented since the Second World War.

This crisis, whose repercussions are particularly severe for the countries of the third world, is the main cause of the worsening of the problems of indebtedness, balance-of-payments deficits, widespread dependency on technology, unemployment and deterioration in living conditions that are being experienced by these countries.

How can one not be troubled, even to the point of dispair I might say, when one realizes that the developing countries, which, according to the estimates of experts, are burdened by a global debt of $1,045 trillion in 1986 and probably $1,085 trillion in 1987, find themselves condemned to austerity and privations for still another year without even glimpsing the end of the tunnel?

Such are the terms, in all their desolating magnitude, of the thorny problem of indebtedness of the third world, which is today compelled to repay more than it receives. These so-called net negative transfers have thus risen from $11 billion in 1984 to $26 billion in 1985 and to almost $29 billion in 1986.

The sudden collapse in oil prices, in combination with the decline in the value of the dollar, has aggravated the difficulties of many oil-producing and oil-exporting countries in Asia, Latin America and Africa.

The idea that this decline in oil prices would benefit oil-importing developing countries did not take into account the dependence of those countries on commodities, which, being the principal form of their resources, have, as is known, suffered a depression that in the opinion of many observers has reduced commodity prices to the level of the 1930s.

This situation is even more disturbing for the African continent, which has the largest number of States classified as LDCs which are struggling with enormous structural obstacles and are economically vulnerable.

Added to this picture is the difficult situation experienced by the countries and peoples of southern

Africa, the daily victims of the Pretoria régime's destabilizing initiatives.

Faced with this general situation, numerous countries of Asia, Latin America and Africa have, as you know, started rigorous corrective, rehabilitation and economic recovery programmes, which are often costly in social and political terms.

However, the efforts and sacrifices made are not producing the expected results owing to the persistence of a hostile international environment based on an unjust and unbalanced international division.

How could one be indifferent to such a tragic situation?

As the African Ministers of trade have said, "We are gravely concerned by the fact that each session of the United Nations Conference on Trade and Development produces consensus between developing and developed countries only in a very small number of areas".

Everyone agrees, however, that the creation of UNCTAD marked a new era in the formulation of a strategy of development for the countries of the third world.

The early 1970s were marked by important successes, as can be seen from the adoption of such resolutions as those concerning:

The Declaration and the Programme of Action on the Establishment of a New International Economic Order;

The Charter of Economic Rights and Duties of States;

The launching of continuous global negotiations on international economic co-operation and the major problems encountered in the fields of commodities, energy, trade, development, monetary systems and finance.

However, not only has the implementation of these resolutions encountered marked reluctance and the absence of firm commitments, but even the meagre results achieved are incessantly contested, as shown by the stoppage in the North-South dialogue, and the disappointing results and negative tendencies observed at the sixth session of the Conference.

It is here that I wish to express our sincere gratitude to the statesmen, the States and the international organizations that have given the efforts deployed by the countries of the third world their constant support and encouragement; their solidarity points to the ways of the future, that is, the interdependence of nations and continents.

It is not a matter of generosity, nor is it a simple moral question; what is at stake are the long-term interests of our States and our nations.

Is it still necessary to convince the States of the North of the imperative need for a new economic order and the urgency of working for its establishment?

The seventh session of the Conference can and must become a decisive, historic turning-point by veritably sounding the alarm for resumption of the process of bringing about a new international economic order. History teaches us that it is the times of crisis which must generate the most resolute decisions, for otherwise the decision-makers lose control of events. That is why

---

[1] *Proceedings of the United Nations Conference on Trade and Development*, vol. I, *Final Act and Report* (United Nations publication, Sales No. 64.II.B.11), Final Act, para. 1.

we place great hope in these meetings, which examine questions that are vital for a more humane future because they are questions of solidarity. And that is why we have followed with much attention, interest and hope the Venice Summit Meeting of the seven most industrialized countries of the Western world.

The conclusions of the work seem encouraging, from the point of view of the burning problems of the third world. I am referring to those concerning support for commodity prices, official aid to development and, lastly, protectionism.

It is a step to be welcomed and encouraged. But, as we have already stressed, what will really count are the concrete actions that follow. And it is by the yardstick of their practical attitude that we shall measure the determination of our partners in the North.

That is why it is worth repeating our proposals for a wholesome and stable economic environment. They are much the same as the concerns reflected in the agenda of the current session. In essence they are:

Questions relating to commodities;

Financing of development and mobilization of resources;

Action against protectionism;

The distressing problems of the LDCs.

I add the question of indebtedness and the vital problems of the environment.

The correct handling of these questions necessarily requires the immediate resumption of global negotiations in accordance with the formula accepted by practically the entire international community.

As regards the particularly critical situation of Africa, we greet and warmly welcome the initiatives taken by a number of countries and international organizations in favour of the effective implementation of Africa's Priority Programme for Economic Recovery 1986-1990, and of the United Nations Programme of Action for African Economic Recovery and Development 1986-1990.

At the same time we earnestly appeal to the entire international community truly to mobilize and convert into action the commitments it has undertaken by adopting this programme in a situation of economic crisis, which, need it be said, means urgency.

I take this occasion to reaffirm the close solidarity of Africa with the other countries and peoples of the third world faced with the challenges we have stressed.

The problems of Africa and the necessity of solving them have been emphasized in recent months because it is now a question of urgency, of acting in good time, if we wish to spare Africa the spectre of widespread poverty, of mendicity and of political obliteration. Everyone now agrees, and the facts prove it, that Africa is the most stricken continent and that it must be given appropriate emergency treatment. That is one of the objectives of the representations we have been making for a year now, and we are gratified by the understanding and sympathy of the other groups of States regarding these concerns, which, in substance, reflect those often evoked in UNCTAD, the non-aligned movement and the Group of 77.

What our countries expect from meetings like this is a consensus on practical measures to help rectify and stabilize the world economy by:

The renewal of growth;

The dismantling of protectionism;

A reform of the international monetary system that takes extensively into account the crucial development problems of the countries of the third world;

A policy of lasting stabilization of commodity prices at sufficiently remunerative levels;

A better approach to the question of the indebtedness of developing countries; and

Increased ODA.

It is important to stress that there is no peace without equity, and no real equity without the balanced and harmonious development of the international community.

In these times of widespread crisis, the major risk is that of self-absorption, of egoism, of the illusion of havens of prosperity. Peace and prosperity are incompatible with the idea of withdrawal to an island sanctuary.

We, peoples who are looking for a future, believe firmly in the virtues of multilateralism and interdependence, and we earnestly hope for fruitful international economic co-operation. That is why we open our doors to the North for co-development. Let us not justify those who dream of an inevitable rupture of the chain of solidarity that joins men beyond frontiers, beyond cultures and beyond levels of development.

**Summary of the statement made at the 203rd plenary meeting, 10 July 1987,
by His Eminence Cardinal Roger ETCHEGARAY, President of the Pontifical Commission
"Justice and Peace"**

1. Cardinal ETCHEGARAY said that in a world in crisis, in which the gap between rich and poor was even wider than in the past, he wished to bring to the Conference a message of hope, a hope fortified by the keener awareness today of the equal dignity and shared responsibility of all mankind. Countries should not be prompted to recognize their interdependence solely out of economic or political necessity; only an ethical sense of genuine co-responsibility would enable them to open up practicable paths to justice in the world and respect fully their joint commitments. In that spirit, the Conference could resolutely address the important issues on its agenda, including those concerning resources for development, debt servicing, commodities and inter-

national trade. It was clear that the valiant development efforts of the least developed countries would achieve nothing without the constant, full support of all.

2. The problem of the external debt of developing countries had just been examined, at his request, by the Pontifical Commission "Justice and Peace", which he hoped would inspire the various partners to agree to share equitably adjustment efforts and the necessary sacrifices, bearing in mind the priority needs of the most disadvantaged populations. The most affluent countries had a responsibility to accept a larger share of that effort.

3. It was UNCTAD's exacting task to re-examine the financial, monetary, production and trade mechanisms of the world economy, which proved unable to remedy the injustices of the past or to meet the urgent challenges of the present. At the same time, it was also an exalting task, for the human being was central to its concerns. There was a growing awareness that development could not be equated with economic growth alone or a mere copying of the models of the industrialized countries, but that developed and developing countries alike must seek the full development of the individual. Development was neither spontaneous nor instantaneous and could be neither decreed nor granted, but should be espoused, of their own free will, by the peoples themselves, patiently prepared for the time when they could control their own destinies. The seventh session of the Conference provided an opportunity not to be missed. Expectations ran too high and the needs were too pressing for States members of UNCTAD to fail to enter into fresh commitments and to demonstrate the political will to honour those commitments.

Statement made at the 204th plenary meeting, 13 July 1987, by Mr. TIAN JIYUN, Vice-Premier of the State Council of the People's Republic of China*

It is a great pleasure to have the opportunity to attend the seventh session of the United Nations Conference on Trade and Development. Permit me, on behalf of the Chinese Government and in my own name, to extend our warm congratulations upon the convocation of this session and to you, Mr. President, upon your election. The current session is being convened at a time when the North-South dialogue has long remained at a stalemate. It is expected that this session will play an important role in advancing that dialogue and improving North-South relations.

The world today is confronted with two major issues, which are closely related to each other. One is peace and the other is development. Peace is the prerequisite for development, while development in turn helps maintain peace and stability. Since the beginning of the 1980s, the world economy has seen slow growth. The inequitable international economic order has not been properly adjusted. The external economic environment of the developing countries has further deteriorated and their economic progress has been severely retarded. If this situation is allowed to continue, the poor countries will become poorer and the rich richer. The development of the third world has become a serious problem facing the peoples of the world, and its solution constitutes an inevitable historical task for the international community.

The post-war period witnessed the rise of the third world countries. They have formed an independent and significant force in the international political arena. Nevertheless, they are still suffering from the inequitable North-South economic relations, and remain underdeveloped economically. As interdependence among different economies has further intensified, the economic development of the third world has become increasingly important to the economic growth of the developed countries and the revitalization of the world economy as a whole. In order to sustain their economic growth, the developed countries have to turn to the developing countries for energy, raw materials, market and capital outlets, etc., whereas the developing countries, to accelerate their development, also need assistance from the developed countries in terms of capital, technologies and managerial skills. It is therefore necessary for both sides, the North and the South, to enhance their co-operation and make joint efforts to resolve the existing problems. This is an issue of great importance which has a direct bearing on their common and long-term interests.

However, recent years have seen little progress in the North-South dialogue. North-South economic relations have been evolving in a direction that is unfavourable to international co-operation. The proliferation of protectionism in the developed countries has increasingly restricted the export markets of the developing countries, thus reducing their share of total world exports. Weighed down by the heavy debt burden, the developing countries have experienced, for the first time since the war, a net financial outflow to the developed countries. The transfer of technology to the developing countries has encountered a series of obstacles. With such an unfavourable external environment the developing countries cannot but sharply reduce their imports and readjust their economies through retrenchment, resulting in a set-back to their economic development. Facts have shown that the developed countries, while developing their newly emerging and technology-intensive industries, have failed to readjust their traditional industries in favour of the developing countries. As a result, they have little to import from the developing countries and the developing countries, in turn, have been unable to increase their export earnings and therefore have no way to expand their imports from the developed countries. This state of affairs has not only seriously hindered the economic development of the South, but also stunted the economic growth of the North. Economic co-operation between the North and the South has become more and more difficult. There is

_____
* Initially issued as TD/L.304 and Corr.1.

no doubt that such international economic relations should not continue any longer.

The international community has the important task of reversing this situation and re-establishing North-South economic relations on an equitable, co-operative and mutually beneficial basis. To this end, the developed countries should adopt effective policies to expedite the structural readjustment of their domestic industries and to open their domestic markets to the developing countries. Meanwhile, they should also provide the developing countries with financial resources and transfer technologies on more preferential terms, creating favourable conditions for the structural readjustment of the developing countries. In co-ordinating macro-economic policies among themselves, the developed countries should take full account of the needs of the developing countries and create an external environment favourable to the latter's economic development. So long as the developed countries respond positively to the developing countries' readjustment, and establish their economic relations with those countries on a fair, co-operative and mutually beneficial basis, the developing countries will be able to achieve prosperity and offer a huge market for the capital, technologies and products of the developed countries. Such North-South mutually beneficial and dynamic economic relations will then pave the way for world economic development and prosperity in the next century.

The fundamental solution to the development problem of the third world lies in the establishment of a new international economic order that is fair and equitable. This requires our continuing and strenuous endeavours. We believe that, in considering such agenda items as international trade, commodities, resources for development and the problem of the LDCs, we should take account not only of the current pressing needs of the developing countries but also of their long-term development objectives. Only in this way can these problems be properly solved.

Protectionism in the developed countries has become the main obstacle to expanding North-South trade and has undeniably obstructed the development of manufacturing industries in the developing countries. China is opposed to protectionism and holds that international trade should be conducted on the basis of equality and mutual benefit. We support the developing countries' urgent demands for better trade terms for their commodities, manufactures and semi-manufactures and the expansion of their share of international markets. We believe that the developed countries should eliminate the protectionist measures aimed at the developing countries' exports, further improve the generalized system of preferences, reduce or remove tariff and non-tariff barriers, open their domestic markets to the developing countries and provide them with more preferential treatment. In this way, the manufacturing industries of the developing countries can be promoted and the South's share of world exports increased. UNCTAD should play a positive role in the new round of multilateral trade negotiations. It should urge the new round to give full consideration to the interests and demands of the developing countries and help bring about an improvement in the current international trading system so as to contribute to the development of the developing countries and the revitalization of the world economy.

The continuing decline in commodity prices has greatly reduced the export earnings of the developing countries and consequently impeded their development process. It has been caused not only by cyclical and structural factors, but also by the protectionism and oligopolistic practices of the developed countries. This problem requires comprehensive solutions. At the seventh session, the Conference should adopt effective measures to speed up the full implementation of the Integrated Programme for Commodities and urge those great Powers which have not yet done so to ratify the Agreement Establishing the Common Fund so as to put it into effect at an early date and help stabilize commodity prices. The international community, and in particular the developed countries, should assist the developing countries to strengthen their capacity to process primary products and help them to achieve diversification in the production, processing and exporting of commodities. In this way, the unfavourable position of the developing countries in world commodity trade can be changed.

The third world is now plagued by inadequate financial resources for development and a heavy debt burden. The developed countries should increase their capital flows to the developing countries in various ways and reach the ODA targets set by the United Nations as soon as possible. The developed economic Powers, especially those with a huge trade surplus, should make a greater contribution in this respect. We believe that creditors, international financial institutions and private banks ought to share responsibility for resolving the debt problem with the debtors. The solution of the debt problem should be based on acceleration of the economic development of the debtor countries. What is of paramount importance today is to alleviate their debt-servicing burden and improve their terms of trade so as to achieve a steady increase in their export earnings, thus establishing favourable conditions for the solution of the debt problem.

The problem of the LDCs calls for special concern on the part of the international community. The crucial need at present is fully and effectively to implement the Substantial New Programme of Action for the 1980s for the Least Developed Countries and the relevant resolutions adopted by the General Assembly and in UNCTAD. The Chinese Government and people, within their capabilities, have always shown sympathy for the destiny of the LDCs, actively supported their efforts to develop their national economies and provided them with assistance. At the current session the Conference should take the special needs and interests of these countries fully into consideration when discussing the other items on the agenda and taking action.

China is a socialist as well as a low-income developing country. In order to accelerate our modernization drive, we have since 1979 pursued a policy of reform, invigoration of the domestic economy and opening up to the outside world. In this connection, great progress has been made. For several years China's economy has achieved sustained and steady growth. This policy is a basic State policy which will remain unchanged for a long time. Our open policy is directed towards all parts of the world. With the further development of its economy and the continuing reform and opening up to the outside world, China will further expand, both in depth and in breadth, its economic co-operation with various countries in the fields of trade, technology and finance.

UNCTAD is an important forum for discussing and resolving problems in trade and development. For more than 20 years UNCTAD has done a great deal of work in resolving international trade and development problems. The tasks and functions entrusted to UNCTAD by the General Assembly should therefore not be weakened but should, rather, be enhanced. Together with other countries, the Chinese Government is willing to exert efforts to enable UNCTAD to play a greater role in international economic affairs and in the promotion of multilateral economic co-operation and development. It stands ready to make a further contribution to the revitalization of the world economy and the expansion of international trade.

I wish the seventh session of UNCTAD great success.

Statement made at the 207th plenary meeting, on 14 July 1987, by Mr. Robert G. MUGABE, Prime Minister of the Republic of Zimbabwe and Chairman of the Non-Aligned Movement

I consider myself greatly privileged that for the second time I have been invited to address this forum. Four years ago, when I first addressed this Conference in Belgrade, I was very much convinced, as I still am, that once nations of the world set themselves, determinedly, to overcome the constraints on human progress, whatever might be their cause, nothing could make them fail. Faith in the capacity of man to liberate himself from poverty and put himself on a sustainable course of progress, freedom and security, was indeed the very attribute which inspired the nations of the world meeting in this historic city in 1964 to inaugurate the first session of the Conference. As we meet here again today it is as if fate has brought us back where we began to review progress and assess our collective achievements against the background of the vision and aspirations which guided us during the first session. Now after 23 years we are back again travelling the same terrain, so we can regain our sense of direction and try to reassure ourselves that we were right at the beginning.

Mr. President, your country is immensely proud that one of its own citizens has been called upon to preside over this historic Conference. A large part of your professional career has been dedicated to the advancement of international economic co-operation. Through your dedication and that of your colleagues in the Secretariat this organization has achieved much that we can all be proud of. It is, therefore, fitting that a man who was part of the UNCTAD vision as its inception should preside over this Conference. As a development crusader, you are extraordinarily equipped to comprehend the complexities of the development process, and the capacity of UNCTAD to make a contribution to the cause of peace and development.

It is not usual in human history, that the torch of enlightenment is passed on to a select group of persons who possess a rare combination of intellect, statesmanship, foresight and full commitment to the progress of developing countries. Indeed, it has been given to only a very few amongst us to bear such responsibilities. It is in this context that we welcome Mr. Kenneth Dadzie to his first session of the Conference as Secretary-General. We regard his elevation to the stewardship of this organization as an honour paid to all developing countries and especially to Africa. The Secretary-General, like his able and illustrious predecessor Gamani Corea, is no stranger to the field of development. He is one of the few people to whom the eradication of poverty on a global scale, and the strengthening of the machinery for international economic co-operation, have been a special vocation.

UNCTAD is as much an embodiment of the political emancipation of the developing countries as it is an intellectual product of third world men and women of unparalleled excellence. Such individuals laid the first bricks and laboured throughout their lives to immortalize their vision and dreams of a world free of hunger, war and inequities. One of them was Manuel Pérez Guerrero, the second Secretary-General of UNCTAD, who passed away on 24 October 1985. That great son of the developing world and a native of Venezuela always saw possibilities for progress and advancement, no matter how minute. His greatest virtue was patience. He was a believer in the capacity of the developing countries to evolve beneficial economic co-operation among themselves, as an element of their quest for a new international economic order. To him, as to UNCTAD, those processes were and should indeed always be self-reinforcing.

Under Guerrero's inspiring leadership, the principle, among many others, of special and differential treatment of the developing countries and that of non-reciprocity, found expression in the ideals on which the generalized system of preferences is based. It is a worthy tribute to the man, his vision and his work that a permanent link exists between the Generalized System of Trade Preferences among Developing Countries and the Pérez Guerrero Trust Fund. For Pérez Guerrero was a visionary to whom every programme of action must have corresponding means to enable implementation and evaluation and to mobilize political support. It is, therefore, not surprising that today we remember him as the father of the Caracas Programme of Action, an effective instrument for collective self-reliance.

Few individuals can claim to be both theoreticians and institutional builders, as was Raúl Prebisch, who unfortunately died on 29 April 1986. In the context of the political environment, in part made possible by the

Movement of Non-Aligned-Countries, UNCTAD emerged as the idea of one man, Raúl Prebisch, who developed it, implemented it and laboured to perfect it. The UNCTAD concept, in his report at the first session of the Conference, provided a blueprint for this organization.

On behalf of the member States of the non-aligned movement, permit me to place on record our indebtedness to the true servants of the Charter of the United Nations, Raúl Prebisch and Manuel Pérez Guerrero. They were rare personalities. We extend and pledge ourselves to sustain their vision by preserving and defending this institution, bequeathed by them to the poor of the world. Through you, Mr. President, we convey our profound sense of loss to their bereaved families and to their Governments and countries.

We are gathered here, as representatives of nations, young and old, great and small, capitalist and socialist, poor and rich, to address the pervasive state of global economic malaise that has accentuated poverty and unemployment levels the world over. This is no ordinary Conference session. The mood of the Conference, therefore, should not be that of business as usual. We are in the throes of a severe economic crisis, the worst ever in the post-war era. It is also a crisis of confidence in ourselves to face this challenge through multilateral economic co-operation. Indeed, it is a crisis of our human civilization.

The theme of this Conference, "revitalizing multilateral co-operation for growth and development", underscores the fact that the world has become an integrated web of interlocking financial and trading transactions, one in which political and geographical barriers have been shattered by phenomenal advances in science and technology. Such is our world in which the fate of one nation has become inseparable from that of others. Inspired by this view of the current world, the Eighth Conference of Heads of State or Government of Non-Aligned Countries, held in 1985 at Harare under Zimbabwe's chairmanship, underscored the imperative of multilateralism as the only road towards our common survival. I am pleased to note that the same sentiment has also been echoed by the recent summits of Warsaw Treaty member States and the OECD. This Conference is indeed an opportunity for the nations of the world to assume the obligations imposed on all by the integration of the world economy, albeit on unequal terms.

The countries of the non-aligned movement have for a long time been warning that the post-war Bretton Woods institutions are not fully equipped to cope with economic problems in a world in which imperialism and colonialism have been defeated. We have been calling for multilateral institutions to be transformed into effective instruments for achieving a new international economic order. The present economic difficulties only serve to underline the urgency of this call.

The tight global liquidity situation has choked the development process in the developing countries, and the existing multilateral financial institutions have become net recipients of financial flows from the less developed countries, including crisis-ridden sub-Saharan Africa, instead of taking an anti-cyclical position. In the area of international trade, GATT is at its weakest point while trade disputes are being settled out of it. The volume of world trade conducted under its discipline is decreasing. GATT is undoubtedly structurally constrained to be able to deal with comprehensive aspects of trade. However, an immediate application of standstill and roll-back provisions of the Punta del Este Declaration might just improve the prospects for global economic recovery.

Few scourges in human history can claim so many victims as today's debt crisis. It is largely responsible for the reversal of the development course of many nations. Although on the surface it appears to be a monetary phenomenon, it is in fact essentially a crisis of our institutions' inability to cope with the consequences of an interdependent world economic system. We have to recognize the fact that the dynamics of global economic growth and structural adjustment are a result of interactions in the spheres of monetary and trading relations.

A few years ago, the major monetary problems were inflation and the recycling of excess liquidity. The latter burden was relegated to private financial institutions, which efficiently transformed that liquidity into debt. At that time it was argued that the level of government intervention in the economy and budgetary deficits in many a country were responsible for the inflationary spiral. On the basis of that analysis governments retrenched expenditures, deregulated and privatized some of their economic sectors. According to conventional wisdom these, then, were the pre-conditions for non-inflationary growth.

With unquestioning faith in the miracles of market forces, developed countries aggressively pursued restrictive monetary policies at home and abroad, which combined to kill inflation and deflate the world economy. That ushered the era of unprecedented high interest rates, which in turn provoked disorderly movements of capital and exchange rate instabilities. These developments, instead of promoting structural adjustment and growth of output, created economic uncertainty, exacerbated external imbalances which in turn heightened protectionism, increased trade tensions and curtailed the volume of world trade—particularly that conducted under multilaterally agreed disciplines.

The changed economic conditions were that debt had to be repaid at higher interest rates at a time when the capacity for servicing it had been severely curtailed. Resources for debt servicing could only come from fresh loans, trade, concessionary and other intergovernmental flows. The private sector was the first to bolt out of the liquidity-creating business when the risks of insolvency increased. Meanwhile, the collapse in commodity prices and restricted market access in the developed economies aggravated the balance-of-payments situation of many developing countries.

As the deflation continued, the external economic environment increasingly became a negative factor in the development process. Nothing was in place to counteract the configuration of procyclical national macroeconomic policies. Not even the World Bank or IMF could be allowed to counteract those tendencies.

From this account, the debt crisis emerges as nothing but an element of a multifaceted development crisis from which no developing country is immune. It mirrors a breakdown in the machinery of multilateral economic co-operation and the success of developed countries in creating and cushioning themselves against a negative external environment.

Efforts to deal with this crisis have hitherto been piecemeal. Almost every initiative from the North has been designed to make debt collectable, even if it meant, in the words of a recent UNICEF report, sacrificing our children on the altar of structural adjustment. Africa's elder statesman, Mwalimu Julius Nyerere of the United Republic of Tanzania, has asked: "Shall we starve our children in order to pay the debt?" I pray that no one here would want to see the Conference drifting in that tragic direction.

Those whose policies and practices have led to this crisis do not want to alleviate it, but insist instead that the plight of the developing countries is a result of suppressed market forces. The LDCs, and in particular those on the African continent, have submitted to that view, but with no positive results whatever. Instead, the flow of concessionary resources to these countries has stagnated at a time when they are undertaking massive structural adjustment programmes. More commodities are being produced, but for which rock bottom prices are being paid. The LDCs are also being urged to liberalize their trade and exchange rate régimes, again at the time when market access is being blocked and their external payments situation cannot finance essential imports. Whatever little current-account surplus they may have generated to finance debt was achieved at the detriment of their development needs. The cumulative effect of devaluation, mounting debt, declining commodity prices and stagnant concessionary flows has reversed the direction of capital inflows in favour of developed countries and IMF and the World Bank.

Unless global economic growth is accelerated, the present economic downturn, in both the North and the South, will continue unabated. The North deceives itself if it thinks that it will be immune from the negative impulses from a bankrupt South. Poverty and unemployment have now crossed the North-South divide. Only growth and development-oriented policies could alter the course. Indeed, the measurement of success for this Conference would be the extent to which the shared perception of the global economic malaise could speedily be translated into policies and measures designed to correct anomalies in the different sectors of economic activities, whose sum total constitute the world economy.

Developed countries have a special responsibility to contribute towards the stabilization of the external economic environment. Time has come for them to appreciate that their privileged status in the world community can no longer prevent the redistribution of income by resisting structural adjustment through protectionism. Such policies have already done much harm to the prospects of the global economy. Time has come for the North to play fair with us of the South. So far, it has been the South that has borne all the costs of the recurrent crisis in the capitalist-dominated world economy. However, the South's resilience has also now been broken, so much so that even its environmental resource base has never before been so precarious. We need not

have waited for the enlightening Brundtland Commission report, *Our Common Future*, to know that, "a world in which poverty is endemic will always be prone to ecological and other catastrophes".

Since its inception, UNCTAD has been concerned with the problems of commodity producing countries. It is ironical, at this juncture that, after the conception of an integrated framework for protecting the incomes of producer countries, and after agreeing on financial modalities and mechanisms for stabilizing commodity prices, commodity prices should be at record low levels since the Great Depression. I would here pause to congratulate and compliment the Soviet Union for lending its support and signature to the Common Fund. I hope that example can be followed by many so that the Common Fund becomes a reality. I wish also in this regard to place on record our deep appreciation for the clear proposals for action, painstakingly worked out by the Group of 77 under the able chairmanship of the Minister of Trade of the Republic of Cuba.

The proposals, now before this Conference, certainly point the way and direction for the world economy to move forward. Surprisingly, in the face of great adversity, the Group of 77 was able to frame moderate and realistic suggestions in the spirit of trying to rekindle the North-South dialogue. The non-aligned movement lends its support to this noble initiative. Indeed, the Group of 77 and the non-aligned have tried to offer the world an alternative to a world economic situation characterized by unemployment, poverty, tension and division. What is now urgently needed is a world consensus towards the revitalization of development, growth and international trade through multilateral co-operation.

In 1964, the nations of the world, inspired by the purposes and principles of the Charter of the United Nations, adopted General Assembly resolution 1995 (XIX). This was a monumental decision, which gave institutional content to the desires of nations to overcome poverty through international co-operation. Thus, UNCTAD was born to be an instrument for promoting international trade, with a view especially to accelerating economic development, trade between countries at different stages of development and also between developing countries with different economic systems. It was also hoped that UNCTAD would formulate principles and policies on international trade and related problems of development, make proposals for putting the said principles and policies into effect, and initiate action in the United Nations forum for the negotiation and adoption of multilateral legal instruments in the field of international trade.

That was the UNCTAD of the founders: an UNCTAD born of the conviction that principles of economic liberalism were in real life thwarted by structural market failures. For this reason, appropriate political institutions and creative policies had to be formulated so as to make the development process a creative and deliberate process for the advancement of human progress and the elimination of poverty the world over. The theology that trade aspects of development could be relegated to tariff cutting exercises is hollow. In the real world, there is no economic homogeneity between North and South, for there are structural differences and there is also an entrenched dependency of the South on the economic fortunes of the North, which in turn feeds on the sweat, toil and sacrifices of the South. Hence, non-discrimination, non-reciprocity, special and differential treatment of all developing countries are not incidental to UNCTAD, but are, in fact, at the core of this organization's philosophy and future development.

In a nutshell, UNCTAD's mandate was to correct the asymmetries in international economic relations between North and South. It was perceived then, as now, that the Bretton Woods institutions were obsolete in an era when imperialism, occupation and colonialism had become things of the past. From UNCTAD, policies and legal instruments have been negotiated that have sought to redistribute global incomes in favour of the poor of the South. The UNCTAD of today, and that of tomorrow, must continue to be a purveyor of new ideas as well as a defender and promoter of the development process as seen by the developing countries themselves. That is the challenge before the secretariat and, to that end, it can count on the full support of the non-aligned movement and other developing countries.

As a universal forum, UNCTAD should aim at harnessing the energies of all the economic systems to the service of the development aspirations of the developing countries, without imposing any form of social and/or economic system on its diverse members. Such domestic policies should remain what they are, although they should not be pursued at the expense of the economic welfare of other countries. UNCTAD-should, therefore, keep under surveillance the impact of trade and monetary policies that are likely to be inimical to the development prospects of the developing countries.

UNCTAD should be true to its mandate to promote a Code of Conduct on the Transfer of Technology, to evolve a blueprint for a future comprehensive international trading system, to promote a framework for making commodity production remunerative, to redress unequal exchanges in international trade and propose mechanisms to stop the haemorrhage of financial resources from developing countries.

We would be deluding ourselves if we believed that faith in economic liberalism alone will restore economic growth and promote structural adjustment in the North. For, in the real world, there are numerous tactics with which economic liberalism can be rendered ineffectual by the developed countries. They can also distort prices in agricultural markets and call such distortions income support programmes. They can physically limit imports from developing countries and simply call that exercise voluntary export restraint arrangements. In special situations where an entire sector just cannot survive the test of the market, then all of it can be excluded from GATT. In that particular situation, economic liberalism ceases to be a universal ideology and becomes a restricted legal concept which excludes agriculture and textiles from agreed disciplines.

I would like to conclude by observing that the biggest irony of our time, or a tragedy perhaps, is that our proud civilization, with such unparalleled scientific and technological progress, should have also produced so much poverty, deprivation and misery for so large a part of humanity; should have caused so much concern about world peace and security and, indeed, so much anxiety about the very survival and future of man himself. What future has this race when, despite so much material and intellectual resources, about 280,000 children die every week from malnutrition and preventable diseases around the world? What are we to make of a generation which, even though it fully understands the devastating capacity of the nuclear bomb to bring about the extinction of humanity and its civilization, yet continues to develop that destructive capacity even much further? Our sense of morality and human values has certainly lost its proper orientation in relation to the values of our civilization. How else can one explain the raging nuclear arms squandering of billions of dollars in the face of growing poverty? It demonstrates an uncaring attitude to the problems and needs of the weak and the poor which should be the most urgent concerns of our time. It also graphically underlines for us that the struggle for peace is inseparable from that of socio-economic development.

Once again, may I say that I feel highly honoured to have had this opportunity to put across the views of the non-aligned countries, as I perceive them.

Statement made at the 212th plenary meeting, 27 July 1987, by His Royal Highness Crown Prince HASSAN BIN TALAL of the Hashemite Kingdom of Jordan

I welcome the opportunity to address this Conference. I view the invitation extended to me by the Secretary-General of UNCTAD as a recognition of the importance of the region I come from, and as an honour to my country.

This session derives its importance from a host of factors, paramount among which is the fact that the world economy is now set on a crucial path. It is beset by major problems which threaten its continuity and fundamental security. The decline in international commodity prices, the unbearable but undiminishing burden

of international debts, the isolationist trends in international trade and the disruptions in international monetary flows are the major manifestations of the serious situation of the world economic order.

This session is also important because it provides a valuable opportunity to make progress towards a consensus on the responses to the major economic threats. A reorientation of global negotiations is urgently needed. The hope that the world community can reach resolute decisions should be nurtured by our commitment to keep international institutions, such as

UNCTAD, operating at the most effective level. It is my sincere hope that despite the well-known difficulties, the Conference will succeed in arriving at a package of rational solutions which will enable UNCTAD to contribute effectively to world economic reform.

The same ingenuity that the world community demonstrated decades ago at Bretton Woods is needed now to rise to contemporary challenges. Institutions as well as attitudes must evolve with the times just as international responses to common problems must keep pace with developments.

Of late, however, certain unhealthy developments have begun to mar international co-operation. The rise of myopic and self-centred interests are dampening the international spirit of co-operation. They are also adversely affecting the international and interregional agencies, some of which are now labelled "pro-South" and others "pro-North". These agencies are judged and supported or denied support accordingly. If we believe that international co-operation cannot survive without its institutional vehicles, then we must act decisively in support of established institutions. To reinvigorate the international economic system, indolent or cosmetic solutions bear no serious promise. They mean, at best, postponing matters for a more painful adjustment later.

I come from a relatively small country which has succeeded, despite its scarce resources and a conflict-torn region, in achieving sustainable growth. We have benefited a great deal from our deep affinity with international institutions. Our conduct has been internationally acknowledged: we have paid our dues, respected agreed norms and utilized whatever funds were made available to us in the most rewarding ventures. We take a strong stand on maintaining the international system in a fully operative condition.

I would like to use this forum to propose the establishment of a mixed commission composed of eminent persons of international repute to reassess the performance of the international economic system in the light of the challenges we all face. The terms of reference for such a commission or working group would be to prepare a comprehensive executive report on the major economic issues which hamper international co-operation and to suggest formulae and alternative approaches which can be adopted by the respective authorities in order to rehabilitate the world economic order and its institutions. I am sure that the report of the Secretary-General of UNCTAD, and those produced by other competent international and regional bodies, will be of fundamental value to this undertaking.

The proposed impartial group would be guided in its work by a number of axioms: first, there is a need for common action derived from the latent faith in the unity of the world bound together by common problems. Secondly, a healthy world economic order cannot survive on charity or unidirectional action: it must embody fruitful exchange on the basis of mutual interest. Thirdly, existing international institutions must be enabled to discharge their duties within their areas of competence in the most conducive environment, and their performance should be judged on merit and scientific criteria. Fourthly, there must be recognition of the

most urgent problems to resolve in order to restore our faith and confidence in a truly international community of States. Fifthly, the proposed group must be guided by the seriousness of its mission. There are inherent conflicts which need to be resolved, and a built-in system of sacrifice and redistribution must be formed. Should its mission be successful, the group would have significantly assisted the world community in its efforts to replace harmful inertia by synergetic action.

The deliberations which have been taking place at the seventh session of the Conference have been on the whole healthy and frank. Yet I cannot help detecting a certain negative tone on the part of some of the representatives in blaming developing countries, especially those in debt, for failing to take the necessary steps to remedy their ailing economies. It is said that developing countries are asking for concessionary assistance which will not solve their internal economic and social problems. I beg to disagree with this line of argument. To illustrate my position, I shall point out four major dilemmas which face the developing world in various degrees of intensity.

First, many developing countries have inherited, through a historically cumulative process, socio-economic problems that are difficult to resolve. At first they were encouraged to mount ambitious resource-related development efforts based on economies of scale and comparative advantage. Once these projects were implemented, their costs were found to be exhorbitant in terms of both allocation preferences and international indebtedness. These projects are now operating below capacity at a debilitating cost and selling at internationally depressed prices. The whole growth momentum in these countries was weighted on these ailing projects. Even if one allows room for bad management and exaggerated capital expenditure, the basic problem still remains. The dilemma which these countries face has negative implications for their growth potential. If they opt to close down these industries, they still have to find ways and means of grappling with the consequences of closure, i.e. the repayment of debt and rising unemployment. Should they maintain production, they have to sustain losses with financial effects similar to those of closure.

Most of the resource-based industries are export oriented. As long as international prices are low and demand, particularly in developed countries, is below potential supply, the problem threatens to grow to a catastrophic magnitude both in economic as well as in social and political terms.

Secondly, the world is currently undergoing a broad recharting of the division of labour map as a result of the technological strides taken by the industrialized countries. Thanks to advances in the fields of information, computers, the space industry and aeronautics, biotechnology and others, the developed countries have turned to basically brain- and skill-intensive and energy-saving undertakings. Moreover, they have become increasingly self-sufficient in food production, to the extent that some are crowding out developing countries from the international market. In addition, the population growth in the North is stagnant and the average age is increasing while, in the South, the contrary is happening. None of these trends is helpful in promoting co-operation between developed and developing countries.

Additionally, there is competition among technology producers which may result in the domination of a few mega-transnationals in the technology trade. At the same time, older and obsolete industries are gradually being transferred to other lands which are either highly populated with an existing market, or to energy-intensive countries where costs can be controlled. This naturally leaves many medium-sized and small countries on the periphery of the international economy. What can these countries do? How can they adjust to external pressures over which they have no control whatsoever?

Thirdly, there are more than 40 regional armed conflicts going on in the world. Although there is participation by proxy of others, the conflicts are being waged essentially among developing countries. They have a protracted nature and their imminent resolution is not foreseen. Their cost is immense and their toll is not confined to the parties directly engaged in the conflict. The negative impact of these wars is embodied in the wasted lives, the resources which are committed and the reallocation of necessary funds away from basic needs.

The level of armament can hardly be described as traditional. It is difficult to believe that these wars have not caused a reverse flow of funds from the developing to the developed world. Under the guise of strategic defence interests, the leading countries of the world have been directly or indirectly involved. If and when the combatants decide to turn their swords into ploughshares, the whole world community must share in the reconstruction efforts. What efforts must be pledged to end wars and fight the ill-effects of their aftermath?

Fourthly, despite technological breakthroughs and signs of plenty, poverty and famine haunt many impoverished parts of the world. Such poverty is not voluntary as some would say; it is not only misfortune but also an abhorrent lack of infrastructure. The plight of sub-Saharan Africa is still fresh in the memory. The existence of poverty and what it does to our children is a poignant reminder of the gap that separates rich from poor.

The solutions which are offered to cope with the overall situation are far from adequate. They are mostly *ad hoc*, unstructered efforts which use philanthropy alone as the driving force. What is needed is a complete development package which would enable the least developed countries to tap their resources and set themselves on a self-sustainable growth path. To demonstrate the validity of such an argument, I would remind you that the drought-stricken countries had bumper crops in 1986 and are expected to have the same again in 1987. Yet famine persists. The affected countries need storage and transportation facilities. It is disheartening to see plenty coexist with penury while millions of our fellow human beings suffer.

We cannot address the problems of these countries simply by calling on them to engage in policies of adjustment. While the technology-rich countries are engaged in dealing with problems emanating from the need to cope with rapid change, poor countries of the world are still fully engrossed in securing their basic needs. To imagine that the poor of the world can resolve their poverty by balanced budgets, floating interest rates and devalued currencies would be an exercise in futility. The poor are not asking for charity. They have sufficient resources which, once developed, will be a major addition to total world wealth. How fast can we move forward on this issue before the problem of poverty reaches unwieldy magnitudes?

It is clear that the chronic difficulties which developing countries face are global and they call for global action. Yet, looking into the near future, I must mention two dimensions that have received insufficient attention due to time constraints. I hope that they will occupy prominent positions on the agenda of future sessions of the Conference.

The first relates to the exchange of human capital. It is expected that international expertise will be the primary item of exchange in the international market. Advanced countries may therefore engage in selective recruitment from the developing countries, thus aggravating the brain-drain even more. Moreover, the decline in population in the advanced economies may create a demand for semi-skilled labour. The lure of foreign exchange remittances may put labour-exporting countries into direct competition.

A decade ago, in this same hall, I submitted to the sixty-third session of the International Labour Conference the idea of the creation of the International Labour Compensatory Facility (ILCF) to help labour-exporting countries to absorb their excess labour in gainful ventures at home. This idea helped to pave the way to the adoption of General Assembly resolution 32/192 of 19 December 1977 asking the Secretary-General of the United Nations to commission a full study of human resource flows. The Secretary-General instructed UNCTAD to carry out the study. The ILCF was the theme of many studies sponsored by UNCTAD, ILO and other regional organizations, but unfortunately, it was never implemented. I feel that the ILCF should be given a fresh chance as a rationale for the continuation of the international resource flows on more equitable grounds. Human resources should occupy the eminent position they deserve, particularly within UNCTAD circles.

My second point relates to technology transfers. It should always be remembered that technology offers a major opportunity for advancement in developing countries provided it is adopted and harnessed to reach new growth frontiers, and not merely for the expansion of trade in new technological consumer goods. What makes new technology of special importance is its profound effect on the direction of world trade, the division of labour and foreign exchange distribution. A decade ago pressure was applied to recycle "petro-dollars". A similar assertive demand must now be made to redistribute what I may call "techno-dollars".

May I, at this juncture commend most warmly the decision of the Government of Japan to recycle substantial funds. Let us hope that other industrialized countries will follow this example.

Clearly, technology-related trade will continue to take the lion's share of world financial resources. It would, therefore, be helpful to establish an International

Technology Transfer Facility (ITTF) whose resources would be tapped by those developing countries which seek to develop or purchase tech-products and services for their development and for the enhancement of their absorptive capacity. The facility may be created through a designation plan of special drawing rights specifically for financing technology transfers. I am sure that this proposal will meet the "mutual benefit" criterion, especially in view of the subsidies allotted by advanced countries to the promotion of their exports.

The problems which are faced by the developing countries are by no means homogeneous: they vary in nature and intensity. Yet they have common attributes which call for common action. The vicious circles, some of which are induced rather than inherent, must be broken. Adjustment should not continue to be a precondition for development, especially if the socio-economic trade-off is very steep. The same logic applies to choices between armament and development, repayment of debt and seed money to meet urgent development. The world seems to suffer from a lack of a financial breathing space which would enable countries to move ahead.

The world at large has adequate assets from which it can draw to satisfy its needs and some of its aspirations. I specifically refer to the advancements in technology and the growing willingness by technology owners to exchange it. The quantum jump in food production and a greater awareness of environmental threats are encouraging signs. The recent serious attempts at resolving regional disputes can all be cited as an encouraging start towards ending the destruction of life and wealth, and setting the world on a new path leading to peace and prosperity.

In conclusion, we must recognize the emergence of new trends which should capture our immediate attention. The unbalanced population growth in the world is creating new realities in countries with zero and with high-population growth. Technological achievements are basically confined to the rich countries and an overwhelming majority of the potential users live in the others.

The exchange of both hardware and software may be a unidirectional pattern. All these developments can either take a healthy course and thus encourage international economic co-operation, or they may lead to extreme mercantilistic practices. The choice is ours and it must be made now if we are to have a better future. Let us resolve to join global resources to global willingness to struggle together for mutual benefit and common prosperity.

B. COUNTRIES

Summary of the statement made at the 216th plenary meeting, 29 July 1987, by Mr. Mohammad Khan JALALLAR, Minister of Commerce of Afghanistan

1. Mr. JALALLAR said that the developing and least developed countries had suffered a great deal from the arbitrary economic policies of the developed market-economy countries, and particularly from their restrictive business practices, protectionism, non-tariff measures and high interest rates, and must therefore strengthen their co-operation in the economic and trade fields to escape those uncertainties and foster their individual and collective self-reliance. UNCTAD could promote that process through its work on trade and development problems, which were inseparable from monetary and financial issues. The developed countries, for their part, should try to fulfil their ODA commitments to the LDCs more scrupulously and agree to the establishment of· a link between development finance and special drawing rights.

2. Despite their obligations under the International Development Strategy for the Third United Nations Development Decade and the Charter of Economic Rights and Duties of States, some developed market-economy States were continuing to use the GSP as an instrument of political and economic coercion against certain countries, including Afghanistan. Nevertheless, in the context of trade and economic relations among countries with different social and economic systems, Afghanistan had maintained mutually advantageous relationships with the USSR, the socialist States of Eastern Europe and other countries. A radical restructuring of international markets was required in view of the deterioration in the terms of trade for developing countries, commodity price instability and market access difficulties; in that respect, the initiatives taken by UNCTAD were to be welcomed, particularly the development of the Integrated Programme for Commodities and the establishment of the Common Fund. The principle of non-reciprocal exemption and the other special concessions granted by the international community to the LDCs should always be borne in mind in the implementation of various plans and programmes relating to commodities. In respect of market access, too much emphasis had been placed on liberalization measures rather than on positive arrangements, such as sharing a percentage of the profits in protected markets. Short-term and long-term agreements and protocols between States could also be concluded, and would be of particular interest to land-locked and island developing countries. He expressed concern about the activities of large TNCs which, through their arbitrary manipulation of the market, often infringed the legitimate and sovereign rights of States and distorted relations between countries.

3. Referring to the debt problem that was having an increasing impact on the developing countries, he pointed out that, first of all, the implementation of projects using foreign capital could exert serious pressure on the balances of payments, and particularly those of the LDCs, well before positive effects made themselves felt through the economy in general. Secondly, the most important problem was not debt servicing in itself, but rather the proportion of foreign currency receipts it swallowed up in developing debtor countries. Thirdly, it was clear that the developing countries could service their debts only if their export products had free access to world markets. Failure by the creditor countries to bear those three points in mind would result in a steadily increasing outflow of the real resources of the developing countries in the direction of the developed countries, and their balances of payments would deteriorate steadily. For that reason, it would be well for the debtor countries and creditor countries to meet under UNCTAD auspices and embark on a constructive dialogue on the debt crisis and possibly consider the establishment of a debt relief fund for the most severely affected countries.

4. The problems of the land-locked developing countries were not confined to administrative and technical matters involved in co-operating with the transit countries; the basic question was that of their right, which had long been recognized but was not yet respected in practice, to free access to the sea, as an essential condition for their economic and social development. It was most regrettable that in recent years the international community had lost interest in the problems of land-locked countries and that the Special Fund for Land-locked Developing Countries had been arbitrarily done away with.

5. Under the provisions and principles of the Substantial New Programme of Action for the 1980s for the Least Developed Countries and the Havana Declaration, the Government of Afghanistan had embarked on a comprehensive programme to mobilize and utilize the human and economic resources of the country with a view to accelerating social and economic development. In that context, it was applying a policy of reconciliation, unity and peace. The Government, conscious of the close links between peace and development, had recently adopted a series of measures affecting both the public and private sectors, and had promulgated a new law intended to stimulate private enterprise by encouraging domestic and foreign capital investment. Studies had also been carried out with a view to the in-

tegration of domestic and foreign markets, with special emphasis on the role of small and medium-sized enterprises.

6. In view of the widening gap between the level of economic development of the LDCs and that of the other developing countries, as well as the absence of political will and practical action, his delegation proposed that the problems of the 40 LDCs should be examined in depth by UNCTAD and other competent United Nations authorities with a view to ensuring rapid and full application of all the special measures intended for such countries, and particularly those in the

Substantial New Programme of Action. In the context of world interdependence, the developing countries now formed a dynamic community whose economic and political influence could no longer be ignored. Their aspirations to economic and social progress, their participation in economic decision-making at the international level and their place in the new international economic order were indispensable factors for the well-being of the developed countries themselves and for economic and political stability in the world. It was beyond doubt that the Conference, in acknowledging the principle of the close interdependence of all nations, would achieve positive results of benefit to all.

Summary of the statement made at the 206th plenary meeting, 13 July 1987, by Mr. Kostandin HOXHA, Deputy Minister of Foreign Trade of Albania

1. Mr. HOXHA said that assessments of the world economic crisis and suggested methods of overcoming it that had been put forward at the sixth session of the Conference in Belgrade n 1983 had not stood the test of time and reality. The crisis had persisted and the developing countries' expectations regarding a solution to many of their problems had remained unfulfilled. He hailed the developing countries' efforts to co-operate in promoting the development of their economies and to utilize their national potential for the benefit of their own independent development.

2. Reviewing the current critical world economic situation, of which he considered the LDCs were the principal victims, he said that the current and future state of the world economy could not be seen in isolation from the prevailing global political situation. Economic difficulties were aggravated by political tension and war, by the super-Powers' policies of militarism, hegemony and neo-colonialist expansion and by their violation of the sovereign rights of other countries and peoples. The developing countries were suffering, in addition, from protectionist measures and other barriers applied against their export products, especially primary commodities, by developed countries. As a consequence, world prices of primary commodities had fallen to very low levels and the developing countries' terms of trade were worsening.

3. The Albanian delegation considered that the legitimate desire and efforts of peoples to create more favourable conditions for co-operation and equality in world economic and trade relations could not be realized unless the super-Powers and other imperialist Powers ceased such activities and policies. In order to achieve the independent and stable economic development of countries based on their national assets, to eliminate the debt burden, to realize a fair balance of trade and to build direct relations of co-operation and equality among States, a change must be made in ex-

isting international economic relations, which were based on imperialist criteria of production and distribution. Those new relations must be founded on complete equality, mutual benefit and interest and must take account of the legitimate and vital interests of all countries so as not to encroach on their dignity, freedom, independence and national sovereignty. His delegation was in favour of the development of world trade free from measures of protectionism, customs tariffs and quota restrictions and from the dictates of the super-Powers and policies of restriction and closed markets.

4. Albania, once one of the most backward countries of Europe, could now boast an advanced industry and agriculture and ever-expanding social emancipation, based on the work of the people and on the channelling and utilization of its own resources in accordance with a clear and consistent economic policy for socialist construction. High economic growth rates were conducive to a perceptible increase in the volume of foreign trade, with exports in a leading position. The volume of exports would be between 44 and 46 per cent higher in 1990 than in 1985. Self-reliance had never prevented the Albanian economy from benefiting, on a basis of reciprocity, from trade and co-operation with other countries.

5. Difficulties and blockades had convinced the Albanian people that freedom and political independence, national sovereignty and dignity could not be guaranteed without a developed and independent national economy. That was not inconsistent, however, with the further development of relations with other countries in fields of mutual interest and continued support for the struggle of peoples for national liberation and social emancipation. He said the delegation of Albania was ready to make its contribution to the successful outcome of the current session of the Conference.

Summary of the statement made at the 208th plenary meeting, 14 July 1987, by Mr. Mohamed ABERKANE, Minister of Trade of Algeria

1.   Mr. ABERKANE said that the seventh session of the Conference was taking place in a context of deeply disturbing tension in which political and economic stability was threatened by a number of paradoxes. First, colonial situations persisted in Palestine and Namibia, as well as the policy of *apartheid* in South Africa. Secondly, the gap separating the North from the South was widening at a time when nations were becoming increasingly interdependent. Thirdly, human, material and financial resources were being wasted on an absurd arms race at a time when the developing countries were having great difficulties in satisfying the basic needs of their populations. Fourthly, the ideals of justice and respect for human rights were being reaffirmed while the accommodating attitude to the inequalities characterizing the international economic system was being reflected in poverty, illiteracy, unemployment and disease for most of mankind.

2.   The major economic indicators bore witness to the depth of the crisis and confirmed the diagnosis made at the sixth session of the Conference in 1983. Since then the negative trends had been accentuated as a result of the decline in co-operation and the calling into question of the international consensus on development. The developing countries had experienced disappointing growth rates since the beginning of the decade. Some of them had even recorded negative growth rates. The fall in export earnings, the instability of exchange rates, persistently high interest rates, the drying-up of sources of development financing and the debt-servicing burden were seriously thwarting their development efforts. In the industrialized countries, the low growth rates recorded in recent years, monetary instability and increased unemployment clearly showed that the recovery begun in 1983 had not been lasting. The forecasts for the coming years were hardly optimistic.

3.   The persistence of the world economic crisis confirmed the inadequacy of the approach adopted so far, which ignored economic interdependence and did not allow for the concerns of the developing countries, which were condemned to suffer the consequences of macro-economic decisions over which they had no control. In addition, the approach failed to take into account the interrelation between different problems, so that positive action initiated in one sector was often frustrated by measures adopted in others. The approach was also limited to contingency planning, whereas there was every indication that the crisis had its roots in the structural imbalances generated and maintained by the existing international economic system. Experience had shown that partial measures, whatever temporary advantages they might have for a particular group of countries, were not likely to solve the crisis, the persistence and extent of which confirmed the need for a democratic, global and integrated approach taking into account the interrelation between problems and the economic interdependence of countries.

4.   The appeal made at the New Delhi summit for solidarity and the proposals for the initiation of global negotiations reiterated at the Eighth Conference of Heads of State or Government of Non-Aligned Countries, at Harare in September 1986, were all based on the conviction that prosperity was indivisible and that no country or group of countries could solve its problems in isolation. The developing countries wished to initiate a responsible dialogue in order to seek, with their partners in the developed countries, lasting solutions in conformity with the requirements of the new international economic order. Any delay in starting such a dialogue would only aggravate the world economic situation and increase political and social tension.

5.   One of the major challenges to be taken up by the Conference was the mobilization of financial resources for development in particular for dealing with the developing countries' debt problem. The approach adopted so far had been inappropriate because it could not ensure repayment of the debt and serve development objectives simultaneously, because it meant that the greater part of the adjustment burden had to be borne by the debtor countries alone, and because the adjustments it involved were likely to threaten the social and political stability of the debtor countries. The solution lay in the initiation of a political dialogue for the formulation of a global strategy based on co-responsibility and aimed at growth and development. The seventh session of the Conference provided an opportunity for starting such a dialogue and for formulating general guidelines for Governments, international financial institutions and private banks.

6.   The solution of the developing countries' debt problem was connected with their capacity to mobilize the financial flows needed for resuming the development drive, with the extent to which they had access to the markets of developed countries, and with the level of their export earnings. It was therefore unlikely that the debt could be repaid in the prevailing circumstances, in which a number of developing countries were recording a net transfer of resources to the developed countries, protectionism was damaging the most dynamic sectors of their economies, and commodity prices were at their lowest level for 50 years. The developing countries had suffered the consequences not only of technological changes but also of the macro-economic policies pursued by the developed countries. There had even been an attempt to call into question what had been achieved for the commodity sector at previous sessions of the Conference.

7.   The Conference must preserve the advantages of the Integrated Programme for Commodities and the Common Fund and decide upon appropriate measures to accelerate progress towards the attainment of its objectives. The decisions taken by the USSR and Côte d'Ivoire to sign the Agreement Establishing the Com-

mon Fund for Commodities were important steps towards making the Fund operational.

8. The situation in commodity markets showed how much the trade position of the developing countries had worsened as a result of recourse to unilateral or bilateral measures, violations of multilateral commitments, and the proliferation of retaliatory measures and restrictive practices, which had increasingly hampered the developing countries' access to markets. His delegation hoped that the developed countries would take advantage of the session to give specific content to their commitments regarding standstill and roll-back and to improve the GSP. In addition, UNCTAD should promote the development of trade relations among countries with different economic and social systems. The Conference was well placed to contribute to the establishment of a universal, non-discriminatory and stable trade system. In that connection it should follow closely the Uruguay Round of trade negotiations and formulate recommendations on particular aspects of those negotiations.

9. The LDCs were particularly hard hit by the crisis, on account of their greater vulnerability. UNCTAD should continue to pay special attention to their situation. They were legitimately expecting the current session to reaffirm and to formulate in more specific terms the commitments entered into by the international community under the Substantial New Programme of Action, particularly the commitments concerning the mobilization of resources on liberal terms. He hoped that the Conference would adopt concrete, concerted and unselfish measures for solving, in the interests of all, the problems he had mentioned.

Summary of the statement made at the 214th plenary meeting, 28 July 1987, by Mr. Bernardo GRINSPUN, Secretary of State for Planning of Argentina

1. Mr. GRINSPUN paid a tribute to two former Secretaries-General of UNCTAD, namely his compatriot Raúl Prebisch and Manuel Pérez Guerrero of Venezuela. Referring to the consensus agreements reached on the issues before the Conference at its seventh session by the Group of 77 at its Sixth Ministerial Meeting, he said that Argentina intended, at the current session—as it had done at previous sessions—to join forces with the group in promoting a sincere dialogue, finding ways of collectively overcoming the obstacles to economic and social development among the Group's members and devising effective policies to correct disequilibria in the world economy.

2. The crisis affecting the world economy reflected profound transformations in the social and international division of labour, which, having not yet settled into a clear trend, had rendered investment choices difficult to make and heightened the uncertainties inherent in economic planning.

3. Even before the crisis, developing countries had faced the need to industrialize as a means of ensuring their long-term development and to accumulate sufficient capital to purchase modern technology, enhance their competitiveness and raise the living standards of their peoples. Following the commodity price slump, by which they had been severely affected, they had had to borrow funds at a time when international financing was abundant and stimulated indebtedness without subjecting it to criteria that would guarantee the capacity to repay.

4. To counter the crisis, industrialized countries had adopted adjustment policies which had given rise to new forms of disequilibria on international markets and exacerbated the already precarious situation of the developing countries. Commodity prices had consequently collapsed, the prices of manufactures had declined, and the most efficient developing countries had been supplanted as a result of the production and export subsidies granted by the developed countries. Despite declining export earnings, developing countries had had to service steadily rising external debts at very high interest rates while adjustment at the international level had reduced external financial flows to those countries. Conventional adjustment policies normally led to extremely high domestic interest rates which slowed production and discouraged investment. The capital stock thus became increasingly outdated, a factor which affected the capacity for growth over the medium and long term. Moreover, any trade surpluses achieved by debtor countries despite the practices of the industrialized countries were absorbed by debt servicing. Consequently, the transfer of resources to creditor countries attained levels far superior to the 1 per cent of GNP target which developed countries had committed themselves to transfer to the developing world, a situation which underscored the perversity of the traditional economic adjustment system.

5. In the circumstances, the developing countries could hardly hope to mobilize the capital necessary to sustain growth in proportion to their needs. The economies of the major industrialized countries for their part, were expanding at very moderate rates and it was unlikely that they would have any appreciable ripple effect at the international level. Nor were interest rates expected to decline significantly or protectionist pressure to abate. Moreover, owing to their shrinking import capacity the developing countries were unable to contribute to recovery in activity and employment in industrialized countries.

6. The debt problem was therefore a result of the policies adopted by developed countries and constituted not only the main obstacle to economic growth in the developing world, but also a barrier to growth in the industrialized countries. The Argentine Government considered that creditors and debtors were jointly responsible for the debt burden, which was a political issue, and that it was in the interest of all to initiate a political dialogue leading to the expeditious adoption of corrective measures. Reverting to an idea suggested by President Alfonsín at the 73rd session of the International

Labour Conference, in June 1987, he expressed the view that debts should be consolidated over the long term by tailoring interest rates to the real debt-servicing capacity of the developing countries. Once the problem had thus been solved, capital flows and economic growth should resume their normal course in the interest of all.

7. By virtue of its universal and multilateral nature, UNCTAD was the ideal forum in which to study questions raised by the growing interdependence of countries and the greater integration of the monetary, financial and trade sectors. The international community should use that forum to engage in a constructive dialogue leading to the negotiation and adoption of specific and consistent measures concerning the debt burden, commodities, trade and international finance. As a prerequisite, UNCTAD must be provided with appropriate institutional and operational structures, a matter which the Trade and Development Board should consider on a priority basis.

8. The Argentine Government hoped that, in parallel with the Uruguay Round, work would be undertaken to design a general system of international trade that was non-discriminatory, universal and oriented towards growth and development, and one in which the developing countries would receive preferential and more favourable treatment. First and foremost, developed countries should comply strictly with the

commitments made on standstill and roll-back in the Punta del Este Declaration and with multilateral rules in that respect.

9. As for the Uruguay Round itself, the Government of Argentina hoped that the UNCTAD secretariat would periodically assess progress and provide technical support to participating developing countries. With regard to negotiations on services, their principal objective should be the promotion of economic growth and the autonomous development of the developing countries, taking into account the domestic policy and legislation of those countries in the field of services and ensuring that transactions in services did not become a further cause of external disequilibrium. In that respect, the UNCTAD secretariat should continue to compile sectoral reports and studies on the analysis and formulation of domestic policies.

10. The Argentine Government was making every effort to promote the restructuring of international relations and foster economic co-operation among developing countries by participating more actively in South-South trade, advocating the establishment of a global system of trade preferences and endeavouring to strengthen the various regional economic integration agreements. In that respect, it also committed itself to supporting the Conference's recommendations at the current session on the problems of the LDCs.

**Summary of the statement made at the 213th plenary meeting, 27 July 1987,
by Mr. Alan Robert OXLEY, Permanent Representative of Australia to the United Nations Office at Geneva**

1. Mr. OXLEY noted that the need to reappraise ways of expanding trade and speeding up development was recognized by all groups of countries, which seemed to be in agreement about the desirable features of a system that would promote development and prosperity, namely, acknowledgement of the dynamism of economies and of the need for flexibility in the economy, optimal allocation of resources, recognition of the role of the price mechanism in effecting such allocation and the creation of an environment conducive to the mobilization of resources. All those factors implied structural changes, the need for which had long been recognized. However, a new idea was emerging, namely, that all countries without exception must act in concert to bring about those structural adjustments.

2. In the Asian-Pacific region, that new perception of development was already widely held. For its part, Australia was in the process of restructuring its economy to make it more open, because it had become aware that protectionism had been harmful to its manufacturing sector. It was attempting to reduce protection, particularly of manufacturing, but also in some areas of agriculture, to liberalize its financial markets and to attract foreign investment.

3. In agriculture, the burden of adjustment must be borne primarily by those countries that had caused the

greatest distortions on the international market, above all the United States of America, Japan and the European Community. In subsidizing their agricultural production, those countries placed a heavy burden on their own consumers and were creating unfair competition for other exporting countries by artificially lowering world market prices. His Government welcomed the commitment made by those countries at the Uruguay Round to liberalize their agricultural trade and the proposals for the removal of all obstacles to such trade.

4. The collapse of most commmodity prices was a disturbing trend that could not be eliminated through the short-term stabilization machinery of the Integrated Programme or the Common Fund for Commodities. Long-term trade-liberalization measures were required to facilitate structural adjustments; compensation for shortfalls in earnings in commodities should be paid against the criteria of general balance-of-payments considerations, rather than on the basis of earnings by commodity.

5. The Uruguay Round had clearly highlighted the link between basic trade and development problems and the liberalization of trade.

6. Owing to the lack of resources, ODA had remained inadequate to meet existing needs, and it was therefore important to reduce protectionism and trade-

distorting measures and to improve access to markets in order to stimulate the development of the third world and enable it to meet its debt commitments.

7. In future, national economies would be classified in two broad categories: the dynamic economies, whether developed or developing, which pursued a policy of growth and efficiency and applied an outward-oriented strategy, and economies characterized by structural rigidities and a distorted allocation of resources. Clearly, the poorest countries would find it quite difficult to put the dynamic policy of the first category into effect and would still require direct external assistance,

but such assistance would not relieve them of the responsibility to strive to become more dynamic.

8. UNCTAD must make clear the need to adopt an outward-oriented strategy. Its work programme should focus on the examination of those elements which had contributed to successful development efforts and assist developing countries in adapting them to their individual needs. It must also examine the cost of policies and measures which hampered structural adjustment and development, and particularly the impact on development prospects of protectionism and trade liberalization.

Summary of the statement made at the 208th plenary meeting, 14 July 1987, by Mr. Heinrich NEISSER, Federal Minister in the Federal Chancellery of Austria

1. Mr. NEISSER said that past approaches to the issues before the Conference had suffered for far too long from frustration caused by the dimensions of the problems and illusions as to how real progress could be achieved. The serious economic situation had far-reaching implications for the future of international relations to which no single State would be immune. The challenge therefore had to be met by a corresponding realism based on the recognition that the many millions living under unacceptable conditions were entitled to expect the international community to show solidarity. However, if poverty called for solidarity, interdependence called for partnership. That meant explicit recognition of the fact that the economic environment for development was determined, albeit in differing degrees, by the national policies of developed and developing countries alike as they interacted with one another. Interdependence could therefore be effectively managed only in a spirit of partnership and constructive co-operation. There was no alternative to an open multilateral world economic system, with effective international institutions and mutually accepted rules and disciplines in trade, finance and investment. Only through that system could better access to the markets, finance and techology needed for development be secured.

2. Major changes had taken place in the pattern of world economic development since the 1970s. The serious economic problems facing the world, particularly the developing countries, called for increased international co-operation aimed at reactivating global growth and development. Group B countries recognized their responsibility for the world economic environment, as had been made clear at the OECD Ministerial Meeting held in May 1987. Efforts to improve economic policy co-ordination and to strengthen multilateral surveillance were being undertaken. Developing countries, according to their capacities, would in turn have to pursue appropriate macro-economic policies in order to contribute to, and benefit from, improved conditions for sustained and stable economic growth on a global scale.

3. However, there was a growing awareness that macro-economic policies alone could not succeed unless

they were combined with structural adjustment policies. That applied to developed and developing countries alike. Accelerating technological change and new patterns of consumption, production and trade, as well as far-reaching developments in financial and commodity markets and growing pressures to preserve the environment called for a more efficient functioning of economic systems on a world-wide scale. All countries, including Austria, faced the challenge of structural change, with the difficult decisions, social costs and great determination which such change implied. Every country was free to choose its own economic and social system, but there was evidence to show that a system recognizing the role of market forces and of signals for the efficient allocation and use of resources could not be matched by any other system.

4. The LDCs suffered from basic economic rigidities. Their problems could be overcome only if they themselves pursued a persistent policy in the framework of the Substantial New Programme of Action to activate their own resources and if their own national development efforts were supported by adequate and sustained ODA. The African countries had impressively demonstrated their determination to carry out reform, which deserved continued support in accordance with the decisions taken at the special session of the General Assembly on Africa.

5. The LDCs had priority in Austria's bilateral development co-operation. Austria's contribution to multilateral institutions had been increased threefold in the period 1983-1985, and the LDCs were again accorded special attention. Austria supported the highest possible replenishment of IDA resources and the allocation of up to one half of their amount to sub-Saharan Africa. It also intended to use 50 per cent of the funds allocated under the current co-financing agreement with the World Bank to help the LDCs.

6. Everyone had failed to recognize in time the decoupling of economic growth from inputs of raw materials. The result was a sometimes dramatic oversupply of most commodities, with little prospect of an early return to equilibrium. In addition to maintaining the commitment to improve the functioning of commodity markets, it was important to address the struc-

tural and development dimension of dependence on commodities, focusing on the horizontal and vertical diversification of commodity-dependent economies and the creation of new productive structures. A much broader approach to commodity problems was therefore needed. In activating resources for development, adequate attention should be paid to the development of human resources, to the contribution to be made by the private sector, and to the creation of a climate of confidence conducive to a renewed flow of capital.

7.   Many developing countries were burdened with a heavy debt. A growth-oriented strategy based on co-operation among debtor and creditor countries, international financial institutions and the private banking sector and aimed at finding the appropriate solution for each case was being implemented. Structural adjustment, adequate financing and an improved international economic environment constituted its essential elements. The adoption of growth-oriented adjustment programmes by many debtor countries was a major step forward. Much had been achieved, but serious difficulties remained and in some respects were intensifying. By some intensive co-operation and by the use of innovative and flexible approaches in financing, it should be possible to overcome existing difficulties.

8.   For the poorest debtor countries, especially those in sub-Saharan Africa undertaking structural adjustment programmes, additional action to reduce the debt-servicing burden and the provision of adequate concessional finance were essential. Austria welcomed proposals to that effect and was participating actively in the efforts of the Paris Club to secure more realistic rescheduling terms for the poorest debtor countries. Austria had also cancelled debts on ODA loans in accordance with Board resolution 165 (S-IX). It was, furthermore, in favour of a substantial increase in the capital of the World Bank and had already participated in substantial increases in the capital of regional development banks and funds and of IDA.

9.   Finance alone did not, however, suffice to promote development. International trade was also needed. It was important for supporting external financing and debt-servicing, and the promotion of trade was indispensable for the process of structural adjustment. Protectionism was harmful to developed and developing countries alike and inevitably led to inefficiency, structural paralysis and unemployment. The Uruguay Round of trade negotiations offered a unique opportunity to reverse protectionist trends. The full implementation of standstill and roll-back commitments was of crucial importance for restoring confidence in the open multilateral trading system. The issues to be negotiated in the particular interest of developing countries included those concerning tropical products, agriculture and the plans to restore General Agreement discipline for textiles. An efficient multilateral system also had to be constantly adapted to new realities and new trade flows. Austria therefore supported any necessary enlargement of the scope of the GATT system.

10.   No single one of the diverse problems and policy issues to which he had referred could be considered as being of concern to any one country or group of countries only. Consequently, there was no substitute for partnership. Nobody stood to gain, and everybody stood to lose, from confrontation.

Summary of the statement made at the 208th plenary meeting, 14 July 1987, by Mr. Karim AL-SHAKAR, Permanent Representative of Bahrain to the United Nations Office at Geneva

1.   Mr. AL-SHAKAR said that multilateral co-operation and mutual solidarity had become essential in a world that was becoming increasingly interdependent as a result of the technological revolution, the volume and speed of financial transactions and their effect on exchange and interest rates.

2.   The period between the sixth and seventh sessions of the Conference had been marked by numerous crises brought about by rapid economic, social and technological changes which, unfortunately, had not led to any real improvement in the economies of the developing countries. The causes of the current imbalance in the world economy had been correctly identified in the Havana Declaration. However, since the sixth session, the world economy had been affected by further severe fluctuations in exchange rates, a decline in the flow of financial resources from the developed to the developing countries, an increase in protectionist trends and a collapse of the prices of commodities and raw materials, including petroleum. There had also been a recent trend towards a net transfer of financial resources from the developing to the developed countries.

3.   The world-wide recession had severely aggravated the imbalances from which the developing countries were suffering as a result of currency fluctuations, high interest rates, inflation, reduced foreign investment, balance-of-payments deficits, increased indebtedness and deteriorating terms of trade. Whereas 1986 had witnessed an economic upturn in the industrialized countries, the economic indicators showed that the developing countries could expect little improvement in 1987, in spite of the sharp drop in petroleum prices and the decline in inflation, interest rates and the value of the United States dollar. In fact, the decline in the value of the dollar had aggravated the situation brought about by the drop in oil prices from more than $30 per barrel in 1982 to less than $10 in 1985, which had had an extremely adverse effect on the economies of the petroleum-exporting countries, whose revenues had declined by 60 per cent during that period. That had inevitably reduced the generous assistance that they had previously been able to grant to other developing countries. OECD had estimated that the industrialized countries had benefited from the decline in the prices of their petroleum imports to the tune of more than $63 billion in 1986. However, none of

those gains had as yet been used to promote development in the developing countries.

4. The international community had a duty to find a solution to the critical situation brought about by the accumulated debts of the developing countries, which had amounted to about $1 trillion in 1986. Since very few of the developing countries were able to pay the high rates of interest on their debts, the developed countries, and particularly those with a financial surplus, should make greater efforts to promote development by reducing interest rates and augmenting their loans and bilateral and multilateral assistance to the developing countries. International financial institutions, such as the World Bank and IMF, should provide those countries with the assistance that they needed and UNCTAD should also play a role in the quest for realistic solutions to help the indebted countries through an improvement in international economic and financial relations.

5. In the LDCs and island developing countries, particularly in Africa, the population's standard of living had declined between the 1970s and the 1980s as a result of rapid population growth and unprecedented droughts, famines and natural disasters. However, the principal cause of the problems facing the LDCs lay in the weakness of their economic and social structures, which made them particularly vulnerable to the effects of the world-wide economic crisis. Accordingly, the international community should make a special effort to achieve the objectives set forth in the Substantial New Programme of Action.

6. As an island developing country, Bahrain felt that the international community, the United Nations agencies, and particularly UNCTAD, should take steps to assist island developing countries in accordance with United Nations resolutions, with a view to facilitating the economic restructuring needed to further their economic growth and self-sufficiency.

7. It was distressing to note that, in spite of the critical international economic situation, world-wide military spending on armaments amounted to more than $1 trillion per year, while two thirds of the world's population were suffering from various forms of poverty, famine and socio-economic backwardness.

8. In the early 1980s, the international community had undertaken to combat backwardness and poverty and to promote socio-economic justice through the international Development Strategy for the Third United Nations Development Decade. Accordingly, it was essential to reach agreement on effective international policies and measures aimed at the achievement of economic recovery and stability through multilateral co-operation. UNCTAD was the appropriate international forum for dialogue between the developed and the developing countries with a view to solving socio-economic problems. However, that could be achieved only through the adoption of international measures that would promote economic stability, growth, development and recovery through the establishment of a more equitable new international economic order.

Summary of the statement made at the 208th plenary meeting, 14 July 1987, by Mr. Mohammad ABDELMUNIM, Minister of Commerce of Bangladesh

1. Mr. ABDELMUNIM said that since the sixth session of the Conference the world economic situation had considerably deteriorated, being characterized by recessional trends, high rates of unemployment, high interest rates, rapidly accumulating debts in the developing countries, and rising protectionism. The developing world had been facing a crisis of unprecedented gravity caused by a collapse of commodity prices, an unbearable debt burden, and a reduction of the net flow of financial resources, including ODA. The multilateral trading system had been greatly undermined. Despite international negotiations for the proper management of the increasingly interdependent world economy, the international economic crisis was more complex and deeper than that of the 1930s. The LDCs were the worst affected.

2. The developing countries themselves had, of course, the primary responsibility for their own development. However, it was beyond their capacity to compensate for the deterioration of the external economic and trade environment. Neither their own efforts nor market forces alone could provide a solution unless a supportive climate was created by the macro-economic policies of the major actors, particularly in the area of trade and finance. The seventh session of the Conference offered an opportunity to devise an interrelated multilateral strategy for revitalizing development, growth and international trade in a more predictable and supportive environment through multilateral co-operation.

3. The developing countries had suffered a net outflow of funds and lower prices for their commodities and energy. ODA flows from the developed countries had reached barely half the internationally agreed targets, and their quality had also deteriorated. The critical situation had forced many developing countries to compress imports and investment in order to reduce balance-of-payments deficits and to service their debts, and as a consequence employment and growth prospects were poor in those countries.

4. In the early 1980s the developing countries had been informed that further trade liberalization could be considered only after the industrialized world had succeeded in overcoming the effects of the economic recession. Now, however, they were witnessing a resurgence of sophisticated protectionist trends covering almost all sectors of importance to them, the most striking example being the upsurge of restrictive measures against imports of their textiles. Even the LDCs had not been spared. For instance, Bangladesh, a least developed country with formidable structural problems and a large pool of unemployed labour, had launched a bold programme of structural adjustments but had been faced with severe quota restrictions on its exports of ready-

made garments. The commitments made by the industrialized countries to halt protectionism were yet to be fulfilled.

5.   In view of the crisis in the economies of the LDCs in 1981 the international community had adopted the Substantial New Programme of Action to help them to overcome their difficulties and to bring about the structural transformations needed for self-sustained growth. In fact, however, the number of LDCs, far from decreasing, had actually increased. Though handicaped by internal and external constraints, they had undertaken fundamental policy reforms consonant with the Substantial New Programme of Action. The imperative need of the moment was the adoption of policies and measures to accelerate the implementation of the Substantial New Programme of Action. President Mitterrand's call for a high-level conference to consider and adopt a substantial new programme of action for the LDCs for the 1990s and France's offer to host the conference were greatly appreciated.

6.   There was no need to evolve an agreed assessment of the unprecedented disarray in international economic relations, for its root causes were well known. What was needed was immediate action to reverse current trends and to put the world economy back on the path of co-operation, growth and development. A positive and constructive dialogue should be held with a view to reaching a consensus on the vital issues and to adopting, immediately, an integrated set of policies in areas of critical importance to the developing countries, and to the least developed in particular. Those policies should lead to the restructuring of world economic relations that was needed for the establishment of the new international economic order. The Sixth Ministerial meeting of the Group of 77 had assessed the situation and had formulated a set of short-term and long-term policies and measures designed to produce reasonable and practical solutions to current world economic problems on the basis of reciprocal interests. Those proposals, contained in TD/330, had his delegation's full support and should be the subject of sincere negotiations.

7.   His delegation welcomed the decisions of the USSR and of Côte d'Ivoire to sign the Agreement Establishing the Common Fund for Commodities and hoped that important decisions in other sectors would also be forthcoming in the course of the session.

**Summary of the statement made at the 215th plenary meeting, 28 July 1987,
by Mr. E. Evelyn GREAVES, Minister of Trade, Industry and Commerce of Barbados**

1.   Mr. GREAVES said that the seventh session of the Conference was being held at a time when a number of problems—such as the continued falling off in investment and trade, deteriorating terms of trade, volatile exchange rates, high real interest rates, the debt problem, depressed commodity prices and rising protectionism—were undermining the efforts of developing countries to achieve economic growth. Those problems also affected the developed countries; some of them had, in self-defence, adopted an isolationist attitude, refusing to recognize the interdependence not only of nations but also of monetary, financial and trading systems. Such an attitude could admittedly be advantageous to them in the short term, but it considerably worsened world economic problems and made the process of structural adjustment even more difficult.

2.   Global interdependence highlighted the need to co-ordinate national policies and ensure that they were in line with world economic development objectives. It was therefore essential to adopt an active multilateral co-operation programme based on political commitment by both developed and developing countries to seek joint solutions to world economic problems. The seventh session of the Conference offered the international community an opportunity to agree upon such a programme of multilateral co-operation incorporating a number of specific measures relating to areas of common interest.

3.   In order to create an international economic environment favourable to development, growth and trade, the first task of a multilateral co-operation grogramme was to include specific commitments from both developed and developing countries. The following measures ought to be expected from the developed countries: policies for expanding their economies, assistance in strengthening the production capacity of the developing countries, improved access to their markets for the exports of the developing countries together with a commitment to making the necessary structural adjustments in their own economies, an increase in the public and private flow of funds to developing countries and assistance in reversing negative growth rates of such countries. The developing countries, in turn, should undertake to increase their efforts to mobilize their human and financial resources for development, to create domestic conditions that would attract funds from outside and to make better use of domestic and external resources. In his view, the adoption of such a package of measures would give new impetus to multilateral co-operation for development.

4.   In the 1980s, the flow of resources to developing countries had been so meagre that many of them experienced a net transfer of resources to the developed countries; in many others, such as the LDCs, positive net transfers had declined. As a result, many developing countries had had to curtail imports and investments, with adverse implications for their own development as well as world economic growth. The growing number of countries designated as least developed made international action a matter of urgency. In addition, the so-called middle-income countries and even some less developed countries in the Caribbean found themselves in difficulties; because they no longer enjoyed an inflow of funds at concessional rates as a result of application of the graduation principle, they no longer had access to commercial loans and their debt burdens went up as their export earnings went down.

5. The members of the international community had a duty not only to combat poverty but also to prevent it. To that end, creditor countries and international financial institutions should offer debtor countries more concessional terms and increase the resources available to institutions such as the World Bank. It was important that the Conference should achieve a consensus on the allocation of further public and private resources to developing countries to enable them to restructure their economies in such a way as to encourage growth and overcome their debt problems. Participants in the seventh session had an equally important duty to find ways of improving the international debt strategy. Any such strategy must be tailored not only to the capacity of developing countries to repay their debts without damaging their development prospects but also to the need to spread the financial costs equitably among debtors and creditors.

6. As for commodities, the developing countries faced steadily falling prices and a declining share of world export earnings as a result of competition from synthetics and substitutes and the protectionist policies of developed market-economy countries. It was essential for the Conference to take urgent steps to correct the situation. In that context, he reaffirmed the validity of the objectives of the Integrated Programme for Commodities and fully endorsed the proposals for implementing them put forward by the UNCTAD secretariat (see TD/328).

7. Healthy international trade was a presequisite for development; the international trading system had been under severe pressure for some time. Existing rules, traditional GATT procedures and the MFN principle were no longer respected, the machinery for the settlement of disputes was ineffective, there was no consensus on a comprehensive system of safeguards, and Governments had difficulty in converting multilateral rules and principles into national legislation. Despite the many statements made in favour of freer trade, protectionist measures had proliferated, often resulting in depressed economic activity and increased unemployment in developing countries. In the final analysis, the protectionist policies of the developed countries had denied

their most basic rights to millions of those living in developing countries, since by cutting back exports from such countries they denied them access to the resources required to fund social programmes and create jobs. Many developing countries were, moreover, being called upon to carry out structural adjustment without being given the means to do so. That process of adjustment was, furthermore, supposed to go hand in hand with the liberalization of their import trade. That would allow the developed countries, whose industries enjoyed economies of scale and access to the latest technology, to flood the markets of the developing countries with low-cost products, thus precipitating the failure of many emerging local industries.

8. The purpose of the Uruguay Round was to develop an open and lasting multilateral trading system that would benefit developed and developing countries alike. One priority goal of the Round should be respect of the standstill and roll-back commitments made at Punta del Este.

9. The seventh session of the Conference offered an opportunity to give a new political impetus to the negotiations undertaken under GATT auspices and to draw up a complementary programme of concrete measures for implementation by UNCTAD. Such a programme should include work on facilitating structural adjustment in both developed and developing countries, evaluation of proposed protectionist measures in terms of their impact on the economies of various countries, consideration of ways of bringing trade in textiles and agricultural products fully in line with General Agreement rules, provision of technical assistance to developing countries in the context of the Uruguay Round, assistance to developing countries to help them assess more accurately the contribution made to the development process by the services sector and to strengthen their capacity to develop that sector.

10. The realities of interdependence and the vital need to embark on multilateral co-operation for development were such that the Conference could not allow itself to fail the millions of people looking to it for a better future.

Summary of the statement made at the 212th plenary meeting, 27 July 1987, by Mr. H. DE CROO, Minister of Communications and Foreign Trade of Belgium

1. Mr. DE CROO said that his country's views on the seventh session of the Conference had already been expressed to a large extent by the Danish representative speaking on behalf of the European Community, whose member States had adopted a constructive and realistic approach intended to help bring the debate to a successful conclusion.

2. Since the end of the Second World War, Belgium had been resolutely pursuing the goal of multilateral co-operation, and it had been one of the first countries to aim at the establishment of relations of solidarity and trust between the industrialized and the developing countries. It was therefore particularly interested in the activities of UNCTAD which, in its view, was in a

privileged position to promote a genuine dialogue between North and South. However, the seventh session was taking place in a highly uncertain and unstable world economic climate, marked by radical change, quickening technological developments and growing interdependence. Such an environment posed a real challenge to the very survival of UNCTAD as an international organization although, paradoxically, the gravity of the situation seemed to be the Conference's main asset in its efforts to achieve a common approach and a new solidarity.

3. The international community had to acquit itself of the following tasks in the near future: it must restore international monetary stability, enhance and reform

commodity markets, remove the threat of protectionism, preserve free trade and reconstruct the foundations of international co-operation so as to achieve growth and development in the world. The consensus on multilateral trade negotiations reached at Punta del Este must now be maintained and expanded, and UNCTAD must support the developing countries which were taking part in the current negotiations. International trade had a beneficial effect on development, provided that it could take place with as few hindrances as possible in a stable monetary environment.

4.   Belgium paid particularly attention to the financial crisis facing many developing countries, particularly the poorest and most indebted countries, and was aware that, despite the rigorous adjustment programmes to which a number of them had been subjected, their situation had continued to deteriorate. The international community must draw the necessary conclusions and adopt concerted and co-ordinated measures to respond to the most immediate needs of those countries. Belgium actively supported the action taken by international financial institutions, and in particular the project to increase the resources of IMF and the World Bank Group for financing structural adjustment in the poorest developing countries. In addition, the Belgian Government was most interested in the idea of using part of the development co-operation budget to alleviate the hard-currency debt burden of certain developing

countries. That would entail the establishment of funds into which debtor countries would pay the local currency equivalent of their hard-currency debt. Such funds would be used to implement structural adjustment plans by the public sector. Belgium intended to increase its assistance to small and medium-sized agricultural and industrial enterprises by opening lines of credit on concessional terms in development banks with a view to promoting co-operation between Belgian enterprises and enterprises in developing countries. Belgium had also decided to grant quick-disbursing loans for structural adjustment, which would complement the operations of the World Bank and should allow enterprises to obtain the inputs they needed to develop their activities.

5.   He was optimistic about the results that the Conference might be expected to achieve, having regard to the desire for moderation and realism shown by those who had prepared it, the competence and sense of responsibility of those who were in charge of it and the understanding and unrelenting search for harmony which were evident in the debate. In view of the limited time available to the Conference, it would clearly not be possible to arrive at definitive solutions; however, it was essential to do something to prepare the basis for genuine international co-operation in the service of development.

Summary of the statement made at the 211th plenary meeting, 24 July 1987, by Mr. Girigissou GADO, Minister of Commerce, Crafts and Tourism of Benin

1.   Mr. GADO said he regretted that the objectives set at the sixth session of the Conference had not been achieved in the preceding four years and that nothing had been done to implement the few encouraging resolutions that had been adopted by consensus. He hoped that the powerful countries would see the seventh session as an opportunity to agree to the need to lay the foundations for a more human and equitable economic system by implementing a concerted and sustained programme for economic recovery and rapid development, bearing in mind the characteristic interdependence of world economic relations.

2.   The situation of the developing countries had by no means improved, but had grown even worse as commodity prices had dropped steadily and reduced the real value of export earnings and as the price of the manufactures and capital goods they required for their development projects had soared. The worsening of the terms of trade was reflected not only in the chronic balance-of-payment deficits of the developing countries, particularly in Africa, but also in the third world's inability to pay back its debt. According to a recent World Bank study, the average annual growth of the terms of trade had been constantly negative from 1970 to 1984 for low-income African countries. For the People's Republic of Benin, the figure had been − 5.3 per cent on average and, from 1983 to 1986, export earnings had covered only 53.6 per cent of import expenditure. The total debt of the low-income African countries ac-

counted for 74 per cent of their GDP and 349 per cent of their exports. Most of those countries, including Benin, had great difficulty servicing their debts and the current situation offered no hope for greater solvency, despite the introduction of national adjustment programmes.

3.   Doomed to insolvency, since their debt-service payments were far higher than their external earnings, the developing countries also faced the obstacle of the protectionism practised by the industrialized countries, despite the many resolutions calling for trade liberalization, and thus had no hope of solving their problems through international trade.

4.   Moreover, ODA was at a standstill and financial flows from the industrialized countries, which continued to earmark considerable sums for military expenditure in total disregard for mankind's desire for disarmament, had been tragically cut back, at the expense of the low-income African countries in particular. A World Bank study estimated that, between 1986 and 1990, the needs of those countries for concessional finance would amount to at least $35.3 billion, or $11.6 billion per year. Such an amount was virtually impossible to mobilize. The deficit would therefore stand at some $2.5 million per year. Such a grim prospect required strong action. UNCTAD must be given the authority to seek solutions to the problems submitted to it for its consideration, regardless of the fact that they might fall within the mandate of specialized institutions such as IMF, the World Bank or GATT. It must also

not be believed that there was nothing the Governments of the industrialized countries could do and that market laws were all powerful. If the developing countries were to take part on an equitable basis in international trade, the participants in the seventh session of the Conference had only to demonstrate responsibility and objectivity, forswearing selfishness and hegemonism. That approach would enable them to seek effective solutions within the framework of international co-operation that would take account of all the factors known to stand in the way of a climate of security and stability, namely, the worsening terms of trade, the decline in resources for the financing of development, external debt and protectionism. Owing to their complexity and interaction, those four factors must be regarded as a whole that required comprehensive solutions. It was therefore clear that world economic recovery and, in particular, the survival of the developing countries should be seen in terms of interdependence, not only of issues, but also of nations. Genuine solutions could come only from the members of the international community, which should work together in a spirit of solidarity and dialogue to identify the characteristics and mechanisms of an international economic system based on the principles of equity, harmony and universality and designed to promote development, growth, employment and social progress. UNCTAD had a major role to play in achieving those objectives and his delegation urged all the groups represented at the Conference and all international organizations to ensure that the seventh session would be an opportunity to take account of the proposed solutions formulated by the African Group and the Group of 77 during the preparatory meetings held in Addis Ababa in March 1987 and in Havana one month later. If the seventh session was to produce tangible results, the member countries of UNCTAD, particularly the industrialized countries, had to demonstrate the necessary political will to forge ahead in revitalizing development and establishing a more equitable and human new international economic order.

Summary of the statement made at the 209th plenary meeting, 15 July 1987, by Mr. Tobgye S. DORJI, Permanent Representative of Bhutan to the United Nations Office at Geneva

1. Mr. DORJI (Bhutan) said that the factors in the critical world economic situation affecting the developing countries included the collapse of commodity prices and deteriorating terms of trade, the intolerable debt burden and costly adjustment programmes which restricted development, the stagnation of ODA and sharp contraction in financial flows, the net transfer of resources from developing to developed countries, the proliferation of protectionist and distorting measures impeding exports and obstructing structural adjustments, the erosion of the multilateral trading system, and the aggravation of the structural problems of the LDCs, including the land-locked and island developing countries. Little had been done to deal with that worsening situation, which threatened international stability, on the basis of shared responsibilities. The developing countries remained on the periphery. It was clear that world economic relations would have to be reconstructed, through a new and bold approach, on the basis of universality, equity and interdependence, with a renewed commitment to multilateral co-operation.

2. The rise in the number of LDCs, of which Bhutan was one and which were particularly hard hit by the economic crisis, reflected the increasing plight of developing countries as a whole. It was regrettable that, although some donors to the Substantial New Programme of Action for the 1980s for the Least Developed Countries, including Denmark, Netherlands, Norway and Sweden, had commendably exceeded the ODA target of 0.15 per cent of GNP and others had attained that target, bilateral and multilateral development assistance to the LDCs had decreased overall during the 1980s and had not attained even half of the target. His delegation urged those which had not met that target or doubled their ODA to those countries to make every effort to do so.

3. It was unfortunate that the majority of the main donor countries did not recognize the land-locked developing countries, which were among the very poorest of the developing countries, as a special category of countries requiring a separate assistance programme. The assistance provided and measures taken to implement the resolutions relating to those countries were still inadequate. In providing technical and financial assistance to least-developed land-locked countries, donors should concentrate on capital input in infrastructural development. International bodies, especially UNDP and the regional commissions, should continue to support those countries with measures to alleviate their specific transit-transport and communications problems.

4. The LDCs had themselves taken a number of measures to improve their economic situation, including the adoption of policies to mobilize domestic resources, expand food and agricultural production and develop external trade, and, for the most part, had designated focal points for the implementation, follow-up and monitoring of the Substantial New Programme of Action. It was necessary to implement fully and expeditiously all the recommendations adopted as a result of the intergovernmental mid-term global review of the Substantial New Programme of Action, along with other measures included in the Programme. Progress had so far been painfully slow and the situation of the LDCs was still critical. As the end of the decade of the 1980s was approaching, the Conference should begin considering a new programme for the LDCs for the 1990s. His delegation welcomed the invitation extended by the President of France to host the 1990 conference on LDCs.

5. The developing countries, keenly aware though they were of their own responsibility for promoting the socio-economic development of their people, were seriously handicapped by a number of external constraints which left them no room for manoeuvre. It was for that reason that they were seeking development

assistance and advocating a more responsible world economic order, involving commitment, political will and flexibility on the part of all, in particular the developed countries. The global economic system should be restructured and the implementation of the International Development Strategy for the Third United Nations Development Decade was of paramount importance.

6. His delegation fully supported the assessment and proposals by the Group of 77 (see TD/330), which were realistic and balanced and showed that the developing world was playing and would play an impor-

tant part in global economic and financial recovery. It welcomed the decision of the Soviet Union to sign the Agreement Establishing the Common Fund for Commodities, and urged those countries which had not signed or ratified the Agreement to do so. It welcomed the announcement that Cote d'Ivoire would sign the Agreement.

7. The Conference could exert a significant influence on future trends in the world economic situation and in political relations and, it was hoped, would play a constructive part in seeking practical solutions to the acute economic problems of the world.

Summary of the statement made at the 216th plenary meeting, 29 July 1987, by Mr. Raúl ESPAÑA-SMITH, Permanent Representative of Bolivia to the United Nations Office at Geneva

1. Mr. ESPAÑA-SMITH said that UNCTAD had, for almost a quarter of a century, acted as a universal forum where countries at different levels of development and with different economic systems could engage in a dialogue and negotiations with a view to instilling into international economic relationships the minimum amount of rationality and equity needed for all human beings to be able to live in comfort and dignity.

2. Despite the far-reaching transformations taking place in the international eocnomic system, the considerable gulf separating North and South, namely, the rich and poor countries, remained a threat to world stability. In that respect, UNCTAD had, over the previous 20 years, largely contributed to emphasizing the interdependence of trade, finance and development, as demonstrated by the adoption of the GSP, the Agreement Establishing the Common Fund for Commodities and the setting up of a system of economic co-operation between countries in the southern hemisphere. However, as the Group of 77 had clearly indicated in the Havana Declaration, some alarming signs of economic collapse were emerging such as the fall in commodity prices to their lowest level for 50 years, the threat to international trade from persistent protectionism and the extremely worrying international financial situation. Appropriate measures must therefore be taken at the seventh session of the Conference.

3. The fate of the Latin American countries depended directly on the outcome of the two crises affecting the developing countries, namely, the foreign debt and commodity crises. New solutions must be found to the foreign debt problem, which constituted a heavy burden on the developing countries, in order to encourage financing and investment in proportion to the real capacities of the debtor countries and their development needs. It would, indeed, be surprising if the great Powers which, 60 years previously, had been able to find reasonable ways and means of alleviating their war debt burdens, now proved unable to produce suitable policies to help solve what was a serious problem for the developing countries. The Bolivian Government had proposed a novel solution, consisting in providing incentives for private creditors to convert their loans into development investments, which would enable them to recover their capital.

4. His Government welcomed the initiatives taken to set up a permanent market information exchange mechanism for commodities. However, even if price fluctuations were indeed factors that played an important role in the economy, the influence of social and institutional problems on the adjustment processes proposed was not always sufficiently taken into consideration. Development was reflected not only in the volume of production, but also in the time taken by the economy to react to market developments. Not only were the developing countries hampered by the lack of diversification of their production, but they also had greater difficulty in adapting production to changes in market conditions. For that reason, market stabilization agreements should be sought more actively, and the revival of interest in the Integrated Programme for Commodities and the Common Fund was to be welcomed.

5. The efforts made by the developing countries to react to the drop in the prices of their main export products and to diversify their production—or to increase it in those rare cases where prices had remained stable—had encountered the major obstacle of protectionism. In that respect, it was precisely the countries that had noised abroad the advantages of free market competition that were the most protectionist. Could it be that the Governments of those countries thought that the free competition principle was effective at the domestic level, but was not applicable to international trade relationships? The Bolivian Government was of the opinion that the advantages of a free market both domestically and internationally were obvious. The dire effects of the world crisis on the developing countries could not be eliminated by domestic measures alone and, in the absence of equitable international co-operation, they would continue to be merely pointless sacrifices.

6. Bolivia, which had been particularly affected by the collapse of the tin market and the drop in the prices of petroleum and other mineral products, had embarked upon thorough structural readjustment and had been able, over a period of two years, to reduce its inflation rate from 24,000 per cent to 10 per cent annually and to achieve an increase of 2 per cent in its GDP,

following a drop of 25 per cent. Continuation of that major effort, undertaken at enormous social cost, naturally depended on international economic conditions and the support of the world community.

7.   But since the establishment of UNCTAD, the Bolivian Government had attached particular importance to measures in favour of the land-locked developing countries, whose geographical situation hampered their economic development. The matter was of special importance to Bolivia as a Latin American developing country which was at a level very close to that of the so-called "least developed" countries, but which did not receive international aid under that heading. Moreover, Bolivia's lack of a Pacific coastline was attributable to a war of occupation, and the Bolivian Government would

continue to do everything possible to settle the dispute peacefully, in accordance with international law and the principles of the Charter of the United Nations and the Charter of the Organization of American States, so that the country could derive full benefit from the resources that belonged to it and thereby eliminate a serious obstacle to its development.

8.   The Bolivian Government and people hoped that the Conference at its seventh session would make an effective contribution to the search for a multilateral solution to the crisis affecting the world, and that the community of industrialized countries would continue not only to provide development aid, but also to improve the fabric of trade, in the direction of fraternity and equity.

Summary of the statement made at the 217th plenary meeting, 29 July 1987, by Mr. Roberto COSTA DE ABREU SODRE, Minister for External Relations of Brazil

1.   Mr. COSTA DE ABREU SODRE said that since its creation UNCTAD had made great efforts to increase the share of the developing countries in international trade, especially with the establishment of the GSP and the launching of the Integrated Programme for Commodities and that, in spite of the difficulties encountered, it had an increasing role to play in enhancing international economic co-operation.

2.   The developing countries were in a state of acute crisis and external conditions were impeding their economic recovery efforts. They were, indeed, the first victims of the instability of international economic relations and of the fiscal, monetary, financial and commercial imbalances which hampered growth and world trade. For the first time since the Second World War, growth had slowed down in practically all the third-world countries. Commodity prices had plummeted to even lower levels than during the crisis of the 1930s. Protectionism hindered the developing countries' access to markets where their exports had proved to be competitive, and a large number of them were now in the untenable situation of being net exporters of financial resources.

3.   The debt problem continued to place a heavy burden not only on the third world but also on the world economy as a whole. There was still a refusal to tackle that problem from the political standpoint, taking into account the needs of the debtor countries and the joint responsibility of creditors and debtors alike. An attempt was being made, moreover, to confine the benefits of the technological revolution to a handful of countries, thereby producing a new international division of labour not between the producers of primary commodities and the industrialized countries, but between countries which produced and those which consumed new technologies, the latter being dependent on the former.

4.   The picture offered by international trade in commodities was extremely discouraging. Prices had dropped to an all-time low, causing staggering losses in terms of the export earnings of the developing coun-

tries. Some disturbing trends were emerging in that vital sector, leaving producers at the mercy of speculative manœuvres and brutal fluctuations. It was essential for exporters and importers to assume their responsibilities and in that regard the early operation of the Common Fund, as part of the Integrated Programme for Commodities, must be one of the major goals of the countries represented at the Conference.

5.   Interdependence had not led to a more harmonious and equitable international system and matters would not improve as long as policies aimed at maintaining hegemonic relationships were maintained. The creation of UNCTAD and the Group of 77 had precisely been inspired by the need to reorganize international economic relations. The objectives pursued by the Group of 77 had lost none of their validity; quite the contrary. The problems of industrialized countries—unemployment, low rates of growth, etc.—were due in part to the lack of outlets for their products. Yet the developing countries could very well evolve into the required markets for such products, if only they had the means to do so. In other words, the leading economies had a stake in the increased prosperity of the less affluent nations.

6.   The proposal of the Group of 77 for a new international trading system was not as radical as it might seem. It involved replacing the existing system, which no longer served development requirements, by a new system allowing for market expansion and economic growth in the third-world countries. UNCTAD could play a decisive role in that regard.

7.   Brazil attached great importance to the proposals made by the Group of 77 with a view to strengthening the GSP, above all in the light of the unilateral changes recently introduced in some national GSP schemes. The international community must firmly oppose attempts to undermine the GSP and convert it into an instrument of economic pressure. Regarding the Uruguay Round, it was essential for all countries, in particular the developed nations, to respect their standstill and rollback commitments. Brazil, for its part, would spare no

effort in contributing to the success of those negotiations.

8. The international community should continue to give particular attention to the LDCs, which found themselves in a critical situation. All countries should combine efforts to ensure full implementation of the Substantial New Programme of Action for the 1980s for the Least Developed Countries. Brazil, despite its limited resources, was doing its utmost to assist the LDCs and hoped that the Conference would contribute to strengthening co-operation in that regard.

9. Reducing the role of UNCTAD would jeopardize North-South co-operation, which was of crucial importance in the current period of crisis. Brazil had contributed actively to the formulation of the proposals submitted by the Group of 77 to the Conference; they were constructive proposals aimed at finding solutions to the benefit of all nations. The Conference offered all members of UNCTAD the opportunity to agree on a set of measures to improve international economic relations in the interest of development and peace. Failure to seize that opportunity would be a serious mistake on their part.

Summary of the statement made at the 218th plenary meeting, 30 July 1987, by Dato' Paduka Haji Selamat BIN HAJI MUNAP, Deputy Minister of Development of Brunei Darussalam

1. Dato' BIN HAJI MUNAP said that, at the current stage of the general debate, he simply wished to state his country's position on certain agenda items. His delegation shared the conviction of other delegations that UNCTAD and its multilateral approach, aimed at revitalizing development, growth and international trade in a more predictable and supportive environment, offered the best opportunity of devising a lasting solution to world economic problems. No country, whether rich or poor, developed or developing, large or small, could escape the adverse effects of the deteriorating world economic situation, but it was clear that the developing countries suffered the most. The indebtedness of most of them was one of the most serious problems, and an increase in the flow of capital from outside would not in itself be sufficient to resolve it. All the parties concerned must draw up comprehensive growth strategies, not only to respond to the immediate needs of the developing countries, but also to support their long-term development programmes.

2. In view of the growing trade difficulties encountered by developing countries in the 1980s, his delegation was concerned about the erosion of the fundamental principles of non-discrimination and non-reciprocity embodied in the GSP and considered that the use of per capita GNP to determine the applicability of a graduation scheme under the GSP was unfair and unrealistic. The liberalization and expansion of trade were essential for the promotion of development, in the interest of all countries. Protectionism was harmful to both developed and developing countries and inevitably led to inefficiency, waste and economic decay. In view of the collapse of commodity prices, his delegation wished to reaffirm the validity of the directives and measures of the Integrated Programme for Commodities. As for the LDCs, it was comforting to note that no one ignored or denied the special problems faced by those countries, but the fact remained that the developed countries must commit themselves to accepting responsibility for supporting their development efforts.

3. His delegation supported the views expressed by the Group of 77 in its proposals on the adoption and implementation of a coherent set of measures covering critical areas where the needs of developing countries were most pressing. It was grateful to the other countries members of the Association of South-East Asian Nations, as well as Switzerland, for their words of welcome on Brunei Darussalam's admission to UNCTAD.

Summary of the statement made at the 203rd plenary meeting, 10 July 1987, by Mr. Hristo HRISTOV, Minister of Trade of Bulgaria

1. Mr. HRISTOV said that, in an increasingly interdependent world, the problems facing mankind could not be solved by policies based on arms superiority and confrontation; they could only be dealt with by genuine partnership and mutually supportive efforts by all countries. A stable, peaceful, political environment, with significant balanced reductions in armaments and the consequent release of additional resources for economic restructuring and development could lead to a new level of global economic interaction as a basic factor for renewed growth. The positive response of world opinion to the recent initiatives of the Soviet Union and the other socialist countries along those lines reconfirmed the relevance of such an approach.

2. UNCTAD had established itself as a leading international forum for developing forward-looking strategies and approaches fostering international economic co-operation. Modern technologies against a background of greater political and economic security offered new, historic opportunities for overcoming imbalances in the world economy in the common interests of mankind. The report by the Secretary-General of UNCTAD represented a significant effort to focus at-

tention on the key issues, the most urgent of which was perhaps that of the indebtedness of the developing countries, for the service of their debt was a drain on resources that should be devoted to their development and jeopardized their economic and social viability. It was the joint responsibility of debtor and creditor countries to find a durable solution to the debt problem, by strengthening the productive capacities of debtor countries through appropriate modern technologies, progressive economic restructuring and access to international markets on favourable terms.

3. Depressed commodity prices accentuated the difficulties of the developing countries. In a context of reductions in the use of raw materials and the spread of technological innovations, the terms of trade of commodity exporters could no longer be significantly improved by reliance on classic market trends; the need was for integrated approaches and harmonized programmes for the diversification and upgrading of commodity production, including the necessary transfer of technologies and capital investment supplemented by traditional price stabilization schemes backed, if necessary, by joint financing arrangements.

4. He stressed that protectionism and restrictive business practices were inappropriate responses to the changes being wrought by modern technology in the manufacturing, raw materials and agricultural sectors. Co-ordinated action to liberalize trade and promote structural adjustment was needed, and in that regard the Uruguay Round had a particularly important role to play. UNCTAD itself could make a most important contribution through recommendations adopted on the basis of periodic reviews and analyses. It should be possible to identify significant additional opportunities for trade and economic co-operation among countries with different socio-economic systems on the basis of

complementarity of economic structures and common interest.

5. Bulgaria, which was undergoing major economic and social change, aimed to enhance social equity on the basis of a more efficient economy, through accelerated technological innovations and decentralized decision-making, self-management and self-financing at the enterprise level. Trade was being expanded through an overall market orientation of business activity. In recent decades, Bulgaria had stepped up its trade and economic co-operation with developing countries, offering assistance for modernizing agriculture and industrial production through technical assistance and supplies of engineering services and equipment on favourable terms. By concentrating on projects relating to infrastructure and small and medium enterprises, more efficient use was being made of local resources, skilled manpower resources were being developed and export capacities expanded. In 1986, the total volume of Bulgaria's economic assistance to developing countries had amounted to over $350 million, or 1.23 per cent of Bulgaria's GNP. Steps taken to reschedule the repayment of Bulgaria's credits granted to a number of LDCs had been coupled with new investments in projects in the raw materials, agriculture and manufacturing sectors of the countries concerned.

6. Bulgaria had been pursuing a consistent policy of increasing trade and economic exchanges with developed market-economy countries, providing new opportunities for direct contacts and business with Bulgarian enterprises on the basis of mutual interest and equal rights and obligations. Bulgaria had also applied for accession to GATT and was negotiating a trade and economic agreement with the European Community. It was actively involved in the restructuring of the mechanisms of CMEA and various forms of economic integration, which should also result in increased opportunities for trade with countries outside the CMEA.

**Summary of the statement made at the 211th plenary meeting, 24 July 1987,
by Mr. Mohamadou TOURE, Minister of Commerce and People's Supply of Burkina Faso**

1. Mr. TOURE, drawing attention to the shocking inequalities and contradictions present in today's world, where the misery of hundreds of millions of human beings stood out in stark contrast with the planet's enormous wealth and technical potential, welcomed the fact that the seventh session of the Conference was being held at a time when multilateral co-operation among all States was finally being recognized as the only viable path to follow.

2. The way the monetary and financial system now worked was preventing trade expansion and cancelling out all the efforts being made by the developing countries by depriving them of the necessary financial resources. Inadequate national savings, the decline in export earnings and monetary depreciation had saddled the developing countries with a critical debt burden. It was therefore essential to reform the international monetary system, which was being seriously threatened

by the debt of countries that were always in greater need of liquidities. Such a reform would require a reorganization of the commodity market, where prices had followed a steady downward trend since 1980 as industrialized country demand had been deliberately compressed by the emergence of substitutes and the rise of protectionism. Some countries, such as the United States, the members of the EEC and Japan, subsidized their products quite heavily, thereby making those of the developing countries less competitive. In view of that situation, Burkina Faso had chosen to absorb a large part of its production domestically, a policy which also boosted employment. The Burkina-Be had set up cottage industries to process the country's raw materials. They, like other peoples of the world, were aware of the collapse of the international capitalist system. The current serious crisis should induce all developing countries to affirm their determination to undertake economic reorganization in such a way as to satisfy the material and other needs of their peoples, the sole masters of the fate of mankind.

3. To fulfil its historical role, UNCTAD had to identify and find practical solutions to the problems of peoples. The concept of peoples should be given paramount importance in any analysis. The peoples of the third world would not be in the tragic situation they now faced if they had taken account of that reality and had avoided following a model of society and development approaches over which they had no control. There was no point in asking for the support of the developed countries, since they had helped to implement economically and socially unviable projects of which they had taken advantage to market their own products while offering suicidal credit to the developing countries. The only path to salvation for the developing world was to follow the will of its peoples. In Burkina Faso, basic economic, cultural, legislative and political choices were made by the people as a whole and the National Revolutionary Council was responsible for ensuring their implementation. Four years had elapsed since the Revolution and the country was now on the right course. It had reduced its trade balance deficit and set up economic interest groups to improve distribution networks, a unique experiment in Africa. Burkina Faso maintained good relations with all countries that respected human rights and shared its ideals of justice and peace.

4. If it was to survive, UNCTAD would have to take account of the aspirations of all peoples. Burkina Faso therefore attached particular importance to the Agreement Establishing the Common Fund for Commodities and congratulated the Soviet Union for having signed it and urged all countries which had not yet ratified it, such as the United States, to do so.

5. While advocating free trade, the developed countries relied more and more heavily on protectionism and their transnational corporations prevented the expansion of the developing countries' trade. Burkina Faso believed that UNCTAD had a key role to play in negotiating and implementing international trade measures in promoting the establishment of a new international economic order—unwelcome though it might be to those who profited by the current situation—and in fostering solidarity among all its members.

6. Despite the measures adopted since 1981 under the Substantial New Programme of Action, the situation of the LDCs, whose ranks had grown from 31 in 1981 to 40 in 1986, had continued to worsen and urgently required a special programme of action to introduce measures to cancel the debt burden, increase ODA to the level set in the Programme of Action and improve compensatory financing mechanisms with more favourable provisions for the LDCs.

7. Burkina Faso hoped that the seventh session of the Conference would be a milestone in the search for genuine equity in relations between North and South, which were mutually in need of each other. Their economic interdependence made it imperative for them not only to harmonize national policies, but also to work together to manage the world economy.

Summary of the statement made at the 218th plenary meeting, 30 July 1987, by U TIN TUN, Permanent Representative of Burma to the United Nations Office at Geneva

1. U TIN TUN said that, since the sixth session of the Conference and despite the efforts of the international community, the world economy had been experiencing an unprecedented crisis by which all countries, but especially the developing countries, had been affected. In many of the latter, per capita income had fallen below the levels of 10 years before, the prices of their export commodities in real terms had dropped to the lowest level in 40 years, their access to export markets had been reduced and the debt burden had reached alarming proportions. In almost all of them the development process had been impeded; that had resulted in a reduction in their import capacity, a consequent drop in exports for the developed countries, and, eventually, a slump in world economic activity as a whole. The Burmese delegation considered that an effective and enduring recovery of the world economy called for determined efforts to revitalize the development process and the fundamental restructuring of the world economic system. The Conference's agenda was geared to those objectives, and all countries must work together to transform their aspirations into specific measures and action programmes.

2. The Burmese delegation attached special importance to some of the main agenda items before the Conference. Burma, which depended on commodities for its export earnings, was most concerned by the alarming situation on world commodity markets. Swift and concerted international action, focusing first of all on ensuring just and remunerative prices for those products, was needed to overcome the current crisis, which had not only severely disrupted the development efforts of developing countries, but had also had considerable repercussions on the entire world economy. The crisis could not, therefore, be considered a problem for developing countries alone, but must be seen in the wider context of the prosperity of the entire international community. Any solution must entail financial support for the developing countries so that they could diversify their commodity production and exports. One possibility would be to guarantee them, by means of international co-operation measures and mechanisms, a greater share in the processing, marketing, transport and distribution of their products. Tariff escalation and other protectionist measures applied to processed and semi-processed products from developing countries

must cease, and such countries must be given support and assistance in the financial and technological fields and in manpower training so as to enable them to improve the competitiveness of natural products. Although compensatory financing facilities had been somewhat liberalized, efforts must continue and the introduction of an additional facility to compensate for the export earnings shortfalls of the developing countries should be speeded up.

3. Referring to the subject of resources for development, he said that developing countries were obliged to bear a heavy debt burden as a result of external circumstances beyong their control. They had presented mutually supportive measures to overcome the debt crisis, including the implementation of an appropriate debt strategy, an increase in the flow of financial resources to developing countries and a reform of the international monetary system. His delegation hoped that, of the measures proposed, particular attention would be given to the appeal for greater efforts to attain, as quickly as possible, internationally agreed ODA targets and implementation of the proposal for a new allocation of special drawing rights linked to the needs of developing countries. In addition, ways should be found for developed countries to forego their share of profits in favour of developing countries in need of reserves. Any progress in the developing countries would help to revitalize the economy of developed countries.

4. On the subject of international trade, he said that his delegation had noted a growing disregard for the fundamental principles and international commitments on which such trade was based. Rising protectionism, the increasing number of trade barriers erected against exports from developing countries and the search for

bilateral solutions to trade problems outside the framework of multilateral rules and principles were all becoming common practice. There must, first of all, be an agreement to halt and roll back protectionism and encourage the liberalization of tariff and non-tariff barriers and other export restraints. Measures should then be taken to improve and strengthen the international trade system and draw up programmes that would facilitate structural adjustment and thus improve market access for developing countries.

5. The overall socio-economic situation of the LDCs had continued to deteriorate, despite the increased attention paid by the international community and international organizations to the search for a lasting solution to their problems, mainly by the adoption of the Substantial New Programme of Action in 1981. The GDP and per capita food production of the LDCs as a group had declined, and the situation with regard to external payments and terms of trade had deteriorated for most of them. Those difficulties had been compounded by increasing protectionist measures and a reduction in ODA and other types of capital flows. His delegation endorsed the specific measures suggested by the developing countries to alleviate the severe economic and social difficulties faced by the LDCs and hoped that they would be swiftly implemented, particularly through the adequate implementation of the Substantial New Programme of Action and the resolutions on LDCs adopted by the General Assembly and in UNCTAD. His delegation hoped that the international community would take full advantage of the opportunity offered by the seventh session to consider the interdependence of the world economy and devise a coherent multilateral strategy to revitalize development, growth and international trade.

**Summary of the statement made at the 216th plenary meeting, 29 July 1987,
by Mr. Vassili I. PESHKOV, Permanent Representative of the Byelorussian Soviet Socialist Republic
to the United Nations Office at Geneva**

1. Mr. PESHKOV said that at its seventh session the Conference, during its consideration of the vital subject of revitalizing development, growth and international trade, could and must contribute to promoting international economic co-operation which, for many reasons, was experiencing major difficulties. The general debate offered an opportunity for in-depth exchanges of views and for developing joint approaches that would lead to constructive decisions, and particularly decisions that could strengthen the role of UNCTAD.

2. His Government, like others, was concerned by an international situation made increasingly complex by the intensification of the arms race, especially the nuclear arms race, by increasing imbalances in international economic relationships, the destabilization of economic, trade, monetary and financial relationships between States, and by the deterioration in the economic situation of the developing countries. In its report (TD/328), the UNCTAD secretariat also

noted that the international economic situation had deteriorated during the 1980s and that long-term economic indicators were becoming less and less reliable. The report by the Secretary-General of UNCTAD (TD/329/Rev.1) also pointed to a number of adverse factors, particularly exchange rates, interest rates, commodity prices and protectionism. In addition, it indicated that military expenditure was swallowing up enormous resources while at the same time representing a threat to the survival of mankind itself.

3. In the circumstances, ways must be found of solving the problems of the world economy in an effective and coherent manner, and in that respect the proposals made at the Conference were extremely useful. A particularly serious problem currently was the foreign indebtedness of the developing countries, which appeared to reflect many aspects of the economic and political situation in those countries.

4. In their statement on the elimination of underdevelopment and the establishment of a new inter-

national economic order, the States parties to the Warsaw Treaty had stressed that the debt problem of the
developing countries had global economic, political and
social causes and global economic, political and social
consequences; they had recommended that an international forum should be convened to examine, as a
whole, issues of economic security, the establishment of
a new international economic order, the development of
co-operation in trade, in science and technology and the
elimination of all factors straining international
economic relationships. The Byelorussian SSR fully
shared the concerns expressed by the non-aligned and
developing countries which were calling for a solution to
the debt problem that was based on equality and would
not affect economic growth. It also supported proposals
to restructure the international financial and monetary
system in a manner that took account of the interests of
all States and was of the opinion that action along
those lines should be examined by an international conference that could be convened under the auspices of the
United Nations or by any other representative international forum, with the participation of all interested
countries. It should be possible, in order to alleviate the
difficulties being experienced by the developing countries, to strike a balance between the role of the State
and that of the private sector in economic development,
and to emphasize that the State, even in the context of
current economic difficulties, was often in a better position to solve a number of economic and social problems
which were beyond the control of private enterprises.

5.   The adverse effects of militarization on international economic relationships were also obvious: many
developing countries have been deprived of their
sovereign rights over their natural resources and currently a considerable proportion of the material wealth
produced by the labour of the masses was being used to
manufacture weapons of destruction. It was clear from
the general debate that practical efforts to reduce
military budgets would release a significant amount of
material and financial resources that could be used for
peaceful and constructive purposes, such as the elimination of underdevelopment in many regions of the world
and the solution of problems of indebtedness.
UNCTAD must play a leading role in the elaboration of
principles governing the use of the resources released by
reductions in military budgets for the benefit of
mankind, and particularly of the developing countries,
and it was to be noted in that respect how important the
International Conference on the Relationship between
Disarmament and Development would be.

6.   The socialist countries had formulated a set of
proposals to develop international co-operation and
create a new climate of peace and security in the world,

thus demonstrating their new political thinking. Those
proposals, which had received broad support at the
forty-first session of the General Assembly, concerned
military, political, economic and social security and
were designed to eliminate confrontational attitudes,
establish new humanitarian norms and bring about a
climate of openness and confidence, conducive to the
maintenance of peace and security in the world. In that
way common values would be better respected and all
peoples would have freedom of choice in the social,
political and ideological spheres.

7.   The question of international economic security
was of the greatest importance, as the General Assembly
had stressed in its resolutions 40/173 and 41/184, and
UNCTAD must play an important role in that connection. The concept of security, which was based on
stability and harmony in economic relationships, should
not replace the idea of establishing a new international
economic order; rather, its purpose was to satisfy the
wishes of all States, and particularly the aspirations of
developing countries as formulated in the Havana
Declaration and by the Declaration of the Eighth Conference of Heads of State or Government of Non-
Aligned Countries, held at Harare.

8.   On the occasion of the seventieth anniversary of
the October Revolution, steps had been taken in the
Byelorussian SSR to speed up the pace of economic and
social development; a programme for the radical reform
of economic management had been adopted and a new
system that would have far-reaching effects on all
aspects of daily life had been introduced. Moreover, the
purpose of the recent law on national enterprises was to
bring about far-reaching changes in the country's
economic structure and accelerate economic development by restructuring enterprises and improving the
quality of industrial production. The State was promoting scientific research in all sectors, and during the
previous year industrial production had increased by
7 per cent, agricultural production by 6.2 per cent and
housing construction by 4 per cent. The results already
achieved under the 1986-1990 five-year plan clearly
demonstrated the progress made in all economic sectors.
Particular attention was being paid to new forms of international economic co-operation, and particularly to
the establishment and management of joint enterprises
which would contribute to the stability of long-term
economic co-operation in a climate of mutual confidence and respect.

9.   UNCTAD had, ever since its establishment,
endeavoured to strengthen international economic co-
operation, and was the best-placed international body
to continue seeking solutions to the complex problems
of the world economy.

**Summary of the statement made at the 210th plenary meeting, 24 July 1987,
by Mr. Michael Elangwe NAMAYA, Secretary of State for Trade and Industries of Cameroon**

1.   Mr. NAMAYA said that his delegation welcomed
the fact that revitalization of development, growth and
international trade had been made the objective of the
Conference. It reaffirmed its support for the United

Nations as the pre-eminent multilateral negotiating
forum where all nations could exchange views in order
to arrive at equitable solutions to problems of common
interest. UNCTAD was the body in which trade and

development problems could be discussed globally and rationally.

2. The current international economic environment had caused an unprecedented crisis in developing countries, many of which, particularly in sub-Saharan Africa, had recently recorded the lowest growth rates, with complete stagnation in some of them.

3. That situation was largely due to the well-known external factors which were analysed in reports before the Conference (TD/329 and TD/328) and which, through their combined effect, had led to the debt crisis, growing poverty, a fall in living standards, high unemployment rates and cut-backs in social services.

4. The world economic crisis had brought home the facts of the interdependence of nations, the need for developed countries to co-ordinate their macro-economic policies, the sovereignty of States in their search for solutions and the need for multilateral co-operation and international solidarity.

5. The deflationary policies of developed market-economy countries, characterized by low demand and monetary stringency, had enabled those countries to curb inflation. However, the combination of low demand and financial instability exerted a negative influence on international trade. Because of the low demand there had been a rash of protectionist measures, the prices of raw materials had dropped, and as a consequence developing countries had been unable to market their exports, improve their terms of trade or acquire goods and services produced in developed countries.

6. The developed countries should co-ordinate their macro-economic policies in order to stimulate and maintain growth in the interest of all concerned. His delegation therefore welcomed the co-ordination process begun by the major developed countries in recent months, particularly at the Venice Summit in June 1987. Such co-ordination should be used not only to reduce trade imbalances between the developed countries but also to reduce real interest rates and stimulate overall growth.

7. Economic adjustment measures should not be imposed from outside but should result from a careful analysis of the economic and social situation in individual countries. As to the need to reinforce multilateral co-operation and international solidarity with a view to restoring stable growth and development, he said that the proposals of the Group of 77 (TD/330) were cogent.

8. Cameroon was deeply concerned about the sharp fall and instability of commodity prices. The Conference offered a useful opportunity for exploring ways of increasing the contribution of commodities to development. His delegation reaffirmed its commitment to the Integrated Programme for Commodities, whose objectives remained valid, and called for its full implementation, together with urgent attention to the effective operation of the Common Fund. Cameroon, which itself had long before ratified the Agreement Establishing the Common Fund, welcomed the decision of the Soviet Union and Côte d'Ivoire to sign that Agreement.

9. It was paradoxical that instead of a flow of financial resources from the rich countries to the poor countries, debt repayments were causing a reverse flow. The Conference should therefore adopt a comprehensive approach to the debt crisis, taking account of the basic economic needs of debtor countries and suggesting solutions that would enable them both to honour their obligations and to promote growth.

10. The need for increased participation by developing countries in world trade should be recognized and the GSP should be made a more effective instrument of trade policy by a broadening of its product coverage. In addition, the international trading system should be adapted to current realities and its constraints and inadequacies should be removed. The Uruguay Round of multilateral trade negotiations offered an opportunity for such action. Governments should fulfil the standstill and roll-back commitments entered into at the GATT Ministerial Meeting at Punta del Este.

11. The particularly difficult situation of the LDCs called for increased and urgent international assistance to those countries. He therefore welcomed President Mitterrand's announcement of France's readiness to host the international conference to be held in 1990 to review the implementation of the Substantial New Programme of Action.

12. Like most developing countries, Cameroon was hard hit by the world economic crisis. It had, for example, suffered a deficit of well over $700 million in its export earnings in 1986-1987. To remedy that state of affairs, the Government was taking steps to cut down State expenditure, lay stress on stringency in economic management, re-evaluate public and semi-public enterprises, privatize some State corporations, stimulate production, encourage small and medium-sized enterprises and industries and reorganize the public service. To be effective, however, those measures would need to be supported by assistance from the international community. He hoped that the necessary political will would be forthcoming for the adoption by the Conference of renewed multilateral co-operation policies and measures that could revitalize growth and development.

Summary of the statement made at the 209th plenary meeting, 15 July 1987, by Mrs. Monique LANDRY, Minister of External Relations of Canada

1. Mrs. LANDRY said that the principle of constructive internationalism, which was the corner-stone of Canadian foreign policy, meant support for multilateral institutions, close co-operation with Canada's main economic partners and an unshakeable commitment to development in the third world. The seventh session of the Conference was considered a key element in the continuing dialogue in which both

developed and developing countries participated. By her personal experience in the course of official visits to many third world countries, including African countries, she had become more convinced than ever of the need for developed and developing countries alike, and for UNCTAD as an international body, to work together to maintain a constructive dialogue leading to workable solutions to complex development issues, in particular, and, more broadly, to the global economic problems which threatened world economic and political stability.

2. Financial flows from developed countries remained of crucial importance. Aid targets brought a message of hope to the developing countries and inspired donors to maintain the flow of resources to those countries even in times of financial stringency. Concurrently, efforts should be intensified to make the most efficient use of scarce resources, to co-ordinate the aid provided more fully and to channel more resources to the poorest countries. Her Government stood committed to its overall ODA targets; it would maintain the level of its ODA at 0.5 per cent of GNP—such assistance having exceeded $Can 2.5 billion in the previous fiscal year—and was aiming to reach 0.7 per cent of GNP by the year 2000. The target of 0.15 per cent of GNP for flows to LDCs had already been reached, and flows to Africa had been increased. So far as multilateral institutions were concerned, she said it was most desirable to strengthen the key roles of the World Bank, the regional development banks and IMF, which should have the resources to support necessary changes and stimulate growth in developing countries. At the same time, the developing countries, being primarily responsible for their own development, should focus on making optimum use of their domestic savings and investment, ensuring greater efficiency in the public sector and promoting the role of the private sector in the strengthening of the economy.

3. Speaking on the subject of external debt, which was of concern to both developed and developing countries, she said that the heavily indebted middle-income countries, whose economies had considerable potential, should realize how important it was to restore their creditworthiness; for the purpose of correcting imbalances they should apply policies which, though difficult to carry out, were crucial to their future. In the case of the poorest countries, it was now well-nigh universally agreed that more needed to be done. The crucial problem for those countries was not so much debt management as development. In Canada's view, there were several key elements to be taken into account in dealing with their debt. In the first place, some way should be found of reducing their indebtedness towards IMF and the World Bank, for they could hardly be expected to repay more than they received from those two institutions. Secondly, future assistance in support of the adjustment efforts of those countries should be more concessional. Thirdly, their public external debt should be rescheduled for longer periods and on easier terms. Fourthly, countries which had not already waived or deferred repayment of their ODA should do so as soon as possible. Fifthly, flows of ODA should be increased and development strategies should be more effectively co-ordinated. Last but not least, the

beneficiary countries themselves should make sure that their own economic policies were both realistic and appropriate.

4. For 25 years international trade had been the driving force responsible for the world's economic growth. In recent years, however, trade had not been making the same contribution to development as in the past. Trade disputes, protectionist pressures and tension between developed countries, and between them and developing countries, had a direct bearing on the debt problem. Confidence in the GATT system should be restored and progress should be made in the Uruguay Round in dealing with the restrictions and distortions that affected trade. In the common interest, an improved set of rules should be devised in the context of the multilateral trade negotiations in order to meet the challenges of the times. One of Canada's major concerns was trade in agricultural commodities, which was threatened by a potentially destructive subsidy war. It was now generally recognized that fundamental reforms were needed in the agricultural sector of international trade, and she hoped that the multilateral negotiations would achieve their objectives in that respect.

5. The fluctuation and decline in commodity prices had a direct impact on development, particularly, but not exclusively, in the developing countries. As a large exporter and importer of primary commodities Canada had a direct interest in the trade in commodities; it was convinced that problems arising in connection with that trade were best dealt with in the context of relations between producers and consumers. Several factors should be taken into account in devising a practical common approach to those issues. First, policies and practices with distorting effects on commodity markets should be avoided. Secondly, the developing countries should endeavour to diversify their economies, taking advantage of the opportunities offered by domestic, regional and international markets, and such opportunities should be safeguarded and expanded through the multilateral trade negotiations. Thirdly, a more sustained producer-consumer dialogue would be the most effective way of settling problems, enhancing market transparency and enabling producers to respond better to market signals.

6. UNCTAD faced a great challenge in the changing world. Steady, high rates of economic growth could no longer be taken for granted. Additional countries had become key players on the economic scene and former relationships had altered. The global division of labour between developed and developing countries was changing fast under the influence of technology and market forces. Moreover, technology had altered patterns of production in the manufacturing and services sectors. With the progress made in telecommunications, isolation in international and domestic capital markets was no longer possible or desirable. Commodity prices were no longer linked to world economic growth. The diversity of the developing countries was increasingly reflected in their different needs. Growth performances that differed from one country to another showed how important it was to make a judicious choice of development strategies and policies. The potentially positive role of the private sector in the creation of wealth and in

the improvement of efficiency was now recognized. Major demographic shifts were exerting previously unforeseen pressures on development. The role of women was increasingly recognized as a significant factor in economic growth. The extent, complexity and implications of global interdependence were becoming more and more clear. UNCTAD had the capability of helping countries to adjust to those changes, of producing new ideas and strategies, and of suggesting realistic approaches and viable solutions, by identifying and evaluating long-term structural changes and trends and contributing to the consensus-building process that made productive negotiation possible. UNCTAD should give substance to the concept of partnership and co-operation between developed and developing countries.

7. Canada took the view that a significant document should be produced by the Conference that would influence the economic debate. The message to be conveyed by the Conference should frankly indicate areas of agreement and areas of disagreement, reaffirm the commitment and determination to build on common views and spell out how it was proposed in practice to bridge existing differences.

Summary of the statement made at the 212th plenary meeting, 27 July 1987, by Mr. Luis ESCOBAR CERDA, Permanent Representative of Chile to the United Nations Office at Geneva

1. Mr. ESCOBAR CERDA, referring to the debt problem, said that in the opinion of his delegation and according to studies undertaken by Chile as a debtor country, it seemed impossible, in view of anticipated rates of economic growth, current population growth rates and interest rates trends on international markets, that developing countries would be able to repay their debts; they would probably not even be in a position to pay all the interest. That situation was entirely due to the deterioration in the terms of trade of debtor countries which, in the case of Latin America, had fallen by more than 30 per cent between 1974 and 1986 and, in the case of Chile, by almost two thirds between 1970 and 1986. Had terms of trade remained at the level of the 1970s, Latin American debts would now be negligible. The countries of the region, including Chile, therefore considered that a political approach or decision was required to resolve the problem, namely, a deliberate decision by the creditor countries to find a solution in collaboration with the debtor countries. The so-called case-by-case approach that had been adopted so far had not, in the opinion of his delegation, produced the intended results, although it had succeeded in preventing an international crisis over the preceding five years. It had caused per capita income to fall in some countries and stagnate in others, to the detriment of consumption, investment and living standards. A world which devoted more to arms expenditure in one year (1985) than the entire outstanding debt of all the developing countries should be capable of finding a formula which would allow the developing countries to pursue their economic growth and to raise living standards in a reasonable space of time.

2. As for the relationship between debt and trade, he pointed out that, since Latin America's creditors were mainly private banks, it was vital that Latin American countries should increase their exports and reduce imports in order to achieve a sufficiently large trade surplus to service their external debt. Such a policy of course reduced consumption levels and economic growth rates and therefore also affected the growth rates of creditor countries. Consequently, in order to reverse that process and allow the debtor countries to continue to increase sales and reduce imports, certain countries must eliminate or reduce their trade surpluses. That role had been assumed so far by the United States of America which, however, now had to balance its trade, if possible, by increasing its foreign earnings by some $190 billion a year. With the addition of the deficit of developing countries, the other developed countries would have to reduce their trade surplus by more than $200 billion a year; he wondered whether other countries would actually take steps to do so or simply rely on the free interplay of international market forces. Traditional measures, based on the devaluation and on stimulation of demand, might well encounter structural obstacles that would prevent the achievement of the desired objective, at least within a politically acceptable period. Initiatives designed to stimulate demand (by facilitating credit, reducing taxes, etc.) in countries such as Japan and the Federal Republic of Germany were likely to fail because of the population's low marginal propensity for consumption. What was required above all was a political decision outlining the desired course of events, followed by negotiations to define ways of implementing that decision—a task in which Governments would have a primary role to play.

3. It was disturbing to note that trade in goods had been hampered by a growing number of non-tariff measures, which had been adopted in spite of the standstill and roll-back commitments undertaken at Punta del Este. The Chilean delegation considered that the Conference should emphasize the need to do everything possible to reverse those trends. It welcomed the recent proposal made by the United States in GATT to do away with all major protectionist programmes entailing quotas, subsidies and tariffs in agricultural trade, so that professions of free trade could be translated into reality. It was well known that the total cost of such protectionist programmes was enormous. Chile hoped that the United States initiative, which was one of the measures required to move in the right direction, would be supported by the other industrialized countries.

Summary of the statement made at the 211th plenary meeting, 24 July 1987, by Mr. Samuel Alberto YOHAI, Director, Institute of Foreign Trade of Colombia

1. Mr. YOHAI said that, 23 years after the first session of the Conference, the time had come to draw up a balance sheet on which to base discussions at the seventh session. Although the first four sessions had led, respectively, to the establishment of the Conference's institutional framework (1964), the introduction of the GSP (1968), the adoption of special measures in favour of the LDCs (1972) and the strengthening of the Integrated Programme for Commodities (1976), the fifth and sixth sessions could hardly be described as successes, even though the fifth had led to the establishment of the programme of economic co-operation among developing countries. At the seventh session the Conference had to deal with the same concerns and problems as at previous sessions and still faced the need for the establishment of a new international economic order. Although no one would deny the fact that the wealthy nations should concern themselves with the problems of the developing countries, where the majority of the world's population lived in extremely precarious conditions, the international co-operation policy that was needed for the rapid development of those countries still did not exist.

2. UNCTAD's recommendations, like those of most United Nations bodies, were not binding, but they were none the less a moral commitment in view of the legitimate aspirations of the developing countries, particularly as far as their relations with the developed world were concerned.

3. He recalled that, at the first session of the Conference, the former President of his country, Mr. Restrepo, had emphasized that disagreements were sometimes more about means than about ends. The industrialized countries therefore had to understand that the Group of 77 had sought to find common ground for the conciliation of divergent ideas and aspirations. Obviously, differences of opinion had always existed and were not about to disappear. Frequently, the so-called facts which underlay recommendations by the industrialized countries were no more than the implicit or explicit expression of specific interests. World economic recovery and the balanced development of financial, monetary and trade relations were the responsibility of all countries, not that of the developing countries alone. The deteriorating living standards of their inhabitants showed that they had already made enough sacrifices and that their future was still uncertain. The problems identified at the first session of the Conference had still not been solved because the rules governing international trade still did not take account of the structural differences between industrialized and developing countries or of their consequences, namely, the steady worsening of the terms of trade and the increasingly inequitable distribution of world income. The Group B countries continued to claim that the worsening of the terms of trade was temporary, whereas the developing countries, particularly the Latin American ones, had always been convinced that the opposite was true, and history had shown that they were right. Few problems had been solved on a lasting basis while others had emerged, such as the external debt, which had become a major obstacle to any improvement in living standards in developing countries and had destabilized the international financial system.

4. In keeping with its ideals of peace, justice and equity, Colombia preferred to transcend differences of opinion and seek a consensus based on clear rules leading to collective action for the promotion of international trade and the full development of the developing countries. History showed that what first appeared to be a dream sometimes became a reality. The Conference should therefore consider five major issues with a view to reaching a consensus that would require special efforts on the part of all groups of countries and, above all, the generosity of the members of Group B. Those issues were the liberalization of international trade, the search for new external debt recycling mechanisms, the dynamic transfer of resources and the international financing of trade and development, monetary and fiscal discipline and the strengthening of enterprise management.

5. With regard to the first issue, it must be recognized that protectionism had increased, particularly in the United States and in the EEC. Countries that had failed in the 1960s and 1970s to ensure a place for their products on industrialized country markets would find it very difficult to do so now and those that had succeeded would have to struggle not to lose their foothold.

6. The economic and social future of the developing countries depended on the solution to those five issues and on the establishment of closer and more confident trade relations among all countries. The international community had 12 years in which to ensure that the twenty-first century would be an era of stability, growth and prosperity and to establish the new international economic order rightly being called for by the developing countries. The seventh session of the Conference provided an opportunity to pave the way for that new era and it was to be hoped that it would lead to the consensus of opinion necessary to strengthen international trade and give the developing countries a real chance to raise the living standards of their populations and build a more prosperous future for all.

**Summary of the statement made at the 210th plenary meeting, 24 July 1987,
by Mr. Said KAFE, Minister for Foreign Affairs, Co-operation and Foreign Trade of the Comoros,
President of the Commission of the Indian Ocean**

1. Mr. KAFE said that at a difficult time of crisis and instability in the international economic system, when most of the world's population was struggling for mere survival, the Conference assumed special importance, for it offered renewed hope of greater understanding and solidarity. The crisis was characterized by disarray in the international economic system, the growing indebtedness of developing countries, sharp falls in commodity prices and constant aggravation of the catastrophic situation of the LDCs, including his own. Being a small island country, lacking mineral resources and suffering from many structural problems, the Comoros faced great difficulties in carrying out its development plans. It suffered from poor sales, and low prices of products accounted for more than 90 per cent of its export earnings, a more than twofold increase in its debt-servicing burden in less than three years, an uncompromising attitude on the part of its creditors, a decline in real terms in its export earnings, and failure by some of its partners to provide the assistance pledged at the first round table of donors held at Moroni in July 1984.

2. Despite those many constraints, his Government continued to make considerable efforts to sustain growth and improve the living conditions of the people. Since 1979, it had been carrying out a restructuring programme, particularly in its productive sectors, accompanied in 1982 by a number of measures for the reorganization and adjustment of the public financial sector and the para-public State sector.

3. That policy had produced some appreciable results in the period up to 1983, during which the multiplier effects of the recovery programme had enabled the country to attain an overall economic growth of 6 per cent per annum and an annual increase of 1.7 per cent in real per capita income. Since then, however, the domestic efforts had been frustrated by the deterioration in the international environment, the sharp fall in commodity prices and the rise in debt-servicing charges as a result of the inordinate rise in interest rates.

4. His Government was determined to continue its campaign against underdevelopment, but that difficult task called for growing and sustained assistance from the international community. He therefore appealed to participants to show their solidarity by offering their valuable assistance.

5. Membership of regional and subregional groupings, as had been reaffirmed in the recommendations of the Lagos Plan of Action and Final Act, was one means of helping to ease the difficulties and one of the main priorities for his country. Accordingly, his Government was committed to promoting regional and subregional co-operation. Comoros was one of the founder members of the Preferential Trade Area, whose members included 18 countries of East and southern Africa and the Indian Ocean. Above all, the establishment in 1982 of the Commission of the Indian Ocean,

comprising Madagascar, Mauritius, Seychelles, Réunion and the Comoros, gave grounds for hoping that a subregional common market would soon materialize. The Commission offered an opportunity of establishing a new economic area capable of ensuring the long-term harmonious development of the subregion. Despite the will and determination of the countries concerned, however, the Commission had insufficient resources to make it the essential tool for the rapid growth of their economies without substantial assistance. Apart from that generously provided by the Commission of the European Communities, no assistance had so far been forthcoming to support such subregional co-operation. As President of the Commission of the Indian Ocean, he appealed to the international community to take an active part in financing the projects envisaged by the Commission.

6. In a world of constant change in which co-operation and solidarity were being sacrificed to protectionism, there was an urgent need to restructure the international economy in the interest of greater justice, more equitable trade relations and a revitalization of growth, international trade and development.

7. Extremely high real interest rates, exchange rate instability, growing indebtedness, falling commodity prices, the decline in official assistance, chronically deteriorating terms of trade and the worsening situation of the LDCs had led to continued uncertainty, sluggish investment and growth, high unemployment and social regression. His delegation therefore fully endorsed the proposals made by the Group of 77 in the Havana Declaration. The time had come to lay the foundations of a world of justice, progress and solidarity; but that called for increased interdependence between rich and poor countries. No country was sheltered from the crisis, and no State, however powerful, could extricate itself by its own efforts. Strengthened solidarity was the key to success in the pursuit of a durable development of the world economy.

8. His delegation welcomed the Japanese Government's decision to devote some of its trade surpluses to financial assistance for the developing countries. That gesture of solidarity should serve as an example to be emulated by other partners among the developing countries. He likewise welcomed President Mitterrand's proposal that an international conference should be convened in France in 1990 to review the implementation of the Substantial New Programme of Action for the 1980s for the Least Developed Countries.

9. There could be no rapid or durable economic growth unless sufficient resources were available to finance investments and relieve or eliminate the debt burden. The establishment of a mechanism for the regulation and stabilization of export earnings in the form of a Common Fund for Commodities was a practical manifestation of North-South co-operation. He urged developed countries of East and West to contribute to its establishment.

10. The Conference had produced evidence of a unanimous will to enlist the intelligence and know-how of mankind in the service of development and progress. That noble ideal must give real hope and renewed courage to the hundreds of millions of people who aspired to a better life. Everything possible must be done to replace words by deeds, and egoism and intolerance by brotherly love.

Summary of the statement made at the 215th plenary meeting, 28 July 1987, by Mrs. Muni FIGUERES de JIMÉNEZ, Minister of Foreign Trade of Costa Rica

1. Mrs. FIGUERES de JIMÉNEZ after paying a tribute to the memory of Raúl Prebisch and Manuel Pérez Guerrero, the farsighted founders of UNCTAD, said that currently, when the optimism that had prevailed on the establishment of the organization appeared to be giving way to pessimism, there was a need for a new source of critical thought capable of tackling the problems of trade and development from a new global standpoint.

2. In the course of the preceding few decades, Costa Rica had embarked on a process of social and economic development based on a stable and thoroughly democratic political system and aimed at reducing social imbalances and improving living conditions. However, recent changes in the international environment had revealed the extreme vulnerability of Costa Rica's economy and the urgent need to diversify and modernize its system of production. At a time when the import substitution process undertaken within the framework of the Latin American Common Market was being completed and political crisis was convulsing Central America, Costa Rica had been compelled by the limited prospects offered by its traditional export markets and declining financial inflows to review its development strategy. The threat of economic crisis was evident from changes in indicators such as GDP, the rate of inflation and the exchange rate; the Government had therefore made the necessary internal adjustments to meet that threat with the support of the major international financial institutions. However, in order to restructure its economy in the longer term and pay off its foreign debt, Costa Rica needed external resources that it could obtain only by increasing its exports, in particular of goods not its traditional exports, to markets outside Central America.

3. Since the success of its recovery efforts depended primarily on access to outside markets, Costa Rica was concerned by current distortions in the workings of international trade. It was particularly worried by tariff and other barriers to the import of goods vitally important to developing countries. It hoped, however, that in the Uruguay Round the developed countries would fully honour the standstill and roll-back undertakings given at Punta del Este. It was vitally important for Costa Rica, as for many other developing countries, to remove all barriers to trade in tropical products, agricultural commodities and natural resource-based products. In the context of the Uruguay Round Costa Rica would, together with the other developing countries, endeavour to have discriminatory measures against the export of goods produced by the textile and garment industries lifted and to have a clearer definition of the rules governing trade in such goods drawn up. It would aim at improving market access for goods from developing countries and strengthening the compensatory financing facilities currently in force. One of the main tasks of the seventh session of the Conference was to determine the contribution the developed countries and international financial bodies were prepared to make in those fields.

4. In order to resume economic growth and thus revitalize social progress, the developing countries should be able to count on international co-operation to reschedule their financial liabilities and provide additional capital to supplement domestic savings and maintain the balance of payments. It was important to adapt debt servicing to borrowers' capacity to pay and to find a lasting solution to the debt problem. And it was essential to halt the negative transfer of resources by developing suitable machinery for recycling the surpluses of the developed countries on conditions acceptable to the developing countries. Costa Rica endorsed the view of the Group of 77 that the developed countries should guarantee a supply of adequate liquidity on an assured, continuous and predictable basis. In that context, it was satisfying to note that at the Venice Summit, the industrialized countries had for the first time given a written undertaking to increase ODA to 0.7 per cent of GNP.

5. With regard to the stabilization of commodity prices, Costa Rica considered it was not enough to strengthen commodity agreements such as those on coffee, cocoa and bananas; efforts should also be made to reach the targets of the Integrated Programme for Commodities. Costa Rica, for its part, undertook to take the necessary steps to ratify the Agreement Establishing the Common Fund for Commodities. She appealed to the developed countries to make a substantial increase in their contributions to the Common Fund and urged all countries to take the necessary steps to bring the Fund into operation.

6. Recalling the words of President Mitterrand,* who had highlighted the economic interdependence of peoples, she expressed the hope that the seventh session of the Conference would see the victory of consultation over confrontation and thus contribute to the establishment of peace and prosperity throughout the world.

_____
* See sect. A above.

Summary of the statement made at the 207th plenary meeting, 14 July 1987, by Mr. Nicolas KOUANDI ANGBA, Minister of Commerce of Côte d'Ivoire

1. Mr. KOUANDI ANGBA said that the seventh session of the Conference was being held at a time when the economic, monetary and financial environment was a source of great concern for all countries. Although the crisis was world-wide, it affected industrialized and developing countries in different ways. In many developing countries, it had halted completely the process of growth. The flow of financial resources to the developing countries had been considerably reduced, and there was currently a net outflow of capital from them. That situation was due to the dramatic reduction of export earnings resulting from speculation in the prices of commodities and to the excessive growth of the debt-servicing burden, caused mainly by an unacceptable rise in interest and exchange rates. It was not surprising that a situation in which a large proportion of the world's population was doomed to suffer the effects of an unfair system of international economic relations might imperil the foundations of peace.

2. The seventh session of the Conference provided an opportunity to make positive proposals and to adopt bold measures for sustaining and improving the international trading system and promoting a true reactivation of the economies of all countries. At its meeting at Havana, the Group of 77 had prepared a moderate negotiating document, the conclusions of which had his delegation's support. In any case, every effort should be made to implement the measures contained in the Substantial New Programme of Action adopted for the benefit of the least developed countries.

3. In the past few years the world economy had been characterized by the collapse of commodity prices, the rise in interest rates and the instability of the exchange rates of the major currencies. The developing countries had lost export opportunities as a result of the growing protectionism in all markets. At a time when ODA was falling sharply and when it was becoming increasingly difficult to borrow private capital on the international markets, the developing countries had to service a debt which was growing from day to day. The African countries had been particularly hard hit, and the efforts which they had made to redress their economies had so far been in vain. For almost a decade most developing countries had been pursuing, without significant results, austerity policies under structural adjustment programmes. Such policies could not continue indefinitely without endangering political and social stability. In order to procure for the developing countries the resources which they needed to finance their development, the Conference had the historic responsibility for adopting a number of effective corrective measures, including the fixing and stabilization of remunerative prices for commodities, the grant of long-term financial assistance subject to fewer conditionalities in order to finance the development of the third world, and the indexing of the developing countries' debt servicing to their export earnings. The international monetary system would also have to be restructured with a view to

reducing interest rates and further stabilizing the exchange rates of the major currencies.

4. International trade was suffering from a proliferation of protectionist measures, with the result that trade wars among partners took place, often in violation of GATT principles. The international community had a duty to put an end to that suicidal trend. Protectionist barriers should be dismantled and all the factors impeding the access of commodities and manufactures from the developing countries to the markets of the developed countries should be studied. The GSP should urgently be extended to all goods which the developing countries were capable of producing. The Uruguay Round of negotiations would provide an opportunity to establish a freer and fairer multilateral trading system, with due regard to the GATT provisions relating to the special treatment of the developing countries.

5. Because of the vital importance of commodities for many developing countries, the international community had established international agreements based on the idea that the commodity-exporting countries of the third world should be able to finance their development from the resources extracted from their territory and that they should not be too brutally confronted with the realities of the international free trade system. Unfortunately, over the preceding 20 years no agreement had succeeded in bringing world commodity markets under control or in stabilizing commodity prices. The incessant changes in prices placed producer countries such as the Côte d'Ivoire in a disturbing situation. In 1987 alone, his country might lose $1.8 billion of its export earnings, with the result that it would be deprived of a large part of the resources needed to service its debt. Its investment budget, drawn up only a few months previously, was no longer sufficient to carry out effectively the projects essential for the country's development. The same was unfortunately true for most other developing countries, whose exports over the period 1980-1986 had increased in volume by 11 per cent, while their export earnings had fallen by 20 per cent. That situation prevailed despite the implementation of certain agreements which his country had signed out of solidarity but whose effectiveness it had always doubted. The main reason why they were ineffective was the lack of real political will to defend commodity prices among some of Côte d'Ivoire's partners, who had always rejected the principles of a remunerative floor price for the producer. Systems of compensation and earnings stabilization had been adopted to correct the deficits caused by the collapse of market prices but, like Stabex, they were of only limited effect. For example, Stabex had recently been able to compensate only 11 billion CFA francs of a loss of over 200 billion CFA francs on commodity export earnings. The effectiveness of the Common Fund for Commodities was also doubtful, in view of its inadequate capacity to meet the enormous demands on it to be made by most producer countries. Despite those defects in the various compensation and stabilization schemes, his delegation had been re-

quested by President Houphouët-Boigny to sign the Agreement Establishing the Common Fund for Commodities; ratification would follow as soon as possible. Côte d'Ivoire hoped that the seventh session of the Conference would serve not only to correct the distortions in international trade, but also to find the most appropriate remedies for the commodity price problem, particularly in relation to the debt problem.

Statement made at the 202nd plenary meeting, 10 July 1987, by Mr. Ricardo CABRISAS RUÍZ, Minister of Foreign Trade of Cuba, as representative of the Head of State of the Republic of Cuba to present the results of the Sixth Ministerial Meeting of the Group of 77

I should like, first of all, to express our appreciation to the people and authorities of Switzerland, the permanent headquarters of the Conference secretariat and the place where the Conference met for the first time, and our most sincere thanks to the Secretary-General, the officials and the entire staff of UNCTAD for their preparatory work and arrangements.

To you, Mr. President, we extend our congratulations on your election to this high office; it is a tribute to your personal qualities and to the people of Zimbabwe, whose struggle for national independence and against racism is an example worthy of admiration. We are convinced that with your well-known experience you will facilitate the success of the negotiations that are to take place in the framework of this session.

As the representative of the President of the Republic of Cuba, Commander-in-Chief Fidel Castro Ruz, I have the honour, on behalf of the Group of 77, to present to this Conference the Havana Declaration. The Declaration is the result of extensive deliberations during the Sixth Ministerial Meeting of the Group of 77, which was held in our country last April, and is an expression of the unity of objectives and solidarity of the developing countries in their just aspirations and demands.

This session is taking place at a time when mankind finds itself faced with the alternative of arriving at appropriate formulas for solving the grave economic and social problems confronting the developing countries or of continuing on the road of their impoverishment and destitution until there is no viable solution possible other than political and social explosions of enormous and unforeseeable consequences.

We do not think it necessary to dwell on the diagnosis of the present international economic situation, for it is only too well known to all of you and has been confirmed by the excellent documents prepared in that regard by UNCTAD's own secretariat, as well as by the studies of other institutions specializing in this field, most of which cannot be classified as partial to the developing countries.

A retrospective analysis of the problems of the developing world raised and discussed from the first to the present session of the Conference, and of the concrete measures taken to solve those problems brings us to the painful conclusion that the problems are essentially the same, though considerably worse, and that the solutions have been meagre and their effects minimal.

The picture presented by the international economy as a whole and the situation facing the world in all areas of life have today become even more complex and urgent.

The most prominent feature is the third world's enormous external debt, which had reached the astronomical sum of more than a trillion dollars and has become a permanent drain on the third world's economies and an insurmountable obstacle on its road to development.

This debt, basically attributable to the irresponsible and selfish financial policies of the great centres of capital and to the contraction of international trade, especially in commodities, has become an unrelenting reality of our times. Without its elimination, it is not possible even to think about true alternatives for the well-being of our peoples; it is, in short, a development crisis which is unprecedented in its scope and intensity.

From the financial angle, the process which created this indebtedness of the developing countries has been characterized by high floating real interest rates, reductions in ODA and the sharp contraction of financial flows to third world countries, which were recipients of the devalued capital generated by the inflationary conditions of the world economy during the previous decade.

At the same time, the economic and trade environment has become a prime culture medium for the growth of our countries' external debt.

Thus, the current purchasing power resulting from the prices for the commodities—food, agricultural raw materials and minerals—on which the developing countries depend for two thirds of their export earnings is at its lowest level recorded since the times of the Great Depression of the 1930s. Their average annual decline in real terms has been 20 per cent in the last five years while the volume of exports of these products has risen by only 11 per cent over the same period. Oil prices have likewise fallen considerably and, although this benefits fuel importers, it is a serious blow to the exporters.

The main factors influencing this behaviour of the commodity markets are both cyclical and structural in nature.

Among the cyclical factors, the preponderant influence has been the deflationary policies of the developed countries and the resulting contraction of their economies. From the structural point of view, the commodity market is confronted by measures engendered by the macro-economic policies of the developed countries, primarily subsidies and price-support systems, protectionist measures, technological breakthroughs and substitute products.

International trade is plagued with protectionist pressures manifested in new laws and restrictive measures put into effect by the developed market-economy countries. These measures are characterized by their disregard for principles and concepts agreed upon multilaterally, their arbitrariness and their systematic breach of international commitments. All this creates a climate of true anarchy in which bilateral arrangements predominate rather than multilateral co-operation.

The major countries impose their criteria unilaterally on international trade and arrogate to themselves the right to take measures of reprisal against the trade of developing countries, in most cases in response to the national policies applied by these countries in non-trade areas, e.g. direct foreign investment, the protection of intellectual property and services.

The same Governments that obstinately refuse to apply economic sanctions against the racist régime of South Africa—despite the General Assembly's condemnations in this regard—have applied and continue to apply trade sanctions against developing countries for political reasons.

Significantly, while the developing countries' share of exports in international trade has continuously declined, their economies still offer a potential market for the developed countries' exports. The grave problems facing the developed capitalist countries—unemployment among them—can only be alleviated if the third world increases its buying power. Therefore, without a solution to the problems of the third world, there will be no sustained or stable development of the world economy.

What is more, we are beginning this session at a time when the indissoluble link between peace and development has never been more evident. It is impossible to achieve lasting peace among nations without eliminating the underdevelopment that is smothering a large part of our planet.

As our President, Comrade Fidel Castro, said on opening the Sixth Ministerial Meeting of the Group of 77:

"It is axiomatic that without peace there can be no development, but it is also axiomatic that without development for eight tenths of the world's population there can be no peace. Consequently, to struggle for our development is to struggle for peace and for the welfare of all the peoples of the world."

Now, when there are hopes of achieving—at least in Europe—a significant reduction in nuclear-missile weapons, we must turn our thoughts to the vast possibilities that would be offered by ending the arms race and thereby freeing enormous human, material and financial resources for use in the struggle for development. These resources would help, among other things, to cancel the external debt that is crushing our peoples; and this, in turn, would contribute to the building of a lasting and just peace of all.

In April, the Ministers of the Group of 77 adopted the Havana Declaration for the reactivation of development, growth and international trade, which we, on behalf of the Group, request should be distributed and submitted to the Conference for consideration.

Likewise, I request you to distribute a draft resolution* on the difficult situation endured by the Palestinian people, especially in the territories illegally occupied by the Israeli invader. This painful and difficult state of affairs has been recognized and denounced on many occasions by the international community, including General Assembly resolution 39/223 of 18 December 1984. We hope this draft receives total support.

The Group of 77 considers that we should not limit ourselves to an assessment of the international economic situation, but that we should look for the best ways and means of reactivating it and promoting the cause of development in our countries. To this end, the Ministers gathered in Havana drafted proposals on policies and measures to be adopted with regard to each of the items of the Conference agenda. Those proposals will be presented by the representatives of our Group in the various working bodies of the Conference with a view to achieving concrete results from our meeting. The proposals outline our approach to a harmonious and equitable reconstruction of international economic relations aimed at ensuring development and employment for all.

In drafting the proposals on the different topics, we based ourselves on the interdependence of every aspect that enters into the international economic environment. The urgent needs of developing countries can be successfully met only through the implementation of a series of coherent measures applied by all, including, in the first place, the adoption of simultaneous macroeconomic policies aimed at considerably reducing interest rates, stabilizing and correcting exchange rates, reducing protectionist pressures, broadening trade and financial flows and reversing the downward trend in commodity prices.

Allow me now to refer to the Havana Declaration.

The Ministers of the Group of 77 believe, as they say in their Declaration, that the 1980s have been a lost decade for development.

The world economic crisis, reflecting the persistent stagnation of economic growth, has retarded economic and social progress and, in some cases thrown it into reverse. The inadequacies and inequities of the international economic system have provoked a stifling of trade, development and employment, in which developing countries have been hardest hit.

This situation, beset with economic, political and social tensions, poses a serious threat to democracy, social stability and international peace and security. Its reversal requires the political commitment and co-operation of all nations in a collective effort to establish the new international economic order.

This effort must be founded on observance of the inalienable right of every State to economic and social development, to choose its socio-economic system and to promote the welfare of its people in accordance with national plans and policies.

Just as the members of the Group of 77 assume their responsibilities to strive for their own development and

---

*TD/L.295.

to continue to strengthen their mutual co-operation, they expect the developed countries to assume their responsibilities in the present world economic crisis and to realize that, by supporting the development process of our countries they can contribute effectively to revitalizing the world economy.

The Group of 77 considers that the present economic crisis is structural in nature and has been aggravated by the developed countries' long-term macro-economic policies, which negatively affect the international economic environment, weaken the demand for developing countries' exports, put downward pressure on commodity prices and aggravate the debt problem.

Moreover, there is a spreading trend among developed countries to show preference for bilateralism in their external economic relations, resorting increasingly to such policies for political purposes, reducing multilateralism, hardening the stalemate in economic negotiations between developing and developed countries and weakening multilateral co-operation.

It is important to point out that while demands are made for payment of our external debt and the adoption of domestic policies onerous for the welfare and development of our peoples, the debtor countries do not receive the external resources indispensable for implementing the economic policy reforms and adjustment programmes they are persuaded or forced to undertake.

The economic interdependence of all countries has intensified owing to the increased share of foreign trade in their economic activity and the internationalization of production and capital. The increasing interaction among countries with different economic systems cannot be denied.

The gigantic TNCs enjoy unprecedented economies of scale. Along with this, new technologies are radically altering demand, production and trade patterns, and, by their concentrated control are creating new international economic relations and making the world economy more complex.

We are convinced that unless external constraints are removed and the required systematic changes made there will be no sustained expansion of world trade and growth in the foreseeable future. At the same time, we consider that the post-war international economic system has not achieved its stated objectives of promoting world-wide economic and social progress.

As stated in paragraphs 17 and 18 of the Havana Declaration:

There has not been a meaningful and comprehensive policy initiative to enhance global economic co-operation, on the basis of interdependence, equity and shared responsibilities. Instead, a new tendency has emerged in some quarters of the developed countries to play down the influence of the external economic environment on the development process and to insist on the primacy of domestic policy reform based on the efficacy of spontaneous market forces alone. This approach, not even applied by its major proponents, is inadequate to address development problems, carries the seeds of social and political instability and ignores the complexity of the contemporary world economy. This approach enables the transnational corporations to move freely goods, raw materials, services, data and capital across national frontiers, at their discretion.

The international community should join its forces and engage in dialogue to work out the characteristics and mechanisms of a comprehensive international economic system, based on the principles of equity, justice, harmony and universality and on the sovereign rights of States. Development, growth, employment and social progress should be its central objectives. The system should give full recognition to the interdependence between money, finance, trade and development.

In this sense, the expansion and diversification of trade, including trade among developing countries and among countries having different economic and social systems, on a non-discriminatory basis and in the framework of mutual co-operation among States, would contribute to these objectives.

At the same time, we reiterate our desire to further economic co-operation among developing countries as an important instrument in our Group's efforts to promote a restructuring of international economic relations, in which the Generalized System of Trade Preferences (GSTP) constitutes the most important component, from which we can already perceive concrete and substantial progress.

Our appraisal of the current international economic situation and our approach to the harmonious and equitable reconstruction of international economic relations aimed at ensuring development and employment for all are criteria that we trust are shared by the other participants in this Conference.

Twenty-three years ago, UNCTAD as an institution was born out of the international collective desire to contribute to the ordering of international economic relations, especially in the fields of trade and development. Today's conditions demand that we strengthen its efficiency and its capacity to respond to present and future problems, that we preserve the integrity of its mandate and functions, and that we give it the means it needs and the political support of all member States to carry them out.

The seventh session of the Conference gives us an opportunity we must not waste. The eyes of hundreds of millions of human beings are turned on us, especially those that each day see their children die for lack of food, for inhuman living conditions, and for the extreme poverty resulting from underdevelopment. It is very difficult—in fact it is impossible—to make them understand that the selfishness and lack of political will of the States with the greatest economic power have prevented the adoption of concrete measures to raise their standards of living and to help base the economy of our common habitat on more just and equitable conditions. On their behalf, on behalf of the peoples of the 127 countries that comprise our Group, I call upon all to ensure that our meeting ends in a really fruitful manner. I invite you to remember that 13 years have elapsed since the General Assembly adopted the principles of the new international economic order, so violated and disregarded today.

Summary of the statement made at the 217th plenary meeting, 29 July 1987, by Mr. Ricardo CABRISAS RUÍZ, Minister of Foreign Trade of Cuba

1. Mr. CABRISAS RUÍZ said that the third world countries were the first victims of the world economic crisis and were suffering on account of the lack of genuine international co-operation. Cuba had not been spared: over the past few years, the prices of its main exports, in particular sugar and nickel, had experienced a catastrophic decline from which the country, despite its efforts to diversify production and exports, had still not recovered. The prices of its imports, on the other hand, were continuing to rise. The deterioration in the terms of trade with the capitalist countries had been underscored by the President of the Republic in his inaugural speech at the Sixth Ministerial Meeting of the Group of 77. Recently, the Cuban economy had also suffered from the depreciation of the dollar as the prices of its main export products were fixed in that currency, whereas imports, because of the economic blockade of the United States, were paid for in other currencies which, on the other hand, had appreciated.

2. Despite the international economic crisis, Cuba, thanks to the efforts of its people and Government and to the fruitful trade relations it maintained with the other socialist and developing countries, was nevertheless continuing on the path of economic and social progress. It believed that the global system of trade preferences negotiated within the framework of the Group of 77 would contribute to the development of trade among third world countries, but that there was also a need to intensify economic relations with the developed capitalist countries on the basis of equality, respect and mutual advantage.

3. Some developed capitalist countries were advocating economic liberalism and claiming that the only way to resolve the serious problems of trade and development consisted in allowing the free interplay of market mechanisms, yet paradoxically they were following increasingly protectionist policies by creating more and more barriers to trade, in particular non-trade barriers, and by granting larger subsidies to producers and exporters, thus restricting access to their markets even further. Even the limited advantages now granted under their schemes of preferences were diminishing, if not being nullified. In addition, countries such as Cuba and Nicaragua were subject to a form of differentiated and non-reciprocal treatment that was anything but advantageous: namely, an economic blockade. It was in March 1962 that, after breaking off diplomatic relations with Cuba and attacking the country, the United States of America had decided to suspend all trade with it—including the supply of medicines, foodstuffs and other essential goods—as well as to take measures against enterprises in third countries which traded with Cuba and to paralyse the financial operations of the Republic by prohibiting the use of United States currency. That economic and commercial blockade had thus been in existence for 25 years and the United States authorities had recently even gone so far as to take the absurd decision of prohibiting the use of credit cards in and tourist trips to Cuba.

4. The granting of subsidies and the development of substitute products had dealt a serious blow to the international sugar market, resulting in structural change that harmed a large number of developing countries which exported that product, particularly Cuba. Such subsidies were inadmissible; as for measures involving technological developments, those had to be subject to international disciplinary rules and take account of the interests of the developing countries concerned.

5. Those problems were compounded by the increased debt burden of the developing countries and the monetary and financial problems created by the deflationist macro-economic policies of the capitalist countries—such as exchange rate fluctuations, higher interest rates, the contraction of credit facilities and the diminution of external capital inflows. Those problems left no third world country unaffected and were causing a decline in demand and investment that was having a generally negative effect on growth rates. The external debt of the developing countries had assumed intolerable proportions and a solution would have to be found urgently if development in the third world was indeed to be reactivated and trade, growth and employment in the developed countries stimulated. As Fidel Castro had predicted as early as 1979, cancellation of the debt of the LDCs had become inevitable and creditors must assume their responsibilities. It was also essential to realize that peace and economic progress were closely linked and that disarmament would make it possible to release resources that should be devoted to the development of the third world countries and, above all, to the solution of the debt problem.

6. Other measures should be taken at the same time to remedy the imbalances and injustices which characterized international economic relations. The establishment of a new international economic order was a necessity and not a dream. How could the developed countries reactivate their economies without sustained growth in the third world countries, which were potentially the most dynamic force in the world economy? UNCTAD could, in view of its experience and its universality, contribute in a decisive manner to strengthening multilateral co-operation for development, and its role must be enhanced rather than reduced.

7. The Conference afforded an opportunity to analyse all those problems and to identify a solution. Unfortunately, the statements made by the representatives of the developed capitalist countries failed to reveal any real desire to negotiate. The Group of 77 had adopted a constructive attitude conducive to dialogue with those countries. Some of them had nevertheless shown that they were open-minded and the socialist countries of Group D and China had generally supported the position of the Group of 77. But the intransigence and obstinacy of a small group of States had created difficulties which prevented agreement from

being reached and threatened to undermine the very foundations of UNCTAD. The time had therefore come for all countries, and in particular the developed countries, to make a determined effort to reach agreement on specific measures aimed at relaunching multilateral co-operation and finding a solution to the serious economic problems of the time which placed the developing countries in a dramatic situation.

Summary of the statement made at the 216th plenary meeting, 29 July 1987, by Mr. Michael MICHAELIDES, Minister for Trade and Industry of Cyprus

1. Mr. MICHAELIDES said that the gravity of the international economic situation and the magnitude of problems called for serious efforts by all countries, large and small, rich and poor, developed and developing. The unprecedented economic crisis affecting the entire world had had an adverse impact on growth rates and development programmes in developing countries, particularly the LDCs, which were feeling the effects of depressed commodity prices, reduced export earnings, high interest rates, fluctuating exchange rates, a reduced flow of ODA, limited access to international capital markets, aggravation of the foreign debt problem and protectionism by the developed countries. In that respect, the seventh session of the Conference offered a unique opportunity to examine outstanding problems and to decide what measures should be taken to ensure observance of the principles of equity, justice and solidarity—a necessary condition for a resumption of development and growth. To that end, the issues of financial resources, commodities and international trade, as well as the problems of the LDCs, must be examined collectively by the developed and the developing countries.

2. In the case of resources for development, including financial resources and related monetary questions, the objective must be to set up an effective mechanism to provide a global and lasting solution to the debt problem of the developing countries. At the same time, financial flows to the developing countries must be increased through the reform of the international monetary system. Particular attention should also be paid to commodity markets, which were of vital importance for the LDCs. The developed countries should modify their macro-economic policies affecting the supply and demand for individual commodities, and the developing countries should be provided with technical and financial support for training, research and marketing, and a system of compensatory finance for export earnings shortfalls should be set up. The liberalization of international trade would alleviate the debt problems of a large number of developing countries, and the industrialized countries should fulfil their commitments to eliminate tariff escalation and non-tariff barriers, and thereby help to resolve the problems of land-locked and island countries.

3. Measures along those lines alone would bring about the rapid recovery of international trade because the developing countries would not have the necessary earnings to increase their imports from the industrialized countries if they were unable to export their products. In view of the interrelationship of the world's economic problems, multilateral and international co-operation must be strengthened with a view to restructuring international economic relationships in order to resolve the problems of development and employment in the framework of a system based on equity, justice, harmony and respect for the sovereign rights of States.

4. The seventh session of the Conference was a unique occasion for setting up a non-discriminatory, universal and balanced trading system that would allow for specialization in the use of resources on the basis of comparative advantage.

5. UNCTAD should continue to be supported in its efforts to give impetus to multilateral co-operation and resolve the problems of development and of unemployment in the developing and the developed countries. It was to be hoped that the eighth session of the Conference would be held in a better climate of economic growth and development.

Summary of the statement made at the 207th plenary meeting, 14 July 1987, by Mr. Bohumil URBAN, Minister of Foreign Trade of Czechoslovakia

1. Mr. URBAN said that the seventh session of the Conference was taking place against an international background of political and economic confrontation and growing expenditure on arms, resulting in a low level of political confidence among States in practically all fields. The foremost task of the international community was therefore to reduce international tension, to restore confidence in inter-State relations, and to safeguard a lasting peace.

2. International security, disarmament and development were unquestionably interrelated. It was gratifying to note that the issue had been taken up by representatives of a number of developing and other countries at the Eighth Conference of Heads of State or Government of Non-Aligned Countries held at Harare in September 1986 and at the Sixth Ministerial Meeting of the Group of 77, held at Havana, in April 1987.

3. There had been no major improvement in the world economic situation since the previous session of the Conference at Belgrade. The development of international economic relations was complicated by the high level of indebtedness of developing countries, by

considerable instability in monetary and financial relations, and by other negative phenomena, including intensified protectionism. Despite the adoption within UNCTAD and GATT of significant decisions aimed at liberalizing and enhancing international trade, practically no tangible results had been achieved so far. Protectionist trends were greatest in the economically strongest countries. The resulting measures had often been applied in a discriminatory way, especially against the socialist countries, including Czechoslovakia, and a number of developing countries. Such a state of affairs was unacceptable, since it conflicted with the existing principles and rules of international trade. The rights of all countries must be respected, and obligations contracted within UNCTAD and GATT must be complied with. That was why Czechoslovakia had given its support to the implementation of the progressive measures laid down in the Declaration and the Programme of Action on the Establishment of a New International Economic Order and the Charter of Economic Rights and Duties of States.

4. Trade relations among countries having different economic and social systems were of major importance. UNCTAD should continue its work in that area, since it was practically the only organ of the United Nations system where the problems of all world trade flows could be considered in an interrelated way. It would be very useful to negotiate, at the seventh session, a new set of measures on that aspect of UNCTAD's activities, possibly on the basis of the proposals which the secretariat had submitted to the Trade and Development Board in September 1986 and of some other measures on which agreement had already been reached at the sixth session of the Conference.

5. The heavy indebtedness of a number of developing countries had assumed such proportions that it had become a world-wide problem with political and social consequences. It had to be dealt with in accordance with the interests of all countries concerned and as part of the restructuring of international economic relations on a just and democratic basis. Concrete measures that might be useful included a reduction of the excessively high interest rates, the stabilization of exchange rates, and the elimination of protectionist measures, especially those that restricted exports by developing debtor countries. Appropriate measures should also be taken to deal with the outflow of resources from developing countries.

6. As far as the LDCs were concerned, he pointed out that the Substantial New Programme of Action for the 1980s was being put into effect at a very slow pace. The Conference should enhance international co-operation with a view to promoting the socio-economic development of those countries.

7. Using both traditional and certain new forms, Czechoslovakia had been striving to increase the volume of its economic assistance to developing countries. By the end of 1986 it had built in developing countries, on financial conditions favourable to them, almost 600 major plants, 55 of them in the LDCs. The work done by Czechoslovak experts in developing countries and the training of personnel from developing countries in Czechoslovakia had also been important. In 1986 the total volume of assistance provided by Czechoslovakia to developing countries had amounted to 1 per cent of its national income.

8. Despite the growing complexity of international economic relations, Czechoslovakia had been making an effort to expand its foreign trade. However, the development of its trade with developed market-economy countries would be facilitated by the abolition of protectionist measures against its exports and of the prohibitions restricting its imports. Czechoslovakia's interest in developing co-operation with all countries of the world had been confirmed in major political and economic decisions recently adopted by the Government and in the new changes currently being prepared for the restructuring of its internal economic mechanisms with a view to strengthening the responsibility and powers of enterprises and to increasing the country's economic efficiency and promoting the development of profitable, mutually beneficial, co-operation with all partners.

Summary of the statement made at the 205th plenary meeting, 13 July 1987, by Mr. Choi Jong GUN, Minister of Foreign Trade of the Democratic People's Republic of Korea

1. Mr. GUN said he was convinced that the current session would be a good opportunity for improving international economic relations and revitalizing global growth, development and international trade. The position of the developing countries on the topics on the Conference agenda was clearly stated in the Havana Declaration adopted in April 1987.

2. The serious world economic crisis resulting from the inequitable international economic order had placed those countries in a more unfavourable situation than ever. They were forced to suffer heavy economic loss under inequitable terms of trade, to sell their natural and human resources cheaply and to buy manufactures at incomparably high prices. In 1987 alone they had suffered a loss of more than $100 billion. The prices of commodities, on which two thirds of their export earnings depended, had fallen to their lowest levels since the great economic crisis of the 1930s. Price stabilization and the increased commodity export earnings for which they had hoped were still unattained and they were finding it difficult to develop their national industries and foreign trade because of protectionist and other discriminatory measures applied by the developed countries. The share in world exports of the developing countries, which possessed some 80 per cent of the world's human and material resources, had continued to decline, having fallen from 28 per cent in 1980 to 22.9 per cent in 1985.

3. The harsh world economic situation and inequitable international trade relations had led to

decreases in the food and commodity production of most developing countries, in particular the least developed among them. Their national income had fallen to the level of the 1970s and their capital accumulation and investment had diminished, with the consequence that their economies had radically deteriorated. Many of them suffered substantial losses from high interest rates and exchange rate fluctuations, and growing indebtedness. The wealth gap between the developed and developing countries was widening steadily. In those circumstances, vigorous steps were needed towards the establishment of a new and equitable international economic order in response to the aspirations of the developing countries.

4. All due support should be given to the Havana Declaration and resolutions adopted by the Group of 77 at its Sixth Ministerial Meeting, and the Conference should take action-oriented measures based on them.

5. The Integrated Programme for Commodities, the Common Fund and resolutions designed to increase the export earnings of the developing countries should be implemented with a view to stabilizing commodity prices. Structural adjustment should be expedited in order to check protectionism and provide free access for the products of developing countries to the developed markets through expanded multilateral trade negotiations, thus enhancing the role of the developing countries in trade and shipping. The international monetary and financial system should also be adjusted for their benefit, interest rates should be reduced, exchange rates of major currencies fixed and ODA and financial and technical support expanded.

6. The current external debt crisis, which was a direct outcome of the old international economic order, not only had a severe impact on the economic and trade development of the developing countries but threatened world security and impeded the healthy development of international relations. The international community had a duty to find a correct solution to the debt problem of the developing countries. One appropriate solution might be for debt repayments to be rescheduled and interests frozen until the developing countries achieved their own independent national economies and the capacity to repay, following comprehensive consultation between debtors and creditors.

7. The active pursuit of South-South co-operation would contribute to the early establishment of a new and equitable international economic order. Such co-operation did not exclude North-South co-operation, for the developed countries still had a historical responsibility to facilitate and help in the development of the developing countries. As the leader of the Korean people had said, South-South co-operation was a noble undertaking for achieving the economic independence of the developing countries through mutual economic and technical assistance and mutual accommodation, and represented new international economic relations based on the common aspirations and interests of those countries. At their Extraordinary Ministerial Conference on South-South co-operation held in Pyongyang in June 1987, the non-aligned countries had undertaken to establish a new and equitable model of international economic relations through economic and technical exchanges and co-operation designed to safeguard their mutual interests. Policies and specific measures for substantial South-South co-operation, and a plan of action, had been adopted at that Conference.

8. If the developing countries used their vast potentialities for South-South co-operation to the full, their bargaining power in international economic relations would be enhanced, a favourable environment for the economic growth of the North would be fostered and the North-South dialogue could go forward. The developed countries should make a substantial contribution to South-South co-operation through the development system of the United Nations and other international organizations.

9. Peace, disarmament and development were closely interlinked, and economic growth could only be assured in a peaceful and co-operative atmosphere. The arms race should be halted at once and urgent disarmament measures taken so that the much-needed human, financial and technical resources could be mobilized in the cause of economic development.

10. He hoped that UNCTAD would be further strengthened as a major forum for the solving of international economic issues of trade and development and that the Conference would be a turning-point for improving international economic relations and promoting the progress and development of the developing countries. He wished it every success.

**Summary of the statement made at the 213th plenary meeting, 27 July 1987,
by Mr. Abdullah Saleh AL-ASHTAL, Permanent Representative of Democratic Yemen to the United Nations**

1. Mr. AL-ASHTAL said that negotiations on the new international economic order had made scant progress for want of good will on the part of most capitalist countries and that the gap between developed and developing countries was widening. It was important, in the interest of all, for the third world to be able to increase its production capacities, diversify its economy and freely sell its products on the market. It was also essential to restructure the international monetary system, taking into account the deficit in the balance of payments of developing countries and easing their debt

burden. In sum, the international economy must be based upon justice, equity and interdependence. In such a system, the developing countries must participate in the decision-making process, instead of being its victims. The policies of capitalist countries led to unemployment, inflation and a decline in ODA. Special thanks were therefore due to those industrialized countries that had started to pursue a positive policy to increase the percentage of their ODA. Assistance of the third world must not be hampered by linkage, hence the importance of the Substantial New Programme of Action for the 1980s for the Least Developed Countries for the expansion and rationalization of such assistance.

2.   Democratic Yemen was one of the LDCs that had suffered most from the effects of the crisis: continuous deterioration of the terms of trade, fluctuation of commodity prices and protectionist policies of the industrialized countries, decline in ODA, increasing interest rates on loans and exchange-rate instability.

3.   Economic recovery and international peace, stability and security were inseparable. Part of the resources devoted to the arms race could therefore be redirected towards economic development.

4.   It should be possible to make the Common Fund for Commodities a reality rapidly, now that the Soviet Union had given an example that other countries should follow by signing the Agreement on Establishing the Fund.

5.   Mindful of the importance of international co-operation, the countries of the third world had striven to develop collective self-sufficiency as a way of bringing about change in the international economic order. They needed to be encouraged by the industrialized

countries in that effort. For its part, Democratic Yemen was pursuing a policy of economic planning. It was preparing its third five-year plan, which focused on light industry, agriculture, exploration for minerals and for underground water. It was being assisted by Arab countries, other socialist countries and international organizations. It was trying to strengthen co-operation at the national and regional level, because that was a way of achieving a degree of equity in economic relations and of avoiding any foreign interference masquerading as assistance.

6.   Some peoples were still under foreign domination or deprived of their legitimate right to self-determination and sovereignty over their national resources. The international community must support those who were fighting for their independence in Palestine, southern Africa and elsewhere, because colonialist and racist régimes were a danger to world peace and security and to international co-operation.

7.   The current session of the Conference must enable all peoples to achieve their aspirations and lead to a fruitful dialogue between developed and developing countries.

Statement made at the 202nd plenary meeting, 10 July 1987, by Mr. Uffe ELLEMANN-JENSEN, Minister for Foreign Affairs of Denmark*

As Denmark holds the Presidency of the Council of European Communities for the remainder of 1987, I have the honour to address the Conference on behalf of the European Community and its member States.

It is with great pleasure that I congratulate you, Mr. President, on your election to this important post. Your great skill and experience are well known and I am confident that you will lead this Conference to a successful outcome.

In a world of growing interdependence UNCTAD, as a universal forum, has an important role to play in promoting international co-operation with a view to reactivating world growth and development. This, in turn, would also contribute to global stability to the benefit of all nations and peoples. The acute difficulties in the world economy, which are particularly affecting developing countries, render international co-operation essential. The alternative is fragmentation of the world economy to the detriment of growth and development and to the detriment of the well-being of all countries represented here.

To transform a general commitment to increased international co-operation into concrete and realistic action is, however, a demanding task. It requires first and foremost, the political courage to put aside ideological and extreme positions and instead concentrate on promoting constructive co-operation. In this context a common assessment of the new realities in the world economy is important.

This opportunity to reach consensus on the necessary domestic policies and international co-operation to

revitalize growth and development must not be lost. Such a consensus would be a positive outcome of the Conference and constitute a new beginning for international co-operation in the field of trade and development. It would also, I believe, increase confidence in UNCTAD and set a new path for the organization by reactivating its role. This is the challenge for all of us. It is the challenge for the seventh session of the Conference.

The European Community and its member States fully accept the particular responsibility of the industrialized countries in ensuring a better international environment by promoting stability and growth.

Important progress has already been made in many developed countries in strengthening the underlying conditions for sustainable, non-inflationary growth. We realize that further efforts are necessary to overcome the internal and external structural imbalances, *inter alia*, through more effective international co-ordination of economic policies. It is essential to continue and intensify the structural adjustment policies. The Community has already initiated such policies in particular in the field of the Common Agricultural Policy and by its efforts to achieve a single internal market and to reinforce economic and social cohesion. Fostering vigorous economies in the developed world contributes significantly to the development process.

At the same time, it must be stressed that the domestic policies of developing countries are of crucial importance for their own development. Many developing countries have already courageously embarked on the process of adjustment. We fully recognize the difficult conditions under which this process is undertaken. But

---

* Initially issued as TD/L.296.

there is no realistic alternative to sound and stable macro-economic policies and to better allocation of internal and external resources. We also believe that increased efficiency in the public sector and a greater role for private enterprise would make a major contribution to adjustment with growth. Furthermore, development of human resources as well as social, demographic and environmental problems must be given due attention.

However, the provision of adequate external resources remains essential for development, particularly for the poorer and least developed countries.

Resources for development are scarce and globally insufficient. Parallel to the efforts of developing countries themselves to establish a sound development process there is a clear need to step up and diversify external financial flows by the timely provision of adequate financing on appropriate terms to support these efforts. The contribution of technical co-operation to the development of human resources is equally important. Both bilateral aid and multilateral institutions play a considerable role in this respect.

The Community and its member States are already large donors. However, we realize that further efforts are needed in order to meet as rapidly as possible the ODA target of 0.7 per cent of GNP, as adopted under the International Development Strategy.

We also recognize the need to enable the multilateral institutions to play a greater part in promoting more satisfactory growth, effective adjustment and mobilization of resources. These organizations have responded in a flexible and efficient way to the needs of developing countries. But we must ensure that they continue to be equipped with the resources and instruments required to fulfil their tasks.

We are fully aware of the serious debt-servicing problems faced by many developing countries. Dealing with these problems is one of the most important tasks confronting the international community. Debt problems differ according to the type of loans obtained and according to the cause of the difficulties for servicing foreign debt. Furthermore, a distinction has to be drawn between the heavily indebted middle-income countries and the poorest countries. Enhancing co-operative action on a case-by-case basis by the parties involved—whether debtor and creditor Governments, the international financial institutions or private banks—will help to reduce the strains in the growth-promoting environment and restore the credit-worthiness of the developing countries.

It is also essential to underline the role to be played in this context by direct investment, including non-debt-creating foreign investment.

Even more constraining are the debt problems among low-income countries. Proposals have recently been made by developed market-economy countries for additional action to reduce the debt-servicing burden of the poorest countries undertaking growth-oriented adjustment programmes. The adjustment of debt renegotiation terms in the Paris Club clearly shows our acceptance of the need for exceptional measures for the most heavily indebted among the poorest countries which are making adjustment efforts.

UNCTAD has a leading role regarding international co-operation in the field of commodities.

Although some progress has been achieved since the adoption in 1976 of the Integrated Programme for Commodities, the overall results must be characterized as limited. At the same time the current situation in most commodity markets poses serious problems for developing countries that are highly dependent on commodities. The need for international co-operation in the field of commodities is therefore more pressing than ever.

Although the continued validity of a number of elements in the Integrated Programme for Commodities is fully recognized, future action should be based on the experience gained and the actual situation for each commodity in order to achieve constructive results.

The international community must support the structural adjustment efforts of developing countries in the form of vertical and horizontal diversification of their economies.

The Integrated Programme and the Common Fund call for measures to support the commodities economy. The Community and its member States express their willingness, in the context of an appropriate financial arrangement, to support new efforts for research, development and diversification regarding commodities and to provide financing for this purpose on a voluntary basis in fulfilment of the pledges made for the Common Fund's second window.

Reducing uncertainty by increased transparency and improving the operation of commodity agreements, consistent with long-term market trends, are, I believe, also common objectives.

The European Community has for a number of years through its Stabex arrangement contributed significantly to stabilize commodity export earnings of the ACP countries. We will continue to do so and call on other industrialized countries to be guided by our efforts in providing special assistance in this area.

There is clear scope for renewed and realistic international co-operation in the field of commodities. The European Community and its member States are ready to engage in a serious dialogue in order to set the priorities for the future.

Liberalization and expansion of trade for the promotion of development are in the interest of all countries and require concerted efforts.

Only if all parties concerned undertake to adhere to multilateralism will positive results be obtained. In this process the diversity of the developing countries must be borne in mind. Rights and obligations must be differentiated according to levels of development, not least in order to meet the needs of the LDCs.

The Uruguay Round provides the only framework for achieving the objective of developing a more open, viable and durable multilateral trading system. The conduct and the implementation of the results of the negotiations must be regarded as forming a whole in order to ensure the mutual advantage of all participants and bring them increased benefits. The European Community remains firmly committed to the objectives and undertakings of the Punta del Este Declaration. The commitment to standstill and roll-back, which applies to all Uruguay Round participants, must be met. We recognize the importance of trade in tropical products to a large number of developing countries. We are also fully aware of the commitment that negotiations in this area shall receive special attention as provided for in the Punta del Este Declaration. Consequently, the Community is preparing a proposal to be presented at an early stage of the negotiations in GATT.

This session should clearly define how UNCTAD can make a useful contribution to the Uruguay Round while respecting the proper role of all concerned in the process under way.

The particular problems of the LDCs and the need to take special measures in support of their development efforts were fully recognized by the adoption of the Substantial New Programme of Action for the 1980s for the Least Developed Countries in 1981. Many LDCs have taken impressive action in fulfilment of the commitment undertaken in the Programme. For these efforts to succeed, it is imperative that the international community as a whole also lives up to its commitments towards the LDCs. In particular the achievement of the ODA target of 0.15 per cent of GNP as adopted in the Programme remains very important.

The European Community and its member States have long been the principal trading partner of, and the main source of external assistance for, the LDCs. They are granted preferential treatment in the framework of the Lomé Convention. Furthermore, in December 1986 the Community created a system analogous to Stabex for the benefit of LDCs, which are not signatories to the Third Lomé Convention.

The external debt situation of the LDCs is a source of increasing concern. Their debt-servicing obligations must be alleviated substantially. We therefore call upon those countries which have not yet done so to implement Board resolution 165 (S-IX) of 11 March 1978.

The European Community and its member States have come to this Conference with an open and constructive mind in order to contribute actively to a successful outcome. The seventh session should result in a major step forward by promoting common perceptions and effective policies and by giving impetus to further progress in UNCTAD itself as well as in other international forums. We do not underestimate the difficult task ahead of us. But we trust that all participants share our aim for a successful outcome and will work towards this end in a spirit of compromise and realism.

Summary of the statement made at the 208th plenary meeting, 14 July 1987, by Mr. F. Daniel SUAZO, Minister Counsellor, Interim Permanent Representative of the Dominican Republic to the United Nations Office at Geneva

1. Mr. SUAZO said that in an interdependent world economy the international community was faced with the challenge of new economic and social pressures stemming from an ever-changing situation. World trade, the flow of private resources and movements of migrant workers across national frontiers were evolving on a scale unprecedented in history. The resulting problems could not be solved by dogmatic, ideological approaches. Pragmatic economic strategies leading to positive action were called for. In the 1970s endless debates had taken place on the evils of the international trading system and the deterioration of the developing countries' terms of trade. Multilateral trade negotiations had not succeeded in reversing protectionist trends in the industrialized countries. The spectre of the external debt had emerged, accompanied by a fall in capital flows to the developing countries, while direct investment in those countries had been slow.

2. As a result of protectionism and debt, Latin America had practically collapsed. The general deterioration in the quality of life had led to strong social pressures and was threatening political structures. The Latin American countries' narrow-based economies had been compressed even further by structural adjustment programmes, and the region had become one of the world's principal exporters of capital.

3. Submerged by such an avalanche of adversity, Latin American countries had taken concrete action to find solutions to the debt problem, as in the Cartagena Consensus, aimed at starting a high-level dialogue based on the co-responsibility of debtors and creditors. However, the industrialized countries, the large international financial groupings and the multilateral financial institutions had not been sufficiently receptive. The Baker plan had proved to be ineffective owing to the reluctance of the banks to supply new funds to debtor countries and to the inadequacy of private investment. In the United States of America, Senator Bradley's determination to help the debtor countries had not been favourably received in financial circles. In any case, the problem would not be solved by stop-gap measures or further restructuring of the debt by means of the injection of fresh funds with which to pay the interest. The pressure on the debtor countries had to be relieved in a context of economic development and stable credit markets. A solution would be found once creditors realized that the third world's debt presented a dilemma of long-term economic solvency rather than a need for short-term liquidity.

4. In the case of the Dominican Republic, payments on its four-billion-dollar debt accounted for more than 100 per cent of its exports, greatly reducing its growth possibilities and leaving no funds to pay for imports of vital items such as medicines and food. The object of his Government's policy with respect to the external debt was to attract a positive flow of capital through multilateral credit institutions. It would honour its international commitments to private banks only in so far as it was able to do so. It sought a rescheduling of the debt that would provide for an extension of grace periods, reductions in interest rates and a substantial

lengthening of maturities. Like other Latin American countries, his country wished to repay its external debt, but on honourable terms that did not jeopardize its development or lead to a social conflict of immeasurable dimensions. Responsibility for economic development lay, of course, with governments, even when they were encumbered by debt, but debt reduced a democratic government's margin of manœuvre.

5. The capacity of small countries like the Dominican Republic to honour their commitments to private banks, Governments and international institutions, as well as to their own population, largely depended on the sale of their products on the international markets. With a few exceptions, international trade in commodities had been depressed during the 1980s. For example, as a result of the increasing reduction of the sugar quota of some producer countries in the preferential markets and of the considerable fall in reserves and the restrictions placed on sources of finance, trade in commodities had continued to deteriorate, to the detriment of most producer countries. The Dominican Republic, despite being a beneficiary of the GSP and of other arrangements, as well as of bilateral and multilateral trade agreements, had not yet managed to overcome the constant deficits in its balance of trade, which had amounted to over $500 million in recent years. Owing to the drastic fall in its sales of coffee, to the reduction of its preferential sugar quota in the United States market and to the increase in the average price of petroleum, the outlook for 1987 was not auspicious. In such circumstances, some small countries were seeking new markets for their exports and tending to co-operate with countries with which they had not had traditional trade relations in the past. That was the case of the Dominican Republic, which might very soon initiate a special trading relationship with the countries of the socialist group.

6. The historical legacy of unequal world development continued to manifest itself in the disproportion between the economic capacity of the developed countries and that of the developing countries. The agenda for the seventh session provided the international community with an excellent opportunity to draw up a coherent multilateral strategy for reactivating the world economy. At the previous session, the Common Fund for Commodities had been approved. However, the commodity sector, which was of crucial importance for the long-term growth of commodity producers, needed to be strengthened further. It would be unfortunate if a commitment to adopt concrete measures within UNCTAD's sphere of competence were again postponed. Action was needed to overcome the barriers to stability in trade of all types and so to promote a sustained expansion and diversification of economic relations among the different groups of countries. It was clear that the Conference could not solve all development problems, but if the main actors could co-operate with one another more closely and effectively, the prospects of making greater progress would be substantially improved for the benefit of all.

Summary of the statement made at the 211th plenary meeting, 24 July 1987, by Mr. Galo LEORO FRANCO, Permanent Representative of Ecuador to the United Nations Office at Geneva

1. Mr. LEORO FRANCO said that the purpose for which the international community had established UNCTAD had lost absolutely none of its validity. In the early days, despite prevailing problems, UNCTAD had made some strides in international economic co-operation with a view to reducing inequalities between the various regions of the world, but it had now reached a deadlock and the advances promised by its major achievements, such as the establishment of the GSP and the adoption of the Integrated Programme for Commodities, had been jeopardized. As the sole universal forum for the discussion of all the complex problems related to trade and development, UNCTAD was the focal point for ideas concerning the formulation of multilateral policies and actions to halt the alarming deterioration of the world economy. Although it was pointless to regret that certain measures had not been taken to avert the recent economic crisis, it was useful to recall the impact of some of the economic developments that had occurred in the preceding 10 years.

2. Inflationary trends that had originated in the industrialized countries had spread internationally in the 1970s, thereby causing inflation and ushering in world recession. The upward spiral of price of manufactures combined with stagnating commodity prices had led to the worsening of the developing countries' terms of trade. The entire world had felt the effects of excess international liquidity and floating exchange rates, which had destabilized balances of payments and hampered economic activity in developing countries. Anti-inflationary measures and their impact on employment, investment and production as well as the international financial market slump, had had serious consequences for commodity-exporting and capital-goods-importing developing countries. That situation, which had already been identified at the sixth session of the Conference in 1983, continued to cripple the growth and development of the third world countries. Slow growth in the developed market-economy countries was the result of the macro-economic policies they had adopted to combat inflation, with no consideration for the overall impact those policies would have on the international economy. Inequalities between the various regions in the world had thus been exacerbated and the injustice of the international economic system compounded. Protectionism, which was now widespread, was contrary to international rules and seriously restricted developing country market access and foreign currency earnings.

3. Debtor countries such as Ecuador, which could not save and invest, were reduced to spending the few foreign currency resources they had in order to continue importing essential goods. Unfavourable external factors prevented them from diversifying their output and increasing their productive capacity. They had conse-

quently experienced a trade shortfall of $96 billion in 1986 and registered a $24 billion net outflow of financial resources. Ecuador was a case in point. It had suffered a 50 per cent slump in export earnings owing to the rapid downward pressure of oil prices in 1986 and its earnings from banana, coffee and cocoa exports had shrunk by 40 per cent. Its debt had soared to $8,159 billion (including $59 million in private debts). Its trade had been hampered by tariff barriers and other types of more or less transparent or discriminatory restrictive measures. The trend towards the use of substitutes and synthetics and restricted access to the GSP were making the situation worse.

4.   Despite all those problems, Ecuador had implemented adjustment programmes at the cost of very great economic and social sacrifices, since debt servicing absorbed 30 per cent of its export earnings. It would be difficult for Ecuador to do more in the light of the fact that its external debt had reached an unprecedented level as against its GDP and export earnings, as was the case in many developing countries. Solving a problem of that magnitude was clearly the shared responsibility of debtor and creditor countries, commercial banks and multilateral finance institutions. The debt crisis was not a temporary situation, but a deep-seated problem resulting from the structure of the international financial system and the existence of trade imbalances. The developing countries were calling for a political dialogue that would lead to the implementation of a global strategy in which debt-servicing payments would be tailored to a country's real disbursement capacity, taking into account its requirements in terms of growth and

economic and social progress. Such a global strategy should apply both to commodities and to trade.

5.   Growing protectionism might well be the greatest threat, since it stood in the way of structural adjustments in the industrialized countries and thus affected the developing countries. A liberal trade system, geared towards development and growth with differential and more favourable treament for developing countries, was essential to ensure equality and justice in international economic relations. The industrialized countries would therefore have to meet their commitments concerning the standstill and gradual roll-back of trade restrictions and acknowledge the importance of competitive exports for GDP formation, trade balances and employment in the developing countries.

6.   In the area of multilateral co-operation, the Integrated Programme for Commodities should be strengthened through price stabilization and market regulation on the basis of individual agreements. The long-awaited implementation of the Common Fund was also essential. In that connection, the announcement of the ratification by the Soviet Union and several developing States of the Agreement Establishing the Common Fund was to be welcomed.

7.   The seventh session of the Conference provided a unique opportunity to find solutions to the pressing problems of the international economy as a whole and to offer renewed development possibilities for the countries of the South. The international community had to be pragmatic in the choices it made and avoid economic upheavals that would be detrimental to all nations.

Summary of the statement at the 214th plenary meeting, 28 July 1987, by Mr. Yousri MUSTAFA, Minister of Economy and Foreign Trade of Egypt

1.   Mr. MUSTAFA noted that there were few international institutions such as UNCTAD that were specifically responsible for tackling trade, finance and development problems in terms of their interrelationships at the global level. UNCTAD's universal nature also made it an ideal forum for North-South and East-West dialogue on those problems. The importance of reviving that dialogue was currently greater than ever before since no country, however powerful its economy, was by itself able to overcome the impact of the world crisis.

2.   The problems confronted by developing countries, especially the debt burden, the inadequacy of financial flows and the commodity price slump, had been thoroughly examined by the Conference. Many developing countries, including Egypt, had initiated structural adjustments in an effort to improve their economies and attract foreign investment. However, the results had fallen short of expectations owing to the persistently unfavourable international environment. In the final analysis, there was not much they could do to offset deteriorating terms of trade, declining export earnings, fluctuating exchange rates, a lack of markets for their products and increasing protectionism in the developed countries. No one denied that each country

was primarily responsible for its own development and that its economic choices determined its domestic prosperity and the living standards of its population. Yet it was clearly up to the industrialized countries, in proportion to their international economic influence, to bring about appropriate changes in the world economic system.

3.   States should therefore explore, before the end of the current session, specific possibilities of facilitating the solution of developing country problems and, more generally adopt decisions of principle that could form the basis of a long-term strategy to revive economic growth and development throughout the world. The final document of the Sixth Ministerial Meeting of the Group of 77, held at Havana, could serve as a basis for such negotiations.

4.   Conference participants seemed to be in agreement on the need for concerted action with respect to the debt problem. The Government of Egypt considered that the most urgent priority was to relieve the debt burden by reducing interest rates and, more generally, by rescheduling payments to bring them more into line with the debt-servicing capacity of developing countries. In the longer term, the international community's efforts should focus on the issues of exchange rates and

developing-country liquidity needs, in other words, the reform of the international monetary system, in which Egypt was prepared to join.

5. The only hope for a lasting solution to the problems of indebted countries was continued development efforts. It was therefore vital for creditor countries and multilateral finance institutions to maintain financial flows to those countries. External assistance should be geared to the projects adopted by debtor countries with a view to the development of economic sectors capable of increasing their export earnings, such as textiles, agricultural products and manufactures. UNCTADthus had a key role to play with respect to commodities, especially within the framework of the Integrated Programme for Commodities, which constituted the only international means of stabilizing commodity prices. He expressed the hope that the number of accessions to the Agreement Establishing the Common Fund for Commodities would soon be sufficient to enable the Fund to begin operations because, through the activities financed under its two accounts, the Fund was destined to become the Integrated Programme's essential instrument.

6. However, producer countries had to secure access to foreign markets. Members of the international community should therefore honour their commitments to put an end to protectionist measures. It was one of the functions of UNCTAD, GATT and the Uruguay Round to foster international trade liberalization and improve market access.

7. The IMF Compensatory Financing Facility should also be improved and supplemented with other measures, since its current scope was too limited for the effective compensation of the export earnings shortfalls of the developing countries.

8. He expressed the hope that the Substantial New Programme of Action for the 1980s for the Least Developed Countries would be fully implemented since the countries for which it had been created had been hardest hit by the world economic crisis. Since the majority of those countries were in Africa, it was also important to implement all the provisions of the United Nations Programme of Action for African Economic Recovery and Development 1986-1990.

9. The number of ministers—and, even more importantly, of heads of State and Government, including President Mubarak—present at the Conference's seventh session underscored the importance that the international community attached to UNCTAD and its expectation that the Conference would take practical and decisive action.

Summary of the statement made at the 207th plenary meeting, 14 July 1987, by Mr. Gebre Kidan TADESSE, Minister for Foreign Affairs of Ethiopia

1. Mr. TADESSE said that, at a time when malfunctions in the international trading, financial and monetary systems inimical to growth and development were worsening, the socio-economic situation in the developing countries continued to be very precarious. In general, there was no real growth in output. The prices of commodities, in real terms, were at their lowest levels since the Great Depression of the 1930s. In 1986 alone the developing countries had lost $100 billion as a result of the continued deterioration of their terms of trade. The hardest hit had been, as usual, the low-income countries. The debt-servicing obligations of the developing countries, particularly the least developed among them, had reached alarming proportions. For some of them debt-servicing obligations exceeded annual export earnings, owing to the unprecedentedly fast accumulation of debt resulting mainly from high real interest rates.

2. The very sharp decline in the flow of much-needed private and official development resources to developing countries had created a very serious gap in the resources available for development. In 1985 the total net flows of concessional development finance had not been higher than in 1981. IMF had become a net recipient of funds from developing countries. The ratio of ODA to GNP had remained below half of the 0.7 per cent target set by the international community. The reaffirmation, at the Venice Summit, of the need to achieve that target was encouraging, as was the commitment to raise the resources of the Structural Adjustment Facility to SDR 9 billion.

3. For many low-income countries the 1980s had compromised the achievements of the 1970s. Social contradictions had been accentuated and political tension sharpened, with dire implications for international peace and harmony. It was now widely acknowledged that the problem of the developing countries should be tackled coherently be increasing financial flows, resolving their external debt problems, diversifying their economies away from excessive dependence on commodities, and improving the international monetary and trading systems in order to revitalize growth and development through multilateral co-operation in a more predictable and supportive environment. The seventh session of the Conference provided a unique opportunity to work out policies and measures to that end.

4. By the end of 1986 Africa's foreign debt had been estimated at $200 billion. Debt servicing now accounted for more than 30 per cent of GDP. In 1986, while debt-servicing obligations had continued to rise, export earnings had fallen by $19 billion. The international community's commitment to the United Nations Programme of Action for African Economic Recovery and Development 1986-1990 was still to be implemented. The International Conference on African Economic Recovery and Development held in June 1987 in Nigeria had rightly expressed the legitimate concern that the efforts of African Governments to grapple with their multifaceted problems might be jeopardized unless that commitment was implemented fully and effectively.

5. Special attention should be given to Africa so that structural changes could be made that would enable the African countries to embark upon self-reliant and self-sustaining growth and development and to secure their rightful place in the society of nations.

6. Since most African and other low-income economies, particularly those of the LDCs were heavily dependent on one or two commodities and were exposed to intolerable external shocks, the expected adoption by the Conference of policies and measures aimed at compensating them automatically for losses arising from a deterioration in their terms of trade, the early institution of the Common Fund and the launching of diversification, processing and marketing programmes for their structural transformation in the medium and long term would do much to combat their underdevelopment. Such programmes would need to be supported by sufficient investment capital from bilateral and multilateral sources. Special facilities could be created for that purpose in the World Bank group, IMF and the regional and subregional development banks. An indispensable component of the programmes should be the conscious upgrading of absorptive capacities in the low-income countries through technical assistance and the creation and strengthening of institutions basic to self-reliant and self-sustaining development. UNCTAD could play a catalytic role in preparing global and country-specific studies on the potential and limitations of international markets, the transfer of technology, and ways and means of insulating the economies of the low-income countries from avaricious predators. A system of consultations between developing countries, donor Governments and international development institutions could also be organized under the auspices of UNCTAD.

7. Since its inception UNCTAD had been particularly concerned with the problems of the LDCs. The alarming nature of their predicament was manifested by high illiteracy rates, low levels of nutrition and health, very low per capita incomes, high rates of population growth, extremely low agricultural productivity, very low levels of exploitation of natural resources, small industrial sectors, very weak infrastructures, acute shortages of skilled personnel, and an alarming degree of environmental degradation. The adoption of the Substantial New Programme of Action for the 1980s for the Least Developed Countries in 1981 had appeared at the time to be a breakthrough. However, the measures envisaged to help those countries to achieve acceptable minimum standards of nutrition, health and income, including a transfer of official development resources amounting to 0.15 per cent of developed countries' GNP or doubling the level thereof by the end of the programme period, had fallen far short of expectations. In fact, in the 1980s the situation of the LDCs had deteriorated further at an alarming rate. The interna-

tional community should take prompt and decisive action to support development if a crisis of the magnitude of that which had occurred in Africa in 1985 was to be prevented.

8. The destruction wrought on the ecosystems of many LDCs as a result of the misuse or over-use of land, leading to desertification, required particular attention. The life-supporting capacities of lands in those countries had been severely undermined by population pressures and mismanagement. Although the preservation of the existing environment and its protection from further deterioration was crucial in those LDCs where deforestation and soil erosion had already seriously compromised environmental conditions, the restoration of the ecosystem was also important. The international community should therefore envisage mounting massive environmental protection and rehabilitation programmes.

9. The fact that the number of LDCs had increased from 32 to 37 was a clear indication of the deteriorating conditions of the low-income countries. Given the current international economic climate and the gloomy prospects, more countries would join that category. The international community should therefore accelerate the pace of implementation of the Substantial New Programme of Action. A high-level international commission should be established under United Nations auspices to monitor and oversee its implementation. In a broader context the commission could be mandated to monitor the programmes, commitments and actions of multilateral organizations and donors. On the basis of its assessments, the commission would be expected to recommend further action to be taken by the international community or by specific organizations to achieve the objectives established by the international community for the benefit of the low-income countries. Action in good time was always better than post-mortem examination. The Ethiopian Government was in favour of holding a conference at the end of the programme period to review the implementation of the Substantial New Programme of Action and to work out a strategy for the 1990s. The offer made by President Mitterrand for France to host such a conference was therefore welcome.

10. He earnestly hoped that the seventh session of the Conference would not be characterized by an impasse similar to those of the past. The world could not afford a continuation of the destabilizing effects of the existing trading, financial and monetary systems, which were grossly unfair to the developing countries. The Conference should therefore be in a position to adopt policies and measures that would help to curtail the further erosion of the international economic climate and help to maintain peace through development.

**Summary of the statement made at the 215th plenary meeting, 28 July 1987,
by Mr. Pertti SALOLAINEN, Minister of Foreign Trade of Finland**

1. Mr. SALOLAINEN said that, despite the efforts made to encourage sustained economic growth, recovery had been less vigorous than expected in the in-

dustrialized countries, while the problems of debt and shrinking resources had worsened in the developing countries. It was essential that the seventh session of the

Conference should contribute to a shared understanding of international economic problems and to the search for solutions to them.

2. The need to promote global well-being ought to incite all countries to manage their interdependence properly by adopting more co-ordinated policies aimed at strengthening growth, correcting imbalances, improving market access, lowering real interest rates and increasing financial flows to the developing countries. In addition, changes in consumption, production and trade patterns called for structural adjustments in both developed and developing countries. In the light of its own experience, Finland considered that adjustment policies should be adapted to the situation prevailing in each country and to the changing international economic environment. It therefore favoured multilateral co-operation based on a differentiated approach.

3. International trade was one of the main motors of economic development. It was thus essential to halt and reverse protectionism and to liberalize and stimulate trade. Finland, a small country with an open economy, was well placed to appreciate the importance of the multilateral trading system, which should be maintained and improved by a process of multilateral trade negotiations. It recognized the responsibilities of developed countries in that respect, but considered that developing countries too should take an active part in the Uruguay Round, which provided an ideal framework for dismantling protectionist measures, particularly in the developed countries. Although their economic difficulties currently made many developed countries unable to undertake any major trade liberalization measures, those which were or were about to become competitive exporters could assume a greater share of responsibility for the multilateral trading system. UNCTAD, which had an important part to play in several sectors of international trade, should follow the Uruguay Round negotiations in order to support GATT in its work.

4. With regard to commodities, market stabilization depended largely on opening up the multilateral trading system and on sustained economic growth. The need for short-term remedies was clear, but flexible and pragmatic solutions were also required to longer-term structural problems and in connection with the diversification of exports from developing countries. In that context, Finland looked forward with interest to the probable entry into force of the Agreement Establishing the Common Fund for Commodities. Encouragement should continue to be given to UNCTAD's work to achieve a better understanding of the factors affecting commodity markets and market operation in order to ensure greater stability and more reliable forecasting of

commodity markets. Another topic that UNCTAD could study was the role of development assistance in diversifying and developing third world economies.

5. Since the early 1980s, the net flow of resources to developing countries had declined sharply. In view of the severe effects of that trend on the development prospects of the countries concerned, the Finnish Government was prepared to make every effort to reverse it. Finland hoped that, in the context of the strategy for tackling the debt problem, many countries would support a significant increase in the resources of IMF's Structural Adjustment Facility. It supported the World Bank's plans to establish a special action programme for debt-distressed African countries. Those initiatives, intended to assist the poorest and most indebted countries, ought to be supplemented by increased assistance from multilateral institutions and donor countries. In view of the success of the new tools and techniques used to alleviate the debt burden of middle-income countries, it was to be hoped that the commercial banks would co-operate fully in management of the debts of such countries.

6. As for the situation of the LDCs, the Finnish Government considered that the international community and those countries themselves should make greater efforts to implement the Substantial New Programme of Action. The best option for such countries remained an increase in ODA and other forms of concessional aid. In order to help the LDCs make better use of the resources available to them, the Finnish Government had decided to allocate the equivalent of $2 million to the UNDP National Technical Co-operation Assessments and Programmes (NATCAP), with a view to strengthening the administrative structures and capabilities of the LDCs. It also endorsed the provisions of Trade and Development Board resolution 165 (S-IX) recommending that LDC debt should be written off as ODA. In addition, it welcomed the recent decisions of the Paris Club and other bodies on methods for dealing with LDC debt.

7. The management of global interdependence called for effective international institutions responsive to emerging challenges and needs and capable of preparing appropriate guidelines. UNCTAD remained a unique forum for studying the interrelationships between financial resources, commodities and intertional trade. However, there still appeared to be room for improvement in its methods and practices. It should be possible to make better use of the skills and other resources available at sessions of the Conference, and in other UNCTAD bodies, in order to give practical support to the development process.

Summary of the statement made at the 217th plenary meeting, 29 July 1987, by Mr. Georges CHAVANES, Minister responsible for Commerce, Craft, Trades and Services of France

1. Mr. CHAVANES said that the work of the Conference must lead to a joint analysis of problems and the elaboration of constructive measures acceptable to the entire international community. The economic results

achieved since the start of the decade had not been as good as might have been hoped and the developing countries were still experiencing serious difficulties. Concerted action to improve the situation was needed from all States, including the industrialized countries, since they each bore their share of responsibility.

2. The developing countries should resolutely pursue rigorous adjustment programmes to reduce their deficits, combat inflation and capital flight, develop their productive sectors, streamline public enterprises and improve investment conditions in the private sector in order to improve the health of their economies and establish the bases for sustainable and balanced growth.

3. There should be no illusions about the fact that those efforts to adapt would require a great deal of time and sacrifice. The industrialized countries, therefore, must seek to create an economic environment conducive to growth and mobilize adequate financial resources for development. Some progress had been made recently in that direction. In particular, it was encouraging to note the commitments made to reduce budget deficits, the opening of a new round of multilateral negotiations under the auspices of GATT, the action taken by some industrialized countries with the largest surpluses to stimulate domestic demand and the decision taken at the Tokyo and Venice summits on improving the co-ordination of economic policies to promote stronger, non-inflationary and sustainable world growth.

4. The Louvre Agreement marked a decisive step forward in that regard: the major western Powers had reaffirmed their desire to ensure more stable exchange rates and had undertaken to set up a multilateral system of performance monitoring with IMF assistance. That concerted action was bound gradually to prove fruitful and benefit the international community as a whole. Regarding the Uruguay negotiations, it was to be hoped that all participants would resist the temptations of protectionism and would seek through negotiation to establish favourable conditions for the balanced expansion of world trade. France intended to participate actively in the negotiations in all areas, including agriculture.

5. Despite those positive developments, there were a number of outstanding problems which urgently required a solution, such as low rates of growth, the high level of real interest rates, the very appreciable drop in commodity prices, and the decline in net inflows of resources to the developing countries, which were all factors that in part explained the acute nature of the debt problem of some countries and the gravity of the situation of many raw-material producers. France believed that priority should be given to assistance to the poorest countries, which must be supplied with a geater volume of resources on concessional terms. It was equally important to study ways of augmenting multilateral and commercial banking assistance to middle-income countries and to pursue debt-rescheduling efforts.

6. The situation of the most disadvantaged countries of sub-Saharan Africa called for special attention. Those countries were the main victims of the falling prices of commodities, their main source of income, which seriously jeopardized the success of their courageous adjustment efforts. Their indebtedness, moreover, was reaching intolerable limits. The General Assembly in 1986 had adopted a special programme of action for Africa, which clearly showed that the interna-tional community was aware of the particular difficulties being experienced by that continent. It was essential to adopt a pragmatic approach in efforts to stabilize commodity prices. France attached great importance to the Common Fund for Commodities and hoped that it would very soon be brought into operation.

7. Despite some positive accomplishments, such as the Eighth Replenishment of the resources of IDA, financial inflows to the most disadvantaged countries clearly remained insufficient to sustain their growth efforts. It was thus essential to speed up consideration of all possible means of increasing the flow of resources on concessional terms to those countries. France has submitted several proposals on the subject, aimed in particular at making the conditions of IMF's Compensatory Financing Facility more flexible or establishing a new facility for refinancing a substantial proportion of their debt-servicing costs at concessional rates. Other formulas were no doubt possible, and France was prepared to consider them in an open-minded spirit. The Managing Director of IMF had proposed tripling the resources of the Fund's Structural Adjustment Facility; that was an excellent initiative and France, for its part, was ready to contribute some $500 million over the coming three years. It was also essential to bring current negotiations on the replenishment of the African Development Fund's resources to a successful conclusion as soon as possible.

8. The Paris Club, for which France provided the secretariat services, had already taken steps to reschedule the debt of the poorest countries, extending the periods of grace and time-limits for repayment. Regarding middle-income and large debtor countries, the Paris Club, like the commercial banks, had shown great flexibility over the past few years.

9. France recognized the merits of many of the proposals formulated in the Havana Declaration. On others, however, it had serious reservations as they would be more detrimental than beneficial to development. For example, to limit debt servicing to a fixed percentage of export earnings would be unreasonable since that might have extremely undesirable effects, such as cutting off resource flows.

10. The multilateral development banks could play a key role. In the preceding two years, they had granted an increasing volume of rapidly disbursable loans to support the implementation of adjustment policies. But their room for manœuvre was generally too limited by the amount of resources currently available to them. An overall increase in the capital of the World Bank would have to be made as soon as possible. It would also be desirable to bring current negotiations concerning the Inter-American Development Bank to an early conclusion. Countries with surpluses could usefully increase their refinancing operations with those institutions, as advocated by the World Bank.

11. He appealed for understanding, imagination and generosity on the part of the international community to promote further progress in the field of development and North-South co-operation. In 10 years, attitudes had changed considerably and people in

the developed countries, particularly young people, were becoming increasingly sympathetic towards citizens of the third world. France, which enjoyed privileged links with many African countries, was ready to play its role in exploring new mechanisms of co-operation. It fervently hoped that the Conference would be successful and would do its utmost to contribute to that success.

Summary of the statement made at the 205th plenary meeting, 13 July 1987, by Mr. Gerhard BEIL, Minister of Foreign Trade of the German Democratic Republic

1. Mr. BEIL said that, as was stated in the message addressed to the Conference by Mr. Erich Honecker, the General Secretary of the Central Committee of the Socialist Unity Party and Chairman of the Council of State of the German Democratic Republic,* world-wide trade and economic co-operation offered genuine opportunities for deepening relations among States and peoples in the interest of détente and the safeguarding of peace; he expressed the hope that at the current session a major impetus would be given to the development of international trade, increased confidence and a more stable peace.

2. In view of the wide-ranging tasks of the Conference, the German Democratic Republic attached great significance to the session and expected it to produce results that would help to strengthen UNCTAD's role in accordance with its mandate. In order to solve the problems facing them, all participating States should show common sense and realism. The strained world political situation and the fact that a move towards the normalization of international economic relations was still awaited made dialogue and co-operation all the more imperative. The protracted crisis affecting international economic relations had particularly dramatic repercussions for the developing countries, whose aggravated domestic and external economic situation had rightly been stressed in the declarations of the Eighth Conference of Heads of State or Government of Non-Aligned Countries and the Sixth Ministerial Meeting of the Group of 77. Economic growth in most developing countries was virtually at a standstill, with drastic socio-economic implications for them.

3. His country concurred with all those who expected that the Conference's discussions on problems of financial and other resources for development and related monetary issues would produce tangible results. By virtue of its mandate UNCTAD had undoubted competence in that field.

4. The developing countries were suffering from a massive external debt and a net outflow of financial resources. The situation was being used by international monopoly capital in its efforts to dominate and exploit the third world. As a consequence international economic relations as a whole were destabilized, the ability of developing countries to participate in world trade was restricted and the continued expansion of mutually advantageous economic ties with other countries, including his own, was hampered. The German Democratic Republic favoured the reshaping of international economic, financial and monetary relations on a just, equitable and democratic basis and supported the idea of preparing for an international conference on money and finance within the United Nations system and with universal participation.

5. His country had noted with concern a growing violation of the basic principles of world trade, particularly the principles of non-discrimination and MFN treatment. The fundamental issues of international trade policies should be discussed and dealt with constructively within UNCTAD. Discriminatory embargoes imposed by some industrialized capitalist countries on technology exports, together with increased import restrictions by Governments and restrictive business practices by private monopolies must be examined. Such restrictions, which interfered with his country's exports, particularly in the machine-building, metallurgical, chemical, textile and consumer goods industries, were being used to exclude foreign competitors from domestic and third-country markets. The German Democratic Republic had actively supported the adoption of the Set of Multilaterally Agreed Equitable Principles and Rules for the Control of Restrictive Business Practices. However, the effective implementation of those rules and principles was being obstructed by the TNCs. The universal application of the progressive rules and principles of international trade included in the final documents of the first session of UNCTAD —which were not in need of revision but remained fully valid—would help to make international economic relations more stable, reliable and predictable. UNCTAD had a specific contribution to make in that regard.

6. There could be no international economic security unless the crisis in world commodity markets and its harmful impact on the commodity-exporting developing countries could be overcome. His country, which favoured the long-term stabilization of commodity markets, considered the strengthening of the sovereignty of developing countries over their commodity resources to be a decisive step in that direction. That could only be done by involving Governments and strengthening the role played by the public sector in that area. His delegation would welcome the improvement of existing multilateral commodity agreements with market-regulating mechanisms and the negotiation of new ones under UNCTAD auspices.

7. Mutually advantageous economic co-operation and the safeguarding of world peace were interdependent. The decisions adopted by the Warsaw Treaty States at the latest session of their Political Consultative Committee offered an opportunity to arrive at far-reaching arrangements on arms limitation and disarma-

---

* TD/L.278 (see volume I, annex IV).

ment, provided that all concerned followed a common sense, circumspect and goodwill approach. His delegation endorsed the declarations of the non-aligned States characterizing the arms race as a principal obstacle to socio-economic progress for it inflicted enormous damage on world trade and, in particular, had a devastating impact on developing countries. The practical implementation of the disarmament-for-development principle would not only increase confidence and security in international relations but would allow part of the released resources to be used for economic and social progress. His delegation expected the forthcoming United Nations Conference on the Relationship between Disarmament and Development to produce action-oriented decisions to that effect.

8. The basic purpose of his country's economic strategy up to the year 2000 was to achieve stable and dynamic economic and social progress. Socialist democracy in the German Democratic Republic was reflected in the universal participation of the working people in the planning and management of State, social and economic affairs. Productivity and efficiency in all sectors of the economy would be substantially boosted by combining the advantages of socialism with the achievements of the scientific and technological revolution. Between 1986 and 1990, national income was to be increased by nearly 25 per cent and both net output and labour productivity were to rise by 50 per cent. The necessary conditions for reaching those targets had been created on a long-term basis, taking account of new internal and external conditions.

9. His country's continued active and reliable participation in world trade was ensured by its economic strategy and its long-term economic, scientific and technological relations with the other countries members of CMEA. Between 1980 and 1986, its foreign trade turnover had increased by 51.5 per cent. Despite growing protectionist barriers, it had, by 1986, gradually raised its foreign trade turnover with industrialized capitalist countries to 28.2 per cent of its total foreign trade turnover. High growth rates had been achieved particularly with France, the United Kingdom, Italy, Austria and Canada. Its trade with developing countries had also steadily increased.

10. It also intended to expand its economic, scientific and technological co-operation with developing countries in a planned, equitable and mutually advantageous manner. Despite the complicated international environment, it had continued to provide assistance to developing countries and national liberation movements in 1986, to a volume equal to 0.89 per cent of its national income. In order to expand mutually beneficial trade and economic ties with industrialized capitalist countries and developing countries, it would have to make increased use of highly dynamic types and methods of co-operation in the future.

11. His country would continue to uphold the principles of equality, non-interference and MFN treatment and their unreserved application in international economic exchanges, regardless of differences in economic and social systems.

**Summary of the statement made at the 217th plenary meeting, 29 July 1987,
by Mr. Martin BANGEMANN, Federal Minister of Economics of the Federal Republic of Germany**

1. Mr. BANGEMANN said that, in view of their economic interdependence, nations should act together and must all take measures to adapt to the rapidly changing global economy if they did not wish to fall behind.

2. The developing countries presented a contrasting picture. The most advanced of those countries could now hardly be distinguished from some industrialized nations. The next group comprised middle-income countries, which the developed countries could assist above all by opening their markets to their products and by providing them with financial and technical assistance. Lastly, there was the group of the LDCs, especially those of sub-Saharan Africa, which greatly needed assistance to be able to satisfy their basic needs and set themselves on the road to economic development. It might well be asked whether the assessment of the economic situation and perspectives presented by the Group of 77 at the Sixth Ministerial Meeting at Havana really took account of that highly differentiated picture.

3. The moderate but sustained growth experienced by the world economy over the preceding five years had no doubt been more beneficial to the developing countries than a short-lived economic boom. It had been ac-

companied by a certain stabilization of prices in the industrialized countries and by a decline in interest rates, which had meant lower debt-servicing costs. The GNP of the developing countries had increased by more than 3 per cent per annum in 1985 and 1986 and trade flows had begun to adjust to the global economic changes. However, that should not be allowed to obscure major outstanding problems such as depressed commodity prices, which placed developing country producers in a critical situation.

4. The world economic situation would not improve on its own and a major effort was required by both the developed and the developing countries. At the OECD ministerial meeting and at the recent economic summit, Governments had agreed that the challenges of the future could be tackled only through a policy of stability and growth that was conducive to adjustment. The Federal Republic of Germany was against cartels and protectionism, which were not to the advantage of any country, and was actively seeking to facilitate competition and to open its markets further. It had already lowered the tax burden and would give an extra boost to the performance of the private sector by a reform of its tax system that would take effect in 1990. Its monetary and fiscal policies remained geared to the objective of

stable prices, and a declining public sector would also contribute to improving the prospects for growth. Imports and exports were moving towards equilibrium as a result of the appreciation of the deutsche mark and the process of external economic adjustment was well under way.

5. The Federal Republic of Germany was endeavouring to help the developing countries to participate more actively in world trade and become more closely integrated into the international division of labour, without in any way interfering with their sovereignty. They had the right to organize their economies as they wished. Experience showed, however, that liberalism and market-economy principles were ever more successful in promoting economic growth and paving the way for structural adjustment—an opinion shared by an increasing number of developing countries.

6. It was the responsibility of the industrialized countries to contribute to the development of the third world. The Federal Republic of Germany was devoting 0.43 per cent of its GNP to development assistance. Its trade in goods and services with the developing countries was traditionally in deficit and had amounted to some $3 billion per annum over the preceding three years. The developing countries must, however, look for ways to improve their domestic investment conditions in order to prevent a flight of capital. Regarding the debt problem, priority should be given to assisting the poorest countries, and efforts must be made to promote growth in the debtor countries, especially by granting credits through international financial institutions and commercial banks. It should be possible to arrive at a consensus by the end of the year on what measures should be taken in that regard.

7. The developing countries producing raw materials were in a very difficult situation, and had to be helped to market their commodities more effectively and to diversify their national economies. The Federal Republic of Germany had already announced that it would voluntarily make available DM 50 million for the Second Account of the Common Fund. In view of the discouraging experience acquired with commodity agreements, it had more confidence in market-oriented

support measures such as research, training, substitution and improvement of marketing infrastructures.

8. Development in third world countries called for increasing participation in international trade flows. The principal outlets for the developing countries' exports were the markets of the industrialized countries, to which they therefore needed broader access. An ever-increasing number of developing countries were, however, playing an active role in international trade. That was true mainly of those that had been able to diversify their exports, had allowed the private sector greater latitude and given free rein to market forces. The most successful among them, namely, the newly industrialized countries, would now increasingly have to submit to the very rules from which they had benefited, and assume their own responsibilities under the system of free international trade.

9. For many developing countries, trade in farm products was of major importance. Efforts were therefore needed to ensure that world agricultural markets functioned better and that agricultural production was adapted to demand. Further liberalization was also required in the tropical products sector. There was likewise a need to intensify and liberalize trade among the developing countries themselves, a task to which UNCTAD should devote particular attention.

10. The objective of the Uruguay Round of negotiations under GATT auspices was the further liberalization of markets, particularly for the benefit of the developing countries, and should be actively supported. UNCTAD could play a useful role in promoting those negotiations through analyses and technical assistance. Lastly, he noted that his country had decided to allot the sum of DM 450,000 to UNCTAD in 1987 and 1988 for training courses on the GSP and related questions to be held in Nairobi, Abidjan, Dhaka and Panama.

11. The discussion at the Conference had shown that the improvement of international relations required efforts by all countries. Success in one part of the world was of benefit to all other parts. Growing integration within the EEC was having a positive effect on the world economy and the same was true of the improvement of East-West relations. The Conference should help to strengthen co-operation between all States in all fields.

Summary of the statement made at the 212th plenary meeting, 27 July 1987, by Mr. Kofi DJIN, Provisional National Defence Council Secretary for Trade and Tourism of Ghana

1. Mr. DJIN said that the Conference was meeting during the deepest world economic crisis since the Second World War. The 1980s had been characterized by considerable uncertainty and risks—the collapse of commodity prices, the proliferation of protectionist measures, a general tightening of financial and monetary markets and an unprecedented increase in the debt burden of developing countries—and the interaction of those factors had greatly reduced the volume of trade and production and had stifled growth, particu-

larly in the developing countries. In addition, Africa had experienced a severe drought that had caused a major famine and a rapid deterioration in living standards. The developed countries themselves had been affected by the instability of the international economic situation, which demonstrated the growing interdependence of all countries of the world and the reciprocal effects of all development issues. Everything seemed to indicate that the problems of the world economy could be resolved only by a multilateral approach.

2. In view of the crucial role played by commodities in economic and social development in the developing countries, his delegation was seriously concerned by the slow progress being made in the implementation of important international initiatives in that sector—the Integrated Programme for Commodities, the Common Fund and compensatory financing for export earnings shortfalls—and considered that the Conference should agree on further measures to accelerate the process. In addition, developing countries should be encouraged to participate in the processing, marketing, transport and distribution of the commodities they exported.

3. His delegation was concerned by recent developments in biotechnology. The use of substitutes and synthetics instead of natural products was becoming so widespread that it posed a real threat to the already fragile economies of the many developing countries which were dependent on natural commodities. It was clear that urgent international action was required to co-ordinate and discipline research in that sector, so that both developed and developing countries might benefit from it.

4. Developments in the financial and monetary sector were a further source of concern. Although the developing countries bore the primary responsibility for their own development, and were making every effort to mobilize the necessary resources, the general sluggishness of the world economy, which had had a negative effect on the exports of most of those countries, made it necessary to assist them by increasing the volume of external financial aid made available on concessionary terms. Yet severe cut-backs in the flow of external resources, together with high interest rates and increased debt-servicing costs, had led to a negative transfer of capital from many developing countries to a small group of developed countries, which prevented the former from achieving any meaningful development.

5. It was equally urgent to alleviate the crushing debt burden of the developing countries and distribute the responsibilities and costs of global development more equitably among debtors and creditors. If the seventh session of the Conference could be used to draw up a realistic and viable debt-reduction strategy, it would help to ensure that debt servicing did not block growth and development.

6. Moreover, in view of the growing disregard for the principle of multilateralism in international trade, his delegation considered that GATT, with its limited membership and field of action, could not resolve the fundamental problems in that area on its own. Although GATT had an important function to perform during the Uruguay Round, it was UNCTAD—by virtue of its universality and mandate—that should assume a major and dynamic role by conducting an in-depth study of the international trade system from the standpoint of its contribution to development.

7. As for the problem of the LDCs, the consensus on the Substantial New Programme of Action adopted in 1981 had not prevented the growing marginalization of those countries in world trade and development. The intolerable situation of those countries and the enlightened self-interest of the entire international community should encourage the Conference to draw up measures to integrate the LDCs into a broader strategy aimed at revitalizing development and growth.

8. It was clear that the crisis in the world economy was of a structural nature and was undermining the foundations of the economic fabric of developed and developing countries alike. The seventh session of the Conference was both a challenge and an opportunity to move from analysis to practical action in order to solve those problems. His delegation was confident that the Conference would be remembered not as yet one more missed opportunity, but as an occasion on which new hope and vitality had been breathed into multilateralism in the service of development.

**Summary of the statement made at the 216th plenary meeting, 29 July 1987,
by Mr. Yannos PAPANTONIOU, Deputy Minister of National Economy of Greece**

1. Mr. PAPANTONIOU said that the world economy was experiencing acute difficulties, which were in particular affecting many developing countries. Sluggish growth in the industrial countries had had an adverse effect on the development and adjustment processes taking place in the third world. Given slow growth, poverty and uncertainty about the future, international co-operation was indispensable as no country could cope on its own with the complex problems created by the situation. However, international co-operation was a difficult endeavour, requiring of all countries the political will to re-examine their traditional view of the world. Nevertheless, despite divergent views and interests, the Conference could undoubtedly help bolster confidence in the international community's ability to devise new and realistic plans for the future.

2. Referring to the question of resources for development, he noted that most developing countries had, since the beginning of the debt crisis, introduced adjustment policies which had severely affected growth, income distribution and employment. Even though some countries had largely succeeded in overcoming their difficulties, the collapse of living standards was a threat to social and political stability in others. The situation therefore remained very worrying.

3. The success of the international debt strategy adopted in the 1980s depended on three conditions: first, internal adjustments and policy reforms in the developing countries; second, adequate external financing; and, third, favourable conditions on world markets. As the second and third conditions had not been fulfilled, developing countries had experienced

considerable difficulty in implementing their adjustment programmes. Commodity prices had fallen, reducing their export earnings, and the international banking system was reluctant to provide new loans to indebted countries.

4.   IMF and UNCTAD statistics showed that commodity prices in real terms had reached their lowest
point since the Second World War. Moreover, price instability continued to disrupt commodity markets with
far-reaching implications for development planning and
social stability in exporting countries.

5.   The international community had long been
aware of the problems created by the secular decline in
commodity prices and their instability, and was in broad
agreement that the decline was mainly due to structural
factors, namely, technological changes, industrial
restructuring and changes in consumer preferences.
UNCTAD had at its disposal a framework for action
based on the conclusions adopted in 1985 by the Committee on Commodities, and it was to be hoped that
they would continue to be used as the basis for practical
efforts to draw up commodity agreements or arrangements adapted to the specific situation of each
country. A lasting solution to the problems encountered
by many developing countries owing to their
dependence on exports of a few commodities implied
far-reaching changes in their production and export
structure. Given the limitations of commodity-based
economies, external support was of the greatest importance. Although the Second Account of the Common
Fund was not a cure-all, it would improve the situation,

and it was to be hoped that it would soon become operational.

6.   It was widely recognized that foreign trade could
contribute to growth and development. However, decisions in that area were strongly influenced by increasing
uncertainties in the economic environment, which were
themselves due to the foreign trade imbalances of some
major industrialized countries, exchange-rate volatility
and the indebtedness of the developing countries. The
link between trade, monetary and financial matters was
therefore obvious. The Uruguay Round and the structural adjustment efforts made in most developing and
developed countries could help improve the trade environment by reducing uncertainties and creating new
trade opportunities.

7.   The LDCs had been the most affected by commodity price movements and their foreign debt had
reached a critical level, thereby reducing their ability to
implement adjustment programmes. The international
community had, since 1981, tackled those problems and
had stressed the need for special measures to support the
development efforts of the countries concerned.
Moreover, the President of the EEC Council had recalled the measures taken by the Community to keep the
promises it had made under the Substantial New
Programme of Action.

8.   His delegation was convinced that all participants
in the Conference would demonstrate the political will
needed to find a common basis for revitalizing growth
and development in the world.

Summary of the statement made at the 218th plenary meeting, 30 July 1987, by Mr. Antonio PALLARES-BUONAFINA, Permanent Representative of Guatemala to the United Nations Office at Geneva

1.   Mr.   PALLARES-BUONAFINA   said   that
UNCTAD had been designed to facilitate direct
dialogue and creative negotiations on trade and
development in order to promote development and
economic growth and to guarantee the transparency of
international trade. There was nothing simple about
those objectives, and it was paradoxical that, at a time
when the most industrialized countries were making
considerable scientific and technological progress, the
majority of developing countries should be experiencing
structural imbalances, jeopardizing the growth rates
that were indispensable if the people of those countries
were ever to live better lives.

2.   International co-operation was more necessary
than ever before in the campaign against poverty,
hunger, need, over-indebtedness and inadequate market
access. In order to reconcile economic development and
social justice, preserve international peace and security
and close the gap between the privileged and the disadvantaged, it was essential to devise a strategy for which
the entire international community would be responsible. The four basic issues that had been considered at
the current session of the Conference were closely interlinked. Third world countries had to speed up the
pace of their development once again; that required a

coherent strategy—as well as the necessary resources to
implement it—namely, a universal, active and stable
trade system and a guarantee of the necessary assistance
for the LDCs. The same was true of the commodities
sector, although very useful instruments were already
available, such as the Integrated Programme for Commodities and the Common Fund, which should begin
operation soon. The import and debt-repayment capacity of the developing countries depended on their income
from commodity exports. It was thus clear that external
debt negotiations must be more realistically directed
towards an overall strategy based on the principle of the
joint responsibility of debtor and creditor countries,
financial institutions and commercial banks.

3.   Different countries had had very different ideas
of the progress and results to be expected from the
seventh session of the Conference. The developing
countries, and some developed countries, had spared no
effort to achieve the desired results. Although the final
score was not as negative as some countries thought, nor
as positive as the third world countries had hoped, it
was clear that UNCTAD was still the right forum for
dialogue, analysis, negotiation and the conclusion of
agreements in its areas of competence. The great majority of participants recognized UNCTAD's usefulness

and value. Despite its shortcomings and failures, it offered the best—and the only—way of achieving true international solidarity. The attainment of the objectives for which it had been established depended on its member States, individually and collectively. And it was for that reason that his delegation reaffirmed its faith in a system which was becoming more stable and which, with the support of all, could be further improved.

Summary of the statement made at the 208th plenary meeting, 14 July 1987, by Mr. Kory KONDIANO, Secretary of State for Trade of Guinea

1. Mr. KONDIANO said that since the sixth session of the Conference the international economy had been suffering the most severe crisis since the Great Depression of the 1930s. No effective remedy had yet been found for the world's economic ills. The imbalance of the world economy was endangering stability and clouding the development prospects of developed and developing countries alike. In the developing countries external factors had intensified inflationary pressures and worsened balance-of-payments problems.

2. Appropriate measures were therefore needed to reactivate the world economy. The industrialized countries should implement economic policy measures, the costs of which should not, however, be passed on to the developing countries. A responsible and adequately funded approach was required in order that the necessary structural adjustments and reforms could be carried out by the developing countries, subject to the proviso that as far as possible the economic, social and political costs and the inflationary effects of those reforms could be contained.

3. Unfortunately, it was becoming more and more difficult for the developing countries to mobilize the resources needed for their reform, adjustment and economic development programmes. Indeed, in recent years there had been a massive transfer of funds from the developing to the industrialized countries, while the level of transfers of resources from North to South and the export earnings of the developing countries were falling. For example, in the case of sub-Saharan Africa, net flows of resources from IMF had fallen from $1,554 million in 1983 to $118 million in 1985. To rectify the situation, measures such as those prescribed by IMF and the World Bank had to be applied, but an approach more adapted to sub-Saharan countries was needed, in the form of a "Marshall Plan" for that particularly hard-hit part of Africa. IMF and the World Bank were giving sympathetic treatment to the developing countries, but their resources fell short of the needs, and the conditionalities to which their use was subject were so strict that in the final analysis those resources were found to be too costly, especially for the LDCs, which consequently needed resources from elsewhere in order to finance their development.

4. The commodity problem was of great importance for the developing countries, particularly those in Africa. In more than 15 of those countries, a single raw material, excluding petroleum, accounted for at least 50 per cent of export earnings. The case of Guinea was sufficient to illustrate the situation. One tonne of Guinea's bauxite was sold on the international market at approximately $36, but one tonne of the aluminium needed for its factories cost $1,750. The relationship was unjust.

5. Guinea had already ratified the Agreement Establishing the Common Fund for Commodities and wished to congratulate the USSR and Côte d'Ivoire, which had just signed it, and to invite those member States which had not yet done so to take the necessary steps to make the Fund operational as soon as possible, particularly since commodity prices were falling, on average, at a rate of 5 per cent a year. The consequent decline in export earnings was obliging the developing countries to borrow more and to make rescheduling a major factor in the repayment of debts. For example, in 1985 Africa's export earnings had amounted to $61 billion, but in 1986 they had fallen to $44 billion. Faced with such a situation, the African countries were compelled to make drastic cuts in imports of goods in respect of which they had no comparative advantage, with the result that the standard of living and the rate of investment and job creation were badly affected.

6. More attention should be given to the LDCs. The Substantial New Programme of Action adopted in 1981 made provision for a series of measures designed to create new mechanisms for mobilizing and increasing the transfer of financial, technical and technological resources to those countries. It would be desirable that donors who had not yet attained the target set in Conference resolution 142 (VI) should do so without delay. Some of the economic policies pursued by developed countries had had disastrous repercussions on the economies of the LDCs, the number of which had increased from 31 in 1981 to 40 in 1986. Another conference, similar to that held in 1981, was therefore necessary. His delegation therefore appreciated President Mitterrand's initiative in offering to convene a conference in Paris to review the situation.

7. Guinea, a least developed country, had taken important policy and economic decisions to build a viable economy, including a rectification of its monetary and financial system, and had instituted structural, legislative and administrative reforms in order to create conditions conducive to economic development. The implementation of such an ambitious programme required substantial resources, part of which had already been obtained from certain international financial institutions and from certain countries, whose help was greatly appreciated. Investors and all other national or international financial or banking institutions were invited to follow that example, which had produced encouraging results.

8. The trade results for 1985 had been disappointing for most developing countries. Their exports had fallen by 5.5 per cent and their imports by 0.5 per cent in that year, and their share in the aggregate value of world

trade had been shrinking steadily since 1981. In recent years some developed countries had been insisting on linking trade in goods with policy changes in the developing countries and had erected barriers to imports of the developing countries' commodities and industrial products. Trading partners in the North should respect the rules and principles of multilateral trade. Above all they should grant more favourable preferential treatment to the countries of the South and comply strictly with their commitments on standstill and roll-back. Unfortunately, that had not been the case so far.

9.   The Uruguay Round of trade negotiations was very important for the future of world trade. The UNCTAD secretariat should therefore continue to provide technical assistance and guidance to developing countries in order to enable them to participate more effectively in those negotiations.

10.   It was greatly to be hoped that the Conference would adopt measures and decisions for settling the developing countries' monetary and financial problems, especially their indebtedness. While welcoming the decision taken at the Venice Summit regarding the rescheduling of the debt of developing countries, his delegation would like to see part of their public debt converted into grants. Decisions should also be taken designed to stabilize commodity prices at fair and remunerative levels and to eliminate all barriers preventing the developing countries from having access to the markets of the developed countries.

11.   The situation in southern Africa was a source of concern. The courageous struggle of the Namibian people under SWAPO required continuous and unconditional support.

12.   President Lansana Conte of Guinea addressed a message to the Conference expressing his hope that the results of the session would reflect the common will to build a peaceful and prosperous world free from social injustice.

Summary of the statement made at the 208th plenary meeting, 14 July 1987, by Mr. Gervais CHARLES, Deputy Permanent Representative of Haiti to the United Nations Office at Geneva

1.   Mr. CHARLES said that the current session of the Conference was taking place at a critical moment. The five-year-old expansion recorded in the North had not led to an automatic reactivation of the world economy, and the convergence of views achieved at the sixth session had not produced results capable of halting its continuous deterioration. Despite a few cases of undeniable success, the third world's distress had become more acute. No category of countries had been spared, and the statements made at the current session bore witness to what were often spectacular reverses. The socio-economic parameters pointed to stagnation or a reduction in real per capita incomes which, in some of the most severely affected regions, were on average at their 1970 levels. As the World Bank and the Secretary-General of UNCTAD had pointed out, the Third United Nations Development Decade appeared to be a lost decade. The multiplication of disquieting signals called for an examination of the extent to which the International Development Strategy, as it had been implemented during the crisis years, had failed, and for further collective reflection on the functioning of the international trading, financial and monetary systems, which, taken together, had undeniably had the effect of halting growth in the countries of the South.

2.   As far as finance and trade were concerned, the countries of the North had, for the most part, failed to adopt measures that might have promoted a sustained economic recovery in the countries of the South. Apart from certain courageous initiatives, in North-South relations little or no account had been taken of the interdependence of the world economy. The result had been an increasing deterioration in the developing countries' terms of trade. The flow of ODA was barely one half of the targets established 25 years previously. As a result of the repeated postponement of the entry into force of the Common Fund for Commodities, it had not been possible to regulate commodity markets on a sounder basis and to stabilize the export earnings of the third world. In that connection, he specially deplored the protectionist measures adopted in the industrialized countries, for they penalized the developing countries in areas in which they had a comparative advantage and they increased their already excessive rates of unemployment and underemployment.

3.   Half-way through its period of implementation, the Substantial New Programme of Action for the 1980s for the Least Developed Countries was failing, as was shown by the fact that two thirds of those countries had lower incomes than at the beginning of the decade. The fall in ODA, the decline in food production, a record deficit in the balance of payments, and a mounting external debt called for an urgent reactivation of the Programme of Action along the lines of its 1981 objectives.

4.   The revitalization of trade, growth and development implied new forms of solidarity. In a world whose interdependence was recognized by all, opportunities for sustained and predictable growth had to be created. The document submitted by the Group of 77 contained a set of proposals which had his country's full support. A solution to the third world's debt problem had to be found, on terms that would facilitate an increased mobilization of flows of private and public capital for investment. Haiti supported all proposals to that end, particularly the proposals made by the EEC for the low-income countries. Every effort should be made to promote a further expansion of world trade through the elimination of protectionism. The Conference provided an opportunity to demonstrate the lucidity and political courage needed to establish a more equitable international economic order.

**Summary of the statement made at the 219th plenary meeting, 30 July 1987,
by Monsignor Justo MULLOR GARCÍA, Apostolic Nuncio, Permanent Observer for the Holy See
to the United Nations Office at Geneva**

1. Monsignor MULLOR GARCIA said that while the Conference had been deliberating, the world population had attained the 5 billion mark. The implicit message of the birth of the five billionth child was twofold. First of all, the child was born into an interdependent world; and second, respect for that child's human dignity and political, civil, economic and social rights would be a matter of concern to all people everywhere. Those two considerations lay at the heart of the bold yet difficult decisions that the world expected of the Conference.

2. Applied to resources for development, those two basic considerations should guide responsible efforts to find an equitable solution to the debt problem and create a new climate of confidence that would ensure co-operation in the search for long-term solutions guaranteeing the participation by all countries in the establishment of a new economic order. There was an urgent need to promote effective measures to control excessive currency fluctuations and correct trade imbalances. With political will and foresight, at least a first step could be made in that direction. The world's resources should be shared more equitably, and economic and social structures created or readjusted to meet current needs. Special attention should be given to the crucial question of interest rates and monetary fluctuations. Agreement should be reached on resolving the problem of the huge external debt of the developing countries and preventing its resurgence in the future. All those concerned—creditors and debtors, but also banks, politicians, businessmen, promoters of development programmes, technical advisers, managers and investors—should accept their share of responsibility for dealing with the debt. His delegation hoped that the "ethical approach to international indebtedness" published on 27 December 1986 by the Pontifical Commission Justitià et Pax would be found useful by the international community.

3. On the subject of commodities, he said that only an increased awareness of interdependence and human dignity could guarantee compliance with rules that were not merely based on the profit motive. Only a global policy based on the principles of a universal ethic and directed towards introducing effective methods of preventing the anarchy currently prevalent in commodity markets could, as well as being sound economically, render justice to the millions who toiled in producing those commodities.

4. The same two principles—interdependence and human dignity—should also form the basis of international trade. Although some progress had been made within GATT, the absence of certain important countries from negotiations and the protectionist policies pursued by others had resulted in deadlock rather than co-operation. International trade had entered a new phase, and could be used to direct—or misdirect—development in the poorer countries. Hence trade likewise should be based on the principle of international social justice.

5. Lastly, the principles of interdependence and human dignity should guide all international decision-making concerning the least developed countries. Interdependence meant a sharing of both material and spiritual assets. The deliberations at the Conference showed that there was broad agreement in principle on the need to translate the unity and solidarity of the international community into reality, and yet numerous difficulties remained when it came to doing so, no doubt because of the considerable interests at stake. That challenge must be taken up. As Pope John Paul II had said in his message to the Conference, it was not sufficient for countries to recognize their interdependence out of economic or political necessity, and only an ethical sense of genuine collective responsibility would enable them to progress towards international justice and to respect their commitments.

**Summary of the statement made at the 205th plenary meeting, 13 July 1987,
by Mr. Tibor MELEGA, Deputy Minister of Foreign Trade of Hungary**

1. Mr. MELEGA said that the main theme of the Conference—revitalizing development, growth and international trade—was of crucial importance for all participants. The success of their discussions would depend on their ability to arrive at a consensus on the action needed.

2. Although there were differing views on the underlying causes of the world economic problems, and differing approaches to their solution, there was a shared recognition of the increasing interdependence of the world economy. The serious problems besetting the world economy were the erosion of the international trading system, the application of protectionist industrial and agricultural policies, the exorbitant subsidization of agricultural exports, tension in the international monetary system, the critical debt situation of many developing countries and the financial consequences of the arms race. All those factors impeded growth and development and disrupted international trade and economic relations.

3. The source of the unfavourable trends and tension in the international trading system lay in the application of national policies and practices inconsistent with its principles and rules. The trading system itself could not be held responsible for its malfunctioning. Normalization of trade relations should take place

within that existing trading system, with full respect for its basic norms. The developing countries should obviously be given differential and more favourable treatment to help them realize their development objectives.

4. The external indebtedness of many of the developing countries was one of the burning problems of the world economy. The debt crisis could only be solved by agreed and co-ordinated measures by debtor and creditor countries. National efforts to that effect should be supported internationally by providing increased access to markets, greater exchange rate stability and additional financial resources. Multilateral financial institutions could also play an important part in improving the liquidity of debtor countries by increasing resources and loan facilities.

5. International trade was not only distorted by impediments of an economic nature but trade relations were used for other purposes such as the application to high technology trade of restrictions that adversely affected the trade interests of exporting and importing countries alike. Confidence-building and the strengthening of security in international economic relations were therefore among the priority tasks.

6. There was an obvious link between arms expenditure and economic development. The development process could be accelerated and the necessary structural adjustments made more speedily and harmoniously if military budgets could be cut.

7. Increased interdependence also meant an interrelationship among the various trade flows. Trade and economic relations within the CMEA were a stabilizing factor for Hungary. In addition, Hungary's trade relations with developing countries were being intensified, its imports from those countries having increased by almost one third between 1983 and 1986. It also intended to increase its trade with Western countries. The steady and harmonious development of all those relations could enhance Hungary's capacity to help in solving the economic problems of developing countries.

8. The current session offered an opportunity to show a willingness to preserve and strengthen UNCTAD as the most universal forum for reviewing all aspects of trade and development. His delegation would co-operate actively in that exercise, which should lead to more open and secure international economic relations.

Summary of the statement made at the 202nd plenary meeting, 10 July 1987, by Mr. P. Shiv SHANKER, Minister of Commerce of India

1. Mr. SHANKER said that the unprecedented disarray in international economic relations had led to strains in the trade and payments system, characterized by the lowest commodity price levels in real terms since the Great Depression, a significant deterioration in the terms of trade of most developing countries, a proliferation of protectionist measures and policies in developed market-economy countries, stagnation in concessional and non-concessional financial flows to developing countries, massive reverse flows from major borrowers and a heavy toll on developing countries, which had been forced by the acute debt crisis to adopt recessive adjustment policies. The entire international financial network was endangered.

2. The unco-ordinated monetary and fiscal policies of the major economies, together with speculative activities, had led to major capital transfers, which in turn had caused fluctuations in the exchange rates of major currencies. Those policies had caused instability in international interest rates, which had remained high in real terms, and misallocation of world savings. Such disarray had been the main reason for stagnation, deceleration of growth and even negative growth in developing countries, which were finding it increasingly difficult to pursue self-reliant development for the alleviation of poverty and unemployment and progressive modernization of production. The 1980s had so far been a period of lost development.

3. The development consensus of the 1960s, when UNCTAD had been created, had been severely shaken and there was now a virtual crisis in development co-operation. The objective conditions providing the basis for the system had been fundamentally transformed, with greatly increased interpenetration of national economies and a world economy characterized by multipolarity. There was increasing interaction among the various economic systems. Market structures had become ever more oligopolistic and the TNCs were relentlessly seeking to extend the scope of their economic activities, while the concentrated control of new forms of technology and the lack of equitable conditions of access to the technologies in question threatened to create further strains in international economic relations.

4. Despite the unprecedented interdependence of nations and systems and the increased need for a new consensus for the harmonious and equitable reconstruction of international economic relations, there was a distinct retreat from multilateralism. UNCTAD had been severely criticized in recent years, its political and institutional foundation had been called in question, and its permanent machinery had been in constant stalemate since the previous session of the Conference. The tendency to restrict its role was paralleled by the vigorous efforts being made in some quarters to enhance the role of GATT far beyond the present scope of the General Agreement. At the same time, the international monetary and financial institutions appeared to be pursuing a joint strategy concentrated on adjustment by developing countries through contractionary measures, liberalization of import régimes, devaluation of their currencies, diminution of the public sector and consequent imposition of inequitable socio-economic policies. It was ironical that those propounding the newly respectable ideology of leaving things to market forces followed it only when it was in their own interests

to do so. Unless the international community was determined to correct it, that trend could only further accentuate the inequity and asymmetry of the international economic power structure.

5. The only countervailing force available to developing countries new to the international economic scene was the strategic exercise of their political sovereignty through such co-operative mechanisms as the Group of 77, the progressive pursuit of collective self-reliance and a co-operative and mutually beneficial interaction with the rest of the world; it was a universal willingness for such interaction that had inspired the development consensus of the 1960s. The challenge currently facing UNCTAD was to develop a countervailing force that could bring about an equitable and harmonious reconstruction of the old order of international economic relations. The Havana Declaration of the Group of 77, which had assessed that challenge, covered the broader issues in a long-term perspective, sought enduring solutions based on such fundamental principles as the recognition of the sovereign right of developing countries to pursue their own social and economic policies, multilateralism based on co-operative interaction of sovereign States and recognition of development and employment as the universal and prime objectives, and provided the rationale for all negotiations concerning development co-operation. A separate document of the Havana Ministerial Meeting of the Group of 77 included a detailed assessment of the relevant economic trends and specific proposals on policies and measures in all the various areas requiring negotiation with a view to finding speedy solutions to pressing problems. He fully endorsed the proposals of the Group of 77, seeking agreement on issues of immediate concern which required specific action in UNCTAD and elsewhere and joint action on systemic issues in the medium term. He urged the Conference to concentrate on negotiations on those proposals. What was required for serious negotiations was a recognition of common interests rather than prior agreement on assessment. The inescapable fact of interdependence should lead to the recognition of such common interests, and it was in the common interest of all States to deal with the current crisis.

6. The seventh session of the Conference was of unique urgency. UNCTAD provided a universal and comprehensive forum for the North-South dialogue and negotiations, for in hardly any other forum was such a dialogue in progress. The results of the seventh session would have an important influence on the attitude of developing countries towards piecemeal or sectoral negotiations elsewhere. The international community could not afford to await another chance, for the deepening crisis would not wait. Failure of the Conference would have serious consequences for the developing and developed world alike. Interdependence called for a joint effort to build a new consensus on development co-operation and to produce firm agreements on specific measures.

Summary of the statement made at the 213th plenary meeting, 27 July 1987, by Mr. Ali WARDHANA, Co-ordinating Minister for Economy, Finance, Industry and Development Supervision of Indonesia

1. Mr. WARDHANA underscored the persistence of protectionism among the numerous problems affecting international trade already referred to at the sixth session of the Conference. The commitments of the developed countries regarding standstill and roll-back had not been adequately followed up. The principle of non-reciprocity and differentiated and more favourable treatment of developing countries was not being implemented any better. The facts were in contradiction with the principle of liberalization. The results of the Uruguay Round had to be implemented and compliance with the principles of the General Agreement ensured the interest of the multilateral nature of trade.

2. The collapse of commodity prices, which had considerably reduced the export earnings of many developing countries, was due in part to weak demand and the import-substitution policies of the industrialized countries. The implementation of the Integrated Programme for Commodities, and particularly the Common Fund, had to be speeded up if that situation was to be remedied.

3. The debt situation of many third world countries had been aggravated by developments beyond their control, such as volatile exchange rates in the creditor countries and the sharp rise in real interest rates. The deterioration of the terms of trade—a consequence of the collapse of commodity prices—also aggravated the debt-servicing problem. Although the debtor countries must restructure their economies, the task of debt management had to be shouldered by lenders and borrowers alike. Debtors and creditors, commercial banks and international financial institutions must devise a comprehensive strategy focusing on growth and assistance to debtor countries in their adjustment efforts.

4. Indonesia had initially been protected against the world crisis by its financial and monetary reforms and import cut-backs. More recently, however, and despite greater efforts to tackle structural problems in its economy, its development plan had suffered a major set-back as a result of external factors such as the decline in the prices of oil and other export commodities, volatile exchange rates and high interest rates. Non-oil exports had been severely affected both by weak demand and by protectionism on the part of importers.

5. If the adjustment effort of the developing countries was to succeed, the overall international economic environment must be changed. Accordingly, the central task of the Conference was to ensure the proper management of interdependence among nations and to revive international co-operation with a view to revitalizing development.

6. Owing to the inherent structural deficiencies of their economies, the LDCs were the ones that had suffered the most as a result of the crisis. His delegation therefore called for the speedy implementation of the Substantial New Programme of Action for those countries.

7. The talks held between various groups of countries had given rise to cautious optimism about the ability of the Conference to reach a consensus on the need to reactivate international co-operation in the monetary and financial fields, to solve the debt problem and to reverse the net outflow of resources from the developing countries; it was also to be hoped that an understanding could be reached on measures to resolve the commodity crisis and stimulate international trade.

8. The Conference was duty-bound to make international trade an instrument of development with a view to creating a more just and equitable world economic order, in keeping with the spirit in which UNCTAD had been established in 1964.

Summary of the statement made at the 212th plenary meeting, 27 July 1987, by Mr. Ali Akbar VELAYATI, Minister for Foreign Affairs of the Islamic Republic of Iran

1. Mr. VELAYATI expressed the hope that the Conference would succeed in formulating policies that would mobilize sufficient resources to ensure world economic growth and in particular the economic development of the developing countries. Although the efforts made by UNCTAD since its establishment to stabilize and develop international economic relations had been successful in some areas, much still remained to be done before equitable relations would be established. Indeed, the determination of certain developed countries to impose their views and policies in the context of those relations constituted the main obstacle to the realization of the desired objective. If the Conference was to be more efficient, it should supplement its consideration of the agenda items by an evaluation of what had been done in the past and determine whether the various problems, inadequacies and failures that it had identified at its six previous sessions had led to any improvement in international economic relations or persuaded the developed countries to take an interest in improving the chaotic situation of the world economy and to abandon their dominant position.

2. The modern world was facing one of the worst economic crises it had ever experienced—caused, in the opinion of the Iranian delegation, by the one-sided, profiteering and hegemonistic policies of certain developed countries. The fall in commodity and raw materials prices, the increase in interest rates and exchange rate fluctuations were partly due to the unjust nature of the international economic decision-making system, which had prevented the developing countries from freely deciding how to manage their economies and exploit their resources. The unjust nature of their relations with other countries had hampered their economic growth, upset their balance of payments, increased their debts and led to a transfer of capital from poor to rich countries. As a result, the developing countries had been obliged to adopt economic austerity plans and belt-tightening measures that rendered the implementation of their education, health and social welfare programmes virtually impossible.

3. The protectionism introduced by certain developed countries was another obstacle to international co-operation and had contributed to the drop in production and export earnings which, in a vicious circle, had created foreign debt repayment problems. The failure of IMF to create sufficient international liquidity and to control payments imbalances had paralysed the international payments system.

4. The adverse effects of that situation had not only prevented the entire world economy from enjoying ideal rates of expansion, but had also accentuated economic inequality and increased poverty. Currently, more than one billion people were suffering from malnutrition. At the same time, direct military expenditures in the world amounted to almost $1,000 billion per year, or more than 20 times total approved ODA. Developing countries had devalued their currencies in the hope of improving their terms of trade, but they had finally been obliged to export more commodities; nevertheless, export earnings had declined and the debt-service ratio had increased. Since 1984, those countries had become net exporters of capital, and that trend would continue for at least another three years.

5. The problems that had disturbed the international economic order could not be resolved by quantitative measures, since further injustices had made the situation a great deal worse. It was essential that payments and transactions should be effected in an atmosphere free from political disputes, and should be based on equality, justice and non-discrimination.

6. Stockpiling and other methods of manipulating the oil and commodity markets had altered the terms of trade in favour of the industrialized countries; in 1986, the GNP of commodity-exporting developing countries had declined by 3.5 per cent. The period 1980-1986, in which commodity prices had fallen by 35 per cent, could be compared with the Great Depression of the 1930s. In addition, exchange rate movements had become disorganized, higher interest rates had hampered capital formation and available capital had been transferred abroad: those developments reflected the inherent contradiction between imposed austerity measures and economic growth. Developing countries were thus confronted with two crises at the same time—the debt crisis and the growth crisis, which they had to resolve simultaneously. Adjustment might well bring about economic growth if it took the form of increased export capacity, savings and efficiency, but no efforts could have the desired results unless they were accompanied by adequate financial resources, an expansion of markets and appropriate interest and exchange rates.

7. The victims of the debt crisis so far had been the poorest population groups in the developing countries, since Governments had reduced social welfare budgets. Statistics showed that public expenditure on welfare, housing, education and health had fallen to less than 1 per cent of the GNP in some of those countries, whereas it amounted to between 10 and 25 per cent in the developed countries. Solidarity and greater economic and technical co-operation among developing countries played an important role in the implementation of their self-sufficiency policies, and the Islamic Republic of Iran advocated the expansion of that type of co-operation.

8. His delegation wished to make a number of proposals intended to stabilize international trade, in accordance with the principles and decisions agreed upon at the previous sessions of the Conference and in other economic bodies of the United Nations. Those proposals were the following: the policy of commodity stockpiling should be replaced by other policies designed to ensure a sustained income for exporting countries; the international economic system should be free of domineering pressures and the principle of national sovereignty over natural resources and production policy should be duly respected; protectionist or discriminatory regulations should be replaced by agreements and conventions designed to strengthen multilateral relations; the Common Fund for Commodities should become operational as soon as possible and immediate steps should be taken to expand it; the decision-making process in the world economy should be based on fairness and non-discrimination; economic transactions and negotiations should not give rise to restrictions or tension and should be free from the influence of political groupings; developing countries should participate on an equal footing in the planning and management of the international monetary and financial system; and more attention should be paid to international efforts to reduce military expenditures and allocate at least some of the resources saved to development. If the forthcoming International Conference on the Relationship between Disarmament and Development enjoyed the co-operation of all States, it would offer a favourable opportunity to work towards that objective.

Summary of the statement made at the 217th plenary meeting, 29 July 1987, by Mr. Qubais Saied ABDUL FATAH, Deputy Minister of Trade of Iraq

1. Mr. ABDUL FATAH said that it was high time for all the members of the international community to combine their efforts to surmount the economic crisis that was affecting every country. That crisis, characterized in particular by a slow-down of growth, problems of financing, weak demand and the serious disruption of the international monetary and financial system, was due in large part to the macro-economic policies followed by the developed market-economy countries. Those policies were undermining the developing countries' efforts to strengthen their national economies and improve living conditions.

2. In those countries, average rates of growth had been less than 1 per cent between 1980 and 1984, owing in particular to a decline in exports and serious debt problems. The indebtedness of the third world had assumed intolerable proportions and debt-servicing payments often exceeded capital inflows to the debtor countries. The debt crisis threatened the entire international monetary system and the developed countries must take urgent action to find a solution.

3. The fall in oil prices during the last quarter of 1986 had had a serious impact on the oil-exporting developing countries. Their export earnings had declined and the assistance given by OPEC members to other countries of the third world had also diminished. The prices of primary commodities, which accounted for two thirds of the developing countries' export earnings, had fallen sharply over the preceding few years compared to the prices of manufactured goods. The commodities market had been influenced by both cyclical factors (sluggish demand, fluctuation of exchange rates) and structural factors (technological developments, protectionism, subsidies to producers in developed countries, etc.). The international community must therefore redouble its efforts to improve and stabilize prices, providing fresh impetus to the Integrated Programme for Commodities and giving earlier effect to the Common Fund. Existing difficulties were compounded by major monetary and financial problems, which had an adverse effect on international trade and placed the developing countries in a critical position.

4. The third world countries, aware that they would have to be the main architects of their own development, were sparing no effort to restructure their national economies and overcome a crisis for which, moreover, they were not responsible. Economic co-operation among those countries was intensifying—a trend that should be encouraged—but could only supplement North-South co-operation, which was essential for the recovery of the global economy. The developed market-economy countries must come to their assistance and take concerted action to build up a solid international monetary system for the benefit of all States, to revitalize trade and development throughout the world and to find a solution to the debt problem.

5. In the course of the previous 15 years, Iraq had launched three development plans, drawing upon all of its resources, and had made considerable progress in all areas. It had been able to achieve a marked improvement in the prosperity of its people and the national income had increased ninefold between 1938 and 1985.

6. It had to be realized that peace was essential for growth and development. War exhausted a nation's financial and human resources, which should be

devoted instead to economic and social progress. Problems therefore had to be resolved through peaceful means and it was essential to ensure full application of all the United Nations resolutions which advocated the strengthening of peace and respect of the right of peoples to development.

Summary of the statement made at the 215th plenary meeting, 28 July 1987, by Mr. Sean CALLEARY, Minister of State, Department of Foreign Affairs of Ireland

1. Mr. CALLEARY said that, in a world of increasing interdependence UNCTAD, as a universal body, had an important role to play in promoting international co-operation in trade and development. It was the tangible expression of the conviction that all peoples should share in the benefits of economic growth, especially those who had in the past been denied their fair share. Despite the current world economic crisis, he shared the view of the Secretary-General of the United Nations that there was enough momentum to revitalize development, growth and international trade. The challenge to be met by the Conference was thus to determine how to take advantage of recent favourable developments to reactivate international co-operation so as to breathe new life into the world economy.

2. Ireland had not been spared by the economic crisis. The slow-down of trade had contributed to an increase in unemployment, and Ireland's growing debt burden had forced the Government to cut public spending drastically. It was not easy in a democracy to make such economic adjustment acceptable to the population because of its effect on the standard of living. However, the consequent restrictions were by no means comparable to the hardships endured by the peoples of developing countries, especially the LDCs of sub-Saharan Africa. He paid a tribute to the Governments of developing countries, which had embarked courageously on economic reform under difficult conditions. He understood the reproaches addressed by the representatives of many developing countries to the developed countries, which have the main responsibility for revitalizing world economic growth, for their failure to make that effort.

3. A heavy debt burden clearly stifled the development capabilities of many third world countries, whether they were heavily indebted middle-income countries or among the poorest. The debt problem highlighted world economic interdependence, since high interest rates increased the debt burden, while depressed commodity prices and sluggish trade reduced debtor countries' ability to pay. The Conference should seek a clear commitment from the countries and institutions most directly concerned to continue unremitting efforts to alleviate third world indebtedness. From that standpoint, the seventh session would contribute to a consensus on measures for settlement of the debt problem in the interest of both creditors and debtors.

4. It was clear that domestic resources were the most important for a country's development. It was for each developing country to mobilize its own resources with support from the international community; some of the countries represented at the Conference had done so admirably despite difficult circumstances. He noted that the people of a developing country were its greatest resource, and drew attention to the role of women in development activities, especially in food production. Ireland, which had a young population, clearly understood the problems encountered by many developing countries in endeavouring to achieve the rate of economic growth required to keep pace with population increases.

5. External resources were a vital complement to domestic resources, but it was for each country to decide for itself the kind of external resources which suited it best. It was vital to increase the amount of assistance provided in the form of grants or on concessional terms. There was also room for non-concessional resource flows or direct non-debt-creating foreign investment. Ireland had contributed to the replenishment of IDA resources and was in favour of increasing the capital of the World Bank. Recalling that Irish bilateral aid was solely in the form of grants, he emphasized that Ireland was committed to achieving the ODA target of 0.7 per cent of GNP under the International Development Strategy for the Third United Nations Development Decade. Nevertheless, owing to its economic difficulties, it was unable to make as rapid progress as it had wished towards that goal.

6. With regard to trade in commodities, he noted that recent price trends had added considerably to the difficulties of many countries that were over-dependent on one or two commodities. International co-operation in that respect, directed for example towards diversifying the economies of exporting countries, was thus more urgent than ever. The principles of the Integrated Programme for Commodities remained valid even though the action to be taken on each commodity should be based on experience and long-term market trends. Ireland's ratification of the Agreement Establishing the Common Fund for Commodities and its announcement of a voluntary contribution to the Second Account of the Common Fund indicated its determination to play an active part in that process. Ireland also recognized the need to make further efforts to stabilize the export earnings of developing countries on the lines of the Stabex system established by the EEC.

7. The Uruguay Round offered an opportunity to establish a more open, viable and durable multilateral trading system. It was important to embark on those negotiations bearing in mind the interests of all participants and taking the needs of developing countries into account. In that context, although the poorest developing countries should continue receiving special treatment, the more advanced developing countries should assume responsibilities under the multilateral trading system commensurate with their economic weight. The seventh session of the Conference would undoubtedly make an important contribution to

strengthening the will to implement the commitments contained in the Punta del Este Declaration.

8.   Ireland was concentrating its bilateral assistance programme on four countries in sub-Saharan Africa, three of which were among the LDCs. It was therefore particularly well informed about the problems of the LDCs and remained convinced of the need to take special measures on their behalf in conformity with the Substantial New Programme of Action. In particular it was important that the ODA target of 0.15 per cent of GNP under the Programme should be reached as soon as possible. The debt burden of the LDCs should be alleviated considerably and Trade and Development Board resolution 165 (S-IX) was particularly relevant in that context. It was particularly important, at the current session, that the developed and developing countries should renew their commitment to the LDCs and to give practical expression to that commitment when measures relating to resource transfers, commodities and international trade were under consideration.

9.   The seventh session of the Conference offered participants a unique opportunity of showing a united front on development, growth and international trade problems. It was therefore to be hoped that it would achieve a broad consensus that would serve as a basis for a practical strategy to revitalize growth and development. Through constructive dialogue, participants could also impart fresh vigour to UNCTAD and to the work of its permanent machinery.

10.   He expressed the hope that, on the conclusion of the Conference, participants would be filled with a new determination to work together for a better world.

**Summary of the statement made at the 216th plenary meeting, 29 July 1987,
by Mr. Itzhak MINERBI, Assistant Director-General for Economic and International Co-operation,
Ministry of Foreign Affairs of Israel**

1.   Mr. MINERBI said it was clear that during the 1980s, development in most developing countries had suffered a serious set-back. Indeed, the hopes entertained 25 years previously, when UNCTAD had been established as an organization devoted to progress, the improvement of economic conditions and the elimination of poverty, famine and other scourges affecting the third world, had hardly been realized. For that reason, before formulating new proposals and making new plans, lessons should be drawn from the past and the reasons why the results had been disappointing examined. Admittedly the record contained a number of positive elements, such as the implementation of the GSP, the establishment of targets for ODA and for the transfer of other financial resources. Yet very little progress had been made since then, mainly because UNCTAD had tended to regard the developing countries as a monolithic, homogeneous whole, and, secondly, because it had attempted to deal with matters which fell within the competence of other international organizations.

2.   Concerning the first reason, differences in levels of economic development were often greater between the developing countries than between many of the more advanced developing countries and most of the developed countries. That monolithic view of the third world had fortunately been discarded by the developed countries as well as the developing countries themselves, which had finally recognized that there were various groups of developing countries whose problems were different and called for different solutions. It had taken years for UNCTAD to abandon that unrealistic attitude, and the initiative for abandoning it had come from outside. Indeed, the Substantial New Programme of Action for the 1980s for the Least Developed Countries had been elaborated at a special conference convened by the United Nations in 1981, and the United Nations Programme of Action for African Economic Recovery and Development 1986-1990 had been drawn up at a special session of the General Assembly in 1986.

3.   With regard to the second reason, the agenda of the Conference was telling in that it included an item on monetary questions despite the fact that UNCTAD's competence in that field was necessarily limited. On the other hand, it was essential for UNCTAD to examine much more closely problems which did not fall within the competence of other organizations, or which other organizations had failed to resolve, particularly the problem of primary commodities. At the time of UNCTAD's establishment in 1964, it had been widely recognized that other organizations had been unable to solve that problem and that there was an urgent need for collective and concerted action. However, it had not been until 1976, 12 years later, that UNCTAD had completed the first stage of its endeavours by approving the Integrated Programme for Commodities. Unfortunately, the Programme had not prevented commodity prices collapsing, and new measures were therefore required.

4.   For its part, Israel, despite its extremely limited financial resources, was making efforts to improve the economic situation of the developing countries, particularly through technical co-operation and by developing human resources in areas where it had gained considerable experience, such as agricultural techniques and rural planning. In almost 30 years of co-operation with 110 developing countries, Israel had welcomed 28,000 trainees and had sent over 9,000 experts abroad to transfer the technical know-how that had been acquired during the building of the State of Israel. Israel was particularly proud to be in the vanguard of those combating desertification.

5.   At the thirteenth special session of the General Assembly, Israel had stressed that it was essential to expand vocational training in the rural areas of Africa and had undertaken to continue its technical co-operation with the countries concerned. At the GATT ministerial meeting in September 1986, Israel had set out its programme of technical co-operation with the Latin American countries. The Government of Israel

remained convinced that the main beneficiaries of UNCTAD's activities must be the LDCs, particularly in Africa.

6.   Foreign trade was of vital importance to Israel as it amounted to nearly $25 billion annually; the Government was therefore most interested in expanding world trade. Only the liberalization of international trade and the promotion of the comparative advantage of all countries could lead to a resurgence of economic growth in the developing countries that would increase investment and reduce unemployment. Resolute steps must therefore be taken to reduce protectionism and eliminate all forms of discrimination, not only between developed countries but also between developing countries.

7.   The GATT contracting parties had undertaken to implement their roll-back and standstill commitments, and progress had been made in international trade in agricultural products. When the General Agreement had been negotiated in 1947, most of the developing countries, which at that time were not yet masters of their destinies, had been unable to ensure that their interests were taken sufficiently into account. During the current Uruguay Round, developing countries must participate in the process from the outset and must have at their disposal all the means they needed to develop their service sectors for both domestic and export purposes.

8.   Israel had been one of the first countries to become aware of the dangers of the excessive indebtedness of the developing countries and had proposed, as early as the first session of the Conference in 1964, that a multilateral guarantee facility linked to an interest subsidy scheme should be adopted in respect of loans contracted by developing countries. At the third session, Israel had proposed the establishment of an international export credit guarantee facility and, at the fifth session, it had proposed setting up an expanded co-financing scheme; all those proposals had been intended to meet the specific needs of various groups of developing countries.

9.   The debt-service problem was currently undoubtedly the principal problem faced by the developing countries. There again, it would be neither realistic nor rational to seek across-the-board solutions applicable to all developing countries alike. Exceptional measures must first be taken in favour of the LDCs, particularly in sub-Saharan Africa. A number of major creditor banks in developed countries had recently announced that they had set aside more than $20 billion to cover possible non-repayment of their loans by developing countries. The result had been a sharp drop in profits for the banks in question and therefore an immediate and drastic reduction of their tax burdens. In other words, a large part of the cost of that new banking practice was being borne directly and immediately by the Governments of the countries where the banks were located, owing to the loss of tax receipts. It might perhaps be better for Governments to assume part of such distressed loans and notify the debtor countries that, for the time being, they were willing to accept debt-service payments in local currency. The banks would thus no longer have to write off all outstanding

debts and might therefore be more willing to extend further credit to developing countries. The mechanism could well take various forms, and it was gratifying to note that the Belgian Government had announced that part of its technical co-operation budget would be used to alleviate the debt burdens of certain developing countries.

10.   The matter could be examined thoroughly in an appropriate forum which might also consider other possibilities. It should not be forgotten that in the 1980s, commercial banks had fulfilled an important function which the international organizations had been unable to perform, namely, the recycling of petro-dollars. It was now time for the main beneficiaries of that recycling to accept their share of responsibility. It was also obvious that the huge sums spent on armaments in both developed and developing countries could usefully be devoted to other purposes and bring about a considerable improvement in the situation of the developing countries.

11.   Although it was not the remit of the Conference to deal with the political conflicts going on in the world, and although its competence was restricted to the economic problems of developing countries, some delegations of the Arab countries had found it appropriate to make unfounded and misleading statements concerning Israel. He therefore wished to draw attention to a few basic facts presented in official United Nations documents. Thus, according to a report on industrial and economic trends in the West Bank and the Gaza Strip issued in December 1981 by ECWA, the GDP of Judea and Samaria in 1965 had amounted to the equivalent of $140 million and the per capita GDP had been $205 per year. According to the figures published by UNCTAD in July 1986 in document UNCTAD/ST/SEU/1, GDP 20 years later—in 1984—had been $806 million and per capita GDP $1,037. The economy of the region, including foreign trade, had therefore made considerable progress. According to the same sources, the figures for the Gaza Strip were a 1966 GDP equivalent to $40 million and a per capita GDP of $103: the territory had at that time been one of the poorest in the world. By 1984, GDP had reached $278 million and per capita GDP $555 per year. The progress made was not yet sufficient, but the Gaza Strip could no longer be called a least developed area. The Israeli administration had therefore largely contributed to the economic progress of those territories, progress which some non-oil-producing Arab countries might doubtless envy.

12.   Some Arab countries at the Conference had revealed the real purpose of their manœuvres, refusing dialogue and not even recognizing Israel's right to exist. It might be thought that the Conference had to deal with matters other than the Israeli-Arab conflict; nevertheless, it would shortly be called upon to vote on a political resolution—a malicious and biased resolution—concerning the territories administered by Israel. The blackmail practised by the Arab countries threatened consensus, but the Israeli delegation would nevertheless continue to spare no effort to contribute to the success of the work of the Conference.

Summary of the statement made at the 212th plenary meeting, 27 July 1987, by Mr. Francesco CATTANEI, Under-Secretary of State for Foreign Affairs, External Commerce and Co-operation of Italy

1.   Mr. CATTANEI said that in view of the major changes taking place in the world, the need for international understanding and co-operation was once again vital, both in political as well as economic relations. In the present context, it was futile to try to resolve the increasingly complex problems being encountered by Governments and society on the basis of ideological platforms which hampered dialogue, encouraged unilateralism and increased the risk of isolationism and dissension. In that respect, UNCTAD had become the focal point of world economic co-operation at a crucial moment for the revitalization and consolidation of its institutional role. The difficulties encountered by the Conference owing to the failings of the international economic system had led Italy to make efforts to contribute to its revitalization, in accordance with its stated position of working for the efficient operation of multilateral bodies.

2.   The agenda for the seventh session was at the same time a medium-term programme of work which dealt with the major sectoral topics of growth and development in the general context of structural adjustment. However, it was also the task of the Conference to bring about a better harmonization of world economic analyses, in order to achieve a consensus on the national policies to be followed—in accordance with each country's responsibilities and capacities—as well as on the general nature of the increasing international efforts called for in the key sectors mentioned in the agenda. A joint analysis and, above all, compatible national policies would enable the international community to reduce current serious imbalances and tension.

3.   His delegation considered that the commitments assumed at the Venice Summit as well as their concerted implementation were of vital importance. Some of the conclusions reached on that occasion affected agricultural policy and other major topics covered by the trade negotiations conducted within GATT. The industrialized countries' special responsibility for encouraging stability and growth and improving the international financial and trade environment must be co-ordinated and meshed with the parallel efforts being made by the developing countries to base their long-term development process on sound and sovereign foundations. Italy appreciated the bold policies pursued by many developing countries, and supported them in its own co-operation policy; its funding had increased fivefold over the past few years, and many new types of assistance had been introduced.

4.   On the question of resources, the sharp decline in the flow of capital to the developing countries was due to various factors: the extent of their debt, which tended to make both lenders and borrowers of private capital cautious; the levelling-off of ODA and the decline in guaranteed export loans as a result of budgetary constraints; and the downturn in direct investment, which was due to lack-lustre growth prospects, the uncertainty of trade relations and the shortcomings of absorption policies. The uncertainty of the situation had led to a tightening of monetary policy and, consequently, to an increase in interest rates, which clearly formed a vicious circle.

5.   Given the crucial problem of the negative transfer of resources, which was connected with the debt-servicing burden and different in every case, it was essential to promote policies and efforts to ensure that those payments were compatible with investment and international trade requirements. Italy, with its European Community partners and in consultation with all the industrialized countries, encouraged as much flexibility and innovation as possible in debt management in the various categories of developing countries, as it had done in October 1985 by supporting a plan to implement a growth-oriented debt strategy and, more recently, by launching a selective debt relief initiative in respect of several African countries.

6.   The current unease among the most vulnerable banking institutions made action to break the deadlock imperative. It was equally clear that the role and resources of the competent international organizations must be strengthened in order to promote the flow of capital to the developing countries. Italy had contributed actively to initiatives such as the establishment by the World Bank of the Special Facility for sub-Saharan Africa and the Eighth Replenishment of IDA and once again called for a considerable increase in the World Bank's capital and the resources allocated to the IMF Structural Adjustment Facility.

7.   The commodities issue—having regard to the role played by UNCTAD in the launching of the Integrated Programme for Commodities and in efforts to establish the Common Fund—was currently particularly acute as a result of the decline in commodity prices, by an average of some 35 per cent over the past six years. Although the weakness of the world economy had no doubt contributed to that decline, it was mainly due to structural factors resulting from technical innovation—in both supply and demand—and developments that created excess production capacity while depressing prices. Vigorous, co-ordinated and universal action must be undertaken in various fields in order to (a) stabilize commodity prices under existing agreements by means of better market supervision; (b) make the multilateral compensatory financing machinery for export earnings shortfalls, particularly the IMF compensatory financing mechanism, function more equitably and efficiently; and (c) reduce, as a matter of priority, the overdependence of many developing countries on the export of one or two commodities, by diversifying their economies. UNCTAD must work towards the establishment of the Second Account of the Common Fund—for which Italy reaffirmed its support—and advocate an increase in the resources allocated to such diversification in both bilateral and multilateral development aid programmes.

8. International trade seemed to be advancing relatively slowly and at a different pace in different developing countries: the structural situation varied in each of those countries, owing to macro-economic and micro-economic factors and institutional and historical conditions. As for the objective of strengthening the multilateral trade system, Italy and its European Community partners had supported the launching of the Uruguay Round of negotiations in order to achieve more open markets and greater discipline in policy and practice in the mutual interests of all the contracting parties of GATT.

9. With specific reference to the LDCs, new international initiatives had recently been put forward, and

Italy supported them actively. The volume of Italy's ODA had increased in 1986 by 67 per cent over the 1985 level which, in absolute terms, made Italy the fifth largest donor among the industrialized countries and had enabled it to reach the target of 0.15 per cent of GNP. Italy also supported the relevant multilateral institutions by concentrating, in particular, on the aid given to the LDCs in the key sectors of agriculture, health, vocational training and technical assistance.

10. He hoped that the Conference would do more than merely express acute concern and end with a message of confidence springing from the greater awareness of the need for more active and better co-ordinated management of interdependence.

Summary of the statement made at the 203rd plenary meeting, 10 July 1987, by Mr. K. G. Anthony HILL, Permanent Representative of Jamaica to the United Nations Office at Geneva

1. Mr. HILL expressed confidence that a better understanding of the dynamics of global interdependence would be achieved through exchanges at the seventh session of the Conference and that negotiations undertaken in a climate of mutual trust would result in concrete agreements and so increase economic growth rates and revitalize economic development in the developing world. That common endeavour required the full support and co-operation of the developed market-economy and centrally planned-economy countries alike. The countries in the Group of 77 were determined to play their part in the dialogue and negotiation process, as attested by the assessment and statement of policies and measures submitted to the Conference (TD/330).

2. The first theme on which he wished to comment was the responsibility and role of Governments in implementing policies and measures designed to raise the living standards of their people, and in creating the conditions which fostered and supported economic and social initiatives. Governments must re-establish the consensus on the proposition that growth and development flourish best in conditions of stability and equity.

3. He stressed, secondly, that the structures of production and trade had changed so profoundly that conventional theories had become obsolete and that new policies and measures had to be applied for dealing with the changed situation. The transition from the prosperity of earlier decades to the current stagnation had caused great harm to the economies of the developing countries. Much innovative effort and entrepreneurial activity would be needed to meet the challenges and make use of the opportunities of the future. No country was safe from external shocks, and the question was how now to exploit the interdependence of all countries to their common benefit. The answer must surely reside in the adoption of consistent and coherent policies and measures in the interrelated fields of trade, commodities, money and finance geared to the development of the developing countries.

4. Thirdly, many Governments, including his own, had responded to the radically changed circumstances in

the world economy by implementing strong adjustment measures, despite the high price that had had to be paid and despite an unfavourable external environment. Jamaica had learned from that experience that sound domestic policies for growth and development were necessary though not sufficient, that market signals for the efficient allocation of resources were indispensable though not exclusive, and that an unfavourable external environment could compromise and destroy those policies and distort market signals. Having adjusted its economy in order to achieve growth and maintain social and political cohesion, Jamaica now needed a predictable and supportive external environment; it was contributing to the creation of such an environment through progressive trade liberalization and investment policies.

5. Fourthly, it was urgent that the developed market-economy countries should correct their massive imbalances and co-ordinate their macro-economic policies in a multilateral framework so as to stimulate overall growth at a faster rate, and above all that they should face up to their responsibilities with regard to the international debt crisis. Statements by the industrialized countries recognizing the interdependence of the developed and developing economies were encouraging, but as yet the developed market-economy countries had done little to forestall the threat of another recession.

6. Fifthly, the socialist countries and China stood to gain from a prosperous world economy, in which they could and should play a fuller part. Their increased openness and readiness to engage in dialogue reflected their perception of the mutual benefits to be gained from greater economic exchanges with the rest of the world. Developing countries members of the Group of 77 expected the socialist countries and China to increase their imports of products from those countries and to take other measures to provide resources for development.

7. Sixthly, on the subject of the debt crisis, he referred to a proposal by the Prime Minister of Jamaica, which was based on the recognition that debtor and creditor Governments, the commercial banking com-

munity and international financial institutions would need to work together in framing solutions for their mutual benefit. The main objective was to ensure that debtor countries would receive the necessary and sufficient financial resources in order to be able to grow out of the current crisis, since manifestly they would be unable to continue to borrow. The Jamaican proposal was based on the acceptance of the widely recognized growth-and-development oriented strategies, and its key element was the targeted reduction of debt ratios to sustainable levels over a programme period which would release sufficient disposable resources to achieve targeted growth. A multilateral facility bringing together the co-responsible partners must necessarily lead to realistic solutions of benefit to all partners.

8. The Jamaican delegation expected, as a minimum, a number of understandings and agreements to emerge from the current session. The results of the session should reflect the common interest and common stake of all States members of UNCTAD in an interdependent world. Immediate action was required, in which each party accepted responsibility for pursuing growth policies co-ordinated within an improved multilateral framework. Policies and measures should be designed that would ensure a significant increase in the flows of resources for development targeted to achieve sustainable levels of growth, including urgent multilateral action to resolve the external debt problems of developing countries and improve their terms of trade through fair prices and by increased processing, marketing and distribution of commodities. Action was needed to liberalize and expand international trade in a way that would increase the developing countries' share

in world markets and give an impetus to the GATT round of multilateral trade negotiations. In addition, measures were urgently needed for dealing with the special problems of the LDCs. The States members of UNCTAD should commit themselves to taking appropriate action, nationally or internationally, in fulfilment of their commitments and agree that UNCTAD would review the action taken by governments. He thought that understandings and agreements on the points he had indicated might best be reflected in a single coherent policy document. The policy conclusions drawn in the Secretary-General's report (TD/329) were in line with the growing consensus on the need for co-operation among all countries in adapting and strengthening the systems, structures and institutional arrangements which underpinned international economic relations.

9. The world economy had entered a new phase. Experience showed that growth, development and full employment could not be taken for granted, but required sound economic policies and a favourable external environment, in which the growth performance of the developing countries was a crucial factor. In an interdependent world, much was to be gained from mutual co-operation and much to be lost from unilateral policies such as protectionism. On the eve of the third millennium, opportunities must not be ignored. The seventh session of the Conference was an ideal forum for engaging in a constructive political dialogue and agreeing on specific policies and measures for revitalizing development, growth and international trade.

Summary of the statement made at the 212th plenary meeting, 27 July 1987, by Mr. Tadashi KURANARI, Minister for Foreign Affairs of Japan

1. Mr. KURANARI said that, since its creation, UNCTAD had tried to find ways of promoting development and prosperity in the developing countries. Although the gulf between North and South had sometimes prevented the establishment of a dialogue that would make it easier to search for appropriate solutions to the problems which had arisen, it was now essential, in view of the major changes taking place in the world economy, to undertake more realistic and constructive action along those lines. Before the end of the seventh session, the Conference had to arrive at a common concept of the issues affecting the world economy and draw up effective measures to resolve them in a spirit of solidarity.

2. Given the current great interdependence of the international community, the Japanese Government was sure that if the developing countries failed to achieve social stability and economic development, the rapid development and expansion of the world economy as a whole would be impossible. The developed countries had a duty to support the developing countries' efforts, and Japan considered that one of its most important obligations towards the international community was to contribute as constructively as possible to the develop-

ment of the developing countries, using its economic capacity and technology. The Government had quadrupled its ODA over the previous 10 years, and was determined to increase its efforts to promote co-operation with those countries. However, the modalities of that co-operation were becoming increasingly complex and varied; given the structural changes taking place in the world economy, developing countries were themselves obliged to seek and resolutely to implement new methods of action in the economic and social fields. Each country should adopt the development policy most suitable for its level of development and its situation, making the most of its own resources and external aid—both of them limited—and basing its actions on a sound appraisal of the current structural changes in the world economy. For their part, the donor countries must strengthen and refine their co-operation in response to such diversified needs.

3. Since sustained growth of the world economy was essential not only for the industrialized countries but also for the developing countries, Japan wished to contribute actively to it and, in co-operation with other developed countries, to correct external imbalances and to stabilize exchange rates, in accordance with the

agreements reached at the recent ministerial meeting of the Council of OECD and the Venice Summit. The various "emergency economic measures" announced by the Government of Japan in May 1987 also reflected that desire. One of their key components was the expansion of domestic demand by means of fiscal incentives which, together with the co-ordinated general policy efforts of other countries, should contribute considerably to world economic growth. Another major component was a new programme to recycle financial resources directly to the developing countries. That programme, which had been adopted at a time when the flow of capital to those countries was beginning to level off, was intended to facilitate structural adjustment and the revitalization of economic growth in the countries concerned, while helping them to overcome their debt problems by means of an increased flow of financial resources. Over the next three years, more than $30 billion would be provided in the form of non-tied aid from both public and private sources, either through multilateral development banks or on a bilateral basis.

4. As for the LDCs (including those in Africa), in respect of which the recycling of private funds was more difficult, Japan had decided to adopt specific support measures, for instance by increasing aid in the form of grants (approximately $500 million over the next three years) and by considering debt-relief measures. In particular, the Government intended to provide a new kind of grant-in-aid not tied to specific projects, which would enable them to finance the import of goods urgently needed for their structural adjustment.

5. Japan also intended to continue its efforts to increase the proportion of its GNP devoted to ODA by making increasing use of flexible and diversified methods of assistance (financing of local expenditure and revitalization of existing projects, for example) in order to satisfy the various needs of each country. Moreover, in order to promote the transfer of technology, it had been decided to take steps to expand technical co-operation, particularly by seconding experts from both the public and the private sectors. The aid supplied through multilateral organizations represented more than 30 per cent of Japan's ODA, mainly because of the efforts made to increase the amount of aid provided to distant regions such as sub-Saharan Africa.

6. The problems caused by the increasing debt burden of developing countries not only hampered their development, but jeopardized the entire world economy. It was therefore imperative that all the parties concerned should display greater flexibility and take concerted action to deal with those problems. The recycling and grant-in-aid measures adopted by the Japanese Government were also intended to support international efforts in that field, including those undertaken by the debtor countries using their own resources. The flow of private capital must also play a role in that process, provided that it met the same flexibility and diversification requirements (debt-equity swaps, co-financing with international financial institutions, etc.).

The provision of non-debt generating capital, and in particular direct foreign investment, was most desirable. Japan had recently signed the Convention establishing the Multilateral Investment Guarantee Agency, and hoped that the Agency would become operational in the near future. As for the increasing foreign debt of the LDCs, his Government continued to apply to the letter the measures agreed upon by UNCTAD in the past, and it was in favour of the further rescheduling of official debts which had already been rescheduled—an idea that was currently under consideration by the Paris Club.

7. In order to resolve debt problems, it was essential for debtor countries to improve their internal economic situation by means of appropriate investment policies, and at the same time to expand their exports with the support of the developed countries. Japan considered that the maintenance and consolidation of a free trade system was the only way of achieving sustained growth and the revival of the world economy, and it had tried to improve access to its markets by expanding and improving its preference scheme. In addition, it would do everything in its power to contribute to the success of the Uruguay Round of negotiations by devoting as much attention as possible to questions of interest to the developing countries.

8. The slump in commodity prices was just as important a problem as the increased burden of foreign debt. Japan had participated actively in the negotiations on various international commodity agreements, and was a party to most of those in force. However, depressed commodity prices were due not only to cyclical factors, but also to structural factors which affected both supply and demand. There was, therefore, a need to improve market mechanisms and particularly, in the longer term, to increase the extent to which commodities were processed, so that the countries dependent on them could diversify their economies. If the Common Fund was established, the activities envisaged under its Second Account would have a major role to play in that respect.

9. He wished to make the following proposals: first, that an independent group of wise persons should be set up with the support of interested countries and the relevant international organizations, to examine ways and means of encouraging the flow of financial resources to developing countries; secondly, that a round table should be organized on the initiative of UNCTAD and with the participation of the relevant international organizations and other interested parties to enhance the degree of processing of commodities, particularly in developing countries which were highly dependent on them. The purpose of the round table would be to draw up a series of "sample country case programmes" and recommend measures that such countries might take in collaboration with developed countries and the relevant international organizations. If those proposals were adopted, the Japanese Government would be prepared to support them by providing a proportion of the human and financial resources required.

Summary of the statement made at the 206th plenary meeting, 13 July 1987, by Mr. Jonathan NG'ENO, Minister for Commerce of Kenya

1. Mr. NG'ENO said that the external environment facing the developing countries had deteriorated to such an extent that their own efforts must be complemented by a fundamental change in the approach and policies of the industrialized countries. In the common interest, an agreement must be reached on measures and policies that would ensure the revival of growth and development.

2. No effective strategy had so far been devised to resolve the debt crisis affecting many developing countries. The share of interest and redemption payments in the Kenyan Government's total expenditure had risen from less than 12 per cent in 1980/81 to more than 27 per cent in 1985/86—a proportion that was expected to increase still further. Kenya's total external public debt had grown at an average annual rate of 25 per cent since 1981, an increase that was jeopardizing the maintenance of appropriate levels of investment for sustained growth. Development investments had declined steadily from nearly 32 per cent of total expenditures in 1980/81 to about 18 per cent in 1985/86 as a consequence of the sharp decline in net external resources available for financing investment. In 1985/86 the Government of Kenya had become a net exporter of capital for the first time since independence. That example showed that there was an urgent need for measures to be taken by the creditor countries to alleviate the situation of debtor developing countries, including substantial rescheduling of repayment periods taking into account the repayment capacity of debtor countries without affecting either the implementation of their economic growth programmes, their independence in choosing their development priorities or new financial flows from creditors. Creditor countries should seriously consider converting into grants the debts owed in respect of ODA, especially in the case of the low-income developing debtor countries.

3. The measures devised should ease liquidity shortages and conditionality criteria and lead to increased credit to the indebted developing countries in support of increased output and exports. His delegation supported the proposals for the establishment of a mechanism for recycling the large current-account surpluses of some developed countries for use by the developing countries.

It also supported the proposal that developed countries and international financial institutions should increase the flow of resources in real terms to African countries in accordance with the United Nations Programme of Action for African Economic Recovery and Development 1986-1990, and the proposal that the IMF Compensatory Financing Facility should be improved in order to respond positively to the deterioration in international commodity prices.

4. The developing countries, most of which relied on earnings from the export of commodities, were concerned about the decline in demand for commodities and the host of problems besetting commodity trade. It was most disheartening that, since the adoption of the Integrated Programme for Commodities, efforts to implement the Programme had been frustrated mainly because of lack of support by some major countries. Immediate and full implementation of the Programme was needed in order to stimulate the growth and development of the developing countries.

5. In the area of international trade, there had been a sharp deterioration in the terms of trade, because the system of open, multilateral trading had been disrupted by protectionist measures and the standstill and roll-back commitments had not been implemented. The hopes of business communities the world over were pinned to the outcome of the seventh session of the Conference and should not be disappointed. A clear signal should go out from the Conference that the international community was determined not only to uphold the open and multilateral trading system but also to take specific measures to liberalize it further.

6. UNCTAD, by reason of its universal character and unique cross-sectoral and interdisciplinary approach to development issues, had contributed positively to international economic relations, and its continued importance depended on the firm commitment of its member States to implement its resolutions and decisions. The seventh session provided an opportunity not only to seek initiatives that would enhance multilateral co-operation for development but also to improve the effectiveness and responsiveness of UNCTAD itself as an institution.

Summary of the statement made at the 213th plenary meeting, 27 July 1987, by Mr. Salem Jaber Al-Ahmad AL-SABAH, Permanent Representative of Kuwait to the United Nations Office at Geneva

1. Mr. AL-SABAH said that the situation in the developing countries, severely affected by the crisis, was being further exacerbated by the restrictive monetary practices of the industrialized countries. That posed a danger for the future of the world economy, and a revival of development would be in the interests of all countries, both advanced and developing.

2. The developed countries bore a heavy responsibility, because their economic policies affected the entire world economy. They must therefore redouble their efforts by increasing their ODA in order to attain the agreed target 0.7 per cent of GNP for all developing countries and 0.15 per cent for the LDCs by supporting the international financial institutions, by backing pro-

grammes for export credit and by financing investments in the third world.

3.   World economic recovery required a revamping of the international monetary system, which must be stabilized and better adapted to the needs of the third world. That was primarily the duty of the developed countries, which had long exploited the resources of developing countries and were profiting from the decline in the price of raw materials.

4.   Monetary reform must go hand in hand with a reform of international trade. The exports of developing countries must be encouraged by guaranteeing them fair and stable prices and eliminating protectionism in the industrialized countries. It was also necessary to do away with the subsidies paid by those countries in artificial support of their local production and to consolidate the GSP. All measures tending to open up export markets would help developing countries to repay their debts and to pay for their imports.

5.   Israel's policy in the occupied Arab territories was aimed at exploiting the market and manpower of those territories. Kuwait approved the resolution of the

EEC granting preferential treatment to Palestinian products and requested UNCTAD to urge implementation of Conference resolution 146 (VI) on the economic situation in the occupied territories.

6.   Kuwait was firmly convinced of the need for economic co-operation among developing countries, as was demonstrated by the creation in 1961 of the Kuwait Fund for Arab Economic Development and the support given to development activities bilaterally or within the framework of OPEC. The contribution of the OPEC countries had enabled some developing countries to balance their payments. Aid granted by Kuwait, Saudi Arabia, the United Arab Emirates and Qatar had been particularly large.

7.   Despite the fall in oil prices since 1982, Kuwait had devoted 4.6 per cent of its GNP to ODA in 1982 and 3.8 per cent between 1983 and 1985. In addition to the difficulties in the oil sector, violations of freedom of navigation in the Gulf had hampered international trade in a region rich in natural resources. Kuwait had therefore been led to sign trade contracts with a number of countries in order to stimulate its foreign trade.

Summary of the statement made at the 206th plenary meeting, 13 July 1987, by Mr. Maligna SAIGNAVONGS, Director, Department of International Organizations, Ministry of Foreign Affairs of the Lao People's Democratic Republic

1.   Mr. SAIGNAVONGS said that the current unprecedented world economic crisis had particularly serious consequences for the developing countries. The dramatic fall in commodity prices, the steady deterioration in the terms of trade and the overwhelming external debt burden of those countries were symptoms of the existing unjust international economic order. Many developing countries had been forced to adopt adjustment programmes—and in doing so had had to pay a high political and social price—and were unable to repay their debt in the prevailing circumstances and in the absence of sustained economic development. In the common interest, creditor and debtor countries should engage in a political dialogue to find a global, definitive solution to the debt problem in accordance with the principles of collective responsibility and the right to development and without prejudice to the debtor countries' sovereign rights to make their own political decisions regarding their economic situation, including debt servicing. His delegation was in sympathy with the recent decision by Brazil to defer interest payments on its external debt.

2.   The coercive economic measures which continued to be applied by the imperialist countries through their TNCs were in flagrant violation of recognized principles of international law, including Conference resolution 152 (VI). The adoption by the Group of 77 at its recent ministerial meeting in Havana of resolutions supporting Cuba, Nicaragua and the Libyan Arab Jamahiriya, the main victims of imperialist coercive economic measures, reflected its active solidarity with those countries. There was an urgent need for effective measures by the international community to put an end to the use of such measures against the developing countries.

3.   It was important for the international community to reactivate its efforts to apply fully the recommendations which had emerged from the intergovernmental mid-term review of the implementation of the Substantial New Programme of Action for the 1980s for the Least Developed Countries. His delegation considered that the developed countries should redouble their efforts to attain the ODA target of 0.15 per cent of their GNP by the end of the decade, either by means of grants or loans on favourable terms or by increased financing of the local expenditure and operating costs of their development projects. They should furthermore convert ODA loans to developing countries to grants or agree to reschedule private debt repayment periods, cancel debt-servicing payments or cancel the debt itself.

4.   Land-locked countries were in a particularly difficult position. Contrary to the United Nations Convention on the Law of the Sea, Conference resolution 137 (VI) and Trade and Development Board resolution 319 (XXXI), some transit countries charged the land-locked countries exorbitant storage and transport fees. Special attention should be given to land-locked countries, particularly the least developed among them, and the transit countries should enter into genuine co-operation with those countries to that effect.

5.   Keenly aware as they were of their responsibility for promoting and guaranteeing their own development, the developing countries attached particular importance to South-South co-operation, as had been demonstrated by the Movement of Non-Aligned Countries at the Extraordinary Ministerial Conference in June 1987 in Pyongyang. At the same time they were endeavouring to develop multilateral co-operation,

which was adversely affected by the misguided macro-economic policies adopted by some developed market-economy countries, rendering the international economic environment unpredictable and unfavourable to growth and development. As had been affirmed by the Group of 77 at its ministerial meeting held in Havana, the developed countries were expected to accept their share of responsibility for the prevailing unprecedented world economic crisis and review their policies with a view to rendering the external environment more predictable and more supportive of growth and development, thereby helping to revitalize the world economy and in so doing resolve their own economic problems, including high levels of unemployment. Concerted international action should be taken to establish a viable system of international economic relations. UNCTAD's task was to promote multilateral co-operation in the service of development, and the seventh session of the Conference provided an opportunity for devising a coherent multilateral strategy to revitalize development, growth and international trade in a more supportive environment. It was to be hoped that the developed countries would display the necessary political will to ensure that it achieved that objective.

Summary of the statement made at the 219th plenary meeting, 30 July 1987, by Mr. Salim NAFFAH, Permanent Representative of Lebanon to the United Nations Office at Geneva

1. Mr. NAFFAH drew attention to some of the main features of the report by the Secretary-General of UNCTAD which reflected the most critical of the world's current economic problems. In a world in which the number of countries whose policies and economic achievements exerted an influence on the global economy was growing, the gap in per capita income between developing and developed countries was widening. Technological progress reduced manpower needs and the demand for commodities. The huge rise in debt-service payments, combined with an unprecedented fall in commodity prices, had substantially curtailed resources available for development. The growing interdependence in international economic relations was not, however, reflected in a perception of common interests, the establishment of equitable relations or a sharing of responsibility for reform. Trade restrictions, including closed markets and protectionist barriers, and the high cost of technology compounded already existing inequalities. The prevailing situation of crisis and uncertainty called for responsible dialogue and concerted action as the only way to achieve just and equitable development.

2. As a result of the war, the once-flourishing Lebanese economy, based on economic liberalism and largely dependent on the service sector, was in a state of acute depression and extreme poverty, aggravated by steeply rising inflation. The sharp fall in the levels and growth rates of production and national income, the contraction of investments, the unprecedented depletion of material and human resources resulting in a substantial decline in productivity, the brain drain, the huge public sector budget deficit and the decline in public sector income, were all problems shared by other developing countries but were particularly acute in Lebanon.

3. That situation was aggravated by the fact that Lebanon had involuntarily become a battlefield for others. He appealed for peace to be restored to his country, which could not undertake to develop its own natural and human resources unless its territorial integrity, political independence and sovereignty were respected. Peace was the priority for Lebanon; development would follow.

Summary of the statement made at the 218th plenary meeting, 30 July 1987, by Mr. Moletsane MOKOROANE, Minister, Trade and Industry of Lesotho

1. Mr. MOKOROANE said that the continuing deterioration of the world economic situation—as revealed by exchange rate fluctuations, higher interest rates, the reinforcement of protectionist policies and problems of international liquidity and debt—was particularly alarming for developing countries. In that context, neither developed nor developing nations could be indifferent to the growing interdependence of the world economy. The seventh session of the Conference, as a universal forum, had an important role to play in the promotion of international co-operation designed to reactivate growth and development and encourage global stability.

2. The international community, aware of the particular problems faced by the LDCs, had adopted various measures in their favour, including the Substantial New Programme of Action. His delegation appealed to delegations attending the seventh session of the Conference to take appropriate measures to ensure that the Substantial New Programme of Action and the conclusions and recommendations of its mid-term review were fully implemented. In addition to all their other problems, many LDCs in Africa suffered from the additional handicaps of geographical isolation and a lack of access to the sea. That was the situation of Lesotho which, like all other land-locked developing countries,

would not be able to overcome its problems unless it received support and assistance from outside. For that reason, it was imperative that the flow of aid to those countries should be increased considerably and provided on a continuing and predictable basis. The external debt problem still weighed heavily on developing countries and particularly on the LDCs, most of which were in Africa, and was the main obstacle to recovery and sustainable growth in those countries. Creditors and debtors must engage in a political dialogue in order to reach a common understanding on ways of solving the problem, which must be based on economic development in the debtor countries.

3.   The continuing decline in commodity prices, together with the devaluation of the United States dollar, had exacerbated the difficulties of many third-world commodity producers, whose economies were heavily dependent on export earnings. His delegation was sure that, when the Common Fund for Commodities began operation, it would help to bring some stability to international trade in commodities. His delegation found it encouraging that some countries had

acceded to the Agreement Establishing the Common Fund for Commodities at the current session, and hoped that many others would follow their example.

4.   The terms of trade of the developing countries had deteriorated and their share in world exports had declined considerably as a result of the protectionist measures imposed on their exports by the developed countries, although developing countries had continued to import from industrialized countries on a large scale. The open, multilateral trade system had therefore not operated in favour of growth and development in the developing countries. Moreover, the developed countries had not yet honoured their standstill and roll-back commitments. His delegation could only hope that at the current session the Conference would adopt specific measures to strengthen and liberalize trade, promote better understanding between developed and developing countries and emphasize the need for a genuine and continuing dialogue aimed at the revitalization of growth and development and, utlimately, the acceptance of multilateralism.

Summary of the statement made at the 214th plenary meeting, 28 July 1987, by Mr. Farhat Salah SHARNANH, Secretary of the General People's Committee for Economy and Trade of the Libyan Arab Jamahiriya

1.   Mr. SHARNANH, referring to the global economic crisis and various measures needed to redress the situation, recalled that the terms of trade had considerably deteriorated following the slump in world commodity market prices which had severely depressed the value of exports crucial to raw-material-producing developing countries. Countries dependent on crude-oil export earnings had also been adversely affected by the price slump and consequently many of them had had to cancel projects essential to their economic and social development. Despite the slump, developed countries had not lowered the prices of their exports to developing countries. On the contrary, they had advanced rising production costs as a pretext to increase prices. In the circumstances, it was important to devise an international strategy to establish a balance between developing and developed country export and import prices.

2.   The protectionist measures applied by developed countries, such as tariffs and domestic production and export subsidies, were contributing to the steady decline in commodity prices. Every effort should be made to defeat those practices and set up product-specific programmes.

3.   Constantly rising interest rates coupled with fluctuating major currency exchange rates had also had the effect of exacerbating the balance-of-payment deficits of the developing countries and restricting their resources when they needed capital to finance their development programmes. It was high time to restore the sound and equitable basis of the international monetary and financial system. External debts had grown to such an extent that they were no longer serviceable by most developing countries. Whilst

acknowledging the danger of the situation and its possible impact on the world economy, the international community had failed to take adequate measures to correct it. An international conference should be convened to study the matter.

4.   The situation was particularly critical in Africa, where even subsistence was barely possible in many countries. The international community should implement the Substantial New Programme of Action in order to increase aid to the LDCs and honour its commitments under the United Nations Programme of Action for African Economic Recovery and Development 1986-1990.

5.   International political tension such as the expulsion of the Arab people from Palestine and the establishment of Zionist colonies in that region, the racial discrimination practised in South Africa and the repression of Namibians struggling for independence, the acts of aggression committed by imperialist countries, particularly the United States, and the embargo imposed by that country on trade with Libya, all constituted further obstacles to international trade and social and economic development in the world.

6.   The crisis affecting the world was clearly of unprecedented proportions and the international situation remained characterized by instability and insecurity. In the circumstances, it was vital to establish a world economic system based on justice and equity. States participating in the Conference's seventh session must engage in a sincere dialogue, strive to improve international relations and work towards constructive cooperation among all countries in the interest of pro-

gress. The Conference should devise solutions acceptable to all. In that respect, the proposals and recommendations put forward by the Group of 77 in the Havana

Declaration provided a good point of departure. Participating States should also respect all the resolutions adopted by the Conference.

Summary of the statement made at the 213th plenary meeting, 27 July 1987, by Mr. Robert GOEBBELS, Secretary of State for Foreign Affairs, External Commerce and Co-operation of Luxembourg

1.   Mr. GOEBBELS stressed the complementarity and interdependence of national economies. UNCTAD should not duplicate the work being done by specialized agencies; its true role was no doubt to determine how trade could be made the driving force of development.

2.   The world economic situation had changed considerably over the preceding 25 years; emergence of new centres of economic activity, and integration of financial markets and national economies. Expansion had been followed by recession, provoking pernicious protectionism. In the expansion-recession cycle between 1980 and 1985, some countries and regions had been more successful than others, particularly South and South-East Asia.

3.   Since then, greater importance was being given to such matters as food, health, human resources and the environment. In industrialized market-economy countries, inflation had been checked, but unemployment, exchange-rate chaos and balance-of-payments distortions persisted. Understanding was only just emerging of the interdependence between development, trade, finance and commodity trade. For the industrialized countries to be able to continue their development aid, they would have to solve their own problems, and to do that, a resumption of growth was essential.

4.   They had made a major financial effort. In 1986, the members of OECD had furnished $26.5 billion in aid, and the EEC had spent more than ECU 40 million in 89 third world countries on development projects, to whose financing Luxembourg had made the highest per capita contribution.

5.   Indebtedness continued to be a major problem whose solution demanded co-operation between debtor and creditor Governments, international financial institutions and private banks. Luxembourg was prepared, along with the other members of the Community, to do more to alleviate the indebtedness of the poorest countries that were determined to adjust their

economy so as to stimulate growth. Steps had to be taken to achieve financial stability, allow debtor countries access to export markets, and reform their economies to prevent the flight of capital and mobilize savings, so that the developed countries could provide financial support.

6.   Luxembourg welcomed the stated intention of the contracting parties to GATT to revitalize international trade through negotiations in the Uruguay Round and hoped that they would be successful in strengthening and liberalizing the system of multilateral trade and in meeting their standstill and roll-back commitments regarding trade barriers. The depression of the commodities market since 1980 was due to both cyclical and unforeseen economic and political factors. Luxembourg regretted that the Agreement Establishing the Common Fund for Commodities had not yet entered into force because it had not been ratified by a sufficient number of countries. The countries of the EEC, which had been the first to sign it, had set up a second window, consisting of voluntary contributions to development assistance. The Fund was the corner-stone of the Integrated Programme for Commodities and was well suited to the needs of the third world.

7.   The Substantial New Programme of Action for the 1980s, for the Least Developed Countries, created in 1981, called for both an economic rationalization effort in those countries and increased financial aid to them. In that area, Luxembourg was participating in the special efforts that the contracting parties to GATT were making in favour of the LDCs.

8.   The encouraging results achieved since the beginning of 1986 in the international co-ordination of macro-economic policies would be consolidated by the Uruguay Round and the special session of the General Assembly on Africa. UNCTAD had a role to play in the co-operation between developed and developing countries.

Summary of the statement made at the 205th plenary meeting, 13 July 1987, by Mr. Kok WEE KIAT, Deputy Minister of Trade and Industry of Malaysia

1.   Mr. WEE KIAT said that the recent political and economic changes, as a consequence of which the international community had become more interdependent than ever, should be viewed in a realistic spirit. It had to be recognized that the economies of developing countries were fragile, though some were more resilient than others. Those countries, like the developed countries, wished to be masters of and improve their destinies. To

ensure the success of the Conference, the participants should adopt a pragmatic approach and show a will to co-operate for the common good.

2.   The recent success in negotiating the second International Natural Rubber Agreement under UNCTAD's auspices and the launching of the Uruguay Round of multilateral trade negotiations showed that

the system could work provided that such positive attitudes existed. The Rubber Agreement was intended to benefit both producers and consumers of natural rubber, and a successful follow-up to that Agreement would show the continued usefulness of the multilateral system.

3. A solution to the debt issue was of critical importance for the developing countries. Recent developments, in a deteriorating international economic environment, intensified the need to strengthen the debt strategy. In view of the slower growth in the industrialized countries, increased trade protectionism and the sharp decline in the prices of oil and other commodities, debtor countries still faced debt-servicing difficulties, despite lower interest rates. Most countries had merely contained the debt crisis with policies geared to import compression and demand restraint rather than to the desired revival of investment and economic growth. As a result, there was an increased flight of capital and a greater reluctance on the part of creditors to provide additional financing. Moreover, since the inception of the Baker plan in October 1985, few practical efforts had been made to solve the debt problem, and owing to the limited impact of that plan, many developing countries had difficulty in obtaining bank financing. The problem was aggravated by the sharp slow-down in official lending, but what was most disturbing was that even the international monetary institutions had been receiving more in repayments than they had lent, while private investment flows to debtor nations had fallen far short of expectations. The fall in oil prices had added to the anxieties of some countries. At the same time, commercial banks were more reluctant to provide new funds until there was firm evidence of success in the adjustment programmes of debtors. More innovative methods of tackling the indebtedness problem were clearly called for.

4. The developed countries should commit themselves to increasing net financial flows to the debtor nations, for they could hardly be unaware of the dangers of a contraction in liquidity that would occur when debtor nations were prevented by lack of finance from importing from the developed countries the capital goods needed to execute their development plans and programmes. The debtor countries could only control their debt problems by earning the necessary foreign exchange from exports and by economic growth. As a counterpart to such a commitment by developed countries, the developing countries and other borrowers for their part would have to make the necessary economic adjustments to strengthen the confidence of creditors by pursuing prudent financial policies such as liberalizing exchange control regulations and maintaining market-oriented rates. What was required was a combination of increased concessionary lending by the multilateral institutions, improved access to markets and a more forthcoming attitude among creditors towards debt restructuring and rescheduling.

5. An alarming feature of the economic recession of the early 1980s had been the persistent decline in the prices of most primary commodities, which in the period 1981-1985 had averaged 7 per cent below the 1980 level and had in fact fallen to their lowest levels since the Great Depression of the 1930s. As a leading

producer and exporter of such commodities as palm oil, natural rubber, tin, tropical timber, cocoa and petroleum, Malaysia urged all developing countries that were producers of primary commodities to work together in order to check the slide in commodity prices and make them stable and remunerative. There was a need for greater sincerity and a political determination to work together in dealing with major commodity-related problems, including those related to changes in the macro-economic policies of the industrialized nations, new technology and innovations leading to increased efficiency, and reduced use of raw materials that were replaced by substitutes.

6. His delegation reaffirmed the importance it attached to international commodity agreements as a means of fostering greater understanding and improved relations between producers and consumers in their efforts to stabilize commodity prices. It urged producer and consumer countries that had not yet done so to sign and ratify the new Rubber Agreement. The decision of the Soviet Union to sign the Agreement Establishing the Common Fund for Commodities was a welcome move that would augur well for the future of the international commodity trade. It was disturbing, however, to learn that some major industrialized nations had yet to sign and ratify that Agreement and were unable to support the Second Account, which was intended to benefit developing commodity producers in upgrading their research and development and market development activities.

7. The problems of the LDCs remained a serious cause of concern for the international community. Within the limits of its resources, Malaysia had, since 1980, been implementing a programme of technical assistance to developing countries, particularly the least developed. It had extended various forms of technical co-operation, including the provision of scholarships, training facilities and study visits and was confident that other better-placed developing countries would offer similar assistance, and hoped that their example would stimulate the developed countries to fulfil their commitments under the Substantial New Programme of Action for the 1980s for the Least Developed Countries.

8. Participants in the Conference were aware of the tasks ahead and would doubtless seek to enter into constructive dialogue, in the common belief that the existing economic scenario benefited no one. All countries were affected when international economic relations were in a state of disarray, although some more badly than others. All member States had a shared interest in change and a common objective in seeking to overcome the prevailing global economic crisis.

9. What distinguished the seventh session from earlier sessions of the Conference was that its agenda could, for the first time, provide member States with the opportunity to promote consensus on the critical issues—a consensus that could be achieved provided that member States worked and negotiated in a constructive spirit of goodwill and understanding. It would give a tremendous boost to the multilateral trading system if, as an outcome of the session, UNCTAD could be given new life and a new direction that it could successfully follow.

Summary of the statement made at the 219th plenary meeting, 30 July 1987, by Mr. Abdul Sattar Moosa DIDI, Minister of Fisheries of Maldives

1. Mr. DIDI said that the gap between the developing and developed countries continued to widen and the self-centred and piecemeal solutions proposed by the developed countries worsened the economic situation of developing countries. The latter had to contend with huge debts, declining commodity prices, reduced inflows of development capital and adverse terms of trade. Yet, in an increasingly interdependent world, it was essential that they should be given the opportunity for ensuring economic recovery and growth. Prospects for the near future were gloomy, and it was necessary to reiterate the call for an open and non-discriminatory multilateral trading system that would ensure a stable global economy.

2. Although the success of the LDCs' development programmes depended largely on their own efforts, substantial economic and social progress could not be achieved without a favourable economic environment and the support of the international community, as part of an overall approach to multilateral co-operation for development. The plight of the LDCs was particularly severe, and only through concerted efforts by the international community could their complex problems be alleviated and could progress be made towards self-sustained growth. As a least developed country, Maldives was anxious to see the measures agreed to in the context of the Substantial New Programme of Action, as well as other resolutions in favour of the LDCs, fully and effectively implemented without delay.

3. One of the most serious problems faced by those countries in developing their industries was their limited local production for small domestic markets, which added to their import burden. With their narrow export base, they were at the mercy of world markets for their export earnings. Moreover, some of those countries, including Maldives, had been afflicted by natural disasters, which had compelled them to concentrate on relief and rehabilitation work to the detriment of development programmes. He expressed his appreciation of the sympathy shown and assistance given by many friendly countries and international and regional bodies in connection with the recent disasters experienced by his country.

Summary of the statement made at the 213th plenary meeting, 27 July 1987, by Mr. Victor J. GAUCI, Permanent Representative of Malta to the United Nations Office at Geneva

1. Mr. GAUCI said that current problems were hardly different in nature from those discussed at the previous session of the Conference; they had simply become worse. It was not so much the previous analysis of the economic situation or projections, but rather the action taken on them that had been wrong. It was futile to prescribe remedies if there was no intention of applying them. There was no question of changing course but of making up for time lost through inactivity. It was therefore encouraging to note that a consensus had emerged at the Uruguay Round on the need to remove obstacles to trade. However, a number of questions had perhaps not received the attention they deserved. For its part, Malta had consistently applied the principles governing trade, co-operation and mutual respect in its regional and international relations. It had accordingly supported the establishment of the Committee for Programme and Co-ordination in the United Nations and had come out in favour of the concept of the common heritage of mankind with regard to the peaceful use of the ocean floor; furthermore, it had always supported the principle of regional action.

2. The per capita GNP was outmoded as a criterion for measuring economic results at the international level, because GNP was primarily a yardstick of national growth. A fairer criterion would take into account a much broader spectrum of economic factors, such as natural resources, the ratio of exports to imports, the degree of dependence on imports and hence on imported inflation. Many countries did not feature at all in international statistics because they were too small to influence major trends in world trade, despite the fact that they were greatly influenced by the world economy. Many of them were small island developing countries. According to a recent study by the Commonwealth Secretariat, they were considered to be the most vulnerable of all, most of them having less than a million inhabitants, and although widely dispersed, they had many features in common. They created no problems for world trade but inherited all the system's major problems. Despite their natural disadvantages and the meagre amount of foreign assistance they received, their average economic performance was twice that of other developing countries. They had succeeded in making judicious use of the assistance received and in pursuing a policy conducive to foreign investment and tourism development. In view of their success, the flow of funds in their direction should be maintained in proportion to their absorptive capacity so that they could continue to develop their economy and exploit the potential of their exclusive economic zone on the sea bed.

3. For its part, Malta greatly appreciated the assistance it had received, and which it had put to productive use, but it had still not attained self-sufficiency. Gross capital formation had declined in all developing regions since 1981, particularly in southern Europe, where Malta was situated. The slow growth of the market economies was one of the principal reasons for

the decline in Malta's exports. Total ODA flows from market-economy countries, however impressive, were inadequate to boost growth.

4. The interdependence of the world economy implied equitable economic progress between nations. The factors of production must be allowed free play, and unused land, labour and capital throughout the world must be put to use through measures to facilitate direct foreign investment in the developing countries and to increase the transfer of technology. All those measures would help to reduce unemployment and stimulate consumption and all countries, developed and developing alike, would benefit.

5. Development aid was not entirely disinterested, because it served in part to finance the imports of developing countries. The markets of the developed countries for manufactured goods were clearly saturated, and the immense third-world market offered good prospects for stimulating growth. In the circumstances the developing countries intended to participate on an equal footing in managing economic development.

6. It was time to go beyond the stage of theoretical studies and take concrete action offering tangible proof of the international community's commitment to multilateralism. The seventh session of the Conference should be the driving force behind that action.

Summary of the statement made at the 214th plenary meeting, 28 July 1987, by Mr. Héctor HERNÁNDEZ CERVANTES, Secretary for Commerce and Industrial Development of Mexico

1. Mr. HERNANDEZ CERVANTES observed that recent world economic trends were far from encouraging. Growth in 1986 had fallen short of expectations in the developed countries and had declined in the developing countries. Persistently high interest rates, declining and unstable commodity prices and export market and external finance trends had compelled most developing countries to adopt swingeing structural adjustment measures. Whilst enabling some to achieve modest trade surpluses, those measures had nevertheless had an adverse impact on development in general, since per capita income had dropped below 1976 levels.

2. Those structural adjustment measures in the developing countries had constituted the linchpin of the debt burden relief policies of those countries, but without the parallel and co-responsible participation of the industrialized world, they had failed to live up to expectations. The Governments of the developed countries had not tried hard enough to create an international economic environment conducive to growth, international financial institutions had not adequately monitored the policies of the major industrialized countries or provided the necessary resources to developing countries, and compensatory financing mechanisms had not sufficiently attenuated the impact of the commodity price slump. A fresh start, based on more equitable foundations and the unequivocal commitment of all those concerned, was needed, and a lasting solution to the debt problem which would correct the shortcomings of the current strategy, had to be found. Structural adjustment had not, *inter alia*, improved the export earnings/debt burden ratio in the 15 most indebted countries, nor had it revitalized growth or promoted a return to voluntary credit. Machinery to reduce the debt burden and the net outflow of capital from developing countries was therefore required. A facility could be set up, for example, to enable those countries to benefit from debt adjustment measures negotiated on secondary markets. The Japanese Government's recent initiative to increase financial transfers to developing countries and the idea of creating new recycling mechanisms were steps in the right direction.

3. Developing countries had to increase their export earnings if they were to meet their debt-servicing requirements over the longer term. However, they were encountering a resurgence of protectionism. Over 30 per cent of their exports of manufactures to industrialized countries had been subject to non-tariff restrictions in 1986. Although it was generally agreed that protectionism hampered world economic recovery, certain countries continued to adopt measures that encouraged it; examples included the trade legislation adopted by the United States Senate and House of Representatives, the EEC's agricultural policy and the non-tariff restrictions applied by Japan on imports. States must undertake to put an end to protectionism and respect the Punta del Este commitments on standstill and roll-back.

4. If international trade was to contribute to development, a stable and predictable trade system equally beneficial to all parties had to be established. That implied abandoning arbitrary and discriminatory unilateral trade measures such as the voluntary export restriction agreements and preferential régimes applied by industrialized countries. Lastly, all countries should contribute to the joint effort. Mexico applied a maximum import duty of 40 per cent, the weighted average being 13 per cent. Only 30 per cent of all imports, including agricultural products, were subject to non-tariff restrictions.

5. Further signatures and ratifications of the Agreement Establishing the Common Fund for Commodities indicated the international community's eagerness to see the Fund begin operations as soon as possible. Mexico had ratified the Agreement several years earlier and had allocated the necessary funds for its entry into force. Countries that had not yet ratified it should understand that the Fund could promote a concerted solution to the problems underlying the severe commodity price slump. The manifold reasons for that slump admittedly included technical progress and change in consumption patterns, but industrialized-country subsidies of uncompetitive production were also in part responsible for the situation. To make matters worse, world commodity prices were set in dollars and the decline in that currency

had neither stimulated demand nor reduced end-consumer prices. Market fluctuations were another contributing factor. Developing countries understandably attached great importance to commodity market revitalization coupled with stability. Another priority should be to relax conditionality criteria and facilitate access to the IMF Compensatory Financing Facility. Concerted measures were also required in the field of commodity trade and transport.

6. Participants in the Conference were responsible for defining UNCTAD's role in coming years. In the opinion of the Mexican Government, UNCTAD should continue to buttress the structural adjustment efforts of the developing countries. It should establish a co-operative programme in the services sector to provide developing countries with technical and financial assistance and help them to determine how the sector could contribute to development, particularly through research at the national level and the improvement of statistical methods. UNCTAD should analyse the issues

raised in connection with the need to define a multilateral framework for international trade in services and study their impact on the economies of the developing countries. In the case of the Uruguay Round, UNCTAD should help developing countries to participate effectively in meetings, particularly in non-traditional fields, and provide technical support for the negotiating groups. Lastly, UNCTAD should not only study the interdependent questions of money and finance, debt, commodities and development and trade, but also closely monitor the evolution of the situation and guide domestic policies in those areas.

7. The Mexican Government was confident that UNCTAD's member States would demonstrate, through the measures adopted at the seventh session of the Conference their determination to base international economic relations on the principles of justice and equity. It was essential, in that respect, that the commitments assumed should be honoured by all.

Summary of the statement made at the 204th plenary meeting, 13 July 1987, by Mr. J. DULMAA, Minister of Foreign Trade of Mongolia

1. Mr. DULMAA said that the years since the sixth session of the Conference had been characterized by an intensification of structural disequilibrium, irregular economic development, a decline in the growth rates of industrial production and international trade, and a crisis of ever-increasing proportions in the monetary and financial systems. Meanwhile the arms race had continued, destabilizing the international environment and diverting huge resources from peaceful, creative purposes. In such circumstances the main task of the Conference at its seventh session would be to shed light on the underlying causes of the current unsatisfactory situation, to bring new thinking to bear on the acute problems of the day, and to adopt bold, original recommendations for dealing with them.

2. The prevention of nuclear war and the adoption of specific measures to ensure lasting peace and security were unquestionably the main conditions for stable economic development and equal and mutually beneficial international co-operation in trade and economic matters. The socialist States were striving to achieve those objectives, as was evidenced by the USSR's proposal for the elimination of nuclear and other weapons of mass destruction and the decisions adopted by the States parties to the Warsaw Treaty at their meeting in May 1987 in Berlin. The socialist countries' conception of international economic security, designed to stimulate the search for common elements in various approaches to the solution of world economic problems, was gaining ground. World economic security presupposed the strengthening of confidence and mutual understanding among States in the economic field and was incompatible with a policy of using international economic relations to interfere in the internal affairs of sovereign States.

3. The developing and non-aligned countries were continuing to make serious efforts to eliminate the scandalous injustices and inequalities in international economic relations, to escape from the burden of indebtedness, and to stop the outflow of financial resources. The debt problem, which had arisen as a result of the economic recession in the industrialized countries of the West, the deteriorating terms of trade of developing countries and high interest rates were clear signs of the disorders existing in the world economy. The severity of the debt problem was due not so much to the size of the debt as to the amount of the yearly payments to be made at exorbitantly inflated rates, which led to the haemorrhaging of the developing countries' economies.

4. Mongolia considered that in the prevailing circumstances it was necessary to make headway towards achieving the objectives set forth in the Declaration and the Programme of Action on the Establishment of a New International Economic Order, the Charter of Economic Rights and Duties of States, and in other basic United Nations decisions and documents on the restructuring of international economic relations. The initiatives taken by the socialist countries on disarmament and the restructuring of international economic relations on a just and democratic basis, and the proposals made by the developing and non-aligned countries for the holding of "global negotiations" under the auspices of the United Nations on the most burning world economic problems, for the convening of an international monetary and financial conference, and for negotiations on the elaboration of a code of conduct for TNCs and the transfer of technology pointed to effective ways of solving the problems facing mankind in the field of development and international economic rela-

tions. The forthcoming International Conference on the Relationship between Disarmament and Development would also play a positive role.

5. The difficulties currently being experienced by the capitalist economies were leading to an unprecedented increase in protectionism and discrimination. His delegation took the view that recourse to political pressure by means of trade, credit and technology blockades, embargoes, boycotts and protectionist arrangements had no place in international economic relations. The developing countries should be given free access to international markets, and a just correlation between prices for raw materials, agricultural produce and manufactures should be established. The experience of many countries showed that social and economic development required a complex approach, economic independence, and the establishment of a rationally structured economy. Of no less importance was the training of skilled personnel. In that connection the Economic and Social Council had recently adopted pertinent resolutions on the role of the public sector in the economic development of developing countries and the development of human resources.

6. For the preceding 66 years the Mongolian People's Republic had been successfully endeavouring to bring about profound economic changes. The new five-year plan for 1986-1990 laid down important objectives for the further development of the country's economy and culture. Those objectives would be achieved through Mongolia's participation in the implementation of CMEA's programme of scientific and technological progress* and through measures provided for in long-term bilateral programmes for economic, scientific and technological co-operation with other socialist countries. The arrangements included trade agreements under which the country's foreign trade would increase substantially. New forms of economic co-operation, especially the establishment of joint undertakings, would be further developed, and direct links would be extended.

7. As was stressed in the message sent by the Chairman of the Council of Ministers of Mongolia to the participants in the Conference,** Mongolia actively supported UNCTAD's work to expand all flows of international trade on a basis of mutual advantage, non-discrimination and equality. It noted with satisfaction UNCTAD's contribution to the formulation of new ideas concerning ways of restructuring international economic relations on a just and democratic basis. If the necessary political will was shown by all member States and if a new approach to the pressing problems of international trade and economic relations was developed, UNCTAD could successfully fulfil its task of promoting the development of trade relations among all States, especially among countries with different social and economic systems, and of accelerating the economic progress of the developing countries.

---

* See A/39/323.

** TD/L.277 (see volume I, annex IV).

Summary of the statement made at the 204th plenary meeting, 13 July 1987, by Mr. Abdellah AZMANI, Minister of Commerce and Industry of Morocco

1. Mr. AZMANI said that, like other developing countries, his country had been severely affected by the world economic crisis. He described the programme of structural adjustment which his country had undertaken in response to the crisis, for he thought that Morocco's experience might serve as an illustration of the preconditions that had to be fulfilled in order that the process of growth and development could be revitalized.

2. In 1983, Morocco's external financial situation had reached its lowest point and as a consequence the authorities had had to take Draconian measures to restrict imports and internal demand. The external debt had reached $11.2 billion, equivalent to almost 85 per cent of the country's GDP. The budget deficit had amounted to 12.2 per cent of GDP. Only 57 per cent of imports had been covered by exports, while the current-account deficit on the balance of payments had amounted to 8 per cent of GDP, after having reached over 13 per cent in 1982. That situation, which was not peculiar to Morocco, had resulted from a number of mainly external factors, including the deterioration of the commodity markets, the erratic behaviour of the major currencies, the high cost of energy, the application of protectionist policies against manufactures and agricultural produce, the rise in interest rates, and the exceptional drought which had hit Africa, including Morocco. The persistently adverse international economic environment, the progressive drying-up of external sources of finance for the investment needed to counter demographic pressures and rapid urbanization had constrained the Government to undertake a searching reappraisal of its economic policy within the framework of a structural adjustment programme.

3. In designing the new policy, the Government had based itself on a number of facts, particularly the structural nature of the stagnation characterizing the markets for the country's commodities, whose real prices were now barely at the level which they had reached in the 1920s and 1930s. Moreover, the policies implemented by the industrialized countries had disturbed the price structure, reduced demand for raw materials and permitted the costly development of substitute products whose comparative advantages were due only to the artificial manipulation of prices, tariffs and other factors.

4. Furthermore, the technological progress achieved over the preceding two decades had seriously disturbed the structure of comparative advantages, adversely affecting the international division of labour. Modern technology was, of course, beneficial to mankind as a whole, but it had been introduced only by sealing off domestic markets from external competition, including competition from Moroccan products, which were very

labour-intensive. The technological changes which had upset the structure of world trade in certain branches had occurred without any transitional period at a time when owing to the debt crisis Morocco had been virtually unable to obtain access to the new technologies. To remain competitive, Morocco had to increase its external indebtedness in order to purchase equipment and know-how; it also had to sacrifice employment, which remained the focal point of its economic policy. The country's margin of manœuvre to design a coherent set of economic measures for developing its competitiveness, promoting employment or self-sufficiency in food was shrinking. With a volume of foreign trade representing over 45 per cent of GDP and a debt-servicing burden which, after rescheduling, absorbed an equivalent proportion of its exports, the slightest decision by the industrialized countries on budgetary, monetary or international trade matters produced disproportionate effects on the Moroccan economy. The unpredictability of the world market and its effects on the developing countries were disruptive of their economy and society.

5.   In those circumstances the Government had had to alter its development plan in an attempt to achieve greater self-sufficiency through the priority mobilization of resources for the benefit of the rural sector, a strategy for the promotion of small and medium-size enterprises that offered employment opportunities, and a structural reform of incentives to permit a more efficient allocation of rare resources, especially to promote exports. Those objectives were being achieved through a new approach to planning: rigid investment programmes covering a number of years were being replaced by more flexible arrangements. The principal measures being applied in keeping with the new approach were: a progressive liberalization of foreign trade allowing for the gradual introduction of foreign competition in domestic markets so as to strengthen Morocco's competitiveness on world markets, exchange rate adjustments to eliminate the handicap facing export industries, a revision of interest rates to raise the level of domestic savings, and a reform of the system of taxation.

6.   Those and other measures had made possible a remarkable recovery in Morocco's economic and financial situation. In 1986 GDP had grown by approximately 6.5 per cent as a result, in particular, of an exceptional advance in agricultural output. The rate of inflation had been contained within limits of 7 to 8 per cent. The budget deficit had been reduced to less than 7 per cent of GDP, and the current-account deficit in the balance of payments to less than 2 per cent of GDP. Coverage of imports by exports had been 65 per cent, and was expected to approach 70 per cent in 1987. That performance was certainly not attributable solely to the structural adjustment measures implemented. It had also benefited from the fall of the dollar, the fall in petroleum prices, and the exceptionally good cereal harvest recorded in 1986. The application of Morocco's adjustment policy indicated at least that the revitalization of growth was possible and completely manageable and that it could not be produced by the will of the State alone but was a matter for everyone.

7.   However, Morocco's promising experiment, which had been conducted in close collaboration with its financial backers and international financial institutions, might in the short or medium term be frustrated by the inadequate mobilization of external resources to finance growth. Paradoxically, at a time when the developing countries were resolutely committed to restructuring their economies, the flow of resources needed to finance the restructuring had been reversed to a point where those countries had become sources of finance for the public deficits of the industrialized world. That state of affairs was all the harder to bear as the severity of structural adjustment was straining the limits of social tolerance. Paradoxically again, at a time when the developing countries were being requested to improve their competitiveness and increase the supply of export goods, ever more sophisticated protectionist barriers were being erected against their products.

8.   Many inconsistencies characterized the international economic environment, but it was clear that certain conditions had to be fulfilled if there was to be a durable recovery of growth in the sorely-tried developing countries. A number of African countries had initiated a bold and innovatory process of transformation and reform. Their act of faith ought to be supported by the international community in accordance with the commitments which it had entered into in the United Nations Programme of Action for African Economic Recovery and Development 1986-1990. Four conditions had to be fulfilled if the impetus was not to be lost and the future of the continent in particular, and of the developing world in general, was not to be irremediably compromised. First, in managing the developing countries' external debt, the main objective should be to arrange for debt-servicing payments to be in keeping with the repayment capacity of the economies concerned, subject to allowance for investments on a scale sufficient to guarantee minimum growth and to keep the social cost of adjustment measures within tolerable limits. In addition, buffer mechanisms needed to eliminate net transfers of resources to creditor countries should be established. Secondly, protectionist measures curbing the access of developing countries' products to the markets of the industrialized countries should be dismantled immediately. Thirdly, the measures approved in UNCTAD for stabilizing commodity markets and halting the deterioration of the developing countries' terms of trade should be implemented without delay. The entry into force of the Agreement Establishing the Common Fund for Commodities would be a test case in that regard. The effective operation of the mechanisms of the Common Fund should open the way for their extension to other products. Fourthly, it was necessary to establish machinery for permanent multilateral consultations on and monitoring of macro-economic policies of both developed and developing countries and the impact of those policies on various interrelated aspects of development. Above all, however, his Government considered that what was needed most was the willingness to engage in a dialogue without ulterior motives, replacing anathemas and sterile confrontations by consultation and solidarity. UNCTAD provided the appropriate framework for such a dialogue.

Summary of the statement made at the 217th plenary meeting, 29 July 1987, by Mr. Daniel G. TEMBE, Deputy Minister of Commerce of Mozambique

1. Mr. TEMBE said that the world was experiencing a major economic crisis. Since 1982, the flow of resources to the third world—official aid, bank lending, direct foreign investment and export credits—had decreased considerably and the developing countries were now transferring more money to the developed countries than they were receiving from them. In 1985 and 1986 alone, that net inverse transfer of financial resources had amounted to $48 billion.

2. Meanwhile, the debt-servicing burden of the developing countries had grown considerably to reach an awesome $900 billion. The countries of sub-Saharan Africa now devoted nearly 4 per cent of their GDP to interest payments, as against less than 2 per cent in the late 1970s. A solution to that problem urgently needed to be found, not only through moratoria, debt rescheduling on concessional terms or outright cancellation, but also by exploring ways of reducing the short- and long-term interest burden. Another approach might be to convert some loans into grants. There must be recognition of the fact that current levels of foreign liabilities were unbearable for developing countries and a drag to the world economy.

3. The problem was compounded by sizeable losses in commodity export earnings as a result of falling prices and deteriorating terms of trade. The developing nations had lost $65 billion in 1985 and $94 billion in 1986, and although some had been able to increase the volume of their exports in 1986, their earnings had been much lower than in the past. Any solution must take account of the fact that fundamental changes had occurred in the consumption of raw materials in the developed countries, that technological innovations had accelerated the use of substitute products, and that the developed countries had moved towards greater economy in the use of raw materials in their processing industries.

4. There had also been a steady shift from the production of goods to services. Goods-producing sectors had accounted for 35 per cent of GDP in the developed market economies in the 1960s, but they now accounted for less than 30 per cent, whereas the share of services had increased from 56 per cent to 62 per cent. The share of agricultural commodities in world trade had declined by one half. The entry into operation of the Common Fund would greatly alleviate the situation with regard to commodities and the signing of the Agreement Establishing the Common Fund by the Soviet Union was to be welcomed.

5. There had also been an increasing trend towards protectionism, especially against developing countries' manufactured exports. Tariff measures were severely impeding the import of processed goods, and non-tariff measures and restrictive business practices had fre-

quently been used to limit exports from third world countries and to thwart competition.

6. Mozambique was confronted with an extremely difficult economic situation brought about by both internal and external factors which seriously hampered its development. The country had been considerably affected by natural disasters over the preceding 10 years and had also been the victim of a destabilization campaign financed by South Africa. Terrorist bands in the pay of the *apartheid* régime were ravaging the country and had recently massacred 380 Mozambican citizens in the village of Homoine, the victims including women, children, elderly and sick people. The acts of aggression perpetrated by the Pretoria régime were also causing considerable material damage that was estimated at more than $5 billion, or almost double Mozambique's external debt.

7. That dramatic situation had led to the convening of an emergency conference by the Secretary-General of the United Nations in March 1987 with a view to seeking greater support from the international community to help the more than 4 million Mozambican citizens who had been obliged to leave their homes by the terrorists' destructive activities. Although the international community had responded generously to the Secretary-General's appeal, it was important to underline that only the creation of conditions conducive to the economic rehabilitation of Mozambique would enable the country to improve the lot of its people. Mozambique had recently adopted a recovery programme, but its success depended to a large extent on the support given by the international community and particularly by the developed countries.

8. Pretoria's aggressiveness was not confined to Mozambique alone. It was part of *apartheid*'s general policy of regional destabilization through direct and indirect aggression aimed at maintaining the States members of the Southern African Development Co-ordination Conference in a state of dependence. Those countries were thus forced to allocate a considerable percentage of their scarce resources to defence, to the detriment of national programmes aimed at economic emancipation and development. Mozambique was convinced that peace and development would not be possible in southern Africa as long as the *apartheid* régime continued to exist.

9. Viable solutions had to be found to overcome the international economic crisis and enable the developing countries to trade with other States in conditions advantageous to all countries, irrespective of their economic, political and social systems. Mozambique was prepared to co-operate with all the countries represented at the Conference in the adoption and implementation of decisions.

Summary of the statement made at the 214th plenary meeting, 28 July 1987, by Mr. Nihat AKYOL, United Nations Council for Namibia

1. Mr. AKYOL observed that Namibia had a typically colonial economy, which functioned exclusively in response to foreign capital needs and demands, exporting virtually all of its primary production. Three primary sector activities, namely, mining, agriculture and fishing, together accounted for over two thirds of GDP and over 90 per cent of exports while employing more than 80 per cent of wage earners. In its economic relations, Namibia was entirely dependent on South Africa, which regarded the territory as a fifth province, a reservoir of natural wealth for it to appropriate and exploit together with various TNCs and financial institutions. The latter were attracted to Namibia by the prospect of extraordinary profit made possible by the extension to its territory of the system of *apartheid*, which guaranteed an abundant and cheap labour force. By using licences issued by South Africa to exploit Namibia's territory, TNCs and international banking groups directly supported the *apartheid* régime, thereby strengthening its determination to block implementation of the United Nations plan for the independence of Namibia, set out in Security Council resolution 435 (1978, and to defy the advisory opinion of the International Court of Justice and numerous Security Council and General Assembly resolutions. The Council for Namibia urged the international community to take strong measures to end the illegal occupation of the Territory by the racist régime of South Africa.

2. The Council was endeavouring to protect Namibia's economic interests in view of its future in-

dependence. In 1974 it had promulgated Decree No. 1 for the Protection of the Natural Resources of Namibia, aimed at preventing foreign economic interests from stripping Namibians of their wealth and heritage. That legal instrument committed the Council's member States to adopt legislative and other appropriate measures to ensure its implementation. The Council also endeavoured to elicit from the international community increasing political, moral and financial support for the Namibian people's needs in terms of food, health, training and housing.

3. Lastly, and in the longer term, the Council was striving to prepare Namibia for independence. Pursuant to General Assembly resolution 37/223, the United Nations Institute for Namibia had in 1986 published a study on the various social and economic aspects of economic reconstruction and planning in Namibia after independence. The study consisted of a national planning outline and the Council would request UNCTAD for technical assistance in connection with follow-up activities. In the past, UNCTAD had carried out a limited study on economic planning in the territory following independence. Further specific action would be desirable, particularly further studies on Namibia's economy, the employment of Namibians as trainees in the UNCTAD secretariat and, more generally, training opportunities for Namibians in the fields of trade and economics.

Summary of the statement made at the 215th plenary meeting, 28 July 1987, by Mr. Prakash Bijaya THEBE, Minister of Commerce of Nepal

1. Mr. THEBE said that the current world economic crisis was occurring at a time when the interdependence of developed and developing countries was becoming more pronounced. The international monetary, financial and trading system clearly no longer met the needs of multilateral co-operation for development, negotiations aimed at global solutions were deadlocked and the principle of multilateralism was itself under severe strain.

2. Such adverse external conditions had halted or even reversed economic progress in many developing countries, where increasing unemployment and underemployment went hand in hand with steeply falling revenues. The LDCs were particularly ill-equipped to develop their economies. Figures revealed a real decline in their economic performance; their share of world exports had fallen, while average annual growth in GNP (2 per cent during the first half of the 1980s) had not only remained well below the target of the Substantial New Programme of Action for the 1980s for the Least Developed Countries but was also considerably less than the 4 per cent actually reached in 1970.

3. Land-locked and island developing countries, which accounted for over one half of the LDCs, faced additional difficulties as a result of their geographical handicaps. It was therefore vital that transit countries and donors should increase their co-operation with the land-locked LDCs to help them overcome their special problems.

4. The LDCs recognized that they had primary responsibility for their own development. Many of them had, moreover, embarked upon the task of improving their economic management and making structural adjustments. Nepal had itself, as part of its overall national development objectives, adopted a number of measures including improvement of the tax system, mobilization of domestic savings and encouragement of private development initiatives. In the social sector, it had launched an extensive programme aimed at meeting the basic needs of its people by the year 2000. In view of the scale of those activities, Nepal was obliged to seek a large part of the necessary funds from outside sources.

5. It was an undeniable fact that international assistance remained an essential adjunct to the national

efforts of the LDCs. The Substantial New Programme of Action was the most important of the UNCTAD programmes for the LDCs and provided a firm foundation for continuing co-operation among those countries and their partners in development. Nepal therefore considered that steps should be taken as a matter of urgency to ensure that the Programme was fully implemented. He thanked President Mitterrand for his offer to host a conference in France in 1990 to review implementation of the Programme of Action. In addition, it was perhaps time to give some thought to preparation of a further Substantial New Programme of Action for the LDCs in the 1990s.

6. In view of the growing interdependence of national economies, the developing countries ought to be treated as full partners in world development. Instead, preference was currently being given to unilateral or bilateral action that would only lead to the erosion of the international system. The sole viable solution to current economic difficulties was world economic growth to help expand markets, reduce protectionism and stimulate national growth in both developed and developing countries. Such a move would, of course, depend on reversing current trends as well as correcting imbalances in the international monetary system, reducing real interest rates, strengthening commodity prices, increasing liquidity, stabilizing exchange rates and introducing a debt strategy geared to development.

7. While recognizing that a process of structural change could lead to sustained economic growth in developing countries, he recalled that the lack of alternative income-generating activities forced many such countries to rely on commodity exports to finance those changes. Their adjustment possibilities thus remained restricted in the absence of urgent action on commodities. It was therefore to be hoped that the decision of the USSR and Côte d'Ivoire to sign the Agreement Establishing the Common Fund for Commodities and the steps taken by Madagascar, Peru and Thailand to ratify that Agreement would accelerate the coming into operation of the Common Fund. Another requirement was to strengthen the aims of the Integrated Programme for Commodities, which continued to be fully valid.

8. UNCTAD was the most universal of the bodies with responsibilities in the area of trade and development; the seventh session of the Conference provided an excellent opportunity not only to review international economic co-operation in order to revitalize development, growth and international trade, but also to strengthen the organization itself and enable it to function more effectively. That unique opportunity should not be allowed to slip by since the future of international co-operation depended upon it. A prosperous and economically just world could be built only upon solidarity, reciprocity and shared benefits of growth.

Summary of the statement made at the 204th plenary meeting, 13 July 1987, by Mrs. Yvonne van ROOY, Minister for Foreign Trade of the Netherlands

1. Mrs. van ROOY said that most people would agree that the North-South dialogue in its traditional form had reached a deadlock and that new and more effective methods for UNCTAD's deliberations and negotiations should be devised. In that respect she shared the analysis made by the representative of Pakistan (202nd plenary meeting). In the past, there had been countless mammoth meetings at which delegations had tried to reach world-wide agreement on a great variety of items with an ever-growing number of countries. Those countries had been subject to strict group discipline, although differences in their interests, views and economic capacities had become increasingly apparent. Quite often the conferences had resulted in disappointment and frustration, or even confrontation. By carrying confrontation too far, delegations had frequently undermined the possibility of reaching a consensus.

2. Some bitter lessons had been learned. She was sure that most delegations would now subscribe to the view that little or nothing had been gained by the proliferation of resolutions, most of which had not been implemented. As a consequence the credibility of such conferences had diminished to the point where they had become irrelevant to Governments, to the business community, and to the public at large. The time had come for a fundamental change in approach. The opportunity offered by the seventh session of the Conference, should be seized in order to try to rebuild the North-South

dialogue on trade and development on more promising ground, aiming at a common assessment of the main problems.

3. Analysis and assessment were, however, not enough. UNCTAD should promote down-to-earth discussions, and on the basis of a common assessment it would be able to negotiate and formulate concrete policies and recommendations. Instead of adopting an avalanche of ineffectual resolutions, the Conference should aim at embodying its conclusions in a single final document. The policies and recommendations adopted should be implemented by Governments and by UNCTAD and other international organizations.

4. In view of the fast-growing diversity among developing and developed countries alike, general solutions would no longer be adequate and differentiated policies were required. Moreover, development necessarily implied the involvement of all sectors of society, including not only Governments but also private organizations such as trade unions and employers' organizations. While emphasizing the crucial role of the private sector, the Conference should not lose sight of the fact that in developing countries Governments had an essential role to play in all stages of development. Dr. Okita, in his Prebisch lecture,*

---

* Third Raúl Prebisch Lecture, entitled "Emerging Prospects for Development and the World Economy", delivered on 9 July 1987 by Dr. Saburo Okita of Japan.

had made some thoughtful comments on the difficult issue of finding the right balance between the private and the public sector; she welcomed particularly his plea for planning with rather than against market forces. She suggested that the UNCTAD secretariat might be invited to undertake an analysis of the respective roles of the public and private sectors in developing countries and their impact on economic development and growth.

5. As far as the debt problem was concerned, she considered that progress could be made only when debtor countries, creditor countries, private banks and international financial institutions assumed their responsibilities. Her Government hoped that the Conference would adopt a consensus statement on the debt problem.

6. The financial problems of the major debtor countries in Latin America were primarily a matter for private capital markets. Since there was no real alternative to private finance for those countries, her Government welcomed the use of new private financial instruments, although direct investment would also have to play a key role in the development financing of the middle-income countries.

7. For many years her Government had advocated special measures for the least developed debtor countries. In their case the prime responsibility clearly lay with Governments. In every instance an increase in the volume of aid had to be the starting-point. More bilateral and multilateral finance would be needed to support adjustment programmes in Africa, and a leading role in that effort should be given to the World Bank.

8. Official development assistance targets had not lost their relevance. The commitment made by participants in the recent Venice Summit of the European Community countries to raise their ODA to 0.7 per cent of GNP was to be welcomed. For many years the ODA of the Netherlands had amounted to 1 per cent of GNP, and her Government intended to continue to provide such assistance at that level.

9. As far as the poorest countries were concerned, her Government welcomed the proposals on debt rescheduling for African countries made in the Paris Club. Since 1973 the Netherlands had cancelled all ODA debts of the LDCs and had announced the cancellation of the debt-service payments of other low-income countries in Africa for five years. The Netherlands already surpassed the ODA target of 0.15 per cent for the LDCs and was willing to accept a further increase. It also fully supported the Substantial New Programme of Action for those countries. It was to be hoped that other countries would agree to similar measures.

10. She endorsed the remarks made by previous speakers regarding the need to liberalize international trade and enhance multilateral discipline in the context of an improved open multilateral trading system. A hopeful sign was the Punta del Este agreement to launch a new round of trade negotiations. That implied decisions on standstill and roll-back, textiles and clothing, safeguards and technical assistance to developing countries. Her Government was in favour of an early implementation of agreements on subjects of special importance to the developing countries, such as

tropical products and tariff escalation. A successful outcome of the GATT negotiations on agricultural products should strengthen the production and export capacities of developing countries. The activities to be undertaken by UNCTAD should prepare the way for the active participation of the developing countries in the new round and so contribute to a successful outcome. Her Government did not expect material concessions from the LDCs in the new round. UNCTAD's complementary role in that respect might include analysing the nature and causes of the differences in economic performance of developing countries in order to formulate a differentiated approach to their position in international trade; examining the impact of new and emerging technologies on the dynamics of comparative advantages; further analysing the role of the service sector in the process of development and identifying the interests of developing countries in the area of services; exploring the possibilities of a greater reliance on the private sector and on more co-operation between small and medium-size enterprises in order to establish viable export capacities in developing countries; and supporting efforts to increase trade and economic integration among developing countries.

11. Falling commodity prices had clearly had a negative impact on the economic situation of many commodity-exporting developing countries. The commodity problem was no longer exclusively a North-South issue, since a major developing country had become a net importer of commodities. Yet all countries had a strong interest in redressing current imbalances, rigidities, interventions and distortions in commodity markets. It would be an illusion to expect a quick recovery of prices for stocks were abundant, there were excess production capacities and demand was stagnant. A pragmatic, market-oriented approach was needed in dealing with commodity problems, with due regard for what had been learned from past experience. Special emphasis should be given to strengthening the competitiveness of individual commodities through measures in the field of research and development, marketing and diversification, and the provision of financial resources for those purposes on a more regular basis; improving market transparency through the establishment of study groups for individual commodities; improving the operation of international commodity agreements aiming at price stabilization; helping to diversify the economies of developing countries in order to diminish their dependence on exports of primary commodities; and supporting the early resumption of consultations on compensatory financing with a view to improving the functioning of existing facilities.

12. The Netherlands had ratified the Agreement Establishing the Common Fund for Commodities at the sixth session of the Conference in 1983 and welcomed the announcement by the USSR delegation concerning the Soviet Union's intention to become a party to the Agreement.

13. Her Government was firmly committed to UNCTAD as an indispensable forum for analysis, assistance and negotiation and was willing to play its part in rebuilding the organization into a more effective instrument for solving the pressing North-South problems facing the world.

Summary of the statement made at the 203rd plenary meeting, 10 July 1987, by Mr. Alejandro E. MARTÍNEZ CUENCA, Minister of Foreign Trade of Nicaragua

1. Mr. MARTÍNEZ CUENCA said that deliberations at the Conference should focus not on a diagnosis of the current international crisis—on which developing and developed countries would find it difficult to agree—but on a plan of action. The foreign debt problem affected developed as well as developing countries, and the necessary sacrifices should be equitably shared. The huge external debt, foreign trade imbalance and budget deficit of the United States of America, were fraught with serious consequences for all nations, in terms of the stability of the dollar, interest rates and protectionism. In a context of interdependence, the economic situation of no single group of countries could be seen in isolation. Proposals for dealing with the third world debt, such as the Baker plan had proved unrealistic and ineffective and had moreover been used to interfere in the internal affairs of the countries concerned. The fact that developing countries were unable to repay debts contracted in the 1970s and 1980s was beginning to be recognized by the international banking system itself. Meanwhile, the United States of America failed to make the necessary internal adjustments that would redirect more resources towards development. Responsibility for such situations must be accepted, as must the reality of interdependence, as a preliminary to effective measures to meet the challenge of the survival of all peoples and to replace confrontation by co-operation, stability and development.

2. The steps taken to ease the environment of confrontation through specific proposals for disarmament conducive to a new era of détente that would open a way to a new economic order based on co-operation among all nations were welcomed as a major move towards assigning substantial resources to aid, development and social stability. Within such a framework, peoples could be asked to make internal economic adjustments, the cost of which would be equally shared by the developed nations, irrespective of their political ideology. He supported, and urged others to support, the proposal that a world conference on external debt be convened at the earliest opportunity under the auspices of UNCTAD.

3. Also related to political polarization in a world struggling for survival were the issues of stability of commodity prices, protectionism and the use of illegal economic pressure. The Conference should therefore make a firm pronouncement in favour of ideological, political and economic détente. It was regrettable that the Common Fund for Commodities had not yet begun to function; protectionism had intensified and coercive measures continued to be used in violation of contractual agreements and international law, and the United States Government continued to attempt to undermine the process of dialogue among Central American nations. The Conference should contribute to the overcoming of mutual distrust among countries with different economic systems.

4. The developing countries members of the Group of 77 had agreed to bring to the Conference a plan of action addressing different aspects of the problems facing those countries. They suggested that during the last week of the Conference a round-table meeting of delegations, including ministers, should be arranged which would discuss proposed actions and thus break through the barriers of distrust. The crisis of international confidence was serious, and the Conference offered the opportunity to remedy that situation. Although a political price might have to be paid, the potential benefits would open up prospects for co-operation and development for which future generations would be grateful.

Summary of the statement made at the 216th plenary meeting, 29 July 1987, by Mr. Nouhou AMADOU, Minister of Commerce, Industry and Transportation of the Niger

1. Mr. AMADOU said that the seventh session of the Conference was being held at a time when the foundations of the world economy were being shaken, and when all States had to demonstrate solidarity and engage in a concerted effort in the context of international economic interdependence.

2. Although the countries of the North had made progress in the fight against inflation and rising interest rates, their success had been achieved at the cost of higher unemployment and lower demand, and consequently a lower volume of international trade. Most of the developed countries had accordingly adopted protectionist measures, and the terms of trade for the countries of the South, and in particular for the African countries, had steadily deteriorated. Per capita income in Africa had declined by 12 per cent between 1980 and 1985, food imports had increased by 640 per cent over a 20-year period, and foreign debt had risen from $150 billion in 1983 to about $200 billion in 1986. In response to those difficulties, the African Governments had adopted the United Nations Programme of Action for African Economic Recovery and Development 1986-1990, approved by the General Assembly in 1986. Yet although most African countries had attempted, at great cost, to carry out structural reforms in their economies, the international community had not always demonstrated the necessary political will to mobilize the resources needed for their economic recovery. Recovery implied close co-operation between banks, debtor countries and creditor countries, increased assistance from international and regional aid bodies, and resources

enabling banks and creditor countries to assist debtor countries in overcoming their temporary lack of liquidity.

3. Since 1982, the Niger had, despite the immensity of its needs, made major strides towards economic recovery. It had also, in order to bring its balance of payments closer to equilibrium in the medium term and to achieve a rate of growth compatible with its development imperatives, concluded three stand-by arrangements with the IMF, enabling it to reschedule a large part of its foreign debt, and had, with World Bank assistance, drawn up a structural adjustment and investment programme.

4. At a time when the pace of technological change was increasing, it was appalling to note that the number of disadvantaged countries, euphemistically termed "the least developed", was increasing with every passing day. The Niger enjoyed the doubtful privilege of being such a country. The adoption of the Substantial New Programme of Action had aroused great hopes throughout the world and in the African countries in particular, but the mid-term review in 1985 had indicated that much remained to be done to attain the objectives of the Programme. The first area in which significant progress should be made was in rescheduling the long-term debt of the LDCs, which were often exporters of commodities for which prices had dropped sharply during recent years. As for debts resulting from ODA, substantial write-offs would be desirable. The second area involved increasing ODA to the LDCs to more than 0.15 per cent of GDP. In that respect, donor countries might pay particular attention to non-project-related assistance to support the balance of payments, and to finance local costs and project operating expenses. The third area concerned stabilization of the prices of raw materials and complete compensation for commodity export earnings shortfalls. The international community, and the developed countries in particular, should aim at the earliest possible entry into force of the Agreement Establishing the Common Fund for Commodities and ensure that the provisions of the Substantial New Programme of Action were applied in full.

Summary of the statement made at the 207th plenary meeting, 14 July 1987, by Mr. Alhaji Samaila MAMMAN, Minister of Trade of Nigeria

1. Mr. MAMMAN said that the developing world was facing a crisis of unprecedented gravity. For most developing countries the development process was either in limbo or in a state of severe retardation. A crushing debt burden had stifled any minimal progress. Prices of commodities had plummeted to their lowest levels for several decades. Real interest rates were still unbearably high. Exchange rates remained volatile. Financial flows, including ODA, had virtually dried up and for the first time, owing to the crippling debt-servicing burden, developing countries had become net exporters of capital to the rich industrialized countries. As a result of the debt burden, investment in infrastructure, machinery and human resources had been drastically cut. Societies and political systems were under acute strain. The LDCs were even worse off because of their structural vulnerability.

2. The preceding two years had seen a sharp decline in oil prices, which had facilitated substantial savings by the industrialized countries. However, no attempt had been made to recycle the funds so saved for development purposes. Nor had there been a corresponding reduction in the prices of manufactured goods exported by the industrialized countries. Together with the fall in prices of commodities in real terms, those factors had enabled the industrialized economies to keep their own inflation rates low without stimulating growth in the developing countries.

3. The continuing financial haemorrhage suffered by practically all developing countries had produced some very disquieting side-effects. Developing countries were thus compelled to resort to import compression, involving the abandonment of imports vital for the maintenance of industrial output. As a result, there was serious unemployment and a deterioration of living standards in developing countries, which had accentuated social tension in many of them.

4. Developing countries were confronted by growing difficulties in their trade. Market access for products of export interest to them was being continually blocked by new and more sophisticated restrictive measures adopted by industrialized nations in increasing violation of the commitments on standstill and roll-back which they had made as recently as September 1986 at Punta del Este. Protectionist measures in developed countries had virtually choked off commodity markets, with results bordering on total catastrophe for commodity-dependent economies, particularly in Africa. The increasing resort to subsidies, particularly in agriculture, by developed countries had sharply eroded the competitiveness of products of export interest to developing countries. In sectors such as textiles, the comparative advantage formerly enjoyed by developing countries had been wiped out by an array of quantitative restrictions. The benefits of the GSP were being eroded by unjustified linkage to new conditionalities in a gross violation of the principle of non-reciprocity.

5. The seventh session of the Conference provided a unique opportunity to reverse the negative trends in the interrelated fields of money, finance, trade and development. First of all, however, the increasing tendency in certain quarters to question the very basis of multilateralism and of UNCTAD's approach must be reversed. The Conference should reject current attempts to focus debate on the autonomous development policies pursued by developing countries, most of which had undertaken a painful structural adjustment programme at considerable social and political cost and still needed concrete assistance to set their economies on a path of sustainable growth and development. UNCTAD

had, and must continue to play, a decisive role in the formulation, negotiation and implementation of measures relating to international trade and its interrelation with debt, money and finance in a development context, since it was the only forum in which a truly non-discriminatory, universal and comprehensive trading system could be forged. Its unique cross-sectoral and interdisciplinary approach was ideally suited to developing such a trading system as part of the harmonious and equitable reconstruction of international economic relations. The developing countries had not deviated from their faith in the basic UNCTAD approach to growth and development, as was evident from the Havana Declaration adopted by the Group of 77 in April 1987, in which realistic and concrete proposals were put forward for remedying the ills of the global economy.

6.   The Conference would find a durable solution to the debt problem only if it acknowledged the fact that debt was a major impediment to recovery in most developing countries and a destabilizing factor in world financial markets, and that it distorted trade flows and forced the developing countries to reduce vital imports. The prevailing net flow of resources from developing to developed countries must be reversed. There was an imperative need for a political dialogue aimed at implementing a new, comprehensive debt strategy based on growth, development and shared responsibility, taking into account the close interrelationship of monetary, financial and trade issues as well as General Assembly resolution 41/202. A start could be made by tailoring debt-servicing costs to debt-servicing capacity, significantly expanding capital flows in multilateral financial institutions, easing conditionalities for borrowing by developing countries, cancelling or transforming into grants the ODA debt of the LDCs and those of sub-Saharan Africa, significantly lengthening consolidation, maturity and grace periods and reducing bank margins to a minimum in debt reschedulings, expanding the IMF Compensatory Financing Facility, and inviting States members of UNCTAD to support the early convening of an international conference on money and finance with universal participation for the purpose of reforming the international monetary and financial system.

7.   The critical situation in the commodity sector confirmed the continuing validity of the objectives and international measures agreed to in Conference resolution 93 (IV) on the Integrated Programme for Commodities, which, in view of the obvious link between the fall in earnings from commodity exports and the accumulation of debt, needed to be urgently implemented in full. Thanks were due to the USSR and Côte d'Ivoire for their decision to sign the Agreement Establishing the Common Fund for Commodities. It was to be hoped that those countries which had not yet done so would sign and ratify the Agreement. There should be improved access to markets in the major market-economy countries for products of export interest to developing

countries. Developed countries could contribute to the success of the seventh session of the Conference by entering into a political commitment to ensure the total liberalization of trade in tropical products and products derived from natural resources. The further expansion of the product coverage of the GSP without impairment of the principles upon which the system was based would also be seen by developing countries as a renewed commitment to the doctrine of interdependence.

8.   The economic ailments affecting developing countries had had their gravest impact in Africa. One full year after the adoption of the United Nations Programme of Action for African Economic Recovery and Development 1986-1990 large tracts of the continent were stagnating economically. In 1986, the first full year of the recovery programme, Africa's GDP had risen by only 1.2 per cent as compared with 3 per cent in 1985. In 1986 African Governments had made considerable efforts to escape from the crisis. In Nigeria, for example, agricultural producer prices had been freed from statutory controls in order to provide more incentives for achieving higher productivy. Food and fuel subsidies had been either drastically reduced or eliminated. Several enterprises in the public sector were undergoing far-reaching reforms and the country had embarked upon the most ambitious forms of trade liberalization and rationalization. Several other African Governments were treading the same path, all at great social and political cost.

9.   Nevertheless, the international community's response to Africa's economic plight was far from encouraging. Earnings from the continent's exports had fallen sharply, while payments on its debt had escalated. Commercial bank flows had dropped by more than two thirds. When the reduction in aid to sub-Saharan Africa was added to those considerations, it was not surprising that participants in the International Conference on Africa held at Abuja in June 1987 had concluded that Africa's continental famine and drought of 1983-1985 had been replaced by financial famine through the failure of the international community to implement its commitments. Unless African Governments were supported with adequate external resources, there was a clear danger that the growth-oriented reform process already begun would flounder, with grave economic and political consequences. It was in the interest of both the developing debtor countries and the developed creditor countries that the developing countries should grow and develop so that the resources needed for debt repayments were generated. A situation in which the debts of developing countries had to be written off because of those countries' inability to pay them could be avoided.

10.   UNCTAD should respond positively to the severe development crisis through the formulation of durable policies and measures. Either growth and development were revitalized, or else the world would slide further into economic stagnation.

**Summary of the statement made at the 214th plenary meeting, 28 July 1987,
by Mr. Thorvald STOLTENBERG, Minister for Foreign Affairs of Norway**

1. Mr. STOLTENBERG said that the progress made since UNCTAD's first session had been far from satisfactory. The field of development financing had paradoxically been characterized by a net outflow of resources from developing countries. That trend had to be reversed rapidly as a prerequisite for real progress in other areas, particularly those of debt management and economic development and diversification in countries dependent on the production of raw materials. In that connection, it was encouraging that the Venice Summit communiqué mentioned an ODA target of 0.7 per cent of GNP. Many States considered that they had done their duty by merely achieving that objective, but charity was not enough. If the problems confronting the international community were to be solved, a co-ordinated approach along the lines of the Marshall Plan would have to be adopted. That Plan had been successfully applied in post-war Europe and there was no reason why the international community should not be able to achieve equally satisfactory results at the global level in current circumstances. He supported the proposal made at the current session by the Foreign Minister of Japan to set up an independent group of eminent persons to study means of increasing financial flows, both public and private, to developing countries, bearing in mind the mandates of the international financial institutions.

2. The fact that the debt problem stemmed from a shortage of resources should suggest the changes to be made in the international community's strategy to remedy the problem. In that respect, there was an urgent need for a political dialogue. Its aim should be to identify the co-ordinated action needed to lower interest rates, ease the liquidity shortage, stabilize exchange rates, raise commodity prices and further open developed-country markets to developing-country products. Furthermore, as strong World Bank and IMF financial support had not been accompanied by any significant new financing from the commercial banks, current policy towards heavily indebted countries needed to be reassessed. A substantial increase in World Bank capital was urgently required. New allocations of special drawing rights and an upward revision of IMF quotas would also be highly desirable. Lastly, the LDCs and other low-income countries, in particular those in sub-Saharan Africa, should benefit from more radical debt-relief measures in the form of concessional finance. Specifically, debt-rescheduling conditions should be improved by lengthening the amortization period and lowering Paris Club interest rates with a view to making terms correspond better to the actual payment capabilities of those countries. Governments should also write off remaining bilateral development credits and consider, for example, creating under World Bank auspices a multilateral facility to provide special assistance to the poorest indebted countries, including possible relief from their debt to financial institutions.

3. The current situation in commodity markets was particularly detrimental to developing countries that relied on commodity exports as their main source of foreign exchange earnings. Norway therefore welcomed the likelihood that the Common Fund for Commodities would soon enter into operation, 11 years after the adoption of the Agreement by which it had been established. In 1976 the Government of Norway had already pledged $25 million to the Fund and in 1983 it had provided $5 million to cover the capital subscription for 10 developing countries. All States that had not already done so should, as a matter of urgency, complete their ratification procedures and accede to the Agreement. Although the Fund's Second Account would constitute an important source for the funding of product-linked projects, the commodity situation was nevertheless so complex that no single measure, such as the Common Fund, was likely to redress it. Norway therefore supported the appeal made by the Secretary-General of UNCTAD in his policy paper calling for interrelated and mutually supportive measures in the commodity sector. In that respect, a new round of intergovernmental consultations should be instituted to revive co-operation between producers and consumers and devise adequate remedies for each commodity. Further work should also be undertaken on a facility to compensate for commodity export earnings shortfalls and diversification programmes should be initiated for the economies of commodity-based developing countries. Lastly, UNCTAD should encourage Governments participating in the Uruguay Round to speed up commodity trade liberalization.

4. It was generally recognized that trade played a vital role in growth and development and that wider market access for developing-country exports was therefore of paramount importance. It followed that GATT and UNCTAD action should be complementary. UNCTAD could provide developing countries with technical assistance in the form of increased support in analysing the international trade situation. There was also a need for further action in favour of LDCs, perhaps including measures going beyond what was foreseen in the GATT Enabling Clause. The international community should, as a matter of urgency agree on the measures necessary to ensure that the efforts made by LDCs to reorient their domestic economic policies along the lines of the Substantial New Programme of Action were successful.

5. The international community, which comprised more than 160 countries, had before it an agenda in which all issues were of paramount importance for every nation and every region. It should therefore seek to solve its problems through multilateral action and the reinforcement of international institutions. Above all, it must act without delay.

Summary of the statement made at the 212th plenary meeting, 27 July 1987, by Mr. Ahmed bin Abdul Nabi MACKI, Under-Secretary, Ministry of Commerce and Industry of Oman

1. Mr. MACKI said that the agreement reached on the agenda and related understandings was an important step that bore witness to a growing awareness of the worsening world economic crisis which had affected trade, financial and monetary sectors. As a result of the growing interdependence of States, the economic policies of the great Powers, in particular, had a considerable influence on the economy of other countries, and above all, on that of the developing countries.

2. Oman was fully aware of the important role played by existing economic organizations, which formed an essential complement to multilateral economic co-operation, and was co-operating constructively with several of them in common areas of activity.

3. The understanding adopted at the same time as the agenda specified that consideration of economic and financial questions should not prejudice the competence of other international financial institutions and emphasized the role of the private sector in development. Oman attached great importance to the latter, since its own development was based on a free economy. His Government also considered that UNCTAD's integrated approach to development and trade had, since its establishment, constituted an important element in international economic relations and that therefore the Conference, at its seventh session, should examine the problems created by the world economic crisis. The symptoms of that crisis were growing world indebtedness, falling commodity prices which brought about a deterioration in the terms of trade of producer countries, the proliferation of protectionist measures which hampered the establishment of a trade system based on the principle of the comparative advantage conferred by human and material resources, exchange rate fluctuations, and a reduction in the flow of capital to developing countries. The consequences had been tension in international economic relations, a slowing down of world economic development and a decline in per capita income in the developing countries.

4. The only positive development appeared to be that the industrialized countries had succeeded in curbing inflation. However, on closer inspection, it became clear that commodity- and oil-producing countries had suffered greatly as a result: their loss of income had af-

fected their ability to carry out their development programmes, stabilize their balance of payments and obtain the equipment they needed for production and development. The trend had a negative impact on employment in the industrialized countries, where unemployment levels were likely to rise even more if the international community failed to take the measures necessary to stimulate the world economy. The developing countries, which took approximately one third of the combined exports of the United States of America, the European Community and Japan, had lost a large part of their purchasing power since the crisis had begun.

5. Moreover, the oil-producing countries not only contributed to world demand for goods and services, but also provided a source of financing for other countries, particularly developing countries, by means of various types of assistance, direct investment or the employment of foreign labour. Unfortunately, the decline in oil prices and the depreciation of the dollar had led to balance-of-payments deficits for those countries and thus affected their ability to help the developing countries.

6. It was essential to realize that all countries had a common destiny and that a crisis affecting one would have negative effects on the others as well, because of the integrated and interdependent nature of the world economic community. The only possible course in that context was multilateral development, which would create equitable conditions reflecting the interests of all concerned. It was essential to embark upon a constructive dialogue and show flexibility in order to agree on policies which would make it possible to tackle the world economic crisis before it was too late. The adoption and implementation of such policies would require a strong international will. The industrialized countries would have to bear much of the responsibility for that process and should contribute actively to the creation of an economic environment favourable to the revitalization of trade, development and growth. For their part, while the developing countries must certainly adopt the internal measures needed to reform their economies—that was their responsibility—it was clear that such measures, despite their high social cost, would not bear fruit in the current economic crisis.

Summary of the statement made at the 202nd plenary meeting, 10 July 1987, by Mr. Mahbub UL-HAQ, Minister for Commerce, Planning and Development of Pakistan

1. Mr. UL-HAQ said that instead of considering the unspecific agenda before the Conference, he wished to speak on the subject of UNCTAD's survival as a viable forum, since without its revival, vigorous renewal and rebirth, a general discussion of the agenda would be a largely meaningless exercise. The question he would consider was why an organization created so enthusiastically 23 years earlier was faced with a survival

crisis, and what had gone wrong. In his view, three fatal errors had been made during its brief history. The first was that UNCTAD had become a partisan secretariat for the third world rather than an honest mediator between developing and developed countries and had come to be viewed by the latter as an advocacy forum rather than a serious and trustworthy negotiating forum. Although there was nothing wrong in pleading the cause of third world development, UNCTAD's skill lay in convincing the developed nations that reasonable solutions could be found through reasonable dialogue. Even continued support for UNCTAD by the developing countries depended on its effectiveness.

2. The second fatal error had been that UNCTAD had concerned itself with the wrong issues. Its only real initiatives had been taken in the early phase, with the establishment of the ODA target of 1 per cent of GNP, the GSP and the framework for multilateral commodity agreements for individual commodities. The 1970s and 1980s had been largely dominated by non-issues. Much energy and political capital had been spent in the 1970s on the establishment of an unsound common fund, as if the most important issue for the developing countries had been the stabilization of their commodity prices. It was ironical that such a priority had come from an organization that should have been seeking trade expansion and diversification rather than the stabilization of past patterns of specialization. By the time it had stumbled on to some real issues of development, such as an orderly framework for reducing protectionism, promoting adjustment through growth and restructuring of debt profiles, other institutions had already taken the policy initiatives that should rightfully have come from UNCTAD.

3. The third fatal error had been that developed and developing countries alike had been content to use UNCTAD as a debating society rather than a serious negotiating forum. No international forum could remain effective for long without a defined mandate to negotiate between nations, and without financial backing for its advice. UNCTAD's effectiveness would depend on the specific role allocated to it in the implementation of the Baker plan for debt relief or any other international action on indebtedness, and on whether it controlled any specific adjustment facility or whether it shared such control with another international institution. The fact that UNCTAD was to have no negotiating role in the Uruguay Round, even in the trade and services areas directly within its competence, was sadly indicative of its declining fortunes.

4. All those fatal errors were closely interconnected. If UNCTAD was to be revived as a viable forum, a small ministerial-level task force must be established to seek a consensus of leading nations on its future role and direction.

5. While UNCTAD was being restructured as a more effective forum, it was also necessary to pursue a programme of change. There were six areas in which action could be taken if an international consensus through constructive dialogue could be arrived at. First, a debt refinancing facility should be established under the auspices of the World Bank and IMF, funded by new special drawing rights, to restructure the third world debt profiles through a number of viable schemes such as zero coupon bonds, debt-service capping and the linking of future debt payments to increases in trade.

6. Secondly, the end of 1988 should be accepted as a time-limit for identifying and implementing an integrated package of early action proposals under the Uruguay Round, covering, for example, agricultural protectionism, reciprocity, dispute settlement, safeguards and services.

7. Thirdly, the compensatory finance facility should be enlarged to compensate developing countries more liberally for the prolonged slump in their commodity prices. The existing IMF facility should be expanded for the coming two years, during which the establishment of a supplementary facility in UNCTAD should be considered.

8. Fourthly, the World Bank should once again become a major net lender to developing countries, particularly in Latin America and East Asia, and should sever its lending rate from the unpredictable fluctuations in commercial markets, finance adjustment through growth by more non-project lending and resume its role as a development bank.

9. Fifthly, the concessional funds of IDA and other multilateral and bilateral sources should be earmarked almost exclusively for the long-term development of the poorest nations in Africa and of the LDCs while a new intermediate facility should be established for the resurgent nations of South Asia and China.

10. Sixthly, Japan should be encouraged to find a suitable institutional mechanism for recycling its accumulating foreign exchange surpluses to the developing countries.

11. In all those areas international efforts should be made in the appropriate forums, but a new atmosphere of confidence could be created if the discussions in the Conference were used to seek a growing consensus on proposals for action. The major question of UNCTAD's real mandate remained, however, and a satisfactory answer to it must be found during the session. It was essential to make a new beginning; the developing countries should show their interest in seeking sensible solutions for their genuine trade and development problems rather than merely criticizing the North, and the developed countries should show theirs in using UNCTAD as a negotiating forum with a defined mandate, rhetoric being replaced by serious and respectful dialogue. A continuation of the existing atmosphere of confrontation would end whatever remained of UNCTAD's original promise. That must not be allowed to happen, since UNCTAD symbolized the hopes and dreams of billions of people in the developing world.

Summary of the statement made at the 218th plenary meeting, 30 July 1987,
by Mr. Marcos A. VILLARREAL, Permanent Representative of Panama to the United Nations Office at Geneva

1. Mr. VILLARREAL said that UNCTAD, by its nature and the instruments at its disposal, was in a position to contribute to a consensus between countries on the issues before it at the current session of the Conference. That consensus might generate progress in areas beyond purely economic growth, although such growth was a necessary adjunct to other types of growth in the various spheres of human endeavour. The Panamanian delegation was aware that the crisis in the world had brought the viability of UNCTAD's activities into question. It therefore wished to reaffirm, by its presence and participation as a State member of UNCTAD, the need for international co-operation in the various fields of competence of UNCTAD, whose existence, activities, potential and results depended on the good will of all member States.

2. Some of the items on the agenda of the seventh session related to Panama's special concerns, while others referred to problems which Panama shared with the other developing countries. In respect of resources for development, Panama considered that external indebtedness had created an inverse flow of resources which paralysed growth in all developing societies. The international financial institutions must understand that the problem had passed from the purely economic sphere to the political and social sphere, and that concerted efforts would be required to resolve it. External debt was a shared responsibility which required the creditor countries to understand that debtor countries could not keep up their efforts at the cost of a deterioration in social relations that could threaten the very stability of the Government as well as the institutions and mechanisms of fraternal coexistence.

3. On the subject of commodities, Panama's concerns were the same as those of all the other countries which depended on exports to honour their external financial commitments and finance their development plans and programmes. The effective implementation of the Integrated Programme for Commodities and the entry into force of the Agreement Establishing the Common Fund for Commodities were necessary preconditions for the beginnings of a solution to the intolerable situation of the developing countries. As for international trade, a kind of irrational fear that the developing countries' problems would spread throughout the world had given rise to many forms of protectionism, which were also nurtured by the national or regional egoism that was partly responsible for the current crisis. Trade had always promoted brotherhood among peoples; if that fact was overlooked, a valuable instrument for promoting international peace would be lost. For that reason, it was essential to adopt multilateral trade instruments that would facilitate market access and, at the same time, give all countries an equal share in permanent and flexible trade arrangements without any obstacles but those imposed by nature.

4. The difficult economic and social situation of the LDCs kept them in a state of crisis, which gave rise to constraints that placed the people of those countries at the mercy of disease, ignorance, hunger and many other evils. Panama had consistently stood by those countries, and reaffirmed its desire to do everything possible to help solve their problems. Considerable efforts would have to be made before the end of the current session, but he was sure that the results achieved, which were the responsibility of all participants, would show that the moral obligations imposed by the crisis had received some response.

Summary of the statement made at the 218th plenary meeting, 30 July 1987,
by Mr. Samuel ABAL, Assistant Secretary, Department of Trade and Industry of Papua New Guinea

1. Mr. ABAL said that his Government attached great importance to its membership of UNCTAD and hoped that at the current session the Conference would adopt policies and measures to address the adverse factors threatening the world economy and aggravating the crisis. Like many other developing countries, Papua New Guinea was heavily dependent on a few commodities, which accounted for a large proportion of the national income. The instability of commodity prices affected not only government revenue but also, and above all, the living conditions of thousands of small commodity producers. For that reason, Papua New Guinea supported any measure likely to promote the stability of the international commodity sector, and particularly the Integrated Programme for Commodities. It had signed and ratified the Agreement establishing the Common Fund for Commodities five years previously, and welcomed the recent signature of the USSR, Côte d'Ivoire and Peru.

2. Referring to the subject of financial resources, he said that capital flows to the developing countries must be increased if the objective of structural adjustment for growth, advocated by the Conference, was to be achieved. Although Papua New Guinea had enjoyed relatively bright prospects in the past, the situation had deteriorated over recent years, and its external debt was now relatively high in comparison with its GDP. The Government had attempted to reduce the debt by making no provision for new borrowing in the current budget; it remained to be seen what effects that policy would have on growth.

3. Papua New Guinea welcomed the Japanese Government's intention to recycle its surpluses to the

developing countries. It also welcomed any increase in private investment in order to provide an impetus for growth. However, his country believed that financial assistance should be only a short-term measure and that, in the long term, it must be replaced by trade. A just, equitable and stable international trading system would allow countries to find their place in the world. For Papua New Guinea, trade was the only way to achieve sustained growth, and the Government had therefore liberalized trade and was trying to manage an open economy. A healthy trade environment could only encourage growth and development; it was essential that the Governments taking part in the Uruguay Round should not forget the vital link between trade and development.

4. Turning to the question of the least developed of the land-locked and island countries in the Pacific subregion, he said that Papua New Guinea supported the position of the Group of 77 on measures in favour of those countries. The special situation of the Pacific island countries, some of which were LDCs, called for particular attention. The factors which distinguished them—small markets, geographical isolation, high transport costs, an economy dependent on a single commodity, vulnerability to natural disasters and remoteness from cheap sources of supply and export markets—had a direct effect on their growth and development. His delegation therefore hoped that the Conference would take due account of those factors when adopting international measures. It also expressed its gratitude to the European Community countries and

countries of the Pacific region, such as Australia, New Zealand and Japan, for their continued assistance, which should, however, be supplemented by more predictable assistance in order to ensure the economic diversification of island countries.

5. Despite the apparent lack of political will at the current session of the Conference and the fact that the issues under discussion were hardly new, it was to be hoped that the seventh session would achieve the success that was needed to reaffirm UNCTAD's role as a key international forum. A firm date for the entry into force of the Common Fund for Commodities would be a good thing, but specific commitments on capital flows and international trade, as well as commitments towards the LDCs were also required.

6. Papua New Guina noted with satisfaction that a symposium for the private sector had been held before the current session; that was a welcome development, since the private sector and TNCs were an integral part of the international trade system. Their practices affected trade and development in developing countries, and more should therefore be done to advise and assist Governments in that respect. His country also appreciated the enormous amount of work done so discreetly by the non-governmental organizations, which complemented the development activities of Governments, particularly in rural areas. His country wished to express its appreciation of UNCTAD's work and the assistance it had provided in some vital areas, particularly in connection with the GSP.

**Summary of the statement made at the 216th plenary meeting, 29 July 1987,
by Mr. José LEY-ELIAS, Vice-President of the Institute of Foreign Trade of Peru**

1. Mr. LEY-ELIAS said that UNCTAD's principal objective was to promote the establishment of a stable economic system that met the concerns of the developing countries; unfortunately, UNCTAD's recommendations had not been applied in a concerted and consistent manner by the developed countries and had therefore not had the desired results. His Government opposed any action likely to transform UNCTAD into an academic forum that would lose sight of the basic principles of international solidarity and mulitateralism. The current unprecedented economic crisis constituted a very real threat to the economies of the developing countries in particular and was widening the gap between rich and poor countries even further. For example the prices of commodities other than petroleum had dropped 30 per cent in real terms between 1980 and 1986, falling to the lowest level since the 1930s, and World Bank and IMF forecasts for the year 2000 hardly presaged improvement.

2. The debt problem was even more serious. Extremely high interest rates and stringent debt-service conditions had entailed an enormous increase in indebtedness, which had risen from the equivalent of 130 per cent of the export earnings of developing countries in 1980 to 213 per cent in 1986. For that reason, many developing countries were experiencing large net

outflows of capital to the developed countries, and the world was in an intolerable situation where the poor countries were financing the economies of the industrialized countries. In the circumstances, his Government had been obliged to restrict repayment of its foreign debt to the equivalent of 10 per cent of its export earnings so as to permit the resumption of economic growth in the country.

3. Apart from the problems of commodity prices and indebtedness, the developing countries were still hampered in their efforts by the resurgence of protectionist measures imposed by the industrialized countries in violation of their international undertakings.

4. Unless practical steps were taken urgently, it would become quite impossible to close the steadily widening gap between the developed and developing countries. In the commodities sector, the prices of the developing countries' exports should be fixed at a fair level, and in that connection the Peruvian Government attached great importance to the implementation in full of the objectives in the Integrated Programme for Commodities, and was pleased to announce that it would that very day deposit its instrument of ratification of the Agreement Establishing the Common Fund for Commodities with the Secretary-General of UNCTAD.

5. In international trade, the developed countries had recognized the existence of a link between trade and development and had clearly affirmed, in the Ministerial Declaration adopted at Punta del Este, that the developing countries, and particularly the most indebted countries, needed a better trading environment to enable them to meet their international obligations. They had also given undertakings in respect of standstill and roll-back measures and it was regrettable that a few months later certain industrial countries had violated them by imposing restrictive measures. The multilateral machinery for monitoring standstill and roll-back commitments must be brought into play to help correct disparities in international trade.

6. Developing countries which benefited from the GSP were now being required to grant concessions if they wished to continue taking advantage of the system; such requirements were in flagrant violation of the principles of non-discrimination and non-reciprocity. UNCTAD must, in that respect, draw attention to the original intent of the system and take steps to ensure that third world countries derived the greatest possible benefit from it.

7. The foreign debt burden was a considerable constraint on the development of debtor countries. The problem must therefore be solved as a matter of urgency by all those concerned in the context of a political dialogue based on recognition of the right of all countries to development and taking into consideration the debtor countries' real capacity to pay. The implications of indebtedness were the responsibility of creditor countries as well as of debtor countries, and the cost of a return to stability should be borne by both groups alike.

8. The international community was aware that the situation of the LDCs was deteriorating from day to day and that their very survival was threatened. For that reason the policies and measures adopted in their favour must be applied as rapidly as possible. The principles of non-discrimination and free access to markets in the developed countries must also be respected, and a more equitable financial and monetary system established.

9. The developing countries would certainly benefit from the Common Fund for Commodities when it started operation, as well as from the recycling of financial surpluses proposed by the Japanese Government. Nevertheless, those steps forward were not sufficient, and it was to be hoped that genuine commitments would be forthcoming concerning concerted and effective international action in the area of development resources, commodities, international trade and the problems of the LDCs.

Summary of the statement made at the 209th plenary meeting, 15 July 1987, by Mr. José D. INGLES, First Under-Secretary of Foreign Affairs, Department of Foreign Affairs of the Philippines

1. Mr. INGLES said that in the common quest for growth and development in a predictable and supportive international environment his delegation sought co-operative action in resolving the problems confronting all countries; the purpose of the Conference was to unite member States in efforts to work out agreed and practical solutions to the world economic crisis. Although his delegation would press for the adoption of the set of policies and measures proposed by the Group of 77, it would be prepared to examine in an accommodating spirit other solutions that it considered to be in the common interest. His delegation attached great importance to the Uruguay Round as an opportunity for halting the drift towards disorder in international trade and restoring momentum to trade liberalization and expansion. UNCTAD could play an important role in fostering an international trade régime based on the principles of universality and non-discrimination, and on non-reciprocity and special differential treatment with respect to developing countries. He hoped, furthermore, that the concern expressed by some developed countries about rising protectionism and non-compliance with standstill and roll-back commitments would be reflected in proposals for correcting the asymmetrical patterns of growth and development.

2. His delegation appealed to the OECD countries to translate their encouraging declarations, notably those made at the Venice economic summit, into concrete action, for instance by renewing intergovernmental efforts to broaden the as yet limited scope of compensatory financing and by using their influence within the World Bank group to increase lending for agriculture-based industries in developing countries.

3. The Philippines was experiencing difficulties in servicing its foreign debt. Hence it attached the greatest importance to the pursuit of a coherent policy for an effective and just solution to the grave debt problem. Although much remained to be desired in the proposals put forward for increasing the resources of the IMF Structural Adjustment Facility and the capital of the World Bank, they were steps in the right direction, as was the recent decision by Japan to make more resources available to developing countries. He hoped that the Conference would agree on an appropriate mechanism for putting those proposals into practice without delay. It was gratifying to note that it was generally agreed that the development efforts of the LDCs should be supported by the international community through full and effective implementation of the Substantial New Programme of Action for the 1980s for the Least Developed Countries and other complementary measures. The positions with respect to the current world economic crisis adopted by the socialist countries of Eastern Europe, including the Soviet Union, as well as the position adopted by China, and the decision by the Soviet Union to join the Common Fund for Commodities, reflected a recognition of the continuing validity of the proposals of the Group of 77. It was not

enough, however, to recognize their validity; they should also be adopted and implemented. To that end, the co-operation of the Group's negotiating partners was necessary. Because such co-operation had been lacking in the past, the very existence of UNCTAD itself as a forum for the accommodation of differences had been placed in doubt.

4. His delegation hoped that agreement would be reached on an international debt strategy, which might include the following features: improving rescheduling exercises by extending repayment, grace and consolidation periods and taking account of the export earnings of developing countries; differentiating existing debt from new credit for the purpose of determining interest rates; establishing a new, expanded IMF credit facility with a view to alleviating the debt-service burden; expanding the Compensatory Financing Facility; pursuing and improving the enlarged access policy; advancing the ninth review of quotas; enhancing flows of foreign investment to developing countries; halting the net transfers of resources from developing to developed countries and international financial institutions, and restoring and increasing net financial flows to developing countries through greater international co-operation in the monetary and financial fields.

5. The outcome of the Conference would be judged by the extent to which it succeeded in achieving the objectives he had outlined.

Summary of the statement made at the 203rd plenary meeting, 10 July 1987, by Mr. Andrzej WOJCIK, Minister for Foreign Trade of Poland

1. Mr. WOJCIK said that the seventh session of the Conference was the most important forum for a debate on economic issues in 1987. It also had a political dimension, for peace and security were the precondition for harmonious economic development and growth, and for that reason the Conference was followed with close attention by Poland and other socialist countries. He voiced the hope that the recent Polish proposal for reducing armaments and building confidence in Europe, known as the Jaruzelski plan, would contribute to an easing of tension in East-West political relations.

2. Among the issues on the agenda that were critical to the revival of international trade and world economic growth, he commented more specifically on those concerning international trade and resources for development. Since the performance of the world economy in the 1980s was obviously insufficient to reduce poverty and unemployment in the world, internationally compatible policy actions were badly needed, and the seventh session of the Conference provided an opportunity for co-ordinating those actions which, given the necessary political will, could launch the process of change. The function of international trade as the major vehicle for revitalizing development and growth was unfortunately not reflected in the policies of all countries. It was regrettable that in response to external challenges a number of countries turned to greater protectionism and more inward-looking policies which effectively precluded the operation of the market mechanism in several product sectors. Trade in those sectors was being managed in ways that favoured the stronger partners and limited or stifled structural adjustment; moreover, restrictions were sometimes imposed for purely political reasons. His own country had suffered from such restrictions. Such attitudes to trade and structural adjustment were criticized from within the developed market-economy countries as well, as was attested by the OECD study entitled *Costs and benefits of protection*, published in 1985. A change in thinking was needed to ensure the success of the Uruguay Round.

3. The question of resources for development was directly connected with the international trade issue and protectionism. Poland was one of the debtor countries and considered that unhindered access to other countries' markets, especially those of developed market economies, and just solutions of debt repayment issues were indispensable for the purpose of generating the necessary resources for development.

4. He considered that a favourable external environment for development should be supplemented by effective internal efforts in all countries; the form which such efforts might take could vary from country to country. His Government was in favour of pragmatic solutions. The economic reform process initiated in Poland in the early 1980s was based on the transfer of economic decision-making from the State to firms and a better use of market mechanisms to enhance the efficiency of the national economy. Policy objectives concentrated on the attainment of higher productivity and the speeding up of scientific and technological progress and structural change, contributing to an expansion of the role of foreign trade and so fostering the development of the Polish economy and providing necessary earnings for debt servicing. It was his Government's firm policy to develop trade relations, on a basis of non-discrimination and mutual benefit, with all countries, in particular the developing countries, and it was hoped that the structural changes under way in those countries, including the diversification and expansion of their exports, would be reflected in their trade with Poland.

5. The seventh session of the Conference upheld the tradition of universality and set out to assess world economic issues and formulate appropriate policy recommendations. The revitalization of international trade, development and growth was in the common interest of all, and his Government and delegation would spare no effort in contributing to the achievement of those goals.

Summary of the statement made at the 215th plenary meeting, 28 July 1987, by Mr. Fernando A. SANTOS MARTINS, Minister of Industry and Trade of Portugal

1. Mr. SANTOS MARTINS said that the seventh session of the conference was the first in which Portugal had taken part as a member State of the EEC; in that capacity it had taken an active part in the preparation of the proposals submitted by the Community to help the Conference reach a successful outcome. The Community had an exemplary record in trade and development as was evidenced by the effectiveness of the Lomé Convention; during the negotiations on the Protocol extending the Convention, Portugal had made considerable efforts to meet the wishes of the African, Caribbean and Pacific countries.

2. Apart from its participation in the Community's efforts, Portugal was continuing its bilateral activities, such as those on behalf of the African countries with Portuguese as their official language. Despite the problems of structural adjustment involved in adapting to the Community, Portugal was making every effort to help those countries solve their acute difficulties. Concerned by the critical situation in the African countries, Portugal had endorsed the conclusions of the special session of the General Assembly on the subject. It had at the same time drawn attention to the need to correct existing imbalances in such countries, for they could exacerbate a state of tension that was incompatible with hopes for international peace and prosperity. Among means for assisting African economies, attention should be drawn to the importance of regional co-operation and in particular to the Southern African Development Co-ordination Conference, in which Portugal participated with great interest.

3. The situation of other developing countries in Asia and Latin America also gave cause for concern. In Latin America, increasing attention was being paid by the EEC to finding new and more creative means of assisting development.

4. A major item on the agenda of the seventh session dealt with resources for development, both as a whole and from their financial, human and technical aspects. Such resources were of key importance and were closely linked to all other variables influencing economic growth. It was therefore important that the international community recognized the need for concerted action to deal with the problem of external imbalances and its repercussions on the indebtedness of the developing countries. Such action should facilitate access by such countries to an adequate level of external investment on appropriate terms. In any event, the solutions adopted would have to take account of the economic, social and political features of each country concerned and satisfy the rules governing the international economic and financial system.

5. In order to promote sustained economic growth, countries that had built up large external deficits would have to make a determined effort to achieve structural reform and to mobilize all possible domestic savings with a view to productive investment. A number of developing countries had already embarked on such a

course. Although primary responsibility for domestic adjustment lay with the countries concerned, such adjustment could succeed only if it enjoyed appropriate international technical and financial assistance, provided either on a bilateral basis or through international development aid bodies. In that regard, he stressed the importance of private investment and integrated programmes of co-operation based on technical assistance aimed at making better use of the human and natural resources of the developing countries.

6. Portugal was not a major producer of commodities but it was profoundly aware of the adverse effects depressed commodity prices were having on the economies of the exporting countries. It considered that the difficulties faced by those countries should be tackled jointly by producers and consumers. It further believed that horizontal and vertical diversification of the economies of the commodity-producing countries was the only way to overcome their over-dependence on commodities and to combat the instability of commodity markets, which should work towards complete transparency and a better balance between supply and demand. The Portuguese Government, for its part, had decided to lose no time in ratifying the Agreement Establishing the Common Fund for Commodities, which should help to bring about structural change in the sector. Portugal considered that there should be a case-by-case evaluation of individual commodity agreements to remove certain adverse effects that had become apparent in recent years and that current market trends should be taken into account in that connection. Producers and consumers should take joint action to establish machinery to increase the transparency of commodity markets.

7. In recent years, on the basis of its membership in the European Community, Portugal had been engaged in a process of domestic deregulation and of opening up to external access that was virtually unequalled among the market-economy countries of the Northern Hemisphere. At an intermediate level of development but belonging to one of the largest and most developed economic zones, Portugal was well placed to appreciate the advantages offered by closer economic and trading relations between various countries and regions. At the international level, an event of the utmost significance was the Uruguay Round, in which action against protectionism was associated with measures for structural adjustment. Those negotiations should lead to a radical change in international economic relations, which should in the final analysis ensure the future well-being and full development of all countries. Portugal was pledged to the success of the Uruguay Round and reaffirmed its support of the Punta del Este Declaration. The ultimate success of the Round would depend on concerted action by all participating countries within the limits of their capabilities and in accordance with the graduation principle.

8. With regard to the LDCs, Portugal, which had very close relations with some of them, considered that

the international community had a duty to help them find ways to promote economic growth. However, the primary responsibility for their development lay with the LDCs themselves; they should therefore adapt their institutional structures and procedures to make the best use of external assistance. As part of its bilateral assistance to a number of LDCs, Portugal had set up various co-operative programmes to promote the social and economic development of the countries concerned and quickly improve the living conditions of their peoples. Those programmes were supplemented by providing an ongoing stimulus for both public and private enterprises, for example by encouraging the establishment of joint undertakings in economic sectors of prime importance to national development. As part of its financial co-operation, Portugal had for a number of years been promoting loans on particularly favourable terms to a number of the LDCs. It had also rescheduled commercial debts and consolidated other debts in a manner highly advantageous to the recipient countries.

9. The seventh session of the Conference had shown that although all were determined to lay the foundations for development, views differed on the best way to proceed. The United Nations, by virtue of its universality, provided an ideal setting for a useful exchange of view on the subject even though the designation of specific measures would have to be left to specialized bodies.

Summary of the statement made at the 210th plenary meeting, 24 July 1987, by Mr. Kwang Soo CHOI, Minister for Foreign Affairs of the Republic of Korea

1. Mr. CHOI said that among UNCTAD's major contributions to world economic progress were the establishment of the GSP, the adoption of the Integrated Programme for Commodities, its contribution to the adoption of the Substantial New Programme of Action for the 1980s for the Least Developed Countries, and the part it had played in drawing public attention to various issues and influencing policies and action in national capitals and international institutions.

2. One distinctive feature of the international economy was a growing interdependence among various economic sectors. Interdependence among countries was also increasing as a result of international trade and the expansion of capital flows. The survival and prosperity of any one country had become interlinked with the survival and prosperity of others. The world economy could not be revitalized by developed countries alone: their efforts must be co-ordinated with the development efforts of developing countries. He therefore reaffirmed his Government's strong support for the activities of UNCTAD, which must continue to play a vital role in world economic development and must be given every support.

3. The global economy in the 1980s was characterized by a sharp decline in commodity prices, a proliferation of protectionist trends, instability of exchange rates, rises in real interest rates, serious debt problems and low economic growth. Despite all the efforts to co-ordinate the macro-economic policies of the major economic Powers, it was difficult to find an effective solution to such problems. The prevailing situation affected most severely the developing countries, whose access to markets was, moreover, impeded by ever-rising protectionism in some developed countries.

4. The deterioration of terms of trade due to declining commodity prices had reduced the development resources of the developing countries and their capacity to service external debts, with the consequences that many of them had been forced to cut back their development projects. As a further consequence they had sharply reduced imports from the developed countries, which in turn had thereby suffered an increase in unemployment.

5. Although it was the primary responsibility of developing countries to develop their own economies, the magnitude and complexity of the problems besetting the prevailing international economic situation were such that those countries were unable to achieve development by their own efforts alone. Only effective multilateral dialogue and co-operation among all countries would make it possible to initiate practical and effective policies and measures to cope with the problems. Despite the difficulties, a new impetus could be given to UNCTAD's activities if all countries participating in the Conference made every effort to reach desirable and practical solutions.

6. The growing protectionist trend was impeding the smooth expansion of world trade. Instead of restructuring their own industries, many developed countries often adopted restrictive measures against imports of various products for which the developing countries had comparative advantages. He was particularly concerned at the concentration of protectionist pressures on a few developing countries that had withstood difficult economic situations. That trend appeared to be based on the so-called graduation concept, a concept which hampered the sustained growth of the developing countries concerned at a time when they needed to grow in order to be able to service their debts and pay for further development projects. The graduation concept, which could be interpreted to mean that developing countries should always remain underdeveloped, would introduce confrontation rather than co-operation into future North-South relations.

7. It was the developing countries that had the primary responsibility for solving the current world economic problems. It was argued in some quarters that a greater share of that responsibility should be accepted by the newly industrializing countries; actually, those countries were doing their utmost within their economic capabilities to preserve an open world trading system.

8. The major trading countries were making increased use of bilateral negotiations instead of seeking multilateral solutions to current trade problems. He hoped that the outcome of the Uruguay Round would be fair to all sides and would contribute to the expan-

sion of trade through the establishment of an improved multilateral trading system. All countries should endeavour to maintain the momentum of the Uruguay Round and halt the deterioration in the trade environment by honouring their standstill and roll-back commitments. Matters of particular concern to developing countries should be fully reflected in the negotiations with a view to establishing a viable and durable trading order that would favour the expansion of world trade and promote exports from developing countries.

9.   Trade between countries having different economic and social systems needed to be encouraged as part of efforts to ensure a balanced growth of world trade. It was for that reason that his Government had been applying an open-door policy towards all countries since the early 1970s; it had, for example, been according most-favoured-nation treatment to the socialist countries since 1982.

10.   The serious worsening debt problem of many developing countries had resulted in a net outflow of their already scarce resources, with the consequence that many of them had had to scale down their development projects; such action had in turn given rise to increased economic and social tension. Despite international efforts, no satisfactory solution to the debt problem was in sight. A joint effort among creditor and debtor countries, international financial institutions and private banks was needed, supplemented by an increased flow of direct investments, ODA and development credits to developing countries from developed countries.

11.   The persistent decline in prices of commodities which accounted for a large share of the exports of many developing countries, had substantially reduced the export earnings of those countries and added to the difficulties affecting their development efforts. The stabilization of commodity prices would ultimately benefit all countries, and the implementation of the Integrated Programme for Commodities, together with the early entry into operation of the Common Fund, was thus vitally important. His Government had ratified the Agreement Establishing the Common Fund in 1982

and had pledged itself at the sixth session of the Conference to contribute voluntarily to the Second Account of the Fund.

12.   The current international economic environment most severely affected the LDCs, whose number had increased from 31 in 1981 to 40 in 1986. He urged that the Substantial New Programme of Action should be implemented fully and expeditiously and that the financial flow to those countries should be significantly increased, primarily in the form of grants or highly concessional loans.

13.   Despite its unfavourable economic situation, shortage of natural resources and external indebtedness, his country would continue to pursue its liberalization policy by opening its market, reducing tariff and nontariff barriers, liberalizing its rules governing foreign investment and readjusting its exchange rates, in line with the global efforts to improve the international economic environment and expand world trade. It had endeavoured to contribute to the development of developing countries by sharing with them the experience it had accumulated in its own national development process over the preceding 25 years.

14.   His Government had provided training in various fields for persons from developing countries and had sent out Korean experts and consultants. South-South economic and technical co-operation had become an integral part of its foreign policy, and it had established an economic development co-operation fund for the purpose.

15.   In the pursuit of common prosperity, what was required was not confrontation but mutual co-operation and immediate and specific action. The existing economic difficulties were a major challenge to mankind. Successful collective efforts to meet the challenge could provide the necessary stimulus to further progress. He hoped that participants in the Conference from both South and North would usher in a new era of sustained economic growth and prosperity by formulating and implementing an imaginative programme, based on mutual understanding and co-operation.

Summary of the statement made at the 208th plenary meeting, 14 July 1987, by Mr. Ilie VADUVA, Minister of Foreign Trade and International Economic Co-operation of Romania

1.   Mr. VADUVA said that the message sent by the President of Romania* eloquently reflected the importance which his country attached to UNCTAD's work. The session was being held at a time when the world economic crisis was continuing unabated and was even deepening, with harmful effects for all countries. Growth in the developing countries was being curtailed by the maintenance and intensification of protectionist trends, the substantial fall in commodity prices, the deterioration of the terms of trade, the reduction of financial flows and the alarming increase in external indebtedness, high real interest rates and unstable exchange rates. Instead of shrinking, the economic and

technological gaps between developed and developing countries were widening. In fact, as the Sixth Ministerial Meeting of the Group of 77 had concluded, the 1980s could be considered a lost decade for development.

2.   Economic progress required that the developing countries should intensify their efforts to implement national economic and social development programmes, but the world had become so interdependent economically that those efforts needed to be supported by international co-operation based on equality and respect for the sovereignty and independence of every country. However, international co-operation was flagging, action to implement important recommendations adopted in the United Nations, including UNCTAD, was lacking, and there was a disquieting tendency for

---

* TD/L.280 (see volume I, annex IV).

some developed countries to replace the universal framework of the United Nations by forums with restricted participation.

3. In such circumstances it was more than ever necessary to intensify multilateral co-operation for development and to build the new international economic order. UNCTAD's role and effectiveness needed to be strengthened, perhaps through the establishment of a special commission which, on the basis of proposals made during the session, would prepare specific proposals for the solution of general economic problems. The President of Romania, Mr. Nicolae Ceausescu, had stressed the need for rich and poor countries to settle their problems together. The proposals made by the Ministerial Meeting of the Group of 77 held at Havana were a source of inspiration in the search for solutions acceptable to all countries.

4. A major topic of the Conference was the external indebtedness of the developing countries, for the purely technical and selective approaches adopted in recent years had not provided an appropriate and lasting solution. The problem called for a political and economic solution in a global framework, and such a solution could not be found without the participation of all countries, both developed and developing, and of IMF, the World Bank and other international financial institutions, as well as the commercial banks. The solution should be based on criteria and principles that took into account the level of development of the debtor countries, their repayment capacity, and the efforts which they had to make to promote their economic and social progress. In particular, it should envisage the cancellation of the debt of the poorest countries, a substantial reduction in the debt of other developing countries, the long-term rescheduling of the debt at reduced rates of interest or even without interest, the limitation of debt-servicing payments to a given proportion of export earnings, a reduction of interest rates for loans received in the past, and the granting of new loans to developing countries on generous terms. Disarmament would

release resources that could be used for financial assistance to the developing countries. Concrete measures were necessary to secure a general reduction in interest rates, including those charged by the World Bank and IMF, and to restructure, with the participation of all countries, the international monetary and financial system so that it would stimulate economic growth.

5. The Conference should contribute to the efforts being made to halt protectionist trends, to liberalize international trade, and to strengthen and improve the world trading system. For that purpose it would be desirable to reaffirm the earlier commitments concerning standstill and roll-back of restrictive measures. Also, the Trade and Development Board might evaluate the proceedings and results of the Uruguay Round of multilateral trade negotiations, as had been done in the case of the Tokyo Round. If the objectives of the GSP were to be achieved, it was essential that it should be substantially improved and that the principles of non-discrimination and non-reciprocity should be strictly applied. UNCTAD should also reaffirm the need to abolish the practice of imposing trade restrictions and sanctions for political reasons, which was incompatible with the principles of international law and with resolutions adopted within the United Nations, including UNCTAD. The international trading system should be based on the effective implementation of most-favoured-nation treatment, non-discrimination, and preferential treatment for the developing countries. Specific recommendations should be adopted for the implementation of the Integrated Programme for Commodities, based on the legitimate interests of all countries, as well as specific measures to implement the Substantial New Programme of Action for the 1980s for the Least Developed Countries. The assistance granted to all developing countries should be increased.

6. He pledged his delegation's co-operation in concerted efforts to achieve positive results at the current session.

Summary of the statement made at the 215th plenary meeting, 28 July 1987, by Mr. Soleiman EL SALEEM, Minister of Commerce of Saudi Arabia

1. Mr. EL SALEEM said that the seventh session of the Conference gave grounds for hope that the countries of the North and of the South, meeting once again, would be able to learn lessons of a realistic and responsible nature from the past, give a new lease of life to UNCTAD and adopt a joint course of action to facilitate attainment of the objectives of international co-operation.

2. Regardless of differences of opinion on the nature and causes of the economic crisis, all the countries affected should as a matter of urgency do everything in their power to overcome it. In addition, the members of the international community, and in particular world market leaders, should undertake to establish a stable and transparent external environment

in which the principles of free trade and equity prevailed.

3. Like other developing countries, Saudi Arabia had been affected by changing external economic conditions that had forced it to make internal adjustments and to adopt appropriate economic and financial policies. As a result of such adjustment, it had emerged from the period of depressed economic activity without any significant set-back and could now discern indications of recovery. Saudi Arabia owed its good fortune to active co-operation and mutual support between the public and private sectors, the latter having been given practical incentives to join in national development. Through its growth—with an output of no less than 53 per cent of real GNP—diversification and keen sense of

responsibility, the private sector had undoubtedly made a major contribution to the success of the development process in Saudi Arabia. Saudi experience also showed how important it was to create favourable conditions for external and domestic investment and to encourage such investment by, for example supporting the financial market and the banking sector. With three development plans successfully completed and a fourth in the course of implementation, Saudi Arabia had been able in the context of a balanced growth strategy, to achieve many goals including diversification of the economy and development of the industrial, agricultural and mining sectors.

4. Unfortunately, its efforts to establish a petrochemincal industry and diversify its economy had been hampered by the protectionist practices of the major industrialized countries; such practices were incompatible with the principles of free trade and recent undertakings given in international forums. He therefore hoped that the Uruguay Round, given positive encouragement at the seventh session of the Conference, would reach a consensus on standstill and rollback measures with a view to encouraging international trade, promoting equitable relations among trading partners and strengthening the multilateral trading system.

5. During the 1980s, commodity markets had been notable for their considerable instability, structural change and steadily falling prices. The oil market had been no exception; the prices of oil products had fallen sharply in 1986, endangering development programmes in the producing countries and exposing the oil industry, and even the entire world economy, to enormous hazards. Saudi Arabia, together with the other members of OPEC, had endeavoured to redress the balance between supply and demand and restore stable prices. Those efforts had been crowned with success in 1987; OPEC had managed, thanks to the solidarity of its members and a continuing process of consultation, to contain the emerging difficulties in the oil market. He was convinced that world economic growth would help to keep the oil market stable and vice-versa. It was self-evident, moreover, that stable oil prices were in the interests of the international community as a whole in view of the interdependence of its component countries and groups of countries.

6. In his address to the seventh session of the Conference, President Mitterrand* had stated that, at the Venice Summit, the industrialized countries had undertaken to increase their ODA to 0.7 per cent of GNP. While welcoming that initiative, Saudi Arabia was acutely aware of the overwhelming needs of developing countries in that field. It was the foremost developing country giving assistance to other developing countries. During the previous five years it had provided over 70 developing countries throughout the world with total assistance in excess of $24 billion, principally to finance long-term development projects. Despite falling oil prices during the preceding two years, Saudi Arabia's total development assistance had increased by 38 per cent between 1985 and 1986. Because it considered implementation of the Substantial New Programme of Action very important, it provided a particularly large amount of assistance to LDCs, mainly in the form of grants. Saudi Arabia was particularly sensitive to the problems of the countries of sub-Saharan Africa and had helped them in overcoming their difficulties, in particular those caused by drought and desertification. The annual amount of development assistance provided by Saudi Arabia had averaged over 4 per cent of its GNP—five times the target set by the International Development Strategy for the Third United Nations Development Decade.

7. Saudi Arabia was aware that, by the end of the decade, the developing countries would have to be provided with the means to make the required economic changes and to achieve a reasonable level of development. For that reason, all members of the international community must contribute to a resumption of growth and expansion of international trade and the developed countries would have to fulfil their responsibilities and financial commitments under the International Development Strategy. The interdependence of nations was quite obvious, as was the need for international co-operation to overcome world economic problems. In that context, it was the international community's duty to restore confidence in international organizations in general and in the work of the United Nations and the specialized agencies in particular. There was cause for hope that current difficulties would stimulate efforts to establish a new international order based on justice and equality.

---

* See sect. A above.

Summary of the statement made at the 205th plenary meeting, 13 July 1987, by Mr. Abdourahmane TOURÉ, Minister of Commerce of Senegal

1. Mr. TOURÉ said that the Conference would prove to be either an opportunity for renewed awareness of the reasons for which UNCTAD had been created, followed by appropriate action, or a further broken appointment with history. Those were the choices before it.

2. The difficulty of the task ahead was evident from the virtually all-pervading air of pessimism attending the opening of the session. There were few who expected any tangible results. One of the many reasons for the pessimism was that UNCTAD had ceased to satisfy some of its members, who had chosen to replace the

climate of constructive dialogue by one of sterile antagonism. UNCTAD's decline, which had become perceptible at the fifth session, had accelerated at the sixth session, and the organization was by now virtually back where it had started. The old international economic order which UNCTAD had helped to shake had largely rallied, and its eclipse appeared to have been a temporary one brought about in the 1960s by the political solidarity of the developing countries and in the 1970s by the action of OPEC.

3.   It was not only UNCTAD as an institution that was under threat but also its most important achievements for international economic co-operation and the development of the disadvantaged countries. That could be seen convincingly in the attacks on two of its major achievements: the GSP, with its principles of non-discrimination and non-reciprocity, and the Integrated Programme for Commodities, with its sound and topical fundamental objectives.

4.   The North-South dialogue, the idea for which owed much to UNCTAD, had become a dialogue of the deaf, who differed in their analysis of the international economic situation. Yet surely, it was not essential to hold identical views on the world situation in order to work for changes that were obviously called for by the deteriorating economic situation in the majority of countries and by the dangerous impact of such deterioration on the stability and growth of the world economy. The facts were there to substantiate the sombre picture, and he proceeded to cite a number of the facts.

5.   The first fact was the steady deterioration of the international market for primary commodities, which deprived most developing countries, particularly in Africa, of the resources they badly needed to discharge their financial obligations. The second was the huge external debt of the developing countries, which constituted a serious danger for the future of debtor countries, the prosperity of creditor countries and the stability of the international financial and banking system. The third undeniable fact was that protectionism had reached so high a level that it threatened the very foundations of the multilateral trade system which had ensured the prosperity of the industrialized countries.

6.   Since those and many other facts were not in dispute, it ought to be possible to seek and find dynamic solutions that would meet the justified concern of the developing countries while safeguarding the legitimate interests of the prosperous countries. Such efforts could only be undertaken, however, if all concerned were fully convinced that the benefits secured by a particular group in open negotiations were not detrimental to another group. Since that condition had not yet been met, efforts of mutual persuasion should be made in that direction.

7.   Despite the prevailing pessimism, the African countries were participating in the Conference with confidence, since the international community had already shown at the thirteenth special session of the General Assembly, on the critical economic situation in Africa, that it could rise to the occasion and take constructive action when circumstances demanded. The adoption on that occasion of the United Nations Programme of Ac-

tion for African Economic Recovery and Development 1986-1990 had raised great hopes among the African peoples, who viewed it as a necessary complement to Africa's Priority Programme for Economic Recovery adopted by the Assembly of Heads of State and Government of the OAU, at its twenty-first ordinary session, in July 1985, and a further means for reversing the persistent and accelerating deterioration of their living conditions. In adopting those Programmes the African countries had undertaken to introduce the reforms necessary for adjusting and developing their economies, while the international community had undertaken to support their efforts by increasing its contributions and promoting a favourable international economic environment.

8.   Although it was still premature to draw up even an interim balance sheet of the operation of the Programme for Africa, the preliminary results hardly encouraged optimism, though there were some heartening signs that things were changing on the African side. In accordance with their commitments, most African countries had undertaken far-reaching reforms in the context of medium-term and long-term economic and financial adjustment programmes, but the results obtained still failed to match the heavy sacrifices made by the people, who bore the major burden of adjustment. There were both domestic and external reasons for that situation.

9.   So far as the domestic situation was concerned, the economic structures of many African countries had admittedly deteriorated so seriously that in many cases any changes carried out would produce their effects only in the medium or long term; but it was the external factors that most severely thwarted the efforts of the African countries. In the first place, the resources promised in support of their reforms had seldom materialized, and when they had, they had been inadequate. Above all, no perceptible effort had been made to render the international economic environment favourable to the structural changes made in the African countries. The prices of African export commodities remained at their historically low levels, tariff and non-tariff barriers continued to be raised against African exports, external indebtedness remained an intolerable burden on the continent's public finances, fresh contributions of resources were falling off, real interest rates were exorbitant and currency fluctuations erratic.

10.   In such circumstances, Africa's economic reforms would take far longer than they should have done and would call for greater sacrifices than ought reasonably to be demanded, without any guarantee of success. It was thus essential, both for Africa and for the rest of the world, to adopt appropriate measures to create an international economic environment favourable to growth and development.

11.   In that connection, he welcomed the action taken by the UNCTAD secretariat to promote the implementation of the United Nations Programme of Action for African Economic Recovery and Development 1986-1990. Such action would be useless, however, unless it was supported and strengthened by resources provided by members of UNCTAD, particularly the

most prosperous countries, and the readiness of those countries to act. Some of them had already taken specific individual action in support of the Programme of Action and they should be encouraged to persevere in their efforts. He also welcomed the USSR's decision to sign the Agreement Establishing the Common Fund for Commodities, which was an essential link in the efforts to stabilize commodities.

12.   The transformation of the international environment called for collective action by the developed countries having most of the decision-making powers and by the developing countries that were the main victims of the prevailing situation. The current session of the Conference offered an opportunity for a dialogue on the revitalization of development, growth and international trade in a more predictable and supportive environment, through multilateral co-operation. Good use should be made of that opportunity by formulating policies and measures that would radically transform the existing situation in the fundamental fields of resources for development, commodities and interna-

tional trade and that would ease the problems of the LDCs. The means were available, but will, too, was needed.

13.   The seventh session of the Conference marked a return to the beginnings of UNCTAD, whose role in international economic relations was unique. It was at a crossroads leading either to its rehabilitation or its continued decline, to the restoration of a climate favourable to a confident dialogue between the prosperous and the poor countries or to renunciation of the common search for solutions to common problems affecting common interests. At the seventh session the Conference faced a challenge: how to live up to the expectations of the founding fathers of UNCTAD. The decisions that would be taken as a result of its deliberations could have as great an impact on the future of international economic relations as those courageous decisions which had for some years made UNCTAD the chosen place for reflection and action on economic development problems. He urged the Conference to rise to the challenge.

Summary of the statement made at the 209th plenary meeting, 15 July 1987, by Mr. Mohamud Said MOHAMED, Minister of Commerce of Somalia

1.   Mr. MOHAMED said that his delegation had come to the seventh session of the Conference in a spirit of understanding and co-operation. Since the growth and development of developing countries and the recovery of the world economy were inseparable, it was unrealistic to assume that the recovery of any one group of nations could solve the economic problems of the developing countries. In order to improve the critical global economic situation, attention should be given to the three important sectors of commodities, trade and finance.

2.   The many commodity-dependent developing countries had been seriously affected in recent years by the decline in commodity prices. He agreed with UNCTAD's assessment that commodities should be thought of as providing the means by which the developing countries could achieve economic growth. Unfortunately, however, the commodity-dependent developing economies had suffered a serious reduction of purchasing power owing to the decline in the prices of their export commodities. It was necessary to give fresh impetus to the Integrated Programme for Commodities, particularly commodity arrangements, the Common Fund for Commodities and price stabilization measures. On the trade front, as a result of the serious decline in real resource flows to developing countries, they depended increasingly on trade. However, owing to protectionist measures applied by developed countries, the commodity-exporting developing countries' income was insufficient to finance their development, and their share in world trade had declined in recent years. In the area of finance, the fall in export earnings, the burden of debt servicing, the contraction of private bank lending and the decline of ODA had resulted in severe liquidity problems for the developing countries and even affected their political stability. Policy-making in a

number of those countries was dominated by a shortage of foreign exchange. In addition, the overhang of their external debt posed a continuing problem.

3.   Accordingly, the developing countries were justifiably disappointed with the performance of the leading international financial institutions. IMF denied the developing countries a mixed economy framework and had imposed a succession of devaluations on the LDCs. The World Bank's structural adjustment programme in Africa had moved from longer-term development issues to the imposition of a conditionality which emphasized adjustment to an already existing structure rather than a structural transformation tending to create a viable growth process while reducing vulnerability to external events.

4.   A reform of the existing international monetary system was needed, including increased participation by developing countries in all decision-making processes of IMF and the World Bank, a strengthening of the role of the World Bank as a development institution, an increase in the IMF Structural Adjustment Facility, and an increased flow of resources in real terms from the developed countries and international financial institutions to African countries, in accordance with the United Nations Programme of Action for African Economic Recovery and Development 1986-1990. There should also be an increase in the lending facilities of the World Bank, regional banks and United Nations technical assistance bodies, especially UNDP. Official development assistance for the LDCs should similarly be increased in real terms in order to meet the objectives of the Substantial New Programme of Action.

5.   The global crisis was compounded by the inadequate flow of resources, particularly those of a concessional nature, high inflation and interest rates, exchange

rate fluctuations and prolonged economic instability, stringent lending policies and protectionism, as well as obstacles to technology transfer, the erosion of the multilateral trading system and unpredictable trade balances. As a result the developing countries had accumulated unmanageable debts and had little hope of being able to create new employment opportunities. Many of those problems were a direct consequence of the reluctance of developed countries to change the international economic order and the structure and functioning of financial and trading institutions. Recognition by some developed countries of the need for change was commendable, but must be matched by specific policy measures. A first step in that direction would be endorsement of an integrated approach towards all relevant issues, as called for by the Group of 77.

6. Somalia stressed the need for immediate measures in favour of the LDCs, which were the most seriously affected by the current crisis and which would suffer disastrous consequences should there be any further delay. Such measures should include balance-of-payments support and total cancellation of their debts; in that connection, he commended the responsible attitude of the countries which had waived their claims on the LDCs.

7. The plight of sub-Saharan Africa was particularly severe and was compounded by the burden of high interest payments on their external debt. Efforts to remedy that worsening situation, such as the Lagos Plan of Action and Africa's Priority Programme for Economic Recovery 1986-1990 of the OAU would come to nothing if they were not backed by massive economic support from the international community. The international response to calls for massive emergency assistance to Africa, including the measures envisaged in the United Nations Programme of Action for African Economic Recovery and Development 1986-1990, had so far been unsatisfactory, and he wished to reiterate that appeal.

8. In response to the problems which severely hampered African countries' ability to meet the demands of a steadily expanding population, African Governments had made significant efforts, at considerable cost, to adjust their policies to meet the guidelines spelled out in the OAU Priority Programme and the United Nations Programme of Action. His delegation strongly supported the establishment of an inter-divisional task force by UNCTAD to implement the recommendations of the United Nations Programme of Action. He associated himself with the words of the Prime Minister of Norway to the effect that the time had come for joint action to create a new partnership between North and South in the fight against poverty and for sustainable development.

Summary of the statement made at the 205th plenary meeting, 13 July 1987, by Mr. Miguel Angel FERNÁNDEZ-ORDÓÑEZ, Secretary of State for Commerce, Ministry of Economy and Finance of Spain

1. Mr. FERNÁNDEZ-ORDÓÑEZ said that the timing of the Conference made it one of the most important events of the year in the dialogue on international economic co-operation in an increasingly interdependent world. The topics for discussion were closely interconnected and of mutual impact.

2. One of the most pressing economic problems facing the world was that of low growth rates. Although increased growth alone could not solve all the problems, it was essential for any progress towards a reduction in poverty and unemployment, an objective which appeared to be within reach for the first time for many years. The situation called for the co-ordination of national economic policies, priority being given to those designed to correct large budget deficits in certain countries and to stimulate domestic demand in countries with substantial surpluses. Obviously, it would be difficult to achieve those objectives so long as there was no improvement in the operation of the multilateral trade, monetary and financial systems.

3. So far as financial resources for development were concerned, he said that what was needed was a more stable monetary and financial system. His delegation therefore supported any action tending to co-ordinate policies and to ensure an equitable regulation of international liquidity. At the same time, however, the developing countries ought to endeavour to increase their dometic resources, particularly savings, and the industrialized countries ought to support those efforts by providing external resources.

4. Spain had resolutely supported the efforts of the multilateral development financing institutions; since the sixth session of the Conference, it had become a member of the African Development Bank and the Asian Development Bank, the Ibero-American Investment Corporation and the Multilateral Investment Guarantee Agency. In addition, Spain had participated in the negotiations on the replenishment of the resources of development institutions, both through the capital window and by concessional funds, as well as such special negotiations as those concerning the Eighth Replenishment of the resources of IDA and the Special Account for Sub-Saharan Africa. It has thus taken the fullest possible part in the community of donor countries in the multilateral financing system and at the same time had updated its bilateral assistance mechanisms. The interaction of multilateral and bilateral factors was reflected in the figures for Spain's ODA. His delegation considered that the targets for such assistance specified in the International Development Strategy for the Third United Nations Development Decade and the Substantial New Programme of Action for the 1980s for the Least Developed Countries should be maintained, and urged the international community to ensure that the aggregate volume of aid would increase.

5. External indebtedness was possibly the most disturbing problem for developing countries, particularly in Latin America—a problem to be dealt with by the combined efforts of debtors and creditors. That was why it was more urgent than ever to work out a concerted strategy for sustained growth in a stable economic environment, with continued adjustment to mobilize domestic resources and with further contributions of public and private external resources. His delegation recognized that there were limits to the adjustment process, owing to considerations of political and social stability, and welcomed the action taken in the Paris Club in rescheduling the debt of heavily indebted countries. Another method of channelling resources to developing countries in a form other than debt was that of encouraging external investment or of converting debt into equity capital.

6. There should be a second phase in which the creditor countries would help to solve the external debt problem, first, by means of contributions made through their financial systems in the more generous rescheduling of principal and the capitalization or, as appropriate, reduction of interest charges; secondly, through an increase in the resources of the multilateral institutions to enable them to expand their financing operations; thirdly, by increased development assistance, and, lastly, through trade liberalization.

7. Spain rejected the idea of a wholesale cancellation of debt, for such action would discriminate against countries that had forgone faster growth or applied stringent adjustment policies, and in addition might destabilize the world economy, with unforeseeable consequences in the developing countries.

8. The current difficulties affecting international trade were reflected in the large imbalances in the trade account of most countries. His country considered that what was needed was a strong multilateral and open international trade system, of which GATT, with some specific changes, would continue to be the central pillar. Accordingly, he reaffirmed his country's commitment to the objectives of the Ministerial Declaration of Punta del Este on the Uruguay Round.

9. Since the previous session of the Conference, Spain and Portugal had signed the Treaty and Act of Accession to the European Economic Community—an important step that had led in Spain to a vigorous process of external trade liberalization, which was, however, adding to the cost of Spain's economic adjustment process, begun in the early 1980s in an unfavourable domestic economic situation of very high unemployment and inflation. In consequence of its membership of the European Community as from 1 January 1986, Spain had become a preference-giving country in the Community's scheme of preferences.

10. His delegation recognized the seriousness of the situation for developing countries that were heavily dependent on commodities. The complex and inter-related factors that had contributed to the fall in commodity prices included cyclical and structural factors, both on the supply side and on the demand side. Machinery to enhance the transparency of markets was therefore needed. More than ever was it necessary to consider, as an important mechanism for development assistance, measures in support of commodity prices that were remunerative for producers and fair to consumers, taking account of the need to stabilize commodity export earnings and of the various international instruments for attaining that objective. For countries seriously affected by the fall in commodity prices, particularly in the Latin American region, firm support for existing international commodity agreements and the early reintroduction, where necessary, of export quotas agreed to between producers and consumers, would be a positive step. In a heavily interdependent international economic situation, that would benefit the entire international economic community.

11. The Integrated Programme for Commodities adopted more than 10 years earlier had many sound features, but because the problems varied from one country to another and from one commodity to another, a case-by-case analysis was called for, as well as a review of the appropriate instruments for counteracting the long-term factors of instability, focusing on the areas of research, development, marketing and diversification. The conditions under which commodity markets were developing called for a careful assessment of the Common Fund. He appealed to the international community to enter into a frank dialogue on that topic in the interest of all concerned.

12. His country was ready to make a voluntary financial contribution, within its capacity, to support activities and programmes in specific commodity fields under the various international agreements, whatever the future of the Common Fund.

13. The LDCs, considered as a group with its own characteristics, should be recognized and supported by the rest of the international community, since those countries had remained in a state of stagnation and chronic economic crisis, with little share in international trade. That situation justified the need for ODA from the prosperous nations to facilitate a substantial transfer of resources and technical capacity in many fields. The serious and urgent problems of the LDCs should become the responsibility of the entire international community, which should co-operate in solving them to the fullest extent possible.

14. The constantly changing conditions of the world economic environment called for a co-operative review of targets and replanning by all countries, developed and developing alike. The international economic system should be redirected towards the equitable distribution of resources and opportunities, the right to development being recognized as the heritage of all peoples.

Summary of the statement made at the 211th plenary meeting, 24 July 1987, by Mr. M. S. AMARASIRI, Minister of Trade and Shipping of Sri Lanka

1. Mr. AMARASIRI recalled that UNCTAD had been established in response to the need for equitable international economic relations. Its mandate had been expanded since 1964 and had become increasingly comprehensive. The stalemate it had recently experienced was primarily the result of a breakdown in international economic co-operation and of attempts to change its mandate. If UNCTAD was to be strengthened and revived, the participants in the current session would have to recapture the spirit that had inspired its founders.

2. The 1980s were already being characterized as the lost decade of development. Few developing countries had been spared by economic stagnation and even recession, with falling living standards and negative growth rates which had had serious social and political consequences. Unless those trends were reversed, the gap between developing and developed countries would continue to widen.

3. The set-back to development had largely been induced by the deflationary external economic environment resulting from the restrictive macro-economic policies of the major market-economy countries. Such policies had not even served the interests of those countries, which had reduced inflation, but had triggered high unemployment rates, external imbalances, growing trade tensions and, above all, negative growth rates. It was, however, the developing countries that had been the hardest hit, particularly the poorest and least developed among them, for which the crisis had meant collapsing commodity prices, worsening terms of trade, intensified protectionist and discriminatory measures, contracting financial flows, unstable exchange rates and monetary markets and the burgeoning debt problem.

4. Uncertainty and unpredictability had become significant factors in international economic relations. International economic co-operation and multilateralism had received a severe set-back. Regrettably, the major developed countries now tended to neglect the potential of mutually beneficial intergovernmental co-operation and to play down the role of the external environment, which was largely responsible for the development crisis. It was nevertheless encouraging to note that they were increasingly aware of the need for greater co-ordination of their macro-economic policies and that they acknowledged the interrelationship between commodities, trade, monetary and financial policies and the gravity of the debt problem. That awareness had to be broadened and deepened and it must be understood that investment in development and the growth of developing-country markets were essential to the world economy and that global peace and prosperity could not be achieved if three fourths of the world's population were excluded. The concept of interdependence therefore had to be translated into specific policies and actions that were capable of revitalizing development, growth and international trade. Account had to be taken of the interdependence of all economic factors, as recommended in the pro-

posals adopted by the Sixth Ministerial Meeting of the Group of 77, held in Havana in April 1987.

5. Since the early 1980s, commodity prices had fallen to their lowest levels in 50 years and there was little hope of any improvement. During the period 1981-1986, the aggregate loss in developing countries' export earnings, as measured against the average of 1980 levels, had amounted to $70 billion. That reverse had been further compounded by the steady deterioration in those countries' terms of trade, which had resulted in a loss of $96 billion for 1986 alone. Sri Lanka had suffered a compression of its export earnings and developing countries as a whole had reached the limits of their capacity to service their external debt and finance their development efforts. Only an integrated approach such as the Integrated Programme for Commodities, whose objectives and principles were more valid than ever before, could improve the situation and the earliest implementation of the Common Fund was therefore essential. In that connection, his delegation welcomed the signature by the USSR of the Agreement Establishing the Common Fund. Commodity stabilization agreements had to be strengthened and improved and shortfalls in export earnings would have to be compensated. The early negotiation of a commodity-specific compensatory scheme was essential. Additional financing should also be provided for diversification programmes in commodity-dependent developing countries.

6. An underlying cause of the development crisis had been the contraction in financial flows to the developing countries and their growing indebtedness. Sri Lanka's debt-servicing burden continued to grow and, unless that trend was reversed, the prospects for sustained growth in developing countries would remain gloomy. A consensus existed with regard to the recommendations made in General Assembly resolution 41/202 concerning measures to alleviate the debt burden of developing countries. Debt reconstruction must replace debt rescheduling and include debt relief and renewed flows of resources to ensure reasonable rates of economic growth. A debt reconstruction facility should be established. In that connection, Japan's recycling of its trade surplus was to be welcomed as a step in the right direction. There should be increased resource transfers and measures should be taken to redeploy resources released by disarmament. It would also be necessary at the same time to ensure expanding trade flows and growth in the world economy.

7. World trade had grown slowly in the preceding two years and the developing countries' share had declined steadily, while their exports to developed-country markets had suffered from restrictive and discriminatory measures. The multilateral trading system had been subject to continuing erosion despite the launching of the Uruguay Round of negotiations, which were aimed at liberalizing world trade and strengthening GATT disciplines. It was to be hoped that those negotiations would succeed in liberalizing trade,

particularly in products of export interest to developing countries which needed to be protected against unilateral and arbitrary trade actions. However, the developing countries were well aware that the Uruguay Round would not be a panacea for all their problems. Parallel and co-ordinated measures therefore needed to be taken by UNCTAD to give more weight to the negotiations and help strengthen and improve the multilateral system. The commitments on standstill and the roll-back of protectionist measures had to be effectively implemented. Co-operative measures to promote and strengthen service industries in developing countries should be undertaken. A programme should also be devised for further promoting trade among countries with different economic and social systems. Com-

mitments under the Substantial New Programme of Action for the 1980s for the Least Developed Countries, whose situation had continued to deteriorate, still had not been fulfilled and the international community therefore had to take urgent remedial measures, including special treatment for those countries.

8. UNCTAD was the forum best suited to adopt and implement measures aimed at revitalizing development, growth and international trade. His delegation trusted that the participants in the seventh session would spare no effort to ensure the success of the Conference and that they would not miss the opportunity it provided to overcome common concerns in a mutually rewarding way.

Summary of the statement made at the 217th plenary meeting, 29 July 1987, by Mr. Abdel Magied Ali HASSAN, Permanent Representative of the Sudan to the United Nations Office at Geneva

1. Mr. HASSAN said that all countries had the right to adopt the economic and social system of their choice but had to take account of the interdependence of nations and adapt to changes in the world economy, and particularly in the international division of labour. The members of the international community must clearly recognize their joint responsibility and work together to find ways of solving the serious economic problems of the time.

2. The developing countries belonging to the Group of 77 had made considerable efforts to adopt a common approach to the Conference. They had prepared themselves actively for the seventh session over a number of months and had finally been able to adopt a declaration at Havana setting out principles that for them were fundamental. Unfortunately, the developed countries did not seem to have shown the same seriousness in their preparations and had not adopted a sufficiently flexible attitude; that was having a negative effect on the work of the Conference. It was to be hoped that that situation was not a sign of lack of political will. The role of UNCTAD should not be taken lightly or minimized. UNCTAD, in fact, was making pioneering efforts in providing technical assistance to the third world countries to accelerate their development and could make a major contribution to the improvement of international economic relations.

3. There was good reason to welcome the initiative taken by the Japanese Government, which had decided to devote part of its financial surplus to aid the developing countries, in particular the LDCs. The other industrialized countries would do well to follow that example and take specific measures to accelerate development and promote trade recovery. Some had already embarked on that path, like the Soviet Union, which had recently signed the Agreement Establishing the Common Fund for Commodities. France, for its part, had agreed to hold a conference in Paris in 1990 to evaluate the Substantial New Programme of Action and

the Minister of Development of Norway had made constructive proposals in that regard. He also fully approved the analysis of economic problems made by the Crown Prince of the Hashemite Kingdom of Jordan in his statement to the Conference,* as well as the proposals he had submitted.

4. The debt problem was only one symptom of the grave crisis within the international economic system. It was essential for all interested parties—creditors, debtors, international organizations and commercial banks—to show genuine political will and combine their efforts to relieve the burden on the third world countries. The LDCs were going through an extremely difficult time in that regard, and their currency earnings were not enough even to cover half of their debt-servicing costs.

5. The economic situation was particularly serious in Africa, a continent which comprised 27 of the 40 LDCs. Participants in the twenty-first ordinary session of the Assembly of Heads of State and Government of the OAU had agreed to take energetic measures and the General Assembly, at its special session devoted to the problem of Africa, had adopted the United Nations Programme of Action for African Economic Recovery and Development 1986-1990. Unfortunately, the international community had not lived up to its commitments, and attainment of that programme's objectives appeared to be in grave jeopardy. It was therefore imperative to redouble efforts for its full implementation.

6. More human and financial resources had to be mobilized and used to good effect in order to revitalize growth and development and to improve the world economy. National efforts should be supplemented by international co-operation as a prerequisite for their success.

_____
* See sect. A above.

Summary of the statement made at the 212th plenary meeting, 27 July 1987, by Ms. Anita GRADIN, Minister of Foreign Trade of Sweden

1.   Ms. GRADIN said that, although national economies—irrespective of their level of development or their social and economic system—were closely interlinked, that fact had still not been acknowledged and translated into decisive measures which would allow appropriate action to be taken. In the past, indeed, short-sighted policies and the inability to co-operate had served merely to aggravate the economic and social crisis in the world.

2.   As for the problem of world economic growth, it was clear that the potential for expansion was not being fully exploited. That was the main obstacle to a lasting solution of the debt crisis and to the efforts of countries to adjust and diversify their economies and improve social conditions. All countries clearly had a duty to create favourable conditions for the resumption and acceleration of economic growth, but it was also clear that the major industrialized countries must assume the main responsibility for co-ordinating their economic policies more effectively, in order to reduce the large external imbalances which currently threatened both growth and stability and the future of an open trade system. However, all countries, in their search for ways to stimulate world growth, should pay due attention to environmental constraints.

3.   On the subject of resources for development, she said that the ultimate aim of development was to improve living conditions; at the same time, meeting essential needs constituted true leverage for long-term development. It must be borne in mind that the term ''human resources'' covered both men and women, for the role of the latter in development was all too often ignored or underestimated.

4.   With regard to capital flows, it was unacceptable merely to note that prospects for an increase in aid in the next few years were hardly encouraging. Net transfers of resources to the developing countries must be resumed in order to support their structural adjustment and economic reform programme, and private lenders and investors should make joint efforts to increase such transfers. Moreover, the 0.7 per cent target which had been reaffirmed at the Venice Summit must be followed up by specific measures in countries by which it had not been achieved, particularly the major industrialized countries. The Swedish delegation noted with satisfaction that Japan intended to increase its aid to a figure more in line with its economic power. The multilateral institutions should also be provided with enough additional funds to fulfil their important role; her Government welcomed the IMF proposal to strengthen considerably the Structural Adjustment Facility. The world debt situation and prospects of consolidating international debt strategy were of crucial importance for the Conference. A strategy was needed to extend and supplement the case-by-case approach, and it must involve all the parties concerned. However, special efforts must be made as a matter of urgency in the poorest and most indebted countries.

5.   Referring to the question of commodities, she said that, in view of developments in commodity markets, multilateral co-operation must assume new dimensions. Developing countries should diversify their economies so that they were no longer dependent solely on commodity exports, but they lacked the means to take long-term action. They must, therefore, be provided with increased technical and financial assistance, and the machinery for stabilizing export earnings must be improved. Some countries would, nevertheless, remain heavily dependent on commodity exports, and UNCTAD must promote multilateral co-operation in that field. Steps must also be taken to improve market transparency and strengthen the long-term competitiveness of commodities. Sweden noted with satisfaction that the Common Fund would probably soon begin operations; there was an urgent need for commodity development projects, and her Government expected the Second Account to stimulate multilateral initiatives in that field.

6.   International trade was an essential vector of growth and development, and it was therefore imperative to roll back protectionism, liberalize international trade even further and strengthen the multilateral trade system, which was currently in a very bad state. The Uruguay Round of negotiations had been launched with a view to contributing to the realization of those objectives and it was therefore of crucial importance if any progress were to be made in the trade sector. As the Secretary-General had indicated, UNCTAD could help developing countries to derive greater benefit from the negotiations. Given UNCTAD's knowledge of developing countries' trade problems, it must use its competence for analytical studies and technical assistance and, at the same time, play a supporting role by analysing the implications of the current negotiations for developing countries. It could also evaluate the costs of protectionism to national economies and the consumer. UNCTAD had done a great deal, through the GSP, to expand the exports of the developing countries. The GSP should continue to be based on principles recognized at the multilateral level, and its stability must be preserved for the sake of long-term investment and export planning. The provision of technical assistance, particularly through the International Trade Centre, UNCTAD/GATT, was also essential in order to improve the export competitiveness of the developing countries. On a more general point, she wondered why it had not so far been possible to reach agreement on trade problems which had been the subject of intensive negotiations during the previous two years and there had seemed to be some convergence of views on the inadequacies of the international trade system and on the measures needed to resolve them. States must seize every opportunity, both in the field of trade and in the work of UNCTAD in general, to throw a fresh light on the debate by exchanges of experience which would make the positions of the various groups more flexible.

7.   The need for solidarity on a global scale was nowhere more obvious than in the case of the LDCs.

Their tragic economic situation was sometimes further aggravated by external political troubles, particularly in the front-line States of southern Africa. The LDCs were especially dependent on the provision of aid on concessionary terms and the commitments which other States had assumed towards them must be fulfilled through multilateral financial institutions so that they could carry out their internal adjustment policies. In addition, they should be offered additional opportunities of increasing their export earnings. Since the beginning of the year, Sweden had undertaken to admit all exports from countries covered by its preference scheme duty-free. Apart from the unilateral measures it had taken to alleviate the indebtedness of certain countries, her Government had advocated international action to resolve the debt problem of the poorest and most indebted countries. It supported the steps being taken in

that direction by the Paris Club, for example, and considered that forceful and decisive action in respect of both repayment periods and interests rates was necessary.

8.   Sweden was convinced that only by strengthening multilateral co-operation could the problems encountered by North-South relations and the dangers threatening the world economy be tackled. Those difficulties could be overcome only by far-sightedness, wisdom and solidarity. For the moment, there were signs that a broad consensus might be achieved on additional measures and efforts to be undertaken in the framework of existing multilateral instruments. That opportunity of making progress and bringing the session of the Conference to a fruitful conclusion must be grasped.

Summary of the statement made at the 208th plenary meeting, 14 July 1987, by Mr. Jean-Pascal DELAMURAZ, Federal Counsellor, Head of the Federal Department of Public Economy of Switzerland

1.   Mr. DELAMURAZ said that the seventh session of the Conference was being held at a time when both developing and developed countries were having to take difficult economic decisions. The session would be judged by the capacity of participants to recognize the facts and to co-operate with one another in a concerted fashion.

2.   There was some ground for confidence. Every country had a heightened awareness of its own responsibilities and of the fact that interdependence called for co-responsibility and solidarity. For some time the principal market-economy countries had displayed a clear will to reach agreement on economic and monetary matters. Some of the effects were already discernible particularly in the form of more orderly exchange rates. All countries were confronted with the growing need to adjust their economic structures to current changes. It was important that the necessary adjustments should be carried out in full awareness of the constraints and also of the opportunities resulting from increasing economic interdependence. Many developing countries were making considerable efforts to restructure their economies in a difficult environment. Switzerland, which was itself engaged in restructuring, was giving those efforts almost daily support in the form of an economic policy geared to balanced growth, an extensive opening of its markets, active participation in debt-rescheduling operations, and the full use of export guarantee mechanisms. Its private sector was also participating in the search for solutions that would permit enhanced growth in the developing countries.

3.   Switzerland particularly wished to show its solidarity with the poorest countries and to reorient its official assistance along the lines of the Substantial New Programme of Action. The doubling of Switzerland's official assistance to the LDCs in recent years was one of the ways in which it had responded to their acute needs.

4.   Much, however, remained to be done. Accordingly, the Conference should arrive at a common diagnosis of the situation and make recommendations on the policies to be pursued. In particular, it should call for a more open response to structural adjustments, better-balanced budgeting and financial accounting in the countries having the most weight in the world economy, the utilization of existing margins of manœuvre in order to sustain long-term demand, determined efforts to reduce the distortions arising from easy-going monetary and budgetary policies and dangerously interventionist trade policies, and an increase in, and rationalization of, assistance to the poorest countries.

5.   Joint efforts were currently being made to find lasting solutions for the debt problem. Most debtor countries had confirmed their intention to honour their commitments, even though changes had had to be made in the terms initially agreed upon. In general, the creditor countries had responded favourably. All parties had agreed to face up to their responsibilities out of concern for their own and the general good. Nevertheless, a great deal remained to be done if the original objectives of transferring additional resources to the developing countries were to be achieved and if flows of productive private investment to them were to be resumed. Those two developments, together with a recovery in economic growth, should create the conditions needed to defuse current tension. Productive private investment was particularly important in that respect, on account of both its volume and its capacity to generate employment and technological progress.

6.   Switzerland had long since waived its claims on the poorest countries and would continue to take an active part in the search for solutions to their private debt problems. The Conference should urge the appropriate circles, especially the Paris Club, to take prompt action for dealing with the indebtedness of the poorest countries.

7. In view of the link between international trade and development, the growing participation of the developing countries in trade in manufactures and services and the will displayed at Punta del Este to strengthen the open multilateral trading system—an essential prerequisite for the creation of reliable, predictable and equitable market conditions—were particularly encouraging. The Uruguay Round of trade negotiations should take place in a credible and reassuring context. It was therefore essential that all parties should respect their commitment to a trade truce. The developing countries' intention to play a more important role in such negotiations was gratifying. The common objective of strengthening the multilateral trading system was serving to increase co-operation among all countries, irrespective of their stage of development. In the negotiations, developed and developing countries alike should display real solidarity with the poorest countries by instituting or improving preferential tariffs for them. UNCTAD had a role to play in contributing to greater consistency in approaches to ways of promoting the function of trade in development.

8. Commodities and the part they played in financing development were a source of great concern. It was becoming increasingly clear that the fall in commodity prices, occurring at a time when economic recovery should have caused prices to rise, was due to profound changes in world economic activity. As a result, a solution to the dilemma faced by the producer countries, particularly countries heavily dependent on their exports of commodities, inevitably involved the diver-

sification of their economies and the general restructuring of commodity trade through a greater respect for market forces. It was to be hoped that the Conference would lay the foundations of a strategy involving a return to meaningful international prices, the elimination of price distortions, co-operation between producers and consumers to counteract short-term price instabilities, an active policy of diversification, and the opening-up of markets. In the Uruguay Round of trade negotiations a major effort would also have to be made to liberalize trade in tropical products and to improve the market access of processed commodities. The decisions taken by the USSR and Côte d'Ivoire to sign the Agreement Establishing the Common Fund for Commodities were, he hoped, a prelude to the Fund's entry into force.

9. The strategy he had outlined was intended for all countries, although the poorest countries needed special support. Switzerland had followed with great concern the fate of the poorest countries that depended on a single commodity. Like many other countries, Switzerland considered that the resources earmarked for offsetting shortfalls in export earnings should be allocated directly to economic diversification. In the period 1987-1990 his country, in support of the international community's compensatory financing effort, would commit up to 40 million Swiss francs to help to diversify the economies of commodity-dependent LDCs that had suffered the heaviest falls in the value of their commodity exports to Switzerland.

Summary of the statement made at the 211th plenary meeting, 24 July 1987, by Mr. Montree PONGPANIT, Minister of Commerce of Thailand

1. Mr. PONGPANIT said that the seventh session was being held at a very critical juncture in terms not only of the future of the Conference itself, but also of the livelihood of billions of persons throughout the world.

2. When UNCTAD had been established, the world economy had been enjoying relative peace, prosperity and harmony. Over 20 years later, very little had been achieved by the body in which world leaders had placed such high hopes and the number of persons living in abject poverty was constantly growing. That situation might be attributed to the fact that what the international community lacked above all was the will to work in the interests of all. Co-operation was the corner-stone of organizations such as UNCTAD, the only forum where all development issues could be dealt with comprehensively. Every effort should be made to ensure that the seventh session of the Conference would enable nations to chart future paths to common growth and development. Interdependence had become a fact of economic life, which was now characterized by the growing role of foreign trade, increasing interlinkages among financial and capital markets and extremely rapid advances in international telecommunications.

3. The action of one nation inevitably had repercussions on the economies of others, especially if that na-

tion was a powerful one. The situation was therefore untenable where the gap between developed and developing countries continued to widen, for it was bound to create political, social and economic tension that would make progress impossible.

4. Countries had attempted to solve problems among themselves. The Group of Seven for example, had tried to redress trade and exchange rate imbalances among its members, but, in so doing, had failed to take account of the impact of its actions on smaller countries whose economies were linked to initiatives by the countries of the North. Economic prosperity in the North could not be sustained without the South, which provided raw materials and market outlets.

5. Genuine co-operation required an effective multilateral framework. The growing interdependence and complexity of economic relations among countries created an even greater need for a set of rules or disciplines to ensure that countries treated each other fairly and reasonably. Bilateral relations would naturally continue, but would have to be conducted, in so far as possible, under the disciplines of the multilateral framework. The use of unilateral power to impose the will of one country on another, as was, unfortunately, all too often the case today, should be avoided at all costs.

6. All those concepts, which were not new by any means, were the very ones that had led to UNCTAD's establishment. To recall them might, however, help to foster more action-oriented results.

7. Thailand, which followed a policy of export-led development, was extremely concerned about the erosion of faith in the multilateral trading system, the rise of protectionism in the major industrialized countries, the use of bilateral and, in some cases, unilateral action, the adoption of grey-area measures and the intensification of agricultural subsidies. It attached great importance to the Uruguay Round of negotiations. Its areas of special interest included trade in agricultural and tropical products, dispute settlement, subsidies, countervailing measures and safeguards. It urged all participants in the Uruguay Round to abide strictly by their standstill and roll-back commitments and hoped that Governments would spare no effort to speed up the negotiations. UNCTAD had a significant role to play in improving and strengthening the trading system. The commitments made at previous sessions should be reaffirmed and their full and expeditious implementation ensured. UNCTAD could also facilitate the expansion and diversification of the developing countries' production and their trade not only with the industrialized countries, but also with the socialist countries of Eastern Europe and even among themselves under the Global System of Trade Preference among Developing Countries. It could furthermore increase technical assistance to the developing countries participating in the Uruguay Round.

8. One of the major obstacles to world trade was the lack of willingness on the part of some industrialized countries to restructure their industries. Textiles and clothing were a classic example of a sector that

developed countries were trying to make artificially competitive, whereas it should be allowed to phase out gradually. Another case in point was agriculture, which, in some countries, benefited from subsidies that distorted competition on world markets. He sometimes wondered whether World Bank structural adjustment loans should not be directed towards the industrialized countries rather than the developing countries.

9. In the past, it had been thought that commodity price fluctuations were of a cyclical nature and therefore required measures designed merely to avoid extreme highs and lows. However, a more recent analysis had shown that the problem was of a long-term structural nature, with the downswing in prices lasting longer and longer and a persistent downward trend in demand. There were many underlying causes and it was clear that emphasis would have to be shifted from price stabilization to development projects capable of increasing productivity, expanding and diversifying end-uses, introducing a higher degree of processing and improving marketing and distribution systems. Whatever the strategy adopted, however, world commodity markets would continue to be depressed if surplus stock disposal by industrialized countries was not strictly regulated. UNCTAD was, once again, a perfect forum in which to develop such disciplines.

10. His Government had taken the necessary legislative steps to ratify the Agreement Establishing the Common Fund for Commodities.

11. His delegation welcomed Brunei Darussalam and Saint Kitts and Nevis as new members of UNCTAD. It expressed the hope that all participants would co-operate fully to ensure that the seventh session of the Conference was a success.

Summary of the statement made at the 207th plenary meeting, 14 July 1987, by Mr. Basdeo PANDAY, Minister of External Affairs and International Trade of Trinidad and Tobago

1. Mr. PANDAY noted that for days, the Conference had been listening to cheerless statements on the economic adversities, or perhaps absurdities, affecting the world. Suggestion after suggestion for effective remedial action had been made, but acceptable solutions remained elusive.

2. The stagnation characterizing international economic relations was attributable principally to misperception of long- and short-term interests resulting in the debilitating, counter-productive and myopic North-South confrontation, unworthy at a time of enhanced awareness of interdependence. As the late Prime Minister of Sweden, Olaf Palme, had pointed out at the sixth session of the Conference, dialogue and consensus were needed to overcome the economic crisis. Rigid and inflexible positions were non-productive and States would need to make firm political commitments to act on the basis of an interdependent approach. Any serious acceptance of the concept of interdependence must be accompanied by a realization that actions based on the idea of an immutable North-South divide were

negative in the extreme. There were, of course, serious regional structural imbalances and many of the economic policies pursued by States in the North militated against the development goals and aspirations of their counterparts in the South. However, his Government's faith in interdependence was such that it preferred to emphasize the self-evident truth that in the long term the North would need the South as much as the South currently needed the North. Realistic approaches had to be formulated by consensus.

3. Trinidad and Tobago was a small island developing country faced with the need to increase its exports and win access to markets. However, the realities of depressed prices and protectionist devices were stultifying, and the simplistic concept of the interplay of market forces could not be relied upon entirely if the much-needed change was to occur. Some of his country's principal products had been subjected to anti-dumping and countervailing duties making them uncompetitive in the markets they had secured. The call for standstill and roll-back of protectionism was

therefore logical and intimately pertinent to progress. Trinidad and Tobago fully supported the Integrated Programme for Commodities and, more specifically, the establishment of a Common Fund. The GSP was fundamental to the development of the foreign trade of developing countries. It was therefore perplexing to see a variety of transparent subterfuges being employed to circumvent the provisions of the scheme. Particularly disquieting was the policy of graduation being pursued by some countries. The proponents of that principle argued that dues must be paid by those able to do so. However, the use of the per capita income principle to determine the applicability of a graduation scheme was unrealistic and unjustifiable.

4. In the 1980s international trade had been seriously affected by intensified protectionism, a steady fall in commodity prices, the debt burden of several States, high interest rates, exchange rate fluctuations, import substitutions due to technological advances, and the non-observance of GATT rules and procedures. Those negative features had been mainly responsible for the decline in the share of world trade recorded by most developing countries, the LDCs being the most affected. There were no facile solutions to those problems. Even so, it was clear that with political will substantial progress could be made in eliminating some of them and diminishing the negative effect of others. Trinidad and Tobago therefore supported the call for a reduction and elimination of protectionist measures against products of export interest to developing countries and for the opening-up of markets to them and endorsed the plea for a review of trade legislation and regulations relating to anti-dumping and countervailing duties. The Uruguay Round of trade negotiations held out much promise for the future of international trade, but those negotiations, too, would fail if rigid positions were adopted and if some contracting parties to GATT sought to implement a policy of trade-offs between trade in goods and trade in services.

5. There was an interrelationship between money, finance, trade and development. Consequently, a comprehensive review of the international monetary system should be undertaken to take account of the case of the developing countries. More particularly, there should be a substantial increase in special drawing right allocations in IMF, a change of the conditionality criteria, an extension of repayment periods and an expansion and improvement of the IMF Compensatory Financing Facility. The decline in IDA's resources should be reversed and the role of the World Bank strengthened through an increase in its capital and a change in its graduation criteria.

6. UNCTAD had his delegation's full support, but it must be allowed to do what it was geared to do and must not be made to feel that its *modus operandi* was in question. The desire of some countries to place greater emphasis on GATT in trade matters and on IMF in monetary matters need not lead to any erosion of UNCTAD's areas of competence. UNCTAD's functions should include the formulation, negotiation and implementation of measures in the sphere of international trade and development and the interrelated issues of debt, money and finance. A strengthening of the negotiating and co-ordinating function of UNCTAD was desirable. In the area of services, given the limited expertise or complete lack of it in some developing countries, it seemed imperative that UNCTAD should continue to be involved in the preparation of studies and be able to assist developing countries with the formulation of their national policies for services. His delegation fully supported the proposal that the secretariat should examine the implications for developing countries of the issues being raised by the developed countries in the context of trade in services and that it should analyse the wider implications of any international régime governing trade in services.

7. The external debt continued to be one of the major problems of several developing countries. Given the drain on their resources which debt servicing occasioned and the corrective action which some countries had found it necessary to take, it had become obvious that some form of political dialogue should be initiated between creditors and debtors. The dialogue should be based on the principle of co-responsibility and the debtor countries' capacity to repay. As was emphasized in TD/330, the magnitude of the problem was such that an increase in external financial loans alone would not be sufficient for its solution. Parallel and co-ordinated action was needed in order to lower interest rates, ease the liquidity shortage, raise commodity prices, achieve exchange rate stability, and increase access to developed countries markets for the products of developing countries. Those views had the support of Trinidad and Tobago, which was determined to join with others in making every effort to achieve dialogue and consensus, understanding and equitable compromise, for the benefit of existing and future generations.

Summary of the statement made at the 216th plenary meeting, 29 July 1987, by Mr. Habib KAABACHI, Director of Multilateral Relations, Ministry of Foreign Affairs of Tunisia

1. Mr. KAABACHI said the entire international community recognized that the world economy was experiencing a crisis that was seriously affecting the developing countries. However, although opinions about the causes of the crisis were not always unanimous, differences of view should not be an obstacle to the adoption of policies and measures directed at growth and development.

2. In Tunisia, the aggravation of the world economic situation had slowed economic and social progress. Although resolute measures had been taken to cope with domestic difficulties, sharp fluctuations in exchange rates and the collapse of commodity prices had made the situation worse; foreign debt had reached an alarming level and the debt-service ratio had almost doubled between 1981 and 1986. In the circumstances,

an economic recovery plan had been launched in 1986 with World Bank assistance. It was aimed mainly at liberalizing foreign trade, promoting exports, adjusting the exchange rate and liberalizing credit and interest rates. The plan also provided for a reduction in public expenditure. Positive results had already been achieved, and the Tunisian Government hoped that its bilateral and multilateral partners would continue to support it in implementing the objectives of the 1987-1991 economic and social development plan.

3. Given the interdependence of the world economy, only a global approach could promote common interests and allocate responsibility in an equitable manner. UNCTAD had a central role to play in that respect as a forum for dialogue and joint action, and a number of encouraging results had already been obtained. It was gratifying, for example, that the USSR and Côte d'Ivoire had signed the Agreement Establishing the Common Fund for Commodities and, it was to be hoped that the developed countries would follow the example of Japan, which had announced that it would recycle $20 billion of its trade surplus as development assistance, and that that initiative would benefit all the developing countries concerned. In addition, the industrialized countries were adopting an increasingly positive attitude and the developing countries were to a greater extent undertaking to adopt appropriate adjustment and growth policies.

4. The structural adjustment programmes recommended for developing countries could yield results only if they were supported by measures on the part of the developed countries and drawn up in the light of the capacity of individual developing countries and the social cost of adjustment. Moreover, the international community as a whole had to agree on measures for the transfer of financial resources on favourable conditions, on a concerted solutions to the debt problem, on effective application of the Integrated Programme for Commodities on improving market access for products from the developing countries and on implementing the Substantial New Programme of Action for the 1980s for the Least Developed Countries, and the African countries in particular. In seeking a solution to the debt problem, the real capacities of the debtor countries and the need to avoid hampering their development should be taken into consideration. Debt service should therefore take account of export earnings, import needs, the growth in GDP and financial inputs from abroad.

5. With respect to the African countries in particular, the measures in the United Nations Programme of Action for African Economic Recovery and Development 1986-1990 should be implemented as a matter of urgency and the debt problem tackled with an eye to the fragility of the economic and social structures of the countries concerned. He hoped that, in the interest of growth and development, a genuine North-South dialogue would take place.

Summary of the statement made at the 215th plenary meeting, 28 July 1987, by Mr. Ali BOZER, Minister of State of Turkey

1. Mr. BOZER said that since the sixth session of the Conference, international economic relations, like approaches to economic problems, had undergone far-reaching change. The world had become increasingly polarized on many fronts and economies more interdependent; such changes had led to many complex problems as well as to converging views on the solutions to be adopted.

2. Despite the onset of recovery in 1983, the aggregate growth of the industrialized countries had not been great enough to solve the problems of trade, financial flows and debt. In early 1986, major adjustments in exchange rates, a sharp drop in the price of oil, falling inflation and declining interest rates had revived hopes of a resumption of economic growth in the OECD area. The world economy in general and the industrialized countries in particular had, however, failed to seize that opportunity. Investment had continued at a low level, international imbalances among the major industrialized countries had worsened, protectionist tendencies had hardened, the terms of trade of developing countries had continued to deteriorate, and the international debt problem had grown increasingly intractable. Large profits had admittedly been made in industrialized countries in the wake of falling inflation and declining commodity and especially oil prices, but had not led to an increase in demand because preference had been given to structural change and a contraction of economic activity.

3. Despite a slight easing of interest rates, renewed protectionism and stagnating export markets compounded by a drastic decline in commodity prices and in the transfer of resources had compelled debtor countries to pursue adjustment programmes at the expense of growth and social development. Furthermore, falling oil prices had restricted demand in the oil-exporting countries. Deflationary trends in developing and industrialized countries had thus reinforced each other.

4. In his view, the long drawn out period of slow growth was the source of many of the difficulties assailing the world economy, and the developing world in particular; nevertheless, a high growth strategy would not solve all problems. International co-operation was the only way of dealing effectively with the problem of slow growth. Under current conditions, growth should be initiated in the developed countries, bearing in mind that the decline in the relative weight of the major countries in the world economy made an increase in global demand essential. Countries with a balance-of-payments surplus should use it to increase their domestic demand and recycle the balance.

5. Yet the roots of the evil went much deeper. Currently, the industrialized countries appeared to fear that

a high level of demand would generate inflationary pressures. To judge from post-war experience, the political response to inflation was rather to promote structural adjustment by squeezing demand. Although such policies had had the effect of shifting resources to more productive areas and removing some inflexibilities, the resultant low level of world economic activity had militated against the process of structural adjustment by encouraging protectionism and hampering new investment. It was time to recognize the need for an expansionist economic policy based on supply as well as demand; to avoid fuelling inflation, such a strategy would require an earlier and more extensive dismantling of protectionist measures than that provided in the Punta del Este Declaration.

6. The developing countries too should endeavour, by means of adjustment, to contribute to improving world economic growth. By taking specific action to solve the debt problem, the international community could ease their task and thus encourage global growth. Should such growth reach satisfactory levels, the scope of the measures aimed specifically at the developing countries could be curtailed, except perhaps in the case of those intended for the LDCs.

7. With regard to the Integrated Programme for Commodities, he considered that instead of an inquiry into its validity it would be preferable for the major producing and consuming countries to join in seeking the conditions required to prepare and implement commodity agreements. In view of the difficulties caused to developing countries by depressed prices for the commodities on which their economies depended, he considered that the problem could be solved in part by diversification of production. Increased growth in in-

dustrialized countries and a commitment to open world markets more widely were needed to stabilize commodity prices. He welcomed the progress that had been made towards bringing the Common Fund for Commodities into operation, and reported that the Agreement Establishing the Common Fund had been submitted to the Turkish Parliament for ratification.

8. In the context of the Uruguay Round, he considered that the recent situation, particularly with regard to trade in agricultural commodities, highlighted the urgent need for standstill and roll-back measures. The success of the Uruguay Round depended on an appreciable improvement in the international economic environment. Turkey, which followed a free trade policy, was increasingly suffering from the protectionism of its trading partners and considered that the industrialized countries should move towards freer trade practices in line with market requirements.

9. The LDCs should be accorded special treatment even if international growth resumed. In his view, the industrialized countries should set aside 0.15 per cent of their GNP as ODA for such countries; it was equally important to channel those resources to productive fields. The proposals for alleviating the debt burden of the LDCs, including writing off bilateral concessional loans, appeared fair. Global projects were also useful. Indeed, Turkey had recently initiated a programme of that nature for the benefit of a number of countries in sub-Saharan Africa.

10. He expressed the hope that the industrialized and developing countries attending the Conference would display the mutual trust and the political will required to solve current severe economic problems.

Summary of the statement made at the 218th plenary meeting, 30 July 1987, by Mr. Israel KAYONDE, Deputy Minister of Commerce of Uganda

1. Mr. KAYONDE said that the seventh session of the Conference was taking place at a time when the world economy was going through a crisis in the development process. For the developing countries, that meant considerable indebtedness, the collapse of commodity prices, an excessive rise in real interest rates, volatile exchange rates for the principal world currencies and a reduction in the inflow of financial resources, including ODA. In response to those problems, the countries of the Group of 77 had submitted proposals that seemed quite reasonable, particularly those on the debt crisis. The same was true of the measures that the developed countries and multilateral financial institutions had been called upon to take in order to help developing countries diversify their export production and contribute to the stabilization of their export earnings.

2. One of the fundamental reasons for underdevelopment was the structural interdependence of the economies of developed and developing countries on a basis of inequality. The high level of commercial interest rates, unpredictable exchange rates, inappropriate

criteria for capital lending and the high incidence of protectionism were all factors in the development crisis over which many developing countries had no control. Another reason for the centuries-old underdevelopment of Africa was the steady haemorrhaging of resources from the developing countries to the developed countries, which reinforced the traditionally peripheral role of the developing countries in the world economy.

3. Developing countries themselves could not be held responsible for their current economic plight, which was largely due to the effects of a vicious circle of economic underdevelopment rooted in colonial history. For that reason, the former colonial Powers and the international community as a whole had a moral obligation to help developing countries to emerge from the current cycle of poverty and stagnation. One of the most urgent issues was to stabilize the prices of the agricultural commodities exported by developing countries; Uganda urged countries which had not yet done so to sign and ratify the Agreement Establishing the Common Fund for Commodities as soon as possible.

4. Referring to the consequences of the civil war that had taken place in his country and the destruction it had caused, he said that the Ugandan Government had succeeded, first and foremost, in guaranteeing the freedom of the individual, maintaining law and order in the country and protecting the human rights of every citizen—measures that it regarded as prerequisites for recovery and development. At the economic level, priority had been given to the restoration and full utilization of production capacity in the agricultural and industrial sectors and to the rehabilitation of the economic and social infrastructure. A currency reform had been carried out and strict fiscal and monetary policies introduced to boost the economic recovery process, increase overall production and diversify agricultural production. Uganda was one of the developing countries which suffered the most from commodity price fluctuations. For that reason, measures had been taken to broaden the export base of the agricultural sector and increase production of both traditional and non-traditional crops. Uganda was also one of the LDCs, and had thus benefited from the Substantial New Programme of Action. In order to ensure that its economic recovery policy enjoyed international support, the Ugandan Government had held intensive consultations with the World Bank and IMF with a view to achieving agreement on the main elements of a medium-term macro-economic framework. He wished to thank the member States and financial institutions which, at the recent World Bank consultative meeting in Paris, had responded positively to Uganda's appeal for financial support to meet the country's needs, as well as African and Arab donors, who had also made a valuable contribution.

5. Although the problems of the land-locked developing countries did not appear on the agenda of the current session, the Ugandan delegation wished to point out how serious those problems were; in the case of Uganda, they were even more alarming because the country was both land-locked and one of the LDCs.

6. The arms race had a number of consequences, including the waste of resources which could otherwise be used for development and the persistence of armed conflits in many developing countries. His delegation would continue to support any measures aimed at redeploying resources that were currently used for the arms race to finance the pressing needs of national economic development, and appealed to the international community to put an end to the *apartheid* régime, which was the very antithesis of the development efforts of African countries. Every effort should be made at the international level to create a peaceful atmosphere conducive to the growth and development of the developing countries and the establishment of equitable international economic relations.

7. The Ugandan delegation hoped that the deliberations at the seventh session of the Conference would yield positive and tangible results that could be fully and effectively implemented by the entire international community.

Summary of the statement made at the 219th plenary meeting, 30 July 1987, by Mr. Andrei A. OZADOVSKI, Permanent Representative of the Ukrainian Soviet Socialist Republic to the United Nations Office at Geneva

1. Mr. OZADOVSKI said that discussions at the Conference, which had been conducted in a spirit of frankness, had made for a deeper understanding of the problems facing the world economy and, despite differences in opinion, had demonstrated a stronger will to take concerted action and seek common approaches towards solving those problems, which were particularly acute in the developing countries. The assessment made by the Group of 77 in TD/330 was an accurate one and reflected the concerns voiced by a number of delegations. The developing world was beset by crisis, faced as it was with declining and even negative growth, adverse terms of trade and indebtedness that jeopardized not only the economic but also the political independence of the countries concerned.

2. The interdependence of all countries could no longer be ignored, and economic problems were indissociable from other factors. For the developing countries, interdependence continued to be reflected in their growing dependence on developed market-economy countries. Particularly alarming was the ever-growing net outflow of resources from developing countries—especially in the form of interest payments and repayments of other credits—at a time when inflows, especially on concessional terms, should really be increased.

3. A new approach and radical solutions were required to solve development problems. The object of the socialist countries, which had repeatedly made proposals to that effect, was to ensure international economic security through the expansion of mutually beneficial international co-operation in protecting the environment, ensuring the use of space and the oceans for peaceful purposes, combating hunger, disease and poverty, and developing a global programme for co-operation in the field of science and technology. A basic component of the proposed international economic security system was the normalization of international economic relations, free of political discrimination, economic blockades and sanctions that were not specifically provided for in recommendations adopted by the international community. A fundamental goal was to work together to find a solution to the problem of indebtedness and establish a new international economic order guaranteeing equal economic security for all States. The proposed concept of international economic security was in no way intended to replace the relevant United Nations decisions and documents on the

restructuring of international economic relations and the establishment of a new international economic order, but was designed to give impetus to the search for common features in different approaches to world economic problems, to build confidence in international economic relations and to bolster economic stability and predictability. An important initiative in that connection was the proposal by the Soviet Union to convene a world forum to discuss all the problems of international economic security, the establishment of a new international economic order and the development of trade and scientific and technical co-operation.

4. Recognition of the close link between disarmament and development was shared by the members of the non-aligned movement and the Group of 77 and expressed in the documents of their conferences held, respectively, in Harare and Havana. Lasting peace was the basic prerequisite for social and economic progress, and disarmament alone could release the resources needed for development. The determination of the socialist countries to take practical steps to achieve disarmament, détente and security was reflected in the recent initiatives of the Soviet Union, including the proposed programme for the full, universal elimination of nuclear weapons by the year 2000 and the proposed moratorium on any increase in military spending by the NATO and Warsaw Treaty member countries.

5. Domestic policy in the Soviet Union reflected that desire for peace and economic and social development. In the Ukrainian SSR, as in the rest of the Soviet Union, a process of economic and social restructuring and renewal was under way and had already borne fruit. In 1986, productivity had increased and national income had risen by 3.6 per cent, while the volume of industrial production had increased by 4.4 per cent. Various laws and instruments relating to restructuring had recently been adopted in the Soviet Union, including the "Basic provisions for a fundamental reform of economic management" (see TD/337). Those measures would promote international co-operation and an improvement of international relations, as would the measures taken to promote foreign economic and trading activity of domestic enterprises of the USSR with developed market-economy countries as well as with developing countries.

6. As a result of those developments, the Ukrainian SSR attached even greater importance to UNCTAD's specific role within the United Nations system. That role was, moreover, complementary to that of GATT, each of the two organizations having its own functions and objectives. Their efficiency depended largely on the political will of the Governments concerned to develop and enhance equitable international trade and economic co-operation.

7. A responsible, considered approach to global economic problems was needed. The great potential of a unique, universal forum like UNCTAD made it possible to conduct global negotiations and thereby speed up the development process. The time spent at the Conference had not been wasted. As its deliberations were drawing to a close, it was clear that a fresh impulse was needed in several areas of UNCTAD's activity. First, UNCTAD should become more actively involved in the process of ensuring international economic security. Secondly, it should carry out further studies on indebtedness and outflows of financial resources from developing countries. Thirdly, UNCTAD should make its contributions to formulating principles concerning the use of resources released as a result of disarmament, in order to accelerate development, especially that of the LDCs. He said that misgivings expressed by some delegations about the possible weakening of the role of UNCTAD had proved unfounded, and it was to be hoped that at the next session the Conference would consolidate the achievements of the current session.

Summary of the statement made at the 204th plenary meeting, 13 July 1987, by Mr. Boris ARISTOV, Minister of Foreign Trade of the Union of Soviet Socialist Republics

1. Mr. ARISTOV, after referring to the great importance which the USSR attached to UNCTAD's activities, as indicated in the message addressed by the Chairman of the USSR Council of Ministers to the participants in the seventh session of the Conference,* said that in its deliberations the Conference should reject outmoded political and economic thinking and revise approaches which had failed to work. The new thinking in UNCTAD should find its expression in a transition to broader and constructive co-operation between all groups of countries and a joint search for solutions to global problems. His delegation invited all participants in the current session to demonstrate a far-sighted political approach and common sense and to take up a flexible and realistic position in elaborating joint arrangements.

2. Like most countries, the Soviet Union advocated the restructuring of international economic relations on an equal and democratic basis, adherence to the provisions of the Charter of Economic Rights and Duties of States, and the implementation of the Programme of Action on the Establishment of a New International Economic Order. The concept of the economic security of States was fully in keeping with that Programme and should give fresh impetus to the strengthening of confidence in international economic relations.

3. The issues relating to the establishment of a new international economic order were closely connected with the issues of disarmament and development. Disarmament could release vast additional resources needed to combat disease, hunger, poverty and backwardness and to solve problems of social and economic development. It was not by chance that the developing countries associated the prospects for deliverance from their debt

---

* TD/L.281 (see volume I, annex IV).

burden with the limitation and elimination of armaments and the re-allocation of resources for development purposes. UNCTAD could contribute to the
elaboration of principles for the use of the resources
thus released for the benefit of the international community and for the benefit of the developing countries
in particular.

4. The problem of the external debt had acquired a
truly global character and had surpassed purely
economic bounds and assumed a political dimension. At
the moment, the service of the debt of the developing
countries absorbed up to one third of their export earnings. Among other measures aimed at solving the
problem, the Soviet Union proposed that annual
repayments of external debts should be limited to such a
proportion of foreign exchange earnings as would not
prejudice social and economic development. Protectionism should be resisted, interest rates lowered and exchange rates stabilized in deed and not just in word. The
monetary and financial system should be restructured,
taking into account the interests of all States, and the
financial institutions functioning within it should be
democratized. In considering ways to settle the debt
problem, primarily that of the LDCs, account should
also be taken of other proposals that might lead to a
global solution. UNCTAD could contribute to a solution of the problems by considering them in relation to
development and with regard also to the serious matter
of the outflow of financial resources from the developing countries.

5. The problems of the international monetary
system and the plans for its reform could be discussed at
an international conference on monetary and financial
issues convened on a universal basis under the auspices
of the United Nations, or in some other representative
forum with the participation of all interested countries.

6. The Soviet Union was in favour of UNCTAD
playing a central organizing role in the process of nor-
malizing international commodity trade. It continued to
take the view that for the majority of countries international commodity agreements were the most acceptable
means of regulating trade in commodities. UNCTAD
was making a major contribution to the elaboration of
such agreements and to the introduction of improvements in the mechanisms through which they influenced the commodity markets concerned. That work
should be continued through the enlargement of the
range of commodities covered by international commodity agreements.

7. The Conference should make a businesslike and
constructive examination of ways and means of
developing international trade. At the moment, unfortunately, the basic principles of international trade,
especially the principles of non-discrimination and
most-favoured-nation treatment, were being widely
breached. Protectionist trends were gaining strength
and various non-tariff barriers were proliferating, as
were the restrictive business practices of TNCs.

8. The Soviet Union stood for the adoption, by the
international community, of effective and fair measures
aimed at developing an equal, non-exclusive democratic
and multilateral trading system interlinked by reciprocal
rights and obligations. UNCTAD and other interna-

tional organizations concerned could make a greater
contribution to the elaboration of recommendations
and arrangements for the further development of the
international trading system. The adoption within
UNCTAD of a programme promoting greater trade
and economic co-operation among countries having
different social systems would be of great importance
and would provide additional mutually acceptable
guidelines for the development of co-operation. The
Group of 77 had made the interesting suggestion that
consultations should be conducted within UNCTAD on
the launching of multilateral negotiations concerning
ways of further strengthening trade and economic co-
operation between developing and socialist countries.

9. Considering that the problems of world trade
ought to be dealt with through the joint efforts of all
States concerned, his delegation felt strongly that only
with the participation of such a major trading nation as
the USSR would the Uruguay Round of multilateral
trade negotiations be able to achieve truly effective
results. The Soviet Union's intention to take part in the
Uruguay Round was in line with its policy of eventually
becoming a contracting party to GATT.

10. The international community had a duty to
alleviate the situation of the LDCs, whose social and
economic circumstances continued to worsen. The Conference should analyse the reasons why previously adopted decisions on the problem had been inadequately
implemented and recommend measures which would
facilitate the more rapid social and economic development of the countries concerned.

11. The USSR was pursuing a consistent course of
extending economic ties with developing countries, including the LDCs. Economic assistance was an important integral part of the USSR's co-operation with the
developing countries. In 1986 the Soviet Union's net
assistance to developing countries had amounted to the
rouble equivalent of approximately $24 billion, in-
cluding assistance to the LDCs amounting to the rouble
equivalent of $3.2 billion.

12. The year 1987 would see the seventieth anniversary of the Great October Socialist Revolution, an
outstanding event which had profoundly changed the
world. The seventieth anniversary was being celebrated
at a time when revolutionary reforms designed to accelerate the progress of socialist society were under way
in the USSR. The reforms were also aimed at extending
the USSR's participation in the international division of
labour, thus effectively promoting the development of
international trade. Moreover, the anniversary came at
a time when the future of the world depended on joint
efforts to eliminate the threat of a thermonuclear war.
Life under conditions of security, independence and
progress in all areas, including the economic area, could
and should be ensured for all nations. In that respect
not everything depended on the USSR, but it would do
whatever was in its power. As Mr. Gorbachev had
pointed out, the current situation was a historical
challenge, and both ideological and political differences
should recede before the common destiny of the human
race, before the priority of life and of values common to
all mankind. It called for courageous and urgent action
by all people concerned about the future of civilization.

13. Before concluding his statement, he had an important announcement to make. In view of the recent instability of commodity markets, the question of putting into effect the Agreement Establishing the Common Fund for Commodities, worked out under the auspices of UNCTAD, had become particularly urgent. The movement of non-aligned countries and the Group of 77 had appealed to countries which had not yet joined the Agreement to do so, if possible by the seventh session of the Conference. The Soviet leadership had carefully considered the question and it had been decided that the USSR should become a party to the Agreement, which he was authorized to sign in the course of the current session of the Conference. His Government hoped that the implementation of the Agreement would contribute to greater stability and predictability in world commodity markets in the interests of both importing and exporting countries and to ensuring the economic security of States and the practical implementation of the Programme of Action on the Establishment of a New International Economic Order.

Summary of the statement made at the 205th plenary meeting, 13 July 1987, by Mr. Saif Ali AL JARWAN, Minister of Trade and Economy of the United Arab Emirates

1. Mr. AL JARWAN said that he welcomed the opportunity to represent his country at the Conference, which was an effective forum for dialogue and exchange of views on contemporary world economic, trade and development problems.

2. His delegation reiterated its support for the Havana Declaration adopted by the Group of 77 at its Sixth Ministerial Meeting. There was widespread recognition of the need for increased international cooperation and greater interdependence based on respect for national sovereignty and more harmonious international relations, since all were equal partners in the development process and equal members of the international community.

3. The Conference was meeting at a time when the world was undergoing a prolonged and dangerous crisis, marked by a disappointing performance of the world economy, deteriorating terms of trade for the developing countries, declining commodity prices, renewed inflation, currency speculation, and a decline in oil prices which had reduced the capacity of oil-producing countries to assist developing countries. The latter's export earnings had amounted to only 22.9 per cent of total world exports in 1985, even though they accounted for more than two thirds of the world's population. The developing countries nevertheless continued to receive a third of the exports of industrialized countries, which, however, had intensified their protectionist measures against exports from developing countries, and particularly against high-quality manufactures offered at competitive prices. Petrochemical products from the Gulf countries, for example, were denied access to the markets of developed countries, while the Gulf countries themselves were pursuing a free trade policy, offering an open market for world products without any discrimination. The Conference should urge the developed countries to respect the UNCTAD resolutions calling for the revision of their protectionist and anti-dumping legislation, to liberalize imports of products from developing countries and to expand their system of trade preferences to those countries.

4. The collapse of the international monetary system had led to political and social upheavals in many debtor developing countries. That system was in urgent need of reform to enable IMF to provide loans to as many of those countries as possible. His delegation supported the idea of convening an international conference for the purpose.

5. Resources should be distributed equitably, and developed countries should be more generous in their dealings with the poorer countries. Despite the United Nations resolutions urging the developed countries to devote 0.7 per cent of their GNP to development assistance, their total assistance had amounted to no more than 0.25 per cent of their aggregate GNP. The developing countries should be helped to help themselves. The oil-producing countries had granted them bilateral loans on preferential terms in an amount of $19.4 billion between 1974 and 1978 and $33.4 billion between 1980 and 1984, while the Islamic Development Bank and other banks and funds in the area had together provided $21 billion between 1974 and 1985.

6. His country had assisted over 50 developing countries. Between 1974 and 1984 the assistance it had provided through the Abu Dhabi Fund for Development had amounted to 5.2 per cent of GNP. It had, in addition, contributed $4.5 billion through international organizations during the same period, while its Head of State had made personal donations and grants to various developing countries.

7. Those countries were confronting some extremely serious problems, including the problem of external indebtedness. Unless a solution could be found, their indebtedness would lead to serious imbalances affecting the entire world economy.

8. To help the international community to achieve harmonious development, the developed creditor countries should, first, distribute the extra income which they had earned as a consequence of the decline in oil prices to the developing countries in the form of grants and the cancellation of debt. Secondly, the process of rescheduling of debts through the Paris Club should be revised and made more realistic. Thirdly, the export earnings of developing countries should be increased through trade preferences established under GATT and developed countries should abandon their protectionist policies. Fourthly, General Assembly resolution 41/202 should be complied with and the developed countries should devote 0.15 per cent of their GNP to assistance to the LDCs. Lastly, developed countries should encourage commercial banks to continue to provide credit to the developing countries.

9. The drought in Africa was becoming ever more widespread, with devastating effects for 34 African countries, despite the world campaign to tackle the food problem. The Conference should do everything possible to ensure the implementation of the resolutions of the special session of the General Assembly on Africa. His country and other members of the Gulf Co-operation Council had provided direct assistance to the affected countries, and a drought-relief plan had been established in the Islamic Conference. His delegation considered that long-term development programmes should be devised to enable the African countries concerned to overcome their difficulties.

10. The Iran-Iraq war was a threat to world peace and an obstacle to the region's development. He urged the international community and the members of the Security Council to do everything possible to put an end to that destructive conflict. Iraq had adopted a praiseworthy position in its readiness to respond to peace initiatives.

11. The economic situation of the Palestinian people in the occupied territories called for a firm stand if the people concerned were to regain their legitimate rights. He drew attention to the relevant resolutions of the Conference, the General Assembly and the EEC concerning the obstacles placed in the way of access by Palestinian products to international markets as a result of Israel's occupation of the territories. UNCTAD should do everything possible to facilitate such access. He welcomed the EEC resolution according preferential treatment to Palestinian products and denounced Israel's refusal to allow them passage through the port of Gaza. He hoped that UNCTAD would continue to show concern for the economic situation of the Palestinian people; he drew attention in that connection to Conference resolution 146 (VI).

12. The *apartheid* policy practised by the white minority Government in South Africa was a serious violation of the Charter of the United Nations and a monstrous act of aggression against human rights, and the occupation of Namibia was an affront to the conscience of mankind. Member States should give effect to the sanctions provided for in Chapter VII of the Charter. UNCTAD should do everything possible to ensure compliance with Conference resolution 147 (VI) on the granting of assistance to the South African and Namibian peoples. He hoped that the Conference would serve the cause of peace and help to establish a better and more unselfish world based on co-operation.

Summary of the statement made at the 214th plenary meeting, 28 July 1987, by Mr. Alan CLARK, Minister for Trade, Department of Trade and Industry of the United Kingdom of Great Britain and Northern Ireland

1. Mr. CLARK said that the United Kingdom, like other developed countries, was aware of the need to tackle vigorously the problems of financial and trade imbalances, but also to ensure that developing countries enjoyed a better economic environment, in which they could achieve their full potential. Participants in the OECD Ministerial Meeting and the Venice Summit had shown that they were adopting sound macro-economic policies coupled with necessary structural adjustment. However, each country faced a different mix of structural difficulties. The United Kingdom, confronted with the erosion of competitiveness in several key industries, had endeavoured to make the economy more responsive to market forces through deregulation, changing the balance between the public and private sectors and restoring personal initiative. The path it had chosen had proved fully justified, since growth had remained steady with low inflation over the preceding four years, and unemployment was beginning to decline. Many other countries had succeeded in maintaining fairly stable growth. Some of them, particularly a number of developing countries with expanding manufacturing sectors, had been able to sustain relatively high levels of external trade. Many other developing countries had the capacity to achieve stable economic growth. Although the options available to the poorest among them were perforce limited, many of those hardest hit by declining commodity prices were nevertheless striving to create a more secure base for themselves through investment in human resources and diversification.

2. The future was therefore possibly not as gloomy as depicted by Conference participants. However, many developing countries would have great difficulty in carrying out the adjustment process without external assistance. The United Kingdom currently provided all bilateral aid to the poorest countries in the form of grants and had implemented Trade and Development Board resolution 165 (S-IX) of 11 March 1978 by relieving past aid debt in the amount of £1 billion. The practice of converting past aid loans into grants had proved of great value, particularly in the context of adjustment, and should be more widely adopted by developed countries. At the multilateral level, the United Kingdom supported a general capital increase for the World Bank and welcomed the initiative taken by IMF to expand its Structural Adjustment Facility. The United Kingdom was also participating actively in negotiations to replenish the resources of the various regional development banks and funds. Its total contribution to the Eighth Replenishment of IDA resources amounted to over £500 million.

3. With respect to the debt problem, the strategy pursued for some years by the international community remained basically valid and required no fundamental change. Countries were applying it with an increasing degree of flexibility and were showing a willingness to resolve problems on a case-by-case basis, taking into account each debtor's specific situation. The United Kingdom considered that to be the only feasible way of tackling debt issues. However, there was again little hope of the poorest countries being able to service their debt, even in the medium term, unless special measures were taken to alleviate their burden. That was why, at the latest joint meeting in Washington of IMF and the

World Bank, the Government of the United Kingdom had submitted specific proposals aimed at relieving the debt burden of the poorest, most heavily indebted countries in sub-Saharan Africa which were pursuing sound economic policies. It would continue to press for reduced Paris Club interest rates, since that was the best way to stop the debt burden rising in an unsustainable manner. Several African countries were already benefiting from longer Paris Club rescheduling terms.

4. However, whether the issue under consideration was debt servicing or development itself of the poorest countries, no amount of external support could replace appropriate domestic policies, which alone were capable of mobilizing financial support both from within and from outside. The Group of 77 had rightly stressed that the primary responsibility for development rested with the developing countries themselves. Those who made an effort to provide the right climate for foreign direct investment could count on support from the international community. Several countries were already taking advantage of assistance from international financial institutions to create an attractive environment for investment. The United Kingdom remained one of the major direct investors in developing countries, its annual average investment amounting to some £1.7 billion.

5. In the field of commodities, it was also important to avoid inhibiting or distorting the operation of market forces. The collapse of the International Tin Agreement showed that it was self-defeating to attempt to maintain prices artificially at levels above those that would otherwise prevail in an open market. The decline of commodity prices in real terms since the 1950s had been brought about by structural factors of supply and demand. The solution therefore lay in adaptation to

market trends and, once again, structural adjustment in developing countries economically dependent on the production of certain primary products.

6. Referring to the Uruguay Round of multilateral trade negotiations, he said that all countries would benefit from the widest degree of trade liberalization. The United Kingdom urged further market-opening by developed countries, but also by the stronger developing countries, to imports from those countries seeking a first foothold in international trade. The considerable economic progress made by a number of developing countries in recent years should also be acknowledged by encouraging wider acceptance by them of the normal obligations of GATT membership.

7. The Uruguay Round covered two areas of particular interest to developing countries, namely, tropical products and agriculture. The European Community had recently indicated that it would honour its commitment to grant priority treatment to tropical products by submitting specific trade liberalization proposals at an early stage. Agricultural over-production had strained the budgets of developed countries and, through pressure on world market prices, had also depressed developing country earnings from the sector. Co-ordinated reforms were therefore crucial. A world agricultural economy where comparative advantage was more justly rewarded could be the Uruguay Round's biggest contribution to growth in the LDCs.

8. He expressed hope that the seventh session of the Conference would lead to action-oriented recommendations that would help the international community achieve the economic and developmental goals to which it was committed.

Summary of the statement made at the 213th plenary meeting, 27 July 1987, by Mr. Daudi N. MWAKAWAGO, Minister for Industries and Trade of the United Republic of Tanzania

1. Mr. MWAKAWAGO said that, like most developing countries, Tanzania was dependent on the export of agricultural commodities, six of which accounted for approximately 80 per cent of its export earnings. His Government had encouraged the cultivation of cotton and tobacco, but following the collapse of prices, the United Republic of Tanzania had only just been able to maintain its export earnings. In the circumstances, it was difficult to satisfy the needs of the population and honour the country's foreign debt obligations. The export earnings shortfall had forced Tanzania to cut back sharply on imports, which consisted primarily of inputs for agriculture, transport and industry. In order to alleviate the socio-economic situation, his Government had concluded a stand-by arrangement with IMF, but was aware that external resources were no alternative to a domestic effort to achieve self-sufficiency.

2. Most developing countries were encountering the same problems as Tanzania. If their economic recovery policy was to be successful, they required remunerative prices for their commodities, better markets for their exports, significantly increased ODA, debt relief and con-

cessional credit. Unfortunately, the attitude of the developed countries was hardly encouraging. Nothing had been done to redress commodity prices or to stimulate demand for products from developing countries; exchange rates remained unstable and interest rates high, and concessional financial flows had levelled off. Moreover, there was a tendency to abandon multilateralism in favour of unilateral and bilateral measures. The resolutions and decisions of UNCTAD and other international bodies remained dead letters, and calculated efforts had even been made to weaken such organizations as UNCTAD.

3. Encouraging exceptions deserved mention. In particular, the Nordic countries were striving to honour their development commitments, despite their own domestic difficulties. Tanzania was grateful for their efforts and assured them that it would make the best use of the resources they provided.

4. That a part of the world should be prosperous and developed while the other vegetated was totally inconceivable. The sole guarantee of sustained development was peace and prosperity for all, and the developed countries must do more for the third world.

It was in that spirit that the Group of 77 had presented its Havana Declaration, which contained proposals for stimulating development, growth and international trade through multilateral co-operation.

5. The international community was more conscious than ever before of the world's economic interdependence. If a universal body such as UNCTAD was to consolidate that interdependence, countries that possessed capital and technology and were therefore responsible for providing leadership must make solemn commitments.

6. One of those countries—the Soviet Union—had just taken a step in that direction by joining the Common Fund for Commodities. It was to be hoped that all the parties concerned, and particularly the United States of America, would make every effort to ensure that the Fund was truly effective.

7. The spectacular economic results achieved in a number of industrialized countries must not conceal the unprecedented difficulties faced by the rest of mankind. A narrow, short-sighted policy might well jeopardize security and peace for all peoples.

Summary of the statement made at the 217th plenary meeting, 29 July 1987, by Mr. Dennis G. GOODMAN, Senior Deputy Assistant Secretary, Bureau of International Organization Affairs, Department of State of the United States of America

1. Mr. GOODMAN said that he would not refer to all the issues on the agenda of the Conference at length, as the United States had already made its position clear in that regard, but instead would concentrate on the way in which work in the economic field was being conducted at UNCTAD and throughout the United Nations system—a matter that, in his view, left much to be desired. It was not without good cause that the United Nations had established the Group of 18 to review the structure of the Organization and that, at its last session, the General Assembly had approved, by its resolution 41/213, a series of reforms of which a large percentage were aimed at rationalizing work in the economic sector.

2. The seventh session of the Conference was drawing to a close: what had been accomplished so far and what could still be done in the remaining two days? There had, exceptionally, been a genuine debate which had perhaps not been as thorough as might have been desired but which had represented a step in the right direction. Unfortunately, as soon as the "drafting" or "negotiating" had commenced, the useful dialogue had largely ended.

3. It had to be recognized that none of the participants in the Conference intended to make fundamental changes in their positions, which had been defined after mature reflection by their Governments. It was to be feared that, once again, they would go no further than producing a paper, cleverly drafted in none too precise terms, giving the impression that they had agreed upon the basic economic problems of the time and on measures to solve them, while in fact constituting nothing concrete. If that was to be the result of the work of the Conference, representatives would have little to feel proud of when returning home, having spent a great deal of their taxpayers' money on their costly stay in Geneva.

4. The time had come, therefore, for all those who were serious about the work of UNCTAD and bodies such as the Economic and Social Council and the General Assembly to examine what was wrong. Moving from the fruitful exchange of views to the drafting of an illusory document because "that was how it had always been done", or because "we could not bring all these Ministers here and not have a declaration for them to sign", was a prescription for the further decline of the Organization. But that was not all. The Conference was working on the erroneous assumption that little or nothing was being done to assist developing countries, or that what was being done was either misconceived or totally inadequate. More importantly, there was a tendency to minimize the achievements that individual developing countries were making to foster development and strengthen the international economy and virtually no recognition was given to existing programmes. The underlying assumption was that each meeting must come up with an entirely new set of proposals.

5. The Conference was also working on the premise that the world was in a perpetual economic crisis. The situation was viewed from a number of different angles, but it was always catastrophic: if OPEC put up oil prices, there was anxiety about the plight of the oil-importing countries, and if prices fell, the drafters turned to the plight of the exporters. Whatever the text, only passing reference was made to the fact that the third world countries were chiefly responsible for their development, but there was a long explanation about how their problems were due to external economic conditions and how the Western countries should act to remedy the situation. The texts refused to acknowledge that some developing countries were doing so well that it was time they assumed more responsibility in the international community. The fact that one major group of countries was doing almost nothing for the developing countries was also completely ignored. No one believed the aid figures that group claimed for itself, but neither did anyone call for the group to account for itself. A kind of double standard seemed to prevail, and that was inadmissible.

6. All too often speakers politicized economic problems. Their explanations changed yearly, of course, but the process was always the same. Everything was blamed alternately on inflation in the West, budget deficits, interest rates, trade deficits, exchange rate fluctuations or the debt crisis. On the latter subject, the only response was to call for the granting of new loans, carefully avoiding the question of how they should be used: that would be interference in the internal affairs of States . . .

7.   Some \$30 million were allocated to the UNCTAD secretariat, but at its seventh session the Conference had virtually ignored the documents produced by that organization, focusing largely on texts prepared by the various country groups. Preparatory meetings had been held throughout the world, but no one seemed able to say what purpose they had actually served. There was an endless list of speakers, yet it was well known that the concentration of listeners faded after a while. Might it not be better to limit statements to five minutes and make the full texts available in print?

8.   Many highly informed persons came to speak but were then allowed to slip away, leaving no time to ask them questions which might produce an extremely useful exchange of views. Documents of a political nature were also allowed, dealing with questions that were not within the purview of UNCTAD.

9.   Those were some of the problems that plagued the work of UNCTAD and most of the United Nations bodies in the economic field. The system was obviously not working well and must be improved. The Group of 18 had worked long and hard to come up with a set of highly useful proposals that provided a very good start, but more remained to be done. Still, it would be unfair to look at only the negative side of things. The Conference had been the framework for a constructive exchange of views, and efforts should be continued in that direction. An encouraging development had also occurred: whereas talk of the private sector a few years ago previously had been all but taboo, today the great majority of members of UNCTAD admitted that the private sector had a major role to play in economic development. However, in the name of the majority of developing countries, a small group of countries continued to put forward proposals that were completely outmoded at the risk of weakening the credibility of UNCTAD and preventing a fruitful exchange of views. The developed countries should remain open-minded to the views of serious and reasonable representatives of developing countries and recognize that many of those countries were making considerable efforts to improve their situation.

10.   Why, instead of wasting time in sterile debate, should the participants in the Conference not recognize frankly that there were differences between them which might not perhaps be reconcilable, at last for the time being, but that in some areas views obviously converged? A beginning had, indeed, been made to identify the essentials of an international consensus. An international strategy had been launched to deal with the debt problems of developing countries on a case-by-case basis and the general view was that there was a need to continue to co-operate in a constructive spirit to restore the economic and financial health of developing countries, placing emphasis on sustainable and non-inflationary growth. In the OECD countries, growth had to be more rapid. It was recognized that economic reforms were essential in the debtor countries, many of which were making considerable efforts, and that those reforms must be supported by additional capital inflows and the repatriation of flight capital.

11.   Regarding commodities, no one contested the fact that prices were at their lowest level in 50 years and it should be possible to agree on the cyclical and structural factors affecting the markets. Agreements should also be possible on the need to take into account the past experience and interests of both producers and consumers. The importance of trade expansion, trade liberalization, transparency in trade policies and structural adjustment in resisting protectionism and promoting growth was clear. All countries recognized the essential role of the Uruguay Round in that regard and believed that the UNCTAD secretariat could help the developing countries participating in the negotiations. lastly, special assistance had to be given to the poorest countries to support their adjustment efforts.

12.   On the basis of the useful discussions that had already taken place and the many papers prepared for the Conference, it should therefore be possible to produce a report that accurately reflected the current situation and views, a report that would set an example for other United Nations bodies. That was the only way for the Conference to reach an honourable conclusion.

**Summary of the statement made at the 205th plenary meeting, 13 July 1987,
by Mr. Enrique V. IGLESIAS, Minister for Foreign Affairs of Uruguay**

1.   Mr. IGLESIAS said that two principles that had been strongly defended by two Latin American former Secretaries-General of UNCTAD—international solidarity and multilateralism, both of which were in a state of crisis—were essential for any improvement in the world situation and could not be sacrificed. The Conference was meeting at a time when the world economy was characterized by monetary fluctuations, low growth rates, macro-economic imbalances and lack of co-ordination in macro-economic policies in the developed countries. The situation was even more serious for the developing countries, for the price of their export commodities—fundamental to their economic development—were at their lowest levels, having declined throughout the 1980s. The situation was exacerbated

by protectionism and restricted access to markets and by an external debt that was so high that some developing countries had to divert more than 50 per cent of their resources to servicing the debt. There had also been withdrawals of public and private capital investment. In such a climate, UNCTAD's message was as valid as ever. It was only through an awareness of the interdependence of the fundamental factors regulating the international economy, and through co-ordinated action, that countries could solve their problems.

2.   There had been some encouraging developments, however, including the Uruguay Round, which had opened so successfully, possibly because it had been realized that a continuing state of conflict was fraught

with danger and that only in a world of open trade exchanges could the situation be improved. After the promising start of the Uruguay Round, the working groups were proceeding with their work and it was hoped that some results would materialize in 1989 that would make it possible to tackle the problems and halt some of the existing protectionist trends and the deterioration in international trade.

3. A further encouraging sign, and an important development for UNCTAD, was that participants in the Venice Summit had confirmed their commitment to free trade. The discussion of agricultural issues and the recent proposal made in that area by the United States had been welcomed, and it was gratifying to note that the various sides had begun to talk a common language, thus raising hopes that agricultural protectionism, which was a major obstacle to world progress, would finally cease. The Uruguay Round had been the first of its kind to take place with the active participation of developing countries and the first to be directed at remedying past shortcomings and considering the economic structure of world trade for the coming decades. Due consideration had been given to ways and means whereby UNCTAD could help to ensure the success of negotiations that were crucial to the future of mankind.

4. His country had taken part in the Cartagena Consensus on external indebtedness, when 11 countries had co-operated in discussing one of Latin America's most serious problems, shared with many countries in other parts of the world. The problem was as yet unsolved but the countries concerned were surviving by making adjustments, and some conclusions were emerging. Indebtedness remained the fundamental problem conditioning all their economic prospects for the coming years. It could only be solved through growth, and not in a climate of depression. There had been some innovative forms of refinancing in such countries as Mexico and Argentina and some success in promoting greater understanding and a more comprehensive view of the problem, in which all countries and financial institutions were involved.

5. His country, and he personally, had faith in UNCTAD which, like all institutions, had its achievements and frustrations. There could be no doubt about its major achievements as an institution whose discussions had for decades illuminated the very concepts of international development and co-operation or

about the major contributions it had made on such questions as commodities, development assistance and preferences, for which it had every reason to be proud. Governments had a responsibility to redefine priorities, identify new areas and invest UNCTAD with renewed vitality.

6. There were three major tasks for which UNCTAD had exclusive responsibility and was uniquely fitted as a universal and global institution. First, it was the forum for the overall political consideration of world economic problems. Secondly, it had to give guidance to the relevant trade and financial forums in an atmosphere of calm and responsible discussion. Thirdly, its field of competence covered certain specific areas, such as structural commodity problems, which called for international negotiation and a reordering of comparative advantages. Many productive systems needed to be revised completely to take account of new features, and only UNCTAD was capable of securing the necessary international co-operation for the purpose. He welcomed the readiness expressed by certain countries to support the Common Fund for Commodities.

7. There had been some talk of catastrophe and of a possible major international crisis, but his delegation was more optimistic, because on past occasions the international community had shown itself capable of facing such challenges. With the maturity and experience acquired since the Conference had last met at Geneva, it was possible to be more hopeful. Profound adjustments were being made in a search for greater efficiency and equity, although regrettably the latter had sometimes been sacrificed to the former. Some ideas, such as the notion that all ills came from outside, had been abandoned. At the same time, however, it had to be recognized that it would be profoundly unjust and would lead to a collapse of the international system if the developing countries were required to make their own economic adjustments without concomitant adjustments on all sides, in the public and private sectors alike. His delegation's belief in a sound, realistic and pragmatic solidarity was based not only on ethical principles but also on a profound conviction that all participants in the Conference had come to it with hope, and believed in UNCTAD as a forum that could fulfil that hope. Uruguay was committed to co-operation and was ready to work in UNCTAD to achieve justice and well-being for all peoples of the world.

Summary of the statement made at the 202nd plenary meeting, 10 July 1987, by Mr. Héctor MENESES, Minister of Development of Venezuela

1. Mr. MENESES said that the Conference was taking place at a time of major structural changes in the world economy, calling for diagnosis and action in the interest of the international community. The world was going through a phase of transition towards a new international order, in response to the emergence of new technologies and the predominant role of service activities against the background of the transnationalization of production. That state of affairs was producing

a new international division of labour backed by a harmful trend towards bilateralism and the conclusion of exclusive agreements among the major economic powers. There was thus a drift away from the principles and practices of multilateralism and co-operation among States. The adoption of national legislation that unilaterally shaped international economic relations, the conclusion of bilateral agreements in conflict with the rules of multilateralism, or the imposition of the interests of a few developed economies as goals for multilateral negotiations were indicative of the systematic exclusion of international forums from the agreement and decision-making process. That was particularly serious at a time when it was not only necessary to find a consensus on the changes taking place but to remedy the inefficiencies of the existing system. The changes were occurring in the context of an economic situation that was deteriorating as never before—a structural, ideological and institutional crisis whose effects had been most damaging to the developing countries and which had eroded the monetary, financial and trade interrelationships of the economic system. Such lack of control over the interdependence of the international economy had been reflected in the erosion of the international monetary system and in the serious problem of external indebtedness and had led to a questioning of the original design and rules of the international trade system and a diminution of the role of trade as a key factor of development, a means of dissemination of technology and a stimulus to production.

2. The crisis of the developing countries affected the entire international community. External indebtedness, for example, threatened not only to paralyse economic growth, hamper the democratization process and disrupt social peace in debtor countries but also to destabilize the entire international financial system. The responsibility for that problem and its solution lay equally on debtor countries, creditor countries, private banks and international financing institutions and was thus of concern to the entire international community. The President of Venezuela had pointed out that debtor countries were making every effort to meet their financial commitments, but the debt problem could not be solved at the expense of the well-being of their peoples, by making the developing countries net exporters of capital or by imposing on them policies that caused recession and unemployment. The developing countries were in effect financing the deficits and adjustments of the developed countries. That situation was not only destructive to their economies but was unacceptable in terms of development as a joint goal of the international community. Some countries had transferred abroad the equivalent of 10 per cent of their GNP and 50 per cent of their export earnings. In Latin America, the consequence had been a substantial fall in domestic investment, increased unemployment, a drastic reduction in imports and a considerable deterioration in living standards, giving rise to social and political tension which threatened the democratic process and the stability of the region.

3. If the world economy and development were to be revitalized, international financial flows must be reversed, but it was also essential to bring about a significant change in the entire economic environment in order to stimulate sustained economic development, since the developing countries would find it extremely difficult to service their debts on the existing terms and conditions, still less to reach acceptable economic and social standards for their population. In that situation there was an obvious need to deal with the instability of commodity prices and to ensure the access of commodities to the markets of industrialized countries. Compliance by the developing countries with their financial obligations was closely linked to their trade expansion prospects.

4. A more favourable world environment could not be achieved merely by the joint action of a few industrialized countries or by piecemeal action in international organizations with limited competence. Owing to the complexity and close interrelationship of the existing challenges, global and multilateral solutions were called for. It was paradoxical that multilateral development co-operation had been subordinated to more immediate problems, to the immediate interests of some developed countries and to bilateralism in international economic relations.

5. The efforts of the developing countries to overcome the existing economic situation and establish the foundations for development called for the firm support of the international community, although the developing countries were aware of their own potential, as reflected in renewed regional and interregional co-operation.

6. His country hoped that it would be possible to reach a joint position at the seventh session of the Conference and to create the conditions conducive to a balanced and sustained development of the world economy. All countries members of the Group of 77 had great faith and interest in UNCTAD which, by reason of its universal membership, its development-oriented approach and its terms of reference, was the only multilateral forum equipped to deal with the interrelated trade, financial and development problems in the interest of all countries. Venezuela therefore endorsed the Declaration and recommendations agreed upon at the Sixth Ministerial Meeting of the Group of 77.

7. A number of prominent Latin American statesmen had devoted their best efforts to UNCTAD and had stated their conviction that multilateral dialogue and agreement were the best means of contributing to the advancement of peoples. UNCTAD had an irreplaceable role to play in confronting the complex issues of the international economy and development, which called for agreement and dialogue.

Summary of the statement made at the 206th plenary meeting, 13 July 1987, by Mr. Dy Nien NGUYEN, Deputy Minister for Foreign Affairs of Viet Nam

1. Mr. NGUYEN said that the seventh session of the Conference assumed particular significance in so far as it succeeded in concerting and mobilizing efforts to devise effective, practical measures for the solution of the economic problems of the 1980s. One of the major factors contributing to the deteriorating economic situation—others were the deterioration of the terms of trade of developing countries, their external debt, and

the instability of currencies—was the application by many developed market-economy countries of policies that tended to shift the burden of their structural economic readjustment on to the developing countries, which resulted in a substantial net transfer of much-needed resources from developing to developed countries. The April 1987 Havana Declaration of the Group of 77 had made an important contribution to the overall assessment of the world economic situation. His delegation urged that a serious examination be made of all the factors impeding the development of developing countries and widening the gap between the rich North and the poor South.

2.   At a time of structural readjustment in a context of growing interdependence among all countries, all economic or political problems could be settled only on a basis of equality and democracy within the framework of a comprehensive security system and rapid economic development for all countries, especially the developing countries. The May 1987 Berlin document of the States parties to the Warsaw Treaty contained principles for dealing with the pressing problems besetting international economic relations, for overcoming under-development and establishing a new international economic order. It was necessary to elaborate further on the international economic security concept in accordance with General Assembly resolutions 40/173 and 41/184 with a view to the realization of a new international order, in line with the Economic Declaration adopted at the Eighth Conference of Heads of State or Government of Non-Aligned Countries, held at Harare in September 1986. No crucial problem had yet been solved through mere bilateral or local settlements; global problems should be solved on a basis of equality, justice, harmony and universality. The Soviet Government's decision to become a party to the Agreement Establishing the Common Fund for Commodities was an important example of such an approach. UNCTAD with its unique universal character could play a constructive role in finding solutions to those problems.

3.   As was stated in the Havana Declaration of April 1987, there could be no peace without development, nor development without peace. Accordingly, it was necessary to create an environment of security, confidence and co-operation for the realization of the principle of disarmament for development; the resources released thereby should be mobilized for the development of the world economy and especially the economies of the developing countries. The Delhi Declaration for a nuclear-free and non-violent world in international relations was an encouragement in that context.

4.   Viet Nam was initiating a process of far-reaching reform, aimed at developing all economic components of society, readjusting economic management on the basis of greater initiative by producers, promoting the principle of socialist business cost-accounting and integrating internal and external markets. Efforts were being made to develop infrastructure in key fields with a view to expanding economic relations with socialist, developing and other countries on the basis of equality and mutual benefit.

5.   Viet Nam faced difficulties similar to those of other developing countries, and in addition had been subjected to attempts to weaken its economy or bring about its collapse. It was none the less succeeding in breaking through the economic blockade, in particular through co-operation with socialist countries and other well-disposed countries, including a number of developing countries. The market shift in the international division of labour confronted his country with many critical challenges, especially with regard to developing its capital and technical potential and industrial processing capacities, and adjusting to fluctuations and new developments in the world economy and international economic relations; but his country was confident of its ability to reduce its vulnerability by taking full advantage of new opportunities that would arise if the international division of labour was boldly carried further. In that spirit, Viet Nam would continue to participate in the common cause of UNCTAD in revitalizing development, growth and international trade in the interests of the international community and primarily for the benefit of the developing countries.

Summary of the statement made at the 208th plenary meeting, 14 July 1987, by Mr. Ibrahim TABAKOVIĆ, Member of the Federal Executive Council, Minister for Co-operation with Developing Countries of Yugoslavia

1.   Mr. TABAKOVIĆ said that as Mr. Lazar Mojsov, President of the Presidency of the Socialist Federal Republic of Yugoslavia* in his address at the opening of the Conference had outlined his country's position with respect to UNCTAD, he would now comment only on a number of specific issues.

2.   He hoped that the Conference would give priority to reaching agreement on concrete policies and measures for ensuring the overall growth of the world economy, and in particular the accelerated development of the developing countries. The general recognition of economic interdependence should lead to the adoption of a final document containing a renewed consensus on development to serve as a framework for policies and measures at the national and international levels and as guidelines and suggestions for international organizations operating in particular areas. Yugoslavia's specific proposals had been incorporated into the final documents of the Sixth Ministerial Meeting of the Asian Group held at Dhaka and of the Sixth Ministerial Meeting of the Group of 77 held at Havana in 1987.

3.   As far as development resources and financial and monetary issues were concerned, at the moment there were three key problems calling for urgent international action: the debt problem had to be solved; the

---

* TD/L.286 (see volume I, annex III).

volume and quality of development resources had to be enhanced; and the functioning of the international monetary system had to be improved. The great majority of debtor developing countries were experiencing stagnation or even negative economic growth. For seven years they had been suffering disinvestment, a contraction in imports, an outflow of already scarce funds, and a sizeable decrease in public outlays on the social infrastructure. The developing countries were also being excluded from the technological adjustment process, with the result that markets for goods, capital and equipment from the developed countries were shrinking. At the same time, frequent and substantial changes in the exchange rates of the main reserve currencies were endangering development and export programmes and destroying productive structures in the developing countries. The result was a steady erosion of the value of national currencies, coupled with uncontrolled inflation, and structural disturbances in international markets.

4. The developing countries' debt problem could not be solved without development, an increase in production, better access to markets, and the stabilization of export earnings. The short-term, case-by-case solutions subject to numerous conditions applied by the creditor countries so far were mainly of a stop-gap nature. Meanwhile, the "debt bomb" was threatening the position of developing countries and creditor countries alike. A political dialogue between creditors and debtors, taking account of General Assembly resolution 41/202 should therefore be initiated as soon as possible. A start could be made at the current session, and subsequent discussions at ministerial level should aim at working out a global framework for a long-term development-oriented solution. The readiness of some developed countries to provide debt relief or to write off part of the official debts of the LDCs, particularly those of sub-Saharan Africa, constituted a positive initial step. However, additional urgent measures were called for to solve the debt problem and to ensure that resources were made available on favourable terms to enable the LDCs to accelerate their development. It was also necessary to seek adequate long-term solutions for the other developing countries, along the lines of the proposals of the Ministerial Meeting of the Group of 77 held at Havana and of the Group of 24 developing countries. Yugoslavia fully supported the view that a committee of ministers from developing and developed countries should be established to consider proposals for the reform and improvement of the international monetary system.

5. In the field of international trade, it was to be hoped that the Conference would make a further con-

tribution to the preservation and strengthening of a multilateral trading system that would promote the accelerated development and diversification of the developing countries' economies and increase their share in world trade. That could be attained through the abolition of all forms of discrimination against exports from the developing countries, the consistent implementation of the obligations undertaken by the industrialized countries in respect of standstill and roll-back, and the preservation, promotion and more consistent application of the principles contained in the GSP and Part IV of the General Agreement.

6. It was to be hoped that the Uruguay Round of trade negotiations would contribute to a significant improvement in the developing countries' position in world trade. Nevertheless, UNCTAD should continue its work on identifying the framework for a universal, non-discriminatory, comprehensive, stable and predictable international trading system and intensify its activities in the field of trade in services.

7. Exports of commodities accounted for the major part of most developing countries' development resources. Since the adoption of the Integrated Programme for Commodities, technological progress and structural changes had taken place in the world economy, with adverse effects on commodity markets. The collapse of commodity prices was, to a considerable extent, the result of erratic developments and speculation in commodity markets. His delegation was convinced that the objectives of the Integrated Programme for Commodities, as well as the instruments envisaged for stabilizing commodity prices, were still valid. The early entry into force of the Common Fund would provide a significant stimulus and would improve the position of commodity exporters in the world economy. His delegation welcomed the decision of the USSR to sign the Agreement Establishing the Common Fund for Commodities and was confident that other countries which had not yet signed the Agreement would do so soon.

8. The gravest problems were those of the LDCs, particularly those in sub-Saharan Africa. It was to be hoped that the Conference would reach full agreement on the measures to be taken to implement, as soon and as fully as possible, the Substantial New Programme of Action and the United Nations Programme of Action for African Economic Recovery and Development 1986-1990. His delegation was confident that all participants would demonstrate the necessary political will, realism and co-operation to make the seventh session of the Conference a turning-point in international economic co-operation.

Summary of the statement made at the 209th plenary meeting, 15 July 1987, by Mr. Kasereka KASAI, State Commissioner for Foreign Trade of Zaire

1. Mr. KASAI said that the current unprecedented world economic crisis had particularly grave consequences for the developing countries, which saw no prospect for recovery. The worsening of the debt situation, the fall in commodity prices, high real interest rates and

volatile exchange rates, the decline in the flow of financial resources to the extent that developing countries were suffering net outflows, and virtually non-existent investment in infrastructure, machinery and human resources had resulted in the continuing impoverishment of their economies, a progressive decline in their share of international trade and their inability to finance development. Notwithstanding multilateral agreements, industrialized countries were evading their historic responsibilities, asserting their faith in market forces and making unrealistic assessments of the developing countries' ability to cope with an unfavourable external economic environment. Multilateralism was gradually being eroded by the developed countries' recourse to protectionist and deflationary measures resulting *inter alia*, in the fall in commodity prices and a reduction of ODA. The seventh session of the Conference provided a timely opportunity for the international community to seek practical, realistic solutions to development problems, bearing in mind the interdependence of all countries. Zaire was convinced that all delegations to the Conference shared the common concern for and interest in development. The report by the Secretary-General of UNCTAD underscored the critical situation of the developing countries, which persisted despite the many international initiatives taken to remedy it. The most recent of those initiatives was the Havana Declaration of the Group of 77, which his delegation had co-sponsored and which it unreservedly supported.

2. Among the issues of special concern to his delegation was the fall in commodity prices, for Zaire earned most of its income from exports of commodities. The various international instruments and arrangements concerning commodity trade, including the Common Fund for Commodities, the Integrated Programme for Commodities and the IMF Compensatory Financing Facility (CFF) had so far produced no tangible results. In keeping with the recommendations made in the Havana Declaration, his delegation hoped that the current session of the Conference might provide the opportunity for all countries concerned to pledge themselves to accelerate the entry into force of the Common Fund and to make the CFF effective. It welcomed the results of the negotiations on a new International Cocoa Agreement, and an International Agreement on Olive Oil and Table Olives, as well as the entry into force of the International Tropical Timber Agreement but deplored the failure of negotiations on a new International Natural Rubber Agreement and the inadequacy of efforts to implement the IPC, particularly so far as it concerned the

processing, marketing and distribution of commodities. United Nations statistics concerning commodity prices and commodity trade painted a gloomy picture. The Conference should make a thorough, realistic assessment of action-oriented approaches designed to enable international commodity trade to play its rightful role in the economic development of the developing countries.

3. The debt crisis and the increasingly heavy debt-servicing burden, which was resulting in net outflows from the developing to the developed countries, posed a threat to the world economy as a whole. Existing strategies and mechanisms had proved ineffective. There was a need to restructure the international liquidity supply system, consistent with the needs of the developing countries. His delegation, endorsing the measures proposed in the Havana Declaration, supported the idea of launching global negotiations on the indebtedness of the developing countries and hoped that IMF and the World Bank would make joint efforts to step up their action in favour of the developing countries and to improve the management of international financial flows.

4. His delegation attached particular importance to any measures that might be taken by the Conference to increase the participation of land-locked and semi-land-locked countries like his own in international maritime transport. It was also hoped that the Conference might lay the foundations for the establishment of a technical assistance programme for the developing countries to help them to derive greater benefit from the Uruguay Round.

5. The international community faced two major challenges—combating the erosion of multilateralism and re-establishing the principle of interdependence. His delegation welcomed the many appeals made at the current session for a broader dialogue and the genuine will to seek solutions to the problems of development. Great hopes were placed in the practical solutions and commitments that might emerge from the Conference. The constructive contribution of the Group of 77 to that end, in the form of the Havana Declaration, should be matched by similar efforts by other groups with a view to achieving positive results on the basis of broad consensus.

Summary of the statement made at the 207th plenary meeting, 14 July 1987, by Mr. J. K. M. KALALUKA, Minister of Commerce and Industry of Zambia

1. Mr. KALALUKA said that the international community was facing unprecedented economic crises which spelt doom for developed and developing countries alike. Fortunately, those crises could be defused if sufficient efforts were made to tackle the problems in a concerted manner at the global level. The root cause of the current economic malaise was the unwillingness of the "haves" to share what they had with the "have-nots" and the insatiable desire of the rich countries to continue to enrich themselves at the expense of the poor developing countries. For example, the prices of primary commodities exported by developing countries to developed countries had continued to decline, while

the prices of developing countries' imports from developed countries had continued to rise. Furthermore, the developing countries could not export their manufactures and semi-manufactures. The time had come to ask whether UNCTAD had achieved its original objectives and, if not, why it had failed to do so.

2. When the International Development Strategy for the Second United Nations Development Decade had been adopted in 1969, the international community had agreed that the developed world should put aside 0.7 per cent of its GNP for ODA to developing countries. That target had been retained in the International

Development Strategy for the Third United Nations Development Decade, adopted in 1980. However, with a few exceptions, notably the Nordic countries, the developed countries had not lived up to that expectation. Over the years most of them had tended to reduce, rather than increase, their ODA. Unfortunately, that step backward had coincided with severe and deteriorating economic conditions in most developing countries, particularly those in sub-Saharan Africa. The decline in the levels of ODA therefore needed to be reversed as soon as possible in order to maintain the momentum of the development process in the developing countries.

3. Governments in the developing countries were committed to a pattern of development whose objective was to satisfy not only the economic needs of their peoples but also their social welfare and political aspirations. Because of their lack of funds to finance high priority development programmes, they found themselves heavily indebted to the developed countries—an issue which UNCTAD should seriously consider at the current session. As the President of Zambia had recently stated, it was not the intention of the developing countries to default on their debt obligations. What they were requesting from their creditors was understanding and co-operation, as well as uninterrupted assistance to enable them to strengthen their capacity to pay their debts.

4. With every day that passed, millions of dollars were spent on the development and manufacture of weapons of mass destruction, at a time when millions of human beings did not have enough to eat. His delegation was therefore pleased to note that the International Conference on the Relationship between Disarmament and Development was shortly to be convened in New York. That, however, should not deter the Conference from sharing ideas on the subject at its current session and from presenting a unanimously agreed recommendation to the Conference to be held in New York.

5. Copper accounted for over 90 per cent of Zambia's foreign exchange earnings and was therefore central to its economic well-being. Zambia's interest in stable and remunerative copper prices was cardinal to its conception of a secure and just international trade régime. The Government of Zambia was, therefore, naturally concerned at the slow pace at which the copper-importing countries approached the question of negotiating an international agreement, as envisaged in the Integrated Programme for Commodities. At times copper prices on the world market fell far below production costs, not necessarily because of the law of supply and demand but because the prices of copper, like those of all other primary commodities exported by developing countries, were manipulated by those who controlled the international commodity markets. He urged the Conference to take up the issues relating to commodities so that an effective mechanism could be evolved to stabilize prices.

6. Well over six years had been spent in trying to put the Common Fund for Commodities into operation. In 1983 and 1984 the Government of Zambia had paid a total of approximately $700,000 as part of its contribution of $1 million. In 1985 parliamentary approval had been obtained for the payment of the balance, but pay-

ment had been withheld because the Common Fund had not yet become operational. Thanks were due to the Soviet Union and Côte d'Ivoire for their announcements regarding their intention to sign and ratify the Agreement Establishing the Common Fund for Commodities. After their noble gestures, it was to be hoped that the Common Fund would become a reality in the not too distant future.

7. The reason why the developing countries were unable to export their manufactures and semi-manufactures to the developed countries was that the latter had surrounded themselves with protective barriers, ignoring the fact that developing countries had comparative advantages in the processing of their raw materials into finished goods in areas like textiles and footwear. The development prospects of the developing countries would be greatly enhanced if only their manufactures and semi-manufactures could gain access to markets in the developed countries.

8. The economic problems being experienced by the least developed, land-locked, and island developing countries, which had been highlighted by President Mitterrand of France in his address to the Conference,* deserved special attention. Those countries faced critical structural problems and needed international assistance. It was therefore gratifying to note that some countries had cancelled all ODA debts owed by the least developed and other low-income countries in Africa. All creditor developed countries should seriously consider the cancellation of ODA debts. Increased assistance to the least developed and other low-income countries should also be given by all those who were in a position to afford it. In addition, international financial institutions should recognize the need for a balanced approach in helping to resolve the debt and structural problems of low-income countries like Zambia.

9. Economic development, especially in southern Africa, could not be divorced from political and social realities. Countries like Zambia were constantly being subjected to acts of wanton destruction. Throughout black-ruled southern Africa, agents of the South African régime were committing murder and blowing up railways, roads, bridges and other installations vital for development. The reason for those actions was those countries' opposition to *apartheid* and support for the patriots who wanted to eradicate it. The Conference should therefore address that issue immediately in order to ensure that the international community was made aware of the dangers which were likely to engulf southern Africa and probably the whole world if *apartheid* was not dismantled immediately. The Conference should endorse the imposition of comprehensive and mandatory economic sanctions against South Africa as the only peaceful way to eradicate *apartheid* and to secure the self-determination of Namibia.

10. The failure of the international community to implement the decisions agreed upon at previous sessions of the Conference could be attributed only to lack of political will on the part of some Governments. The reason was that some countries, especially those in the industrialized world, were enjoying affluence while the rest merely managed to survive in squalid conditions.

---

* See sect. A above.

Only a man of limited vision could insist that the arrangements made over 40 years earlier to govern international economic and financial relations were still valid. The memories of the oil crisis in the mid-1970s should serve as a reminder that the world was interdependent and would remain so. The issues before the Conference should therefore be approached in a concerted and constructive manner for the sake of all.

C. UNITED NATIONS SECRETARIAT

Statement made at the 201st plenary meeting, 9 July 1987,
by Mr. Kenneth K. S. DADZIE, Secretary-General of UNCTAD*

Mr. President, may I say at the outset how pleased all of us in the secretariat are at the prospect of working under your leadership at the present session of the Conference. Your election is both a tribute to Zimbabwe and a measure of the respect in which you are held throughout the international community. But we cannot help taking pride in the fact that you are the first former staff member of UNCTAD to preside over a Conference session. You can count on all of our support in discharging your duties.

It is also an honour for us that this session was opened by the President of Yugoslavia, Mr. Lazar Mojsov. His presence here symbolizes the role of his country at the vanguard of international co-operation.

I take this occasion also to say how privileged we in the secretariat are to have helped prepare the ground for the Conference and to renew our commitment to enhance the effectiveness of the institution as an agent of development and its responsiveness to the demands placed upon it by changing economic realities.

1. *The world economic situation*

The quadrennial sessions of the Conference are the broadest high-level assemblies of economic policy-makers in the intergovernmental calendar. All the national leaders and ministers who gather at these sessions subscribe to at least one common goal: to promote a constant improvement in the well-being of all their people. Their specific objective in coming to the present session is to evolve convergent perceptions of the factors underlying this objective and to agree on effective policies to revitalize, through multilateral co-operation, the processes of development, growth and international trade.

Since the beginning of the present decade, efforts towards this objective have been bedevilled in all countries by the growing complexity and unpredictability of the world economy. Systemic malfunctions and instability have deepened. And policy-makers and entrepreneurs alike have had to contend with the challenges posed by new technologies, by changing patterns of production, competitiveness, trade and consumption, by the erosion of established disciplines, and by the volatility of international finance.

Those in the developing countries, however, continue to face daunting handicaps. All but a few of these countries have been unable to overcome the disability arising from inadequate external support for their efforts but

also from an unfavourable external environment which remains beyond their control. It is this interface, between the national efforts of developing countries and the environment in which they strive, which must be at the centre of our concerns at this Conference.

The inclemency of the external environment for development has recently been the subject of extensive analysis. As this session opens, were are receiving fresh and disturbing evidence of the mounting threat to the health of the world economy stemming from deflationary forces. Growth of investment, output and trade continues to slow. The terms of trade of the developing countries as a whole continue to worsen; as a result of this deterioration, the real income of this group of countries declined in 1986. The debt overhang persists and the prospects of its repayment are receding, while the rules of the game oblige several developing debtor countries to transfer real resources to developed countries. Competitive exports, agricultural and industrial, from developed and developing countries alike, continue to provoke protectionist reactions, often of a discriminatory character. To be sure, there are a number of bright spots in the global economic picture. But they are hedged with question marks concerning their sustainability and their replicability.

These trends are compounding the maladjustments in the world economy and making structural adaptation more difficult for all countries. They are also generating political tension, nationally and internationally, while difficulties in international political relations are in turn constraining the possibilities for enhanced economic co-operation.

2. *Policy responses*

The strength of the deflationary forces moving through the world economy, and depressing growth and development, did not come out of the blue. The policies of the major market economies have been geared predominantly towards disinflation for several years since the beginning of the decade. What is more, these policies were framed without paying full attention to the high degree of interdependence that exists both among countries and among the monetary, financial and trading systems, including the world commodity economy. Cyclical factors were compounded by problems of a structural and systemic character, with the result that most countries were caught in a spiral of declining production, employment and trade. Moreover, the problems thereby generated were reflected in political and social symptoms: social regression, urban unrest and systemic strains in developing

---

* Initially issued as TD/L.276.

countries; chronic unemployment, underemployment and rural distress in developed countries.

These trends were accompanied by shifts in economic philosophies and perceptions of a number of Governments with regard to the capabilities and responsibilities of Governments in national and international policy-making, and to the respective roles of governmental and intergovernmental institutions on the one hand, and of market forces on the other. Substantial changes emerged also in the assessment by these Governments of the complex interactions between domestic policies and the international environment and of the appropriate mix of public and private sector activities in national economies. These shifts were largely based on their view that prevailing economic difficulties resulted primarily from inappropriate policies at the national level. One conclusion therefore was that the emphasis in domestic economic management in developing countries must be shifted towards adjusting national economies to changes in external variables and "putting one's own house in order". Likewise the development issue was seen as a matter much less of improving the external environment than of enhancing allocative efficiency through structural reforms designed to provide incentives for the private sector to become a driving force for development.

Underlying these developments are important political questions relating to the distribution within and among countries of economic power, of incentives to economic activity and of the benefits derived therefrom. Decisions on such questions affect the very fabric of societies and it is now being increasingly accepted that those questions are not amenable to the universal application of one single prescription. This is so not only because of the right of each country to choose its own economic and social system, but also because the relevance of any prescription will vary according to the widely different circumstances of each country, including the social, cultural and even historical context. There is growing awareness, too, that national capacities and options for action—even those of the most powerful economies—are not immune from the impact of policy choices in other countries. Wider acknowledgement is also evident that no country can solve its economic problems in isolation from others, nor can the difficulties of the world economy be resolved through disconnected national actions. These are political realities, the realities of interdependence—an interdependence of highly disparate partners to be sure—but one in which countries have little choice but to coexist.

Indeed, this thinking seems to have inspired the commitments undertaken over the past few years by the Governments of the major market-economy countries to strengthen their co-operation towards sustainable economic growth, to reduce their mutual trade imbalances and to seek stability on foreign exchange markets. Their commitments are indeed commendable. However, in practice their efforts have focused primarily on the correction of their mutual imbalances. Their perception of interdependence has yet to extend in an operational manner to the functioning of the international trade and payments systems and to multilateral co-operation to foster directly the growth and development of developing countries—both of which are no less important as potential areas for closer policy co-ordination.

Thus, the major challenge confronting the Conference is above all a political one and member States need to address it with all the political wisdom at their disposal, together with their economic expertise. After the seventh session, answers will need to be provided to a number of searching questions. Has the outcome of the session of the Conference opened any doors to the enhancement of national welfare? Has UNCTAD as an institution confirmed its utility and relevance to the international community? Have Governments succeeded in translating their particular interests into mutual benefit and common interest? Have they taken significant steps towards the successful management of interdependence in the interests of world economic growth and development, steps which also provide for more effective participation by all groups of countries in global economic decision-making? These are but some of the yardsticks by which the outcome of the session might be evaluated.

3. *A framework for action*

The logic of interdependence—the growing integration of the world economy and the linkages among different policy areas—points to the conclusion that world economic stability and growth increasingly require national policies to be co-ordinated in order both to avoid inconsistencies among them and to ensure their convergence in support of global objectives. This does not detract from the primary responsibility and the prerogative of countries to pursue actions responding to national aspirations, objectives and priorities. Rather, it calls for multilateral co-operation to be an umbrella for national actions, as an instrument for sharpening their effectiveness and promoting their contribution towards common goals.

This Conference accordingly offers an opportunity to agree upon a framework for reviving multilateral co-operation for development, in which specific policy approaches and concrete measures could be inserted in a mutually reinforcing way, without having to redefine, in each case, the understandings on which they rest. Such a general framework could be derived from the concepts of mutual benefit, common interest and collective responsibility, as well as the recognition of the diversity of national paths to development. Its application, in a particular conjuncture, would have to pay due regard to cyclical and structural trends and incorporate both international dimensions and the interactions between those dimensions and national factors and policies. It should also take into account the interrelationships between short-, medium- and long-term problems and solutions.

As indicated in the report which I have submitted to the Conference (TD/329), this framework could include an understanding on the need:

First, for all countries to implement policy measures to improve the environment for accelerated development;

Secondly, for major market-economy countries to adopt co-ordinated expansionary policies, consistent with their declared aims, and to enhance the positive impact on development of measures to deal with their mutual imbalances;

Thirdly, for all developed countries (market-economy and socialist) to contribute to the strengthening of the production potential of developing countries, to improve access for imports from those countries and to undertake the consequential structural adjustments; and also to enhance the flow of public and private resources to developing countries, bearing in mind their particular resource needs: those of the poorer countries, notably the least developed countries and other countries in sub-Saharan Africa, those of the commodity-dependent countries and those of the heavily indebted countries;

Fourthly, for developing countries, in fulfilment of their primary responsibility for their own development and in accordance with their respective national objectives and priorities, to strengthen policies and measures to mobilize domestic financial and human resources, including indigenous private capital and entrepreneurship; to provide an appropriate policy environment for external financial resources, both public and private; and to improve the effectiveness of domestic and external resource use.

An understanding of this nature would help the Conference to agree on policy orientations to unblock the constriction of growth and development through action by countries, collectively and individually, with each country contributing to this objective in accordance with its capacities and its weight in the world economy. It would also facilitate the task of Governments in positively influencing, and accommodating, processes of structural change in the world economy. It would moreover strengthen the co-operation that is urgently needed to adapt and improve the systems, structures and institutional arrangements that underpin international economic relations, so as to provide more effective support for macro-economic management, structural adjustment and the development process.

4. *Elements of an outcome*

The selective agenda for the seventh session of the Conference, and its unifying theme—namely, "Revitalizing development, growth and international trade"—were intended to enable the Conference to concentrate on the key obstacles to development and growth in the current economic situation. The thrust of our assessment leads to the conclusion that the scarcity of resources for development, compounded by the effects of slow growth in the world economy, is now such that significant advances in human welfare are beyond the reach of most developing countries. Ways must therefore be sought of mobilizing development resources, human and financial, and using them more effectively. In this effort, multilateral co-operation has a vital role to play, complementing national efforts and private initiatives.

Following this line of thought, an important focus of attention at the seventh session should be on the awesome accumulation of debt by developing countries and the need to improve the international strategy for dealing with the debt problem. The essence of such improvement is that the strategy must be tailored to

realistic estimates of the capacity of developing debtor countries to repay their debt, within a given external environment, without damaging their development prospects. The readiness of all parties to engage in substantive discussion of the international debt strategy in its entirety is, I believe, one of the keys to a constructive outcome of this session. This discussion must recognize not only the specificities in different debtors' situations, but also their commonalities, including their susceptibility to the external economic environment, the need for equitable burden-sharing among debtors and creditors, and the need for new money to respond to debtor countries' shortages of resources. There is scope for consensus here on desirable improvements in the current debt strategy, which would, of course, be elaborated, implemented and monitored in the competent forums, including UNCTAD as appropriate. Depending on the type of debt and the category of the debtor/creditor relationship, this consensus could encompass differing degrees of concreteness, for instance as regards the applicability of different types and instruments of debt relief within an overall approach to the debt problem.

Another focus of the seventh session of the Conference should be on the weakness of the world commodity economy and the vulnerability of commodity-dependent developing countries—from which not even oil-exporting developing countries have been spared. The Integrated Programme for Commodities was devised to respond to these realities and its objectives remain valid. In the present conjuncture, there is a need for a two-pronged thrust towards those objectives: first, to strengthen markets for individual commodities through a new round of consultations among producers and consumers and, second, to mobilize finance to accelerate the diversification of commodity-dependent economies of developing countries. The entry into force of the Common Fund, for which I hope that this Conference will be decisive, would complement both lines of action, facilitating the conclusion of international commodity agreements and, through its Second Account, financing commodity development activities. In addition, resources available for compensatory financing would need to be augmented.

Another aspect of the agenda for the seventh session which deserves special attention is the promotion of new flows of public and private credits and development finance, including finance for diversification. A number of opportunities to enhance the flow of new money may be explored at this time: for instance, the need to augment the resources available through the World Bank, the regional development banks, and the International Monetary Fund; the possibility of increasing the liquidity of developing countries through an issue of special drawing rights; and measures to recycle the accumulated payments surpluses of major market-economy countries—following the commendable first steps announced by the Government of Japan and inspired by the far-sighted proposals submitted by the UNU/WIDER Study Group under the chairmanship of Dr. Saburo Okita. The Conference may give an impetus to action in these areas, as well as to the improvement of the conditions attached to finance from the Bretton

Woods institutions and the content of adjustment pro-grammes approved by those institutions.

Moreover, in the light of the prospects that are open-ing up for a measure of nuclear arms reduction, it is not too early to begin preparing for the possible release of resources from military budgets, which could become an immensely valuable source of finance for develop-ment and other socially productive uses, if the necessary measures are put in place in good time. UNCTAD could make an important contribution to the examination of the economic consequences and opportunities implicit in current nuclear missile disarmament options.

The treatment by the Conference at its seventh session of debt, development finance and commodities would have to include special provision for dealing with the problems faced by the least developed countries in these areas. There is wide agreement on the need of these countries for official development assistance and for special measures of debt relief, which should be equitably shared by all categories of their creditors, in the context of the necessary overall improvement of the debt strategy. Similarly, many problems of particular concern to the developing countries of sub-Saharan Africa would be covered in these areas.

The promotion of trade, in particular as an instru-ment of development, is central to the raison d'être and indeed the mandate of UNCTAD. However, this par-ticular session of the Conference is convening at the beginning of a new round of multilateral trade negotia-tions. Accordingly, Governments have the opportunity of using the Conference and the UNCTAD machinery to build consensus which will facilitate a satisfactory outcome of those negotiations, particularly in areas of special interest to developing countries, including the least developed countries. I have in mind, for instance, the areas of agricultural trade, textiles, tropical and resource-based products and safeguards, as well as trade in services.

It may therefore be envisaged that, in addition to pro-moting action in support of the Uruguay Round, the Conference will take action in pursuit of UNCTAD's own mandates and programmes in the area of interna-tional trade. In this category, one may envisage: action to reinforce standstill and roll-back commitments, in-cluding the encouragement of national mechanisms to improve the transparency of protectionist measures; a new impetus to trade and economic co-operation among countries having different economic and social systems, including multilateral or plurilateral East-South con-sultations; and processes of review, analysis and consensus-building which would identify elements for strengthening and improving the international trading system and enhance our awareness of the policy implica-tions of the interdependence of all trade flows.

Finally, the Conference is expected to encourage special measures to help the least developed countries maintain and strengthen their national development ef-forts. In doing so, the Conference will wish to bear in mind the Substantial New Programme of Action for the 1980s for the Least Developed Countries, which is under periodic intergovernmental review, while also drawing upon the deliberations in other areas of its agenda. The need in this area is not so much for a new policy framework as for the prompt and effective implementa-tion of agreed approaches and commitments, including in particular a substantial increase in official develop-ment assistance to these countries and special measures of debt relief, as I have already mentioned.

All these possible measures in the different areas of the seventh session agenda are interrelated. They can and should be mutually supportive. They will be all the more effective in a climate of economic growth, for which co-ordinated expansionary policies by the major market economies is a prerequisite—as is recognized by those countries themselves.

5. *Reviving multilateral co-operation for development*

This sketch of possible elements of an outcome of the seventh session complements the more elaborate presen-tation in my report to the Conference, which in turn builds upon the foundations laid by the analytical report by the UNCTAD secretariat on assessment and policy options (TD/328/Rev.1). These documents remain our main substantive contributions to your deliberations and we trust that they will facilitate the attainment of constructive results.

Such results, however, will depend upon the political perceptions, evaluations and constructive participation of all member States. It is for you to grasp the oppor-tunity offered by this Conference to move ahead decisively in dealing with the burning issues facing your national constituents and the entire international com-munity. From this platform, you can generate consen-sus and establish guidelines for action in other institu-tions, as well as in UNCTAD. This opportunity must not be allowed to go to waste. If you do rise to the challenge before you, the entire international commun-ity will stand to reap the benefits of the successful management of interdependence in the global interest. All countries will then be able to look forward to an era of active and fruitful multilateral co-operation for development and to the reinvigoration of the United Nations and of UNCTAD as a major instrument for in-ternational economic co-operation.

**Summary of the statement made at the 208th plenary meeting, 14 July 1987,
by Mr. Peter HANSEN, Executive Director of the United Nations Centre on Transnational Corporations**

1. Mr. HANSEN said that in recent years there had been a reassessment of long-cherished assumptions about development, and the contribution that the private sector could make had been given greater prominence. At the same time, there was now a greater awareness of the limits of direct government intervention to bring about rapid economic change.

2. Despite the fact that many Governments in developing countries had adopted policies closely in keeping with that view, in most developing countries investment had not increased. In a large number of them, it had actually declined dramatically. The domestic private sector was not committing resources to development, and TNCs did not appear to be interested in increasing their investments in developing countries.

3. The reason for that discrepancy was patently that the international environment had not been conducive to the allocation of resources by private agents to productive investments. During the 1980s, the international economy had been characterized by sharp swings in interest and exchange rates and by a protracted debt crisis affecting a large number of developing countries and threatening the survival of the international financial system. In addition, the integration of world markets for manufactures brought about by successive rounds of trade negotiations was being reversed, apparently inexorably, by escalating protectionist measures in all major trading nations. Those factors were not propitious for productive investment.

4. Transnational corporations had tended to concentrate their flows of foreign direct investment in the developed market-economy countries, particularly the United States of America, which had moved from being the largest net investor abroad to being the largest net absorber of foreign direct investment flows. With a few exceptions, the investments made in the United States by both foreign and United States-based TNCs had not represented additions to productive capacity but purchases of existing assets. Among developed market economies, more generally, investments in the financial sector had acquired a prominence which they had not had in more stable days. The integration of world financial markets had led to large-scale foreign direct investments in practically all major financial centres. Since 1981 the total net size of the international banking market had doubled.

5. The growth in international financial intermediation had thus been phenomenal. Even large numbers of industrial TNCs were participating in financial markets more actively than ever before. The unsettled international economic environment encouraged purely financial investment and was seriously discouraging productive investment. For TNCs, the skilful manipulation of the broadening range of internationally traded financial instruments could bring in more profit than productive investments which might require years of patient nurturing and the yield from which was inherently uncertain.

6. The growth of financial intermediation in the industrialized countries, together with depressed domestic conditions in the developing countries, had also contributed to drawing capital away from developing to developed countries. In addition, since the onset of the debt crisis there had been a massive reverse transfer of resources from South to North, resulting in the drying-up of new lending by the transnational banks to the indebted countries, falling commodity prices, and a sharp increase in international interest rates. Owing to the absence of internationally agreed mechanisms for dealing with the debt crisis, most of the burden of adjustment fell on the borrowing countries.

7. A solution clearly had to be found to the complex problems of capital flight and reverse transfers of resources. It had been a mistake to think of foreign direct investment as a possible remedy for the debt crisis, for debt-servicing requirements were so much larger than current foreign direct investment inflows that even very substantial increases in foreign direct investment would have been insufficient. Moreover, in the debtor countries depressed domestic conditions and the drying-up of loan capital from transnational banks had resulted in a dramatic retrenchment in private domestic investment.

8. Accordingly, more stable international and domestic environments were a pre-condition for the revival of productive investment, foreign or domestic. Developing countries must continue to play their part in encouraging investment by adopting appropriate domestic policies. However, any such efforts would be of no avail if the international economic environment continued to exhibit characteristics that inhibited productive investment. Although foreign direct investment was not a panacea, the resumption of foreign direct investment flows to developing countries could play a positive role. In that respect, the adoption of a universally agreed code of conduct on transnational corporations would give greater stability and transparency to the international framework for foreign direct investment. An early conclusion of the negotiations on the code would make it more likely that the badly needed increase in foreign direct investment flows would be forthcoming.

Summary of the statement made at the 215th plenary meeting, 28 July 1987, by Mr. Richard JOLLY, Deputy Executive Director of the United Nations Children's Fund

1.   Mr. JOLLY said it was encouraging that frequent reference had been made in Conference documents and in the general debate to two issues close to this heart. One was the social cost of the recession and of adjustment policies in many developing countries and the other the need to pay greater attention to human factors and the fight against poverty when drafting national and international policy. Decision-makers had long ignored the crushing impact of the 1980s recession on the poor and the effect that essential adjustment measures might have on those most at risk from malnutrition. That attitude was illustrated by the declining share of health and education expenditure in the budgets of many States in African and Latin America between 1979 and 1983.

2.   Some of the reasons for the tendency to make light of human considerations were as follows. Firstly, the lack of any systematic collection of data on changing living standards had resulted in a failure to appreciate the severity of the crisis in the early 1980s. Furthermore, people in the developed countries, protected by unemployment benefit and social security systems that were virtually absent in the developing countries, sometimes found it difficult to grasp the magnitude of the economic difficulties faced by the third world. Even more important was the influence of prevailing economic theory, which only too often led national leaders and international agencies to analyse world economic problems solely in terms of economic growth, which was in their eyes not only a panacea but also a *sine qua non* of social progress. That view, it should be stressed, had never been shared by Raúl Prebisch or any of the other eminent persons associated with the establishment of UNCTAD.

3.   The well-being of peoples in the developing countries, which had made great strides in the 1960s and 1970s, had, as a result of neglect of the human factor, declined in almost one half of those countries, where the 1980s could be considered a decade lost to development. Nutritional status and school attendance rates had declined, sometimes quite spectacularly, in at least 35 developing countries. In a smaller but still appreciable number of African and Latin American States, infant and child mortality rates that had steadily fallen during the 1960s and 1970s had risen during the 1980s. Those attending the Conference—whatever their economic concerns—would surely consider that trend unacceptable.

4.   It was increasingly recognized that deteriorating living conditions undermined the productivity of a working population and irreversibly slowed the physical and mental development of its children, who were the workforce of the future. As the former Managing Director of IMF had said, it was difficult to see how a country could maintain its external balance when a large proportion of its working population had no occupational qualifications, let alone the basic level of health and nutrition needed to produce goods able to compete on world markets. Such a state of affairs was not in-evitable; there was a new approach to adjustment whereby the aims, thrust and implementation of recovery and development policies took explicit account of essential human needs in the fields of nutrition, health and education. That approach, which UNICEF called "adjustment with a human face", was not an abstract formulation; policies developed along those lines had already been implemented during the 1980s in several developing countries, such as the Republic of Korea, Zimbabwe, Ghana and Peru and even, more recently, in a number of the poorest countries in Africa, such as Burkina Faso. Other developing countries had incorporated some components of that approach into their policies but needed additional support from the international community in order fully to realize their ambitions in that regard.

5.   Many of the measures comprising a strategy of adjustment with a human face were not costly (e.g. immunization, oral rehydration therapy) and helped to improve economic efficiency and redistribute income (e.g. public works, loans to the informal sector and to small farmers).

6.   Although national action on its own could produce results, the pursuit and propagation of a growth-oriented strategy of adjustment with a human face required international action to relieve the shortage of foreign currency afflicting many developing countries.

7.   Many Conference participants had dwelt on the measures required to cope with falling commodity prices, a declining volume of trade, protectionism in industrialized countries, the debt problems, shrinking trade cash flows and stagnating development aid. UNICEF considered it essential to take action on all those fronts; however, among the major changes of direction envisaged at the current session of the Conference, three practical steps were imperative to encourage growth in third world countries and ensure the survival of their peoples.

8.   The first was to alleviate the debt burden, in particular that of the poorer African countries, by the long-term rescheduling of the liabilities of the major debtor countries and the granting to such countries of loans on the best concessional terms. An option to be considered was what UNICEF termed "debt relief for child survival". Under that formula, the interest on all or part of commercial or bilateral loans would be paid in local currency and used to finance child survival and development programmes. That method of funding programmes, a variant of which had already been used in Bolivia, had been shown by experience to benefit both recipients and donors, as well as the private banking sector.

9.   The second step concerned the changes proposed in the regulatory machinery, which should, in UNICEF's view, make every allowance for the need to protect groups at risk. The scope of existing mechanisms, such as the IMF Compensatory Financing Facility and Stabex, should be considerably expanded

and their conditions of application to poor countries made more flexible. New regulatory machinery (for example, automatic debt relief or increased allocations of special drawing rights) could be made available to countries where "human indicators" were deteriorating as a result of international instability. The Managing Director of IMF had also expressed his readiness to explore alternatives within the framework of adjustment policy.

10. The third measure considered a priority by UNICEF was to step up technical co-operation among developing countries as a means of promoting exchanges of experience on adjustment with a human face. In that way, the example set by developing countries that had incorporated the human dimension into their policies would prevent neighbouring countries or

countries in other regions from making the mistake of following a conventional approach.

11. It was clear that children were one of the major groups at risk; they were the rising generation and their lives and capabilities would be determined by today's efforts or lack of efforts. Consequently, international policy-makers would have to show them as much solicitude as parents did for their own offspring and take the same care to satisfy their needs. The resources, knowledge and technical capabilities required for adjustment with a human face and the eradication of poverty were already available. It remained for the international community to display the political will and provide financial support required to protect the world's children—its most precious resource.

Summary of the statement made at the 203rd plenary meeting, 10 July 1987, by Mr. William H. DRAPER III, Administrator of the United Nations Development Programme

1. Mr. DRAPER said that times of economic crisis like the present, in which one important factor was the low level in real terms of commodity prices, were times of opportunity, as illustrated by the inspiring policy changes adopted by many developing countries, in the face of considerable political risk, in order to adjust their economies. In that context, it was essential for the international community to give further support, at the national and international levels, to developing countries undertaking adjustment programmes, of which there were 22 in Africa alone. The understandings reached by donors, UNDP and multilateral agencies in the context of the United Nations Programme of Action for African Economic Recovery and Development 1986-1990, for instance, must be respected. If such support were not provided soon, the political will for change would evaporate and the countries in need of structural adjustment would be deterred from pressing forward.

2. UNDP was ready to help countries to identify options for diversifying their production base in order to counter the over-supply of some commodities and was assisting Governments in addressing the adjustment issue at the national level on three fronts, by helping countries to weigh the advantages of new economic strategies and to design their adjustment programmes, by assisting them to develop qualified human resources and efficient institutions to implement such programmes, with the aim of achieving economic growth with social equity and by helping them to manage their social sectors more effectively in order to protect the most vulnerable sections of their population. National actions must be matched by international measures to increase resource flows in support of reforms, through a combination of more bilateral aid, the softening of the terms governing debt, the recycling of surpluses by the major surplus countries and concerted action to raise the level of funds available to multilateral agencies.

3. UNDP was helping countries to enhance economic efficiency—the basic purpose of adjustment—in various ways, for example by advising

several Governments, including those of Kenya, Ghana and Sierra Leone, on how to improve their fiscal and marketing policies and reduce budget deficits, and by advising many developing countries, at their request, on how to formulate appropriate pricing policies and rationalize or dismantle obstructive licensing procedures. Technical assistance in debt management was currently being provided to 16 countries in Asia, Latin America, Africa and the Middle East, with UNCTAD acting as UNDP's partner and executing agency. Such assistance was being followed up by appointing regional or inter-regional debt management teams to assist individual Governments once national policies and mechanisms had been established.

4. Through the Substantial New Programme of Action for the 1980s for the Least Developed Countries, special assistance was being provided to the 41 poorest countries. Central to that effort was the round-table aid review process which had been significantly improved. At the Round Table for the Niger, pledges had exceeded the programme target of $350 million. LDCs were also, of course, priority recipients of UNDP funds.

5. UNDP was also stepping up, at Governments' request, support for private sector initiatives, including the privatization of State-owned enterprises and the creation of the right conditions for private sector operations. Meetings were being arranged for representatives of the private sector and of developing countries, and case studies of failures and successes of privatization measures were being prepared, an important part of UNDP's strategy being to bring together groups of developing and developed countries to exchange ideas and experience. UNDP was looking forward to closer co-operation with UNCTAD in the areas of fiscal policy, economic and debt management and the private sector. Another opportunity for co-operation between UNDP and UNCTAD in order to strengthen the negotiating capabilities of developing countries had materialized through the Uruguay Round.

6. Bold and novel measures were needed for dealing with the world economic crisis and in particular for

relieving the plight of developing countries. What was needed was a dramatic infusion of additional funds to be applied through existing mechanisms to the provision of technical assistance to those most in need—the LDCs. In another forum he had recently proposed that ODA be increased by 50 per cent, to over $50 billion, equivalent to about one half of 1 per cent of the industrialized world's GNP. At that level, ODA would still not reach the long-term 0.7 per cent target agreed upon in UNCTAD in 1968, and would be far less than the 1.3 per cent of the United States GNP set aside in support of the Marshall Plan of 1948. However, the provision of money alone would not be enough under prevailing conditions. Many developing countries re-

quired support in policy-making and management in order to ensure the proper environment for the massive aid input needed. Now was a time of opportunity, for a modest investment made promptly would produce benefits later. He was encouraged by the signs of greater awareness of the need for more balance in development efforts, in the form of national and international actions, for a more sensitive approach to debt problems and structural adjustment programmes, and for greater emphasis on the human dimension, as well as on the physical environment. UNDP joined UNCTAD wholeheartedly in its endeavour to ensure that the countries of the North, in partnership with those of the South, would overcome the difficulties they jointly faced.

Summary of the statement made at the 209th plenary meeting, 15 July 1987, by Mr. Mostafa K. TOLBA, Executive-Director of the United Nations Environment Programme

1. Mr. TOLBA (United Nations Environment Programme) said that there was a growing realization of the extent to which environmental degradation could retard development and prosperity. The state of the environment exerted a critical influence on economic policy and decision-making. Deforestation was a case in point. And yet environmental considerations still did not adequately guide development planning, effective control of trade in scarce natural resources and in hazardous materials was still lacking, patterns of transnational investment and technology transfers continued to be set without reliable information and with an often shocking disregard for environmental safety standards, and renewable resources were depleted. Environmental conservation clearly made good economic sense, for prevention was considerably less expensive than cure. Profit margins, as well as the environment, were adversely affected by the inefficient use of natural resources and inefficient agricultural methods. For instance, UNEP had estimated that $4.5 billion would be required annually for 20 years to arrest desertification in the developing world, whereas $26 billion in potential agricultural productivity was already being lost each year to the encroaching desert.

2. The current imbalance, to the detriment of the developing countries, in patterns of trade, investment and finance had contributed to the inexorable degradation of the poorest nations' environment, which all too often bore the brunt of the cost of deteriorating terms of trade and huge external debt payments. Resource conservation had traditionally been ignored as a legitimate economic consideration, and yet a natural resource used in a sustainable way continued to provide, year after

year, far more than the value it could command as an export commodity.

3. In response to those issues, development cooperation should concern itself more than ever with the long-term improvement of natural resource productivity and environmental conservation, and at the same time should aim at restoring areas already suffering from ecological degradation. The stabilization of commodity prices would give countries more scope for adopting conservation measures. Environmental safeguards should be incorporated as a matter of course into all international trade and commodity exchange agreements. UNCTAD should show greater concern for the environmental impact of international trading patterns and integrate environmental considerations into all international trading arrangements. Governments and international agencies should, as far as possible, promote the transfer of low-waste and pollution control technologies, at concessional prices. Recipient Governments should develop procedures to ensure that imported technologies conformed to established environmental standards and fulfilled legitimate economic and social needs. International financial institutions for their part should reconsider, in bilateral negotiations with developing countries, aspects of foreign debt, structural adjustment and economic reform in relation to environmental protection measures and prospects for sustainable development.

4. It was known that the world's resources were not unlimited. If they were exploited ruthlessly, economic ruin would follow. It was the responsibility of the international community to prove its determination to avert the threat of ecological disaster by guiding international economic relations in the right direction.

Summary of the statement made at the 211th plenary meeting, 24 July 1987,
by Mr. Lal E. JAYAWARDENA, Director, World Institute for Development Economics Research,
United Nations University

1. Mr. JAYAWARDENA said that a study group of the Institute had formulated and proposed a five-year plan to recycle $125 billion of Japan's surplus to developing countries at an annual rate of $25 billion. The plan built on the three-year $20 billion recycling initiative which had been announced by the Japanese Prime Minister in early May and which supplemented the $10 billion recycling programme announced previously. It was to be hoped that other surplus countries, and even developed deficit countries, would be encouraged to follow suit in a manner consistent with their balance-of-payments adjustment objectives and ODA targets. In its report, which the Secretary-General of UNCTAD had acknowledged as relevant to the work of the seventh session of the Conference, the study group had endeavoured to respect three pragmatic limits to what were conventionally regarded as desirable international policy goals. The first related to macro-economic policy co-ordination. The standard means of correcting current-account payments imbalances was for the United States to follow through on the depreciation of the dollar with measures to reduce its domestic fiscal deficit, thereby helping to scale down its current-account external payments deficit. The idea was that countries with large surpluses, primarily Japan and the Federal Republic of Germany, should simultaneously adopt policies to sustain domestic expansion. Such co-ordination, apart from being desirable in itself, was, of course, indispensable for developing countries, whose growth still depended on growth in the developed world. In terms of current-account balances, such an approach meant a reduction in the surpluses of Japan and the Federal Republic of Germany that corresponded to the desired reduction in the United States deficit. However, the Institute considered that the extent to which domestic expansion in surplus countries could offset the deflationary impact of the desirable reduction in the United States deficit was necessarily limited, since domestic expansion could have adverse consequences, such as reigniting inflation in surplus countries, increasing their domestic public debt to uncomfortable levels and creating a risk of destablilizing world economic growth through too rapid a shift from export-led growth to domestic demand-led growth. It was primarily for those reasons that, in Japan's case, the Institute considered that a current-account surplus of $50 billion should be aimed at over the medium term. That objective would require an increase in domestic absorption through fiscal expansion of up to $40 billion annually. The accuracy of the foregoing analysis seemed to have been confirmed by the Japanese Economic Planning Agency's announcement, shortly after the release of the Institute's report in Tokyo, of the adoption of a medium-term current-account surplus target of 2 per cent of GNP, or $50 billion for 1987. A target of that magnitude automatically constrained the degree to which the desired reduction in the United States deficit could be accommodated through domestic expansion in Japan and in other surplus countries. If the United

States was to reduce its current-account deficit by $150 to $200 billion (equivalent to 8 per cent of world exports), as generally urged by policy-makers, without triggering a major world recession, the deficit clearly had to be transferred to one or more third parties, which should, in the Institute's view, be the developing countries. Recycling surpluses to those countries was a means of offsetting the deflationary presure inherent in a substantial reduction of the United States deficit, taking into account the three above-mentioned constraints. That was the practical argument. The moral argument was that excess savings that could not be absorbed by expansion in surplus countries should go where they were most needed, namely, to the developing countries, where they could be used to step up capital formation. A quantitative analysis also showed that recycling Japan's surplus to developing countries was undeniably the best solution. That had been confirmed by an econometric model which consisted of three options and was designed to assess the consequences of recycling on the basis of a three-year programme involving $25 billion a year. Fiscal expansion in Japan—the first option—would reduce the United States deficit by $3 billion in the first year, $2 billion in the second and $1 billion in the third. Recycling $25 billion to Latin American countries—the second option—would reduce the deficit by $11.5 billion in each of the three years. If all non-oil producing developing countries were included and the total amount was split equally—the third option—the improvement in the United States trade balance would work out at $9.5 billion in the first year and $8.5 billion in each of the two subsequent years. The results in the latter case, although less impressive owing to the fact that the two groups of countries did not share the same propensity to import from the United States, were still far better than the domestic fiscal stimulus option in Japan ($2 billion).

2. The second set of limits which the Institute had had to take into account related to the expansion of conventional ODA. Its analysis showed that, to restore the situation prevailing prior to the 1980s, current ODA would have to be tripled to a level of $90 billion. However, that amount would not be enough to expand the import capacity of the developing countries. It was therefore essential to find other sources of capital transfers. The ODA performance of the DAC countries stood at 35 per cent of their GNP on average, with only Norway and, in 1984, the Netherlands reaching 1 per cent. On that basis, it would be a daunting challenge to triple current ODA levels, since all DAC countries would rapidly have to raise their ODA to more than 1 per cent of GNP. The Institute estimated that Japan alone would be able to do so during the period 1985-1990. ODA expansion would therefore not be sufficient in the near term to provide the capital transfers needed by the developing countries. It would be more reasonable to seek funding for interest subsidies on lending to developing countries that could come out of

increments to ODA, a feasible solution in Japan's case. The alternative means of obtaining the required capital sum was to tap private capital markets under various sorts of guarantee mechanisms.

3. The authors of the Institute's report had taken account of a third set of limits relating to the conditions governing lending to developing countries. It had been clear to them that a sizeable fraction of the proposed lending programme should be in the nature of programme finance in the interests of rapid disbursement. The wastefulness associated with the recycling of OPEC surpluses through the private banking sector in the 1970s absolutely had to be avoided, since it had culminated in the current debt problem. What was needed was a kind of long-range policy conditionality typified by World Bank structural adjustment loans (SALs).

4. The concluding section of the report outlined a practical debt reconstruction facility that would remove at one stroke a substantial burden of interest payments now being incurred by developing countries and improve their economic prospects, thereby enabling commercial banks to resume lending to those countries within a framework of long-term conditionality prescribed by a policy co-ordination committee such as the one which was being proposed by the Institute and which would be composed of major donor Governments and commercial banks. The only risk run by a commercial bank under the proposed scheme would be the non-payment of interest and that risk could be neutralized by the long-range policy conditionality prescribed. Experience in India and Sri Lanka had shown that the supervision of a country's economy by a

consortium of donor nations meeting annually and chaired by the World Bank produced excellent results and avoided errors. Other countries should seriously consider the possibility of following that example, since the prolonged austerity measures adopted by debtor nations had only further impoverished their inhabitants, whose living standards had fallen below 1980 levels, thereby creating a political problem. Traditional rescheduling packages had facilitated only short-term adjustment, at best an unsatisfactory solution. The Institute was proposing the establishment of an International Co-operation Committee composed of representatives of major Governments, international organizations and commercial banks. In many cases, the Committee would have only to support the efforts that national economic policy-makers were willing to impose upon themselves. The Committee would also be responsible for defining a type of long-term conditionality that was intermediate between the harsh short-term packages accepted in recent years by debtor developing countries and the total absence of conditionality typical of commercial bank lending.

5. In the light of its findings concerning Japan, the Institute urged that research should be undertaken for other surplus countries and even for developed deficit countries with the economic capacity to meet ODA targets in a manner consistent with their balance-of-payments adjustment objectives. The international community should strive to identify country-specific recycling mechanisms and bring them to the attention of the policy-makers concerned. The Institute remained confident that the seventh session of the Conference would provide the required impetus in that direction.

Summary of the statement made at the 217th plenary meeting, 29 July 1987, by Mr. G. HINTEREGGER, Executive Secretary of the Economic Commission for Europe

1. Mr. HINTEREGGER said that the issues on the agenda of the Conference were regularly examined by all the regional commissions, which were working to strengthen multilateral co-operation for trade and development not only at the regional level but also between regions, in close co-ordination with United Nations bodies, in particular UNCTAD, and the specialized agencies. ECE, which comprised most of the industrialized countries of the world, was actively seeking to strengthen the economic relations of its member countries both among themselves and with other countries of the world. In that regard, ECE programmes affecting countries of other regions had assumed greater importance in recent years as a result of the growing interdependence of the world economy.

2. Trade questions figured prominently on the agenda of the Commission, whose activities, although mainly emphasizing East-West trade, also had important implications for world trade. That was the case, in particular, of "trade facilitation"—namely, the harmonization and simplification of documents and procedures concerning international trade—which resulted in a considerable reduction of costs and much speedier

transactions and deliveries. The ECE Working Party on Facilitation of International Trade Procedures was, in particular, developing universal standards for electronic trade data interchange. Interested Governments from the various regions and all the international organizations concerned were participating in the work to adopt facilitation measures and standards for world-wide application. The other regional commissions had been associated with ECE activities and were kept informed of the results of its work, especially as part of the UNCTAD Special Programme on Trade Facilitation (FALPRO). The specific needs of developing countries were taken into account through FALPRO participation in ECE meetings. The Commission's standardization activities in other areas, such as perishable produce, motor vehicles and building regulations, were also having a major impact on global trade.

3. ECE work in the field of transport had produced more than 40 conventions and agreements, many of which extended to countries in other regions. The well-known TIR Convention, for example, which had greatly simplified goods traffic in Europe, was already in use in Africa, western Asia and Latin America. Conventions

on the transport of foodstuffs, the design of road and rail signals, and many others, were also widely used throughout the world. ECE serviced the Committee of Experts on the Transport of Dangerous Goods of the Economic and Social Council, in which countries from various regions of the world participated. The regulations developed by the Committee of Experts and issued in the so-called "Orange Book" were available in all the official languages of the United Nations and had become a best-seller throughout the world.

4.   ECE also managed, with UNDP financial support, the Trans-European North-South Motorway Project, which would link the Baltic Sea with the Aegean and south-eastern Turkey and which had already stimulated interest in ESCWA. In addition, ECE had undertaken or was studying other projects with the participation of ESCWA and ECA. It was also formulating a joint project among the regional commissions on the problems of transit traffic, which would be submitted to the Economic and Social Council the following year, and was engaged in joint work with ECA on an exploratory study for a permanent link across the Strait of Gibraltar.

5.   At the 1987 summer session of the Economic and Social Council, the regional commissions had submitted a proposal for co-operation on a project to develop further information technologies. The Commission had much to contribute to that project, which would be of great value to the developing countries. Furthermore, ECE was co-operating closely with FAO in both the agriculture and timber sectors, and had set up a joint committee, with FAO and ILO, on forest-working techniques and the training of forest workers which was playing a very useful role. ECE was likewise providing assistance, through specific projects, to promote the transfer of appropriate technology in those fields. Many of the publications issued by the Committee on

Agricultural Problems and the Timber Committee were of considerable value to producers and exporters in other regions.

6.   Work on new sources of energy also lent itself to interregional co-operation, and ECE had organized a number of seminars on the subject. In the field of statistics, ECE had launched a UNDP-funded regional project in 1980 with the participation of 20 countries. Its objectives were, first, to develop software to improve the efficiency of national statistical services and, secondly, to provide training in the development of software products. The results of that project were being disseminated to the statistical offices of developing countries in other regions.

7.   The need for a comprehensive approach to economic development had been emphasized by Mrs. Brundtland in her statement to the Conference* and in the report entitled *Our Common Future* by the World Commission on Environment. That report stressed the interdependence of environment and economic development. The work of the regional commissions covered practically all the aspects of development considered in that document, including environmental issues, and adopted an interdisciplinary approach that was fully in accord with the recommendations of the World Commission.

8.   ECE was prepared to share the results of its work with the other regions of the world. Like the Secretary-General of UNCTAD, he believed that the Conference offered an opportunity to agree upon a framework for reviving multilateral co-operation for development. Regional economic co-operation would have a major role in that regard. ECE could make a large contribution to the success of the endeavour to revitalize development, growth and international trade.

_____

* See sect. A above.

**Summary of the statement made at the 217th plenary meeting, 29 July 1987,
by Mr. K. GUNARATNAM, Chief of the International Trade Division of the Economic
and Social Commission for Asia and the Pacific**

1.   Mr. GUNARATNAM said that the fall in the value of the dollar, the price of oil and interest rates had failed to stimulate growth, as had been expected in 1986, owing to the absence of global policy actions necessary for taking full advantage of the opportunities presented, and instead there was a fear of world economic recession. Despite the attempts to increase policy co-ordination among the developed market-economy countries, huge imbalances persisted in trade flows and international payments. Those imbalances had exacerbated conflicts among the major trading nations, with the developing countries being hard hit as a result. As the debt problem and falling commodity prices became more acute, many developing countries found themselves in extreme predicaments which impeded their adjustment and development efforts.

2.   The policy initiatives recently taken at the global level to deal with some economic issues had not been

vigorous enough to yield the desired results. Efforts to harmonize the macro-economic policies of the major economic Powers and stimulate growth in some developed countries had been limited in scope, providing few benefits to the developing countries, and the Baker plan for growth-oriented adjustment had still not been put into practice. For many major debtor countries, the normal access to commercial sources of credit had not been restored and resource flows to low-income countries had been clearly inadequate. The export performance of developing countries had been poor and their debt-service ratio had risen, despite some relief from the lowering of interest rates. The decision taken at Punta del Este to launch a new round of multilateral trade negotiations nevertheless held out great hope for an improvement in the international trading environment, which was currently bedevilled with increasing uncertainties and a trend towards protectionism, particularly in agriculture.

3. Although the growth performance of the developing countries in the ESCAP region in the early 1980s had attracted attention throughout the world, it had been much less encouraging during the recent past. Hong Kong and the Republic of Korea had certainly accelerated their expansion, but the general pattern of growth had been much less vigorous. The larger low-income economies of China, India and Pakistan had maintained their momentum, but the ASEAN countries, with the exception of Thailand, had experienced sharp deceleration. The least developed and Pacific island countries, however, continued to face dire circumstances. Perhaps the most serious constraint on growth in the region had been the depression of commodity prices, which had emphasized the need for rapid structural changes.

4. Many of the ESCAP countries, especially those with diversified manufactured exports, had benefited considerably from recent changes in the global economic climate, particularly exchange rate adjustments. But those developments had not been entirely, positive. For example, the yen's sharp rise had enhanced the competitiveness of the region's exports but had also substantially increased the burdens of many Asian countries with sizeable yen-denominated debts. Though not yet alarming, the debt-service ratios of many ESCAP countries had been on an upward trend and the region would not be immune to debt problems if the international economic environment failed to improve significantly.

5. In recent years, the developing countries of the ESCAP region had become progressively more integrated with the world economy. They were acquiring significant weight as both exporters and importers, and Asia and the Pacific had emerged as the most important developing region in terms of world trade. It was attracting a large share of foreign direct investment and private bank credit. Subregional economic co-operation was also expanding, with the growth in trade (more than 25 per cent of total exports), financial flows, joint investments and the emergence of important subregional groupings such as the ASEAN, the South Asian Association for Regional Co-operation, and the South Pacific Bureau for Economic Co-operation.

6. ESCAP was attempting to tackle some of the major issues of the world economy. In particular, it had fostered the creation of intraregional trade and monetary co-operation mechanisms such as the Bangkok Agreement, the Asian Clearing Union and commodity groupings among producing countries as in pepper, jute, silk, tropical timber and coconuts. A meeting of the ministers of trade of the ESCAP region had been convened in Bangkok in June 1986 and had issued a declaration* in accordance with which the members of the Commission had pursued activities directed towards the expansion of trade in manufactures and technology, the promotion of foreign investment and joint ventures, the development of human resources in the sector of international trade and the provision of technical assistance in the field of trade policy, the Uruguay Round and commodities trade.

7. Those efforts, however, represented only a fraction of the action that needed to be taken. Participants in the seventh session of the Conference had not only to reach agreement on short-term measures which would help developing countries to cope with their immediate problems of debt, depressed commodity prices, declining terms of trade, protectionism and fragile export flows, but also to launch a longer-term international effort to deal with the structural problems that hindered the growth of the world economy.

8. In view of their interrelationship, problems in the field of money, finance and trade would have to be viewed and resolved in an integrated and non-sectoral manner, on the basis of co-operation between all members of the international community. Improved co-ordination of macro-level fiscal and monetary policies and the observance of commitments to standstill and roll-back of protectionist measures would substantially aid the developing world. The industrialized countries could devote a proportion of their financial surpluses to development assistance, particularly through multilateral institutions, as suggested by Mr. Saburo Okita. Implementation of the agreement reached on the resources of the IDA, improvement and expansion of World Bank lending facilities, flexibility in the conditionalities of IMF loans and enhanced ODA flows would also help to improve the situation.

9. Although, in the longer term, developing countries would have to diversify their economies and process their own raw materials, as indeed they were in the process of doing, the acute depression of commodity prices emphasized the need for urgent international action to assist them, notably through the Integrated Programme for Commodities and early operation of the Common Fund. Liberalization and expansion of the Compensatory Financing Facility and extension of Stabex-type facilities would also help to stabilize export earnings.

10. The adoption in 1981 of the Substantial New Programme of Action had created great expectations among the LDCs. Unfortunately, the overall socio-economic situation in many of those countries had since deteriorated further. The number of LDCs in the ESCAP region had risen from 7 to 10 in the preceding two years and the Commission was attaching more and more importance to assistance for that group of countries.

11. In its resolution 261 (XLIII) of 30 April 1987, ESCAP had requested the Conference to urge the international community to review its efforts to implement the Programme, so as to enable each LDC to achieve a minimum standard of performance in development. It had also invited the Conference to discuss a possible follow-up to the Programme in the 1990s.

12. ESCAP was prepared to contribute fully, at the regional level, to implementation of the decisions adopted by the Conference, which it hoped would be crowned with success.

---

¹ See E/ESCAP/547.

**Summary of the statement made at the 210th plenary meeting, 24 July 1987,
by Mr. Gerald Ion TRANT, Executive-Director of the World Food Council**

1. Mr. TRANT said that the statistics of falling national incomes, reduced export earnings, net capital outflows and adjustment programmes that had engendered reduced economic activity in most developing countries gave little idea of the human suffering, waste of life and lost opportunities for human development caused by increasing poverty, hunger and malnutrition. At their thirteenth session, held in Beijing, Ministers of the World Food Council had concluded that the community of nations was moving further away from the central objective of eliminating hunger and malnutrition and had declared that situation to be untenable.

2. Fundamental policy changes must be made in order to place the improvement of the human condition in the forefront of economic development. That should be central to UNCTAD's discussions and negotiations, and member States should commit themselves to increased and more effective co-operation in the food sector and external support for social policies designed to banish hunger and poverty.

3. In their review of the food security aspects of international agricultural trade, the Ministers of the World Food Council had drawn attention to the harmful effects of protectionism and low commodity prices on nutrition. In their Beijing Declaration, they urged those responsible for trade negotiations to re-establish a healthy and equitable exchange of agricultural products and allow equitable participation by developing countries. Some policy changes had been made by developed countries in accordance with the Punta del Este Declaration, but much more was needed. Concerted, balanced and progressive action was required to strengthen those changes, and the Ministers had strongly urged the OECD countries to put their political will into practice.

4. Many developing countries had made encouraging progress in introducing domestic policy reforms in the food and agricultural sectors. Many Asian countries had long been applying effective policies and programmes in support of the food sector and, despite their difficulties, many Latin American countries had endeavoured to make readjustments in the agricultural sector. As had been recognized at the thirteenth special session of the General Assembly in May 1986, at which the United Nations Programme of Action for African Economic Recovery and Development 1986-1990 had been adopted, the African countries needed increased external assistance to sustain their efforts to restructure their agricultural economies. The Ministers had also recognized the need of other developing countries for additional support.

5. Efforts to improve the situation in the international trade in agricultural products should be accompanied by national policy reforms. The Uruguay Round could help to solve agricultural trade problems within a multilateral framework. In that Round, the contracting parties should give special and differential treatment to agricultural exports of developing countries, particularly the LDCs.

6. The Ministers of the World Food Council had also considered ways and means of ensuring that the existing food surpluses were used to provide technical and financial assistance to accelerate the economic development of developing countries. He suggested that the participants in the Conference might wish to keep that possibility in mind in their discussions under agenda item 8 (*a*).

7. International agricultural trade relations appeared to have moved a considerable way towards agreement in principle on the nature of international trade and related domestic problems, the urgent need for dealing with those problems, and the general direction of the action required. The time had come to translate the agreement into action. The participants in the Conference had a special responsibility for promoting progress in the international agricultural trade, narrowing divergences of view and avoiding action that was inconsistent with declared intentions.

8. UNCTAD and the World Food Council had an important part to play in solving the global food and development crisis. It should be possible to further the co-operative search for improved international economic relations for the benefit of the poor and hungry people of the world. Speakers at the Conference had shown a sense of realism as to the prospects of a more just and equitable economic and development environment, as ably summed up by the representative of Uruguay* in urging participants not to hope too much but to be hopeful nevertheless.

9. The Conference should reconfirm the commitment of member States to improving the human condition as the central objective of development and to taking essential and feasible co-operative action that would eliminate hunger and mulnutrition.

---

* See sect. B above.

*

*   *

Statement made at the 208th plenary meeting, 14 July 1987, by Mr. Gamani COREA, former Secretary-General of UNCTAD*

Let me say first how privileged I feel to have this opportunity to address the seventh session of the United Nations Conference on Trade and Development as a former Secretary-General of UNCTAD. It is indeed a pleasure to be back in these familiar surroundings and to be able to meet so many friends—both former colleagues in the secretariat and those I have known among the delegations. It is, however, sad to recall that this is the first occasion when a session of the Conference convenes without the presence of my distinguished predecessors, Raúl Prebisch and Manuel Pérez-Guerrero. I want to take this opportunity to pay a tribute to their memory, to acknowledge my own debt to them, and to recall their role in the creation and shaping of UNCTAD. Although they are with us no more their leadership and their ideas will continue to inspire and guide us.

Mr. President, let me also say how delighted I am to see you preside over this important session. It was a happy thought to select you for this role of leadership, because of the direct association you have had with UNCTAD over so many years and because of your outstanding qualities and great experience. Your presidency is indeed a good augury for the Conference, and I extend to you all my good wishes for success.

I want also to express my appreciation to the Secretary-General of UNCTAD for his invitation to me to attend the Conference and to address you today. UNCTAD is fortunate to have the benefit of his experience, his judgement, and his sagacity and I wish him every success in the challenging task that lies ahead.

Mr. President, UNCTAD VII convenes in a setting in which the development process in many of the countries of the third world has been virtually halted and uncertainties and imbalances dominate the overall global environment. The documents submitted to you by the secretariat of UNCTAD amply describe this state of affairs. It is not only a state of affairs that prevails today; it is one that has persisted for a number of years—in fact over most of the 1980s. Only the insensitive can fail to sense the dangers inherent in this situation. The "lost decade", as it has already been called, is affecting the economic, political, and social fabric of the countries of the third world and the eventual consequence of this can well be global.

On reflecting on the situation today, I am struck by the unhappy parallel with the sixth session which was held in Belgrade four years ago. I call it an unhappy parallel because the situation in evidence at that time has remained with us to this day. In 1983, the economies of the developed countries were emerging from a recession. Already, at that time, growth in the developing countries had begun to slow down drastically, resource flows had begun to dwindle, and the debt crisis had come to the forefront. The trend towards protectionism in the developed countries was already

sharply evident and commodity prices had plunged deeply.

At that time we in UNCTAD pleaded for timely actions to reverse this state of affairs. We made two basic arguments. First, that the incipient recovery in the industrialized countries was unlikely to be vigorous, extensive, or sustained because there were points of weakness—unstable exchange rates, high interest charges, fluctuating payment balances—that were robbing the recovery of its vitality. We pleaded, therefore, for bolder and more positive macro-economic policies on the part of the industrialized countries to reinforce recovery and to put a sharper accent on growth.

Our second point was no less fundamental. We did not consider that the recovery of the industrialized countries alone, though vitally necessary, would suffice to reactivate—or to revitalize—the development process in the developing countries. We did not believe that the "trickle down" of a recovery in the North would be strong enough to give the required momentum to development. We pleaded, therefore, for further actions aimed directly at getting the development process going again in the countries of the third world. We proposed a number of specific measures in the three critical areas of resource flows, of market access, and of commodity trade. We pointed to the need for special actions in favour of the least developed countries, whose situation was deteriorating despite the hopes raised by the Paris Conference of 1981. We warned also that the management of the debt problem required more comprehensive and more imaginative approaches than were in prospect at the time. We base our arguments on the reality of what we termed the "new interdependence", on the reinforcing character of growth in all parts of the world, and on the common interest of the whole international community in the acceleration of recovery and the reactivation of development.

At Belgrade, we did not get the responses we hoped for. Although there was ample endorsement of the importance of recovery and of development, there was scepticism about the need for actions other than perhaps on a case-by-case basis in exceptional or emergency situations. There was much faith in the developed countries in the locomotive power of the recovery process in their own economies. The recovery, then young and "fragile", should be allowed, we were told, to take its course. It would soon pull up the global economy and provide the momentum needed for development. There was a good deal of misplaced confidence at the time. Most things were "manageable". The debt crisis was manageable, and so was the payments crisis of the developing countries. The need of the hour was "adjustment" on the part of the developing countries rather than action to improve the global environment. If these countries tightened their belts, cut down their budgets, and stopped interfering with market forces, all would be well.

Time has tragically proved the inadequacy of this reasoning and the validity of UNCTAD's analysis. Four

---

* Initially issued as TD/L.298.

years after Belgrade, we find the crisis continuing, even deepening. The industrialized countries are still displaying a halting, faltering, stop-go, kind of recovery, and each year growth forecasts of the previous year are revised downwards. The developing countries continue, for the most part, to stagnate; the debt crisis remains despite numerous rescheduling efforts. The adjustment exercises have not restored strength to the economies of the developing countries; rather, they have undermined the social, political and economic stability of their societies. Developing countries might have no option but to ''adjust'' to harsh circumstances, but on a broader front the need is to get out of a global recession, not to adjust to it. In fact, no amount of adjustment will ensure a return to rapid growth if the global environment remains hostile.

If I detect a change relative to four years ago, it is, perhaps, that there is now a greater awareness that the responses of the past have proved inadequate and a greater sense of unease about the prevailing situation. There is still no lack of signs, of course, of malaise in multilateral negotiations and of stalemate in dialogue. But in certain critical areas such as macro-economic management, debt, and the situation in Africa there appears to be some consciousness of the need for further actions. These developments are, of course, welcome as far as they go. But the critical issue remains the adequacy of the actions that might be undertaken. I am convinced that more positive macro-economic policies on the part of the industrialized countries with an accent on growth are an essential requisite for an improvement in the overall environment. But I do not believe that this is all that is needed to give the necessary momentum to development in the developing countries.

Growth rates in the industrialized countries are unlikely, even if accelerated, to reach the levels of the 1950s and 1960s. Moreover, both structural and technological change has affected the manner in which growth in the industrialized countries is transmitted to the developing countries. This is why it would still be necessary to take actions that are aimed directly at reviving the tempo of development in the developing countries. The case-by-case response to crisis situations needs to be replaced by more comprehensive approaches and actions that would vastly augment the flow of financial resources to the developing countries, eliminate the barriers to their exports, and strengthen their earnings from commodity trade. Such actions will not benefit just one group of countries. They would impart strength and dynamism to the global economy as a whole.

It is not my intention to dwell on the specific actions that might be taken. These have been identified in the documents before you and in many of the statements that have already been made. I consider that the urgent need in the immediate situation is to restore the flow of sizeable financial resources to the developing countries and to utilize the many promising instruments and mechanisms that are available for this purpose. I believe also that it is important to utilize the Uruguay Round of trade negotiations to achieve quick results in the area of improved market access for all countries and particularly for the developing countries. These are not issues upon which I can elaborate today. I do wish, however, to say a word on the issue of commodities because this

has been a major preoccupation of UNCTAD and because the present situation in this field is an important aspect of the crisis facing the developing countries. More than a decade ago UNCTAD launched a major initiative in the form of the Integrated Programme for Commodities that received the endorsement of the international community. In the early years there was momentum behind the programme. A complex negotiation on the Common Fund was brought to a successful conclusion: some individual commodity agreements were negotiated or renegotiated and it seemed that there was a good prospect for establishing, over time, a new régime to govern world commodity trade. In later years, the picture changed. Commodity agreements became increasingly difficult to negotiate or renegotiate whilst the Common Fund did not get established.

This situation seems to have encouraged some negative attitudes. I do not, however, accept the view that the difficulties in negotiations of recent times are proof of the futility of commodity agreements. The issue of market forces versus intervention is an old one and from time to time changing political attitudes can influence the diplomacy of commodity negotiations. But these attitudes do not negate the essential logic of the Integrated Programme or of commodity agreements. Commodity agreements have had a long history of successful operation going back to pre-war times. There are two things about the Integrated Programme that need be borne in mind in the context of the recent experience. First, the Programme has not up to now enjoyed the benefit of the Common Fund which was intended to be its centre-piece or catalyst. Secondly, individual commodity agreements were never intended to deal with a synchronized global recession but rather with the problems of commodity-specific cycles. They have not proved a failure so far on that test. I do not consider that the alternative to commodity agreements based on producer-consumer co-operation is a retreat to completely unregulated markets. The inescapable need would be for the producers themselves to improve their own co-operation and co-ordination in the management of supplies.

Two days ago the Minister of Trade of the Soviet Union announced the decision of his country to join the Common Fund. The Soviet Union has consistently supported efforts at stabilizing commodity markets and I am greatly heartened by this announcement. I am sure that the 94 countries that have already ratified the Fund are deeply encouraged by it. There is now, at last, a good prospect for the establishment of the Fund. Such an event would be the high watermark of years of effort to implement the Integrated Programme. I would like to express my appreciation of the efforts of the Governments of both developing and developed countries and of the UNCTAD secretariat in continuing to press for the establishment of the Fund. I would urge the remaining Governments that have not ratified the Agreement to do so quickly. The changed prospect for the establishment of the Fund has altered the prospects for the implementation of the Integrated Programme itself and has strengthened the credibility of multilateral negotiating processes. I have always felt that the Fund has to be viewed in terms of its potential, of its role as a universal institution with financial resources at its disposal and concerned specifically with the subject of commodities.

I hope that the developments at this session of the Conference will help launch a new and vigorous phase in the implementation of the Integrated Programme. The Programme deals with an important sector of the world economy and with an issue that remains of crucial importance to the developing countries. The current experience provides a dramatic illustration of the link between commodity prices and earnings and the development process. The Integrated Programme was conceived as an exercise in international co-operation between developed and developing countries and between producers and consumers. I cannot think of a better response to the present situation than the speedy implementation of the Programme in all its crucial aspects.

I would like to take the developments concerning the Common Fund as a good omen for the Conference. The Conference has on its agenda the critical issues relating to the world economic situation and the plight of the developing countries. No one would expect complete solutions to all the critical problems to emerge from this session. But it is vitally necessary that a significant beginning be made. If the decisions of the Conference lead to decisive steps in crucial areas and to the creation of a new and more favourable climate for dialogue and for negotiation, the Conference could well mark the beginning of a new and constructive phase. I would hope that after the unhappy experiences of the 1980s a new chapter would open. There are many signs that the time has come to build afresh on the basis of new perceptions. There is now a greater recognition of the need for disarmament and for an end to the debilitating arms race of recent years. Progress in this area will surely have positive implications for the world economy and for the capacity of the international community to support the development process. Recently, the Brundtland Commission highlighted in compelling terms the relationship between development and environment. It pointed to the imperative need for "sustainable development", where there is both growth and the pro-

tection of the resource base. A recognition of this must surely point, not only to national actions, but also to the creation of an international framework that make sustainable development possible.

Some years back I spoke of the need for a new "development consensus", a global consensus, similar to the consensus on full employment in the early postwar years. Such a consensus would recognize that dynamic growth was of crucial importance to the world economy and a condition for stability. It would recognize that the rapid growth of the developing countries is crucial for the strength and stability of the world economy. A development consensus would take us beyond short-term and incremental responses. It would lead inevitably through change, adaptation, and reform to a better international monetary and financial system, a better régime for international trade, and a sounder system of world commodity markets. All countries must participate in moulding this consensus. It must take account of differing needs but must also reflect the common interest in a new and better world. The developing countries must themselves be active in the negotiating processes that lie ahead. They must enhance their unity and their capacity to co-operate with each other. I do not believe that there can be sound negotiating results if the developing countries are weak and divided.

UNCTAD can play a crucial role in the shaping of a better world. The interdependence of issues and the importance of the development dimension in the world economy will gain increasing significance in the period ahead. UNCTAD has, both by its mandate and by tradition, viewed issues in terms of their interrelationship and in a development perspective. UNCTAD has not hesitated to highlight major issues simply because negotiations might prove difficult. All this has made UNCTAD unique among international agencies. I feel convinced that UNCTAD's future relevance lies in retaining its unique character. I feel convinced too that, as events unfold on the world economic scene, all member States will come increasingly to appreciate the value of UNCTAD and that its strength and stature will grow.

D. SPECIALIZED AGENCIES, GATT, INTERNATIONAL TRADE CENTRE UNCTAD/GATT*

Summary of the statement made at the 213th plenary meeting, 27 July 1987, by Mr. Francis BLANCHARD, Director-General of the International Labour Organisation

1. Mr. BLANCHARD said that, during the past decade, all countries had fought vigorously against the crisis, either by combating inflation or by attempting to redress their balance of payments. But interdependence, which all agreed was necessary, was far from being a reality, and much remained to be done to link economic progress to social progress and to start a genuine dialogue among the members of the international community.

2. In the current economic context, ILO wished to draw the attention of the Conference to the consequences of unemployment in the industrialized countries and of underemployment and poverty in the developing regions; far from diminishing, those problems had worsened over the preceding two years. The adjustment measures adopted to tackle the debt problem, bring the world economy on to an even keel once again and to curb inflation had taken a heavy social toll. Peoples might well continue to be hard hit by austerity policies for a long time to come unless, through a judicious combination of national and international policies, the world economy could be revitalized to meet the needs of the world's five billion inhabitants.

3. The Conference would help provide a better understanding of the social dimension of development. ILO would be holding a meeting to consider such structural adjustment and employment problems as the im-

pact of world economic trends and more dynamic adjustment and growth policies on employment and poverty and the resources available to international organizations for promoting adjustment and growth programmes aimed at achieving social objectives. On that occasion, ILO intended to focus on employment, and to draw the main economic actors, i.e. Governments, labour and management and the international organizations, into the discussion. Its own contribution to the debate would consist of its knowledge of the working world and its experience of collective bargaining. The development of human resources would occupy an important place at the meeting, because it was vital to all countries, whether industrialized or not.

4. Convinced that economic progress had no justification other than social progress, ILO would strive to give tangible form to the principles and norms set out in international labour conventions and recommendations. Its work could only succeed if there was a genuine give-and-take between the democratic countries which defended human rights and the rights of workers, and those that gave priority to meeting the needs of their populations. Development was both economic and social, and it would be dangerous to dissociate those two aspects.

5. Looking beyond the short-term measures imposed by circumstances, the international community must attempt to overcome the crisis through longer-term policies, with specific commitments being assumed by all.

---

* Under rule 80 of the rules of procedure.

Summary of the statement made at the 205th plenary meeting, 13 July 1987, by Mr. Edouard SAOUMA, Director-General of the Food and Agriculture Organization of the United Nations

1. Mr. SAOUMA said that at the time of the previous session of the Conference, the world economy had been poised between recession and recovery. It had been hoped that the incipient recovery would be sustained and expanded, that improved demand would boost world trade and reverse the slide in commodity prices, that the burden of debt repayments would be eased and that economic recovery would help to stem rising protectionism. Those hopes had not been fulfilled.

2. The FAO Council had recently reiterated its concern for the deteriorating situation in international commodity markets, with its adverse impact on the export

earnings of developing countries, and had drawn attention to the serious imbalances and increased protectionism in agricultural markets and to the great efforts of many developing countries to service their debts and revive their economies. Those countries had received inordinately low prices for their export commodities, had increasingly been denied access to markets for their agricultural products and had suffered further deterioration in their terms of trade.

3. The agricultural situation was of particular concern for the developing countries, since in many of them 70 per cent or more of the active population depended on agriculture for their livelihood. Those countries had

accorded priority to that sector, and many of them made striking changes, by offering production incentives, reforming outmoded or inefficient institutions and endeavouring to remove the bias against agriculture which had held back rural development.

4.   Their efforts had unfortunately been impeded by fundamental imbalances, heavy external indebtedness and constantly growing protectionism. Development problems were closely linked to monetary, financial and trade problems, and an integrated approach was therefore needed. It was the function of UNCTAD as a world forum to seek consensus on those problems and on proposals for action.

5.   Because of the burden of their debt and the service of the debt many developing countries were in a precarious situation. Their export earnings were inadequate to pay for badly needed imports, their economies were stagnating and inflows of investment resources faltering, so that they found it increasingly difficult to finance the imports they needed in order to revive their economies. That state of affairs harmed their trading partners as well. The most heavily indebted commodity producers among the developing countries had to increase the volume of exports in order to adjust their accounts, but their capacity to earn enough from those exports was limited by weak demand and restricted access to markets. The international community should give high priority to tackling the indebtedness of developing countries and improving the international trade situation through a concerted world-wide strategy.

6.   Measures to improve the agricultural trade environment had figured prominently on the agenda of many international gatherings. The FAO Committee on World Food Security had recently examined the effects of agricultural policies of industrialized countries on world food security, had recognized the paramount importance of those policies for the success of efforts by developing countries to improve their food security through increased food production, and had agreed on the need for gradual elimination of protectionist policies.

7.   Many industrialized countries had insulated their markets for food and agricultural products from world market forces and curbed access for low-cost producer countries. Too often, farm price support policies had not only encouraged uneconomic production but had also led to the institutionalization of incentives unrelated to market demand and to the creation of vested interests for their perpetuation, with the consequence that vast surpluses of subsidized agricultural products had accumulated.

8.   Agricultural support and export subsidies in 1988 were expected to cost the United States, the EEC and Japan more than $70 billion—a sum equivalent to the total agricultural export earnings of developing countries. That, moreover, represented only a part of the true costs, since those entailed by the consequential distortion of international trade and the cost to the consumer must be added.

9.   While developing countries were being forced by circumstances to make radical structural adjustments in their economies, many industrialized countries were not restructuring their own agricultural sectors, and hence the adjustments of developing countries became even more difficult. There were many other paradoxes in the world food and agricultural situation. Although staple food production had reached unprecedented levels and, in the developing countries as a whole, was rising faster than the growth in population, such progress was not uniform. In a world of plenty, large and growing numbers of people were suffering from undernourishment or malnutrition.

10.   When there was a glut in so many agricultural products, it might seem paradoxical to urge that the capacity and competitiveness of the food and agricultural sector in developing countries should be strengthened, but that was fully justified since there would be continued growth in domestic demand for farm products in line with population growth and economic expansion. Moreover, many of the developing countries would continue for a long time to rely on exports of primary products as a source of foreign currency earnings. Progress must be made in those areas, particularly by strengthening research and development and using every opportunity for diversification, both in terms of new products and in terms of processing for export.

11.   There was, fortunately, some evidence, including a more auspicious political climate, that the international community was more prepared to deal with the crisis in agriculture. Welcome prospects had been opened up by the recent Venice Summit. The leading economic Powers appeared to be increasingly determined to launch a concerted attack on the world's major economic ills: slow growth rates, trade imbalances, unstable currencies, growing protectionism, the burden of indebtedness and growing marginalization of the poor. He hoped that that resolve would be put into practice without delay.

12.   He urged donors to grant ODA at levels in keeping with the internationally accepted targets. There had unfortunately been virtually no increase in such assistance since the sixth session of the Conference. In fact, after account was taken both of public and private capital flows, the developing countries as a whole had been net exporters of capital in 1986, for the third year in succession. However, the replenishment of the resources of IDA and IFAD and the example set by certain donor countries gave reason to hope for an improvement.

13.   Certain industrialized countries had taken some, but still inadequate, steps in recent months to halt the over-production of some agricultural commodities, though the potential threat of an agricultural trade war had still not been averted. It was to be hoped that the Uruguay Round of multilateral trade negotiations would offer an opportunity to end the disarray in world agricultural trade. As proof of its determination, the international community should first and foremost fulfil its standstill and roll-back commitments, including those for agriculture. Secondly, rapid progress was needed in the negotiations on agriculture, tropical products and processed commodities as part of a general movement towards trade liberalization. He had assured GATT of FAO's support for the success of the Uruguay Round.

14. Although the eventual liberalization of the international trade in agricultural products would help to reduce price instability, some supply and demand fluctuations could again destabilize the markets and inhibit the orderly trade expansion. Recent developments on world markets for sugar, tea and jute, for example, showed what upheavals could occur, to the detriment of exporting developing countries in particular. Yet there was little enthusiasm for international price stabilization agreements, for they were difficult to operate under conditions of exchange rate instability.

15. In 1986 alone, the loss suffered by the developing countries in their terms of trade was estimated at 3 per cent of their total national income. Little progress had been made in establishing or strengthening machinery to compensate countries for shortfalls of foreign exchange earnings or to deal with the underlying causes of such adverse movements. A praiseworthy exception was the renewal and expansion by the EEC of the Stabex arrangement under the Third Lomé Convention. He urged all developed countries to follow that example with a view to arriving at a global arrangement covering all products of export interest to the developing countries.

16. He hoped that the current session would stimulate renewed multilateral efforts to remedy the causes and effects of market instability. It was most disappointing that as yet the Common Fund for Commodities remained in abeyance, but he welcomed the announcement that the Soviet Union intended to become a party to the Agreement Establishing the Common Fund, and hoped that others would follow that example and that the Fund would soon become operational. The experience of the 1980s had shown that there was a need to improve the productivity and competitiveness of the commodity sector in the developing countries in keeping with the purposes of the Second Account of the Common Fund. When the Fund became operational, it would also become possible to mobilize the resources pledged to the Second Account for the benefit of developing countries.

17. At the moment the world economic environment was unfavourable for developing countries and in certain respects the long-term outlook was hardly encouraging. Recent FAO, UNCTAD and World Bank studies had shown for example, that the prices of most agricultural products were likely to remain low in the medium term, while those of most manufactures would continue to rise. The terms of trade of commodity exporters were therefore likely to deteriorate further.

18. An improvement of living conditions for the masses in the third world would depend on concerted international action being taken on a number of fronts, including action to deal with the debt problem, promote trade liberalization, create a healthy trade environment, revitalize the exports of all countries, and help developing countries in particular to earn a fair return from trade. A new spirit of international co-operation was needed in all those areas.

Summary of the statement made at the 218th plenary meeting, 30 July 1987, by Mr. Amadou-Mahtar M'BOW, Director-General of the United Nations Educational, Scientific and Cultural Organization

1. Mr. M'BOW said he wished to begin with a few words in memory of the Argentine economist Raúl Prebisch, the founder and first Secretary-General of UNCTAD. It was as a result of his decisive efforts that developing countries had become increasingly aware of the crucial importance of trade and international co-operation for economic development. Moreover, his studies of the deterioration of terms of trade had led him to question traditional international trade theories, namely, that a free trade mechanism based on comparative advantage would inevitably lead to equitable distribution at the world level. Raúl Prebisch had been both a theorist and a man of action; he had argued forcefully for the establishment of machinery to protect developing countries from the vicious circle of underdevelopment, and had thus gone on to become the first Secretary-General of UNCTAD.

2. Yet the improvement in the terms of trade of many third-world countries during the 1970s—which had demonstrated the effectiveness of the action taken—had been short-lived, and the current situation was as bad as it had been 30 years before. Two major complementary theories were advanced in explanation of that trend. The first emphasized the technological progress factor, as a result of which the proportion of raw materials used in the production of manufactured articles had steadily declined, as was clear from the current situation in the food and agriculture sectors. The second theory called into question the development policies followed in the past. As the Prime Minister of Norway and President of the World Commission on Environment and Development had stated earlier in the session,* the importance of gaining acceptance for the concept of "lasting development" in various international organizations in order to respond to the hopes, aspirations and priorities of developing countries posed the crucial question not only of the relationship between development and environment, but also of the cultural dimension of development itself.

3. Everyone had realized the limitations of purely economic measures. In view of the increasing number of constraints on developing countries—growing indebtedness, the deterioration of terms of trade, the protectionist policies of the countries of the North—they had no choice but to rally round objectives based on their own resources, their own capacity to master technological tools, their deep-seated aspirations and their own system of values. No one could deny that it

_____

* See sect. A above.

was one of UNESCO's special tasks to contribute to the establishment of favourable conditions for that kind of independent development. UNESCO had the mandate and objective, proclaimed in its Constitution, of

... advancing, through the educational and scientific and cultural relations of the peoples of the world, the objectives of international peace and of the common welfare of mankind for which the United Nations Organization was established and which its Charter proclaims.

There could be no lasting progress in the field of co-operation for trade and development without a parallel reinforcement of the international intellectual and scientific co-operation, that UNESCO had been set up to promote. Education, science, culture and communications, which were UNESCO's fields of activity, provided mankind with the means for its development, provided that the growing interdependence between the peoples of the world served not to aggravate existing disparities but to strengthen the desire of nations to forge links of equity and co-operation based on solidarity. World developments over the past few decades had highlighted the pre-eminent role of science and technology in the economic development of societies. However, although scientific and technological progress, better training and the improvement of information and communications set the pace for material development, the tendency of science and technology to impose uniformity made it more necessary than ever before to respect the uniqueness and resources of individual cultures. Without development, there could be no cultural vitality, but without culture, there could be no real development.

4.   The question was whether a two-track world should be allowed to develop where the wealth of some existed alongside the poverty of the rest. In today's in-terdependent world, peoples were becoming less and less tolerant of inequality of opportunity and glaring differences in their standards of living. In today's world people everywhere declared themselves equal to all others in dignity and responsibility. Ethical and political reasons dictated that development in all countries must be centred on people—a requirement that made increasing economic and technical sense as well, since production was increasingly based on the acquisition of knowledge and information. By acquiring the necessary know-how and learning how to use it in accordance with their own aspirations and the requirements of regional and international co-operation, the peoples of the South could change their status and gradually become the partners of peoples of the North in an increasingly balanced system of mutual exchanges, in which all the parties would have a vital interest in preserving collective peace and prosperity. However, as the natural evolution of market relationships did not tend in that direction, action other than economic—a voluntary act of solidarity—would be necessary to offset the inequitable machinery of the market. The current situation called for a sense of collective responsibility on a world-wide scale, leading to a sort of Marshall Plan for mankind as a whole. Not only the necessary financial resources, scientific knowledge and technical facilities but also the institutional machinery and international experience were available. There was even a greater awareness throughout the world of the need for such action, thanks, in particular, to the continuing activities of United Nations bodies during the preceding 42 years. As the peoples of the world, with many pasts but only one future, approached the third millenium, a collective sense of responsibility was more necessary than ever before.

Summary of the statement made at the 202nd plenary meeting, 10 July 1987, by Mr. Barber B. CONABLE, Jr., President of the World Bank

1.   Mr. CONABLE said that a significant degree of consensus on the nature of the problems facing the world was reflected in the statements of previous speakers. The nations represented at the seventh session of the Conference, which was taking place at a critical juncture for the world economy, would set a course towards either renewed global growth or stagnation and eventual recession. The gravity of the existing situation and the strength of the forces threatening to undo past progress must be acknowledged. Fitful growth, volatile currencies, high real interest rates, heavy debt loads, depressed commodity prices, increased trade barriers and massive payments imbalances had combined to slow earlier rates of advance and even to erode earlier gains of developing societies. The prospect was one of dangerously slow growth in the developed nations and further regression in the developing world. In the absence of co-ordinated international action to reform the existing fiscal, monetary, credit and commercial policies, it was evident that by 1990 per capita income, consumption, imports and investment in most developing nations would be dangerously below the marks set 10 and 25 years earlier. The cutting of per capita consumption in sub-Saharan Africa below its 1965 level and the reduction of per capita investment in the heavily indebted middle-income countries to 60 per cent of its 1980 level could only be described as a disaster, the repercussions of which would be felt not only by the suffering nations but also by the developed economies in the form of losses of export sales and shortfalls in domestic growth.

2.   Parts of the developing world were, however, being reshaped by one encouraging change: out of sheer necessity country after country was beginning to move away from rigid, closed and inefficient economic systems towards freer and more open markets and fewer price-distorting internal subsidies. The structural adjustment, which the World Bank would continue to support vigorously, was a crucial force for improvement. As adjustment programmes helped nations to become more efficient, they also helped to make them stronger international competitors and better credit risks. The adjustment process could, however, impose heavy social costs on fragile societies. Tangible and speedy results were needed to avoid economic stagnation and political unheaval. There was a growing awareness of the need to protect the poor during the adjustment period, and the

World Bank's programmes took increasing account of that need. The adjustment process was far from complete and its success far from assured, but the boldness of the leaders of developing countries and the patience of their peoples should serve as examples to all policy-makers, particularly in the wealthier societies.

3. Success also depended on the political will and determination of the industrial nations to adjust their own practices to the reality of global interdependence. Concerted action was needed on their part to assure significant, steady, non-inflationary expansion of economic activity, to reverse the rising tide of protectionism in their economies, to lighten the debt-service burdens of the developing world and to provide borrowers with substantial new flows of external capital which would lead through reform to stability and growth. There was no real alternative to adjustment, and the industrial countries had a part to play in the adjustment process.

4. Trade reform was an integral part of the adjustment process, which was, however, endangered by the forces of protectionism. High tariffs, inefficient subsidies and a maze of quotas and other non-tariff barriers were depriving the world community of the gains of enhanced global integration. Developed countries in particular were increasingly shielding their non-competitive sectors from free trade. Instead of providing temporary relief during a process of adjustment and rebuilding, many barriers were becoming permanent refuges for powerful political interests unwilling to face new risks. The developed world could not preach free trade with success while at the same time practising protectionism, as in the agricultural trade. Increased protection by the industrial nations could set back economic development for many years and inflict unnecessary suffering on some of the world's poorest people. The fundamental truth that open markets spurred efficient production and expanding prosperity remained as sound as it had been in Adam Smith's time and at the inception of GATT. The World Bank's 1987 *World Development Report* showed that the most outward-oriented developing economies had tended to increase their GNP, real per capita income, savings rates and employment in manufacturing more than most nations which had sought to insulate themselves from global competition and that the more a developing economy exposed itself to the world and adjusted to outside forces the more it prospered.

5. Adjustment to global competition could not await the outcome of the Uruguay Round. The debt-service burdens were so heavy that export expansion was indispensable, and competition in freer markets was a strong incentive for efficient growth. Trade liberalization was therefore critical for restoring the creditworthiness of developing countries and attracting adequate capital flows for their development. Freer and expanding trade was only one of the essential means of achieving global economic recovery and progress, but the Uruguay Round would provide a vital impetus to action and would be the political testing ground of the ability of all countries to act in the common interest and build an effective mechanism for expanding world trade.

6. Although trade liberalization was crucial to the successful development efforts of all developing coun-tries, trade was no substitute for adequate flows of resources for financing and adjustment purposes. Resource flows to developing countries in recent years had been far from adequate; what made matters worse was that many heavily indebted countries had become net exporters of capital to creditor countries at a time when they urgently needed to expand their own domestic investment. Although net disbursements from the World Bank to the heavily indebted middle-income countries had increased by 50 per cent in 1987, multilateral institutions alone could not compensate for the severe shortfall of financial flows from private sources. The World Bank, which had already done much, was ready to assume even greater responsibilities and risks and would shortly be seeking a substantial general capital increase to permit further growth in its lending programme. Commercial banks, export credit agencies and private direct investment had a significant role to play in contributing to increased domestic resource generation in developing countries. The Bank, the International Finance Corporation and the Multilateral Investment Guarantee Agency (MIGA) would actively help to increase the net flow of resources from private sources.

7. In 1986 ODA from all sources to the low-income countries had fallen to about $36.6 billion, which meant that concessional flows had barely exceeded the 1980 levels in real terms despite the increased needs of recipient countries. He welcomed the agreement reached earlier in 1988 on the Eighth Replenishment of the resources of IDA by $12.4 billion and urged all contributing countries to ratify the agreement as soon as possible. Increased bilateral and multilateral assistance was essential if adjustment and growth programmes in low-income countries were to be sustained, and he urged donor Governments to do everything possible to increase their flows of concessional finance.

8. The Bank and IMF had recently arranged an informal gathering of donors and creditors to consider additional urgent measures for alleviating the situation of the most heavily indebted poorest countries, particularly in sub-Saharan Africa, which were undertaking adjustment programmes. That was the first of a series of meetings designed to gain support for a special three-year programme of debt relief and growth-oriented import financing needed by a number of such countries.

9. Renewed global growth and their own self-interest called for further adjustment by developing nations. Above all, however, action was required also on the part of industrialized countries with respect to adjustment, trade and resource flows in order to strengthen their own economies and those of the rest of the world. Adjustment reforms and improved trading prospects could contribute fully to resumed growth in the developing world only if concomitant increases were made in the net external resources available to developing countries. Such combined action could help to turn the world from the brink of a deep recession to a steady course of renewed growth. Only by moving together, with all groups sharing the burden, could rich and poor alike hope to regain the past economic momentum and redeem past hopes of development and social progress. He was confident that the seventh session of the Conference could help to stimulate such action, and he wished the Conference every success.

**Summary of the statement made at the 212th plenary meeting, 27 July 1987,
by Mr. Michel CAMDESSUS, Managing Director of the International Monetary Fund**

1. Mr. CAMDESSUS said that the theme of the Conference was fully consonant with the objectives of IMF in a world economic situation characterized by a reduction in the growth rates of world production and international trade and a deterioration of the external debt situation of third world countries and, consequently, of their development prospects. It was essential to revitalize world growth and remove all the obstacles in its path, beginning with the debt problem—particularly by re-establishing the creditworthiness of indebted countries. That aim could be achieved in the following ways: growth-oriented structural adjustment programmes; financing to relieve over-indebtedness; and universal adjustment efforts, to promote growth.

2. In the case of the first of those methods, IMF's objective was to restore the basis for lasting economic expansion by correcting balance-of-payments disequilibria. Despite the persistence of preconceived ideas to the contrary, IMF had contributed positively to the recovery efforts of the countries concerned. Thanks to IMF support in the implementation of their adjustment programmes, those countries had maintained a level of economic activity far higher than if they had been thrown back on their own resources. The financial support associated with the adjustment agreements ($125 billion since the beginning of the debt crisis) had made it possible to increase the resources available to those countries; it had also been possible to increase the efficiency with which they were used. The growth rates anticipated under those programmes had not been achieved in some cases, owing to slippages in implementation or unforeseen external developments. A detailed review was currently under way, and any suggestions made would be taken into consideration.

3. Offering a definition of growth and its requirements he said that: (a) it had to be durable; (b) it required structural adjustment and therefore a long time to come to fruition; (c) it implied difficult decisions and a lasting political commitment; (d) it was the result of the complex interplay of various forces and was therefore less adaptable than other variables to fixed objectives and timetables; (e) it required the mobilization of adequate resources and, more importantly, the more efficient use of those resources; (f) it also implied the mobilization of people, a process that could be considerably facilitated if care was taken to reduce the social cost of adjustment; and (g) it must be universal if it was not to remain precarious.

4. Those were the seven characteristic features of growth on which IMF based its support for adjustment programmes. In view of the faltering pace of economic development in recent years and the existence of structural obstacles, adjustment programmes must concentrate on supply-enhancing measures that promoted savings, increased export capacity and used resources more efficiently. Such action could bring about real and sometimes spectacular progress, as experience had shown, although the indebted countries should still not relax their efforts.

5. He then took up the question of financing adjustment programmes in countries where domestic savings were inadequate as a result of debt servicing or where the commercial banks were reluctant to increase their exposure in a context where creditor countries were experiencing budgetary constraints which prevented them from increasing their ODA. Despite such difficulties, he was sure that a concerted effort by the parties concerned would do a great deal to enhance the ability of indebted countries to undertake productive investment, make better use of their economic potential and alleviate their debt burden through growth. What was needed was a strategy that concentrated the limited public resources available in areas lacking alternative financing and that ensured that increased efforts on one side would be matched by greater support from the other. A strategy of that kind must, of course, be diversified and adapted to the type of debt and the economic situation of the country concerned. Middle-income countries that were carrying out vigorous adjustment programmes must be able to count on timely and adequate financing from their bankers, particularly on the basis of "à la carte" arrangements that would give the banks a wider range of financing options and help to normalize relations between debtors and creditors.

6. It was essential that the international community should clearly signal its determination to provide more aid to support the efforts of low-income countries to adjust their economies. In view of the serious difficulties encountered by those countries and the inadequacy of the financial assistance currently available to them, he had requested that the resources that could be allocated to them under the Structural Adjustment Facility should be tripled over the next three years (approximately $9 billion instead of $3 billion). He hoped that all countries that were in a position to do so would make a contribution, since in that way low-income countries undertaking major adjustment programmes could receive adequate financial support on concessional terms and for an appropriate period.

7. The expansion of IMF's activities on behalf of the poorest countries had not detracted from its more traditional work. Concern had been expressed about the recent decline in lending under the Compensatory Financing Facility, but he pointed out that it was explained by the increase in recent years of the value of exports in most of the countries concerned as a result of expanded economic activity. That was no longer the case, however, and compensatory financing had regained its importance after the mediocre results of 1986 and the decline of many commodity prices. Indeed, disbursements during the first few months of 1987 had been double the total for 1986 as a whole, which demonstrated that compensatory financing for temporary export shortfalls was still an essential IMF activity.

8. Steps had to be taken to promote adjustment and growth in countries which, owing to their economic importance, controlled the level of world growth. It was

essential to promote a vigorous expansion of demand in the industrialized countries and facilitate access to their markets for the developing countries. The Governments of the industrialized countries must also try to reduce their competitive subsidization of agricultural exports. The UNCTAD secretariat's report had clearly revealed the pernicious consequences of trade restrictions and the urgent need to roll back the current wave of protectionism. The opportunity offered by the Uruguay Round should be seized in order to bring about a more open international trade system. IMF could best contribute to the restoration of a world trade environment more favourable to the expansion of exports from the indebted countries and thus to an improvement in their growth prospects by promoting the effective co-ordination of economic policies among the major industrialized countries in order to maintain a satisfactory rate of economic growth while correcting undue fluctuations in their balance of payments. The agreement reached at the Venice Summit on increased surveillance of the economies of the seven major industrialized countries entailed new and important responsibilities

for IMF: first, to help determine whether the economic policies of those countries were compatible with the medium-term objectives of the group as a whole and, secondly, to examine current trends and identify any significant deviations from the desired course of development.

9. In fulfilling those responsibilities, IMF would continue to pursue three objectives, namely, to provide the countries concerned a frank and objective evaluation of their economic policies; to inform them of the consequences of their policies for others; and to ensure that the interests and aspirations of the rest of the world were taken into account. At the same time, it would do everything possible to ensure orderly and continuing growth. In that context, the maintenance of stable conditions on exchange markets was most important; exchange rates were one of the performance indicators on which IMF should concentrate its surveillance, since their stability and—when necessary—their orderly adjustment could contribute to world economic growth and equilibrium.

Summary of the statement made at the 211th plenary meeting, 24 July 1987, by Mr. Richard E. BUTLER, Secretary-General of the International Telecommunication Union

1. Mr. BUTLER said that it should come as no surprise that ITU was making a statement on the topic of "Revitalizing development, growth and international trade, in a more predictable and supportive environment, through multilateral co-operation", since telecommunication by its very nature required multilateral co-operation and was receiving much greater recognition as a key factor of development. Telecommunication made the information and tools necessary to ensure efficiency, productivity and supply more effectively available. The search for solutions to more pressing problems had taken priority, particularly in the developing countries, and too little attention had been paid to the impact of the information and telecommunication revolutions, including opportunities for lower unit cost technology applications. Growing awareness of insufficient research and investment in the telecommunication sector had been the focus of discussions at the ITU Plenipotentiary Conference held in Nairobi in 1982. The Conference had set up an Independent Commission for World-Wide Telecommunications Development composed of members from a wide range of disciplines. The Commission had issued a report containing suggestions on the priority to be given to telecommunications, taking into account national and international activities to enhance telecommunications for the mutual benefit of all countries, particularly in under-equipped areas. It had also recommended that countries should make appropriate provision for telecommunications in all economic and social development projects and had appealed to all investment authorities to take telecommunications into account, bearing in mind specific national and regional needs. It had urged Governments and international organizations to grant higher priority to telecommunications in their assistance and development programmes and had stressed the importance of increasing telecommunica-

tion resources, facilities and services. In addition, it had sought to promote better understanding of the underlying causes of gaps in the telecommunication sector and its efforts had already begun to bear fruit. The President of the World Bank had announced that investment requests were increasing. There was reason to believe that the reorganization of the Bank towards programmes would help to promote certain telecommunication objectives. ITU had also established contacts with regional development banks.

2. ITU paid special attention to Africa, where the lack of adequate telecommunication infrastructure gave rise to serious problems, particularly during the recent devastation of the continent by natural disasters. In 1985, ITU had convened the First World Telecommunications Development Conference to consider the many recommendations made by the Independent Commission. The Conference had led to the Arusha Declaration on World Telecommunications Development, which had endorsed the major points of the Commission's report and provided special guidance. It had urged all Governments to adopt the Commission's recommendations and had called upon Governments, telecommunication manufacturers and operating entities in developed countries to allocate more financial and technical resources for telecommunications under multilateral and bilateral aid programmes, paying special attention to the LDCs. A number of countries had taken specific action, with the support of UNDP, in particular, to develop master plans relating to the technical aspects of telecommunications over the next 20 years and to investment planning over shorter periods. Special efforts had been made to restructure telecommunication entities so as to provide the necessary autonomy in terms of planning and investment, management, operation and internal self-

financing. However, much remained to be done, since the development of a high-technology sector such as telecommunications depended largely on investments by the industrialized world. The Commission had recognized the importance of special contributions by the international community in favour of countries with foreign currency problems. It had also recognized the needs of the LDCs for financing on concessionary terms, at least in the early stages of the extension of their telecommunication networks. ITU was ready to explore various forms of partnership with those who were interested in making contributions on a multilateral basis.

3. Recent developments in computer technology had created a need for greater multilateral and bilateral co-operation. Initiatives had been taken to bridge gaps in that regard. Feasibility studies had been carried out for the proposed Regional African Satellite Communication System for the Development of Africa (RASCOM), a project that was currently being implemented in co-operation with various organizations. The project served to unify all studies and to provide information on special new telecommunication developments for the coming two decades with a view, in particular, to remedying existing shortcomings stemming from the absence of rural and remote communications. ITU congratulated the Governments of Zimbabwe and Ethiopia for having agreed to meet African

Development Bank conditions as potential guarantors of technical assistance loans, thereby making it possible to carry out the feasibility study, whose cost was estimated at $6 or $7 million. It urged other countries to follow their example and mentioned that two industrialized countries had agreed to contribute completely untied funds for the study. Countries needed such co-operation in order to improve their telecommunication services and in order to stimulate development. Protectionism in the telecommunication industry also had to be cut back. The development of telecommunication networks in several industrialized countries had stimulated local industry. Deregulation and competition had currently taken hold in the sector and the very complex issue of telecommunication equipment supply and market access was already being considered by GATT and was expected to be discussed during the Uruguay Round of multilateral trade negotiations.

4. ITU had decided to convene a World Administrative Telegraph and Telephone Conference in 1988 with a view to regulating the telecommunication infrastructure necessary to convey information or messages of any kind through electronic means. It would therefore closely follow the negotiations on services between the GATT contracting parties in order to avoid any duplication of potentially related international treaty provisions.

Summary of the statement made at the 208th plenary meeting, 14 July 1987, by Mr. Idriss JAZAIRY, President of the International Fund for Agricultural Development

1. Mr. JAZAIRY said that the hardest hit by the current world economic crisis were the rural poor in the developing countries. It might be thought that they lived apart in their pastoral setting, far removed from the trade and financial problems that were shaking the world. That, however, was not the case. Protectionism in the industrialized countries had reduced market outlets for the agricultural produce of the developing countries. Agricultural subsidies granted by industrialized countries and the consequential agricultural overproduction had led to a fall in world prices for foodstuffs and were reducing the developing countries' export earnings even further. The fall in commodity prices was causing a decrease in the volume and profitability of investment in tropical and sub-tropical agriculture. Such a situation discouraged the developed countries themselves from providing the incentives and making the structural reforms needed to improve agricultural performance.

2. At a time when the industrialized countries were considering cuts in their domestic farm support programmes it was surely not unreasonable to ask them to devote a small part of the savings to helping small farmers in the developing countries, or at least in those developing countries that were determined to do their best for their farmers. If the farmers were given the means of improving their production, they could increase their incomes and consume more products from the developed countries. Everyone would benefit.

3. The developing countries had practically ceased to receive inflows of private capital, and ODA had not filled the gap. For the preceding three years there had even been a net outflow of resources from the developing countries to the developed countries, entailing a loss of $2 billion for Africa alone. Something must therefore be done to alleviate the developing countries' debt burden. He suggested that the industrialized countries concerned might authorize the developing countries, especially those in sub-Saharan Africa, to repay part of their debt in local currency. The resulting amounts in local currency might be paid into an international development fund for re-investment in programmes designed to alleviate rural poverty in the countries concerned. The fund might be managed by a multilateral institution such as IFAD, in close consultation with Governments and non-governmental organizations. In that way vulnerable groups would be better protected during the structural adjustment period and outflows of foreign exchange would be avoided.

4. The decline in ODA for agriculture was a particularly serious source of concern. The slackening of net flows of resources to sub-Saharan Africa was especially tragic. African Governments had taken bold steps to adapt their economies to new realities, but unfortunately the industrialized countries had been slow in supplying the additional resources needed to implement the new programmes, particularly in agriculture. The Economic and Social Council in its resolution 1987/90

of 9 July 1987, had urged those donor countries which had not yet done so to contribute to IFAD's special programme for sub-Saharan Africa, so that it could attain its target of $300 million. He hoped that the countries concerned would do so before the closure of the Conference.

5.   IFAD itself had had difficulty in replenishing its resources and was therefore finding it hard to perform its mission of helping small farmers in the developing countries to increase their production. Poverty was just as endemic in Asia and Latin America as it was in Africa. In all those regions IFAD was concerned with stimulating group credit for the purchase of inputs in cases where commercial credit could not be obtained for lack of guarantees. It emphasized the production of traditional crops, the role of women, and the need for small farmers to protect the environment. Quite often landless agricultural labourers deliberately misused land by applying inappropriate methods. For them it was a question of survival, and hence they had no choice. Projects designed to raise the productivity of poor rural areas through the use of low-cost techniques which protected the environment were therefore needed. IFAD was also concerned with reconciling the structural adjustment process with the interests of the rural poor, who were particularly vulnerable to the effects of budget cuts in transitional periods.

6.   UNCTAD had focused on the needs of the LDCs through the Substantial New Programme of Action, with which IFAD had a natural link, since it had lent, on very favourable terms, over $808 million for 88 investment programmes in 35 LDCs, 27 of them in Africa. Under its Special Programme for Africa, IFAD had so far approved six loans of $150 million. In support of the Substantial New Programme of Action, the Fund had committed over $100 million in grants for agricultural research. It had also trained personnel for the management of projects for small farmers in many countries and was planning to allocate $50 million for rural development in countries in the region of the Southern African Co-ordination Conference.

7.   At its Sixth Ministerial Meeting, held at Havana, the Group of 77 had invited the industrialized countries to increase their participation in the third replenishment of IFAD and had urged those developed countries members of the Fund that could afford to do so to increase their contributions. The next replenishment of the Fund provided the industrialized countries with an opportunity to recycle their surplus foreign exchange earnings through IFAD for the elimination of rural poverty. It also provided beneficiary developing countries with an opportunity to make an extra financial effort to support an institution which was, after all, their own and which had taken several initiatives to promote economic co-operation among developing countries, including the use of contributions in the non-convertible currencies of some developing countries to finance research and training in other developing countries, the purchase of goods and services in some developing countries for projects implemented in others, the transfer of project designs from one country to another, and the recruitment of a large number of experts in the developing countries themselves. IFAD, with its unique system of financing, would contribute more effectively to the Substantial New Programme of Action and to South-South co-operation if it had the necessary resources.

8.   The Extraordinary Ministerial Conference of Non-Aligned Countries on South-South Co-operation held in June 1987 at Pyongyang had reiterated the non-aligned countries' support for the establishment of a South bank. That was a very positive development, but it was also to be hoped that the will to promote South-South co-operation in concrete institutional terms would be reflected in an even firmer commitment to preserve existing institutions such as IFAD, in which the developing countries received three dollars from the industrialized countries for every two dollars which they contributed themselves. The support of delegations at the current session of the Conference would be decisive for placing IFAD, as the only concrete institutional expression of the restructuring of international economic relations, on a sound financial footing.

Summary of the statement made at the 203rd plenary meeting, 10 July 1987, by Mr. Domingo L. SIAZON Jr., Director-General of the United Nations Industrial Development Organization

1.   Mr. SIAZON said that the 1980s had been a period of uncertainty, instability and difficult adjustment for the world economy to which the developing countries had been especially vulnerable. Their external debt had reached staggering proportions and the international flow of credit and capital had dried up. The structure of investment and production had been undergoing a fundamental transformation in recent years. Although a number of developing countries had proved capable of producing an increasing range of industrial products at internationally competitive prices, they were experiencing difficulties in finding markets for their products, while having to continue production in order to service their debts. The rate of growth of industrial output in the developing countries as a whole had declined steadily since 1976. Although deregula-

tion, introduced as a measure to revitalize the economy of major industrial countries, had made their industries more mobile in that firms had been relocated away from their original base or were sub-contracting abroad, only a few developing countries with relatively cheap but sophisticated labour had been able to benefit from that globalized production network, whereas most others had been overwhelmed by increasingly severe external constraints on their growth and development. That contraction in world trade posed the most immediate threat to the industrialization prospects of the developing countries as well as to many export-oriented industries in developed countries. Although privatization and deregulation had been extensively debated and adopted as important policy options in many developing countries, the mere shift of ownership from the public to the private sector did not of itself guarantee improved economic performance. The improvement of performance might have to be preceded by a measure of rehabilitation and related investment, including investment in technology, equipment, marketing, management and human skills.

2. UNIDO was receiving an increasing number of requests to assist countries and enterprises in resolving industrial restructuring and rehabilitation problems. Any schemes that it suggested must lead to effective industrial rehabilitation and restructuring, as well as stimulating related new investment. UNIDO had adopted action-oriented approaches and the principle of involvement with the many agents of industrial change. Such co-operation entailed serious attention to small industries geared to domestic consumption which were, however, facing increasingly fierce competition, even in South-South trade, and UNIDO had therefore placed great emphasis on the symbiotic development of small and medium-scale industries with larger industries so as to form part of a dynamic industrial structure. It viewed that new inward-looking strategy not merely in the context of growth with equity, but also in relation to production efficiency or survival strategy, which, in turn, called for renewed efforts to achieve regional and subregional solidarity among the developing countries themselves.

3. UNIDO supported technical and economic co-operation among developing countries in the field of industrial development for it regarded such co-operation as an effective instrument for promoting the rational and efficient use of resources in those countries with a view to achieving their individual and collective self-reliance. In a period marked by a decline in the flow of official external resources to developing countries, a broader innovative institutional mechanism to promote direct foreign investment, mutually beneficial joint venture agreements and technical co-operation was of particular significance. Since 1980 UNIDO had successfully promoted projects worth a total of more than $4 billion. UNIDO was also endeavouring to tap under-utilized resources for industrialization in developing countries by working directly with companies. Industrial enterprises in developing countries were seeking help with their rehabilitation programmes, and private or State firms in industrialized countries made contributions in cash and in kind or became involved in technical assistance projects and rehabilitation programmes from the outset.

4. The value of UNIDO's technical assistance services was expected to exceed the $100 million mark in 1987, and the organization made a point of suggesting realistic, practical solutions for the problems that arose, in the light of the varied national interests of the countries concerned. It had developed the system of sectoral consultations, which provided a unique forum for the identification of key industrial issues, for the elaboration of common approaches by government representatives, industrialists, bankers and professional experts from developed and developing countries, and for negotiations between those countries in specific sectors.

5. The operational programme of UNIDO reflected its serious concern with the situation in Africa, and the organization had devoted nearly 36 per cent of its technical assistance services in 1986 to projects in that continent, with special emphasis on the LDCs. During the previous two years it had also promoted $200 million worth of industrial investment projects in the African region, and since 1980 had carried out a special programme, the Industrial Development Decade for Africa, devoted to meeting the industrial needs of African countries. Convinced that developing countries should be assisted in building their capabilities not only in respect of conventional technologies but also in respect of the industrial application of the most advanced technologies, UNIDO had promoted the establishment of an International Centre for Genetic Engineering and Biotechnology, which had now commenced operations.

6. UNIDO's efforts to identify and solve technically manageable problems in the process of industrial restructuring at the national and international levels were an indispensable element in world economic management. Its new status as a specialized agency should enhance its capacity to act as a focal point for innovation in international industrial co-operation. UNIDO's efforts, which concentrated on sector-specific technical issues and micro-level solutions, could not, however, claim to suffice by themselves to achieve the principal objectives of the United Nations. The growing complexity of the international system presented a continual challenge to its management. The world industrial economy remained in the doldrums, and that situation might worsen unless a determined and concerted move was made towards adjustment and development on a global scale. The world continued to await the emergence of new financial tools, comparable in vision and generosity to the Marshall Plan, to help fuel growth and development, and it was to be hoped that the seventh session of the Conference would be the catalyst for new initiatives.

*

* *

Summary of the statement made at the 214th plenary meeting, 28 July 1987,
by Mr. Arthur DUNKEL, Director General of GATT

1. Mr. DUNKEL commented on three factors of major current importance for international trade and

economic co-operation, namely the Uruguay Round of multilateral trade negotiations, trade in goods and services as a stimulus to growth and development, and the increasingly uncertain environment facing investors and producers.

2.   He first observed that the negotiations launched in Uruguay in 1986 under the General Agreement were progressing under propitious and encouraging conditions. Their objectives had been clearly defined in the Punta del Este Declaration and were firmly rooted in the idea that trade, in conjunction with finance and development, was an essential part of economic policy, that steps had to be taken not only to open up world markets still further but also to strengthen and expand multilateral trade rules and disciplines, and that the negotiations must be based on commitments to a stand-still and roll-back on trade-restrictive and trade-distortive measures. The framework for the negotiations had also been provided in that negotiating groups, 14 concerned with trade in goods and 1 with trade in services, had been set up under a Trade Negotiations Committee. Substantive proposals, some of which were extremely far-reaching, had been submitted by Governments. The ambition and courage demonstrated at the start of the negotiations suggested that worthwhile results would be achieved. A large number of States—nearly 100—were participating in the Uruguay Round. Developing countries had shared fully in defining the objectives and general guidelines of the negotiations and in getting them under way, thereby demonstrating their deep concern that the trading system as a whole should be improved, as the basic prerequisite for the success of any efforts to meet their special needs. The many specific proposals that had been made by developing countries reflected the positive role they could play in shaping the future of the trading system. Participating Governments were undoubtedly highly appreciative of the technical assistance provided by UNCTAD to those participants in the Uruguay Round in need of it. There were numerous possibilities of co-operation with UNCTAD and other international institutions in that area.

3.   With respect to the second factor, it would appear that Governments were recognizing the contribution of trade to development and accepting the challenge of structural adjustment through competition, since they were allowing the market mechanism freer rein, at least domestically. However, a number of countries were not applying to their international policies the principles underlying their domestic strategies, possibly because traders felt that they would be exposed to greater risks on the international level owing to factors over which their Governments seemed to have little or no control. The nature of the topics being taken up in the multilateral trade negotiations indicated that Governments intended to remedy that situation, at least in the area of trade policies, by improving the conditions of competition on international markets.

4.   With respect to the third factor, he noted that the uncertainty of the international economic environment was due partly to self-restraint agreements, market sharing and trade-distortive government interventions. However, it was also attributable to other factors, and particularly macro-economic management problems. Developed countries had almost succeeded in bringing inflation under control, but only at the cost of a sharp slow-down in economic growth. As a result, declining industries no longer benefited from the necessary adjustment margin enabling them to expand at a healthy rate, and protectionist pressure was on the rise. Whatever the experts believed, public opinion, and therefore political circles, viewed current imbalances as indicative of a malfunctioning trade system and thus as posing a threat to liberal trade policies in developed countries and to the gradual market-opening process.

5.   Exchange rates were another source of uncertainty. They were increasingly seen to be determined more by capital flows than by current-account transactions, and exchange rates at variance with economic fundamentals made it harder to interpret world markets through price signals. Decisions on investment were also made more difficult by widely fluctuating exchange rates.

6.   The debt problem also fostered uncertainty. Between 1981 and 1986, the imports of the 16 most heavily indebted countries had declined by about 25 per cent. That contraction of purchases on world markets had had an immediate impact on consumption and living standards in those countries, but declining capital goods imports along with reduced investment also threatened to hamper economic growth for many years to come and had a negative impact on the trading partners of those countries. There was no better demonstration of the trade-finance link. At the same time, banks and financial markets were increasingly reluctant to maintain capital flows to all developing countries, regardless of their debt situation. Many of those countries would, no doubt, be prepared to liberalize their trade régimes, but feared the impact on their balance-of-payment situation. They were also less willing to rely on international sources of financing to overcome temporary balance-of-payment difficulties that might result from liberalization and to meet some of the costs of structural adjustment.

7.   Although the solution to those problems lay in a healthy trading environment, it was nevertheless true that trade policy changes could not, by themselves alone, eliminate existing imbalances in the world economy. That was suggested by the Punta del Este Declaration which emphasized the need for "concurrent co-operative action at the national and international level". The seventh session of the Conference offered yet another opportunity to carry forward the collective consensus in favour of more integrated international action in the economic field. Such a step was all the more necessary since the way ahead was long and difficult. In any event, tomorrow's economic environment would be shaped by current policy decisions.

*

*   *

**Summary of the statement made at the 206th plenary meeting, 13 July 1987,
by Mr. Göran ENGBLOM, Executive Director of the International Trade Centre UNCTAD/GATT**

1. Mr. ENGBLOM said that by reason of its essential function, which was to assist developing countries in expanding their trade, the International Trade Centre was following attentively the deliberations of the Conference.

2. After stagnating for some years, the value of the Centre's technical co-operation programme had grown dramatically, by over 40 per cent, in 1986, and the prospects for 1987 looked satisfactory. That improvement was due to increased contributions from the traditional trust fund donors, from developing countries' own national resources and regional UNDP resources and from the interregional programme of UNDP, and warm thanks were due to all contributors, including the six developing countries that had become contributors to the trust fund, for their invaluable support.

3. In addition to expanding traditional activities, the Centre had been diversifying the range of its services, notably in two new areas. Over the preceding three years, it had been exploring the potential for an expansion of the export trade of developing countries in specific technical consulting services and, with the help of a number of contributors, in particular China, India and Indonesia, had been able to launch a programme of technical co-operation at the enterprise level aimed at improving the competitive position of a number of enterprises exporting specific technical consulting services. It was hoped that the programme could be sustained by continued contributions for the three to five years necessary for participating enterprises to achieve tangible results. The Centre was focusing a sizeable part of its activities on assisting enterprises direct, often with the participation of government services, its aim being to assist enterprises to become successful exporters. Those concerned in both the public and private sectors would be awaiting anxiously the outcome of the seventh session of the Conference and of the Uruguay Round.

4. In the past, the Centre's technical co-operation activities related to commodities had tended to be of an *ad hoc* nature, depending on requests from developing countries and the level and nature of resources available, and had generally concerned specific commodities at particular levels of processing. The Centre's work in stimulating demand for commodities and thus improving the competitive position of and market prospects for certain commodities had been carried out in close co-operation with commodity organizations. Its work on jute and jute products and timber, for instance, had provided the Centre with an opportunity to integrate activities into consolidated programmes of activities. In response to Conference resolution 158 (VI) concerning the strengthening of the Centre, particularly in relation to commodities, the Centre has systematically examined with regard to individual commodities and also to the processed and semi-processed products obtainable from them—technical co-operation needs falling within its mandate, and had engaged in a fund-raising campaign to permit the identification of needs, the development of project proposals and the implementation of technical co-operation projects. As a result, a number of traditional and other donor countries, particularly Sweden and Switzerland, had increased their financial contributions to the Centre's commodity-related work.

5. Efforts had concentrated on commodities covered by the Integrated Programme and on commodities for which the Centre had already accumulated knowledge and experience. Consultations had been held with international organizations and commodity bodies. The result was the continual development of an overall programme of action for specific commodities and of project proposals for technical co-operation based on identified needs, work already carried out and services available from other sources.

6. As a consequence of the realignment of the Centre's programme priorities towards result-oriented projects, an increasing number of projects were being formulated at the level of State-owned or privately owned enterprises, marketing boards, producers' associations, growers' co-operatives and others. The Centre was endeavouring to strengthen and improve the effectiveness of indigenous entrepreneurs by providing them with technical assistance in its areas of competence.

7. He reiterated the Centre's commitment to provide developing countries with a better targeted range of services to meet their needs, both in the Centre's traditional activities and in support of the UNCTAD Integrated Programme for Commodities.

E. OTHER INTERGOVERNMENTAL BODIES*

**Summary of the statement made at the 218th plenary meeting, 30 July 1987,
by Mr. Faris BINGARADI, Senior Economist, Department of Research and Statistics
of the Arab Monetary Fund**

1. Mr. BINGARADI explained that the Fund, which attached particular importance to the seventh session of the Conference because of the role it could play in promoting international co-operation and understanding, had been set up to grant loans to Arab countries on favourable terms and to encourage its member States to liberalize their trade with one another. It was rently also trying to set up additional machinery for financing trade between Arab countries.

2. In view of the difficulties being experienced by the world economy, the results of the seventh session would have a great influence on international co-operation. Three basic problems, namely, the international trade system, the position occupied by the developing countries in that system, and the external debt of the developing countries, had to be tackled if the objective of revitalizing development, growth and international trade was to be attained.

3. Confidence had to be restored in the international trade system by ensuring respect for the agreements in force, adopting measures to liberalize trade and eliminating the barriers put up by the developed countries, mainly against exports from developing countries. The position of the developing countries in the international trade system was far from satisfactory; it must be redefined to enable those countries to enjoy all the advantages of foreign trade and increase their capacity in order to fulfil their external obligations. The current system must be modified so as to bring about greater participation in international trade by developing countries, particularly through measures to stabilize commodity prices and to promote the local processing of commodities. The external debt of the developing countries had reached unprecedented levels; and experience had shown that the debt problem depended not on the way in which they managed the

resources they were given, but on the restrictions imposed on their exports to the developed countries.

4. The objectives of the current session of the Conference could be attained by increased co-operation between all countries, both developed and developing, and a proper understanding of the interests at stake. The problems of the international economy could not be resolved in a fragmentary, case-by-case manner or by one group of countries to the detriment of the others. Only if that fact were realized could a new international system be established on the basis of trust and equitable relations between countries—in other words, on understanding and justice.

5. The developing countries were aware that not all their problems were due to external factors, and they had tried to reform their own systems in spite of the great sacrifices required. However, they had received no help from the developed countries, whose protectionist policies had blocked developing countries' exports and whose provision of concessional aid had declined. All those facts indicated that co-ordinated efforts were needed to resolve the problems of the developing countries.

6. At the seventh session the Conference should be capable of promoting conditions conducive to the revitalization of trade and development, which would mark a turning-point in the history of international co-operation. The reforms undertaken by the developing countries must be matched by the developed countries which must open up their markets to exports from the developing countries, stabilize commodity prices and increase capital flows to developing countries on concessional terms.

7. The Arab Monetary Fund was proud of its co-operation with UNCTAD and was doing its best to expand its relations with other international and regional organizations in order to promote true international co-operation.

---

* Under rule 80 of the rules of procedure.

**Summary of the statement made at the 217th plenary meeting, 29 July 1987,
by Mr. Akira NAGASAKA, Acting Secretary-General of the Asian-African Legal Consultative Committee**

1. Mr. NAGASAKA said that the Consultative Committee and UNCTAD were pursuing common objectives in the sense that both were contributing to the progressive development and codification of international law. The Consultative Committee was working to

define norms and practices aimed at enabling the African and Asian countries to make progress along the path of development in a manner consistent with their political independence and at helping them also to examine the major questions being tackled by the United

Nations and other international organizations, taking into account the evolution of international economic co-operation and trade law.

2. At its Colombo session in 1960, the Committee had decided to carry out an extensive study of questions concerning the international sale of goods and commodities in anticipation of changes in the trading patterns of its member countries. The Committee had simultaneously directed its activities to other areas of international economic co-operation, including foreign investments. That had led it to participate in the work of UNCTAD, and it would be recalled that his organization had played a role in consolidating the position of the developing countries with regard to the Code of Conduct for Liner Conferences in 1974. It was also co-operating closely with UNCITRAL, which had in particular adopted the programme of work it had recommended.

3. The developing countries, which aspired to consolidate their political and economic independence and to be treated as equal partners in development, had emphasized the need to restructure international economic and commercial relations to create a new balance. But their economic situation had continued to deteriorate as a result of the low level of commodity prices, huge imbalances of trade and their large accumulation of debts. The Declaration and the Programme of Action on the Establishment of a New International Economic Order, together with other texts adopted subsequently, had identified priority areas for action and advocated the adoption of specific measures. Particular mention should be made of the Lima Declaration and Plan of Action, resolution 3362 (S-VII) on development and international economic co-operation adopted at the seventh special session of the General Assembly, the Charter of Economic Rights and Duties of States, and the resolution concerning the International Development Strategy for the Third United Nations Development Decade.

4. The global economy was facing an extremely grave crisis characterized by stagnation of growth and even, in some cases, by recession. Financial stringencies, the weakness of demand and glutted markets were all symptoms of that crisis. At its eleventh special session, the General Assembly had recognized the inadequacy of piecemeal solutions based on the strategies of the first two development decades and had called for global negotiations on a wide range of interrelated issues. Although those negotiations had never really got off the ground, there was reason to hope that the members of the international community would recognize the need to adopt appropriate measures to revitalize the world economy. Only long-term planning and policy decisions could bring stability to the world economic system and generate real growth and development. UNCTAD could contribute to the improvement of the situation and of international economic relations, in particular through greater co-operation between the developed and developing countries.

5. After the eleventh special session of the General Assembly, two ministerial meetings had been held under the auspices of the Consultative Committee, one at Kuala Lumpur in 1980 and the other at Istanbul in 1981, with a view in particular to creating a more favourable climate for trade and investment in the developing countries of Africa and Asia. The Committee had also drawn up models for bilateral investment protection agreements, which had been finalized at its Kathmandu session in 1985. In addition, it had organized a meeting in New York, in December 1984, aimed at promoting dialogue between a group of prospective investors and the representatives of interested States on such matters as the investment climate, modalities for co-operation, investment incentives and safeguards. A follow-up meeting had been held in New York in 1985 to discuss the effect of the World Bank's Multilateral Investment Guarantee Agency (MIGA) in promotion of investments, modalities for investment, joint ventures and the role of the private sector in the development of developing countries. The Consultative Committee intended to continue to participate actively in the work of UNCTAD.

Summary of the statement made at the 205th plenary meeting, 13 July 1987, by Mr. Claude CHEYSSON, Commissioner for North-South Relations, Commission of the European Communities

1. Mr. CHEYSSON said he had noted with satisfaction that the information media were devoting considerable attention to the Conference and he therefore hoped that the general public would at last come to understand that the world economy was in disarray, that its future was at stake and that all countries must accept a responsibility commensurate with their economic importance. The alternative was chaos, which would strike at all countries, beginning with the weakest, poorest and least developed, threatening renascent democracy, being used to justify human rights violations, racism and discrimination on the pretext of economic efficiency, and engendering division, despair, revolt and violence in a divided world where those excluded from a better life would not always remain passive.

2. All countries shared the responsibility for past errors and excesses. Indebtedness, for example, would be less burdensome if all sides had refrained from encouraging some questionable and economically unjustified operations that had been poorly monitored, if at all, by the national and international authorities. All were responsible because of the inescapable interdependence of their needs, ambitions and imbalances—an interdependence which had for too long been denied by the strongest. The European Community was more aware than others of that fact because of

the volume of its exports to the oil-producing countries and newly industrialized countries during its economic peak and during its later so-called decline. All countries were concerned because the return to healthy, predictable and durable economic and financial systems could be accomplished only through a joint effort.

3. The industrialized countries had belatedly begun to examine their conscience. With the encouragement of the Secretary-General of OECD in May 1987, and later during and after the Venice Summit, they had identified and listed the major shortcomings and inconsistencies in their own economic, financial and monetary policies, drawn up guidelines, made declarations of intent and announced action to be taken, some of which, such as that in the agricultural sector, had a new ring. There had been some progress with analysis, and discussions had been streamlined.

4. Since all were involved, the analysis and general guidelines had to be made uniform and mutually adjusted, efforts being made to reduce differences in evaluation and to seek a consensus on common interests. There were difficult situations to be tackled in both North and South, and that would take time. The interaction of the trade, financial, monetary and economic fields must be measured globally before individual topics were referred to the appropriate international institutions or Governments.

5. No other forum was as fitted to perform that task as UNCTAD, in which all countries—socialist, capitalist, North and South, rich and poor, producers and consumers, strong and weak—were represented. The opportunity for CMEA countries and market-economy countries to meet was one that must not be missed. UNCTAD was a unique international forum, and its members should seize the opportunities offered by the seventh session of the Conference, despite the prevailing chaos in the world economy. It was encouraging that non-governmental organizations and the media were keenly interested in the Conference and that Governments had sent their most eminent representatives to the session.

6. The Conference would fail to come up to expectations, however, if it went no further than producing an analysis and general guidelines. Practical progress on specific issues was also needed. In his statement on 10 July, the President of the EEC Council* had told the Conference of some of the European Community's commitments in that direction. If everyone followed that example, UNCTAD would achieve good results. In his report, the Secretary-General of UNCTAD rightly invited the Conference to make an analysis and announce constructive measures.

7. The main causes of the international economic disarray had been universally acknowledged, though with shades of differences in analysis. No one could deny that a return to sustained non-inflationary growth was essential. That implied that every country capable of development must have a sound economic policy and that financial resources must remain available to it after it had discharged its external commitments. The stimuli of the market economy must become stable once more,

or at any rate transparent, since transparency generated security. Due account must be taken of market signals, though not at the expense of the weak.

8. One simple factor that was often forgotten was the chain reaction of imbalances. The total of world surpluses and deficits in international trade was, by definition, nil. The United States Secretary of State had recently stated at a meeting of Pacific countries that the desired reduction in the American trade deficit would mean a curtailment of the exports of third world countries to the United States. It would therefore have to be accompanied by renewed efforts by industrialized countries with large surpluses. On the other hand, however, to oblige heavily indebted countries to maintain an enormous balance-of-trade surplus for debt servicing would perpetuate the imbalance in world trade. Brazil, for example, would have to generate a billion dollar surplus a month. A nightmare situation had been created, in which net financial flows were moving from South to North.

9. He referred to another well-known case of a chain reaction: a country with a large budget deficit that wished to avoid inflation and had insufficient savings had to attract foreign capital by very high interest rates. If there was a substantial response, then world financial resources would be diverted from productive investment in industry or services to the benefit of more or less speculative financial markets. Stock exchanges would flourish, debts increase, production stagnate and per capita GNP would fall. That example typified the existing situation.

10. The remarkable speed of technological progress, which had at first been welcomed but which was yet another cause of imbalance, had brought about radical changes with which market forces by themselves could not cope. Technological and biogenetic progress had necessarily created structural surpluses on agricultural markets, which had led to the prevailing disorder. The outlets for most minerals were being reduced by the use of substitutes and by saving and recycling, prices were plummeting and exporters in the developing countries were consequently suffering. The effects of such chain-reaction imbalances were extremely serious for the weak and particularly disturbing when they could not be mitigated by sustained long-term growth.

11. The inference to be drawn was that firm political will must be demonstrated so that a vast international co-operative effort could be made in which all concerned faced up to the difficulties and inevitable changes. Every subject should be dealt with as necessary and every case should be considered on its merits, but in the medium term and long term there must be a global view and all concerned must make adjustment efforts commensurate with their own economic and political importance. Mutual surveillance and economic understandings must be accepted, and the monetary area must be seen to concern all countries of North and South.

12. The States members of the European Community were contributing to the stabilization and development of international economic relations by creating a market—open and without frontiers—of 320 million consumers, by stabilizing exchange rates through the

---

* See sect. B above.

European Monetary System, and by helping weak countries to catch up with the more advanced countries.

13. In its relations with the developing countries the European Community also had other achievements to its credit. The GSP established by the Community in 1971 was helping to develop industries in the developing countries, all of which benefited from the system, but access to the Common Market was even easier for the 78 countries with which it had concluded preferential agreements. The African, Caribbean and Pacific States were linked to the Community by the Lomé Convention, which dealt globally with all subjects—a method that should be commended by the Conference. Financing was guaranteed for several years, and innovative mechanisms such as Stabex had been established. Lomé thus expressed Europe's will to give systematic support to co-operation efforts, or preferably to regional integration as a means of defending common interests. The EEC had concluded agreements with other regional groups such as the Andean Pact, the Association of South East Asian Nations and countries of Central America, and hoped to conclude others in the future with countries of the Gulf, and other regional groups in Latin America.

14. That general approach was significant for the Community's commitments as announced by the President of its Council. The States members of the Community renewed their commitment to the target of 0.7 per cent of GDP for ODA and of 0.15 per cent for assistance to the LDCs. They hoped that the international effort to speed up transfers of aid to African countries that were applying a sound policy of recovery would be intensified. The Community would make its own direct contribution to that effort. In addition, it considered that loans to the LDCs should gradually be replaced by grants, as far as possible retroactively. The Community has begun to apply the GSP and the Multifibre Arrangement differentially in favour of the LDCs and would continue to do so in order to ensure that the facilities offered were not monopolized by industries that had become competitive.

15. The Stabex scheme for stabilizing the developing countries' earnings derived from exports of the main commodities applied to the 66 Lomé Convention countries; in 1986 alone, 230 million ECU had been allocated to the scheme. In addition, the Community had extended the benefit of the Stabex scheme to the LDCs in the rest of the world. The first payments would be made to Bangladesh, Yemen and Nepal, restrospectively to 1987. In view of the unquestionable benefit of the stabilization scheme, which buffered the LDCs against unforeseeable shortfalls in earnings from exports of tropical products, he hoped that all industrialized countries would follow the Community's example.

16. The situation of LDCs which depended on exports of raw materials and commodities was nevertheless a cause for concern in view of the technological progress to which he had referred. Almost all Community Governments had long ago approved and ratified the Agreement Establishing the Common Fund for Commodities, and the last was about to do so. The Community supported efficient commodity agreements, but at the same time and above all it wished to encourage and finance research, diversification and in-

dustrialization. That was the task envisaged for the second window and the Community would shortly implement its commitments in that connection.

17. The Community fully intended to assume its responsibilities. It had admittedly helped to build up the dangerous structural agricultural surpluses and to that extent was partly responsible for the disorder in agricultural commodity prices. Accordingly, it had decided to offer to all third world countries its technical and financial assistance in support of food strategies that tended to promote national or regional self-sufficiency, though that was not enough. The analysis made by OECD and at the Venice Summit and the ensuing recommendations had been essential. Action must be taken at once. Other proposals made in Geneva, though welcome and imaginative, were geared to the long term; the Community was not convinced that they were realistic but would consider them in the context of GATT. The Community was committed to cutting all its output of animal and vegetable products by imposing quotas, ceilings and surtaxes above certain levels and making regular and large cuts in Community markets, and it called upon its competitors to stop outbidding or undercutting the Community's products in export markets. The measures it had taken had already had some effects on dairy and meat production and were to be applied also to the principal cereals and oil-seeds. Such a restructuring of the farm sector took time, and the extent and strength of reactions in interested quarters in Europe showed how far-reaching was the scope of the Community's action. The follow-up of the GATT negotiations would demonstrate the Community's keen determination to act if it met with the same determination from its partners.

18. In that connection, he said, moves to liberalize international trade in goods and services were of interest to third world countries as well as to the Community, which could be depended upon to play a constructive role in the Uruguay Round by affirming multilateralism, denouncing protectionism and seeking a balance between rights and obligations.

19. That was a justified hope of the third world countries. It was essential to increase trade with them and help them to finance their own development. Action should be taken to reactivate export credit, give developing countries the means to monitor the quality and invoicing of their imported products, arrange for the recycling in the developing countries of some of the surpluses of industrialized countries, ensure that debt servicing did not frustrate the revival of economies, develop scientific, technical and industrial co-operation activities in order to undertake more joint ventures, reassure and attract investors and encourage banks to show flexibility and use all their financial ingenuity, and support the action of the regional development banks.

20. The international financial institutions should continue to be the guarantors and monitors of good management and should have the means to act speedily. The 12 Community countries favoured a rapid increase in World Bank capital and welcomed the request by the Director-General of the International Monetary Fund for a substantial increase in the Structural Adjustment Facility.

21. Some of the commitments to which he had referred would be implemented nationally or at Community level, while others would be renewed in international organizations and conferences where the Community would be sitting with countries from the South, which had a shared interest in creating the conditions for stimulating growth, without which the problems of neither side could be solved, injustice would spread and unrest would worsen. The world could not allow such a threat to weigh on the future of its peoples or such despair to be passed on to future generations. The Conference must therefore succeed.

Summary of the statement made at the 213th plenary meeting, 27 July 1987, by Mr. Shridath S. RAMPHAL, Secretary-General of the Commonwealth Secretariat

1. Mr. RAMPHAL said that the Commonwealth Secretariat wished to express its support of UNCTAD and all that it symbolized, namely, the interdependence of the world economy and multilateralism.

2. He welcomed the establishment of the South Commission, whose task was to analyse the major problems facing the third world and to seek practical solutions. Such a body could pave the way for a productive partnership within the international community in all areas of concern to UNCTAD.

3. The current session of the Conference should be an occasion for strengthening the global negotiation process through consensus. Whereas such specific topics as monetary and financial questions or trade must be the subject of detailed negotiations in other bodies, the latter must be guided by the integrated policy framework proposed by UNCTAD.

4. Ideas were currently converging; the developed countries showed signs of a greater willingness to co-operate and to respect multilateralism, and the developing countries a greater willingness to admit their mistakes. That could not fail to encourage UNCTAD in its efforts to achieve consensus.

5. The Commonwealth had always supported multilateralism actively. It had contributed to development co-operation through action and discussions and its North-South studies. The ministerial and summit meetings of the Commonwealth all stressed multilateralism and embraced UNCTAD's concerns. Suffice it to recall that in 1978, the action taken by the Commonwealth ministers had been decisive in breaking the deadlock in negotiations on the Common Fund; all the developed Commonwealth countries had ratified the Agreement Establishing the Common Fund for Commodities. It was to be hoped that the Common Fund would shortly enter into force and that maximum use would be made of the First and Second Accounts. Yet much still remained to be done, particularly in the area of compensatory financing.

6. For many developing countries, export diversification was a necessity, but implied that the developed countries had to open up their markets. It was pointless to process raw materials if they simply came up against the protectionism of the importers. Following the Uruguay Round, agreement must therefore be reached, as a matter of urgency, on a set of measures to liberalize trade, and the Conference must promote that process.

7. The liberalization of trade would be of crucial importance in reviving financial flows to developing countries. In a period of crisis, capital flows were declining and ODA was far from the target of 0.7 per cent of the GNP of the donor countries. The Conference could revitalize the aid process, particularly for the LDCs. If the developing countries were to achieve minimum acceptable growth rates, financial flows would have to be doubled by 1990. Urgent measures were therefore required to strengthen the resources of the multilateral financial institutions, particularly the World Bank.

8. The problem of financial flows was inextricably bound up with that of debt, which for many low-income countries constituted an unmanageable burden. Capital flows on concessional terms must be increased, for example by providing bilateral official debt relief or by following up the proposal made by the Managing Director of IMF to treble the Fund's Structural Adjustment Facility. As a gesture of solidarity, the major creditor countries should grant separate treatment to the low-income countries, just as China and India had done for Africa. The fate of proposals relating to the debt of those countries would be an acid test of the Conference's concern for the LDCs.

9. Technological and economic changes were creating new forms of interdependence in the world, which explained the increased interest shown in multilateral co-operation. It was important for the Conference to pave the way for a revival of international development co-operation, and UNCTAD must resolutely seek to make progress in such specific areas as aid flows, compensatory financing, the debt, commodity trade and protectionism. It must be borne in mind that the results of the Conference should not be assessed individually, but as a contribution to the negotiations and decisions of other international organizations.

Summary of the statement made at the 206th plenary meeting, 13 July 1987, by Mr. M. MARINOV, Deputy-Secretary of the Council for Mutual Economic Assistance

1. Mr. MARINOV, speaking under rule 80 of the rules of procedure, reviewed the current world economic situation and stressed the need for new political and economic thinking and approaches in the common interests of the world community, irrespective of differences in political and economic systems. He said that the CMEA member countries believed that the acute problems of the developing countries could be solved only by the establishment of a new international economic order ensuring the economic security of every State within the framework of a comprehensive system of international peace and security which would harmonize the processes of economic interdependence and build a universally acceptable collective basis for the implementation of multilateral measures. The problem of external indebtedness, which was not only economic but also political, could be solved primarily by restructuring international relations within the wider context of disarmament for development. UNCTAD might play an important role in studying such problems and drawing up practical recommendations. The socialist countries attached great importance to the convening of an international conference on the relationship between disarmament and development, for they considered that such a conference might contribute to the cause of disarmament, to the removal of the threat of nuclear war and to the development of all countries. Such an approach was in line with the ideas contained in the Havana Declaration adopted by the Group of 77 in April 1987. The CMEA member countries advocated the implementation of the provisions of the Charter of Economic Rights and Duties of States, the Declaration and the Programme of Action on the Establishment of a New International Economic Order, and the Economic Declaration adopted at the Eighth Conference of Heads of State or Government of Countries at their meeting in Harare.

2. Measures taken in the socialist countries to develop their own economies and make them more efficient through structural changes in keeping with the requirements of scientific and technological progress, the use of economic management methods and greater independence and responsibility of enterprises opened up new opportunities for the CMEA member countries to play a more active role in international economic relations. It was hoped that that approach would meet with understanding in other States and elicit a similar response, leading to an expansion and improvement of mutually beneficial trade. In view of the acceleration of scientific and technological progress, the CMEA member countries had adopted a comprehensive programme of scientific and technological progress up to the year 2000.

3. Economic growth rates had been stepped up in the socialist countries and more active social and economic policies were being pursued. In 1986 growth rates in all CMEA member countries had been significantly higher than in 1985, with an increase of 4.2 per cent in national income. Foreign trade turnover with all countries in the world had grown by 2 per cent in absolute terms, despite a 3 per cent decline in value resulting from the fall in prices for their exports on the world market. CMEA member countries were seeking to expand their trade and economic ties with developing and developed capitalist countries. Trade with developing States was being developed mainly through the expansion of the practice of long-term agreements and contracts, with an emphasis on specialization and co-operation in production and in deliveries of various kinds of machinery, joint construction and assembly work, etc. Reiterating their intention and readiness to continue to expand mutually beneficial trade, economic, scientific and technological ties with the developed capitalist countries, which depended also on the willingness of those countries to remove barriers to such expansion, the CMEA member countries advocated more efficient use of potential capacities for the development of business co-operation, including specialization and co-production, the creation of joint enterprises and opportunities to expand trade turnover and an exchange of services, know-how and scientific and technological achievements on the basis of equal rights and mutual benefit, non-interference in internal affairs and respect for international obligations.

4. UNCTAD was to be commended for its contribution to the restructuring of international economic relations and to the expansion of economic co-operation among States. UNCTAD's possibilities, within its terms of reference, should be used to a fuller extent, in order that it might consider the problems of the international monetary system, including the foreign debt of developing countries, and make proposals for the cessation of the use of economic relations as a means of exerting political pressure on individual countries. Activities relating to the preparation of new international commodity agreements and the initiation of international co-operation in the processing, marketing and distribution of primary products should be stepped up. He attached great importance to the discussion within UNCTAD of international trade problems: such problems should be solved on the basis of the sovereign equality of States and non-discrimination. An appropriate place should continue to be given in UNCTAD's activities to the subject of trade relations among countries with different social systems, taking into account the increasing interdependence of all trade flows. CMEA member countries advocated the further development of co-operation with UNCTAD both in traditionally established forms and in the search for new forms of relationship between the two organizations.

Summary of the statement made at the 211th plenary meeting, 24 July 1987, by Mr. Behçet TÜREMEN, Secretary-General of the Economic Co-operation Organization

1. Mr. TÜREMEN said that the Economic Co-operation Organization was a regional body composed of Iran, Pakistan and Turkey. It had been established in 1965 and had seen great fluctuations in international economic and political trends.

2. The 1980s had been characterized by economic depression with high rates of unemployment and cuts in social services and productive investment, rising debt-service payments, downward pressure on the export earnings of most developing countries and a general slow-down in international trade. Changes in the world economy had increased the need for greater interdependence among national economies through trade and increased financial integration.

3. His organization considered that regional economic co-operation was an effective instrument of economic policy among like-minded countries in that it facilitated trade, economic growth and development. Such co-operation, which should be viewed in the context of the growth and development potential of the countries concerned, had been strengthened by the need to tackle economic problems. Experience showed that regional groupings were highly beneficial to their member countries.

4. There had none the less been some positive developments in the past few years. For example, inflation had been reduced without any slow-down in the growth of the developed countries and exchange rates had been brought more into line with basic economic factors. However, the correction of the large current-account imbalances of the major countries and the improvement of the economic performance of the developing countries had yet to be achieved.

5. International structural adjustment reforms and increased financial flows to developing countries were essential to the revitalization of development. In the long term, however, it was clear that diversified and increased production and trade had to be the backbone of that process. The developing countries did not have the economic and social capacity to bring about adjustment and diversification alone. The developed countries had to live up to the international community's expectations and assume their responsibilities towards the populations of developing and low-income countries. To do so, they had to step up their adjustment efforts, for distortions and rigidities in certain protected and subsidized areas were compounding macro-economic problems and retarding growth.

6. There was a vital link between a non-protectionist international trade régime and the ability of debtor countries to service their debt while generating sources for their own growth and development. The need to dismantle all protectionist barriers was therefore greater than ever before.

7. His organization considered that UNCTAD had a key role to play in creating a healthy international trading environment and wished to benefit from the activities and expertise it could offer, especially in the areas of economic co-operation among developing countries, commodities, insurance and international trade.

8. The seventh session of the Conference provided an opportunity to discuss with developing countries major problems and general policy issues with a view to promoting common perceptions concerning trade and development, but it was to be hoped that it would also lead to the adoption of action-oriented decisions which would contribute to world-wide economic recovery and help revitalize development, growth and international trade.

Summary of the statement made at the 215th plenary meeting, 28 July 1987, by Mr. Ziga VODUSEK, Executive-Director of the International Center for Public Enterprises in Developing Countries and the International Association of State Trading Organizations of Developing Countries

1. Mr. VODUSEK said that the purpose of the two organizations he represented was to promote economic and technical co-operation in trade and development among developing countries. The Center was an intergovernmental institution open to all developing countries; it engaged in research, training and documentation and provided advisory services. Currently, 37 developing countries were members of the Center and over 50 others took part in its work.

2. The Center's efforts and resources were currently directed to improving the performance of public enterprises in the belief that a vigorous public sector would make a positive contribution to national development in developing countries and to strengthening co-operation among such countries. The Center also endeavoured, in particular in countries with a mixed economy, to investigate possible forms of productive co-operation between the public and private sectors.

3. To give new impetus to public enterprises that were flagging because, for example, of social and economic conditions, many developing countries had embarked on programmes of reform and structural reorganization in the public sector and initiated a reorganization of public enterprises. The Center supported those efforts to the best of its ability without interfering in national decisions.

4. In the interest of improving the viability of public enterprises, the Center had developed an integrated approach to deal with their problems both from a macro-economic standpoint and in terms of individual enter-

prises. The purpose of the studies undertaken was to increase the efficiency, cost effectiveness and productivity of public enterprises and, thereby, to develop their financial independence and sense of social responsibility. Macro-economic analysis revealed the relationship between the performance of public enterprises and variables such as economic growth, employment, income distribution, external debt, balance of payments, efficiency of investment, pricing policies, etc. Conversely, it enabled the effect of public policies on the performance of public enterprises to be determined. The findings of such specialized studies could then be used in drawing up government policy on public enterprises. In addition, the results of looking into the efficiency of various public enterprises had an impact on their performance and could be useful in establishing wage scales and incentives schemes.

5.   The efficiency of public enterprises depended to a considerable degree on the competence of their staff, and especially their senior staff, who were primarily responsible for the organization's performance and determined its adaptability. Technological developments had reduced the competitive strength of low-cost goods produced by cheap labour. In addition, far-reaching changes in national and international economies were posing new problems. It was therefore essential that public enterprises should be able to call on new knowledge and skills at both technical and management levels. For those reasons, the Center invited developing countries and interested organizations to make use of its institutional skills and capabilities in the design of programmes in which public enterprises were to play a leading role.

6.   It was the State trading organizations themselves that had established the International Association of State Trading Organizations (ASTRO), a non-governmental organization with a current membership

of 39 State trading organizations based in 28 developing countries and presenting a total annual turnover of $50,000 million to $60,000 million. The principal purpose of ASTRO was to encourage trade among State trading organizations and to promote trade in general. To that end it had embarked on an extensive programme of work to help member organizations improve the occupational skills of their staff, to facilitate their access to markets, disseminate information on markets and on a number of trading practices such as counter-trading and hold meetings among State training organizations.

7.   ASTRO would in future continue to study the complementarity of trade among developing countries in order to help them strengthen such complementarity and hence to develop communication and co-operation on trade matters among State trading organizations, which had the task of finding other trade outlets than the traditional ones between developing and developed countries and thus contributing to the expansion of world trade.

8.   The UNCTAD secretariat, as well as other agencies such as the International Trade Centre UNCTAD/GATT, the International Center for Public Enterprises in Developing Countries, and UNDP had encouraged the establishment of ASTRO from the outset and helped it to carry out its programme of work in the areas of counter-trade, training, and the convening of meetings and conferences. In order to continue its development, ASTRO needed to increase its membership. He therefore took the liberty of appealing to all developing countries present to encourage their State trading organizations to join the Association. He also urged the international agencies that had sponsored the establishment of ASTRO to continue their support so as to enable the Association to play an increasingly influential role in international trade.

Summary of the statement made at the 210th plenary meeting, 24 July 1987, by Mr. Kobena G. ERBYNN, Executive-Director of the International Cocoa Organization

1.   Mr. ERBYNN said that, despite the mutual interest of cocoa producers and users to ensure some price stability, it had taken over 17 years of arduous negotiation before the first International Cocoa Agreement had been concluded in 1972. That Agreement and the three subsequent Cocoa Agreements had been negotiated and concluded under UNCTAD's auspices.

2.   The characteristics of cocoa as an internationally traded commodity had remained basically unchanged since the conclusion of the first Agreement. It was still produced exclusively in developing countries of the tropical South and consumed mainly in the industrialized countries of the developed North. Many producing countries still relied heavily on earnings from cocoa to finance their economic development. In 1984-1985, the share accounted for by cocoa exports in the total foreign exchange earnings of Ghana had been 68 per cent, Côte d'Ivoire, 40 per cent, Cameroon, 21 per cent, the Dominican Republic, 9 per cent, Papua New Guinea, 8

per cent and Ecuador, 6 per cent. World cocoa bean production had risen from an average of about 1.5 million tonnes in the early 1970s to about 1.96 million tonnes in each of the preceding three years. Global consumption had also increased since the entry into force of the first Cocoa Agreement but demand over the preceding three years had failed to keep pace with expanded production.

3.   Despite its underlying upward trend, world production of cocoa had varied significantly from year to year, having ranged from 1.35 million tonnes in 1976-1977 to an estimated 1.97 million tonnes in 1986-1987. The daily price monitored by the International Cocoa Organization (ICCO) had fluctuated widely, ranging from a monthly average of 44.9 United States cents per pound in June 1975 to 197.8 United States cents in July 1977. Since 1985, nominal cocoa prices had moved in an apparently narrow range between 86 and 108 United States cents per pound, but

real prices had been considerably distorted by the fluctuations in the value of the United States dollar. Since the entry into force of the 1986 Agreement in January 1987, the average ICCO daily price, expressed in constant 1985-1986 special drawing rights and corrected for inflationary and currency distortions, had been lower than that for any year since the inception of the first International Cocoa Agreement in 1973. Short-term and medium-term prices were unlikely to be favourable for producers, and the prospects for countries heavily dependent on cocoa for their foreign exchange earnings, many of which were already burdened with large external debts, were bleak. In such circumstances, the effectiveness of all cocoa Agreements might well be questioned.

4. Throughout the period covered by the 1972 and 1975 Agreements, market prices had remained well above the stipulated maximum. For that reason the export quota provisions had not been activated, and there being no cocoa in the buffer stock, no selling operations in defence of the upper part of the price range had taken place. However, by providing a kind of insurance cover against unacceptably low prices, the Agreements, together with the high price levels of the mid-1970s, had helped to create a more favourable climate for increased investment in producing countries. Because of the ensuing abundant supply, the high cocoa prices reached in the second half of the 1970s had been followed by substantial falls in the 1980s. The considerable excess of production over consumption had arisen partly because most cocoa production policy-makers had underestimated the productivity of the new early-bearing and high-yielding hybrid cocoa varieties and partly because of failure to realize that per capita consumption in traditional markets might be approaching saturation point.

5. The International Cocoa Agreement of 1980 had been the first to bring the price stabilization mechanism into operation. During its 62-month life, the monthly average of the ICCO daily price had been above the minimum for only 32 months and above the lower intervention price for only 10 months. The established price levels in all cases had tended to reflect the relative negotiating strength of the parties concerned, conditioned by market prices observed in the immediate past.

6. In addition to suffering from defective operating rules and from the absence of an effective supplementary mechanism to reinforce the buffer stock, the operation of the 1980 Agreement had been severely impaired by inadequate financing and the gross distortion caused by the fluctuations of the United States dollar. The withdrawal of 100,000 tonnes of cocoa by the ICCO buffer stock had unquestionably supported market prices. It was estimated that between 1981-1982 and 1983-1984, cocoa producing countries had benefited to the tune of between $1,000 million and $1,200 million through increased earnings from the higher market prices resulting from buffer stock intervention; by comparison, the buffer stock's operating costs had amounted to only about $170 million during the same period.

7. The recent conclusion of the International Cocoa Agreement of 1986 was an important milestone in the history of commodity agreements and in international co-operation between cocoa producers and cocoa consumers. It took account of most of the difficulties encountered in previous agreements and showed a marked improvement over them. It was strongly market-oriented and contained a number of pragmatic provisions to help in breaking deadlocks and speeding up decision-taking in the Council. Unlike the 1980 Agreement, it was financially self-sufficient for the purpose of acquiring the maximum buffer stock capacity of 250,000 tonnes. The denomination of the price range in special drawing rights was a radical but necessary step in the right direction, which should minimize distortions in price objectives. It had been shown that the buffer stock mechanism of the new Agreement was capable of operating effectively. In May and June 1987, about 75,000 tonnes of cocoa had been purchased for the ICCO buffer stock when cocoa prices, currently well in the free range, had been well below the intervention price. The second level price mechanism should help to strengthen the buffer stock by keeping surpluses off the market, but only in the short term and medium term. Over the longer term, members of the Agreement would need to seek other methods of ensuring a balanced development of the world cocoa economy. There was a vast potential for strengthening the Agreement's cocoa promotion provisions, particularly in the light of renewed optimism concerning the Common Fund and the possibility of financing such promotion activities through the Fund's Second Account.

8. The success of a commodity agreement depended largely on credibility. The level of participation in the new Agreement, which covered over 90 per cent of world exports and over 60 per cent of imports was encouraging, but he appealed to the United States of America, the world's largest cocoa consumer, and Malaysia, the most rapidly expanding producer, to join ICCO, thereby immeasurably enhancing the Agreement.

9. The International Trade Centre UNCTAD/GATT, which was making an invaluable contribution to cocoa export marketing, had, in consultation with ICCO, recently published a handbook entitled "Cocoa, a trader's guide", which was important not only for the smaller and newer cocoa exporting countries but also for use in training in well-established producing countries. The handbook would be presented to participants in the International Cocoa Council at its meeting in September 1987. He hoped that co-operation between the Trade Centre and ICCO, particularly in the selection by the Trade Centre of new projects in the cocoa commodity field, would be strengthened.

Summary of the statement made at the 210th plenary meeting, 24 July 1987, by Mr. Harbans SINGH, Executive-Director of the International Jute Organization

1. Mr. SINGH said that his organization, which had been established in January 1984 under the International Agreement on Jute and Jute Products of 1982, currently comprised 5 exporting and 26 importing members, accounting for about 98 per cent of world exports and over 65 per cent of world imports. He appealed to all jute importing and exporting countries that had not yet done so to join the organization.

2. The objectives of IJO did not include buffer stocking or price or supply stabilization. Its primary objectives were to improve structural conditions in the jute market, to enhance the competitiveness of jute and jute products, to maintain and expand the existing market and develop new markets, to develop the production, export and import of jute and jute products and to bring about improvements in quality. Those objectives had to be achieved through research and development projects in jute agriculture, industry and market promotion, and IJO was thus primarily a research and development organization.

3. The importance of price and supply stabilization had nevertheless been recognized, and it had been agreed that questions relating thereto should be considered along with other important issues such as competition with synthetics and substitutes; any action in that respect, however, would necessitate an amendment of the Agreement by special vote.

4. At its half-yearly meetings, the International Jute Council reviewed the situation with respect to jute and competition with synthetics on the basis of information provided by the IJO secretariat and FAO. The issue of buffer stocking with a view to stabilizing prices and supplies had been discussed at a special session of the Council and later by an informal working party, but no agreed decision had been reached. There had been an understandable expectation among the various parties concerned that, as a specialized commodity organization, IJO would indeed be involved in price and supply stabilization matters. Exporters and importers alike were agreed that instability of supplies and prices posed the greatest threat to the jute economy, and government representatives had sometimes raised the question, particularly in relation to the over-supply of jute over the preceding two years. Exporters and importers should tackle the problem and seek practical ways of mitigating the harmful effects of frequent and violent fluctuations in prices and supplies.

5. Jute continued to share the problems faced by several other commodities, as had been recognized in the Dhaka Declaration of the Ministerial Meeting of the Asian members of the Group of 77 in March 1987. Competition from synthetics was a serious threat even within jute producing countries, and demand from developed countries continued to decline. Despite production curtailment and price support measures by the major producing countries, prices in 1986-1987 had fallen alarmingly and huge stocks had accumulated. There was thus an obvious need for price and supply stabilization measures.

6. The IJO Council had approved a number of projects in jute agriculture, industry and market promotion. The agricultural projects were designed to develop new and higher-yielding varieties of jute and to improve the quality of the product. The industrial project was aimed at increasing the demand for jute through the blending of jute with other fibres and other processing improvements, while the market promotion projects were aimed at protecting and expanding the market. It was thus hoped to improve the competitiveness of jute and increase demand for the commodity.

7. Three possible sources of financing had been indicated in the International Agreement on Jute and Jute Products of 1982: the Second Account of the Common Fund for Commodities, the regional and international financial institutions such as UNDP, the World Bank and the Asian Development Bank, and voluntary contributions. He welcomed the improved prospects for the future of the Common Fund and hoped other Governments would emulate the decision of the USSR Government so that the Fund could become operational. The necessary arrangements would nevertheless take time and IJO would have to depend meanwhile on the other two sources of finance. There had been an extremely limited response from regional and international institutions in the past, and it had been necessary to depend mainly on contributions from members.

8. A major portion of the cost of agricultural projects, which absorbed the bulk of the funds, was to be met by participating countries themselves in the form of the services of their research personnel and institutional facilities, though some relatively modest costs had to be met through international funding. The total annual amount required from outside funds for the forthcoming five years had been estimated at $2 million, which was not excessive for a commodity with an annual world trade valued at nearly $1 billion. Yet it had not been possible to raise adequate and timely funds for the approved projects. There had been long gaps between project approval and execution, and by the time funds had become available for some of the projects, the estimates had had to be revised to allow for inflation, currency fluctuations and other factors. For about three years to the beginning of 1987, it had not been possible, owing to lack of funding, to execute any agricultural or industrial projects. Some of the market promotion projects had been executed with funds secured by the International Trade Centre UNCTAD/GATT from donors to its Trust Fund and other agencies. That body had been executing market promotion projects for jute and jute products prior to IJO's establishment. Hopes of enhanced market promotion efforts had failed to materialize, total expenditure had declined and programmes had suffered frequent interruptions. The market promotion project in the United States, approved in 1985, had yet to be fully funded and there was no such activity at all in the vitally important markets of Western Europe.

9. If IJO was to fulfil its objectives and justify its considerable administrative expenditure, half of which was being contributed by poor developing countries, there would have to be some rethinking about funding, for which firm arrangements were essential. The Conference should stress that point to interested parties. IJO welcomed the valuable assistance it had received from, among others, FAO, the International Trade Centre, UNIDO and ESCAP.

10. The IJO had been considering the possible renegotiation of the International Agreement on Jute and Jute Products, which would expire on 9 January 1989, and had requested that an evaluation of IJO's performance should be carried out. Any such evaluation should take account of the structural and other prob-

lems that had impeded the achievement of the objectives. The organization had been prevented by lack of funds from making any real headway and it had had to struggle for three years to launch its first project. Its objectives were largely of a long-term nature and no rapid or immediate results could be expected. Its members would no doubt take account of all those factors in their discussions on the renegotiation of the Agreement.

11. The funding arrangements were the crux of the problem. Valuable assistance had been given by some donor countries and by UNCTAD, which had helped to arrange an informal meeting of donors, and he hoped that the countries concerned would expand their support.

Summary of the statement made at the 210th plenary meeting, 24 July 1987, by Mr. P. SOEPARTO, Executive-Director of the International Natural Rubber Organization

1. Mr. SOEPARTO said that a combination of factors, rooted in the structure of the natural rubber industry and in the international economic and political climate of the mid-1970s, had prompted natural rubber producing and consuming countries to come to an agreement for stabilizing the international market price of the commodity. The International Natural Rubber Agreement concluded in 1979—the first international commodity agreement to have been set up under the UNCTAD Integrated Programme for Commodities—had completed five years of operation on 23 October 1985 but had been extended for a further two years. Although the Agreement had entered into force provisionally in October 1980, the organization itself had only begun its buffer stocking operations in November 1981. Subsequent activities up to the end of 1986 had related to commodity stabilization and commodity development.

2. A number of broad conclusions could be drawn concerning the effects of operations under the Agreement. First, considerable stability had been achieved in the movements of the price of natural rubber. Secondly, from the start of the organization's operations in November 1981 until 30 June 1987, the daily market indicative price had been kept in the neutral and ideal range, in which the buffer stock neither bought nor sold rubber, for 58 per cent of the marketing period. Thirdly, when buffer stock operations had been necessary, price stabilization had largely been attained at the higher end of the buying range, at or near the lower intervention price. Only for short periods had the daily market indicative price approached the price level at which the buffer stock had to buy rubber, and the lower trigger price at which action became mandatory had been breached only on three market days immediately before its revision in mid-August 1985. The daily market indicative price had then remained near that price level for only about three months. Prices had thus largely been stabilized well above the lower indicative price provided for in the Agreement.

3. Fourthly, price stabilization for the entire period had been achieved with buffer stock purchases of approximately 378,000 tonnes (within 95 per cent of the normal buffer stock of 400,000 tonnes), and hence without recourse to the contingency buffer stock of 150,000 tonnes.

4. Fifthly, the entire stabilization exercise had related to buying operations only, no rubber being sold out of the buffer stock for stabilization purposes. Judgement on the success of the organization's operations must thus be tempered by the fact they had been limited to one side of market intervention. Although it was possible that the mere existence of the buffer stock had had some influence in preventing prices from breaching the upper intervention price more markedly, the general effects of the organization selling operations on price stabilization were yet to be seen.

5. Sixthly, one of the aims of the Rubber Agreement was to stabilize earnings from exports of natural rubber while also aiming at increasing such earnings through an expansion of export volumes at fair and remunerative prices. In the period 1981-1986, the combined total United States dollar earnings of Malaysia, Indonesia, Thailand and Sri Lanka from exports of rubber had declined by about 6 per cent in current prices and by 13 per cent in constant prices. That decline had been caused mainly by a fall in unit prices of 8 per cent in current terms and 16 per cent in constant terms, but export volume had increased by some 2 per cent. Hence, despite some rise in export volume, the lower unit prices had prevented the Rubber Agreement objective of stabilizing and increasing export earnings, measured in a hard international currency such as the United States dollar, from being achieved for the four countries concerned, though it should be noted that export prices and the value of export earnings would have fallen even more severely without the buffer stock intervention.

6. Seventhly, average annual natural rubber production had risen by over 400,000 tonnes, or 11 per cent, during the six years of the Rubber Agreement's

operations as compared with production during the six preceding years. The long-term upward trend had thus been sustained and it could be inferred that the planting programme undertaken in the 1970s had benefited from the price stabilization achieved by the Agreement in the first half of the 1980s. Such stabilization had also helped to raise world natural rubber output to unprecedented levels, with a reasonable balance between supply and demand along with a maintenance of price incentives.

7. Lastly, little headway had been made with respect to the other measures for attaining the development objectives referred to in article 44 of the Agreement. The Common Fund for Commodities had not yet become operational and the Natural Rubber Council had not succeeded in obtaining financial assistance from other sources for project proposals submitted in the field of rubber research and development and expanded and improved production.

8. A new Agreement had been concluded in March 1987 by the United Nations Conference on Natural Rubber after four negotiating sessions spread over nearly two years. Some 40 countries, accounting for some 90 per cent of world trade in natural rubber, had taken part in the negotiations for reviewing and improving the International Natural Rubber Agreement as an instrument of co-operation between exporting developing countries and importing developed countries.

9. The new Agreement incorporated several new provisions but retained the main objectives of the predecessor Agreement, the most important of which concerned price stabilization and achievement of a balanced growth between supply and demand. A significant difference was the elimination of the provision for borrowing. The buffer stock would remain the sole instrument of market intervention to stabilize prices. Its maximum capacity was unchanged at 550,000 tonnes: a normal buffer stock of 400,000 tonnes and a contingency stock of 150,000 tonnes.

10. The new Agreement would come into force provisionally when it had been ratified by exporting and importing countries accounting for 75 per cent of net exports and imports, and finally when ratified by 80 per cent of both parties. At the United Nations Conference on Natural Rubber in 1985, a resolution had been adopted inviting Governments to deposit instruments of ratification, acceptance or approval before 23 October 1987 or, if unable to complete their constitutional procedures in time, to undertake to apply the Agreement provisionally. He appealed to all Governments concerned to give the resolution serious consideration. As a major producer of natural rubber, Malaysia had delivered its instrument of ratification on 26 June 1987. He hoped participants in the Conference would do everything possible to ensure that the new Agreement entered into force as early as possible.

Summary of the statement made at the 210th plenary meeting, 24 July 1987, by Mr. Alfredo A. RICART, Executive-Director of the International Sugar Organization

1. Mr. RICART said that sugar, particularly as a source of export earnings for developing countries, was facing a serious crisis, world market prices having been well below the accepted production cost for the preceding five years. The structural changes that had occurred both in supply and demand had reduced the likelihood of the substantial rise in prices that might normally be expected once excess stocks had been depleted.

2. Because of the fall in prices and also because of the shrinkage of the market for sugar, the value of total world exports of sugar, which in 1981 had stood at $15 billion, had by 1985 fallen by 40 per cent to $9 billion. The total volume of exports during that period had fallen from 29 million tonnes to 27.5 million tonnes, while the volume in the free market had fallen from nearly 20 million tonnes to 18 million tonnes.

3. Despite those changes, sugar remained second only to coffee, among food products, as a source of export earnings for developing countries and one of the top three among the products mentioned in the Integrated Programme for Commodities as of major export interest to those countries. It was even more important for the many developing countries in which sugar exports were the principal, and in some cases the only, source of foreign exchange.

4. The sugar market was the only one among the commodity markets covered by the Integrated Pro-

gramme to have undergone a profound structural change during the preceding decade—a change triggered by the high prices of 1974-1975 which had encouraged the development of a sugar substitute in the United States of America and Japan. By 1985, the growth of that industry, boosted by a further short period of high prices in 1980-1981, had reduced United States and Japanese imports by two thirds and one third, respectively. The market for sugar had become more sensitive to high prices because, there being fewer high-income buyers and more lower-income buyers, it was less likely that prices would be bid up to the high levels of 1974-1975 and 1980-1981. In addition, developing countries in general had faced severe economic problems in the 1980s, further limiting their ability to bid up sugar prices. The extent of structural change in demand could be seen in the fact that the share of developed countries in free market sugar imports had fallen from nearly 67 per cent in 1975 to 40 per cent in 1985, while that of developing countries had risen from 35 per cent to 60 per cent during the same period.

5. The structural changes had not been confined to the demand side, however. The share of developing countries in free market exports had fallen from 70 per cent in 1974 to 52 per cent in 1985 as a result of rapidly increased production and exports of sugar by the EEC, which currently accounted for over 20 per cent of free market exports. The increased share of sugar produced from an annual crop for export by the EEC had reduced

the time needed to respond to rising prices, while unfortunately making it no easier to cut production if prices fell. The sharply increased output of the EEC was attributable partly to higher yields achieved through technological and agronomic advances in beet culture.

6. Even the most efficient sugar producers could not make a profit at current price levels. However, the most striking evidence of the structural change that had occurred was that if prices began to rise they were damped down either by the inability of developing importers to stay in the market or by an unco-ordinated production response by individual producers who hoped to benefit from higher prices—or by both factors combined. Current world prices were remarkably stable at between 6 and 8.5 cents per pound. Sugar exporters should consider whether they could not improve the average, without greatly reducing demand, by co-ordinating their efforts and managing supplies coming onto the market. Although the new market structure was such that there was little probability of a major price rise, it was conceivable that a crop failure in a major producing country, combined with dwindling stocks, might produce a boom if no co-ordinated effort was made to prevent it by holding sufficient stocks, and such a boom might unleash a further round of structural change.

7. There were, of course, political and practical reasons why sugar exporters had not worked out a co-operative strategy. The economic risks could, however, be reduced and returns increased by co-ordinated action. After the failure in 1983 and 1984 of efforts to negotiate an agreement with economic clauses, informal talks had taken place among the principal sugar exporters in 1985 and 1986, but they had lost momentum, and the International Sugar Organization was currently engaged in negotiations with a view to revising and updating the existing Administrative Agreement and settling the issue of contributions of members to the organization's budget. Once that had been done, it was essential to regain the momentum for negotiating an economic agreement.

8. The International Sugar Organization had consistently maintained a close and fruitful association with UNCTAD. The 1977 Sugar Agreement had been among the first commodity agreements with economic clauses to be negotiated after the launching of the Integrated Programme for Commodities. All the Sugar Agreements had embodied the ideals of fair, remunerative and stable commodity prices advocated by

UNCTAD. He urged participants in the Conference to support the effort to apply those principles to sugar once again within a new International Sugar Agreement.

9. He particularly appealed to representatives of sugar exporting countries for their support. It had been possible in the past to endure low-price periods in the expectation that high-price periods would follow, but owing to the structural changes to which he had referred, any such expectation was unlikely to be fulfilled. Exporters had to seek other ways of stabilizing prices than merely awaiting the next boom. The object of any new International Sugar Agreement should be to increase revenue during low-price periods and yet to prevent the price from reaching a level that would encourage recourse to alternatives. Such an agreement was perfectly realizable provided that all exporters believed in the need for it and worked constructively for its success. He appealed to delegations to help to unify and co-ordinate the efforts of all exporters and all importers to secure fair and stable sugar prices. The Soviet Union's announcement of its intention to accede to the Agreement Establishing the Common Fund for Commodities was a most encouraging and significant development which had come at a particularly appropriate time for all commodities.

10. Price stabilization was an important means of preventing high sugar prices from triggering a further round of damaging structural change, and at the same time it would bring the maximum return to producers. However, it was because of the tight constraints affecting the sugar economy that it was necessary to develop and improve the entire sugar producing process, and in particular to make full use of every by-product, thus reducing the industry's vulnerability to the sugar price and improving overall returns. The International Sugar Organization could co-ordinate and initiate those essential developments. The new technology that had been responsible for the entry of competitors into the market should henceforth be applied for the benefit of sugar. His organization welcomed the prospect of early implementation of the Common Fund. Vertical diversification with the aid of the Second Account provided for in article 18 of the Agreement on the Fund was precisely what was required to ensure the health of the sugar economy within the constraints imposed by structural changes.

Summary of the statement made at the 210th plenary meeting, 24 July 1987, by Mr. B. C. Y. FREEZAILAH, Executive-Director of the International Tropical Timber Organization

1. Mr. FREEZAILAH said that his organization had only 41 members, of which only 18 were producer developing countries. It was nevertheless a very special organization, dedicated to multilateral co-operation as the only way of achieving effective and lasting development in the tropical timber sector by bringing producer and consumer countries together to focus constructively on problems and the steps needed to solve them. Such co-operation in ITTO was unique because of the

organization's small size, its difficult and pressing problems and the common will of its members to succeed. That had enabled it to overcome almost insurmountable obstacles during the negotiations to establish the Tropical Timber Agreement under UNCTAD's auspices. Despite the fact that tropical timber was one of the most diverse, diffuse and heterogeneous commodities in the world, a spirit of good will and co-operation between producer and consumer countries, which had made the Agreement possible, continued to pervade ITTO and to extend to the environmental sector. A recently published history of UNCTAD* had singled out the International Tropical Timber Agreement as one of the most important and innovative features of UNCTAD's efforts to establish commodity agreements that took account of the ecology. It did so by provisions that encouraged reforestation and forest management activities and the development of national policies for the sustained use and conservation of tropical forests and their genetic resources, and the maintenance of the ecological balance in the regions concerned.

2. If ITTO succeeded in contributing to the achievement of a pragmatic balance between the use of tropical forests and their conservation for the welfare of existing and future generations, it would have served the cause of tropical timber and helped to foster what the Prime Minister of Norway and Chairman of the World Commission on Environment and Development had described as the common green conscience.

3. The way ahead was arduous and difficult, however, ITTO needed the financial and technical co-operation of the organizations concerned within and outside the United Nations system. Several United Nations bodies with complementary activities were indeed already co-operating with it. He had stressed at the second session of the Council, that its work philosophy should be to complement rather than compete, to act as a catalyst where work remained to be done rather than

---

* *The History of UNCTAD, 1964-1984* (United Nations publication, Sales No. E.85.II.D.6).

to duplicate, and to play a harmonizing and co-ordinating role in activities relating to tropical timber both as a resource and as a commodity. The work of ITTO had begun only in February 1987, it was far from fully staffed, and the Headquarters Agreement had still to be finalized. Pre-project activities had nevertheless been launched so that the Council could consider full project proposals at its session in November 1987. Several projects would, if approved, be under way as from the beginning of 1988 within the limits of the modest projects budget.

4. The generous voluntary contributions to the Special Account by the Governments of Japan, Switzerland and the Netherlands had provided the necessary boost, but if the organization's objectives were to be achieved, much more would be required not only in funding but in kind, for example by the secondment of technical staff, paid for by donor countries, to augment the small regular staff.

5. He welcomed the Soviet Union's decision to sign the Agreement Establishing the Common Fund for Commodities, since that improved the prospects for the early entry into operation of the Common Fund. His organization looked forward to taking full advantage of the Fund's Second Account facilities for some of its projects.

6. He acknowledged the generous support given by the Japanese Government and the City of Yokohama in providing all the facilities for ITTO's headquarters and funding the costs of all the sessions of the Council and permanent committees, including those convened outside Japan.

Summary of the statement made at the 210th plenary meeting, 24 July 1987, by Mr. Jean PAROTTE, Executive Director of the International Wheat Council

1. Mr. PAROTTE said that the International Wheat Agreement consisted of two Conventions: the Wheat Trade Convention, administered by the International Wheat Council, and the Food Aid Convention, administered by the Food Aid Committee.

2. The objective of the Food Aid Convention was to achieve, through a joint effort by the international community, the World Food Conference target of at least 10 million tons of grain annually for shipment as food aid to developing countries. The first Food Aid Convention had come into effect in 1968, when the minimum annual commitments of donors had amounted to no more than 4 million tons. The Convention had been renegotiated in 1980 and commitments had been raised to 7.5 million tons—a level that remained practically unchanged in the 1986 Convention.

3. In 1986-1987, the 23 members of the Convention had exceeded the target of 10 million tons for the fourth year in succession. Shipments in 1984-1985 had reached almost 12 million tons, partly in response to the food emergency in Africa. Since 1980, donors had shipped about 70 million tons of grain and grain products to about 100 developing countries, mainly as outright donations.

4. Members of the Convention were encouraged to engage in triangular transactions in which a donor purchased grain in one developing country for shipment to another, preferably in the same region. The exporting country thus earned badly needed foreign exchange and the recipient country obtained its staple food without undue delay.

5. The history of international co-operation in grain matters went back at least to the 1920s, when low prices had caused distress among wheat producers in many countries. Governments had decided that concerted international action was required to deal with the global problem of over-supply on world grain markets. Subsequent scarcities and high prices had encouraged Governments of importing nations to join in efforts to improve world food security and grain market stability, but the cycle of surpluses to shortages had continued.

6. During the past 50 years, the International Wheat Council had devoted much of its efforts to seeking mechanisms, involving specific commitments on the part of exporting and importing countries, that could offer protection from the vagaries of the markets.

7. The 1986 Wheat Trade Convention contained none of the traditional substantive economic provisions,

but that did not mean that the Convention or the International Wheat Agreement had been a failure. Although it had been neither politically desirable nor possible to negotiate an agreement with such provisions, the Council had shown remarkable resilience and surmounted all the obstacles to assume a unique place in the world grain economy by moving with the times and adapting to changing circumstances.

8. The 1986 Convention was designed to strengthen international co-operation between grain exporting and importing members and to assist developing members in particular. The fact that its successful negotiation had taken less than one year, at a time when the global environment for the conclusion of commodity agreements had been distinctly unfavourable, was impressive evidence of the value attached by member Governments to the Council as a source of information and a forum for discussion and possibly for even more active co-operation.

9. The provisions of earlier International Wheat Agreements had been limited to wheat and wheat flour, but the Council had found it necessary to take account also of developments concerning other grains, such as maize, barley, oats and sorghum, which affected the world wheat situation.

10. The new Wheat Trade Convention, of 1986, further enhanced the Council's importance as a forum for international co-operation in the grain sector. First, there were the twice-yearly discussions at Council sessions, when standing agenda items provided for a review of the current world grain situation and short-term outlook and for an examination of recent policy measures affecting grain. Participants were able to express their views concerning the impact of measures taken by others on their own agricultural and economic prospects.

11. Members had repeatedly expressed their satisfaction at the benefits they gained from their membership, which had been particularly valuable for developing importing countries. It was generally recognized that, in order that the grain market should function efficiently, buyers and sellers alike should be fully informed of current and prospective developments. Accurate and comprehensive data on the world grain situation could enhance market transparency, while the lack of such data might promote uncertainty and lead to erroneous decisions.

12. The Convention had come into effect on 1 July 1986 for a term of five years, but it could be terminated before its expiry date, and that would be most likely to happen if the Council decided to replace it with a new instrument with economic provisions. The Convention provided that the Council could convene a negotiating conference when it judged that such an instrument could be successfully negotiated. During recent discussions, several Council members had stressed the importance they placed on the convening of such a Conference, which would be held under UNCTAD auspices.

13. Grain production had its ups and downs depending on the weather and domestic policies. Commodity agreements, including wheat agreements, followed the same pattern. Some countries had consistently favoured an agreement with economic provisions while others had been lukewarm and yet others strongly opposed but there were signs of a change of heart among some of the latter, though it remained to be seen whether they were not hopelessly outnumbered.

14. A remarkable degree of agreement existed on the fundamental causes of and solutions to the current agricultural crisis but, despite considerable efforts, there had been no agreement to implement the solutions.

15. It had been suggested at the session of the Council in December 1986 that, as the most important body considering grain issues, the Council should be involved in international policy questions. Its members believed that it could make a valuable contribution without supplanting GATT's decision-making functions. That would not be the first contribution of its kind. The GATT Kennedy Round of negotiations in 1967, to which the Council had made a technical contribution, had led to a memorandum of agreement on the basic elements for a new International Grains Arrangement administered by the Council and including the first Food Aid Convention.

16. The International Wheat Agreement was healthy and could look forward to a bright future as an unrivalled instrument of international co-operation between grain importing and exporting countries, between producers and consumers.

Summary of the statement made at the 214th plenary meeting, 28 July 1987, by Mr. Jean-Claude PAYE, Secretary-General of the Organisation for Economic Co-operation and Development

1. Mr. PAYE said that the most striking feature of the post-war economic environment was the extraordinary development, ease and speed of international exchanges of goods, services and capital. The best example was the capital market, which had been integrated throughout the world and functioned without a break, making it possible to mobilize huge sums almost immediately. The consequence of that spectactular expansion of international trade was the greater interdependence of all countries of the world, which was reflected in the reciprocal influence that national economies exerted on one another, in proportion to their individual weight in the world economy. It was also reflected in the speed at which economic impulses, and disequilibria in particular, were transmitted and amplified, in the pooling of benefits and risks—namely, chances of prosperity and threats of recession at the international level and in the very potent interaction between international competition and technical progress.

2. The positive effect of interdependence among countries was that it gave full rein to comparative ad-

vantage. The world's resources were therefore better employed to stimulate economic growth, and production was being developed where it was most efficient. However, interdependence also had a disturbing effect. Growing fluidity of the world economy was forcing everyone to adjust at an increasingly rapid pace. To stand up to international competition, and use it to advantage, demanded constantly improved performance. Such continuing pressure was possibly the underlying cause of the upsurge in protectionist temptations throughout the world. In that respect, it should be noted that in post-war years countries had succeeded, through a steady collective effort, especially in the framework of GATT, gradually to lower customs barriers and quantitative restrictions on trade in goods. In recent years, however, there had been a resurgence of restrictions, such as grey-area measures and the replacement of multilateralism by bilateralism or even unilateralism, contrary to the trend that all countries purportedly wished to foster.

3.   Several lessons could be drawn from the profound changes that had taken place in the world economy. First, economic policy must be concerned not only with the right macro-economic balance, but also with continuous structural improvements; not only on the management of demand, but also on the quality and vigour of supply. Secondly, control of inflation was the prerequisite for genuine and lasting growth. Thirdly, in spite of its imperfections and long-term unpredictability, the market remained the least harmful guide to economic decision-making since it rewarded the right decisions, punished errors and taught responsibility. That explained the critical reappraisal to which the role of government was being subjected more or less throughout the world. Fourthly, because the ultimate

and true wealth of nations was their human potential, it was crucial to reduce the unacceptable waste inherent in unemployment, to prepare women and men effectively for the tasks ahead, and to create conditions which sustained and rewarded the efforts and ability of each and every one.

4.   The question was whether domestic economic policies took those lessons into account. The economic situation clearly did not lend itself to easy optimism, fraught as it was with slow growth, rising current-account imbalances, widely fluctuating major currency exchange rates, intolerable developing country indebtedness and steadily declining commodity prices. However, over and above differences in economic situations, development levels and social and political systems, nearly all countries were endeavouring, with varying degrees of determination and success, to combine macro-economic and structural policy effectively, beat inflation, extend the role of the market and develop their human potential.

5.   There was thus reason to believe that nations would jointly be able to take up the challenge of economic independence. However, that presupposed that everyone should recognize and accept their share of responsibility for the order of the world, contribute to the elaboration and application of fair rules of the game and fulfil their commitments. It was for States participating in the seventh session of the Conference to demonstrate that such conditions could be fulfilled. It was useful to recall that each country's responsibility was proportionate to the relative weight of its economy in the world. Industrialized countries were therefore largely accountable for the good or bad state of the world economy.

Summary of the statement made at the 213th plenary meeting, 27 July 1987, by Mr. Driss ALAOUI MDAGHRI, Director of the Organization of the Islamic Conference

1.   Mr. ALAOUI MDAGHRI noted that short-term interests and national egoism had a tendency to conceal what was really at stake in the crisis and to impede collective solutions. Such blindness sustained anarchy in the monetary sector and protectionist trends in trade. In such a chaotic environment, the crushing debt of the third world was particularly dangerous, because the adjustment policies which it entailed implied heavy economic, social and political burdens. It would be difficult to reconcile the requirements of adjustment with those of development, and the decline in the export earnings of third world countries had certainly not improved the situation. The Integrated Programme for Commodities had failed to yield the desired results and the collapse of raw material prices undermined the ability of developing countries to reimburse their debt and jeopardized their economic and social development efforts. In addition, the protectionist measures adopted by the industrialized countries had a severe impact on the developing countries. International trade was witnessing the internationalization of markets, the emergence of new technologies producing items that replaced certain

raw materials, and the modernization of production processes that led to the marginalization of the human element. The developing countries were excluded from those transformations, which were decisive for the future of mankind.

2.   Each country, whether industrialized or not, must act to put its own affairs in order, but international co-operation was also important, particularly among developing countries, where it was likely to strengthen the complementarity of their economies.

3.   As could be seen from the number of resolutions and recommendations adopted during its summit conferences and ministerial meetings, the Organization of the Islamic Conference attached particular importance to that question. Institutions, and in particular the Islamic Centre for Development of Trade, had been created to give tangible form to co-operation among Islamic countries in all areas of the economy.

4.   Given the interdependence of the modern world, international co-operation and dialogue were more necessary than ever to resolve the difficulties en-

countered by world trade. It was essential for the developing countries to co-operate among themselves in respect of such trade so that they could be a real negotiating force instead of passively acquiescing to events.

5. The Organization of the Islamic Conference was gratified by its co-operation with UNCTAD. It was to be hoped that the seventh session of the Conference would help define issues more clearly and result in more concerted action.

F. NON-GOVERNMENTAL ORGANIZATIONS*

GENERAL CATEGORY

**Summary of the statement made at the 218th plenary meeting, 30 July 1987,
by Mr. Julien RANDRIAMASIVELO, Afro-Asian People's Solidarity Organization**

1. Mr. RANDRIAMASIVELO said that the interdependence of nations, instead of being certain countries' favourite way of shaping economic exchanges and development to suit themselves, should be seen as a process of mutual and harmonious development based on equitable trade exchanges and mutual advantage, respecting the sovereignty of nations and the universally recognized rules and standards which governed such trade. In fact, however, the over-exploitation of developing countries had led to the ominous and paradoxical situation that those countries, which were already suppliers of raw materials, had become net exporters of capital as well.

2. The various practices under which the developing countries laboured—such as indebtedness, excessively strict lending criteria, protectionism, and the manipulation of import and export prices—were major obstacles to genuinely mutual and harmonious international development and just and mutually beneficial co-operation. Those were just some of the challenges faced by UNCTAD and other bodies, but AAPSO was sure that UNCTAD could and should play an important role in the campaign for the reform and improvement of international relations in its areas of competence. AAPSO was also aware of the efforts that would be needed to put an end to the waste of material, financial, scientific and human resources in the arms race and the militarization of economies and thereby to promote disarmament for development, create and guarantee a system of economic security for nations and promote and support the establishment of a new international economic order. It was imperative to convert military expenditure into civilian expenditure.

3. Developing countries must move towards self-sufficiency by carrying out reforms and making internal changes that were at variance with the interests of their exploiters. At the same time, in order to slough off their role as mere raw material exporters, they should give high priority in their investment programmes to the local processing of commodities, which implied speeding up the pace of scientific and technological research, the development of industrial infrastructures and, consequently, diversifying their exports. Bilateral

and multilateral co-operation among developing countries must be expanded and reinforced on the basis of economic compatibility through co-ordinated development plans, joint projects and measures to control the activities of the TNCs. The collective self-sufficiency which would thus be created would strengthen their hand in negotiations with their industrialized capitalist partners and prevent the emergence of new forms of dependence. The problem of peace and security must play a major part in the pursuit of the common objectives agreed upon in UNCTAD. It was a vital issue that affected the state of international relations and determined the effectiveness of a people's contribution to its own development.

4. African and Asian countries, and the developing countries in general, had great hopes of the current session of the Conference, and AAPSO wholeheartedly supported the common effort to overcome the problems of underdevelopment. UNCTAD was fully capable of giving a decisive boost to those efforts, and it had to do so in view of the magnitude of the development task. He particularly wished to emphasize UNCTAD's important decision to contribute to the implementation of the United Nations Programme of Action for African Economic Recovery and Development 1986-1990.

5. The development issue came high on the list of activities of AAPSO, which was to celebrate its thirtieth anniversary in 1987 and was preparing an international conference in Manila on the relationship between development and disarmament. The conference would be followed by an institutional meeting of the Presidium, which would undertake a thorough analysis of social and economic developments in the world and particularly in the African and Asian countries. In 1988, AAPSO was to hold its seventh congress in India, which would give it another opportunity to evaluate the socio-economic and general development situation and to try to contribute to the solution of problems encountered by the developing countries.

6. Development in conditions of peace must be the recurring theme of all activities concerned with international relations and trade, and it was to be hoped that at the current session the Conference would make considerable progress in that direction.

---

* Under rule 81 of the rules of procedure.

Summary of the statement made at the 208th plenary meeting, 14 July 1987, by Ms. Agnes CHEPKWONY, Commission of the Churches on International Affairs of the World Council of Churches

1. Ms. CHEPKWONY speaking under rule 81 of the rules of procedure and at the invitation of the President on behalf of a large number of non-governmental organizations concerned with development issues, said that those organizations were deeply concerned by the unprecedented scale of the crisis which the majority of developing countries were currently experiencing and which hit the poorest sectors of the population hardest. Internal problems and policy shortcomings in the third world were clearly evident. At the same time, however, debt and destabilization of the economic system were also major causes of the crisis. The situation, which represented a fundamental breach of the security of peoples, raised not purely technical or economic problems, but also political and moral issues. For example, hunger and underdevelopment in Africa could not be considered without taking account of the destabilization in southern Africa caused by the Government of South Africa. A commitment to human rights required the achievement of an equitable economic system improving the basic economic rights of the majority of mankind.

2. The organizations on whose behalf she was speaking strongly supported UNCTAD because of its special position in the international community as a forum in which issues of trade and debt could be considered from the point of view of the needs of the poor. The climate in which the Conference was taking place was marked by an absence of political will on the part of most industrialized countries, whose rhetorical recognition of interdependence was contradicted by their national policies. In all their negotiations and policies, Governments should take account of the interrelationship of people, resources, environment and development. She welcomed the recommendations concerning the protection of the environment conveyed to the Conference by the Prime Minister of Norway.* In addition to environmental issues, the non-governmental organizations would raise, during the session, issues such as the role of women in development, the effects of biotechnology, the control of communications technology, and the link between disarmament and development.

3. Without the necessary financial resources the future development prospects of people in the third world were bleak. The crucial issues at the current session were the external debt of the third world and the crisis in the international monetary and financial system. The Conference provided an opportunity for reviewing constructively the proposals recently made by responsible leaders from North and South for an international monetary conference to evaluate the role and function of the Bretton Woods institutions and the reforms in international monetary and financial policies needed to restore stability to the system. The debt burden would not be eased without a recognition of the co-responsibility of both lenders and borrowers, a positive net transfer of resources to the South, the linking of levels of debt-servicing payments to a mutually acceptable percentage of export earnings, the prevention of capital flight from the South, and the attainment of at least the 0.7 per cent ODA target by all donor countries. The non-governmental organizations further urged the United States of America to accept debt relief measures for low-income countries, including longer grace periods, longer repayment periods and concessional rates of interest on existing debts, as agreed by the other major industrial Powers at the Venice Summit. Whatever technical solutions were proposed for dealing with the debt crisis, their object should be the development of peoples and social justice, not solely to ensure the repayment of loans.

4. The prices of key commodities produced by developing countries were at a historically low level. Since two thirds of the export earnings of developing countries still came from trade in commodities, the collapse in commodity prices had aggravated their debt problem and significantly retarded their development. She urged Governments to show the political will to support price stabilization arrangements that would provide a fair income to third world producers, to establish machinery for compensating for shortfalls in the developing countries' export earnings, and to provide funds for promoting structural change. Many of the difficulties facing commodity-exporting countries in processing, marketing and distribution would not be disposed of by the coming into operation of the Common Fund for Commodities. The Conference should, in addition, find ways of bringing into operation measures which dealt adequately with those difficulties, and in particular it should assist commodity-dependent developing countries to secure an alternative basis for their economic development.

5. The existing international trading system brought little or no benefit to the peoples of most developing countries. Everywhere tariff barriers against third world exports were proliferating. The non-governmental organizations welcomed the standstill and roll-back commitments envisaged in the context of the new GATT Round and hoped that they would actually be implemented. Whereas free market and free trade policies were advocated by developed countries for developing countries, the developed countries themselves practised non-market policies. The use of protective measures, including tariff and non-tariff barriers as well as dumping and export subsidies, particularly for agricultural produce, were evidence of that contradiction. Countries in the North should not expect countries in the South to apply measures, adjustments and policies which they were not prepared to adopt themselves. Governments in the South for their part should ensure that the population was not further harmed by the disparities often caused by increased trade and that the benefits derived from a higher level of economic activity flowed to the poor among the population.

---

* See sect. A above.

6. The non-governmental organizations welcomed the dialogue between enterprises and the UNCTAD secretariat, especially the recognition of the diversity of enterprises active in the South. However, such enterprises could not replace either multilateral co-operation or government activity. Transnational corporations largely determined the global distribution of the production, processing and marketing of third world exports, but they were not sufficiently accountable to peoples, Governments or the multilateral system and their operations were carried on for the sole purpose of making a profit. Transnational corporations should follow the guidelines on development policies laid down by OECD and ILO. In addition, the United Nations Code of Conduct for Transnational Corporations should be adopted and become binding in the near future.

7. The organizations on whose behalf she was speaking supported the Substantial New Programme of Action for the 1980s for the Least Developed Countries adopted in 1981. It was regrettable, however, that although the Governments of LDCs had begun to implement policy reforms, with a few exceptions donors had failed to implement their side of the bargain. All donor countries should attain the 0.15 per cent target by 1990 or alternatively double their ODA. The quality of the aid disbursed to LDCs should be improved along the lines of the Programme of Action. Preferential trade policies to benefit the LDCs needed to be improved to cover the financial gap left by existing compensatory finance schemes and by extending the GSP to all exports from those countries. UNCTAD must deal effectively with the external debt of the developing countries by calling for a write-off of official debts and the conversion of private debts into equity or the creation of a special interest rate subsidy facility. The conversion of debt into local currency for investment in domestic development projects and programmes or in support of non-governmental organizations in the LDCs was also desirable.

8. People in the South could not afford the luxury of political manœuvrings by Governments which did not advance the discussions or offer immediate solutions to the problems facing them. Manœuvres by groups and individual countries seeking to frustrate progress at the seventh session or to defer discussion to some other forum would demonstrate that their primary concern was not for the poor and underprivileged in the South. The self-interest of both developed and developing countries would be best served by concentrating on efforts to eradicate poverty in the world.

Summary of the statement made at the 208th plenary meeting, 14 July 1987, by Mr. Hans KOENIG, Secretary-General of the International Chamber of Commerce

1. Mr. KOENIG, speaking under rule 81 of the rules of procedure and at the invitation of the President, said that since ICC's mission was to help to promote an open world economy with maximum freedom for commercial transactions across national frontiers, it followed UNCTAD's activities with close attention. Being an association of businessmen, it was pleased to note that one of the specific "understandings" reached regarding the agenda of the seventh session was that due attention should be paid to the role of the private sector in development. The Enterprise Symposium organized by the UNCTAD secretariat during the opening days of the Conference had been most fruitful.

2. The seventh session of the Conference was taking place at a time when the deterioration of the world economy was arousing considerable anxiety. What was required was enlightened political leadership to restore business confidence, which was the key to investment and economic growth. The Governments of the industrialized countries must implement, without further delay, their internationally agreed commitments at both the macro-economic and structural policy level.

3. As far as the third world's debt was concerned, the Baker plan had undeniably suffered a serious loss of credibility, but the fact remained that it outlined the elements of a sound strategy that was still valid: faster growth in the industrialized world, a more open trade environment to improve access for the developing countries exports, and new net lending to indebted countries that pursued growth-oriented adjustment policies. What had been lacking was sufficient co-operation and determination by all the parties concerned to make the strategy work. ICC had constantly called upon the commercial banks to maintain their lending to countries which had undertaken effective internal reforms and had urged the banks to display flexibility and a spirit of innovation. The development of the "menu" approach, offering a range of financing options, was a welcome step in the right direction in that it gave greater latitude to both lenders and borrowers. The banks, however, had not had much encouragement from Governments in developed countries. Official development assistance was stagnating at only 0.36 per cent of the combined GNPs of the countries members of OECD, and officially guaranteed export credits were no longer a significant net source of development finance.

4. Banks were commercial undertakings whose primary responsibility was the prudent management of their stockholders' and depositors' funds. They were, of course, well aware that it was in their own interest, as well as everyone else's, to contribute towards a smooth defusing of the debt problem. However, that contribution could not be disproportionately large. In ICC's view, the Governments of developed countries were not pulling their weight as far as ODA and resources for official export credit guarantee agencies were concerned.

5. It was no less important to encourage a greater mobilization of domestic savings in developing countries. ICC had long argued the merits of enlarging the flow of foreign direct investment and had definite views on the conditions which were most likely to attract such investment. Nevertheless, those same conditions were

equally likely to raise domestic savings for productive use; they could, for instance, help to reverse capital flight.

6. The sharply declining trend in commodity prices noted at the sixth session of the Conference had continued since 1983. Such a substantial and sustained price collapse lent strong support to the view that major structural changes had been taking place on both the supply and the demand sides. It was hardly surprising, therefore, that international commodity agreements had experienced a checkered history in recent years. ICC had long stressed the weighty technical drawbacks to arrangements which sought to stabilize prices through buffer stocks and controls on production or exports. It had, however, always recognized the interest of both producers and consumers in ensuring that commodity prices were as stable as possible. As a consequence, it had long advocated a case-by-case approach.

7. Whether or not the Common Fund for Commodities ever became operative, ICC believed that it would, at best, be peripheral to the principal problem facing commodity producers in the developing countries—namely, the steep decline in commodity prices during the 1980s and the structural changes accounting for the decline. The essential policy response lay in the realm of longer-term developmental measures to assist third world countries that were heavily dependent on commodity exports in developing and diversifying their economies. That task should become a top international priority. The overriding need of the commodity-oriented economies in the third world was for a broader productive base plus greater market access for their exports.

8. ICC had always been a stout advocate of an open world trading system, for it was essentially through trade that indebted developing countries could hope to alleviate their burden of external obligations. The business community strongly supported the new Uruguay Round of multilateral trade negotiations, which offered a real hope of curbing the creeping protectionism of recent years and provided the industrialized countries in particular with a golden opportunity to restore credibility to the principles and rules of the international trading system. It would be a test of the success of the Uruguay Round whether it would satisfy the aspirations of the developing countries. A firmer adherence to the standstill commitment by the industrialized countries, rapid and substantial progress in the negotiating groups on tropical products and natural resource-based products towards a reduction of tariff and non-tariff barriers to developing countries' exports, including exports in processed and semi-processed forms, would be required. In addition, the developing countries would derive considerable benefits from early progress in the negotiating group on agriculture towards bringing national trade practices under effective

multilateral control. There must also be a genuine effort on all sides to curb measures which impeded trade in manufactured goods of particular interest to developing countries, not least in textiles and clothing.

9. The World Bank had recently called upon the developing countries to play an active part in the Uruguay Round, noting that they had suffered a setback in previous negotiations by not participating actively while the industrialized countries had concentrated on reducing barriers to products of interest primarily to themselves. ICC strongly endorsed the Bank's view. Experience had shown that the so-called special and differential treatment and the GSP had proved to be a bargain of doubtful worth compared with what the developing world would stand to gain from a successful strengthening of rules and disciplines within the multilateral system, to which it should give high priority in the Uruguay Round.

10. More official multilateral and bilateral aid was needed for the LDCs. Although their capacity to attract foreign private investment was for the time being limited, that did not mean that the private sector's role in those countries was insignificant. They had an abundance of indigenous entrepreneurs with remarkable natural skills. The challenge was how to help those entrepreneurs to become more productive. Among the tasks of government, the maintenance of political stability, the establishment of a sound and equitable legal and administrative system, and the improvement of the physical infrastructure were crucial to the encouragement of a thriving enterprise sector. At the same time, some things could be done by the enterprise sector itself. ICC was collaborating with the International Trade Centre UNCTAD/GATT in a programme to strengthen chambers of commerce in developing countries. There was considerable scope for joint official/private sector initiatives in building up direct technical co-operation between businessmen in developed and developing countries.

11. ICC very much welcomed the signs of a new political climate more favourable to private business enterprise. It was anxious to see, particularly in the LDCs, an expansion and strengthening of national and local bodies which could represent the business community, provide it with support, information and guidance, and serve as a valuable sounding-board for government in the design and implementation of economic and social policies.

12. ICC had long believed in the need to foster a productive "dialogue for development" between government and the private enterprise sector. The political mood almost everywhere was shifting decisively in that direction. As the body representative of world business, ICC was ready to expand its co-operation with UNCTAD and other organs of the United Nations system.

Summary of the statement made at the 218th plenary meeting, 30 July 1987,
by Mrs. Georgina ASHWORTH, Programme Director, International Coalition for Development Action

1. Mrs. ASHWORTH said that her organization had been set up between the third and fourth sessions of the Conference by courageous individuals from North America, Western Europe, Australia and New Zealand, who had been angered by the reluctance of their Governments to negotiate fairly with the countries of the South or to acknowledge that the goal of international conferences and economic dialogue was to bring equity and justice to tea-pickers, small farmers, tin miners, laundrywomen, factory workers and others. Although it was gratifying that the principle of the joint responsibility of Governments had frequently been cited at the current session of the Conference in the context of international debt, the fact remained that the same principle of joint responsibility must prevail in issues which concerned the very future of humanity.

2. Her organization believed in the concept of indigenous, democratic, sustainable and local development which preserved the rights, dignity and economic self-determination of all human beings, both women and men. It rejected enforced adjustment, which increased social inequality or sacrificed one generation for the alleged benefit of another. The International Coalition therefore urged member States and the UNCTAD secretariat to create a production and trade system that would revitalize the physical environment; in particular, all technical agreements on commodities, services, manufacturing activity, etc. should provide for research into their social effects.

3. The greatest inequity and inequality in the distribution of resources in the modern world was between men and women, as was clear from the United Nations system itself. Women were the backbone of the world economy, but they went unnoticed and unrepresented. National debt servicing and structural adjustment increased such inequality, because they assumed the free disposition of women's time in lieu of

financial resources. In 1985, member States had adopted the Forward-looking Strategies for the Advancement of Women, which contained a number of recommendations, including the elimination of exploitation in employment in both manufacturing and the production of commodities for export. In future, all economic conferences should tackle the problem of the world economy's dependence on a population group which did not receive the remuneration it deserved. Member States and UNCTAD must implement the Forward-looking Strategies at all levels.

4. By the next session of the Conference, progress in biotechnology would probably have transformed not only commodity production, but also the shape of world economic relations. Concerted international measures must immediately be taken to ensure that control over simple and free biological resources was not seized by a small number of institutions that could not be brought to account. Before the next session of the Conference member States must take steps to protect the interests of their citizens so as to prevent a dangerous distortion of a world economy which should be democratic, transparent and equitable.

5. Non-governmental organizations had attended the current session of the Conference in unprecedented numbers. Almost all participants had appreciated their work, despite some threats to their freedom of speech and integrity. Throughout the world, those organizations were composed of ordinary people—parents, lawyers, trade unionists, students, peasants, and so on—concerned and often courageous citizens who had come together to defend economic and social justice at both the local and international level. The non-governmental organizations hoped to continue and increase their participation in the assemblies, committees and other decision-making bodies of a strong UNCTAD.

Summary of the statement made at the 219th plenary meeting, 30 July 1987,
by Mr. Edouard LAURIJSSEN, Assistant Director, International Confederation of Free Trade Unions

1. Mr. LAURIJSSEN, speaking under rule 81 of the rules of procedure, referred to the document containing a comprehensive set of policy proposals which the International Confederation of Free Trade Unions (ICFTU) had earlier submitted to the Conference (TD/NGO/30). Those proposals were concerned primarily with the devastating consequences of growing unemployment and poverty in industrial and developing countries alike.

2. The foremost subject of concern in the 1980s was the debt crisis. It was evident that few debtor countries would ever repay their debt in full, and the major issue was no longer whether or not debts should be written off but what form the write-off should take—preferably

not in a piecemeal fashion but by means of a multilateral agreement on specified criteria for debt reduction. Special assistance was required by countries that faced severe economic problems aggravated by the debt burden. They might have to reduce or suspend debt payments, but they should not be further penalized by being declared ineligible for new credits. The central banks of the major industrial countries should take joint action to reduce interest rates and to maintain them at much lower levels than those currently applied. The share of exports absorbed by payment on the debt of raw material exporting developing countries should be reduced in proportion to the fall in commodity prices which had occurred since the date when the loans had been contracted. That formula should be included in rescheduling agreements and be backed by a special new facility of IMF.

3. Moreover, IMF ought to take social as well as financial indicators into account in stipulating the conditions governing its financing programmes for developing countries. Over-emphasis on the injection of private foreign capital was not an adequate alternative for aid and long-term commercial borrowing, although direct foreign investment should be promoted in cases where it was consistent with a country's overall development plans and was based on mutually understood agreements. There was a pressing need for an internationally agreed code defining the duties and responsibilities of TNCs in conformity with the ILO Declaration on Multinational Enterprises. Remaining obstacles to the finalization of the United Nations Code of Conduct on Transnational Corporations should be speedily resolved.

4. The ICFTU urged that, in order to achieve predictability in foreign exchange markets, the major industrialized countries should undertake negotiations aimed at adopting workable systems of managing exchange rates, within agreed but flexible target ranges, and to work for the formalization of such systems through IMF.

5. There was a paramount need for an increase in aid. Trade unions in developing countries were often well placed to advise on the use of aid and should be more closely involved in national decisions concerning its allocation. It was deplorable that the World Bank and the Inter-American Development Bank were not lending up to the full amount of the disbursements they were entitled to make; new facilities should be created within those organizations to increase loans for long-term development.

6. Most developing countries needed to place greater emphasis on policies for agricultural development and the alleviation of rural poverty. Reforms in agricultural price structures should be accompanied by the creation of credit institutions for small farmers, im-

proved marketing facilities, assistance for investment in machinery, fertilizers, seeds and animal husbandry, and extension programmes for training in new techniques. A key element in rural development policies should be the provision of specific support services for rural women, and, in order to increase rural workers' productivity, rural workers' organizations should be developed.

7. The ICFTU, a firm supporter of the UNCTAD Integrated Programme on Commodities regretted that the Common Fund had not yet been set up and that the Integrated Programme did not cover the full range of commodities initially envisaged. Agreement should also be reached on other means of ensuring a fair return to producing nations. As a minimum, developing countries' export earnings should be stabilized. The IMF Compensatory Financing Facility should be enlarged and the resources provided made less conditional. The Stabex agreement was an ideal model, and its principles should be supported by all industrialized countries and extended to all developing countries, with an enlarged product coverage and increased funding.

8. ICFTU fully supported the Uruguay Round objectives calling for concessional treatment for developing countries and pleaded for greater access by developing countries to industrial country markets. It was also in favour of the inclusion of a social clause in the General Agreement and similar international agreements to ensure the observance of minimum labour standards specified by an advisory committee to be established by GATT and ILO. Pressures for increased protectionism would be much harder to resist without such a clause, which should be supported by an international fund as well as by technical advice to assist countries in complying with the specified standards. New international initiatives were long overdue, and it was hoped that the outcome of the Conference would help to restore confidence in the world's economic future and, through a co-operative approach to debt, excessive exchange rate fluctuations and other financial problems, bring the implementation of recovery programmes and exchange rate co-ordination closer to reality.

Summary of the statement made at the 206th plenary meeting, 13 July 1987,
by Mr. Hulas C. GOLCHHA, Vice-President of the World Assembly of Small and Medium Enterprises

1. Mr. GOLCHHA, speaking under rule 81 of the rules of procedure, said that, despite the disturbing state of the world economy, there were positive signs of progress towards mutually acceptable solutions to complex problems. The enterprise sector placed sincere hope in the successful outcome of the Conference and appealed to member States to work towards the creation of a liberal and supportive trading environment leading to the removal of protectionist barriers and restrictive practices, the easing of the debt burden of developing countries and greater access to ODA and concessional lending. The statement of the President of France was most welcome in that connection. Only within such an environment could small and medium enterprises (SMEs) be expected to play an optimal role in revitaliz-

ing growth, generating employment at minimum economic cost and strengthening international trade and technology exchanges.

2. The significant contribution made by SMEs to economic growth and development in developed as well as developing countries was reflected in General Assembly resolution 41/182, which called upon the United Nations system to support the efforts of States in encouraging indigenous entrepreneurs. The success of SMEs hinged on sound policies, political commitment, responsive administrative systems and intrepreneurial dynamism. Such enterprises in several developing countries were now in a much better position to enter into collaborative arrangements with counterparts in

developed countries for technology transfer, foreign direct investments, training and stimulation of exports.

3. Major obstacles to their growth included, however, a lack of access to adequate, timely credit, to raw materials and other inputs and to domestic and international markets. They lacked resources for research and development, and there was a need for increased research and development support and for expanded training facilities. High priority should be given to the introduction and assimilation of updated technology, of which SMEs were important users. In that regard, WASME commended the initiatives taken in recent years by such bodies as UNDP, UNIDO, ILO, UNCTAD and the International Trade Centre UNCTAD/GATT and hoped that further co-operation would be forthcoming. Individual entrepreneurship needed to be adequately nurtured through efficient, helpful administrative systems, and the development of SMEs including informal businesses in rural areas, should receive high priority in national growth strategies.

4. Since its establishment in 1980, WASME had become the focal point of governmental and non-governmental initiatives in both industrial and developing countries to promote indigenous entrepreneurship, strengthen the entrepreneurial base, identify problems and seek solutions and facilitate technical co-operation among enterprises through the dissemination and exchange of data, exchanges of advisers and specialists and the provision of training. To illustrate the activities of WASME he referred to a number of meetings it had organized to promote the role of SMEs, including the first African Symposium on Small and Medium Enterprises in Rabat, which had produced the Rabat Plan of Action. The Plan had been endorsed by the Ministers of Industry of Africa. WASME had also helped to organize the Second International Conference on Small and Medium Enterprises, which had called for the proclamation of 1988 as the Year of Small Enterprises. WASME appealed to the States members of UNCTAD to endorse that initiative. He also drew attention to the Afro-Asian Conference on Small and Medium Enterprises to be held in October 1988 in Istanbul.

5. WASME commended two initiatives taken recently by the Secretary-General of UNCTAD. The first was the convening of an Enterprise Symposium attended by 35 leading businessmen representing all economic systems and enterprise sectors for discussions with the Secretary-General and secretariat officials. The other initiative was that of organizing a press encounter at which six eminent experts and media representatives had shared views on the issues before the Conference. He pledged the support of WASME for the objectives of UNCTAD.

Summary of the statement made at the 219th plenary meeting, 30 July 1987, by Mr. Blaise ROBEL, World Confederation of Labour

1. Mr. ROBEL, speaking under rule 81 of the rules of procedure, said that his organization, whose members were trade unions in 85 countries, including developing countries, attached great importance to the questions of development and economic relations which were UNCTAD's primary concern. He outlined the position of WCL with respect to the main items on the Conference agenda.

2. So far as commodity prices and trade were concerned he said the statistics were truly alarming. According to UNCTAD's estimates, the drop in commodity prices during the period 1981-1985 had cost the developing countries some $93 billion. The causes of that phenomena, as described in the documents before the Conference, were the concentration of markets in the hands of a small group of industrialized countries for several products, changes in consumption habits, the increased use of substitutes, and technological innovation. Moreover, owing to protectionist measures adopted in the rich market-economy countries large surpluses of farm products had been accumulated, with the consequence that prices had dropped disastrously and that any hope which the developing countries might have had of offsetting the lower prices by higher output for export had been frustrated.

3. However, what was of primary concern to his organization was the future of millions of persons living in third world countries who depended on commodities for their very subsistence. In other words, the economic and social development of those countries was closely linked to the trend in the markets for their commodities. Their growth depended on improved earnings from the exports of those commodities which would enable them not only to diversify their economies but also to process the raw materials locally and so to strengthen their position on the world market.

4. Financing to compensate for shortfalls in earnings from commodities was vital for the purpose of redressing the current imbalance in the terms of trade of developing countries exporters of commodities. However, price stabilization, diversification and modernization of production, the processing of basic commodities into finished goods or semi-manufactures, the application of research and development, the improvement in the productivity and marketing of products and all other measures recommended to the developing countries required special, substantial and prolonged financing by the international community.

5. It seemed that the concept of trade liberalization meant different things to different people. The rich countries, far from liberalizing their reciprocal trade, had raised tariff barriers by 20 per cent in the period 1981-1986, because of GATT's powerlessness. At the same time the protectionist measures which affected mainly agricultural and livestock products from the third world as well as primary industrial products such as textiles, clothing, leather, shoes, steel, continued to be applied and were even proliferating.

6. Paradoxically, countries of the third world were being told to abandon their substitution policies and to adopt instead an open-market policy, particularly in the services sector. That was neither equitable nor rational; many developing countries had had to cut imports precisely because of the reduced value of their exports and the fact that they had to devote a large part of their resources to service their foreign debt. Thus, the decline in their imports of industrial and capital goods, which were, after all essential for their development, far from being deliberate, had been imposed from the outside through those negative factors. The only rational solution would be to give the developing countries a purchasing power that would enable them to revitalize their economy, start the development process once again and thus catch up with the growth rate of the industrialized countries.

7. It was well known that the multinational corporations controlled 80 per cent of the world trade in commodities. The interests of those powerful companies did not always coincide with the interests of peoples or of the Governments representing those peoples. It was rather significant that after so many years of discussion the drafting of the United Nations code of conduct for transnational corporations had still not been completed. The influence of multinational corporations in international trade should be analysed in depth, for although international trade was rightly regarded as a means of promoting development, it was also necessary to avoid a situation in which it would become merely an instrument for enriching small groups or consortia. It had been noted on several occasions that some sectoral or regional development programmes served more the interests of multinational groups than those of the socalled beneficiaries.

8. Referring to development co-operation, he said that when IMF and private banks had for well-known reasons decided to reduce radically the flow of financing to indebted countries, it had been expected that there would be an intensification of bilateral and multilateral aid. Unfortunately, that had not been the case. Only the Nordic countries and the Netherlands had allocated more than 0.7 per cent of their GNP for development aid; on the average, other countries had allocated less than half that percentage. The ODA of countries such as the United States and Japan was even below that average. The industrialized countries ought to make great efforts in order to meet their commitments to the developing countries. Similarly, multilateral development banks should increase their credit capacity and soften the terms of their loans to developing countries. IMF should review its policy and the harsh conditions it imposed, so that the countries which required its assistance could bring their balance of payments into equilibrium and maintain an even rate of growth and development.

9. In 1980, when the current recession had begun, his organization had stressed the existing link between human rights and trade union rights, on the one hand, and the expansion of international capitalism, on the other. The World Symposium on Human Rights and Trade Union Action organized at Quebec by his organization in March 1980 had drawn up a depressing catalogue of the fundamental rights denied to workers everywhere, particularly in the poor countries, because of the unjust distribution of the benefits of economic activity. Fighting constantly for the rights and freedoms of workers and peoples, his organization had observed all too frequently that the profound cause of the violations of those rights and freedoms were to be found in the unjust international economic system, the inequalities inherent in the system, the abuses of multinational corporations, and the development models imposed, which were based solely on competitiveness and egoism.

10. With regard to the problem of external indebtedness, his organization called for an immediate and total cancellation of the debts of the LDCs. The problem was more of a political than of a technical nature, and an international conference on debt, bringing together developed and developing countries and various international bodies of the United Nations family, including IMF and the World Bank, should be convened as soon as possible under United Nations auspices in order to find a fair solution that would promote the development of all the concerned.

11. It would not be possible to end the recession and promote the growth of industrialized countries while ignoring the rights of workers, worsening their conditions of life and work and replacing human beings by computers or robots. The economy was in the service of man and society, and productivity was not an end in itself but a means to improve collective social well-being. Nor could the recession be resolved and the development process brought about in the third world at the cost of the misery and hunger of people. For example, the freezing of wages (as required by the austerity programmes proposed by some international bodies) in countries suffering from galloping inflation and low purchasing power would be a threat to the very life of workers and their families. His organization regarded the respect of human rights, trade union rights and democratic freedoms as a *sine qua non* for any adjustment process or economic recovery in general.

12. He expressed the hope that, despite the enormous problems which still existed, the decisions taken at the Conference would lead towards the establishment of a just new international economic order promoting true development and peace.

Summary of the statement made at the 218th plenary meeting, 30 July 1987, by Mr. Ivan MITIAIEV, World Federation of Trade Unions

1. Mr. MITIAIEV said that the Federation's position on the main issues before the seventh session of the Conference was set out in the Memorandum entitled "Trade Unions and Global Economic Relations and International Action for Development", which it had distributed to all delegations at the Conference. WFTU considered that the refusal of the major capitalist countries to implement the Declaration and Programme of Action on the Establishment of a New International Economic Order and the Charter of Economic Rights and Duties of States was the reason for the deterioration in world economic relations since the sixth session of the Conference. The increasing importance attached to profits rather than workers during the previous four years had led to the further militarization of economies, severel cuts in social services and programmes, colossal budget deficits, intensified exploitation of peoples and uncontrolled speculation. It was sad and ironic to note that in 1986—proclaimed the International Year of Peace by the General Assembly in order to promote the idea of "disarmament for development"—military expenditure had reached a record one trillion dollars. WFTU had consistently warned that the militarization of economies would lead to enormous budget deficits, to the detriment of economic stability and social development.

2. It was most disturbing to note that speculation had taken over from production and trade in current economic activity, since it gave rise to serious problems, particularly in the developing countries. It was that unchecked speculation which was the main cause of violent fluctuations in exchange rates and the fall in commodity prices which had had a disastrous impact on the economies of the developing countries and others. The real implications of those trends should, in the opinion of the trade unions, be measured in terms of their social and human costs; the social cost was currently not only huge but unprecedented and outrageous. In the developing countries, millions of people lived below the poverty line, suffering from malnutrition; they were illiterate and had no access to medical facilities, adequate housing or employment. Although the situation in the industrialized capitalist countries was not as serious, it was just as disturbing, with unemployment and heavy cuts in social services and programmes a sad reality.

3. WFTU considered that any serious approach to the question of development must first of all take its human and social aspects into account and create the political will to democratize world economic relations. Co-operation must replace confrontation and exploitation, and people must come before profits. The eleventh World Trade Union Congress, held in Berlin in September 1986, had reaffirmed the determination of the trade union movement to continue its campaign for the establishment of a new international economic order, which would guarantee the maintenance of just and equitable economic relations conducive to development in all countries, particularly the developing countries. WFTU considered that the establishment of the new international economic order required, above all, measures to control and curb the activities of TNCs; it was regrettable that, after more than 10 years of debate, the United Nations had still not succeeded in adopting an international code of conduct for the TNCs.

4. The increased concentration of economic power threw the question of international trade into sharper relief and highlighted the urgent need to reform the existing trade system. The increasing tendency for the industrialized countries, particularly the United States of America, to resort to discrimination, sanctions, embargoes and trade measures as a means of pressure and a political weapon must be stopped. Effective measures must be taken to stabilize commodity prices and promote the implementation of the Integrated Programme for Commodities and the entry into force of the Agreement Establishing the Common Fund for Commodities.

5. UNCTAD should also take appropriate measures to encourage economic co-operation among countries with different economic and social systems, as well as special measures to speed up the implementation of the proposals for economic co-operation among the developing countries themselves, and in particular those made by the non-aligned movement and the Group of 77. The debt crisis must be resolved without delay; however, the prescriptions of IMF and the World Bank provided no real solution. Many trade unions considered that there were economic, social and moral grounds for demanding the cancellation of debts in view of the current outflow of resources and the unjust nature of neo-colonial exploitation. Special consideration must be given to the LDCs in that respect.

6. WFTU supported the proposal by the Group of 77 to convene an international conference on monetary and financial questions as soon as possible with a view to reforming the international monetary system. However, efforts to revitalize development and establish more just and equitable international economic relations would make no progress as long as preparations for war and the development of new and more destructive weapons continued to be the main priority of a number of nations, whose lead the others were obliged to follow. WFTU, echoing the demands of the workers of the world, urged that immediate steps should be taken to stop the arms race and implement effective disarmament measures.

7. WFTU considered that development must be a democratic process entailing broader involvement of the people, and particularly of trade unions, in all aspects of decision-making. Consideration of that aspect by UNCTAD would help in the elaboration of constructive action programmes for development.

Summary of the statement made at the 219th plenary meeting, 30 July 1987, by Mr. Jacques LE DAUPHIN, World Peace Council

1.   Mr. LE DAUPHIN, speaking under rule 81 of the rules of procedure, said that the fundamental objective of UNCTAD was to support and promote the development process. That concerned primarily the developing countries, some of which were in a dramatic situation. However, in view of the crisis, it also concerned a number of developed countries, since there could be no true growth or full employment in one part of the world while another part was suffering from stagnation.

2.   Debt was a cancer for the developing countries and, at the same time, it cut off the developed countries from a solution to the crisis facing them. The debt problem of the developing countries seemed to defy a solution. That reality, recognized in connection with Latin America, was even more manifest in the case of sub-Saharan Africa. It was becoming increasingly clear that earlier endeavours for dealing with the debt problem had come to a dead halt. It was not enough merely to improve rescheduling terms by lengthening repayment periods and by reducing the interest rates applied to such rescheduling, as had been proposed at the recent Venice Summit. Rescheduling of debts only delayed the payment of the capital borrowed, but at the cost of higher ultimate interest payments. Thus, countries were forced to pay more and more in interest without being able to reduce the total amount of their indebtedness.

3.   Several countries were already aware of the contradictions and restraints inherent in structural adjustment policies. The social cost of the policies imposed by IMF and the World Bank was very heavy. A set of immediate measures was required aimed at restricting the amount of annual repayments to a share of export earnings which did not adversely affect development. In fact, however, the cancellation of a large proportion of accumulated debt in respect of which the underdeveloped countries had already paid very large amounts to their creditors was the only way of putting an end to the financial demands which stifled them. Accordingly, what should be envisaged was the cancellation of debts and, at the same time, the injection of new financing that would enable the developing countries to restore and develop their human and material potential.

4.   The treatment of debt could not be isolated from the availability of new financing. However, the difficulties of the countries concerned would not be removed if new financing was made available without resolving the problems of indebtedness. Nor would it be enough simply to wipe the slate clean and to revert to the situation as it had existed in the 1970s. What was really needed was fresh credit that would effectively serve to finance growth, with maturities and at interest rates in keeping with the situation of the developing countries. The burden of debt cancellation and the cost of financing on easier terms could be financed in particular through a reduction in armaments expenditures which were not only sources of insecurity but represented a considerable and scandalous waste of resources. Those considerations added to the importance attaching to the International Conference on the Relationship between Disarmament and Development, to be held in New York shortly.

5.   The recognition of the dual interdependence of the economies of the developing and developed countries should lead to multiple forms of mutually advantageous co-operation. Such co-operation should help each country to create more resources and employment at home in order to improve living conditions and strengthen sectors in which it had a comparative advantage. Each country should enjoy independence of action, and the rules and content of the co-operation agreements should be freely negotiated. Co-operation should also and especially cover services, reduce the cost of material investment and financing, promote training, research, facilitate access to science and high technology, and create employment. Aid through co-operation should therefore not be subject to considerations of profitability.

6.   New credits at low rates and more advantageous price formation for developing countries could be agreed within the framework of such co-operation accords. Such mutually beneficial co-operation would promote relations between developing countries and between developed countries irrespective of their social systems. It would also tend to promote relations between capitalist and socialist countries that would not only yield economic benefits but also tend to improve international relations generally and strengthen détente.

7.   As a consequence fresh momentum could be given to prospects for a new international economic order. Of course, the tasks to be undertaken were vast and difficult. The magnitude and originality of the international dimensions of the crisis created new problems but at the same time offered new potential for joint action aimed at transforming international relations. He was convinced that the lines of thought, the proposals made and the various approaches put forward during the Conference would contribute to the achievement of the desired objectives.

G. OTHER ORGANIZATIONS

Summary of the statement made at the 217th plenary meeting, 29 July 1987, by Mr. Patrick MAGAPATONA, Administrative Secretary, African National Congress of South Africa*

1. Mr. MAGAPATONA said that, while concentrating its efforts on the liberation of the people oppressed by South Africa, his organization was not neglecting world economic problems. The Declaration and the Programme of Action on the Establishment of a New International Economic Order and the Charter of Economic Rights and Duties of States had lost none of their relevance—quite the contrary—and the developing countries desired more than ever the establishment of equitable economic, commercial, financial and technical relations between rich and poor nations.

2. Many developing countries were being crippled by their debt burden and in Africa a large number of them spent their entire export earnings on repaying and servicing debts. Furthermore, institutions such as IMF had imposed austerity measures on the developing world with disastrous consequences. Paradoxically, therefore, the developing countries were now becoming exporters of capital to the developed countries. The latter must be urged to ensure that the ODA target of 0.7 per cent of GNP was met.

3. Peace, stability and, consequently, development would not be possible in southern Africa until the triumph of the liberation struggle of the peoples of South Africa and Namibia. The Pretoria régime was deliberately continuing a policy of destabilizing the front-line States, preventing the economic independence of the countries of the sub-region and keeping them under its heel. Its armed attacks against neighbouring countries and its support for the UNITA rebels in Angola and the MNR rebels in Mozambique were destabilizing those States not only politically, but also economically. Ravaged by terrorist bands regularly sabotaging vital installations, they were obliged to devote a large part of their scarce resources to the protection of their territorial integrity. The racist régime of Pretoria was also continuing to occupy Namibia illegally, in flagrant violation of the resolutions of the United Nations, the non-aligned movement, OAU and

other international bodies, and was also continuing shamelessly to plunder the resources of that country.

4. The African National Congress was struggling to achieve the complete political and economic emancipation of the South African people and the building of a society founded on the basic principles of its programme—the Freedom Charter—and its victory could only be of benefit to southern Africa and the continent as a whole. The South African economy was in deep recession and matters would certainly not improve until there was a fundamental change in the country. The *apartheid* régime was confronted with a growing challenge abroad and external loans had fallen sharply. South Africa's debt was now about $32 billion, the equivalent of roughly 33 per cent of the GDP. Economic mismanagement, monstrous wastage of resources, the state of emergency and building up of the military had brought the country to the verge of ruin. The *apartheid* régime was in an impasse. The only solution lay in the fundamental restructuring of society, based on the will of the majority.

5. The struggle for national liberation in South Africa had intensified. The fascist régime of Pretoria could no longer govern, except by the imposition of the state of emergency and other acts of State terrorism, and Botha had decided to continue the policy of internal repression and external aggression. But even that was failing to stem the rising tide of the people's demands for all their fundamental rights, and there was no doubt that victory was near. The battle being waged by the Namibian people, the heroic struggle of the Palestinian people and that of the African National Congress would be a great contribution to the establishment of just peace and a favourable environment for economic co-operation. Peace and development were inextricably linked and called for co-operation among all nations on the basis of the right of each people to adopt the social system of its choice.

6. He wished to congratulate the Soviet Union and Côte d'Ivoire on signing the Agreement establishing the Common Fund, a gesture that would be welcomed by the developing countries.

---

* Invited to participate pursuant to General Assembly resolution 3280 (XXIX).

Summary of the statement made at the 213th plenary meeting, 27 July 1987, by Mr. Ahmad SULEIMAN ABU-ALAA, Director-General, Economic Affairs Department, Palestine Liberation Organization*

1.   Mr. SULEIMAN ABU-ALAA said that the new international economic order was still far from becoming a reality. However, it was high time to introduce balance and fairness into world trade and to free it from exploitation and domination. Disarmament and peace would be conducive to economic development and the mobilization of resources; the elimination of foreign occupation was a prerequisite for that development, in accordance with article 16 of the Charter of Economic Rights and Duties of States. Peoples deprived of their right to liberty, independence and self-determination, such as those subject to colonialist and racist régimes in southern Africa and in Palestine, were also deprived of the possibility of economic and social development.

2.   The Israeli occupation authorities were expropriating land, establishing colonial settlements, appropriating water resources and practising various other forms of discrimination against the Palestinian people. They had made the economy of the occupied territories dependent on that of Israel, and transformed them into nothing but a market for Israeli goods. They were applying a military and commercial blockade against Palestinian imports and exports and were even preventing the implementation of a decision by the European Community granting preferential access to Palestinian products, on the pretext that such products would compete with Israeli exports on the European market.

3.   The PLO was grateful to the members of the European Community and hoped that it would cancel the preferential treatment granted to Israeli products in the Community as a means of penalizing Israel for disregarding that decision.

4.   The PLO hoped that UNCTAD would assist it in overcoming Israel's obstruction of the building of a commercial seaport in Gaza. Approved by the General Assembly in 1984, the port would be the sole maritime outlet for the occupied territories and would give them direct access to foreign markets. The PLO also hoped that UNCTAD and the International Trade Centre UNCTAD/GATT would assist it in creating a commercial and export centre for Palestinian products.

* Invited to participate pursuant to General Assembly resolution 3237 (XXIX).

5.   The Israeli authorities had confiscated more than half the Palestinian territories, creating settlements there in violation of article 55 of the Hague Regulations and article 49 of the Fourth Geneva Convention. The Security Council had condemned those manœuvres, as well as those aimed at changing the natural and demographic character of the occupied territories. The Israeli authorities had imposed restrictions on the use of water by the Palestinians for the benefit of certain Israeli towns and settlements. Agriculture had been affected by those restrictions, and many farmers had had to emigrate, thus playing into the hands of the Israelis, who were seeking to drive out the Palestinian population.

6.   The Israeli authorities were also attempting to hamper Palestinian industry by placing obstacles in the way of imports of machinery and equipment and forcing businesses to surrender the foreign currency proceeds of exports. They were refusing to license the construction of a cement plant despite the housing shortage brought about by Israel's destruction of dwellings. They were banning the construction of dwellings in the Palestinian camps and had even destroyed homes in Gaza. They were placing obstacles of all kinds in the way of the activities of housing co-operatives, and even refusing to allow them to obtain foreign capital.

7.   At its sixth session, the Conference had approved the creation of a special economic unit to monitor the evolution of the economic situation in the occupied Palestinian territories. That unit had competently carried out its mandate under Conference resolution 146 (VI).

8.   The PLO was grateful for the assistance extended to its people; the best form of assistance would enable them to put an end to the Israeli occupation, to develop their economy freely and to exercise their inalienable right to return to their homeland, to self-determination and to establish an independent State. The PLO was confident that the Palestinian people would triumph in its liberation struggle, as would the peoples of southern Africa in their struggle against occupation, violence and terrorism, *apartheid* and discrimination, which were endangering international peace.

Summary of the statement made at the 219th plenary meeting, 30 July 1987, by Mr. Elliot MFAXA, Member, Central Committee, Pan Africanist Congress of Azania*

1.   Mr. MFAXA said that, as was shown by the deliberations at the Conference, there was a tug of war going on between developing countries and the developed world. The former pleaded for aid and better debt repayment terms, while the latter sought to protect

* Invited to participate pursuant to General Assembly resolution 3280 (XXIX).

its economies and demanded concessions before it granted assistance.

2.   When the Group of 77 had met in Argentina in 1982, the issue of national liberation movements had become vital. SWAPO had been requested to prepare a comprehensive study of the situation in Namibia, for example, to indicate how many firms operated there, to

whom they belonged, the rate of exploitation of human and natural resources, how SWAPO hoped to correct some of the exploitative machinery and what UNCTAD could do to help. That study was to form part of the basis for a meeting of donor countries. PAC and the African National Congress would follow suit at the appropriate time.

3. It was clear that a crisis existed in the LDCs, particularly in the entire continent of Africa, which depended on commodities for its foreign trade. It should be borne in mind that the Conference was dealing with matters that directly affected the living conditions of thousands of human beings. It was his earnest hope that the developed countries would help to save the situation by coming to grips with reality and not magnifying differences. The Pan Africanist Congress hoped that it would be possible for the developed and developing countries to reach a consensus hastening the integration of developing countries into the world economy so that they could share equitably in the fruits of development.

4. During the period 1850-1950, South African capitalists had produced wealth at an extraordinary rate, while the conquered people had suffered from severe poverty. South Africa's agriculture provided one of the highest standards of living for the franchised, while three quarters of the population did not have enough to eat. There could be no equality in a situation where a developed agricultural industry existed alongside an inefficient and wasteful form of subsistence farming.

5. Unemployment in South Africa was structural. With regard to the labour force, he said that in every recession, Africans were easily fired and then were easily hired again in times of expansion. There was a need for collective and immediate action by the international community. As was known, a number of resolutions had been adopted in UNCTAD and other international bodies had also proposed a series of different sets of principles, but none of them signified revolutionary initiatives.

6. When asked why no action was taken, countries replied that they had signed the General Agreement on Tariffs and Trade. What that meant in fact was that partners in a trading relationship would not boycott each other. In his opinion, however, an internationally accepted legal principle could not be used to defend an unjust system and the argument of the countries concerned was merely an excuse for inaction.

7. He took note of the contribution and moral support given to PAC by the neighbouring front-line States. The people of Zimbabwe had given tangible expression to their support by creating a solidarity fund for the vast masses of the Azanian people. He called on the international community to assist the front-line States. PAC also paid a tribute to the PLO and expressed its conviction that the Palestinian people would triumph.

Summary of the statement made at the 219th plenary meeting, 30 July 1987, by Mr. Ben AMATHILA, Secretary for Economic Affairs, South West Africa People's Organization*

1. Mr. AMATHILA urged that in accordance with General Assembly resolution 41/39 C, UNCTAD should grant qualified Namibians an opportunity for in-service training in the UNCTAD secretariat as its contribution to the preparation of Namibian manpower for the future independent State of Namibia.

2. Many speakers had adequately identified the root cause of the current problems affecting developing countries in the field of trade. Some had proposed solutions, and others had demonstrated their determination to solve the problems by signing the Agreement Establishing the Common Fund. He hoped that by the end of the current session of the Conference its four committees would be able to submit proposals for enabling the developing countries to solve their problems.

3. He fully supported the proposals which the Group of 77 had submitted to the Conference (see TD/330). He appreciated the efforts made to improve trade relations between countries, but stressed that those efforts should not extend to the *apartheid* régime of South Africa. Indeed, the General Assembly had recommended economic sanctions against that country because of its *apartheid* policies and its illegal occupation of Namibia.

4. In view of South Africa's defiance of the relevant resolutions of the General Assembly and its refusal to allow the implementation of Security Council resolution 435 (1978), SWAPO had demanded the imposition of sanctions against that country. It had demanded trade boycotts against the Pretoria régime in accordance with Decree No. 1 of the United Nations Council for Namibia, 1974, which forbade the exploitation and export of Namibia's natural resources.

5. SWAPO demanded the total isolation of the South African régime in accordance with the 1971 advisory opinion of the International Court of Justice that South Africa's presence in Namibia was illegal and that Members of the United Nations should do nothing that would imply recognition of that illegal situation. SWAPO had noted with appreciation the action taken by individual Nordic countries to impose trade sanctions against South Africa, including Namibia. It had also noted the decision taken by the EEC to impose selective sanctions against South Africa, but regretted that those measures deliberately excluded Namibia, making it a potential safe haven for South Africa's manufacturers and exporters.

6. SWAPO had applauded the measures taken against South Africa by the United States Congress the previous year, which had led to the withdrawal of some United States companies from that country. It noted with alarm that the Congress was currently considering

---

* Invited to participate pursuant to General Assembly resolution 31/152.

action to withhold financial support to those countries in southern Africa which had stood firm in their support of the oppressed of South Africa. Furthermore, the United States Congress was considering measures to restrict the activities of ANC and SWAPO representatives to certain centres. Under the legislation being considered in the United States Congress, United Nations agencies would have difficulty in receiving funds from the United States if they were intended to support SWAPO and ANC. All those measures were not anti-*apartheid* and placed the United States squarely behind *apartheid*.

7.   South Africa was the greatest single factor in the region, apart from drought and other natural calamities, retarding economic development, growth and social progress through its policies of destabilization and aggression against its neighbours.

8.   He doubted that measures for dealing with the indebtedness and debt servicing problems of front-line States alone would bring progress to those countries or stop South Africa in its efforts to wreck their economies. In his opinion, to try to solve the indebtedness problems of the States in the region without tackling the root cause—and South Africa was a cause—was a contradiction in itself. The purpose of trade sanctions against South Africa was to restore democracy in that country and to secure the abolition of *apartheid*. Trade sanctions against the Pretoria régime would enhance the process leading to Namibia's independence. Economic sanctions would curtail South Africa's abilities to commit or sponsor aggression against its neighbours.

9.   He said that there could be no development or progress in any society in the absence of peace and security. Those who continued to support *apartheid* in South Africa through trade or other means were contributing to South Africa's programme of destabilization.

Part Two

SUMMARY RECORDS OF PLENARY MEETINGS

PART TWO

Summary records of plenary meetings*

201st (OPENING) PLENARY MEETING

Thursday, 9 July 1987, at 4.35 p.m.

Temporary President: Mr. Lazar MOJSOV
(Yugoslavia)

President: Mr. Bernard T. G. CHIDZERO (Zimbabwe)

TD/SR.201

AGENDA ITEM 1

Opening of the Conference

1. The TEMPORARY PRESIDENT, in accordance with rule 16 of the rules of procedure, declared open the seventh session of the United Nations Conference on Trade and Development.

AGENDA ITEM 2

Election of the President

2. The TEMPORARY PRESIDENT invited nominations for the office of President of the Conference.

3. Mr. CABRISAS RUÍZ (Cuba), speaking on behalf of the Group of 77, nominated Mr. Bernard T. G. Chidzero, Minister of Finance, Economic Planning and Development of Zimbabwe.

4. Mr. THUYSBAERT (Belgium), on behalf of Group B, Mr. WOJCIK (Poland), on behalf of Group D, and Mr. SHEN Jueren (China) seconded the nomination.

5. *Mr. Chidzero (Zimbabwe) was elected President by acclamation and he took the Chair.*

6. The PRESIDENT** expressed to the Conference, on behalf of the delegation of Zimbabwe as well, his most sincere and profound appreciation for the honour bestowed on his country, on its people and its Government, in electing him to the Presidency of the seventh session of the Conference.

7. The seventh session was taking place against a background of exceptionally difficult economic problems and intractable issues in a world which had become something of a global village—because science and technology had reduced it to that—and the dynamics of trade and the mobility of factors of production, defying

---

* Incorporating corrections requested by delegations and any necessary editorial modifications.

** The full text of the statement was issued as TD/L.284.

national boundaries, reinforced that historical process of the "villagization" of the globe. Those problems and issues might suggest that the session was taking place at an inauspicious moment. For in the industrialized countries of the West there were the problems of slow growth, high unemployment, large external imbalances and the pressing need for structural adjustment and macro-economic co-ordination; in the developing countries, growth was stymied by exceptionally low and unstable commodity prices, deteriorating terms of trade and declining export earnings, crippling and ever-mounting debt-service payments, escalating trade barriers, negative net inflows of financial resources and growing balance-of-payments deficits.

8. Statistical and other data on all those issues were abundant in the documentation before the Conference and elsewhere, all pointing to the unfavourable external environment and increased uncertainties: no security and no predictability as if market forces had disarmed nations. In sum, the situation was overwhelming. But that was the very raison d'être of the Conference. Now was the time for vision and decisive action.

9. There should be assessment of problems and issues, although there could never be complete convergence of views, let alone unanimity in matters of perceptions. The real challenge lay in finding effective policies and measures. That was the imperative need. It was, therefore, to be hoped that the Conference, within the framework of the most universal of international institutions with such a broad mandate on trade and developmental issues, especially as they affected developing countries, could agree on the broad strategies called for and craft the needed guidelines. It must also generate the momentum for action in UNCTAD itself and in other forums or ongoing exercises such as in the Uruguay Round of trade negotiations. It must regain and espouse the development consensus and breathe new life into multilateralism through which all could confidently confront the problems of an interdependent world.

10. It was a unique opportunity to engage in a genuine process of "revitalizing development, growth and international trade". The route of effective international co-operation was the most efficient and least expensive for the advancement of the common good and enlightened self-interest. Given its comprehensive mandate under General Assembly resolution 1995 (XIX), UNCTAD provided the most representative forum for the consideration and co-ordination of international trade and development issues. Buttressed by sustained and expanding South-South co-operation across the board, as well as by East-West co-operation, North-

South dialogue must lead to concrete actions in the macro-economic management of the world economy for increased growth and world development for the good of all nations.

11. The very carefully selected agenda of the session—a result of prolonged and protracted debate and extensive negotiations over a period of time—focused on four key areas of the development *problématique*:

(*a*) Resources for development, which were patently inadequate: more resources were required and in particular those that would be available to multilateral institutions. Ironically, the resources that were there were encumbered or depleted by the burden of debt;

(*b*) Commodities, whose exceptionally low prices and poor long-term prospects reinforced the validity of the manifold objectives of the Integrated Programme for Commodities, the overall aim of which could be summed up as the generation of export earnings and provision of resources to develop and diversify the economies of commodity-dependent developing countries;

(*c*) International trade, which was impeded by escalating protectionist tendencies and the erosion of trading disciplines; virtually all the adjustment and export-oriented programmes would come to naught unless trade expanded and rules and fair play prevailed in the global trading system;

(*d*) The problems of the LDCs, the majority of which were in Africa. The efforts at economic transformation by that group of countries, aimed at overcoming structural obstacles and promoting sustained development, would not succeed without adequate additional external support.

12. Over and above its selectivity, the agenda had the very important characteristic which must be underlined, namely the fact that the four problem areas were assembled under a single unifying, action-oriented theme:

Revitalizing development, growth and international trade, in a more predictable and supportive environment, through multilateral co-operation.

13. At the sixth session in Belgrade, in 1983, it was recognized that the world economy was going through the most pervasive and dangerous crisis since the Great Depression of the 1930s, and that if the crisis then engulfing the world economy remained unresolved, even greater damage was going to be inflicted on the international economy. Since then, the international economic scene had worsened. There was now a crisis in development of unprecedented proportions.

14. The symptoms of that sad state of affairs had included very high real interest rates and volatile misaligned exchange rates and the effects they had had on debt-servicing; commodity prices that had plummeted to disastrously low levels and the worsening trading situation for developing countries which had been exacerbated by loss of export markets by reason of intensified protectionist pressures and slow growth in their principal markets. All that had led to a fall or slowing down in the growth of the economies of both developing countries and developed countries and in levels of trade, further aggravated by contraction in international liquidity in relation to the volume of trade and in particular the needs of developing countries.

15. At the seventh session, the Conference had the historic challenge to make a decisive contribution to the renewal and strengthening of effective dialogue between the developed and developing countries as well as to revitalize multilateral principles and institutions of international co-operation. Developed countries stood to benefit from such efforts in terms of growth from the otherwise dormant or thwarted demand forces in developing countries; while the latter needed the financial and trade flows emanating from a more rational and more equitable international economic system.

16. On the question of debt, it was now virtually universally acknowledged that debt-service obligations had become so onerous and could not be met without jeopardizing the development process and generating thereby high political and social costs. The enormity and gravity of the debt problem indicated that that problem could no longer be left to the short-term mechanisms of what could be termed the "muddling-through" strategy, if it was a strategy at all. While recognizing those efforts for what they were and the good they had presumably done in isolated cases, there was compelling reason for an improved and comprehensive international debt strategy that would conclude appropriate mechanisms to ensure continued adequacy of resources for development while growing out of debt. The strategy should be accompanied by the provision of adequate financial resources for development, including ODA, commercial bank lending and an enhanced lending role by multilateral institutions. Increased flow of non-debt-creating resources and direct foreign investment would also be called for. To be sure, domestic policies and adjustment programmes would need to be in place in accordance with the circumstances and chosen development path of each country.

17. It should be noted that, despite the general unfavourable external environment, many developing countries had made remarkable efforts to reduce their payment imbalances. In virtually every case that had been at very high cost. The adjustment measures or programmes had led to contraction in imports and entailed reduction in public expenditure (including subsidies), devaluations of exchange rates, and increasing interest rates. Furthermore, the impact of adjustment measures had in given cases led to increased numbers of the absolutely poor and rising levels of malnutrition among children, particularly in Africa.

18. The severity of the austerity which accompanied those measures could be borne or endured only if there was light at the end of the tunnel. Indeed, if those measures were to succeed, and trends in declining consumption reversed, there was clear and urgent need for enlarged and sustained support from the international community and for a supportive international environment.

19. In all those matters concerning increased development resources, the debt burden, the commodity problem, international trade including trade in agricultural products and the issue of subsidies, the views and positions expressed in the Venice Summit Communiqué and in the recent OECD Ministerial State-

ment, as well as in the communiqués of the meetings of the Interim Committee and the Development Committee in respect of the heavily indebted middle-income countries, the low-income countries and the LDCs, were noted with interest. Surely those views and positions would contribute to the emergence of more concrete policies and guidelines at the current session of the Conference.

20. The fundamental challenge was to search for policies and measures, to seek for ways and means, with a view to tranforming the relationships between the developed and developing countries by facilitating the stimulation of growth and development on a global level and in particular in the developing countries. Poverty and indebtedness could be overcome and the forces behind them transformed into growth factors.

21. The success of the Conference would also be measured by its contribution to the creation of a stable and predictable environment for international economic co-operation in which member States, irrespective of their stages of development, size or economic systems, could engage in unhindered processes of co-operation in such areas as trade, finance and technological transfers under conditions of growth, peace and security.

Messages from heads of State or Government

22. The PRESIDENT informed the Conference that messages had been received* from the Heads of State or Government of China, Cuba, the German Democratic Republic, Mongolia, Poland, the Union of Soviet Socialist Republics, and Viet Nam.

AGENDA ITEM 6

Adoption of the agenda

23. The PRESIDENT suggested that, in view of the fact that the Pre-Conference Meeting of Senior Officials had not yet completed its work, rule 8 of the rules of procedure should be waived and the provisional agenda, together with the understandings (TD/327), should be adopted. In that connection, he referred to Trade and Development Board decision 341 (XXXIII), and its annexes I and II, relating to the adoption of the agenda for the seventh session of the Conference. The position taken in the Board at the time of the adoption of that decision was reflected in annex III, paragraphs 4 to 7, of the report of the Board on the first part of its thirty-third session (TD/B/1118).

24. *It was so decided.*

AGENDA ITEM 9

Other business

Periodic review by the Conference of the lists of States contained in the annex to General Assembly resolution 1995 (XIX)

25. The PRESIDENT recalled that at its sixth session the Conference had reviewed the lists of States con-

tained in the annex to General Assembly resolution 1995 (XIX). Pending action by the Conference at its seventh session, the Trade and Development Board had decided that two States which had become members of UNCTAD, Brunei Darussalam and Saint Kitts and Nevis, should be treated as if they were included in the appropriate lists of States contained in the annex to resolution 1995 (XIX), in list A and in list C, respectively. The lists of States revised in conformity with that decision were reproduced in annex 4 to the provisional agenda for the seventh session of the Conference (TD/327). In the absence of any objection he would take it that the Conference endorsed that arrangement.

26. *It was so decided.*

27. The PRESIDENT extended a warm welcome to the two new members of UNCTAD.

Designation of intergovernmental bodies for the purposes of rule 80 of the rules of procedure

28. The PRESIDENT invited the Conference to consider the applications by the International Tropical Timber Organization and the International Textiles and Clothing Bureau for designation for the purposes of rule 80 of the rules of procedure. In that connection, the Conference had before it two notes by the UNCTAD secretariat (TD/L.273 and TD/L.274) containing information on those two intergovernmental bodies. He invited the Conference to designate them as entitled to participate in the work of UNCTAD in accordance with rule 80 of the rules of procedure.

29. *It was so decided.*

30. The PRESIDENT, on behalf of the members of the Conference, welcomed the participation of the two bodies concerned in the work of UNCTAD.

Statement by the Secretary-General of UNCTAD

31. Mr. DADZIE (Secretary-General of UNCTAD) made a statement.*

The meeting rose at 5.55 p.m.

---

* For the full text of the statement, see part one above, sect. C.

202nd PLENARY MEETING

Friday, 10 July 1987, at 9.15 a.m.

President: Mr. Bernard T. G. CHIDZERO (Zimbabwe)

TD/SR.202

AGENDA ITEM 7

General debate

1. Mr. CABRISAS RUÍZ (Cuba) made a statement.*

---

* See volume I, annex IV.

---

* For the full text of the statement, see part one above, sect. B.

2. Mr. SHANKER (India) made a statement.**

3. Mr. MENESES (Venezuela) made a statement.**

4. Mr. CONABLE (World Bank) made a statement.***

5. Mr. ELLEMANN-JENSEN (Denmark) made a statement on behalf of the European Economic Community and its member States.*

6. *The meeting was suspended at 10.40 a.m. and resumed at 11.10 a.m.*

7. Mr. MITTERRAND (France) made a statement.****

8. Mr. UL-HAQ (Pakistan) made a statement.**

9. Mr. MUBARAK (Egypt) made a statement.****

The meeting rose at 12.55 p.m.

** For the summary of the statement, see part one above, sect. B.
*** For the summary of the statement, see part one above, sect. D.
**** For the full text of the statement, see part one above, sect. A.

203rd PLENARY MEETING

Friday, 10 July 1987, at 3.05 p.m.

President: Mr. Bernard T. G. CHIDZERO (Zimbabwe)

TD/SR.203

AGENDA ITEM 7

General debate (*continued*)

1. Mr. DRAPER (United Nations Development Programme) made a statement.*

2. Mrs. BRUNDTLAND (Norway) made a statement.**

3. Mr. NGUESSO (Congo) made a statement.**

4. Mr. HRISTOV (Bulgaria) made a statement.***

5. Mr. HILL (Jamaica) made a statement.***

6. Monsignor ETCHEGARAY (Pontifical Commission) made a statement.**

7. Mr. MARTÍNEZ CUENCA (Nicaragua) made a statement.***

8. Mr. WOJCIK (Poland) made a statement.***

9. Mr. SIAZON (United Nations Industrial Development Organization) made a statement.****

The meeting rose at 6.15 p.m.

---

* For the summary of the statement, see part one above, sect. C.
** For the full text of the statement, see part one above, sect. A.
*** For the summary of the statement, see part one above, sect. B.
**** For the summary of the statement, see part one above, sect. D.

204th PLENARY MEETING

Monday, 13 July 1987, at 11.15 a.m.

President: Mr. Bernard T. G. CHIDZERO (Zimbabwe)

TD/SR.204

AGENDA ITEM 7

General debate (*continued*)

1. Mr. ARISTOV (Union of Soviet Socialist Republics) made a statement.*

2. The PRESIDENT expressed his deep appreciation for the very comprehensive and positive manner in which the USSR representative had faced the issues before the Conference. As a firm believer in the imperative need for concerted international action in the field of commodities, he considered the decision of the Government of the Soviet Union to sign the Agreement Establishing the Common Fund for Commodities to be a landmark in the history of UNCTAD and of multilateral co-operation and to augur well for the success of the Conference. There was no need to stress the political importance of such a decision, which meant that the long-awaited entry into force of the Agreement was within immediate reach. He hoped that its signature by the USSR would soon be followed by ratification, which would bring the total percentage of the directly contributed capital of the Fund accounted for by the ratifying countries to 65.26 per cent, only 1.4 per cent short of the required two thirds. He therefore addressed an urgent appeal to those countries which had not yet done so to sign and ratify the Agreement as a matter of priority during the Conference. In particular, he appealed to the countries beneficiaries of either the OPEC offer or the Norway offer—which together accounted for 2.36 per cent of the capital—to ratify the Agreement if they had not already done so. The necessary arrangements had been made to permit signatures of the Agreement to be effected and instruments of ratification to be deposited in Geneva during the Conference.

3. Mr. DADZIE (Secretary-General of UNCTAD) said that the announcement made by the USSR representative was of great political importance, extending well beyond the Common Fund itself and auguring well for significant progress towards the objectives of the Integrated Programme for Commodities. It also augured well for an ever more active involvement of the USSR in international economic co-operation for development. It was also a great encouragement to all those in the secretariat who had laboured long and hard to negotiate the Agreement and to promote its ratification. He hoped that the positive action taken by the USSR in that respect would boost the prospects for a constructive outcome of the seventh session of the Conference. A signing ceremony would be held the following morning.

4. Mr. AZMANI (Morocco) made a statement.*

5. Mr. TIAN Jiyun (China) made a statement.**

---

* For the summary of the statement, see part one above, sect. B.
** For the full text of the statement, see part one above, sect. A.

6. Mr. DULMAA (Mongolia) made a statement.*

7. Mrs. van ROOY (Netherlands) made a statement.*

The meeting rose at 12.45 p.m.

---

* For the summary of the statement, see part one above, sect. B.

205th PLENARY MEETING

Monday, 13 July 1987, at 3.25 p.m.

President: Mr. Bernard T. G. CHIDZERO (Zimbabwe)

TD/SR.205

AGENDA ITEM 7

General debate (*continued*)

1. Mr. FERNÁNDEZ-ORDÓÑEZ (Spain) made a statement.*

2. Mr. SAOUMA (Food and Agriculture Organization of the United Nations) made a statement.**

3. Mr. TOURÉ (Senegal) made a statement.*

4. Mr. CHEYSSON (Commission of the European Communities) made a statement.***

5. Mr. BEIL (German Democratic Republic) made a statement.*

6. Mr. IGLESIAS (Uruguay) made a statement.*

7. Mr. WEE KIAT (Malaysia) made a statement.*

8. Mr. GUN (Democratic People's Republic of Korea) made a statement.*

9. Mr. MELEGA (Hungary) made a statement.*

10. Mr. AL JARWAN (United Arab Emirates) made a statement.*

AGENDA ITEM 3

Constitution of sessional bodies

AGENDA ITEM 4

Election of Vice-Presidents and the Rapporteur

AGENDA ITEM 5

Credentials of representatives to the Conference:

(*a*) Appointment of the Credentials Committee

Organization of the work of the Conference

Report of the Pre-Conference Meeting

11. Mr. ALFARAGI (Egypt), President of the Trade and Development Board at the thirty-third session and the fifteenth special session, and Chairman of the Pre-Conference Meeting, introducing the report of

---

* For the summary of the statement, see part one above, sect. B.

** For the summary of the statement, see part one above, sect. D.

*** For the summary of the statement, see part one above, sect. E.

---

that meeting (TD/336), referred to the provisions on Board decision 346 (S-XV) on the establishment by the Conference of four sessional committees which, in accordance with past practice, would be open to the participation of all members of the Conference.

12. In accordance with rule 14 of the rules of procedure, and in keeping with past practice, the Pre-Conference Meeting recommended that the Credentials Committee should be composed of representatives of the nine States that had been members of the Credentials Committee at the most recent session of the General Assembly, namely, the Bahamas, China, Fiji, Ghana, the Netherlands, Rwanda, the Union of Soviet Socialist Republics, the United States of America and Venezuela. In accordance with rule 14 of the rules of procedure, the Credentials Committee would elect as its presiding officer the representative of the country that had chaired the Credentials Committee at the forty-first session of the General Assembly, namely, Venezuela.

13. Nominations for the offices of Chairman of the four main Committees were as follows: Committee I, Resources: Mr. M. Taniguchi (Japan); Committee II, Commodities: Mr. Carlos Pérez del Castillo (Uruguay); Committee III, International Trade: Mr. Chak Mun See (Singapore); and Committee IV, Least Developed Countries: Mr. Martin Huslid (Norway).

14. He understood that Mr. Andrei Ozadovski (Ukrainian Soviet Socialist Republic) had been nominated as Rapporteur of the Conference.

15. The following nominations for the 29 offices of Vice-President had been received from the various groups:

Group B:

Austria; Canada; Denmark; Germany, Federal Republic of; Netherlands; Spain; United Kingdom of Great Britain and Northern Ireland.

Group of 77:

African Group: Cameroon; Egypt; Madagascar; Nigeria; Senegal; United Republic of Tanzania.

Asian Group: Bangladesh; Jordan; Kuwait; Philippines; Pakistan; Yugoslavia.

Latin American Group: Argentina; Colombia; Dominican Republic; Jamaica; Mexico; Nicaragua.

Group D:

Hungary; Poland; Union of Soviet Socialist Republics.

China.

16. In accordance with past practice, the Conference might wish to recommend that the co-ordinators of regional groups be associated with the work of the bureau to be elected.

17. The regional distribution of the posts of Vice-Chairman and Rapporteur of the four Committees was as follows:

Committee I, Vice-Chairman from Asia and Rapporteur from Africa;

Committee II, Vice-Chairman from Group D and Rapporteur from Group B;

Committee III, Vice-Chairman from Group B and Rapporteur from Group D;

Committee IV, Vice-Chairman from Africa and Rapporteur from China.

18.   In accordance with the arrangements endorsed by the Board in its decision 346 (S-XV), the President of the Conference would establish a high-level contact group to assist him, when appropriate, in guiding the substantive work of the Conference and promoting agreement on policy issues outstanding from the work of the Sessional Committees. Subject to the decisions of the Conference, the contact group would hold formal meetings with a view to preparing a consolidated text in accordance with item 8 of the Conference agenda. In keeping with past practice, the contact group might be composed on nine members from the Group of 77, six from Group B, three from Group D, and the representative of China and would, as customary, be open-ended. The seven regional group co-ordinators and the sectoral co-ordinators should participate in its work and all Ministers of member States attending the final negotiations would be invited to participate in accordance with paragraph 2 of General Assembly resolution 41/169.

19.   After referring to the allocation of items and outlining the suggestions for the organization of work and the tentative timetable, he explained the arrangements for the preparation of the report of the Conference and designation of a group of "Friends of the Rapporteur".

20.   The PRESIDENT said that the Conference would have before it at its next meeting the report of the Pre-Conference Meeting (TD/336). If there was no objection, he would declare elected the Chairmen of Committees I, II, III and IV and the 29 Vice-Presidents of the Conference as nominated. He would further declare Mr. Andrei Ozadovski of the Ukrainian Soviet Socialist Republic elected as Rapporteur of the Conference.

21.   *It was so agreed.*

22.   The PRESIDENT said that the Conference had concluded its consideration of organizational matters.

The meeting rose at 6.30 p.m.

206th PLENARY MEETING

Monday, 13 July 1987, at 9.20 p.m.

President: Mr. Bernard T. G. CHIDZERO (Zimbabwe)

TD/SR.206

1.   *In the absence of the President, Mr. Kaczurba (Poland), Vice-President, took the Chair.*

AGENDA ITEM 7

General debate (*continued*)

2.   Mr. MARINOV (Council for Mutual Economic Assistance) made a statement.*

---

* For the summary of the statement, see part one above, sect. E.

3.   Mr. ENGBLOM (International Trade Centre UNCTAD/GATT) made a statement.**

4.   Mr. NGUYEN (Viet Nam) made a statement.***

5.   *Mr. Ingles (Philippines) Vice-President, took the Chair.*

6.   Mr. HOXHA (Albania) made a statement.***

7.   Mr. NG'ENO (Kenya) made a statement.***

8.   Mr. SAIGNAVONGS (Lao People's Democratic Republic) made a statement.***

9.   Mr. GOLCHHA (World Assembly of Small and Medium Enterprises) made a statement.****

The meeting rose at 10.55 p.m.

** For the summary of the statement, see part one above, sect. D.
*** For the summary of the statement, see part one above, sect. B.
**** For the summary of the statement, see part one above, sect. F.

207th PLENARY MEETING

Tuesday, 14 July 1987, at 10.05 a.m.

President: Mr. Bernard T. G. CHIDZERO (Zimbabwe)

TD/SR.207

AGENDA ITEM 7

General debate (*continued*)

1.   Mr. MUGABE (Zimbabwe), Chairman of the Non-Aligned Movement, made a statement.*

2.   *The meeting was suspended at 10.45 a.m. and resumed at 11.30 a.m.*

3.   Mr. URBAN (Czechoslovakia) made a statement.**

4.   Mr. KOUANDI ANGBA (Côte d'Ivoire) made a statement.**

5.   The PRESIDENT requested the representative of Côte d'Ivoire to convey to his Government the Conference's appreciation of the demonstration of support which it had just given by announcing its intention to sign the Agreement Establishing the Common Fund for Commodities.

6.   Mr. DADZIE (Secretary-General of UNCTAD) also expressed his appreciation for the announcement made by the representative of Côte d'Ivoire. For several years Côte d'Ivoire had commanded the admiration of many countries for the successes which it had achieved under the wise leadership of President Houphouët-Boigny. In recent years, however, it had been badly hit by the slump in commodities, with devastating effects on its capacity to service its debts. Nevertheless, despite its doubt regarding the effectiveness of commodity agreements in their current form, the Government had

---

* For the full text of the statement, see part one above, sect. A.
** For the summary of the statement, see part one above, sect. B.

decided, out of solidarity with the rest of the developing world, to sign the Agreement Establishing the Common Fund for Commodities. He hoped that other developing countries which had not yet signed or ratified the Agreement, particularly those whose contributions had been underwritten by Norway or the OPEC countries, would do so as soon as possible during the session.

7. Mr. TADESSE (Ethiopia) made a statement.**

8. Mr. PANDAY (Trinidad and Tobago) made a statement.**

9. *Mr. Shen Jueren (China), Vice-President, took the Chair.*

10. **Mr. KALALUKA (Zambia) made a statement.**

11. Mr. MAMMAN (Nigeria) made a statement.**

The meeting rose at 1.20 p.m.

** For the summary of the statement, see part one above, sect. B.

208th PLENARY MEETING

Tuesday, 14 July 1987, at 3.15 p.m.

President: Mr. Bernard T. G. CHIDZERO (Zimbabwe)

TD/SR.208

1. *In the absence of the President, Mr. Makhlouf (Egypt), Vice-President, took the Chair.*

AGENDA ITEM 7

General debate (*continued*)

2. Mr. ABERKANE (Algeria) made a statement.*

3. Mr. JAZAIRY (International Fund for Agricultural Development) made a statement.**

4. Mr. VADUVA (Romania) made a statement.*

5. Mr. DELAMURAZ (Switzerland) made a statement.*

6. Mr. TABAKOVIĆ (Yugoslavia) made a statement.*

7. Mr. NEISSER (Austria) made a statement.*

8. Mr. AL-SHAKAR (Bahrain) made a statement.*

9. Mr. ABDELMUNIM (Bangladesh) made a statement.*

10. Mr. CHARLES (Haiti) made a statement.*

11. Mr. SUAZO (Dominican Republic) made a statement.*

12. *Mr. Neisser (Austria), Vice-President, took the Chair.*

---

* For the summary of the statement, see part one above, sect. B.
** For the summary of the statement, see part one above, sect. D.

---

13. Mr. KONDIANO (Guinea) made a statement.*

14. *Mr. Suazo (Dominican Republic), Vice-President, took the Chair.*

15. Mr. HANSEN (United Nations Centre on Transnational Corporations) made a statement.***

16. Mr. KOENIG (International Chamber of Commerce) made a statement.****

17. Ms. CHEPKWONY (World Council of Churches) made a statement.****

The meeting rose at 7.10 p.m.

---

* For the summary of the statement, see part one above, sect. B.
*** For the summary of the statement, see part one above, sect. C.
**** For the summary of the statement, see part one above, sect. F

209th PLENARY MEETING

Wednesday, 15 July 1987, at 10.40 a.m.

President: Mr. Bernard T. G. CHIDZERO (Zimbabwe)

TD/SR.209

Message received by the Conference

1. The PRESIDENT announced that a message had been received from Mr. Alan García Pérez, President of the Republic of Peru.*

AGENDA ITEM 7

General debate (*continued*)

2. Ms. LANDRY (Canada) made a statement.**

3. Mr. TOLBA (United Nations Environment Programme) made a statement.***

4. Mr. DORJI (Bhutan) made a statement.**

5. *Baron van Voorst tot Voorst (Netherlands), Vice-President, took the Chair.*

6. Mr. KASAI (Zaire) made a statement.**

7. Mr. MOHAMED (Somalia) made a statement.**

8. Mr. INGLES (Philippines) made a statement.**

9. Mr. COREA (former Secretary-General of UNCTAD) made a statement.****

The meeting rose at 1.05 p.m.

---

* Reproduced in volume I, annex IV.
** For the summary of the statement, see part one above, sect. B.
*** For the summary of the statement, see part one above, sect. C.
**** For the full text of the statement, see part one above, sect. C.

210th PLENARY MEETING

Friday, 24 July 1987, at 10.30 a.m.

President: Mr. Bernard T. G. CHIDZERO (Zimbabwe)

TD/SR.210

1.   *In the absence of the President, Mr. Montgomery (Canada), Vice-President, took the Chair.*

AGENDA ITEM 5

Credentials of representatives to the Conference (*continued*):*
(a) Appointment of the Credentials Committee (*concluded*)

2.   The PRESIDENT announced that the Bahamas and Fiji, two of the nine States designated to form the Credentials Committee, would not be attending and that alternative States from the Latin American and Asian regions would have to be nominated. In accordance with rule 14 of the rules of procedure, he suggested that Barbados should replace the Bahamas and that Burma should replace Fiji.

3.   *It was so decided.*

4.   The PRESIDENT said that the membership of the Credentials Committee was therefore: Barbados; Burma; China; Ghana; Netherlands; Rwanda; Union of Soviet Socialist Republics; United States of America; and Venezuela. The Committee would be under the chairmanship of Venezuela.

AGENDA ITEM 7

General debate (*continued*)

5.   Mr. TRANT (World Food Council) made a statement.**

6.   Mr. KAFE (Comoros), President of the Commission of the Indian Ocean, made a statement.***

7.   Mr. CHOI (Republic of Korea) made a statement.***

8.   Mr. NAMAYA (Cameroon) made a statement.***

9.   Mr. PAROTTE (International Wheat Council) made a statement.****

10.   *Baron van Voorst tot Voorst (Netherlands), Vice-President, took the Chair.*

11.   Mr. ERBYNN (International Cocoa Organization) made a statement.****

12.   Mr. SOEPARTO (International Natural Rubber Organization) made a statement.****

13.   Mr. FREEZAILAH (International Tropical Timber Organization) made a statement.****

14.   *The President took the Chair.*

___

* Resumed from the 205th plenary meeting.
** For the summary of the statement, see part one above, sect. C.
*** For the summary of the statement, see part one above, sect. B.
**** For the summary of the statement, see part one above, sect. E.

15.   Mr. RICART (International Sugar Organization) made a statement.****

16.   Mr. SINGH (International Jute Organization) made a statement.****

The meeting rose at 1 p.m.

___

**** For the summary of the statement, see part one above, sect. E.

211th PLENARY MEETING

Friday, 24 July 1987, at 3.25 p.m.

President: Mr. Bernard T. G. CHIDZERO (Zimbabwe)

TD/SR.211

AGENDA ITEM 7

General debate (*continued*)

1.   Mr. JAYAWARDENA (United Nations University, World Institute for Development Economics Research) made a statement.*

2.   Mr. BUTLER (International Telecommunication Union) made a statement.**

3.   Mr. YOHAI (Colombia) made a statement.***

4.   Mr. AMARASIRI (Sri Lanka) made a statement.***

5.   Mr. LEORO FRANCO (Ecuador) made a statement.***

6.   Mr. PONGPANIT (Thailand) made a statement.***

7.   *Mr. Clark (United Kingdom), Vice-President, took the Chair.*

8.   Mr. DADZIE (Secretary-General of UNCTAD) expressed his deep gratitude to the delegation of Thailand, which had announced the forthcoming ratification by its Government of the Agreement Establishing the Common Fund for Commodities. He also welcomed the announcements by the Governments of Madagascar and Peru of the adoption of preparatory measures for the ratification of the Agreement.

9.   Mr. TOURE (Burkina Faso) made a statement.***

10.   Mr. GADO (Benin) made a statement.***

11.   *Mr. Orawika (Nigeria), Vice-President, took the Chair.*

12.   Mr. TÜREMEN (Economic Co-operation Organization) made a statement.****

13.   The PRESIDENT said that the text of the statement by the representative of ECLAC, who had to leave Geneva earlier than planned, would be issued as a Conference document.*****

The meeting rose at 6.15 p.m.

___

* For the summary of the statement, see part one above, sect. C.
** For the summary of the statement, see part one above, sect. D.
*** For the summary of the statement, see part one above, sect. B.
**** For the summary of the statement, see part one above, sect. E.
***** For the full text of the statement, see TD/L.311.

212th PLENARY MEETING

Monday, 27 July 1987, at 10 a.m.

President: Mr. Bernard T. G. CHIDZERO (Zimbabwe)

TD/SR.212

1. *In the absence of the President, Mr. Tabaković (Yugoslavia), Vice-President, took the Chair.*

Message received by the Conference

2. The PRESIDENT informed the Conference that a message had been received from Mrs. Corazon Aquino, President of the Republic of the Philippines.*

AGENDA ITEM 7

General debate (*continued*)

3. Mr. MACKI (Oman) made a statement.**

4. Crown Prince HASSAN BIN TALAL (Jordan) made a statement.***

5. Mr. KURANARI (Japan) made a statement.**

6. Mr. CATTANEI (Italy) made a statement.**

7. Mr. DJIN (Ghana) made a statement.**

8. Ms. GRADIN (Sweden) made a statement.**

9. Mr. VELAYATI (Islamic Republic of Iran) made a statement.**

10. Mr. CAMDESSUS (International Monetary Fund) made a statement.****

11. Mr. DE CROO (Belgium) made a statement.**

12. Mr. ESCOBAR CERDA (Chile) made a statement.**

The meeting rose at 1.20 p.m.

---

* Reproduced in volume I, annex IV.
** For the summary of the statement, see part one above, sect. B.
*** For the full text of the statement, see part one above, sect. A.
**** For the summary of the statement, see part one above, sect. D.

213th PLENARY MEETING

Monday, 27 July 1987, at 3.25 p.m.

President: Mr. Bernard T. G. CHIDZERO (Zimbabwe)

TD/SR.213

AGENDA ITEM 7

General debate (*continued*)

1. Mr. AL-SABAH (Kuwait) made a statement.*

2. Mr. AL-ASHTAL (Democratic Yemen) made a statement.*

---

* For the summary of the statement, see part one above, sect. B.

3. Mr. GOEBBELS (Luxembourg) made a statement.*

4. Mr. MWAKAWAGO (United Republic of Tanzania) made a statement.*

5. Mr. GAUCI (Malta) made a statement.*

6. Mr. OXLEY (Australia) made a statement.*

7. Mr. WARDHANA (Indonesia) made a statement.*

8. Mr. BLANCHARD (International Labour Office) made a statement.**

9. Mr. ALAOUI MDAGHRI (Organization of the Islamic Conference) made a statement.***

10. Mr. RAMPHAL (Commonwealth Secretariat) made a statement.***

11. Mr. SULEIMAN ABU-ALAA (Palestine Liberation Organization) speaking at the invitation of the President, pursuant to General Assembly resolution 3237 (XXIX), made a statement.****

The meeting rose at 6.35 p.m.

---

* For the summary of the statement, see part one above, sect. B.
** For the summary of the statement, see part one above, sect. D.
*** For the summary of the statement, see part one above, sect. E.
**** For the summary of the statement, see part one above, sect. G.

214th PLENARY MEETING

Tuesday, 28 July 1987, at 10 a.m.

President: Mr. Bernard T. G. CHIDZERO (Zimbabwe)

TD/SR.214

1. *In the absence of the President, Mr. Furulyas (Hungary), Vice-President, took the Chair.*

AGENDA ITEM 7

General debate (*continued*)

2. Mr. DUNKEL (GATT) made a statement.*

3. Mr. PAYE (Organization for Economic Co-operation and Development) made a statement.**

4. Mr. CLARK (United Kingdom) made a statement.***

5. Mr. STOLTENBERG (Norway) made a statement.***

6. Mr. CABRISAS RUÍZ (Cuba), speaking on behalf of the Group of 77, said that not only in the initial preparatory stages of the seventh session of the Conference and during its meetings, but also in the proposals it had made in the Havana Declaration, the Group of 77 had demonstrated an open and co-

---

* For the summary of the statement, see part one above, sect. D.
** For the summary of the statement, see part one above, sect. E.
*** For the summary of the statement, see part one above, sect. B.

operative spirit based on the desire to initiate serious negotiations with the developed countries on the policies and measures required to face the economic crisis and revitalize growth and development. However, with only a few exceptions, that constructive attitude had clearly not been matched by the industrialized countries. It was difficult to understand that, on issues such as financial resources, commodities, international trade and the problems faced by the LDCs, which were of interest to all UNCTAD member States, it had so far not been possible to agree on solutions that would, moreover, benefit the entire international community.

7.   UNCTAD was an institution born of the collective will of the international community. Its universal character, as well as its unique, cross-sectoral and interdisciplinary approach, made UNCTAD an important link in the chain of international economic relationships. It was therefore important to place at its disposal the means not only to continue carrying out its mandate, but also to tackle current and future problems more effectively. The Conference's seventh session provided a signal opportunity to strengthen multilateral co-operation for development and thereby to strengthen the institution of UNCTAD itself. The Group of 77 expected its partners, particularly those which had greater economic strength, to muster sufficient political will and seize that opportunity. It should not be forgotten that the results of the seventh session would have an important influence on the attitude of developing countries towards other international negotiations and activities.

8.   Mr. SHARNANH (Libyan Arab Jamahiriya) made a statement.***

9.   Mr. MUSTAFA (Egypt) made a statement.***

10.   Mr. HERNÁNDEZ CERVANTES (Mexico) made a statement.***

11.   Mr. GRINSPUN (Argentina) made a statement.***

12.   Mr. AKYOL (United Nations Council for Namibia), representing Namibia, made a statement.***

The meeting rose at 12.35 p.m.

_____

*** For the summary of the statement, see part one above, sect. B.

215th PLENARY MEETING

Tuesday, 28 July 1987, at 3.25 p.m.

President: Mr. Bernard T. G. CHIDZERO (Zimbabwe)

TD/SR.215

1.   *In the absence of the President, Mr. Faseeh-Ud-Din (Pakistan), Vice-President, took the Chair.*

Expression of sympathy to the people of Hormoine, Mozambique

2.   The PRESIDENT, speaking on behalf of the Conference and on his own behalf, expressed deepest condolences to the families of the 380 victims of the tragic incident at Hormoine in Mozambique.

General debate (*continued*)

3.   Mr. JOLLY (United Nations Children's Fund) made a statement.*

4.   Mr. BOZER (Turkey) made a statement.**

5.   Mr. GREAVES (Barbados) made a statement.**

6.   Mr. SALOLAINEN (Finland) made a statement.**

7.   Mr. EL SALEEM (Saudi Arabia) made a statement.**

8.   Mr. CALLEARY (Ireland) made a statement.**

9.   Mr. SANTOS MARTINS (Portugal) made a statement.**

10.   Mr. THEBE (Nepal) made a statement.**

11.   Mrs. FIGUERES de JIMÉNEZ (Costa Rica) made a statement.**

12.   Mr. VODUSEK (International Centre for Public Enterprises in Developing Countries and International Association of State Trading Organizations of Developing Countries) made a statement.***

The meeting rose at 6.20 p.m.

_____

* For the summary of the statement, see part one above, sect. C.
** For the summary of the statement, see part one above, sect. B.
*** For the summary of the statement, see part one above, sect. E.

216th PLENARY MEETING

Wednesday, 29 July 1987, at 10.15 a.m.

President: Mr. Bernard T. G. CHIDZERO (Zimbabwe)

TD/SR.216

1.   *In the absence of the President, Mr. Isaksen (Denmark), Vice-President, took the Chair.*

AGENDA ITEM 7

General debate (*continued*)

2.   Mr. PAPANTONIOU (Greece) made a statement.*

3.   Mr. PESHKOV (Byelorussian Soviet Socialist Republic) made a statement.*

4.   Mr. MINERBI (Israel) made a statement.*

5.   Mr. MICHAELIDES (Cyprus) made a statement.*

6.   Mr. ESPAÑA-SMITH (Bolivia) made a statement.*

7.   Mr. JALALLAR (Afghanistan) made a statement.*

_____

* For the summary of the statement, see part one above, sect. B.

8. Mr. AMADOU (Niger) made a statement.*

9. Mr. KAABACHI (Tunisia) made a statement.*

10. Mr. LEY-ELIAS (Peru) made a statement.*

11. Mr. DADZIE (Secretary-General of UNCTAD) said it had been most gratifying to hear that the Peruvian Government had confirmed its decision to deposit its instrument of ratification of the Agreement Establishing the Common Fund for Commodities and thanked the Governments of Costa Rica and Portugal for deciding to speed up their ratification procedures. The Costa Rican Government had already indicated its firm commitment to the Common Fund by signing the Agreement in July 1981, and the deposit of its instrument of ratification had been facilitated by the generous offer made by the Norwegian Government at the sixth session of the Conference. Peru's ratification would be the first to be deposited at Geneva on the occasion of the seventh session.

12. Portugal's decision meant that all 12 countries members of the EEC would soon become parties to the Agreement. Those 12 countries together would contribute a total of 20.75 per cent of the direct contributions capital and $92 million to the voluntary contributions announced for the Second Account.

13. Those decisions demonstrated that the three countries in question were deeply committed to multilateral co-operation for development and to the work of UNCTAD in the commodity area; they would contribute to the rapid entry into force of the Agreement.

The meeting rose at 12.25 p.m.

217th PLENARY MEETING

Wednesday, 29 July 1987, at 3.15 p.m.

President: Mr. Bernard T. G. CHIDZERO (Zimbabwe)

TD/SR.217

1. *In the absence of the President, Mr. Grinspun (Argentina), Vice-President, took the Chair.*

AGENDA ITEM 7

General debate (*continued*)

2. Mr. BANGEMANN (Federal Republic of Germany) made a statement.*

3. Mr. HINTEREGGER (Economic Commission for Europe) made a statement.**

4. Mr. ABDUL FATAH (Iraq) made a statement.*

5. Mr. GOODMAN (United States of America) made a statement.*

6. Mr. COSTA DE ABREU SODRE (Brazil) made a statement.*

---

* For the summary of the statement, see part one above, sect. B.
** For the summary of the statement, see part one above, sect. C.

7. Mr. DADZIE (Secretary-General of UNCTAD) said that earlier in the day Mr. Guinev, Deputy Minister for Foreign Trade of Bulgaria, had signed the Agreement Establishing the Common Fund for Commodities on behalf of his Government and had announced that it would shortly deposit its instruments of ratification or acceptance. Other States had indicated that they would deposit their instruments of ratification in the near future. That would bring to 101 the total number of countries which had ratified the Agreement, of which the share of capital represented by direct contributions would reach 66.95 per cent. The Agreement should, therefore, enter into force shortly, a fact which was most gratifying.

8. Mr. CHAVANES (France) made a statement.*

9. Mr. CABRISAS RUÍZ (Cuba) made a statement.*

10. *Mr. Martínez Cuenca (Nicaragua), Vice-President, took the Chair.*

11. Mr. HASSAN (Sudan) made a statement.*

12. Mr. TEMBE (Mozambique) made a statement.*

13. Mr. GUNARATNAM (Economic and Social Commission for Asia and the Pacific) made a statement.**

14. Mr. MAGAPATONA (African National Congress of South Africa), speaking at the invitation of the President, pursuant to General Assembly resolution 3280 (XXIX), made a statement.***

15. *Mr. Suazo (Dominican Republic), Vice-President, took the Chair.*

16. Mr. NAGASAKA (Asian-African Legal Consultative Committee) made a statement.****

The meeting rose at 7.10 p.m.

---

* For the summary of the statement, see part one above, sect. B.
** For the summary of the statement, see part one above, sect. C.
*** For the summary of the statement, see part one above, sect. G.
**** For the summary of the statement, see part one above, sect. F.

218th PLENARY MEETING

Thursday, 30 July 1987, at 10.15 a.m.

President: Mr. Bernard T. G. CHIDZERO (Zimbabwe)

TD/SR.218

1. *In the absence of the President, Mr. Kasrawi (Jordan), Vice-President, took the Chair.*

AGENDA ITEM 7

General debate (*continued*)

2. Mr. MITIAIEV (World Federation of Trade Unions) made a statement.*

---

* For the summary of the statement, see part one above, sect. F.

3.   Mr. KAYONDE (Uganda) made a statement.**

4.   Mr. MOKOROANE (Lesotho) made a statement.**

5.   Mr. VILLARREAL (Panama) made a statement.**

6.   U TIN TUN (Burma) made a statement.**

7.   *Mr. Touré (Senegal), Vice-President, took the Chair.*

8.   Mr. BIN HAJI MUNAP (Brunei Darussalam) made a statement.**

9.   Mr. M'BOW (United Nations Educational, Scientific and Cultural Organization) made a statement.***

10.   Mr. ABAL (Papua New Guinea) made a statement.**

11.   Mr. PALLARES-BUONAFINA (Guatemala) made a statement.**

12.   Mr. RANDRIAMASIVELO (Afro-Asian People's Solidarity Organization) made a statement.*

13.   Mr. BINGARADI (Arab Monetary Fund) made a statement.****

14.   Mrs. ASHWORTH (International Coalition for Development Action) made a statement.*

The meeting rose at 1.05 p.m.

---

* For the summary of the statement, see part one above, sect. F.
** For the summary of the statement, see part one above, sect. B.
*** For the summary of the statement, see part one above, sect. D.
**** For the summary of the statement, see part one above, sect. E.

219th PLENARY MEETING

Thursday, 30 July 1987, at 3.25 p.m.

President: Mr. Bernard T. G. CHIDZERO (Zimbabwe)

TD/SR.219

1.   *In the absence of the President, Mr. Ahmad (Bangladesh), Vice-President, took the Chair.*

AGENDA ITEM 7

General debate (*concluded*)

2.   Mr. LAURIJSSEN (International Confederation of Free Trade Unions) made a statement.*

3.   Mr. DIDI (Maldives) made a statement.**

4.   Mr. OZADOVSKI (Ukrainian Soviet Socialist Republic) made a statement.**

5.   Mr. NAFFAH (Lebanon) made a statement.**

6.   Monsignor MULLOR GARCÍA (Holy See) made a statement.**

---

* For the summary of the statement, see part one above, sect. F.
** For the summary of the statement, see part one above, sect. B.

7.   Mr. MFAXA (Pan Africanist Congress of Azania), speaking at the invitation of the President, pursuant to General Assembly resolution 3280 (XXIX), made a statement.***

8.   Mr. AMATHILA (South West Africa People's Organization), speaking at the invitation of the President, pursuant to General Assembly resolution 31/152, made a statement.***

9.   Mr. LE DAUPHIN (World Peace Council) made a statement.*

10.   Mr. ROBEL (World Confederation of Labour) made a statement.*

The meeting rose at 5.20 p.m.

---

* For the summary of the statement, see part one above, sect. F.
*** For the summary of the statement, see part one above, sect. G.

220th PLENARY MEETING

Monday, 3 August 1987, at 4 p.m.

President: Mr. Bernard T. G. CHIDZERO (Zimbabwe)

TD/SR.220

AGENDA ITEM 5

Credentials of representatives to the Conference (*concluded*):*
(*b*) Report of the Credentials Committee

1.   The PRESIDENT drew attention to the report of the Credentials Committee (TD/346). He announced that the Islamic Republic of Iran wished to be associated with the letter dated 9 July 1987 addressed to the Secretary-General of UNCTAD by the delegations of the Arab Group (TD/342). In that connection, he drew attention to communications addressed to the Secretary-General of UNCTAD from the head of the delegation of the Yemen Arab Republic (TD/349) and the Permanent Representative of Israel (TD/348).

2.   Mr. YAZDANI (Pakistan) associated his delegation with paragraph 7 of the report of the Credentials Committee for the reasons already stated by his delegation at the forty-first session of the General Assembly.

3.   Mr. GEGHMAN (Yemen), speaking on behalf of the Arab Group and as co-ordinator of the members of the League of Arab States, recalled that, in the letter dated 9 July 1987 addressed to the Secretary-General of UNCTAD (TD/342), the Arab delegations had expressed the reservations of their Governments concerning the credentials of the Israeli delegation to the seventh session of the Conference and had clearly explained their position. It would have been only fair to take those reservations duly into consideration and reflect them in the report of the Credentials Committee (TD/346), coming as they had from 21 delegations, or

---

* Resumed from the 210th meeting.

one seventh of the total number of delegations attending the Conference.

4. However, the report, which explicitly referred to the reservations of a number of delegations regarding the credentials of other delegations, as well as the objections to those reservations merely indicated in paragraph 4 that the Committee had before it TD/342 without specifying its contents. His delegation had therefore sent a telegram to the Secretary-General of UNCTAD and to the Chairman of the Credentials Committee conveying the surprise and concern of the Arab delegations at the disregard for their reservations and the reasons for them, namely Israel's violations of the Charter of the United Nations, of the principles of international law, of the rights of the Palestinian people and of the status of the city of Jerusalem.

5. The Arab delegations had then contacted the Chairman of the Credentials Committee, as well as a number of its members and representatives attending the Conference to inform them that they found it unacceptable that their reservations had been thus ignored.

6. That was still the position of the Arab delegations. But prompted by the desire to ensure the success of the Conference, in which the Arab delegations had participated sincerely and enthusiastically, his delegation simply asked that the reservations expressed appear in the record of the meeting and in the report of the Conference.[1]

7. Mr. DAOUDY (Syrian Arab Republic) agreed with the remarks of the representative of the Yemen concerning the report of the Credentials Committee. Paragraph 4 of that document, in addition to merely giving the symbol of the document containing the letter of the Arab delegations without indicating what it contained, also omitted the name of the signatories and avoided mentioning Israel or exposing it to criticism.

8. Most delegations probably could not recall the nature of a communication from its symbol alone, and paragraph 4 of the report therefore should have explained its content. Accordingly, the representative of Yemen had asked the Chairman and some members of the Credentials Committee why the reservations of the Arab delegations had only been referred to in such a vague fashion. In reply, he had been told that the matter was one of form, that the communication had been addressed not to the Committee itself, but to the Secretary-General of UNCTAD, and that the Committee had only learned of it upon its publication as a Conference document. The reply of the Arab delegations to those verbal excuses was unambiguous. The question was within the competence of the Committee, and as soon as it had become aware of it, the Committee could have done one of two things: it could either have mentioned the communication in its report, specifying its purpose and stating to whom it had been addressed, or it could have ignored it, while referring in the report to the formal reasons given for not indicating its content. The procedure followed had been both ambiguous and inappropriate. To say that the principle of consensus should apply in the drafting of the report was neither valid nor convincing. Moreover, any decision that the letter did not require a value judgement by the party to

whom it was addressed should have been left to the delegations concerned.

9. What had happened, however, was that one of the delegations on the Credentials Committee had insisted that there should be no mention either of Israel or of the Arab delegations that had reservations with regard to Israel's credentials. That was why the Committee had adopted such a vague text. While not wishing to incriminate the Chairman of the Committee, his delegation denounced the fact that the Committee had adopted the text of paragraph 4 for fear of a boycott or the withdrawal of the above-mentioned delegation, and drew attention to the regrettable precedent that that situation had created for the work of international conferences, particularly those involving the countries of the third world. On numerous occasions at the current session, when a group of delegations had sought to raise vital issues or delicate matters, it had been accused of attempting to politicize the Conference and introduce polemics that were out of place. When those same delegations had raised economic issues or the problem of the debt and the crisis in commodity prices, they had received replies such as the one made by the United States delegation, which had advised them to leave those questions to other bodies, because that would be better for all concerned.

10. Mr. KHERAD (Afghanistan) referred to the observations of the Chinese and United States delegations with regard to the Afghan delegation in paragraphs 7 and 9 of the report of the Credentials Committee. In response to those observations and the Pakistan representative's ill-intentioned remarks, his delegation reiterated its position as set forth during the forty-first session of the General Assembly.

11. Mr. KOENTARSO (Indonesia) recalled his delegation's position as expressed during the forty-first session of the General Assembly, and associated Indonesia with the position of the signatories of the letter distributed in TD/342.

12. Mr. EL MIRDASS (Saudi Arabia) supported the Yemeni representative's statement concerning the credentials of the Israeli delegation. With regard to the participation of the Afghan delegation in the seventh session of the Conference, he reaffirmed Saudi Arabia's position as recorded in the report of the Credentials Committee of the General Assembly at its forty-first session.

13. Mr. KHOK (Malaysia) endorsed the Yemeni representative's statement concerning the credentials of the Israeli delegation.

14. The PRESIDENT, after noting that all the preceding statements would be recorded in the report of the Conference, said that, if there were no objections, he would assume that the Conference adopted the draft resolution concerning the approval of the report of the Credentials Committee as it appeared on page 3 of TD/346.

15. *The draft resolution was adopted.*[2]

16. Mr. ELIAV (Israel) deeply regretted that the seventh session of the Conference should have been exploited for political reasons to create an unnecessary,

[1] See volume I, part three, sect. F.

[2] See Conference resolution 168 (VII).

unwarranted and unseemly confrontation under item 5. It was superfluous to add anything to his delegation's letter of 29 July 1987 (TD/348) replying to the slanderous attacks against Israel, especially as the Conference had just adopted without objection the report of the Credentials Committee.

17.   The PRESIDENT noted that the Conference had completed its consideration of agenda item 5.

AGENDA ITEM 8

Revitalizing development, growth and international trade, in a more predictable and supportive environment, through multilateral co-operation: assessment of relevant economic trends and of global structural change, and appropriate formulation of policies and measures, addressing key issues in the following interrelated areas:

(a) Resources for development, including financial and related monetary questions

Report of Committee I

18.   Mr. ABHYANKAR (India), Vice-Chairman of Committee I, introduced the report of the Committee (TD(VII)/C.I/L.2), as amended by TD/L.309, which reflected the debates at the Committee's closing meeting. On 27 July, the texts prepared by the Chairman of the Committee had been submitted to the President's Contact Group, in accordance with the decision taken by the Committee at its fourth session, together with a summary of the Committee's discussions. Following intensive consultations conducted under the auspices of the President of the Conference, an agreement had been reached on the important questions that had been placed before the Committee.

19.   The pertinent part of the draft consolidated text of the Conference (TD/L.316/Add.2) contained a number of elements that had a bearing on the way in which the international community treated the vital questions of debt, financial flows and related monetary questions, and also UNCTAD's own role in that key area of international co-operation for development.

20.   The PRESIDENT said that, as he saw no objections, he took it that the Conference had taken note of the report of Committee I on agenda item 8 (a) and that it decided to incorporate its substance, in an appropriate form, in the report of the Conference on its seventh session.

21.   *It was so decided.*[3]

(b) Commodities

Report of Committee II

22.   Mr. TENA GARCÍA (Spain), Rapporteur of Committee II, introduced the report of the Committee (TD(VII)/C.II/L.2), as amended by TD/L.306. The texts considered by the Committee had been submitted to the President's Contact Group. Thanks to the com-

petence of the Chairman of the Committee and the continuing co-operation of all concerned, negotiations conducted in the framework of the Committee had resulted in a broad consensus between the regional groups and China, on several questions connected with agenda item 8 (b). That consensus was reflected in part II B, entitled "Commodities" (TD/L.316/Add.3), of the draft consolidated text of the Conference.

23.   The PRESIDENT said that, as he saw no objections, he assumed that the Conference took note of the report of Committee II and decided to incorporate its substance, in an appropriate form, in the report of the Conference on its seventh session.

24.   *It was so decided.*[4]

25.   The PRESIDENT drew attention to the draft proposal submitted by Cuba on behalf of the States members of the Group of 77, by Poland on behalf of the States members of Group D and by the People's Republic of China, entitled "Commodities: other action by the Conference" (TD/L.317). The Contact Group had agreed to recommend that that text should be approved and incorporated in the first part of section III of the report. As he saw no objections, he took it that the Conference approved that recommendation.

26.   *It was so decided.*[5]

(c) International trade

Report of Committee III

27.   Mr. SEE (Singapore), Chairman of Committee III, introduced the report of the Committee (TD/(VII)/C.III/L.2), as amended by TD/L.303, which reflected the proceedings of the Committee at its closing meeting. At its last meeting, the Committee had decided to annex the documents listed in TD/L.303 to its report. It had also agreed to submit to the Contact Group the text prepared by its Chairman, on his own responsibility, and of the documents of the Conference relating to agenda item 8 (c).

28.   The PRESIDENT said that, as he saw no objections, he took it that the Conference took note of the report of Committee III and decided to incorporate its substance, in an appropriate form, in the report of the Conference on its seventh session.

29.   *It was so decided.*[6]

(d) Problems of the least developed countries, bearing in mind the Substantial New Programme of Action for the 1980s for the Least Developed Countries

Report of Committee IV

30.   Mr. HUSLID (Norway), Chairman of Committee IV, introduced the report of the Committee (TD(VII)/C.IV/L.2) as amended by TD/L.307. The

[3] See volume I, part two, paras. 130-147.

[4] *Ibid.*, paras. 148-161.
[5] For the text, see volume I, part one, sect. A.3.
[6] See volume I, part two, paras. 162-186.

Committee had held four plenary meetings and nine Contact Group meetings to consider draft proposals relating to agenda item 8 (*d*) on the basis of the Chairman's text and proposals submitted by the regional groups. At its closing meeting, the Committee had decided to refer the various draft texts containing proposals relating to agenda item 8 (*d*) for further negotiation by the President's Contact Group. Those drafts had subsequently been considered in informal meetings within the President's Contact Group, and a draft consolidated text had been drawn up. That text had been the subject of further intensive consultations and negotiations under the able chairmanship of Mrs. Anita Gradin. All those efforts had resulted in a consensus text that had been submitted to the Conference in TD/L. 316/Add.5. While expressing pleasure at the successful outcome of negotiations, it was regrettable that it had not been possible to achieve more substantive results with regard to the very acute problems of the LDCs. However, he noted with satisfaction the recommendation to hold a second United Nations conference in 1990 at the invitation of France on the problems of the LDCs.

31.   The PRESIDENT said that, as he saw no objections he took it that the Conference took note of the report of Committee IV and decided to incorporate its substance, in an appropriate form, in the report of the Conference on its seventh session.

32.   *It was so decided.*[7]

ADOPTION OF THE FINAL ACT OF UNCTAD VII

33.   The PRESIDENT introduced the draft consolidated text (TD/L.316 and Adds.1-6), with the agreed amendments, which had been elaborated in the President's Contact Group on the basis, *inter alia*, of the contributions of the Sessional Committees and represented the substantive outcome of the consideration of item 8. The Contact Group had recommended that the text should be entitled "Final Act of UNCTAD VII".

34.   Mr. HILL (Jamaica) recalled that, during the informal negotiations that had led to the finalization of the part of the consolidated text dealing with resources for development (TD/L.316/Add.2), his delegation had on two occasions indicated that the text as it finally emerged did not reflect the instructions his delegation had received, although at a certain stage it had appeared that it would do so. The day before, his delegation had conveyed to the Contact Group the elements that it wished to have appear in the Final Act, which would determine the direction of the future work of the UNCTAD secretariat and the international community in that area. As records had not been made of the meetings of the Contact Group, his delegation felt obliged to repeat itself.

35.   Jamaica—as well as perhaps more than 50 other countries—had not seen its concerns reflected fully in the text on resources. The policy statement by the representative of Jamaica at the opening of the Conference[8] had contained a section headed "Debt and

development: the experience of small middle-income developing countries", and set forth a proposal by the Prime Minister and Minister of Finance of Jamaica which sought to ensure that the developing debtor countries received the necessary and sufficient financial resources to enable them to grow out of the current crisis. The Jamaican proposal built on widely accepted growth and development oriented strategies, and the key element was the targeted reduction of debt ratios to sustainable levels over a programmed period, which would release sufficient disposable resources to achieve targeted growth. The Jamaican delegation believed that if that element were added to the debt strategy, it would allow all developing debtor countries to receive the external resources needed to achieve sustainable growth and thereby development.

36.   He recalled further that one of the documents emanating from the informal negotiations on 1 August 1987 contained a paragraph 4, which read as follows:

"The objective of bringing indebtedness and debt-servicing capacity into line with one another in the context of adjustment with growth can only be realized if all the parties concerned discharge their responsibilities. Such a process requires higher levels of external resources availabilities as investment and import volumes will need to grow substantially."

37.   In the informal negotiations he had stated that that text was acceptable to the Group of 77 and to his own delegation. Subsequently, in another informal setting in which he had not participated, that text had been changed, and the new version was to be found in paragraph 4 of the introduction to part II.A of the consolidated text (TD/L.316/Add.2).[9] His delegation therefore requested that the above text, emanating from the informal consultations—which at that stage had been an agreed text—should be reproduced as an additional formulation to that paragraph of the Final Act.

38.   Paragraph 6 of the introduction[10] stated that the debt problems of both those developing countries with lower per capita income, whose debt was mainly on concessional terms and largely with official creditors, and those with higher per capita income, whose debt was mainly on market terms and largely with commercial creditors were being addressed. He pointed out that the debt problems of those developing countries whose external debt was owed to bilateral and multilateral creditors but on non-concessional terms, and because of their limited access to private capital markets, was not being addressed. He found it difficult to associate himself fully with a text which clearly excluded that category of countries that was now clearly recognized to be in need of consideration by the international community. Although he was not proposing the amendment of that paragraph, he hoped that the problems of those developing debtor countries which relied primarily on bilateral and multilateral non-concessional flows, and with limited access to private capital markets, would be adequately addressed.

39.   In the circumstances, his delegation wished to propose two amendments to the section entitled "Debt problems" in TD/L.316/Add.2—one in paragraph 1 (*j*)

[7] *Ibid.*, paras 187-205.

[8] For a summary of the statement made at the 203rd plenary meeting, see part one above, sect. B.

[9] Paragraph 37 of the Final Act.

[10] Paragraph 39 of the Final Act.

and one in paragraph 1 (*l*).[11] Paragraph 1 (*j*) would be amended by the addition of the following sentence: "Creditor Governments are encouraged to apply flexibility in debt restructuring operations and in providing new loans to developing debtor countries which rely primarily on official and officially guaranteed loans." That amendment did not harm the balance of the text, in view of what was stated in paragraph 1 (*h*), which addressed the concerns of the heavily indebted countries whose borrowings on the private capital market endangered the international financial system. Just as it was appropriate for paragraph 1 (*h*) to be included in the Final Act, so it would be quite in order for the concerns of his delegation to be reflected.

40.   As to paragraph 1 (*l*), which stated that in respect of the ODA debt of poorer developing countries, developed donor countries which had not yet done so should implement in full Trade and Development Board resolution 165 (S-IX) of 11 March 1978, he proposed the addition of a sentence reading: "Consideration should be given to extending the coverage to include those developing debtor countries that rely primarily on loans from official sources and multilateral development banks."

41.   He observed that delegations from a wide cross-section had said that they understood and sympathized with the above amendments. Over the years, the Jamaican delegation had participated in the work of UNCTAD and had contributed to the elaboration of Board resolution 165 (S-IX) in an effort to seek better opportunities for all and not only for Jamaica. But it could not see why the pursuit of the general good should be at the expense of the national good. It had therefore submitted those amendments to the draft final act, and he read the Final Act as encompassing those sections which dealt with the assessment, the policies and measures, and the orientations for the future. For that reason, his delegation wished to see its concerns reflected specifically in the Final Act and not merely accommodated in another section of the report of the Conference.

42.   Mr. THUYSBAERT (Belgium), speaking on behalf of Group B, assured the representative of Jamaica that his statement would be examined with great care by the countries of Group B. The Jamaican proposals, however, referred to issues discussed during the Conference on which agreement had been difficult to reach. It would be both difficult and dangerous to reopen the discussion. Group B was therefore unable to accept the Jamaican delegation's proposals.

43.   Mr. HILL (Jamaica) drew attention to part III, paragraph 5, of TD/L.316/Add.2, which dealt with important and yet controversial issues. In order to differentiate between individual opinions and the general opinion, the wording used was "Most UNCTAD members reiterated . . ." or "Other UNCTAD members . . . continue to believe . . .". In the absence of a consensus on its proposals, his delegation would agree to the reformulation of the amendments it had proposed along those lines. It would even be prepared to accept such wording as "The opinion was expressed that . . .".

44.   Mr. THUYSBAERT (Belgium), speaking on behalf of Group B, said that despite its sympathy with the ideas of the Jamaican delegation, Group B had the impression that at the current stage, it would be dangerous and probably pointless to seek to amend a text that had been accepted by all representatives to the Conference. He therefore asked the representative of Jamaica not to press his draft amendments.

45.   Mr. HILL (Jamaica) said that the previous speaker was going a little too far in saying that such proposals, which as he knew enjoyed the support of many delegations, were both dangerous and pointless. The fact was that, as long as agreement was not reached in plenary meeting, there was no agreement. In view of the negotiations and their conduct, representatives were free to make their views known since the questions at issue were of great importance for many countries. His delegation did not wish to hamper the adoption by consensus of the Final Act, but it was also loath to see a practice established that had the effect of disregarding the concerns of certain delegations and at the same time giving preference to the views of delegations that carried greater economic weight.

46.   He therefore proposed that the Final Act should indicate, in some way or other, that the questions he had mentioned had been raised. That might be done by means of an asterisk, referring to the text of his statement in the report of the Conference.

47.   Mr. THUYSBAERT (Belgium), speaking on behalf of Group B, said that every delegation could obviously express its views on the subject and suggest amendments until a text was adopted. However, the procedure agreed upon in the present case made it clear that the ideas to be presented at the closing meeting were to be decided upon at an earlier meeting of the Contact Group. In order to preserve what had been achieved jointly, it would be better not to introduce any new ideas into the text of the Final Act. It was futile to reopen the discussion which might well lead to the same conclusions as those in the Final Act. He did not object to the inclusion of the Jamaican representative's statement at an appropriate place in the report of the Conference providing that the Final Act was not thereby amended in any way.

48.   The PRESIDENT said he did not interpret the position adopted by the representative of Jamaica as being so inflexible that it might hold up the work of the Conference. He was sure that a suitable place could be found for the Jamaican statement in the report of the Conference. If there were no objections, a reference to it would also be included in the index to observations and reservations in part one, section IV, of the report.

49.   *It was so decided.*[12]

50.   The PRESIDENT announced that the proposals presented by Cuba on behalf of the States members of the Group of 77 (TD/L.312 to 314), as well as the proposal submitted by Bangladesh on behalf of the same States (TD(VII)/C.IV/L.1) had been withdrawn.

51.   The PRESIDENT said that, as he saw no objections, he took it that the Conference adopted in its entirety the text of the Final Act of UNCTAD VII, as it

---

[11] Paragraphs 44 (*j*) and (*l*) of the Final Act.

[12] See volume I, part one, sect. B, and part two, paras. 13-17 and 20.

appeared in TD/L.316 and Add.1-6, together with the agreed amendments he had read out.

52. *It was so decided.*[13]

Statements made on the adoption of the Final Act

53. Mr. CABRISAS RUÍZ (Cuba), speaking on behalf of the States members of the Group of 77, observed that the seventh session of the Conference had been the occasion of a major development: the decisive progress made towards the entry into force of the Agreement Establishing the Common Fund for Commodities. The Group of 77 took note with deep appreciation of the action taken by Peru to deposit its instrument of ratification in Geneva and by the Union of Soviet Socialist Republics, Côte d'Ivoire and Bulgaria to sign the Agreement, and of their firm intention to ratify it very soon, as well as of the announcements by Madagascar that it had completed its ratification procedure and by Costa Rica, Portugal and Thailand of their intention to deposit their instruments of ratification in the very near future. The Group of 77 wished to express its gratitude to Norway and to States members of OPEC for undertaking to provide the contributions on behalf of the LDCs.

54. Those important decisions were of great political significance. Those actions, when completed, would indeed fulfil the remaining condition for the entry into force of the Agreement. They meant that the long-awaited entry into force of the Agreement had practically become a reality. That would represent advancement towards the aims and objectives of the Integrated Programme for Commodities. It was a concrete step forward which augured well for a brighter future for international co-operation in the field of commodities.

55. The Group of 77 wished to express once again its deep appreciation to all those countries which had, before the beginning of the Conference and, for many of them, a number of years earlier, already deposited their respective instruments of ratification, acceptance or approval of the Agreement.

56. The Group of 77 reaffirmed its commitment to the Common Fund and to its principles and objectives and emphasized its importance for the developing countries. It therefore appealed to all those countries which had not yet joined the Agreement to do so as a matter of priority. It also appealed to those countries which had signed and/or ratified the Agreement to accelerate the implementation of their commitment to the Fund so that it could start its operations as soon as possible.

57. When the Agreement Establishing the Common Fund came into force, the Group of 77 hoped that the Secretary-General of UNCTAD would proceed as soon as possible with the mandate given to him under paragraph 2 (*b*) of resolution 2 (IV) of 27 June 1980, adopted by the United Nations Negotiating Conference on a Common Fund under the Integrated Programme for Commodities,[14] namely, to convene the first annual meeting of the Governing Council of the Fund.

58. Mr. THUYSBAERT (Belgium), speaking on behalf of the States members of Group B, said that his Group welcomed the adoption of the Final Act. It appreciated the intensive efforts which had been devoted to the assessment process both before and during the Conference. The fact that those efforts had resulted in a common assessment would be widely welcomed. Naturally, each delegation had its own perceptions, and not all would agree with every word of the assessment. However, it must be recognized that that was all part of an important process leading to better understanding and co-operation in the field of development.

59. He wished to make some observations on issues to which Group B attached particular importance. First, Group B would like to underscore the importance of the Uruguay Round of MTNs for all participants, and it went without saying that the text just adopted in no way impinged on the letter or spirit of the Punta del Este Declaration. The central role of the Uruguay Round in addressing the major problems in international trade had been clearly brought out during the Conference. The improvement and strengthening of the open multilateral trading system and the further liberalization of trade were objectives all shared. In that regard, Group B attached great importance to the continuation of substantive progress, achieved through the active participation of all participants, with a view to a successful and comprehensive conclusion to the negotiations within the agreed time-frame.

60. Group B welcomed the increasing recognition of the vital relationship between structural adjustment and growth and development, for all countries. In that regard, his Group fully supported the continuation of the Trade and Development Board's annual review of protectionism and structural adjustment in the agriculture, manufactures and services sectors, under its existing mandate, but with further improvement in the quality of analysis and a wider and more balanced coverage of regional groups.

61. Finally, having agreed to accept the text in section II.C (TD/L.316/Add.4), on international trade, Group B wished to express, in particular, its reservation on paragraph 19[15] relating to UNCTAD's work on services.

62. Its concern was based on its experience with the use to which work mandated to the UNCTAD secretariat had been put, and with the extent to which that could be used either to delay or to impede the progress and process of negotiations on trade in services in the Uruguay Round. Group B's concerns were justified by its wish to preserve the process of negotiations in the Uruguay Round. In that context, Group B encouraged all participants in the MTNs to participate actively and constructively in those negotiations.

63. Group B attached importance to the completion of the work in the existing mandate as contained in Board decision 309 (XXX) of 29 March 1985, on services, particularly the national studies.

64. Group B hoped that that message would be understood as a positive effort on its part to advance work in the area.

---

[13] See volume I, part one, sect. A.1.

[14] See the report of the Negotiating Conference on its fourth session (TD/IPC/CF/CONF/26), annex.

---

[15] Paragraph 105 (19) of the Final Act.

65. Mr. CHRISPEELS (Legal Adviser) stated that the reservation placed on record by the representative of Belgium did not change the legal status of the text, which stood adopted by the Conference. Nor did the reservation modify the legal basis for action by UNCTAD under paragraph 19.[15]

66. The PRESIDENT said that that was the common understanding.

67. Mr. FREYBERG (Poland), speaking on behalf of the States members of Group D and of Mongolia, said that, in a spirit of realism, dialogue and responsibility for the future of the world economy, the Conference had been trying to find agreements and joint constructive actions or appropriate policies and measures to benefit the entire international community.

68. Group D welcomed the fact that the Conference had reached a consensus on the Final Act. It found it balanced, but was of the opinion that the issue of international economic security, together with confidence-building measures in the economic field, should remain on the agenda of UNCTAD activities.

69. The comprehensive attitude of the Group D countries on all important issues on the agenda was fully presented in TD/333 and had been expressed on various occasions during the general debate and in the Sessional Committees.

70. It was Group D's firm conviction that there was a close relationship between disarmament and development and that all concrete steps on the way to disarmament should be linked with reallocating a portion of the resources to be released to meet the needs of economic and social progress of all countries, in particular developing ones.

71. He regretted to note that that important problem, mentioned on so many occasions during the general debate by various heads of delegation, was not adequately reflected in the operative part of the Final Act of the Conference. UNCTAD had a mandate in that field, which should be fully implemented.

72. Group D agreed that the removal of discriminatory restraints on exports was essential for liberalization. It agreed also that the export interests of developing countries should in particular be taken into account. It was his Group's understanding that such liberalization should be implemented in strict compliance with the respective principles of international trade. With regard to the question of economic and trade sanctions, Group D's position was that they should not be imposed for non-economic reasons, except in the case of those based on General Assembly resolutions.

73. He confirmed Group D's well-known position of principle on fixed targets for ODA, Board resolution 165 (S-IX), as well as on the interpretation of the words "developed countries", and "donor countries". That position had been expressed upon the adoption by the General Assembly of the International Development Strategy for the Third United Nations Development Decade and of the Substantial New Programme of Action for the 1980s for the Least Developed Countries and had been reiterated on several occasions. The socialist countries of Group D would continue strengthening their trade, economic and technical co-operation with developing countries with the aim of promoting their national, social and economic development and assisting them in overcoming economic underdevelopment.

74. Concerning the orientations for the future work of UNCTAD, Group D proceeded from the understanding that UNCTAD's future activities should cover all the main fields of its work programme in accordance with its mandate as contained in General Assembly resolution 1995 (XIX).

75. Mr. ENGEL (United States of America) said that his delegation considered section II.A, on debt, resources and related issues, on balance to be a constructive statement. However, there was one portion he wished to comment on. The United States believed that the international economic environment, described in paragraph 7[16] and as characterized elsewhere in the Conference text, had been substantially more positive than was stated in the paper. Industrial countries' growth had been sustained for five years, market access had been improved, and interest rates had fallen. Those factors had had a positive and helpful influence on the economic prospects of developing countries. He expressed appreciation for the constructive and co-operative efforts and leadership which had resulted in the successful outcome on that item of the agenda.

76. The United States had worked hard throughout the session to reach agreement where possible on issues of substance, and where differences persisted, had sought to have those differences recorded in the text when possible. In the area of commodities (section II.B, TD/L.316/Add.3), he recalled that the United States had voted against Conference resolution 125 (V), which commissioned a study of a new complementary financing facility, as well as resolution 157 (VI), which called for the establishment of an expert group. The United States did not recognize that UNCTAD had a mandate to study and make recommendations on compensatory financing and, as a result, had not and would not participate in the discussions of the expert group.

77. With respect to the conclusions reached by the Conference in section II.C (TD/L.316/Add.4), on international trade, the United States wished to express its appreciation to those who had participated constructively throughout the Conference on the important issues involved. It was because of such co-operation that the United States had chosen, after careful consideration, to join the consensus on that section. In so doing, it wished to make the following points concerning the text.

78. First, it believed that the agreement in no way compromised or reinterpreted the commitments reached in Punta del Este with trading partners on the Uruguay Round of MTNs, which it hoped would be concluded rapidly and with the active and constructive participation of the parties involved.

79. Secondly, with respect to paragraph 19[17] on services, the United States fully supported the declaration made on behalf of Group B and the reservation expressed. Its decision to agree to that particular text had

_____

[16] Paragraph 40 of the Final Act.
[17] Paragraph 105 (19) of the Final Act.

not been easy, none the less, it had joined the consensus in order to demonstrate its constructive attitude, which it hoped was genuinely shared by all concerned. Agreement to the text should in no way be construed as extending an exclusive role to UNCTAD for the analysis of the implications for development of trade in services. The complexity of the issues involved required analysis by many interested in trade in services. The United States did not expect that the agreement would be used to undermine the process nor impede rapid progress in the negotiations on trade in services under way in the Uruguay Round.

80. Finally, with respect to paragraph 23[18] regarding the international trading system, the United States maintained the position that any review or study by the Trade and Development Board should be of a general character and should not be aimed at establishing a new set of rules for international trade.

81. With respect to the LDCs, and in particular with respect to paragraph 12 (section II.D, TD/L.316/Add.5)[19] of that portion of the Final Act regarding ODA targets established in the Substantial New Programme of Action, he recalled the position of the United States on that issue, which had been most recently expressed at the 1985 mid-term review of the Substantial New Programme of Action following the adoption of the report of that Conference.[20]

82. Mr. HUTTON (United Kingdom) said that his Government had throughout been working for a positive outcome to the Conference which would address the very real problems facing developing countries and contribute practically to their solution. Accordingly, it could accept the single final outcome document as a broad statement of the consensus which had been reached. There was, however, a point concerning the Common Fund on which he wished to make the position of his Government clear.

83. As the Minister for Trade of the United Kingdom had said in his statement at the 214th plenary meeting of the Conference, on 28 July,[21] the United Kingdom recognized the seriousness of the problems facing a number of developing countries whose economies were dependent upon the production of certain primary commodities. That was an area to which the United Kingdom had pledged resources both in its bilateral aid programme and through its support for activity by the international institutions. But, as the Minister had also underscored, the solution to the decline in commodity prices in real terms since the 1950s was not to attempt to rig the market or to distort consumer choice. It must lie in the acceptance of change and the readiness to adapt to market trends.

84. Those considerations were especially relevant given the prospect that the Common Fund would enter into force in the foreseeable future. It had been 10 years since the negotiations establishing the Fund had begun. Since then there had been major changes in world com-

modity markets. The United Kingdom believed that it was important to reflect very carefully on the lessons learned from experience in that period. In the light of those changes, States must ask themselves how far the Common Fund could still fulfil the tasks originally envisaged for it.

85. The United Kingdom believed that it was highly desirable that ways should be found in which those aspects could be examined thoroughly before steps were taken to bring the Common Fund into operation.

86. Mr. CABRISAS RUÍZ (Cuba), speaking on behalf of the States members of the Group of 77, referring to economic measures applied for political reasons in order to exert economic and political coercion, stated that the Group of 77 wished to reaffirm its full respect for the inalienable right of all States to ensure their economic and social development and to exercise their sovereign choice in deciding on their economic and social systems, as well as to promote the well-being of their peoples in accordance with national economic plans and policies. It was not acceptable that that right should be restricted by the arbitrary economic measures which other States imposed in order to exert economic and political coercion. They did so to achieve aims which were incompatible with the United Nations Charter and which were a violation both of bilateral and multilateral commitments entered into and of international law. In demanding the revocation of those measures of economic aggression, the Group of 77 reaffirmed its full support for, and solidarity with, the peoples victims of a policy that was directed to retarding their economic development and social welfare.

AGENDA ITEM 9

Other business

Report of the Trade and Development Board

87. The PRESIDENT, drawing attention to the note by the secretariat on the report of the Trade and Development Board (TD/332), said that the Board's report to the seventh session of the Conference consisted of its reports to the General Assembly on the sessions it had held since the sixth session of the Conference. If there were no objections, he would take it that the Conference took note of those documents.

88. *It was so decided.*

Economic situation in the occupied Palestinian territories

89. The PRESIDENT drew attention to a draft resolution on the economic situation in the occupied Palestinian territories, submitted by Cuba on behalf of the Group of 77 (TD/L.295).

90. Mr. ELIAV (Israel) said that draft resolution TD/L.295, which was replete with falsifications, was but yet another exercise of the political and propaganda campaign waged incessantly against Israel by Arab States ever since its inception. It came on the heels of a futile attempt to challenge the credentials of his delega-

---

[18] Paragraph 105 (23) of the Final Act.

[19] Paragraph 117 of the Final Act.

[20] See *Official Records of the Trade and Development Board, Thirty-second Session, Annexes*, agenda item 7, document TD/B/1078, paras. 220-223.

[21] For a summary of the statement, see part one above, sect. B.

tion and had nothing to do with the subject-matters of the Conference. It was the only political resolution, in fact the only resolution at all regarding a specific issue, to be put to the vote. Other resolutions had been adopted at Havana, but they had apparently got lost *en route*. Thus, although the United Nations was based on the principle of sovereign equality enshrined in the Charter, it appeared, again, that there was one cause which, because of the manipulation of an automatic majority, was more equal than others, namely, the singling out of Israel for blame through diplomatic pressure and economic blackmail.

91. The General Assembly might decide, upon the recommendation of the Committee of Eighteen that unnecessary proceedings should be curtailed and the work of United Nations bodies streamlined, the Secretary-General might call for the avoidance of unnecessary confrontation, but a plethora of repetitious resolutions directed against Israel continued blithely to emanate from the Organization, at the behest of those who sought thereby to serve their terrorist purposes. Meetings of the Group of 77 and the non-aligned countries were cynically abused in order to impose those texts, as was the case with the current draft.

92. At the current session, the major problems besetting world trade and development were thus put aside for the all-important goal of Israel's detractors to extract their customary pound of political flesh. Ultimately, the member States interested in the solution of those problems would be the real losers of that cynical squandering of resources, time and energy. The draft would hurt the cause of the Conference rather than that of the State of Israel. Public opinion would not fail to note that regrettable diversion, drawing its own conclusions on the validity and relevance of UNCTAD's work, as had indeed already been the case in the local press.

93. As for the real economic and commercial situation in the territories under Israeli administration, the facts were very different from the situation portrayed in the draft. Israel had submitted full data in proceedings in the General Assembly, the Economic and Social Council, Habitat, UNEP, ILO and WHO and in the Israeli statement in the general debate (216th meeting).[22] The records were there for everybody who wished to know the true facts. The GNP in the territories under Israeli administration had increased by about 400 per cent since 1967, private and public construction had risen 900 per cent and the value of exported goods had increased almost twelvefold, namely, from $34 million to $395 million. In that period, close to 2,500 industrial plants and workshops had been established, the industrial workforce had doubled, and the unemployment rate had dropped from 10 to 3 per cent, while private consumption had risen 230 per cent. All that was notwithstanding the 45 per cent increase in the population since 1967.

94. In its continuing endeavour to improve the living conditions and promote the economy of the territories, Israel more than welcomed international assistance. UNDP was carrying out a most effective

programme in that respect, comprising 13 fully implemented projects and 20 projects under implementation, involving the expenditure $16.6 million.

95. It would be much more helpful for the inhabitants of the territories if international bodies like UNCTAD were called upon to do more in practice to assist in their economic growth, rather than to host sterile debates and pass unnecessary and unwarranted resolutions. That applied even more so to the wealthy Arab States, which really could at least finance the projects for which UNDP was seeking funds (see DP/1987/23).

96. Consequently, instead of belabouring a non-problem of difficulties regarding the export of goods from the territories, it would be much more appropriate to take steps to abolish import restrictions regarding those goods in various countries, partly because of illegal boycott practices. Instead of referring to a white-elephant project of a commercial seaport, conceived for political purposes only, it would be much more advisable to mobilize funds for a fishing port at the same location. Instead of yet another Palestinian unit at UNCTAD, in addition to an ever-growing department at Headquarters, it would be much better to spend the money involved in one of the many projects in agriculture, industry, housing, health and infrastructure in the territories, which still awaited financing.

97. It was highly incongruous, in a conference aiming at human betterment through the promotion of trade and development, to call for co-operation with those whose trade was inhuman terrorism and whose main development activity was to develop air piracy and whose production line included the preparation of explosives to be used in market places, public transport, beaches, restaurants, schools and synagogues.

98. He called upon all member States wishing to promote the real goals of UNCTAD to reject the transparent attempt to distort and politicize the work of the Conference and to vote against the draft.

99. Mr. ABU-KOASH (Observer for the Palestine Liberation Organization), speaking in accordance with General Assembly resolution 3237 (XXIX), said that draft resolution TD/L.295 reflected the views of the Group of 77. He did not consider the statement by the Israeli delegation as directly related to his organization or the Arab Group but rather as an insult to the Group of 77 as a whole. The Israeli delegation should stop preaching wisdom and pretending innocence as if it were not aware of the nature of the Conference. The draft resolution concerned UNCTAD's work, the economy of the occupied Palestinian territories and, particularly, the trade sector. He challenged the Israeli delegation to say why it had blocked the implementation of a seaport in occupied Gaza. Surely the construction of a seaport was related to the question of trade? Such was the sort of assistance the Palestinian people was receiving under Israeli occupation. He also asked, with reference to the decision of the European Community agreeing to give Palestinian products access to the EEC market on a preferential basis because the EEC was very much concerned at the deteriorating economic conditions in the occupied Palestinian territories, as were the other countries of the world, why Israel had stopped Palestinian

---

[22] *Idem.*

products from being exported to the European Community. Was that an act of assistance to the Palestinian people? Was it a logical or an illogical act? International conferences had become used to false statements by the Israeli delegation, which claimed that occupation brought economic development and prosperity. Why, then, had the Conference spent long nights discussing the situation of the world economy and why did the Israeli delegation not submit a resolution advising all delegations to welcome Israeli occupation in order to rid the whole world of deteriorating economic conditions? Recalling the Arabic proverb that he who had not could not give, he said that the Israeli economy was suffering from an extremely critical crisis. It had an external debt of over $22 billion and over $23 billion of internal debt. That was in addition to inflation and a balance-of-payments deficit, and despite the aid given by the United States, which exceeded $4 billion annually.

100. That money was spent on military adventures against the Arab Nation, including the Palestinian people, and for the construction of colonial settlements in the occupied Palestinian territories. The Palestine Liberation Organization was no match for Israeli propagandists but, whatever the fine words used to conceal them, the facts spoke for themselves. There could be no economic development or growth under Israeli occupation. The Israeli delegation had referred to United Nations reports. He noted, however, that such reports described a deteriorating situation. He challenged the Israeli delegation to address itself to the resolution and say why Israel did not agree to implement the EEC decision or agree to the building of a seaport. The Palestinians did not want Israel or Israeli occupation. They wanted to be free from any occupation. He noted that the President was from Zimbabwe, a country which had suffered from alien colonial occupation. He expressed confidence that the Palestinians would one day be full members of UNCTAD, despite the intentions of the Israeli delegation, which must know that the era of colonialism was long past. The time would come for Palestine and South Africa to join the ranks of the independent States.

101. He pointed out that draft resolution TD/L.295 was wholly related to trade matters and appeals for improvement of the conditions of people living under occupation, and was confident that all would support it.

102. Mr. DAOUDY (Syrian Arab Republic) observed that the Israeli delegation's references to happiness and prosperity and to the so-called terrestrial paradise that existed in the occupied Palestinian and Syrian territories created a certain degree of remorse and envy because the rest of the world had been unable to avail itself of such prosperity.

103. The Conference had been told by the Israeli delegation that it was discussing problems which did not exist and, in that connection, he recalled that Mrs. Golda Meier and Mr. Abba Eban had both asserted that the Palestinian people did not exist. Yet when the Israelis wished to kill Palestinians they knew where to find them. If the occupied Palestinian and Arab territories were such a terrestrial paradise, why had the Israeli authorities prevented the United Nations mission entrusted with investigating Israeli practices with regard

to violations of human rights, and the mission inquiring into the health conditions in the occupied territories, from visiting those territories? Why had representatives of churches, of jurists, of legal organizations, and all those who defended and protected human rights been forbidden access to those occupied territories which, according to the Israeli delegate, enjoyed such quality of life? The situation in the occupied territories resembled only what was experienced in South Africa and Namibia at the hands of the *apartheid* régime. That was why those two régimes, the Israeli and the South African, were in sympathy, and why they collaborated, sowed discord and sought to conclude political, military and economic treaties. Those régimes, which defied the Charter of the United Nations and its resolutions, continued to benefit from the support of the greatest Power of the world, namely, the United States.

104. Mr. ENGEL (United States of America) requested a roll-call vote on draft resolution TD/L.295.

105. Mr. DAOUDY (Syrian Arab Republic) supported the United States representative's request.

106. Mr. SACCO (Malta) announced that his delegation would not participate in the vote because, although it supported the attainment by the Palestinian people of their legitimate rights, his delegation considered that the seventh session of the Conference was not the proper forum in which to pursue a purpose that should rather be taken up in the Committee on the Exercise of the Inalienable Rights of the Palestinian People, at the General Assembly and in the Security Council, where Malta would continue to work for the attainment of the Palestinian rights.

107. Mr. DAOUDY (Syrian Arab Republic), speaking on a point of order, objected that, as the vote had started, the representative of Malta had no right to speak.

108. The PRESIDENT considered that the statement by the representative of the Syrian Arab Republic was very pertinent. He himself had thought that the representative of Malta intended to speak in explanation of vote, which he believed was permissible.

109. Mr. CHRISPEELS (Legal Adviser) stated that the representative of Malta had asked for the floor to explain his position on the draft resolution. Once the vote had started, it should not be interrupted, and all other explanations of vote or position should be made after the voting was completed and the result announced. However, to explain positions and votes before the voting had begun was perfectly permissible.

110. *The vote was taken by roll call.*

111. *Suriname, having been drawn by lot by the Secretary of the Conference, was called upon to vote first.*

112. *In favour*: Afghanistan, Algeria, Argentina, Bahrain, Bangladesh, Benin, Bhutan, Bolivia, Botswana, Brazil, Bulgaria, Burma, Burundi, Byelorussian Soviet Socialist Republic, China, Colombia, Comoros, Cuba, Cyprus, Czechoslovakia, Democratic Kampuchea, Democratic People's Republic of Korea, Democratic Yemen, Ecuador, Egypt, Ethiopia, Gabon, German Democratic Republic, Ghana, Hungary, India, Indonesia, Iran (Islamic Republic of), Iraq, Jamaica,

Jordan, Kenya, Kuwait, Lebanon, Libyan Arab Jamahiriya, Madagascar, Malaysia, Mexico, Mongolia, Morocco, Mozambique, Nepal, Nicaragua, Niger, Nigeria, Oman, Pakistan, Philippines, Poland, Qatar, Republic of Korea, Romania, Rwanda, Saudi Arabia, Senegal, Singapore, Somalia, Sri Lanka, Sudan, Syrian Arab Republic, Thailand, Togo, Trinidad and Tobago, Tunisia, Turkey, Ukrainian Soviet Socialist Republic, Union of Soviet Socialist Republics, United Arab Emirates, United Republic of Tanzania, Venezuela, Viet Nam, Yemen, Yugoslavia, Zaire, Zimbabwe.

Against: Israel, United States of America.

Abstaining: Australia, Austria, Belgium, Cameroon, Canada, Costa Rica, Côte d'Ivoire, Denmark, El Salvador, Finland, France, Germany, Federal Republic of, Greece, Guatemala, Honduras, Ireland, Italy, Japan, Liechtenstein, Luxembourg, Netherlands, New Zealand, Norway, Panama, Paraguay, Peru, Portugal, Spain, Sweden, Switzerland, United Kingdom of Great Britain and Northern Ireland, Uruguay.

113. *Draft resolution TD/L.295 was adopted by 80 votes to 2, with 32 abstentions.*[23]

114. Mr. ENGEL (United States of America), speaking in explanation of vote after the vote, stated that his delegation wished to register its profound dismay at the introduction and subsequent vote on draft resolution TD/L.295, and at the fact that such a resolution had found its way into a conference on trade and development. It had voted against its adoption because it dealt with a subject-matter which had absolutely no relevance to the purposes of the seventh session of the Conference. Had there been any question about that, certain of the statements made before the vote should have removed any doubts. The contribution that the seventh session of the Conference had made in finding common understandings on the fundamental issues affecting the world economy had now been flawed. Consequently, UNCTAD's credibility as an ongoing forum for serious economic and development discussions, perhaps its single most precious asset, must now be called into question. All of that because a few countries could not resist using UNCTAD, a forum so potentially important to so many developing countries, to score cheap political points. The United States delegation hesitated to speculate on the implications for the future of UNCTAD of the sorry effort to politicize the session.

115. Mr. ISAKSEN (Denmark), speaking on behalf of the European Economic Community and its member States, stated that they had abstained in the vote on TD/L.295. The EEC found that the resolution went beyond the agreed agenda for the session. Its vote should in no way be taken as an indication of the views of the Governments of the States members of the EEC on the substantive issue. Those views had already been fully explained in the General Assembly, where the question was regularly dealt with.

116. Mr. CAMBITSIS (Greece) said that his delegation had joined the other States members of the European Community concerning draft resolution TD/L.295, for it found the reasons put forward in the Community statement legitimate. That, however, did

not imply any change in substance of the position taken by the Greek Government on the Palestine issue in international forums as well as in the European Community, where it had been recently decided to strengthen the economic ties with the Palestinian people in the Gaza Strip and the West Bank.

117. Mr. RIVADENEIRA (Ecuador) wished to place clearly on record that, in voting in favour of draft resolution TD/L.295, his delegation did so in keeping with an unswerving principle of the international policy of Ecuador regarding the rejection of occupation and the acquisition of territories by force. The Government of Ecuador also considered that the occupation of those territories caused serious economic and social problems for the Palestinian population.

118. Mr. FREYBERG (Poland), speaking on behalf of the States members of Group D and of Mongolia, said that the delegations of his Group and Mongolia had voted in favour of draft resolution TD/L.295. They attached great importance to the socio-economic aspects of the Middle East problem, which required a speedy, just, equitable and comprehensive settlement. They had strongly and consistently supported the inalienable rights of the Palestinian people to self-determination, to national independence and sovereignty and the right to establish its own independent State. It was their conviction that the path to a comprehensive settlement of the Middle East problem lay through the collective efforts of all interested parties, including the Palestine Liberation Organization, the sole authentic representative of the Palestinian people. They would in future continue to support UNCTAD activities that corresponded to those purposes in the socio-economic aspects of the Middle East situation.

119. Mr. ABU-KOASH (Observer for the Palestine Liberation Organization), speaking in accordance with General Assembly resolution 3237 (XXIX), said that he would ignore completely certain remarks made after the vote which, worthless as they were, were not worthy even of an attempt to answer them.

120. He expressed deep gratitude to all the countries which had supported draft resolution TD/L.295. His organization understood the position of the countries which had abstained, although he did not agree with it, and hoped that they would in future be able to support such resolutions. He respected the right of Malta as a sovereign State to take any action it chose; the close relationship between the people of Palestine and the people of Malta would in no way be affected, and he acknowledged the strong support of the people of Malta for the Palestinian people.

121. Mr. ESPAÑA-SMITH (Bolivia) said that his delegation had voted in favour of the draft resolution because Bolivia rejected the occupation and annexation of territories by force. At the same time, he expressed Bolivia's fervent wish for an early and permanent peace in the Middle East.

Review of the calendar of meetings

122. The PRESIDENT said that, during the second part of its thirty-third session, the Trade and Develop-

---

[23] See Conference resolution 169 (VII).

ment Board had approved a revised calendar of meetings for the remainder of 1987, which the Informal Group had reviewed in accordance with the decisions and recommendations of the Conference. As he saw no objections, he took it that the Conference adopted the calendar that appeared in the note by the secretariat (TD/(VII)/CRP.2 and Add.1).

123.   *It was so decided.*[24]

Financial implications of the actions of the Conference

124.   Mr. DADZIE (Secretary-General of UNCTAD) said that the various decisions taken by the Conference, including the adoption of the Final Act under item 8, contained programme indications for the work of the UNCTAD secretariat. He would take those indications fully into account in drawing up in final form, immediately after the Conference, the UNCTAD submission for the 1988-1989 programme budget.

AGENDA ITEM 10

Adoption of the report of the Conference to the General Assembly

125.   Mr. OZADOVSKI (Ukrainian Soviet Socialist Republic), Rapporteur, introducing his draft report (TD/L.300), said that it was a rough draft, to which he must add, in consultation with the group of "Friends of the Rapporteur", a summary of the debates of the current session. The final version of part one of the report would comprise the consolidated text and the text of the resolutions and decisions adopted by the Conference, as well as the index to observations and reservations on the Final Act, resolutions and decisions at the time of their adoption. Those observations and reservations would be included in part two of the report; all delegations that had taken the floor at the closing meeting would have the opportunity to verify the record before the final version of the report was submitted to the group of "Friends of the Rapporteur" for approval. The financial implications of the actions of the Conference would appear in part three.[25]

Preface (paragraphs 1-16)

126.   *The text of the preface was adopted.*

Part one: Action taken by the Conference

127.   *Part one was adopted.*

Part two: Summary of proceedings (paragraphs 17-24)

128.   *Part two was adopted.*

Part three: Organizational and procedural matters (paragraphs 25-57)

129.   *Part three was adopted.*

130.   The PRESIDENT said that, as he saw no objection, he took it that the Conference adopted the draft

---

[24] See volume I, part one, sect. A.4.

[25] *Ibid.,* part three, para. 41.

report as a whole and that it authorized the Rapporteur, as was customary to complete it and make the necessary amendments, in consultation with those concerned, after the closure of the seventh session.

131.   *It was so decided.*

Closure of the session

132.   Mr. CABRISAS RUÍZ (Cuba), speaking on behalf of the States members of the Group of 77, said that his Group saw in the seventh session of the Conference the continuation of a process towards achieving the aims and ideals entrusted to UNCTAD by the international community. The seventh session of the Conference could not have been more opportune, given the serious deterioration in the world economic situation witnessed during the current decade. The persistent stagnation of economic growth for developing countries, caused by the inadequacies of the international economic system, had severely retarded their social and economic progress. Their own national efforts towards achieving their development goals had thereby been seriously affected. He referred in that connection to the Havana Declaration, in which the Group of 77 explained at length the dramatic implications of the world economic crisis for developing countries (TD/335, para. 7).

133.   Particular difficulties were experienced by the Palestinian people, whose living conditions had been deteriorating as a result of the Israeli occupation and who urgently needed to be liberated from their occupation to enable them to develop their national economy. The same could be said of the peoples of southern Africa and Namibia, particularly those of the front-line States, whose painstakingly developed infrastructure and legitimate development programmes were undermined by the South African régime's destabilization policy. Furthermore, the practice of imposing coercive economic measures against developing countries for purposes incompatible with the Charter of the United Nations had been an additional impediment to their economic progress. Again, the wording of paragraphs 3 and 6 of the Havana Declaration was relevant, the latter paragraph stating that the members of the Group of 77 expected the developed countries to assume their responsibilities in the current world economic crisis, and to redesign their policies in order to contribute to an external environment more predictable and more supportive of growth and development.

134.   Observing that revitalizing development, growth and international trade for the benefit of all had been the main task of the seventh session of the Conference, he said that it had been a difficult and long-drawn-out exercise demanding maximum effort from all participants. For more than a year the Group of 77 had seriously and tirelessly committed itself to the preparations for the Conference, through regional Ministerial Meetings in Dhaka, Addis Ababa and Costa Rica, which had culminated in the adoption of the Havana Declaration. The agenda for the Conference had singled out four interrelated and crucial areas in the international economic environment. The Group of 77 sincerely believed that more concrete and far-reaching policies and measures should have resulted from so

much effort, in order to respond adequately to the gravity of the international economic situation. The Group of 77 was fully conscious of the challenge, and faced that challenge pragmatically and realistically. That was evident from the proposals drawn up by the Group and put forward in its negotiations with the other members of the international community. However, the response of some of the negotiating partners had not been commensurate with the gravity of the international economic situation.

135.   Having said that, it was the sincere wish of the Group of 77 that the results of the seventh session of the Conference should herald the beginning of the reversal of the current economic situation. In particular, the Group of 77 felt that, at a time when the interdependence of nations and issues in the economic field was increasing, there was a need to take positive action to exploit the potential of international economic co-operation. That potential could best be realized through multilateral co-operation based on the recognition of the equality of all countries. UNCTAD remained the forum for international economic co-operation and negotiation in the field of trade, development and interrelated areas and could play a unique role in furthering that interdependence.

136.   The Group of 77 was confident that all States members of UNCTAD would endeavour to work in earnest to implement the agreements reached by the Conference, that the political will would be renewed and be made more effective, that all the developed countries would assume their responsibilities in the face of the seriousness of the situation, and that multilateral co-operation for development and economic growth would become a reality.

137.   Mr. SHEN Jueren (China) observed that Governments had attached great importance to the seventh session of the Conference, which had been convened at a time when the North-South dialogue had for a long time remained deadlocked.

138.   Serious discussions had been carried out on the situation of the world economy and trade as well as such other issues as financial resources for development, commodities, international trade and the LDCs. Those discussions were conducive to the promotion of mutual understanding. In the general debate, the majority of countries had expressed the wish for dialogue and co-operation and demanded the establishment of a liberalized multilateral trading system and strengthened multilateral co-operation so as to solve the economic and trade problems they confronted. The developing countries had made a positive contribution to the Conference, and some developed countries had shown sympathy for their plight.

139.   Owing to the efforts of the participants, consensus had been attained on some issues and certain progress had been made which would be helpful to the continuation of constructive dialogue in the future.

140.   The current international economic situation continued to be grim, and the developing countries were confronted with great economic difficulties, as the economies of all States were more and more interdependent, the economic development of the developing countries would become increasingly important to the

economic growth of the developed countries and to the revitalization of the world economy as a whole. The economic development of countries depended not only on their own efforts and correct policies but also on a favourable external environment and international co-operation. It would be detrimental to the developed countries if no help was offered to the developing countries to resolve their current problems and speed up their economic development. China therefore believed that the dialogue between North and South on an equal footing and the strengthening of their economic and trade co-operation would contribute not only to the prosperity of the world economy but to peace and stability as well. For its part, China would continue to pursue a policy of liberalization and adjustment so that it, too, could contribute to world economic growth and the expansion of international trade.

141.   The Conference had proved once again that UNCTAD served as an important forum within the United Nations system for discussing and resolving issues relating to trade and development. That role must be strengthened.

142.   Mr. YOHAI (Colombia) recalled that it had been Colombia's tradition, deeply rooted in its commitment to international peace, justice and equality, not to limit any analysis and action in the international arena to areas of disagreement and structural discrepancies that existed in respect of so many issues, but always to persevere in the search for consensus and for clearly defined ground rules that fostered the collective action of States in favour of international trade and development.

143.   That was precisely what had happened in the course of the present important Conference, and Colombia was amply satisfied with the results achieved.

144.   Geneva had once more proven fertile ground for new ideas and agreements. All had allowed their imagination and generosity to run their course, and he trusted that the seeds sown at the seventh session of the Conference would bear fruit in the not too distant future.

145.   With the support of the industrialized States, UNCTAD could become a forward-looking forum of ideas as well as an effective instrument for action in favour of developing countries. The final outcome would be determnined by how the international agreements subscribed to were implemented in the years ahead.

146.   The work had been hard but interesting. Participants had undertaken their various tasks with integrity, dedication and shared responsibility. History would judge whether what was being proposed and had been agreed to at that session of the Conference would gradually be translated into tangible results and whether current aspirations could become future realities.

147.   Developing countries, far from becoming the sort of "offensive alliance" some had anticipated, had not adopted extreme positions and, in the formulation of their policies, had taken into account the concerns and problems of the industrialized countries.

148.   There were, no doubt, differing viewpoints, but participants had been able to overcome such dif-

ferences. There had also been—throughout the Conference—fundamental disagreements which had continuously threatened consensus. Fortunately, reason and good will had prevailed in the end, as had everyone's most sincere desire to seek the co-ordination and complementarity of various groups' efforts. All that had resulted in the happy ending of the seventh session.

149. Those endorsing the ministerial declaration in the form of UNCTAD VII's "Final Act" had made a historic commitment. Upon signing, they pledged their word, thereby guaranteeing the agreements reached. That ensured that the agenda Governments had agreed on would move forward and without undue delays in their respective jurisdictions.

150. Consensus had been achieved on some truly critical issues: debt, commodities, international trade and the needs of the LDCs. On each of them, Governments had made pledges. If they were fulfilled, the seventh session of the Conference would be remembered as a giant leap forward, and all participants would have the feeling of a job well done. The Conference had supported new forms of recycling for external debt and for the transfer of financial resources; it had agreed on the basis of a dynamic and fair international trading system; it had adopted effective formulas and proposals to improve the outlook of commodities; and it had established the requirements of the LDCs to finance the growth and development they needed to improve their people's quality of life. It could be emphatically stated that, as a result of the agreements at the current session, there was a new awakening for UNCTAD as well as the hope of a more promising future for developing countries.

151. Mr. THUYSBAERT (Belgium), speaking on behalf of the States members of Group B, observed that the opening of the session had been marked by a certain scepticism in many capitals and even a great deal of indifference among public opinion. The results that had been achieved were due above all to those actively engaged in the work of the session. Some found those results modest. He believed that to be appreciated they should be measured not only in quantitative but also in qualitative terms as well as in the longer perspective. What had been achieved was above all the determination of common approaches which would be fruitful in future work. In the case of a problem as important as that of debt, anything that could promote a convergence of views would surely facilitate settlements in specific cases, which was currently of fundamental importance.

152. As to commodities, an area marked by frequent difficulties and confrontations, there were now grounds for hope that discussions leading to arrangements for individual commodities could take place under conditions conducive to success.

153. As to trade, it was important, if not essential, that there should be an assurance that GATT and UNCTAD could each continue to work towards results corresponding to their mandates. Then again, there were also all the measures in favour of the LDCs which had been formulated during the session. In addition, there were the common perceptions achieved with regard to economic strategies. His feeling was that, after

so many years in search of a North-South dialogue, it could be said, to paraphrase Proust, that the foundations had now been laid for the rediscovery of an entente.

154. Mr. FREYBERG (Poland), speaking on behalf of the States members of Group D and of Mongolia, observed that Group D countries had come to Geneva to "revitalize development, growth and international trade in a more predictable and supportive environment through multilateral co-operation". They had come prepared to negotiate in good faith in order to make things better, being deeply concerned at the current economic situation and the challenges facing every member of the international community in the process of development. In the course of the general debate and the work of the Committees the discussion had focused on international trade and development, on the urgency of solving the debt problem, liberalizing trade, diminishing protectionism and stabilizing commodity prices, and on the LDCs. The seventh session of the Conference had proved that UNCTAD was a unique universal international forum mandated to deal with problems of trade and development. The Group D countries had always supported its work, and that support had been demonstrated during the Conference. Group D was pleased that, owing to the political will of all countries, the Conference had been able to reach consensus on almost all important items. That would foster revitalization of development, growth and international trade. It would also contribute to the establishment of international economic security and speed up the negotiating process within UNCTAD. He expressed the hope that the results achieved at the Conference would lay good foundations for sound economic relations in the world and strengthen the role of UNCTAD. Group D was fully committed to working towards that goal.

155. Mr. DADZIE (Secretary-General of UNCTAD), in a very preliminary and personal political assessment of the session, observed that the atmosphere and substantive content of the discussions had been positive; they had not been confrontational; they had been constructive. They had ranged widely over the burning issues facing policy makers in all countries, in particular in developing countries, and they had not been unduly constrained by narrow institutional concerns.

156. Those discussions had led to the adoption of a Final Act which was characterized by a degree of balance and moderation and which was, at the same time, realistic in content. All countries and groups of countries had worked strenuously towards an outcome to which all could rally, even though that outcome gave complete satisfaction to none.

157. The text of the assessment section of the Final Act was a case in point. Each country or group of countries would have written it differently, but all could live with it. It provided the international community with a platform for stronger international co-operation to revitalize development growth and international trade. He believed that the Conference owed a vote of thanks to the President for the skill, mastery and determination with which he had carried forward the assessment exercise and brought it to a conclusion.

158. However, delegations had come to the Conference not simply to assess economic trends and global structural change but to promote decisive action in the interest of world economic growth and development. The question thus arose whether the Conference had indeed taken decisions which would affect the course of the world economy and of international economic relations and benefit the welfare of the people, to whom all Governments were accountable.

159. Against such a yardstick, the results of the session must be evaluated with some caution. Many, perhaps all, would have wished to have gone further. However, he believed that participants could be satisfied that the Conference had achieved constructive and significant advances in the areas addressed by its agenda. Without going into the many specifics, he had in mind, for instance, the emphasis given to the need for sustainable non-inflationary growth in the developed countries and for an environment supportive of accelerated and sustainable development; the recognition in that context of the respective responsibilities of developed and developing countries, based on the consideration that the greater the economic weight of a country, the greater the effect of its policies on other countries and on the external economic environment; the new impetus given to the evolution of a growth-oriented debt strategy; the arrangements for renewed intergovernmental co-operation in the field of commodities, for which the Common Fund will be an important instrument; the realization of the complementarity between UNCTAD and GATT in their efforts to promote world trade, fight protectionism and strengthen the international trading system; and the reaffirmation of the need for more vigorous efforts in support of the development of the LDCs. Those might not be considered dramatic breakthroughs, but they were nevertheless important. What was more, Governments had pledged themselves in good faith to give effect to those results, nationally and internationally, in the competent forums, including UNCTAD.

160. Each participant and each delegation would evaluate the results of the Conference against their own yardsticks or against those suggested in his opening address. For his part, as executive head of the institution, he felt that UNCTAD had emerged strengthened from the process leading up to and including the seventh session of the Conference. He was impressed by the evolution in the attitudes of many delegations, who had come to the Conference in a sceptical frame of mind but who were now preparing to leave convinced that UNCTAD was an institution where they could develop common approaches to issues of international economic co-operation with their counterparts from all States and agree on effective policies which would have an impact at both the national and international levels on the problems under discussion.

161. That result was in large part due to the intensive preparatory process that had been under way for over a year. The preparations had begun with discussions on the agenda and continued through consultations on the documentation and on the issues in the different agenda areas. They had been enriched by a number of sectoral meetings, by visits to and discussions in capitals, and by the contributions of the research

community, the enterprise sector and non-governmental organizations. Their high points were the ministerial meetings of the various regional groups. And they ended with the initial work on assessment. Those interactions had been protracted and, at the intergovernmental level, often difficult, but they had been fruitful and indeed indispensable for the results embodied in the Final Act of the Conference.

162. As to the way in which UNCTAD would evolve, he would not wish it to be said that that session of the Conference was the only basis for the future work of the institution. UNCTAD had been in existence for close to a quarter of a century since its establishment by General Assembly resolution 1995 (XIX). It must continue to build upon all its historical experience and fulfil all the elements of its wide-ranging mandate. Moreover, the scope of that session of the Conference, although broad, had not comprehended all the issues on the UNCTAD agenda. Those issues which had not been directly treated at that session remained important, and they must continue to be given a proper place in the organization's work.

163. On that basis, the secretariat would proceed to analyse and assess the implications of the Final Act of UNCTAD VII for its programme of work for the coming years. It would do so in the light of processes of reform currently under way within the United Nations as a whole. The secretariat would come up with a package of specific work orientations for the UNCTAD of the next few years. That package would include activities involving research, conceptual innovation and policy analysis; information exchanges and consultations; support for intergovernmental deliberations, for negotiations and for the implementation of their outcomes; and technical co-operation. All member States would be able to shape that package through their participation in the work of the Trade and Development Board and the General Assembly.

164. Whatever the shape and content of the package, the organization had a hard road ahead. He gave an assurance that the UNCTAD secretariat would continue to exert itself to respond to the demands and interests of Governments, collectively expressed. It would also spare no effort to enhance the effectiveness of UNCTAD as an instrument of international economic co-operation and as an agent of change in support of development.

165. The PRESIDENT observed that the session of the Conference had been an exacting event, as it was bound to be, given the nature of the agenda, a background of complex international economic problems, a withering development consensus and faltering confidence in the principles of multilateralism. He expressed deep appreciation to the heads of State and Government who had addressed the Conference and had dissipated the clouds of gloom, delivering messages of faith and hope in the future of mankind, and who had underscored the importance of unity and solidarity in efforts to overcome the many problems confronting the world. Similarly, he expressed deep appreciation to the Ministers who had participated in the Conference, and he emphasized that the large ministerial attendance had been a very positive omen for the final outcome. The thoroughness of the preparatory work and the

outstanding quality of the documentation had made a distinct contribution to the Conference, and he paid a tribute to the Secretary-General of UNCTAD and the staff of the secretariat for their unstinting support.

166. He observed that the seventh session of the Conference had in many ways been unique in the history of UNCTAD conferences. The pre-Conference preparations in the Trade and Development Board had marked a point of departure and set a precedent and standard for future conferences. The agenda of the Conference was short and well focused, discussions had been transparent and pointed and held in a nonconfrontational atmosphere. The achievement of a consolidated text, the Final Act of UNCTAD VII, the product of a searching and painstaking exercise, was a milestone in the proceedings of UNCTAD and, indeed, in the conduct of the North-South dialogue. It remained to be seen whether all that would strengthen UNCTAD and its mandate enshrined in General Assembly resolution 1995 (XIX). There was reason to believe that would be so, but there was a need to be vigilant and to maintain the momentum.

167. It would be some time before Governments fully appreciated the results of the Conference. He himself was encouraged because expectations had been tempered by a recognition of the positive results achieved in an environment of patent international crisis as typified especially by the debt burden of developing countries, stunted growth and, of course, misalignment of macro-economic policies, particularly in the major industrialized countries, and the near collapse of multilateral economic co-operation. By the same token, he was disappointed by the modest results in an environment which called for decisive action in the face of the grave international economic problems, given the potential of that forum in contributing to the formulation of joint solutions to the problems of trade and development.

168. He was persuaded to conclude, however, that the clear result of the work of the Conference had been the advancement of multilateralism and the preservation of UNCTAD itself as a unique universal forum for formulating and negotiating interlocking trade and development policy and monetary issues. UNCTAD must be preserved, and there were better times ahead.

169. A serious attempt had been made at revamping the North-South dialogue. A momentum of consensus-building had been launched which would inevitably spill over into other parallel efforts, including those of the permanent machinery of UNCTAD as well as in other forums.

170. It was encouraging that the unifying theme of "Revitalizing development, growth and international trade in a more predictable and supportive environment through multilateral co-operation" had remained a valid beacon throughout the Conference. The policies and measures adopted would provide a momentum, and indeed guidelines, which would nourish that theme in that and other forums until the objectives were achieved. The results marked a new beginning and demanded more effort and political will commensurate with the development challenges of the times.

171. In concrete terms, member States and Governments had only just begun addressing the agenda for the seventh session of the Conference: it was an agenda which would have to continue to be addressed and which all must sustain and enhance in UNCTAD as well as in other organizations. The physicist Isaac Newton had said that scholars, and indeed statesmen, had greater vision because they stood on the shoulders of the giants who preceded them. UNCTAD had its giants, in Governments as well as outside, and so could not fail; it must hold the course that they had set. Ideologies and ideals inspired, but hard-headed management and determination were their handmaid.

172. After the customary exchange of courtesies, the President declared the seventh session of the United Nations Conference on Trade and Development closed.

The meeting rose at 8.10 p.m.